THE GIANT BOOK OF
MURDER

THE GIANT BOOK OF
MURDER

Edited by Jonathan Goodman

This edition published and distributed by
Parragon Book Service Ltd in 1995

This edition first published by Magpie Books Ltd in 1995,
a division of Robinson Publishing

Magpie Books Ltd
7 Kensington Church Court
London W8 4SP

First published as *Masterpieces of Murder*
by Robinson Publishing in 1992

Selection and notes © by Jonathan Goodman, 1992

ISBN 0 75251 020 7

A copy of the British Library Cataloguing in Publication Data is
available from the British Library.

Printed by Griffin Paperbacks, South Australia

CONTENTS

Some Executions – and an Executioner

THE GIANT BOOK OF
MURDER

This book is for
the eleven friends
who have contributed to it,
and for the five other friends
who have let me include
writings that are in their care

INTRODUCTION

I AM SURE no reader of this book will be favourably impressed by its every case and its every telling of a case, let alone consider that all of the cases—or, as for those cases considered rather drab, the enlivening accounts of them—deserve to be called *masterpieces* of murder. But, speaking for myself, never mind: I am sure that the 'one man's meat is another's poison' rule applies—that, of a section of cross readers, say a dozen or so, each will grumble at a different one or two (I hope not more) of the constituents. And if the same dozen or so are at all conversant with the true-crime genre, they will enjoy the one invariable pleasure from this sort of book, which is the spotting of omissions so glaring, considering the title, that the book must be damned on the ground of deficiency. I am not being hoity-toity about such criticising; I do it myself. Let me say, though, of this anthology, that certain authors, or certain works by those authors, are missing against my will.

Exemplifying what I mean by that, nearly three months ago I wrote to a well-known literary agency, seeking permission to use small amounts of work by two dead authors whose literary executors it represents; one of the authors was American, the other was English (he was helpfully kind to me after I had written my first true-crime book, encouraging me to write others, and that had a little to do with my wish to have something of his in this book). A replyless month passed, and so I wrote again. After another replyless month, I phoned and, before I had a chance to say anything, was ordered to hold the line. Overlapping the 'ne' of 'line' (and, it would be nice to think, quite obliterating a 'please'), you-haven't-been-disconnected muzak crackled into my listening ear: the last half of a palm-court orchestra's notion of 'Greensleeves', followed, without intermission, by 'The Londonderry Air', followed, without respite, by 'Clair de Lune'—which, as it is no longer a favourite of mine, I hung up on. Perhaps because I have been spoiled by the comparatively excellent quality of reproduction and repertoire of the muzak at Charlie Butler's pub at Mortlake (close to the spot on the towpath of the Thames where, in the spring of 1879, one of Kate Webster's containers of cooked meat bobbed ashore; I mention that riparian fact only because, though inaugural to Ms Webster's come-uppance, it does not appear in the sketch of the case on page 9), I didn't phone up for a further recital. A couple of days later I got a letter from a magazine, saying that the author of an essay that they had published and that I had hoped to use was represented by the agency that I was angry with. I crossed out the title of that essay from my list of wants—also, while I was about it, the two other titles. This morning—yes, *this* morning—I got a written reply from the agency! The writer, who doesn't specify her job-title, at least says sorry about the delay, and then says that she will be passing my letter to 'the person here concerned with the Estate' of the English author, and will be sending a copy of it to the American publishers of the American author, and then, just above where she claims that she is mine sincerely, unwittingly reminds me of the dichotomous letter from Lieutenant Henry Clark to his wife, quoted on page 15, by extending her very best wishes. In a wonderfully prompt reply to a letter I wrote to those American publishers some four months ago, the head of their permissions department told me to get in touch with the agency that I first wrote to nearly three months ago. Forgive my discourtesy, but I don't intend to write to the agency girl to tell her that—and, fearing that a phone-call will coincide with a recording of the palm-court orchestra's rendition of the theme-music of *Chariots of Fire*, I certainly won't try to speak to her. I admitted to anger just now. Part of the reason for it is that some out-of-print writings that ought to be in print are not.

But still, if the agency were even ten percent efficient, some pieces of this anthology would have had to be left out. I remember Ewen Montagu telling me of how, both before and after he fooled the Nazis by making 'The Man Who Never Was', so many disappointments in his life had turned out to be blessings in disguise—and his moral-making comment, and the beaming smile that surrounded it, and his underlining of the words with the stem of that ever-held but rarely-lit pipe of his: 'Pray for calamities.' Perhaps, along far less dramatic lines, the agency's . . . what shall I call it?—tardiness?—yes, that will do, has been to the betterment of this book: perhaps the pieces occupying the space intended for three others are not merely worthy replacements but worthier ones; perhaps, to readers on the look-out for omissions, they, if left out, would have been more conspicuously absent than are those they have replaced. I don't know.

The main reason for my not knowing is that I can only speak for myself as to what makes a 'good' murder—and I can only do that with regard to particular cases—and, with few exceptions, I can only do *that* in terms of condimental rather than basic ingredients of a case (by saying, for instance—and from now on, whenever I feel that an example will help, I shall refer to a story missing from this book—that the Hall-Mills case is good because of the crab-apple tree's shading of the ecclesiastical victims, the quaintness of one of the witnesses, the 'pig woman', and of one of the suspects, Willie Stevens, and the fact that the trial, itself often picturesque, was the outcome of efforts by a sleazy newspaper-editor to boost his rag's circulation).

A case will stand a good chance of being good if it holds a riddle of some important kind: among them, and as well as the whodunit one, Did the person found guilty really do it? . . . Did a co-murderer or an accessory get away with it? . . . What made the murderer do it? . . . *Was* it a case of murder—or of suicide or accident (I am thinking of Edwin Bartlett, of Starr Faithfull, of Evelyn Foster) or of natural—well, perhaps ever so slightly hastened—death (one or three late patients of Dr John Bodkin Adams)?

An unregarded case may become good many years after the fact, simply because, with the passing of those years, some throwaway lines of the testimony have turned into clues to how it felt to be living in a certain place at a certain time—or because some salient bit of information, unearthed or visible over the years but only now seen to be salient, all of a sudden makes the case remarkable.

The general setting may help, of course: rural murders, such as those of Sarah Alexander (the very fact that the rurality of that case was of Brooklyn adds to the goodness), Régine Fay, Rose Harsent and Maria Marten[1] (it occurs to me that a victim's being female helps as well), have an advantage over urban ones; Alfred Hitchcock must have had them in mind when he said that the sort of murder that most appealed to him was 'like blood on a daisy'.

It is unthinking, I'm sure, to say that any particular type of murderer leaves one cold. I have come close to saying that about mad murderers, saving myself from the silly generalisation by recalling Ronald True—who, *because* he was madder than all hatters put together, made a comedy blacker and more surreal than any that Joe Orton, himself eventually a murder-victim, ever made up. (I have, by the way, discovered the identity of True's mother. The fact that she, a spinster when she bore him, married into a noble family suggests an answer, in the absence of others, to the question of how, though not why, her son was kept out of an asylum till his becoming a murderer left no choice in the matter. I must write about the case again, contradicting some of what I wrote before.)

I have expressed elsewhere my feeling that as soon as murdering becomes a habit, the murderer, nearly always a nonentity to start with, usually becomes a caricature of a human being; that a murder should be as especial an event to the murderer as it is to the victim. But though, therefore, I find most cases of serial-killings humdrum, and of a kind with the sort of suiting that a backstreet tailor is alleged to have foisted by saying, 'Never mind the quality, feel the width,' I shall always enjoy the multicidal exploits of Messrs. Burke & Hare, and of Dr William Palmer, and—still referring to enjoyment, most of all—of George Joseph Smith (any murderer who can drown a fresh bride in the bathroom of a guest-house and, still drying his

---

[1] Richard Whittington-Egan has advised me that, as accounts of two of those cases are hard to come by, I should mention that accounts of all four appear in an anthology entitled *The Country House Murders* (London, 1987, 1989) which I edited.

hands, tiptoe downstairs to concoct an alibi from an all-stops-out playing of 'Nearer My God to Thee' on the harmonium in the parlour, surely warrants universal wonder).

Near the top of my first scribbled list of authors, rather than titles of essays or names of cases—authors who had or have written a number of essays that can be called 'masterpieces of murder'—was the name Edmund Pearson. When I came to a difficult task, that of deciding which one of Pearson's many best essays I should pick, I thought at first of using his 'What Makes a Good Murder?' as well as, or even instead of, an introduction. But by then I had chosen other contents; and a re-reading of the essay reminded me that, according to his ideas of what makes *bad* murders, several of my choices were inadmissible. Partly because the inclusion of his essay *and* the accounts of cases of kinds he rules out might have seemed akin to the prefacing of a Lives of the Saints with an article of anti-faith, I decided that I had better use another of his essays—the other of his edictal essays, 'Rules for Murderesses'.

The further reason for my decision was that, coming to think of them, all but one of Pearson's kind-of-murder exclusions excluded any number of cases, on top of my already-chosen 'bad ones', that, so far as I am concerned, are not just good but very good indeed. I think that he was—or, as for those cases he did not live to know, would have been—delighted with most of them; and I think his tongue was deeper in his cheek than I thought when I first read his essay; and I think that, though he was a *true* crime writer, I pay him a great compliment when I say that the enjoyability of the essay fooled me, and I'm sure many other readers, into unawareness of its strolls into illogic.

I understand that, with certain exceptions, rules are supposed to be proved by exceptions to them; but surely no rule can make sense if the exceptions to it are numerous. The only one of Pearson's rulings-out that I can think of only one exception to is *political assassination*; some students of murder may think that there are exceptions other than that of Lincoln—and I might too were it not that the epidemic of crank-theory writings on the assassination of John F. Kennedy has made it hard for me to concentrate on any writing about any assassination, as my eyes keep flinching in expectation of an exposé. Among Pearson's other rulings-out are the *crime passionel* (which, if the term has as wide a meaning as I think it does—murder arising from a desire to commence, continue or curtail a sexual relationship—includes many more good cases than the couple I have picked) and *murders of complete strangers* (he must have been thinking only of killings by thugs, terrorists and psychopaths, if there is a difference between them, quite forgetting a lot of cases that he liked—for instance, Alfred Arthur Rouse's 'blazing-car murder', intentionally on a Bonfire Night, and intended to give the impression that it was he, the productively satyric Rouse, who had gone up in flames, which was of a total stranger whose identity will never be known).

Having quoted from De Quincey's 'On Murder Considered as One of the Fine Arts' in illustrious support of some of his arguments, Pearson (who seems always to have tried to tell the truth and nothing but the truth in his essays on single cases, which cannot be said of the writer Edward Radin, who accused him of lying about the Borden case) needs to admit that it is 'unexplainable' that De Quincey decried the works of the poisoner—'for of all sly deviltry the art of the poisoner is unsurpassed'.

That just goes to show—yet again, I hope—the truth of the meat-and-poison proverb that I mentioned earlier. All I can say now, at the end of this beginning, is that, in my view, none of the subjects in the following pages is out of place in them—and that, speaking of all but one of the divers dealers with those subjects, each merits your attention.

RULES FOR MURDERESSES
Edmund Pearson

*[As a chronicler of crimes, he made New England as much
his 'manor' as William Roughead made Scotland his. He
and Roughead were pen-friends till his death in 1937;
their admiration for each other's work is understandable,
for in terms of elegance and apt wryness, their styles bear
resemblances, and they shared pet aversions (among those,
of mumbo-jumbo-isms of psychiatrists—or, as Pearson
termed such persons, 'alienists'). He was born at Newbury-
port in 1880, of a family long-established in Massachusetts
(speaking of a line of bakers in his ancestry, he said that
'Pearson's Pilot Bread gave more people happiness than
Pearson's books on murder will ever do. There's no
question which I would choose, if I were on a desert
island.'). After graduating from Harvard with a BA, he
became a librarian, at first in Washington, DC, and from
1914 till 1927 (with a break during the Great War, while
he was in the army) at the New York Public Library, where
he was eventually editor of publications. Meanwhile, as
well as writing about murders and bibliographical oddities,
he contributed a weekly column, 'The Librarian', to the*
Boston *Evening* Transcript; *a generous selection of the
columns was published by the Scarecrow Press, New Jersey,
in 1976, and is, I understand, still in print. No collection
of his murder stories has been published in England since
1964 (in America, I believe, since 1967); adding to the*

8

sadness of that fact, many of his stories have never appeared in books.]

'A WOMAN with fair opportunities,' said Thackeray, 'and without an absolute hump, may marry whom she likes.'

That is an understatement. A woman's privileges are even greater— for if she will observe a few restrictions, she may *murder* whom she likes. It is three to one that she will go scot-free. If she is treated with severity, it is because she has disregarded one of the obvious rules.

I have been looking over the histories of about thirty more or less charming ladies who have chafed under the suspicion of having removed some person or persons from the earth by violent means. They are the more remarkable of the sisterhood, and range in time from 1752, when Miss Mary Blandy fell foul of the law.

The women who appear in my survey have dotted the earth from the rainy Scottish moors, where Katherine Nairn made her home, to the burning plains of the Punjab, where flourished Mrs. Fullam of Agra and Meerut.

Augusta Fullam, although little known to fame in America, was one of the most extraordinary murderesses of all time. It was she who penned that Napoleonic sentence, admirable alike for terseness and decision:

'So the only thing is to poison the soup.'

Eight of the thirty women actually paid the law's highest price. These eight, who perished at the hands of the executioner, chosen as they are from the records of about a hundred and seventy years, are women who disregarded one of the great rules for murderesses. And this brings me back to my remark at the beginning: that the wise murderess will take care to observe a few simple restrictions. She overrides these at her peril. Briefly, the regulations are as follows:

1. *If you decide to murder your husband, you must never act in concert with a lover.*

In comment upon this rule, it must be added that a lover should appear nowhere in the record; not a sign, not a suspicion, not even a shoelace of his. The careful murderess of her husband removes him, unaided, and then proceeds, helped by a clever lawyer, to blacken the dead man's character. This is always successful, and very popular: she usually becomes a heroine.

All women who find their husbands annoying—and it is astonishing how many there are of these—make her cause their own. By the time the trial is over, people are wondering how so wicked a man as the dead husband was allowed, by Heaven, to live as long as he did.

2. *It is inadvisable for a maidservant to murder her mistress under circumstances of extreme barbarity.*

Kate Webster, in England, killed her mistress for the purpose of robbery. Webster was a big, muscular and rather savage-looking woman; her employer, Mrs. Thomas, was small and frail and alone in the house. Webster was heard by the neighbours pounding and chopping, and was afterwards known to be boiling something in the copper wash-boiler.

A day later, she was making calls on her friends and joining them at tea, carrying with her a small black bag. When still later the disappearance of Mrs. Thomas and the flight of Webster began to be investigated, the black bag was found and its contents examined. Thereafter, throughout Great Britain, Kate Webster was regarded with considerable distaste, and this never ceased nor diminished until the sentence of the law was executed.

Webster blundered at every opportunity. She made the mistake of operating in England, instead of America, and of limiting her murders to one. As I hope to show, by further examples, a woman's immunity from severe punishment increases according to the number of persons she murders.

3. *Even in the murder of a father or mother, the astute murderess will take care that no lover appears upon the scene.*

Plain murder is often forgiven by a jury. But murder combined with a love-affair is almost always disapproved. The feeling is that somebody has been having too much fun. The famous Miss Mary Blandy, of Henley-upon-Thames, found certain obstacles in the way of her marriage with Captain the Honorable William Cranstoun, a Scot of ancient lineage. One of these—or, rather, two of them—were the captain's wife and daughter. More serious, however, was her father's dislike of Cranstoun. Still, as Mr. Blandy was old and a man of wealth, and as Miss Mary was his only heir, almost anything might happen. So the captain sent his sweetheart some powders, described as a 'love philtre', and supposed to awake, in the old gentleman, sentiments of warmest affection for military men in general and for Captain Cranstoun in particular.

Miss Blandy administered these powders to her father— in his tea and in his gruel—and continued to administer them, even when, so far from causing him to conceive a liking for the captain, they merely made him very ill. Finally he died of them; Cranstoun fled to Europe; and the officers of the Crown hanged Miss Blandy upon a gallows at Oxford. She died with notable modesty, however, remarking as she climbed the ladder:

'Gentlemen, do not hang me high, for the sake of decency.'

A hundred and forty years later, in Massachusetts, a similar situation arose, but with far different results. A lady of about Miss Blandy's age, and also the heiress of a wealthy father, fell under grievous suspicion of having caved in his head—and also that of her stepmother—with a hatchet. Her name was Miss Lizzie Borden, and the State showed evidence of motive, animus, opportunity and guilty knowledge of the crimes. Indeed, it has been very hard to understand how anyone except the lady could have committed the two murders, at an interval of more than an hour, and escaped unseen.

Some cynical people, weary of the hymns to her innocence chanted by her admirers, suggested that perhaps the old people murdered each other. And a newspaper man offered the sarcastic theory that the shocking wounds on the heads of the victims should be disregarded and, in view of the warm weather at the time of the tragedy, the deaths should be put down to heat-prostration.

One thing, however, the law could not show, and that was the existence of any love-affair. Despite unsubstantial gossip, nothing appears in the record about any entanglement with a man. The jury had a fine disregard for logical proof and preferred to rest on the theory that what seemed unheard of was therefore impossible. The State asked them to believe that the lady-secretary of the Young People's Society for Christian Endeavour had, in broad daylight, and in the manner of a Mohawk warrior, attacked and slain two elderly persons with a hatchet or an axe—one of the sufferers being her own father.

The gossip of some of the townsfolk, in order to account for the mysterious absence of bloodstains on her clothes, went still farther and advanced the fantastic theory that she had given the scene an unusual flavor of indelicacy by stripping herself stark-naked before she commenced the slaughter.

This orgiastic touch does not appear, of course, in the case for the State, but it is a favourite legend, always related when the tale of the crime is told. It is even set down in print, as if it were an accepted fact, by Mr. Algernon Blackwood, the novelist of the supernatural and the *macabre*. And this not in a novel, but in his memoirs—from his recollections of newspaper days.

No lover appeared (except in vague gossip) on Miss Borden's even most distant horizon. The jury promptly acquitted her amid the ecstatic applause of hundreds of persons, who were content with the simple assertion that 'a woman couldn't do such a thing'. The lady retired to a life of affluence: to a pleasant villa, to theatre parties, motor-cars and improving travel. And after thirty-five years of this agreeable existence, she passed on as serenely, and as little troubled by horrific visions, I have no doubt, as any of the rest of us.

A woman couldn't do such a thing . . . How often that is said, even by persons who have heard all that happened on that night in Mr. Snyder's bedchamber when Mrs. Snyder entered with the picture-cord and the window-weight.

4. *If you commit murder for insurance-money or for mere pleasure, make it wholesale. Never stop at one.*

This regulation bears with equal force against men; women are not especially restricted at this point. The person who kills some one obscure individual, who does it quietly and with moderate civility, is in a rather perilous position. There are about three chances in a hundred that he may be sentenced to death.

It is the wholesale poisoner, or the shockingly cruel and unusual murderer, who attracts the sob sisters and sob brothers of the yellow press; causes quack alienists to rally to his defence like buzzards around a carcass; invites the windiest oratory and the most unmitigated flapdoodle from his attorneys; and finally, if he be convicted at all, makes thousands of persons move heaven and earth, slander the living and vilify the dead, in order to keep his precious body alive.

In the 1870s in Connecticut, Mrs. Lydia Sherman confessed that she poisoned three husbands and eight children.

'Of course,' someone will say, 'she was insane.'

There is really no 'of course' about it. She was well aware of what she was doing, and was careful to be furtive and to try to avoid detection. She never acted on an 'irresistible impulse' to kill these people; there was never a time when she could not have controlled herself if she had been observed. The deaths of these persons brought her profit or they relieved her of care and annoyance. The qualities of selfishness and callous disregard for others—qualities present in all of us to some degree—were developed in her to an unusual extent, and she slew people as you or I would kill a mosquito, or as some folk will club an egret to death for its feathers, or shoot a seagull *pour le sport*.

Sarah Jane Robinson of Massachusetts also illustrates the fact that the poisoner, when discovered, is usually no greenhorn at the business. One or two successes always create boldness, and she proceeds upon her career.

Mrs. Robinson did not confine her efforts to her immediate family, but went farther afield. In her enthusiasm for insurance and in her skill with arsenic, she is generally supposed to have included in her attentions a brother-in-law, a nephew, and even her landlord, a gentleman called Oliver Sleeper. These, added to her husband, her son and her daughter, brought her total score up to at least six persons by 1882. It was on account of the death of her brother-in-law, named Prince Arthur Freeman, that the courts at last put an end to her activities. When it came to allowing a lady—'an American mother'—to perish, the Commonwealth of Massachusetts proved as tender as the rest, and Mrs. Robinson was permitted to retire to prison and to loud and sanctimonious professions of religion.

In the same state, Miss Jane Toppan, 'dear Aunt Jane,' arose to a brief but disturbing fame. Miss Toppan, whose real name was Honora Kelly—not all of New England's sins come from Plymouth Rock—was a nurse. She was much in demand for her warm-hearted, motherly, big-bosomed and gracious presence—simply beaming with health and good spirits; the very personification of healing. It is not surprising if death sometimes follows the arrival of a nurse: we do not call in these helpers for trivial ailments. Yet death seemed to follow in strange and perplexing forms when dear Aunt Jane was around. And when investigations began, the startled physicians and officers were suddenly aware that they had pried the lid off a section of hell into which none of them had ever peered.

With a few exclamations, the cover was quickly replaced: Aunt Jane was put in an insane asylum, and the greater part of her history remains unknown to this day. Except to a very few, it was never known. To the established facts, which account for four or five poisonings, a great many robberies and one case of arson, there is added, in legend and gossip, the tale of an enormous list of murders—ten, twenty, forty—which may or may not have any foundation in fact. A nurse's opportunities are many, yet the popular tendency is always to exaggerate.

Four of her murders were committed within forty-eight days, and some of these seem to have had no motive but sheer sadism. Yet the distinguished alienist, Doctor C. F. Folsom, who vouched for her 'moral insanity,' says that from 1892 to 1900—or the last eight years of her career—she had the reputation of being 'the best nurse in Cambridge'. Furthermore, until her crimes became known, 'of all the many people who knew Miss Toppan, there was not one who . . . had the least thought of her being in any form or degree insane or a degenerate, defective, mental or moral imbecile, or, poetically speaking, even a deviate'.

Of Mrs. Belle Gunness, beloved and perpetual heroine of the Sunday newspapers, and of her Indiana 'murder farm' it is unnecessary to speak. Nearly everybody in America has heard of her and her wondrous success in tempting middle-aged Scandinavians and Teutons into putting all their bank-deposits into their pockets and joining her in her rural home: object, matrimony. And of how these trusting gentlemen thereupon vanished from human sight, never to be met with again, until the exhumations began.

Mrs. Gunness never came into conflict with the law. She disappeared in 1908. If she had been arrested, I have no manner of doubt that she could have found a lawyer unscrupulous enough to foul the characters of all her victims and represent her as a lamb of innocence. She could have hired an alienist, or psychiatrist, to testify that she played with dolls as a child and was, therefore, subject to a complex which made it impossible to hold her responsible for anything whatever.

Chocolate creams masked the deadly purposes of the Englishwoman Christiana Edmunds and the American, Cordelia Botkin. Each struck with a cruel disregard of consequences; Miss Edmunds put strychnine in her confections, while Mrs. Botkin adhered to the simple and inexpensive recipe so long favoured by lady-poisoners: powdered arsenic.

In 1871, Miss Christiana Edmunds conceived the brilliant notion of removing her doctor's wife. That lady was practically an-apple-a-day in Miss Edmunds' life, since she was keeping the doctor away from his adoring Christiana. She modestly prepared her sweets and took them with her to tea at the doctor's house. The plan was discovered, however, and both doctor and doctor's wife told Miss Edmunds, quite plainly, that a gift of chocolate creams, plus strychnia, constituted a breach of friendship which they were not disposed to pardon.

How was the rejected one to regain favour in their sight? A happy thought: simply by poisoning all, or nearly all, the chocolates at the local confectioner's and thereby, in the face of a general slaughter of the townsfolk of Brighton, put the blame upon the confectioner. So she slipped her deadly chocolates into his stock. Only one victim perished, however—a little boy—and in spite of the judge's remark about method in her madness, the jury found Miss Edmunds to be mentally incompetent.

A note written in 1895 by Christiana Edmunds to Dr David Nicholson, the retiring Superintendent of Broadmoor Asylum, and his wife. Miss Edmunds is said to have retained her vivacity and her vanity till just before her death, at the asylum, in 1907, when she was seventy-nine.

Mrs. Botkin struck from across the continent. In 1898, her loaded bonbons travelled by mail from California to Delaware and poisoned six harmless people—four women and two children. Two of the woman died. All were unknown to Mrs. Botkin, but one of them was the wife of the Californian lady's lover. Mrs. Botkin, thanks to the uncertainty of the courts and laxity of the law, spent some years—with many privileges—confined in jail. Her husband's name was one of the incongruities of the case. In view of her aversion from him, it is amusing to learn that he was christened Welcome A. Botkin.

Mrs. Fullam of Agra (whose astounding tale was in the English newspapers in 1913) used to write to Lieutenant Clark:

> The way, not mine, O Lord
> However dark it be;
> Lead me by thine own hand,
> Choose out the path for me.
> I dare not choose my lot,
> I would not if I might;
> Choose Thou for me, my God,
> Then shall I walk aright.

She would copy these model verses and add: 'These lines are just what my poor sentiments now express, Harry darling, my own very precious sweetheart.'

All the Fullams and Clarks were queerly inspired when they took pen in hand. The lieutenant used to write to his wife, saying:

'I am fed up with your low disgusting ways, for I am quite sure you don't care a damn what becomes of me.'

Then he would sign himself:

'With fond love and kisses to self, and the rest at home, I remain

Your affectionate husband,
H. L. Clark.'

The four persons in the tangle were Lieutenant and Mrs. Clark of the Indian Medical Service, and Mr. and Mrs. Fullam of the Military Accounts Department. Mrs. Fullam was purely English; the others, I believe, were Eurasian. Clark and Mrs. Fullam, desiring the total destruction of Mrs. Clark and Mr. Fullam, contrived, not without difficulty, and the writing of hundreds of incriminating letters, to slay Mr. Fullam. It was during their campaign that Mrs. Fullam wrote the sentence about the soup which I quoted earlier.

Clark was rather brutal in appearance and manner. He was given, among other more commonplace diversions, to the curious sport of 'duck-fighting', a fact which makes me form a low opinion of his character. The man who forces such agreeable birds into combat seems to be somewhat lacking in the finer sensibilities.

The course of slow poisoning to which Mr. Fullam was subjected was finally ended by Clark. Under pretence of acting as his physician, he killed the wretched man by injections of gelsamine, an alkaloid poison.

A year later, the assassination of Mrs. Clark was carried out by hired murderers in the employ of her husband. The actual perpetrators were Indian natives, *budmashes*, or loafers from the bazaar. Their fee for work of this kind was very moderate; they came into her room at night and killed her with a sword. (The method of a 'brave man,' according to 'The Ballad of Reading Gaol'.)

When Mrs. Fullam's bungalow was searched, the police found all the correspondence with Clark. It revealed the entire plot: all this evidence had been preserved with the same fatuous care with which young Freddie Bywaters kept the letters of Mrs. Edith Thompson.

Mrs. Fullam was sent to prison and soon died there. One or two of the *budmashes* were hanged; and with them, I am glad to say, there also died by the noose, Lieutenant Henry Lovell William Clark, the patron of duck-fights.

SCENES FROM A MURDER TRIAL
William Cooper

[One of the sharpest-eyed—and, partly therefore, one of the most entertaining—novelists of English social life, he was born at Crewe in 1910. After graduating from Cambridge with a degree in physics, and then serving in the RAF during the Second World War, he became a recruitment specialist, working for, among other organisations, the Civil Service Commission, the UK Atomic Energy Authority, and the Commission of European Communities; he was Adjunct Professor of English Literature at Syracuse University, London Centre, from 1977 till 1990. Meanwhile, plays of his were produced, and he published short stories and books of divers genres. His first three novels—published under his baptismal name, H(arry). S(ummerfield). Hoff—appeared before the war. The first of his brilliant Scenes *series,* Scenes From Provincial Life, *appeared in 1950; the fifth, and most recent,* Scenes From Early Life, *in 1990. (The entire series is available, as are too few of his other novels, in hardback and/or paperback.) He lives in Putney, close to the starting-point of the Oxford & Cambridge Boat-Race—and to the spot on the towpath where, in March 1953, J.R.H. Christie was arrested (which, no doubt coincidentally, is close to 12 Roskell Road, the home till October 1944 of Muriel Eady, a respectable one of Christie's cupboard-or-garden victims).]*

'PUT UP Arthur Hosein and Nizamodeen Hosein!' So runs the formula with which the ritual of an English trial begins. At those words, uttered by the Clerk of the Court, the accused make their first, fateful appearance in the dock. The date is 14 September 1970; the place, the Old Bailey.

They stand, awaiting the beginning of a process in which they are presumed innocent until such time as the Crown may have proved beyond all reasonable doubt to a jury of twelve men and women drawn from the common public that they are guilty.

So it is with the trial of the Hosein brothers, two dark-skinned men from Trinidad, well-dressed, speaking English perfectly well (accent apart), brought to trial in Court One, the 'star' court of the Old Bailey.

The Press are fitted mainly into benches on either side of the dock—it is unobtrusively in the far corner of one of these benches that Mr. McKay and his son frequently sit, listening, unable to tear themselves away from it all, no matter how unbearable, because they want to know what, what became of Mrs. McKay.

The brothers Hosein look so different from each other that one would not guess at first sight that they are brothers. They come from a family of tailors at some remove from the lower classes. Their father is in court, a thin, spare, reflective-looking man, wearing a suit that looks too big for him. He is said to be very 'holy'.

The Clerk of the Court reads the charges and asks the brothers if they plead Guilty or Not Guilty. Arthur Hosein: 'Not guilty.' Nizamodeen Hosein (softly): 'Not guilty, sir.'

Arthur is the smaller, plumpish, with the beginnings of an embonpoint that curves over his waistbelt, immaculately suited according to his lights—after all, he is a tailor's cutter by profession. He has handsome large black eyes with dark circles round them, and full cheeks, beautiful bushy black wavy hair, well cut, and a black moustache.

The younger brother Hosein does not watch the jury being called: he quietly, motionlessly, looks straight ahead. He is taller and more athletic in physique, yet his features are softish, amorphous, distinctly Chinesey. He wears spectacles, and has a wad of dark hair combed across his forehead.

The jury are sworn in. With a nod, the Judge tells the

accused men to sit down, and on the front bench of counsel the Attorney-General, Sir Peter Rawlinson, prepares to rise and open the case for the prosecution.

This is the first trial in modern British legal history for kidnapping for ransom. (Our nearest example would appear to be a case in Australia, R.v.Bradley, in 1960.) Furthermore, it is an offence under Common Law here, but not statutory—as it is, for example, in France and the USA—which means that there is no prescribed punishment laid down.

The front bench of leading counsel shows the newspapers to have been wrong. They gave correctly Mr. Barry Hudson, QC, and Mr. Hubert Dunn for Arthur Hosein; but in giving only Mr. Leonard Woodley for Nizamodeen, they omitted Mr. Douglas Draycott, QC. Each brother has a leading counsel. So each brother has a separate defence.

'On the evening of 29 December, last year,' the Attorney-General begins, 'Mrs. McKay disappeared from her home at 20 Arthur Road, Wimbledon. She has never been seen again.' It is a dramatic opening; but although his manner is admirably polished, it is not in the least showy or theatrical.

The Crown alleges: 'This was a brutal and ruthless scheme to kidnap a wife, and by menaces to extort from her husband a vast sum of money.'

(A million pounds—we know that already).

The Attorney-General speaks of days and weeks in which Mr. McKay was subjected to a systematic series of threats by telephone and by letter, threats to execute his wife, threats to kill her. He leans forward a little towards the jury as he delivers straightaway what sounds as if it is going to be the essence of the Crown case for alleging murder:

'We may infer that those who threatened to kill did kill.'

The Attorney-General then launches the statement that the real intention of the kidnappers was to take another woman! She was Mrs. Rupert Murdoch, wife of the chairman of The News Of The World group of newspapers. Mrs. McKay's husband, Mr. Alick McKay, is deputy chairman.

Both Mr. McKay and Mr. Murdoch are Australian, and in the middle of December Mr. Murdoch and his wife went to Australia for a visit. In his absence, Mr. McKay was acting chairman, and as such had use of the chairman's Rolls-Royce, travelling to and fro in it between 20 Arthur Road and the newspaper offices. The kidnappers, tracing the car, thought they were going to take the wife of the chairman. Arthur Hosein, the Attorney-General now tells the jury, had spoken to neighbours, telling them of his desire to become a millionaire.

The story begins, the Attorney-General says, on 19 December — the date on which, unknown to the brothers, Mr. and Mrs. Rupert Murdoch left for Australia —when Mr. McKay began to use the Rolls-Royce.

So we come to 29 December, the day of Mrs. McKay's disappearance for ever. Mr. McKay left for the office in the Rolls; Mrs. McKay went in her own car to fetch the daily help, went shopping, visited her dentist, and then, at 5 p.m., drove the daily help home. The daily help was the last person ever to see Mrs. McKay alive—or dead. At that time Mrs. McKay was wearing a green jersey suit, a black-and-white check topcoat, and cream-coloured leather driving shoes.

At 7.45 p.m. Mr. McKay came home, got no answer to his ring on the doorbell, found the outer door not on the chain, opened the inner door, and saw a desolating sight. . . . Furniture disarranged; the telephone off the hook, the disc giving the number (ex-directory) having been removed; his wife's open handbag with its contents scattered; and some alien objects. . . . The Attorney-General suggests their purpose:

A billhook, such as might have been used for intimidating;

A strip of $2^1/_2$in. adhesive tape, for gagging;

Some baling twine, for trussing. . . .

Mrs. McKay's jewellery was gone, together with a reversible fawn and black topcoat.

Mr. McKay seized the billhook to arm himself, rushed through the house—Mrs. McKay's dachshund was sitting by the fire, and the television was on—and through the outbuildings. His wife was gone. In minutes the Wimbledon police arrived and a search was begun with dogs.

One of Mr. McKay's two married daughters, Diane Dyer, joined him at 11.15 p.m. with her husband David. Shortly afterwards, his other daughter, Jennifer Burgess, arrived with her husband Ian.

'At 1.15 in the morning of 30 December, five hours later, the first approach from the kidnappers reached the house.'

The call was from a public box at Epping—and it was overheard by the operator!

'Tell Mr. McKay it is the M3, the Mafia.'

A detective, listening on an extension, the Attorney-General says, took the conversation down.

'This is the Mafia Group 3. We are from America. Mafia M3. We have your wife.' And then: 'You will need £1,000,000 by Wednesday.' Today was Tuesday. 'We have your wife. You will need £1,000,000 to get her back. You had better get it. You have friends. Get it from them. Have £1,000,000 by Wednesday night or we will kill her.'

There was a second telephone call from M3 on the 30th; and that evening Mrs. Diane Dyer was interviewed on BBC television about her mother's disappearance.

On 31 December, there arrived at Arthur Road a letter, a heart-rending appeal in handwriting identified without doubt as Mrs. McKay's: 'Alick darling, I am blindfolded and cold. Please do something and get me home. Please co-operate or I cannot keep going. I think of you all constantly and have kept calm so far. What have I done to deserve this treatment?'

The letter had been posted in Tottenham, London N.17; and the sheet of paper bears two fingerprints—of, the Crown says, Arthur Hosein.

On 1 January, Mr. McKay's son, Ian, arrived at Arthur Road from Australia. That evening there was the next call, ending at 7.45 p.m., in which the caller asked to speak to Diane—he took to using the family's Christian names, it seems, without the least inhibition.

The Attorney-General mentions several letters from Mrs. McKay received at later dates; but, he suggests, they could have been written earlier and posted by degrees. During that period, he says, proofs repeatedly demanded by the family that Mrs. McKay was alive were refused.

Turning to the situation at Rook's Farm, Stocking Pelham (about twenty miles north of the northern edge of London), where the Hosein's lived, the Attorney-General notes that Arthur Hosein's wife had taken the children on a visit to her relations in Germany on 13 December and did not return until 3 January. . But on 31 December, only 48 hours after the kidnapping, a girl-friend of Nizam's came to stay overnight at the farm: in the Attorney-General's submission, Mrs. McKay must even then already have been dead.

On 19 January came a call ending at 3 p.m. The Attorney-General deliberately reads extracts from the transcript in a moderate tone. It makes unbearable hearing, in the anguish of Mr. McKay and the boasting of the blackmailer. He demands the first half, £500,000. Mr. McKay cries: 'Look, bring a gun here and shoot me rather than ask unreasonable situations!' (In his agonising emotion, grammar fails him.) Mr. McKay suggests a reasonable sum—he can raise £20,000. 'No use. Accept or reject. Half a million.'

The Attorney-General goes on to the next call, on 21 January, taken by Ian McKay, who says his father is now ill. The first discussions of a rendezvous take place. The Attorney-General says Ian had a police officer beside him, helping to suggest probing questions and to keep M3 on the line.

Ian asks what his mother says that proves that she is alive, but all he gets is M3's ranting.

A few minutes later, another call, this time about the date of the rendezvous. Ian had said his father was too ill to come—the police were determined, in case an international gang was at work, to protect Mr. McKay now. The date is to be 1 February. 'We want a million, but the first delivery has got to be half a million!'

The first ransom note arrived on 22 January. It warned the family not to inform the police and reiterated the demand for £1,000,000. It then gave Mr. McKay his instructions—on 1 February to place £½ million in a black suitcase, drive his wife's car along the North Circular Road to the A10 Cambridge road, where he would see a public telephone-box: to enter it and wait for a call at 10 p.m. The black suitcase is to be locked, as it will be collected by a stranger who is paid to do the job; if he is caught, he will not be able to help the police.

At 10.30 a.m. on 23 January, the telephone calls to Arthur Road resumed with growing agitation. On the McKay family side they were handled by Ian, demanding proof that his mother was still alive; M3 sounding pressed and relapsing into menaces. 'We won't be needing the money and you won't be seeing your mum.' Ian says they have a quarter of a million—but they need proof, another letter.

Fifteen minutes later, he is back on the line. Mrs. McKay is saying, he says to Ian, 'Why have they forsaken me?' On 26

January, a letter addressed to Mr. McKay and posted in London, N.22, was received at 20 Arthur Road. It contained two letters written by Mrs. McKay.

'Alick darling—If I could only be home. I can't believe this thing has happened to me. Tonight I thought I see you. But it seems hopeless. You betrayed me by going to Police, not co-operating with the M3 gang. Love Muriel.'

The other: 'Darling Alick—You don't seem to be helping me. Again I beg of you to co-operate with the M3 gang. You do understand that when the. . . .' There is something cut from the letter.

At 9 p.m. on 1 February, the Rolls leaves Arthur Road, driven by Detective-Inspector John Minors dressed as the chauffeur and with Detective-Sergeant Street disguised as Ian McKay. In the car they have a black suitcase containing bundles of false banknotes, each bundle has a genuine banknote on the top—half a million pounds!

The Rolls drives to the telephone box on the A10. 'Ian' duly receives the M3 call, which directs him to another box about forty minutes' drive down the Cambridge road. In the second box, a call comes through quite soon. 'Look on the floor! You'll see a cigarette packet with your instructions.'

They are to go to a place called Dane End—about fifteen miles further—in High Cross, Hertfordshire. There, at the road corner, they will see two paper flowers stuck in the bank as markers for the depositing of the suitcase.

The suitcase is deposited and the Rolls drives back to the first telephone box, following M3's instructions, to hear from Mrs. McKay. . . .

Further down the road from Dane End there is a café where police (presumably working on information steadily radioed from the Rolls) are watching. At 2.30 a.m. the suitcase is still there, and Mr. Minors is instructed to collect it, together with the paper flowers.

In the meantime, a dark-coloured Volvo saloon has passed the café, where two police officers are watching from a taxi. In the Volvo are a driver and a passenger with bushy hair. The rear nearside light of the car is observed not to be working. The Hosein's car, the Attorney-General reminds us, is a Volvo, and when it was examined by detectives ten days later, the nearside rear light was found not to be working.

The Attorney-General returns to 3 February. There were two calls from M3 to Ian McKay. In the first, M3 says he is going to a meeting of the bosses, 'the semi-intellectuals,' to settle the time at which 'your Mum' should be executed. As for the suitcase: 'You know why I didn't even touch it. My boss, the Head Boy, was there. All The Boys were there. We saw cars parked all round there. Did you know they were all police?'

Two hours later came the second call. Another attempt to collect the ransom is on the tapis. 'The Boys' insist on delivery being made by Mr. McKay and Diane. M3 proposes they should bring the money this time in two briefcases. They must go in the Rolls, driven by Mr. McKay, first to a telephone kiosk in Church Street, Tottenham, at 4 p.m.

So, on February 6, Detective-Inspector Minors, made up as Mr. McKay, and a woman police officer disguised as Diane set off in the Rolls. At the first kiosk 'Mr. McKay' is directed to a second kiosk at Bethnal Green—M3 demands to speak to 'Diane' to make sure she is there. They are told to take the Tube to Epping, then go to a specified telephone kiosk there. They drive to Theydon Bois, park the Rolls and get in the Tube—a member of the Flying Squad is in the same compartment.

At Epping they are told by M3 to take a taxi to Bishop's Stortford, stopping at Gates Garage, where in the used-car lot they will see a Minivan, UMH 587F. They are to drop the suitcases beside it.

Five minutes after the two suitcases have been deposited, the watching police officers see a dark blue Volvo, XGO 994G, being driven slowly past the used-car lot; neither of the nearside obligatory lights is working. The driver is alone. He looks out and drives slowly on. The Attorney-General says he has subsequently been identified as Nizam.

At 10.47 p.m. the Volvo comes back, but now with a man in the passenger seat—a man who has been subsequently identified, according to the prosecution, as Arthur Hosein.

At 11 p.m. two well-meaning members of the public drive by. They see the apparently abandoned suitcases, and stop; one gets out to stand guard while the other telephones the local police, who immediately come and take the suitcases away!

On 7 February, having traced the owners of the Volvo, a party of police, led by Detective Chief Superintendent Wilfred Smith, who has been in charge of the investigation with Detective-Inspector Minors as his second-in command, went to Rook's Farm with a search warrant for stolen jewellery, Mrs. McKay's jewellery.

During the search which followed, the police discovered:

An empty Elastoplast tin of the size to hold $2^1/_2$ in. tape;

Six paper flowers in various places—home-made, like those used as markers;

An empty tipped-cigarette packet.

'On further search, six days later,' the Attorney-General adds with devastating effect, 'the police found a pair of trousers belonging to Nizam, in the left-hand pocket of which was a piece of paper giving the number of the Minivan UMH 587F at Gates Garage used-car lot.' In the search of Arthur's workroom, Chief Superintendent Smith took possession of two pairs of tailor's shears; in the kitchen he found a billhook.

The brothers were taken in separate police cars to Kingston Police Station. On the way, Arthur pointed out Sleepy Hollow Farm, home of a farmer-friend who, he says, lent the billhook to chop up a calf that had died.

But there are two billhooks. The other one is the one left at 20 Arthur Road, and it has been traced, the Crown alleges, to Arthur's home.

The Attorney-General reports interrogations.

Nizam gives handwriting specimens. He is shown the billhook from Arthur Road, and starts to shake, closes his eyes; the baling twine—more shaking of the head; then the sticking plaster—he suddenly cries: 'Let me die!'

On the night of 10 February there is a final confrontation between Arthur and Chief Superintendent Smith, in which Arthur furiously says: 'If you've got anything on me, then book me!' A little later, the brothers Hosein are formally charged with the murder of Mrs. McKay and with demanding a million pounds by menaces from Mr. McKay.

The first witness to be called is Mr. Alick McKay.

The Attorney-General examines him, bringing out more detail of the familiar story. His return home, on the evening of 20 December. Photographs of the scene in the hall, as he saw it, are passed round to the jury. The process of identifying the exhibits is begun concurrently with eliciting the story.

There is a moment at which the oppression is lifted from Mr. McKay, as he identifies his wife's handbag. 'It has a special catch.' As he finds it and springs it open, he looks up with a triumphant smile, as if taken out of himself, perhaps taken back to the time when his wife first showed it to him. He identifies the baling twine, the billhook—he can hardly look at it in his hands, though he watches it being passed round the jury.

Mr. McKay goes on with his story. The fire built up, the dog sleeping in front of it. Then his rush through the house: the missing jewellery, valued for insurance at £600. Mrs. McKay had lost most of her jewellery in a burglary the previous September. That was why she was nervous and kept the chain on the front door always.

He describes calling the police, the arrival of his two daughters and their husbands, friends coming round to the house as the news spread . . . The first call, at 1.15 a.m., from M3.

More telephone-calls and the question of identifying the kind of voice, or voices. 'Sometimes softer and deeper,' says Mr. McKay, 'with a stronger American accent.' The conclusion: that they were West Indian.

And so on to the final questions. 'Was there a great deal of publicity?' And, 'All your children were very close to their mother?' Mr. McKay nods. The Attorney-General sits down.

Mr. Hudson, for Arthur Hosein, cross-examines.

We now hear of hoaxes, other police traps and all the rest of it, giving intimations of mountainous detail behind the scenes. Mr. Hudson sits down. And solitarily, almost unceremoniously, Mr. McKay leaves the witness-box.

The morning of 16 September, and the third day of the trial begins with the other members of the McKay family: the two daughters, Diane and Jennifer, with their respective husbands, David Dyer and Ian Burgess: and the son, Ian, who flew in from Australia on 31 January.

The young women have the well-dressed, affluent look one would expect. Their father has an Australian accent: they have not. Their husbands are apparently English. So far as physical resemblance goes, it is only strong between father and son—and there it is very strong. They both have the same heavy build, the same rather pale complexion and small light eyes, the same thinning dark hair.

David Dyer goes into the witness-box first. He took M3's first call: like Mr. McKay, he has heard the tapes so often since that he has to pause and think which is which. Mr. Hudson cross-examines him about whether he thinks call No. 2 and call No. 3 from M3 were made by different voices from that of the call he took. 'Similar,' he says.

Diane Dyer, slender and nervous, with her hair drawn back into a high bunch of curls, has to identify her mother's clothes, the letters, the pieces of material. But the essential part of her evidence is about when she spoke on television, as well as being seen.

(It seems now that both prosecution and defence must believe that the last moment at which they can be certain Mrs. McKay was still alive was shortly after her daughter spoke on TV.)

Ian McKay makes a brief appearance, alert and businesslike — he knows the telephone calls by their numbers and does not need to refer to the transcripts.

Jennifer Burgess, sun-tanned and subdued-looking under a big white felt safari hat, took one of M3's telephone calls. 'I gave my sister's name because he usually spoke to her.' Another vista into the repulsive Christian-name intimacy forced by the blackmailers on the family. 'I wanted to negotiate as quickly as possible.'

More prosecution witnesses followed. Among them, Detective Chief Superintendent Harvey, who led the police expedition to Rook's Farm at 1.45 p.m. on 7 February.

We get a description of the sitting-room at Rook's Farm—photographs are passed round the jury. A biggish room with beams across the ceiling, and a style of furnishing appropriate to what would be called a 'lounge'—an open fireplace, a curved bar with a couple of stools, some sofas, a radiogram, a television set. Incidentally, there is nothing either cheap-looking or inappropriate looking to contemporary dormitory-belt society about Rook's Farm. It is pretty from the outside, eighteenth century, painted white.

Mr. Hudson cross-examines about the extensive searches of Rook's Farm in February and March, also others in June, July, and as recently as 10 August. Police officers galore, police dogs galore.

Mr. Draycott, for Nizam, rises. 'Is it right to say Rook's Farm has been searched as scrupulously as it is possible to search anything?'—'Yes.'

'Every skill has been employed?'—'Yes.'

'And there is no trace of Mrs. McKay having been on that farm?' 'No trace whatsoever.'

No trace whatsoever.

The Attorney-General re-examines about the sheds, the dark outhouses with bales of straw, the calves and the pigs; the surface of the passage—hard—to where the rubbish was dumped by a stream.

There is an intermission in police evidence while Mrs. McKay's doctor testifies to her having been in good health, cheerful, stable and strong-minded.

The police evidence now comes to the two chief men in the case, Detective Chief Superintendent Smith, who led the whole investigation, and Detective-Inspector Minors, who assisted him— also chauffeuring the Rolls in the first ransom-delivering expedition and disguising himself as Mr. Alick McKay in the second. It is mainly due to these two men that the brothers Hosein are now in the dock.

Detective-Inspector Minors comes first. He is a big chap, full cheeked, very fresh-complexioned and blue-eyed, with smooth darkish hair and a moustache. The Attorney-General takes him through what is now the familiar story.

We come to 7 February at Rook's Farm, the search and the findings. Then the drive to Kingston Police Station, Arthur continually discoursing on his universal popularity, his intention of standing for the local council, the influence 'in high places' of his wealthy father. And at the police station the first questions about 29 December and Wimbledon.

The following day, Mr. Minors's examination-in-chief continues. We hear again about the continuing interrogations at Kingston Police Station of Arthur and Nizam alternately about the events of 6 February.

Nizam refused, like Arthur, to sign his statements; and, furthermore, refused to speak into the telephone for recording tests. In the evening Arthur and Nizam were told they were going to be taken to Wimbledon Police Station, where they would be charged. Arthur: 'I have nothing to say, Mr. Smith. You have your job to do.' Nizam made no reply at all.

Then there were the extraordinary scenes, we hear, resulting from Nizam's asking to see Mr. Smith and Mr. Minors without his legal representatives present.

At the second such meeting came Nizam's extraordinary statement: 'I could get out of ninety per cent of this trouble if I put my cards on the table.'

Mr. Smith: 'What do you want to tell us?' After a silence, Nizam replied: 'I want to think . . . I'll leave it till another day.'

Mr. Hudson rises and points out that the brothers were held in custody from Saturday, 7 February, to Tuesday, 10 February, 'assisting the police' without being charged with anything.

Mr. Hudson gets Mr. Minors's assent to Arthur's complete denial of all knowledge of the crime, and comes to the last of his questions raised by what Arthur may say in the witness-box—that Mr. Smith slapped him across the face. Mr. Minors: 'No, sir. That's news to me.'

Now Mr. Draycott slides smoothly and sweetly into a quite different line. 'I have no quarrel with your evidence,' he says: 'I want you to assist me about Nizam. At Wimbledon Police Station, when he was seen on 12 June, he was on the brink of telling you something. He wanted to, but something held him back.' Mr. Minors: 'We felt it did.'

Mr. Draycott: 'Would you agree with me that, having seen these two brothers over a long period, it is abundantly clear, abundantly plain, that Nizam's relationship with his brother is unusual, in that it is based not on brotherly affection but on fear?'

Mr. Minors: 'That would appear to be the case.'

Mr. Draycott, still with most amicable courtesy—why should they quarrel?—says: 'Nizam's fingerprints have been taken. You agree with me, do you not, that there is no evidence of fingerprints to connect Nizamodeen Hosein with Mrs. McKay's home at Arthur Road, Wimbledon?' He eyes the jury sagely. Mr. Minors: 'No, sir.'

Detective Chief Superintendent Smith is called. He is shortish and very strongly built. The Attorney-General examines him on substantially the same points as he did Mr. Minors, since the two men worked together all the time. Mr. Hudson, addressing Mr. Smith as the senior officer in charge of the case, establishes that Arthur Hosein has no previous convictions for violence or dishonesty. He has convictions for speeding offences and was court-martialled for desertion in 1960.

Mr. Hudson points out that after the charges were made, there were seventeen remands until the hearings began at Wimbledon on 8 June. During that time there were further searches; if there was anything to be found, there was a better chance if the brothers were not in possession.

Mr. Hudson goes through some of the details of the investigation for Mr. Smith's agreement. The Aga heater was dismantled. An architect and a builder were consulted about possible secret compartments. Ponds were drained by the fire brigade. The hedges and ditches in surrounding fields were searched, Sleepy Hollow . . .

'Also Epping Forest,' says Mr. Smith wryly.

Finally: 'I now put this to you, personally. I suggest that during some parts of the investigation at Kingston Police Station, you punched Arthur Hosein and slapped him across the face.'

'That is not true.'

Later, Mrs. Liley Mohammed, Nizam's girl-friend, is called. We know already from the Attorney-General that she spent the night of 31 December at Rook's Farm. She is a hospital nurse, a bit short, dressed in a brown-and-white striped suit. She looks frightened. Her face is oval, her hair drawn back from it into a high double bunch of curls like a more African version of Mrs. Diane Dyer's.

The Attorney-General examines. Mrs. Mohammed—she soon becomes known as Liley—says she first spent the night at Rook's Farm on 26 December.

Liley visited the farm, just for the day, in the early part of January, and then about a week later. Mrs. Hosein and the children were there. Liley is now shown a box of coloured tissues with some paper clips. 'It belongs to me.'

The Attorney-General asks about a visit when she took some paper flowers she had made and gave them to Nizam.

Mr. Hudson then cross-examines, beginning with her visit on Boxing Day, when at first she did not want to go.

While she was at the farm she saw only Nizam and Arthur; she did not leave the farm. Mr. Hudson: 'You told us about several subsequent visits to the farm. Did you get the impression on any of those visits that there was anything there to hide?'—'No.'

Mr. Hudson pauses. 'At the farm, did you sometimes go out with Nizam while he was looking after the animals?'— 'Yes.'—'You helped him to skin the calf?'—'Yes.'

Then Mr. Draycott gets a surprising revelation. Referring to Boxing Night, he says: 'I believe there was some trouble between Arthur and Nizam that night. In the course of that trouble, did Nizam get very frightened?'—'He did.'—'And run out?'—'Yes.'—'And when he came back, did he say he'd made a complaint to the police?'—'He did.'

Mr. Draycott pauses. 'Less than seventy-two hours before they were allegedly going to kidnap Mrs. McKay, Nizam called in the police!'

The Attorney-General re-examines.

'Did you know about the workshop?' he asks. Liley did not—not until Mrs. Hosein came back.

'What was the calf cut up with?'—'A long knife. It looked like a chopper.'

'I don't suppose you went to the shed where the dogs were kept?'—'No, I did not.'

The law seems to take a long time, and the impression is not mitigated by the order in which witnesses are called. As we begin the last day of witnesses for the prosecution (21 September), it is difficult to see what order there has been. No doubt they were in the first place put down in an order that matched the development of the prosecution case. But that, for one reason or another—we have been told from time to time that a witness was not available—is not the order in which they turned up.

However, there has been a weekend in which to freshen up.

What is the defence going to be? What on earth *can* it be?

The Attorney-General announces the end of the Crown case. But all is not finished. Mr. Hudson has something more to say. He stands up and tells His Lordship that he wants to make a submission in the absence of the jury.

The jury are sent out. Then Mr. Hudson, with Mr. Draycott associated with him, makes a submission:

That on Count 1, murder, in the circumstances of the evidence before the jury, the case should not proceed further.

Mr. Hudson argues that what became of Mrs. McKay is, on the evidence, the basis not for rational hypothesis but only for speculation.

'There is a prima-facie case, I agree, that she is dead. But I submit there is not one scintilla of evidence that she was at Rook's Farm or met her death at Rook's Farm.'

Mr. Draycott, who has been whispering to his junior, now joins in, to argue that Mrs. McKay could not have been at Rook's Farm—meanwhile, Arthur and Nizam, according to the evidence of Liley, *were* for most of the time at Rook's Farm.

The Judge listens. He looks at them. There is no other rational hypothesis, he tells them, than that those who abducted Mrs. McKay are responsible for the fact that she is not on this earth. There *is* cause for the jury to consider Count 1.

It is the morning of 23 September.

'Members of the jury, there is a great deal more evidence in this case than you have already heard.'

So begins Mr. Hudson in the defence of Arthur Hosein. He leans a little forward towards the jury: 'Arthur Hosein's defence,' he says, 'is that he had nothing to do with this dreadful crime at all!'

Arthur Hosein denies his guilt. It is not enough to say that. In support of his protestation of innocence, he will go into the witness-box, though he is not compelled to.

We all look at the dock, where a warder is opening the side door. Arthur Hosein goes down the steps, walks past the long table in the well of the court, and ascends the steps into the witness-box. He is smaller than I thought, seeing him on high in the dock. And for the occasion he has selected a slightly peculiar garb—at first sight it looks as if he is in a dinner-suit. It is black, single-breasted, with a U-shaped waistcoat that displays a bulging white expanse of chest under a black bow-tie. But the collar and cuffs of the white shirt are black with white polka-dots. 'Selected' is the correct word: he has appeared in a different suit every day, and is reported to own fifty suits. (How does he keep *that* up, as well as Rook's Farm, the Volvo, and all the rest?). We have already heard of his boastfulness; his appearance makes one suspect that he is vain.

In the witness-box he stands a moment under the shadow of the light-oak canopy and against the dreary background of light oak, his hand to his face, touching his moustache. The black and white collar makes it difficult to see which is his neck and which is his shirt. He gives his profession:

'Fashion designer, cutter, etc.'

His counsel, Mr. Hudson, asks: 'Where did you spend Christmas Day?'—'At home in Hertfordshire.' The details of Monday the 29th. 'My usual, awake between 11 and 12. I had a terrible cold. There was a 'flu epidemic. Nizam was up; it was his duty to look after the animals.'—'Did you go out?' 'I buy milk by bulk, so I keep calves—to get rid of the milk. Nizam said we had too much milk, could we have more calves? I didn't mind, said the fresh air might do me good. So we went to Pateman's farm, between 2.30 and 3.30.' Later: 'After Nizam and Pateman put the calf in the boot of the car, we went back to Rook's Farm.'

'What then?' Mr. Hudson asks. Arthur: 'I told Nizam to take care of the rest.'

And then? 'Mr. Coote telephoned between 5.15 and 5.30. I advised Nizam to take any telephone calls about business. Nizam came in and told me it's Mr. Coote, so I spoke to Mr. Coote.'

Mr. Hudson: 'What did you do for the rest of the evening?' Arthur: 'I told him who David Coote was.'—'Did your brother stay?'—'After making me something to eat, coffee and biscuits.' — 'Did your brother stay in the house?'—'I bid him goodnight at 7.30. I took up a bottle of scotch and ginger ale to my bedroom, closed the door. There was I.'

'When you went to bed, did you do something with the telephone? Someone rang up?' Arthur: 'Yes, yes, I knew who it was, at about eight o'clock. I pressed the bell-button to switch off the bell, for Nizam to answer downstairs.'

Mr. Hudson moves on to 30 December.

'Did anyone call at the Farm that day?'

Arthur thinks—he seems disturbed. 'I can't remember!'

Mr. Hudson reminds him of the 31st, when they collected Mrs. Mohammed in the car to come to the Farm. On 1 January, she says he, Arthur, never left the Farm. Can he recall Nizam leaving the Farm? Arthur: 'I think he mentioned a bit of fresh air. I can't give the precise time.'

Mr. Hudson comes back yet again to telephone calls. 'I have two questions: Did you make any telephone calls to Wimbledon?' Arthur: 'I made no telephone calls to anyone at any time.' Mr. Hudson, with his second question: 'Did you hear anyone in your house telephoning?' Arthur: 'Well, sometimes . . . I might be wrong about these telephone . . .'

The Judge asks him to take his hand down, and repeats the question.

Arthur (looking down): 'I believe that during the absence of my wife . . . No, I never heard anyone using my telephone, or any voices.'

Mr. Hudson studies the details of the trip to the tailoring 'finishers'. The schedule is important because of the M3 calls directing the ransom-bringer ultimately to Dane End, calls at 9.55 p.m. and 10.45 p.m., and the Volvo was seen at Dane End at 11.45 p.m.

Arthur and Nizam left Rook's Farm soon after six. The Judge asks how long the journey took to the first finisher. Three-quarters of an hour. Arthur confirms that Nizam borrowed money to telephone. The last finisher they visited was at Hackney Wick, at 7.50 p.m. After that, Arthur sent Nizam into a pub to buy him some cigarettes. 'What did he do?'—'I waited for ten minutes, circulated, assumed he'd gone to his girl-friend.' Then: 'I know my brother can find his way home, so I went home.'

Mr. Hudson: 'What time did you go to bed?' Arthur: 'I sat in the lounge, had a drink, I'm enthusiastic about news—saw the Ten O'clock News. Then we both went to bed.'

Mrs. Hosein was worried about Nizam, who returned at midnight, disturbing the house. 'His clothing was wet. I said, "Take off your clothes or you'll get pneumonia!"' Later Nizam's story comes out: he telephoned Liley, who was not in, so he'd hitch-hiked home. 'He is twelve years my junior, a stranger in a strange land. My duty is to protect him. I didn't want to provoke him. But all the while I had considerable concern about him in this country.'

We pass on to 6 February. (M3 calls the telephone kiosk in Church Street, Tottenham, at 4.45 p.m., in Bethnal Green at 6 p.m., in Epping at 7.30 p.m. Nizam is at Gates Garage at 9.00 p.m.). Arthur and Nizam delivered goods to the tailors that afternoon. Arthur interrupts himself to say to the Judge: 'I've said I made no telephone calls. I meant for the ransom. I made calls about business.'

Then they made for home. Mr. Hudson: 'What time did you arrive at the Raven Pub?' 'I shall remember to my dying day! It was very cold. I sat at the front of the taxi. Between seven o'clock and five past seven.'

Mr. Hudson: 'What time, Mr. Hosein, did you leave The Raven?'— 'At 10.20.' 'What time did the pub close?'— 'Eleven o'clock.' 'What happened then?'—'My brother drove me home. I said goodnight . . .'

Mr. Hudson asks for Arthur to be handed Exhibit 5, a billhook. Arthur handles it possibly with interest, certainly not with revulsion: he touches the blade casually.

Mr. Hudson now asks for him to be handed the other billhook (taken by the police from the Rook's Farm kitchen on 7 February). Arthur behaves in the same way with it. 'Do you use a billhook?' Arthur begins: 'A calf died through mishandling. We were going to bury it.' The Judge: 'Did you chop the calf up?'—'I instructed my brother to.' The Judge: 'Was it fed to the dogs?' Arthur: 'I believe so.'

(What everyone is thinking about cannot be uttered, because there is not the faintest trace of forensic evidence to justify it, not the faintest trace.)

Mr. Hudson's examination-in-chief continues during the afternoon. He asks about Arthur's letter-writing habits, letters to his relations in the West Indies—airmail paper was found at Rook's Farm. 'Did you write the ransom letters?' Arthur: 'Good heavens—I'd be stark staring mad!' Mr. Hudson: 'Did you write the directions on the cigarette packet?'—'No.' 'Have you any knowledge at all about the despatch of these letters and the calls to this telephone?' Arthur: 'I have absolutely no knowledge of these suggestions.' Mr. Hudson sits down. That is the end of that.

Mr. Draycott turns to the album of photographs of Rook's Farm. The tumbledown building used as a dog kennel, the coalhouse with a piece of sacking in place of a door. The work-room, a big room at the front of the house, no curtains to the window so as to give as much light as possible. 'Was Mrs. McKay ever at the Farm?' Arthur: 'I haven't met, seen, or heard of such a person.'

The night of Sunday, 1 February, when Arthur and Nizam parted company. Mr. Draycott persists in dealing with the circumstances in which they parted company. Nizam will say they both drove towards Dane End together. Arthur says he drove home on the A11, alone. (Dane End is on the A10). Nizam will say Arthur told him to plant the paper flowers.

Arthur says he was at home by 9.30. Then there was a quarrel, suggests Mr. Draycott. 'No.' 'Because you told Nizam to go back and pick up the suitcase, and he wanted to know what it was about?'

'There was a row, a fight,' Mr. Draycott goes on, with his quiet, formal intimacy. 'Nizam was tipped out of the car and was on his own. That's why he arrived home soaking wet, after you?'—'I sent him to buy cigarettes and I didn't see him till midnight.'

The Attorney-General turns to the letters and fingerprints. On the 30th, M3 said he had posted a letter to Mr. McKay. 'Were you in London on that day?' Arthur: 'No.' 'The letter arrived. It is said to bear your thumbprint. Did you handle any such letter before it was posted?' Arthur: 'No.' He argues that it would have to be proved that it was his thumbprint and that it had been taken from his home. 'It is possible that my home was used, unknown to me.'

When Arthur realises his last moment in the witness-box has come, he addresses the court:

'Believe me, I have great sympathy for the McKay family. I have a mother myself. I am no murderer even if I am found guilty. These hands'—he holds them out—'are artistic, not destructive. I believe in the preservation of Man. That is what I am living for!'

As other defence witnesses are called, the tiny panorama of English society in the dormitory-belt resumes its unfolding.

Mrs. Hosein makes her way through the court. She is a good-looking woman, bigger than her husband; blonde and blue-eyed. When she returned from Germany on 3 January did she see anything unusual about the Farm? asks Mr. Dunn, Mr. Hudson's junior.—'No.'

Mr. Dunn goes on to 6 February, the night of Arthur's coming home from The Raven. 'He'd had a few. As usual he was very hungry. And then we went to bed.'

Mrs. Hosein now has to face the Attorney-General. He wants to know whether a calf had died while she was in Germany: 'No.' Any more when she got back? One more.

Now we see another Hosein brother: Adam. He is short, stronger and heavier than Arthur, and he has a deep strong voice. He is a businessman, an insurance-broker, living in Thornton

Heath. Mr. Hudson elicits that Nizam turned up at 11.30 p.m. on the night of 29 December in Arthur's Volvo, delivering some trousers and collecting some shirts. His behaviour was normal. He mentioned that some people were helping him to get a permanent visa, but did not say who. He said Arthur was in bed ill.

Locations and routes are checked. Thornton Heath is twenty minutes' drive from Wimbledon. Finally a note Nizam wrote to Adam from Brixton Prison is produced. 'Did you read it?'—'Not really.'—'Did you realise he was asking you not to tell anyone he had been to your home on Monday evening?'—'At the time I didn't understand.'

Now we come to the defence forensic expert and prepare ourselves for an accumulation of minute detail over an inordinate length of time. The defence expert is Dr. Julius Grant, Vice-President of the Forensic Society.

They go over the fingerprints. Then: 'I find a number of similarities in the writing,' says Dr. Grant, 'and I reached the conclusion that there is reasonable doubt that Arthur Hosein wrote the letters. But I cannot exclude the possibility that he did.'

The evidence of Dr. Grant concludes on 25 September. The court momentarily lapses into a short busy spell of re-sorting papers and documents. And then it becomes one hundred per cent attentive. Mr. Draycott is going to call his client to the witness-box.

The warder opens the door of the dock, and Nizam does not glance at his brother as he passes him to go out.

He stands in the witness-box looking nervous, shy, slightly lost. His voice appears to be non-existent.

Finally, the judge suggests one of those small microphones you wear round your neck and Nizam agrees. It is produced from somewhere and he stands submissively while it is hung round his neck.

Mr. Draycott begins with establishing the relationship between the two brothers. Fear . . . 'I was afraid of him,' Nizam whispers. Mr. Draycott probes further. Nizam says in a soft, nearly non-existent voice: 'Whenever I don't do something he tells me to do, he has a go at me.'

We come to 28 December and the visits of the police officers.

Two different lots, one about Nizam's complaint, the other about 'another matter'. 'Did they come regularly?' Mr. Draycott asks. 'Yes, to check if everything is all right.'

Then the 29th. Mr. Draycott: 'As far as you can say, the day began in the ordinary way?'—'Yes, sir.' On the 29th Arthur left in the Volvo—whose lights Nizam knew to be defective—at about 3 p.m. for the finishers. Nizam fed the animals, as usual, at 4 p.m. He next saw Arthur at about 8.15, when Arthur complained of 'flu and went to bed.

When he thought Arthur was asleep, Nizam went to look and saw him under the feather quilt. He then borrowed the Volvo, to go and see first his relatives at Norbury Crescent, and then his brother Adam at Thornton Heath.

One of the next points is the death of the calf while Mrs. Hosein was away and the decision about what to do with it.

Then Sunday, 1 February. Mr. Draycott: 'Did you drive to Dane End?'—'Yes, sir.'—'What did Arthur say?'—'There were two paper flowers on the dashboard. He said I was to stick them in the ground on the corner of the road.'

Instead of driving home, Arthur told him to drive back to London. 'Did he make a further request?' asks Mr. Draycott. 'Yes. He said he would leave the car with me and I would be going back to pick up a black suitcase where I had put the flowers. And I asked him why.'—'Did he make any reply?'—'He asked me if I was going to do as I was told.'

Mr. Draycott goes through the events of 6 February. Nizam had been in London with Arthur, and at Bishop's Stortford Arthur stopped the car and told Nizam to go back to Gates Garage's used-car lot, where he would see two black suitcases opposite a Minivan. He was to pick them up, not to open them, and come to The Raven.

Nizam is asked: 'Did you try and think of an excuse for not picking them up?'—'Yes. I could tell him they were white, not black.'—'Could you have picked them up?'—'Yes, sir.'—'But you didn't.'—'No, sir.'

The suitcases were left there, and Nizam never got an explanation from Arthur of what it was all about. The next day, the police came with the search warrant for some stolen jewellery. Mr. Draycott: 'Had Arthur told you what to do?' Nizam: 'Keep my mouth shut.'

We go on to the police station. Nizam did not realise the situation till Chief Superintendent Smith showed him the paper flowers and the billhook from Arthur Road. Then he was very frightened.

The following day, Nizam is still in the witness-box. Mr. Hudson stands: 'Why didn't you agree to speak on the telephone at the police station, as your brother did?' 'I didn't know what was happening. I was frightened . . .'

Mr. Hudson: 'I suggest what you've been telling us about fear is an invention. You've told us that when you were with the police under interrogation, you were afraid to tell them what you've been telling the court now.' Pause. 'You were brave enough to call in the police on 28 December when you made a complaint?'—'Yes, because Arthur was doing something wrong . . .'

Mr. Hudson pounces: 'What bigger incentive to tell the police than when you were held on a graver charge—why didn't you?' Nizam (cowering): 'I couldn't get myself together . . .'

In time, Mr. Hudson launches into the final gambit. 'I suggest that you are quite capable of dealing with a situation involving violence.' Nizam shakes his head.

'And that you are not afraid of people?' Nizam is soundless.

Now the final cross-examination by the Attorney-General.

He refers to the journey back, through Epping; the call at 1.15 a.m. Nizam: 'I could have been in the area, but I didn't make the call.' The Attorney-General has the transcript of the M3 call handed to Nizam. 'Will you read it? "This is Mafia Group 3" and so on.'

Nizam reads, just audibly, hesitating occasionally.

More questions. 'Were you involved in the fact that Mrs. McKay was missing?' Nizam: 'I was involved with the paper flowers.' Attorney-General: 'Then why should you say "let me die"?' Nizam (on the edge of breaking down): 'Mr. Smith said I'd murdered her. Mr. Smith said it was not a calf I chopped up, it was a woman . . .'

The words are out! The words that have never, so far, been uttered in the court.

The Attorney-General moves to Tuesday, 30 December. After six hours' driving in the early hours about Surrey and Hertfordshire, what else was he doing? Nizam says he didn't feel good.

Was he watching TV? He doesn't remember. Did he see Mrs. Dyer? 'No.' Does he know her Christian name? 'Diane.' The Attorney-General produces transcripts of the next M3 call at 4.30 p.m., and makes Nizam read them aloud. 'Your wife just posted a letter . . . Don't call the police! You have been followed . . . Did you get the money . . .?'

On 29 September Nizam is still in the witness-box. The Attorney-General cross-examining. On Thursday, 1 January, Liley was at the Farm; Liley had wanted to go to a party, but Nizam had to look after the animals. She was scared of Arthur, but Arthur 'had promised not to interfere with her again'. It was important, Nizam agrees, not to leave her with Arthur. Yet he did.

The Attorney-General tries to make him fix the time. There were two M3 calls before 8 p.m. Nizam says 'evening, 3 p.m.' 'You call that evening?'—'In Trinidad we call it evening.' When he left, Arthur and Liley were watching television. 'In the *afternoon*?' (TV does not begin till later. But if it were what we in England call evening, television would have begun.)

Later comes the dreadful call to Ian about his mother being very worried, offering herself to the doctor. Attorney-General: 'Do you realise what a terrible thing it was for a son to hear those words?'—'Yes sir.'—'Did you speak them?'—'I never did.'

The Attorney-General has marshalled his next notes: he begins the final assault. The second ransom-attempt.

The Attorney-General points out that he, Nizam, wrote the name and number of the Minivan on the piece of paper which was subsequently found in his pocket. Nizam says he wrote it down while he was on the Bishop's Stortford road.

Isn't it more believable that he noted down the number much earlier in order to give it over the telephone to Mr. Alick McKay? The Attorney-General hammers it in with one accusing question after another. Nizam looks more frightened.

The Attorney-General moves on to the police arrival at Rook's Farm on the following day, saying first that they were looking for stolen jewellery, then for a missing woman, then for Mrs. McKay. 'You remember being shown the paper flowers by the police? Did you realise then that the suitcases and the paper flowers had something to do with the kidnapping?' Nizam: 'Yes, sir.' 'Why didn't you tell the police?'—'I was scared . . .'

Shortly, tears are in Nizam's eyes.

'You said to Detective-Sergeant Parker, "Oh my God, what have I done? Arthur always gets me into trouble."'

'I didn't know what I'd done!. . .' He is breaking down. 'Was it your desire to die because you knew you'd done something dreadful?' Nizam: 'I'd rather die than be charged with murder . . .' He is unable to speak for weeping. The Attorney-General sits down. Nizam gets out his handkerchief, standing there helplessly.

Eventually the evidence of Nizam is over. He returns from the witness-box to the dock. His counsel calls no further witnesses. The whole case for the defence of both brothers is over.

The Attorney-General's closing speech, like his opening speech, is relatively short.

Standing up straight and tall, he tells the jury, in his untheatrical, man-to-man tone, that he will not be repeating what he has said before. The jury will accept what the Judge says is the law: they will decide what is fact.

Of the brothers, he says that each is trying to saddle the other with some or all of the guilt. 'The crime,' he says, 'was committed by both.'

What is suggested by the Crown, he says, is that those two, calling themselves M3, kidnapped that woman: seeking Mrs. Murdoch, they found Mrs. McKay. He emphasises the jury's role in considering the situation. It is not a matter of law; the Judge will direct them on that. 'No,' he says: 'If you are satisfied there are such circumstances as render the committing of the crime certain, that there is no rational hypothesis except that the crime was committed, then you are entitled to conclude that she was murdered.' He pauses, and then exhorts them to think of the threats to execute, the total silence after the brothers were arrested. There is no rational hypothesis but that she met her death at their hands.

He calls for a verdict of Guilty on all counts for both brothers.

We now come to the closing speeches for the defence.

'This is the last time that I, who am charged with defending this man, Arthur Hosein, shall have the chance to speak to you on his behalf.'

Mr. Hudson has folded up his spectacles and put away his notes. He has begun a speech that will last for many hours.

Having dealt, often in detail, with just about every aspect of the evidence, he comes to 'one last word, which may be of importance in the jury room'. His tone is quieter now that he is on ground where there can be no possibility of anyone being against him. 'All human beings are vulnerable. Don't allow your anger at an ordinary woman being brutally kidnapped, at the anguish of those near and dear to her . . . don't let it affect your reason! Because it has taken place, we all want the people responsible to be brought to justice. But only if you are sure . . . It must be something of which you are sure.'

Finally: 'On all the charges, I submit, there is reasonable doubt. Arthur Hosein has never given any indication, he has emphatically denied, knowing anything about the crime. If there's just a possibility that what he's said so often may be true, you must find him Not Guilty.'

Mr. Draycott, Nizam's counsel, is on his feet, looking small and sturdy, strong-nosed and bright-eyed, ready as ever with lively terrier-like energy to address the jury in his own, special, examining manner.

He exhorts the jury to be careful to consider each man separately, and each count against each one. 'Don't approach it as "the Hoseins", "the brothers", unless the evidence compels you to it. It is a very, very easy mistake to make.'

It is only a few moments before he has his finger on the essential fantasy of the case, the demand for a million pounds; and he is fixing it directly on Arthur. Grandiose ideas, lack of grasp of reality. . . . He quotes Arthur: 'I am very sorry for you, Mr. Smith. You have a very difficult case to solve.'

'The whole thing,' says Mr. Draycott, 'is the plan of a mind that has no understanding or grasp of reality.' Having established Arthur's being thus off his rocker, he goes on: 'So that when Nizam gives you to understand, and the police give you grounds to understand, that the relationship between these two was not a normal one, there was no affection but only fear, that point has been established time and time again.'

Mr. Draycott reiterates some of the most cogent of the defence arguments, linking them with the idea that somebody else must be concerned in the case.

Then he invites the jury to consider Arthur's attitude to Nizam. 'Isn't it a waste of time to say Nizam was not afraid of Arthur, when domination and fear is everybody's evidence?'

Mr. Draycott asks the jury to look at Nizam's attitude to Arthur. 'Put yourselves in his position, with a brother who held him in terror and domination! If Nizam were a party to the kidnapping, is it conceivable that he would do the series of things he is known to have done—ring up the police just before the plan was put into operation, hang about at Gates Garage and so on?'

His Lordship, he says, will tell them about the necessity for considering each case separately, each defence differently; he gives them a final reminder that Nizam was under no obligation to go into the witness-box. Then he sits down.

It is time for the judge to sum up.

His Lordship, Mr. Justice Sebag Shaw, addresses the jury on their duties and their attitude: they have to decide what facts are proved, what inferences they are entitled to draw, applying the same tests to witnesses from whichever direction they come. If in doubt, they must resolve in favour of the accused.

'If you think a view falls from me,' he says, 'you are entitled to disregard it if it's not consonant with your own.'

His Lordship begins with two statements.

(i) Nobody could doubt that Mrs. McKay was abducted—no one has sought to suggest otherwise. There is evidence of false imprisonment, blackmail and threat to murder.

(ii) The charge of murder is on a different footing. Unless and until they come to the conclusion, if they do, that it's proved that one or two of the defendants was party to the kidnapping, no charge of murder can be brought. Only if one or the other is concluded to be party must they begin to consider the charge of murder.

He touches on the event of one of two defendants giving evidence which supports the prosecution case against his co-defendant: they should not act on the evidence of one to the detriment of the other unless they are assured that it comes from a reliable source. And the evidence as it affects each of them is not the same. This makes it imperative to consider each separately and independently of the other.

The judge starts to go through the case detail by detail. He tells the jury he expects to complete his summing up the next morning (6 October).

This, one imagines, is the last day. Three and a half weeks—fourteen and a half working days!

The brothers are put up and the judge continues his summation.

Eventually, he comes to Count 1. 'Unless and until you find either or both of the defendants guilty of kidnapping Mrs. McKay, there is no vestige of a case against them for murder.' He pauses. 'If, however—in order to say what I have to say, I have to make an assumption—if you find one or other guilty of kidnapping, what are the indications that she is dead?' One indication is what the kidnappers were saying, but it doesn't follow that each is guilty of killing her.

His Lordship tells the jury what murder is, narrowing the definition for the purposes of this case: 'Murder means doing an act which causes death when that act is done with intention to kill.'

It is 12.35 p.m., and the jury retires to consider its verdict.

Something after half past four, the jury are rumoured to have sent for their tea and are consequently thought—don't ask me why!—to be nearing a decision.

In fact they are. So, after just over four hours, we all troop back into the court for the last time.

The accused men are put up. The jury file in, their foreman leading. Suddenly there is silence.

'Are you unanimous?' asks the Clerk of the Court.

'Yes,' says the foreman. He stands, healthy-looking, spectacled, thoroughly in command of himself.

And then the Clerk of the Court reads out again, like a litany, the charges for each defendant, count by count. And count by count comes the answer, each time, for each count, the same answer. 'Guilty.' 'Guilty.' 'Guilty.' 'Guilty.'

It is over. But the foreman remains standing. He wishes to say something more. The Judge nods permission. He says the jury unanimously recommend leniency towards Nizamodeen Hosein.

Everyone is expecting an explosion from Arthur. The warders surrounding him must be at the ready. He wants to make a speech, of course. But it begins both bitterly and wittily.

'Injustice has not only been done. It has also been seen and heard by the public gallery'—he waves an arm towards us all—'to be done.'

He addresses himself to the Judge:

'The provocation of your Lordship has shown immense partiality. To his Lordship I would say that from the moment I mentioned Robert Maxwell, I knew you were a Jew.'

He is beginning to work himself up. 'Not that I am anti-Jewish myself,' he adds, thus showing his own absence of partiality. 'You have shown throughout this case,' he tells the Judge, 'that you have directed the jury on only one side, to the Crown. . . . I have produced thirty witnesses, and not once. . . .'

His Lordship watches him steadily on the same level over the well of the court. Arthur goes on:

'You have denied me justice!'

Arthur is now raising his voice in sarcasm to the jury. 'Thank you, members of the jury! It is a grave injustice!' The warders show signs of crowding in on him, and he becomes incoherent and stops.

The sentences are to be passed. Nizam has said not a word.

'On the conviction of murder, the sentence is life imprisonment.' This is for Arthur. For Nizam the same, with a recommendation of leniency 'from another quarter'.

Now the kidnapping. His Lordship makes a short introductory speech to impart that every right-minded person will expect the punishment to be salutary. 'The kidnapping and confinement of Mrs. McKay was cold-blooded and abominable. She was snatched from the security of her home, and so long as she remained alive she was reduced to terrified distress. This crime will shock and revolt every right-minded person. The punishment must be such that law-abiding citizens may feel safe in their homes.'

On the count of kidnapping, he sentences Arthur Hosein to twenty-five years. To Nizam he says: 'I am not sure whether you are in any degree less culpable, but the jury's view is that you were under the influence of your brother and I have to regard the possibility that this was so.' He sentences him to fifteen years.

Coming to the next count, he says: 'There could not be a worse case of blackmail. You put that family on the rack for weeks and months in an attempt to extort money by your monstrous demands.' For this both brothers receive the maximum sentence of fourteen years. For sending threatening letters, each gets the maximum of ten years. The sentences are to run concurrently.

Since the abolition of the death penalty, a Judge has power to recommend to the Home Secretary that the prisoner should not be released for a specified length of time. No such recommendation to the Home Secretary was made by Mr. Justice Sebag Shaw—so it looks as if his Lordship is sending Arthur down for a certain twenty-five years, and Nizam for a certain fifteen years under the kidnapping conviction.

As it is the usual practice to remit one-third of a fixed sentence, provided the prisoner behaves himself, general opinion among the army of reporters seems to be that Arthur will serve just under seventeen years and Nizam ten years if they get their remission.

His Lordship has ordered the two brothers to be removed from the dock. For the last time we hear the cry which begins, 'Be upstanding!' and ends—'God Save The Queen!'

Both brothers put in applications for leave to appeal, Arthur against the verdict and the sentence, Nizam against the verdict.

The applications are heard by Lord Justice Davies, Lord Justice Karminski and Mr. Justice Melford Stevenson.

The brothers are brought in, now handcuffed to warders. There is a marked change in Arthur—he looks terrified, the whites of his eyes showing all round the irises as he glances at the people in the court. Has a short time in prison deflated him so far? And Nizam—he looks just as composed as ever.

Leave to appeal is refused; and refusing Arthur's application to appeal against the sentence, Lord Justice Davies says the maximum sentences were right, 'for no more terrible crime could be conjured up'. Then he says sharply: 'Take them away!'

William Cooper

EDITOR'S NOTE. *In February 1990, Nizamodeen Hosein, who had been a well-behaved convict, was released from Verne Prison, Dorset, and immediately deported to Trinidad. His brother Arthur, who is considered to be mentally unstable, remains in a top-security hospital at Liverpool.*

THE BUSINESS METHODS OF ALPHONSE CAPONE
Frederick Lewis Allen

[A tweedy Bostonian, he spent most of his working life as an editor on magazines: The Atlantic, Century, Harper's. *His 'instant history of the Twenties',* Only Yesterday *(of which the following is an excerpt), was an even more instant success when it was published by Harper & Brothers, New York, in 1931; a reviewer dubbed him 'the Herodotus of the Jazz Age'. Chiefly because the material yielded by the Thirties was, generally speaking, less picturesque, his sequel-volume,* Since Yesterday *(1940), was far less successful. He died in 1954 at the age of sixty-three.]*

> Prohibition is an awful flop.
>   We like it.
> It can't stop what it's meant to stop.
>   We like it.
> It's left a trail of graft and slime,
> It's filled our land with vice and crime,
> It don't prohibit worth a dime,
>   Nevertheless we're for it.
>
> 'Flaccus', quoted in the FPA
> (Franklin P. Adams) column in
> the New York World

IN 1920, WHEN PROHIBITION was very young, Johnny

Torrio had an inspiration. Torrio was a formidable figure in the Chicago underworld. He had discovered that there was big money in the newly-outlawed liquor business. He was fired with the hope of getting control of the dispensation of booze to the whole city. At the moment there was a great deal too much competition; but possibly a well-disciplined gang of men handy with their fists and their guns could take care of that, by intimidating rival bootleggers and persuading speakeasy proprietors that life might not be wholly comfortable for them unless they bought Torrio liquor. What Torrio needed was a lieutenant who could mobilize and lead his shock-troops.

Being a graduate of the notorious Five Points gang in New York and a disciple of such genial fellows as Lefty Louie and Gyp the Blood (he himself had been questioned about the murder of Herman Rosenthal in the famous Becker case in 1912), he naturally turned to his *alma mater* for his man. He picked for the job a bullet-headed twenty-three-year-old Neapolitan roughneck of the Five Points gang, and offered him a generous income and half the profits of the bootleg trade if he would come to Chicago and take care of the competition. The young hoodlum came, established himself at Torrio's gambling-place, the Four Deuces, opened by way of plausible stage-setting an innocent-looking office which contained among its properties a family Bible, and had a set of business cards printed:

ALPHONSE CAPONE
Second-Hand Furniture Dealer
2220 South Wabash Avenue

Torrio had guessed right—in fact, he had guessed right three times. The profits of bootlegging in Chicago proved to be prodigious, allowing an ample margin for the mollification of the forces of the law. The competition proved to be exacting: every now and then, Torrio would discover that his rivals had approached a speakeasy proprietor with the suggestion that he buy their beer instead of the Torrio-Capone brand, and on receipt of an unfavourable answer, had beaten the proprietor senseless and smashed up his place of business. But Al Capone had been an excellent choice as leader of the Torrio offensives; Capone was learning how to deal with such emergencies.

Within three years it was said that the boy from the Five Points had seven hundred men at his disposal, many of them adept in the use of the sawed-off shotgun and the Thompson sub-machine gun. As the profits from beer and 'alky-cooking' (illicit distilling) rolled in, young Capone acquired more finesse—particularly finesse in the management of politics and politicians. By the middle of the decade he had gained complete control of the suburb of Cicero, had installed his own mayor in office, had posted his agents in the wide-open gambling-resorts and in each of the 161 bars, and had established his personal headquarters in the Hawthorne Hotel. He was taking in millions now. Torrio was fading into the background; Capone was becoming the Big Shot. But his conquest of power did not come without bloodshed. As the rival gangs—the O'Banions, the Gennas, the Aiellos— disputed his growing domination, Chicago was afflicted with such an epidemic of killings as no civilized modern city had ever before seen, and a new technique of wholesale murder was developed.

One of the standard methods of disposing of a rival in this warfare of the gangs was to pursue his car with a stolen automobile full of men armed with sawed-off shotguns and sub-machine guns; to draw up beside it, forcing it to the curb, open fire upon it—and then disappear into the traffic, later abandoning the stolen car at a safe distance. Another favourite method was to take the victim 'for a ride': in other words, to lure him into a supposedly friendly car, shoot him at leisure, drive to some distant and deserted part of the city, and quietly throw his body overboard. Still another was to lease an apartment or a room overlooking his front door, station a couple of hired assassins at the window, and as the victim emerged from the house some sunny afternoon, spray him with a few dozen machine-gun bullets from behind drawn curtains. But there were also more ingenious and refined methods of slaughter.

Take, for example, the killing of Dion O'Banion, leader of the gang which for a time most seriously menaced Capone's reign in Chicago. The preparation of this particular murder was reminiscent of the Kiss of Judas. O'Banion was a bootlegger and a gangster by night, but a florist by day: a strange and complex character, a connoisseur of orchids and of slaughter. One morning a sedan drew up outside his flower shop and three men got out, leaving the fourth at the wheel. The three men had apparently taken good care to win O'Banion's trust, for although he always carried three guns, now for the moment he was off his guard as he advanced among the flowers to meet his visitors. The middle man of the three cordially shook hands with O'Banion—*and then held on* while his two companions put six bullets into the gangster-florist. The three conspirators walked out, climbed into the sedan, and departed. They were never brought to justice, and it is not recorded that any of them hung themselves to trees in remorse. O'Banion had a first-class funeral, gangster style: a ten-thousand dollar casket, twenty-six truckloads of flowers, and among them a basket of flowers which bore the touching inscription, 'From Al.'

In 1926 the O'Banions, still unrepentant despite the loss of their leader, introduced another novelty in gang warfare. In broad daylight, while the streets of Cicero were alive with traffic, they raked Al Capone's headquarters with machine-gun fire from eight touring cars. The cars proceeded down the crowded street outside the Hawthorne Hotel in solemn line, the first one firing blank cartridges to disperse the innocent citizenry and to draw the Capone forces to the doors and windows, while from the succeeding cars, which followed a block behind, flowed a steady rattle of bullets, spraying the hotel and the adjoining buildings up and down. One gunman even got out of his car, knelt carefully upon the sidewalk at the door of the Hawthorne, and played one hundred bullets into the lobby—back and forth, as one might play the hose upon one's garden. The casualties were miraculously light, and Scarface Al himself remained in safety, flat on the floor of the Hotel Hawthorne restaurant. Nevertheless, the bombardment quite naturally attracted public attention. Even in a day when bullion was transported in armoured vans, the transformation of a suburban street into a shooting-gallery seemed a little unorthodox.

The war continued, one gangster after another crumpling under a rain of bullets. Not until St. Valentine's Day of 1929 did it reach its climax in a massacre which outdid all that had preceded it in ingenuity and brutality. At half-past ten on the morning of that Day, seven of the O'Banions were sitting in a garage which went by the name of the SMC Cartage Company, on North Clark Street, waiting for a promised consignment of hijacked liquor. A Cadillac touring-car slid to the curb, and three men dressed as policemen got out, followed by two others in civilian dress. The three supposed policemen entered the garage alone, disarmed the seven O'Banions, and told them to stand in a row against the wall. The victims readily submitted; they were used to police-raids and thought nothing of them; they would get off easily enough, they expected. But thereupon the two men in civilian clothes emerged from the corridor and calmly mowed all seven O'Banions with sub-machine gunfire as they stood with hands upraised against the wall. The little drama was completed when the three supposed policemen solemnly marched the two plain-clothes killers across the sidewalk to the waiting car, and all five got in and drove off—having given to those in the wintry street a perfect tableau of an arrest satisfactorily made by the forces of the law.

These killings—together with that of Jake Lingle, who led a double life as reporter for the *Chicago Tribune* and as associate of gangsters, and who was shot to death in a crowded subway leading to the Illinois Central suburban railway station in 1930—were perhaps the most spectacular of the decade in Chicago. But there were over five hundred gang murders in all. Few of the murderers were apprehended; careful planning, money, influence, the intimidation of witnesses, and the refusal of any gangster to testify against any other, no matter how treacherous the murder, met that danger. The city of Chicago was giving the whole country, and indeed the whole world, an astonishing object lesson in violent and unpunished crime. How and why could such a thing happen?

To say that Prohibition—or, if you prefer, the refusal of the public to abide by Prohibition—caused the rise of the gangs to lawless power would be altogether too easy an explanation. There were other causes: the automobile, which made escape easy, as the officers of robbed banks had discovered; the adaptation to peacetime use of a new arsenal of handy and deadly weapons; the murderous traditions of the Mafia, imported by Sicilian gangsters; the inclination of a 'wet' community to wink at the by-products of a trade which provided them with beer and gin; the sheer size and unwieldiness of the modern metropolitan community, which prevented the focusing of public opinion upon any depredation which did not immediately concern the average citizen; and, of course, the easy-going political apathy of the times.

But the immediate occasion of the rise of gangs was undoubtedly Prohibition—or, to be more precise, beer-running. (Beer rather than whisky on account of its bulk; to carry on a profitable trade in beer, one must transport it in trucks, and trucks are so difficult to disguise that the traffic must be protected by bribery of the Prohibition staff and the police and by gunfire against bandits.) There was vast profit in the manufacture, transportation, and sale of beer. In 1927, according to Fred D. Pasley, Al Capone's biographer,[1] federal agents estimated that the Capone gang controlled the sources of a revenue from booze of something like sixty million dollars a year, and much of this—perhaps most of it—came from beer. Fill a man's pockets with money, give him a chance at a huge profit, put him into an illegal business and thus deny him recourse to the law if he is attacked, and you have made it easy for him to bribe and shoot. There have always been gangs and gangsters in American life and doubtless always will be; there has always been corruption of city officials and doubtless always will be; yet it is ironically true, nonetheless, that the outburst of corruption and crime in Chicago in the nineteen-twenties was immediately occasioned by the attempt to banish the temptations of liquor from the American home.

The young thug from the Five Points, New York, had traveled fast and far since 1920. By the end of the decade he had become as widely renowned as Charles Evans Hughes[2] or Gene Tunney. He had become an American portent. Not only did he largely control the sale of liquor to Chicago's ten thousand speakeasies; he controlled the sources of supply, it was said, as far as Canada and the Florida coast. He had amassed, and concealed, a fortune

---

[1] *EDITOR'S NOTE:* Al Capone: The Biography of a Self-Made Man, *Ives Washburn, New York, 1930.*

[2] *EDITOR'S NOTE: Most British readers—even some American ones—need to be told that Hughes was, inter alia, the Republican Governor of New York State from 1906 till 1910; a close second to Woodrow Wilson in the Presidential election of 1916; Secretary of State in the administrations of Harding and Coolidge (1921–26); Chief Justice of the US Supreme Court from 1930 till 1941.*

the extent of which nobody knew; it was said by federal agents to amount to twenty millions. He was arrested and imprisoned once in Philadelphia for carrying a gun, but otherwise he seemed above the law. He rode about Chicago in an armoured car, a traveling fortress, with another car to patrol the way ahead and a third car full of his armed henchmen following behind; he went to the theatre attended by a bodyguard of eighteen young men in dinner coats, with guns doubtless slung under their left armpits in approved gangster fashion; when his sister was married, thousands milled about the church in the snow, and he presented the bride with a nine-foot wedding cake and a special honeymoon car; he had a fine estate at Miami where he sometimes entertained seventy-five guests at a time; and high politicians—and even, it has been said, judges—took orders from him over the telephone from his headquarters in a downtown Chicago hotel. At the end of the Roaring Twenties, he was still only thirty-one years old. What was Napoleon doing at thirty-one?

Meanwhile gang rule and gang violence were quickly penetrating other American cities. Toledo had felt them, and Detroit, and New York, and many another. Chicago was not alone. Chicago had merely led the way.

EDITOR'S NOTE. In June 1931, a federal grand jury in Chicago indicted Capone on charges of income-tax evasion and of conspiracy to violate the Prohibition Laws, and in October he was found guilty of several of the charges of tax evasion, and of contempt of court, and was sentenced to eleven years' imprisonment ('uproar of amazement in court') and ordered to pay fines totalling $50,000 and costs of $30,000 (out of his petty-cash box, presumably); the indictment for violation of the Prohibition Laws was not pursued. Surprisingly, he did go to prison—eventually at Alcatraz. By the time he was released, in 1939, his brain was a shambles and he was partially paralysed; both conditions had probably resulted from untreated syphilis. He was taken to his estate at Miami, where he remained—virtually a recluse; occasionally lucid—till his death in January 1947. It is said that he had once remarked, self-excusingly: 'There's a touch of larceny in all of us.'

ROBERT AND RUBY
Jonathan Goodman

So you think that Bob's a killer?
Don't be silly—he just *couldn't*.
You can say all night, 'twas Robert Wood,
And I'll say Robert Woodn't.

*An anonymous verse that was often
recited during the winter of 1907*

NO ONE WOULD DENY that—whether innocent as the jury at his trial decided, or guilty as most students of the case believe—Robert Wood certainly deserved to be hanged for the murder of Phyllis Dimmock in 1907.

He had as much luck in the final quarter of that year as many men, regarding themselves fortunate, accumulate in a decade or more. He was lucky in being represented by Arthur Newton, possibly the cleverest and almost certainly the most unscrupulous solicitor in criminal practice at that time; he was lucky in being defended at the trial by Sir Edward Marshall Hall, supremely eloquent and ingenious in a case that perfectly fitted his talents as a jury advocate. And, by one of the oddest paradoxes in the annals of crime, he had the great good fortune to have the falsity of his alibi revealed by the person upon whom it depended: to the public, and therefore to the jury, it seemed that he had been betrayed, Iscariot-fashion, for money, and this notion was perverted into an atmosphere of sympathy towards Wood, who became transmuted into the second victim of the case, far more worthy of pity than the wanton Phyllis Dimmock.

Her body was found by Bertram Shaw, the man with whom she had lived, ostensibly as his wife, for some nine months. Shaw was a dining-car chef on the Midland Railway; his working routine was to leave St. Pancras Station for Sheffield in the afternoon, and to return the following morning on a train that arrived in London at about eleven. This arrangement suited Phyllis down to the ground, for it meant that while Shaw was away, she was able to supplement her housekeeping money by having male paying guests at the two-roomed flat in Camden Town which they rented for eight shillings a week.[1] Shaw afterwards professed ignorance of Phyllis's extra-common-marital activities, but it is hard to believe that, even if he did not find out for himself, none of the neighbours in St. Paul's Road[2] apprised him of the nocturnal comings and goings at number twenty-nine, for Phyllis was a popular whore, and it was rare for her to spend a night alone.

On the hot and cloudless morning of Thursday, 12 September 1907, Shaw arrived home as usual, at 11.30. Receiving no reply when he banged on the locked door of the ground-floor flat, he obtained entry with a duplicate key borrowed from the landlady, who lived in the basement. The parlour was a shambles: every drawer had been ransacked and most of their contents strewn about the floor. There were four empty stout bottles and the remains of a meal on the table; places were set for two, indicating that Phyllis had entertained someone to supper. The folding doors to the bedroom were locked, and as there was no sign of the key and no answer to his frantic knocking, Shaw smashed them open. Rushing to the bed, he pulled aside the tumbled and blood-soaked sheets and blankets.

The naked body was lying in a position of sleep, and the face held the expression of a peaceful dream. The head, resting on a pillow, was almost completely severed; only the vertebrae had resisted the knife. Blood had seeped through the flock mattress

---

[1] The 1992 purchasing power of the 1907 £ is reckoned to be about £41.75—and so eight shillings then would have bought roughly what £16.75 does today.

[2] Soon afterwards (presumably at the request of remaining residents) renamed: Agar Grove.

and spilled on to the floor to form an obscene puddle that extended halfway across the room.

When he had recovered from the initial shock, Shaw made a hasty search of the flat and found that some pieces of jewellery and a purse were missing; yet on the chest of drawers, in plain view, were two gold rings. It seemed, therefore, either that Phyllis Dimmock had been murdered by an unobservant thief or that the missing articles had been taken only to simulate the morive of robbery.

One of the dead woman's most cherished possessions, a postcard album that had normally been kept on a small table in the parlour, was lying open on top of a sewing machine in the bedroom; a cursory examination showed that some cards had been torn out, and it occurred to Shaw—and later to the police—that the murderer had searched for, and taken, certain cards that connected him with his victim.

From the degree of rigor mortis, the police surgeon estimated the time of death as between 4 and 6 o'clock in the morning. Neither the landlady nor her husband had heard any suspicious sounds. The landlady had last seen Phyllis Dimmock, with her hair in curlers, at about 7.30 in the evening, and had heard her leaving the house three-quarters of an hour later.

The police were at first unsuccessful in tracing her movements later that night. She had *not* visited the Rising Sun, a pub that had been her favourite rendezvous and the market-place for her trade. But several of the bar-room habitués told the police that they had seen her on more than one occasion recently with a 'rather strange young man'; statements from other witnesses, most of them members or entrepreneurs of the oldest profession, referred to the same young man and extended the period of his acquaintanceship with Phyllis Dimmock to fifteen months. The police distilled the various descriptions into the following:

> About 30 years of age. Height, 5 feet 7 inches. Sallow complexion. Dark hair. Clean shaven. Peculiar difference about eyes. He is a man of good education and of shabby-genteel appearance.

A further distinctive detail was added to this description when a man named Robert MacCowan came forward. According to his

story, he had passed through St. Paul's Road at about ten minutes
to five on the morning of the murder; hearing footsteps behind
him, he had turned to see a man leaving number twenty-nine and
walking away in the opposite direction. MacCowan described
him as a stiff-built man, 5ft. 7 or 8in. in height, wearing a bowler
hat and a dark overcoat with the collar turned up. But what
MacCowan remembered most vividly was the man's walk:

> I noticed a peculiar jerk of the shoulders . . . His left
> hand was in his pocket, or down by his side, and he
> jerked the right shoulder forward as he walked.

Although the police were chiefly interested in tracing the ubiqui-
tous young man of the witnesses' statements, they made every
effort to identify other men who had been beguiled by Phyllis
Dimmock, and it was from one of these, a ship's cook with the
repetitious name of Robert Roberts, that they obtained several
important clues. On the Sunday before the murder, Roberts had
met Phyllis Dimmock in the bar of the Rising Sun, and after a
short discussion of monetary matters, they had left to spend the
night together. Roberts, a truly satisfied customer, had returned
to the flat on the following two nights, Monday and Tuesday,
and, his virility and savings being sufficient, had suggested a
further episode on the Wednesday, only to be told that an
advance booking precluded such an arrangement. Before he had
left the flat on the Wednesday morning, the post had arrived and
the girl had shown him part of a letter, masking from his view
the preceding sentences and a postscript that directly followed.
He remembered the message as:

> Dear Phillis, Will you meet me at the bar of the Eagle at
> Camden Town, 8.30 tonight, Wednesday.
>
> Bert

Phyllis Dimmock had then taken a postcard from the chest of
drawers and handed it to him to look at. On one side was a
picture of a woman embracing a child, and on the other side the
address and the words:

> Phillis Darling, If it pleases you meet me 8.15 p.m. at the
> [here was a cartoon drawing of a rising sun]. Yours to a
> cinder, Alice.

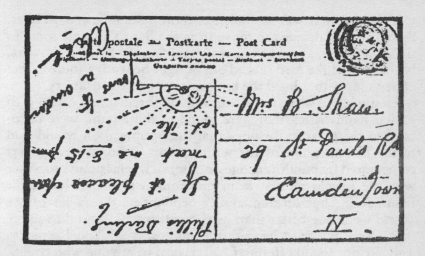

The 'rising sun' postcard.

After replacing the card in the drawer (no doubt with the idea of pasting it into her album at some later date), Phyllis Dimmock had set fire to the letter and dropped it into the empty fire-grate. Roberts, who seems to have had a near-photographic memory, recalled that both the letter and the postcard were written in indelible lead; in his opinion, both were in the same hand.

The police would no doubt have viewed parts of Roberts's story with some suspicion had it not been for two facts: first, he produced a water-tight alibi for the night of the crime, and second, in the fire grate they had already found the charred remains of a letter on which the following syllables were decipherable:

> ill . . . you . . . a of the . . . e . . . Town . . . Wednes if . . . rest . . . excuse . . . good . . . fond . . . Mon . . . from . . . the

The first group of syllables provided perfect corroboration of Roberts's account of the letter received by Phyllis Dimmock, for they fitted exactly into the message he remembered:

> Dear Ph*ill*is, Will *you* meet me at the b*ar of the* Eagle at Camden *Town*, 8.30 tonight, *Wednes*day.
>
> > Bert

The police failed to find the 'rising sun' postcard, but it seems that their search was not all that thorough. A few days later, Bertram Shaw decided to move from the flat to a single room in the same house, and when he was emptying the chest of drawers, he discovered the card tucked out of sight beneath a folded sheet of newspaper that lined the bottom of one of the drawers.

Facsimiles of that postcard, and of three other cards with similar handwriting that were found in the album, were circulated to the press in the hope that their publication would lead to the identification of the writer. Most national newspapers co-operated by publishing one or other of the facsimiles together with the formal request from the Commissioner of Police for information; but on Sunday, 29 September, the *News of the World* went one better than its competitors by reproducing the 'rising sun' postcard beneath the caption 'Can You Recognise This Writing?' and offering £100 reward to anyone who could.

One of the millions of readers of the *News of the World* was a girl named Ruby Young who called herself an artists' model but was actually a member of the profession that had recently lost Phyllis Dimmock from its ranks. She recognised the handwriting on the postcard at once; and not only the handwriting, but also the individual style of the cartoon. They belonged, she felt sure, to a young man whom she had known for about three years; the relationship, professional at first, had gradually become one of mutual affection, even love on her part, but she had seen less of him in recent months and was reconciled to his having discarded her for another woman, or other women.

Ruby Young wrote a letter to the *News of the World*; but it was never posted, partly because the mauve ink of the last few lines was still damp when the young man turned up at her flatlet on an upstairs floor of 13 Finborough Road, Earls Court.[1] His name was Robert William Thomas George Cavers Wood. He lived in

---

[1] Coincidences. For a year or so till 6 March 1922, the basement of the house was occupied by a prostitute whose business-name was Olive *Young*; early on that Monday morning, she was murdered by a madman, Ronald True. Early in May 1948, the first-floor flat of the house two doors away, 17 Finborough Road, was the scene of the murder of another prostitute, Winifred Mulholland—by George Epson, the tenant of the flat and a client of hers.

the St. Pancras district with his father (who, if he bestowed as many names on his other children, must have found it hard to avoid duplication, for Robert, et cetera, had nineteen brothers and sisters). An artist-engraver—and a talented one, whose work had been admired by William Morris—he had well-paid and secure employment with a firm of glass-makers in Gray's Inn Road. In his spare time, when he was not indulging his *nostalgie de la boue* in the sawdust-speckled bars and dimly lit whores' havens of Camden Town and Islington, he did freelance cartoon-drawing for a number of periodicals.

When Ruby Young showed him the letter that was waiting to be posted, he admitted that the 'rising sun' postcard was in his handwriting. He had, he said, been in the bar of the Rising Sun on the evening of Friday, 6 September, when a young woman, a complete stranger, had asked him for a penny to start the mechanical organ grinding. They had got talking, and he had shown her some picture postcards that he happened to have with him, souvenirs of a holiday in Bruges. She had asked him to send her one after writing 'something nice' on it and, on the spur of the moment, he had composed a mock invitation, which she had told him to sign 'Alice', or else 'the governor might cut up rough'. He had put the card in his pocket and, after buying her another drink, said goodbye. The following day, quite by coincidence, he had met the woman in the street, and she had reminded him about the card; he had promised to post it, and had done so on the Sunday evening, afterwards thinking no more about it. On the Monday evening he had again visited the Rising Sun, and had again chatted with the woman and bought her a few drinks. He had not seen her since.

As Ruby Young listened to this story, she must have thought back to her last two meetings with Robert Wood. A week after the discovery of the murder in Camden Town, she had received a telegram from him, his first communication with her for more than a month:

MEET ME AT PHIT-EESI'S TONIGHT 6.30. BOB.

When she had met him outside Phit-Eesi's, which was a shoe shop in Southampton Row, he had said that he needed her help: 'If any questions are ever asked you by anyone, will you say that you always saw me on Monday and Wednesday nights?'

He had given no reason for the unusual request, but she had consented.

Three days later, on Monday, 23 September, she had received a postcard from Wood which contained the message:

> Sweetheart, If it is convenient for you, will you meet me as before at Phit-Eesi's, 6.30, and we will have tea together and then go to the theatre, which I hope will be a little ray of sunshine in your life. Goodbye. R.W.

They had gone to the Prince of Wales Theatre to see *Miss Hook of Holland*, and afterwards, waiting at a bus stop, Wood had suddenly said: 'Don't forget now—Mondays and Wednesdays.'

The reason for the meetings, for the repeated request, for Wood's visit that evening, was now clear, and it seemed to Ruby Young that she was faced with a choice of evils: she could either post the letter or help to concoct a false alibi. She suggested that he should go to the police, but he explained: 'I cannot prove where I was on the Wednesday night—that's why I can't go to them. I was out alone, walking, and no one was with me who could speak for me.' Once again he asked her to stick to the story about the Monday and Wednesday nights, and eventually she agreed.

'The best thing for me to do', she said, 'is to say that I met you at 6.30 at Phit-Eesi's, and we had tea at Lyons's Cafe, and then after tea we went down Kingsway to the Strand and straight on to Hyde Park Corner. Then we'd better say we walked along the park straight out to Brompton Oratory, and got there at half-past ten. We will say that we parted there: you went back by tube to King's Cross and got back home just before midnight.'

And that was how it was left.

Ruby Young might have had second thoughts if she had known that Wood had already enlisted the aid of others in avoiding any connection with the case. Only the day before, a man called Tinkham, a foreman at the glass works, had spoken to him about the postcard and he had admitted that the handwriting was his; he had told Tinkham the same story he told Ruby Young, and the foreman had agreed to say nothing about the card after Wood had told him that his father was suffering from gouty eczema, 'and if it came to his knowledge that I

'Myself'—a sketch by Robert Wood.

was in any way mixed up in the affair, it might have dire results'.

A week before the discussion with Tinkham, Wood had called on his friend Joseph Lambert, a bookseller in Charing Cross Road, and had reminded him that at about 9 o'clock on the vital Wednesday evening they had met by chance in the bar of the Eagle, opposite Camden Town Station. Wood had been with a young woman whom he had introduced as 'Phyllis', and who had apologised for her hair being in curlers by saying: 'I hope you will excuse me for being so untidy, as I have just run out.' Lambert had had a drink with them, and had then left them together in the bar. When Wood had called on Lambert on 20 September, he had said: 'I have seen Mr. Moss, the head man at the works, and he has been talking about the Camden Town murder. If he says anything to you, will you tell him that we had a drink, *but leave the girl out*?' Without asking for further explanation, Lambert had agreed.

Ruby Young saw Wood on two occasions after his Sunday visit, and both times he reminded her of her promise. 'Yes, I'll be true,' she replied abruptly. 'Don't bother me. It's getting on my nerves.'

And it was; soon the secret became too much for her to bear alone and she told a friend—in confidence, of course—of Wood's dilemma. The friend passed the secret on to one of his own friends, who happened to be a reporter, and in no time at all the secret was shared with Inspector Arthur Neil, the detective in charge of the investigation of the murder of Phyllis Dimmock.

At 6.30 on the evening of 4 October, as he was leaving work, Wood was met by Ruby Young, who shook hands with him. It was the signal to Neil, who made himself known to Wood and asked him to step into a waiting cab. 'Very well,' Wood said equably. 'You will allow me to wish my young lady goodbye before I go.' He then turned to Ruby Young and uttered a piece of solipsistic jingoism that must have sounded rather bizarre in the absence of a brass-band accompaniment: 'Goodbye, dear. Don't worry. I have to go with these gentlemen. If England wants me, she must have me. Don't cry, but be true.'

During the drive to Highgate Police Station, Wood insisted that he had made no secret of having written the 'rising sun' postcard. After being cautioned, he told Neil: 'My young brother, or my step-brother, called my attention to the handwriting of the postcard when it came out in the Sunday paper. I told them it was *like* my handwriting, but I knew at the same time that I wrote the card, and the same night I had a chat with my brother Charles, a conscientious sort of chap who lives at Museum Street, and his wife Bessie. I was advised to go to Scotland Yard. But about that time I was very busy at the office with the work of the chief, who was away on holiday at the time. My brother then said that the next best thing to do was to write a letter, addressed to one of us, care of the poste-restante at the G.P.O. We sent the letter, addressed to Charles, and it stated that I acknowledged writing the postcard, and giving my reasons for not coming forward.

Now I want you to get that letter, Inspector, because it shows that I did not conceal the matter.'

What Wood meant by this is anyone's guess; the surprising thing is that not only he, but also his brother and his brother's wife, considered that by writing a letter confessing a secret—a letter that was to be opened only in the event of the secret's being discovered—all secrecy was erased. The letter, signed by Charles Carlyle Wood, Bessie M. Wood and Robert Wood, was obtained by the police from the poste-restante department at the St. Martin's le Grand Post Office. It read as follows:

43 Museum Street,
London, W.C.,
Sunday, Sept. 29, '07

We, the undersigned, make this statement and place it in the charge of the poste restante at St. Martin's le Grand in order to safeguard our good faith in the matter should our course of action be impeached. We, the first two signatories, are aware from his own full avowal that the post card published in the newspapers of September 27th and 28th by desire of the police in order to obtain information in the Camden Town murder case is in the handwriting of, and was written by, Robert Wood, of 12 Frederick Street. We jointly are anxious to help the police in every way possible; but we are also anxious to avoid the publicity and personal trouble occasioned by an immediate communication.

Having regard to the non-reliability of newspaper reports, theories, and comments, and being quite satisfied of Robert Wood's *bona fides* and that his contribution to the matter can aid but little, we consider it wise to await the results produced at the adjourned inquest on September 29th [a mistake: the inquest was resumed on the 30th], and while trusting that the intervention of Robert Wood may thereby be unnecessary, at the same time we determine, should no satisfaction arise from the inquest, to make the avowal of Robert Wood without delay.

The last paragraph, although high-sounding, was actually only a legalistic form of words, a clause that could be conveniently forgotten but that for the time being salved the consciences of Charles and Bessie Wood. Not only was the resumed inquest of 30 September adjourned days before Wood's arrest, but Wood himself admitted that the letter 'was intended to be opened in the event of the police calling on me for an explanation'.

At the station, Wood dictated a statement in which he repeated the story he had told Ruby Young and Tinkham about the three casual meetings with Phyllis Dimmock. And, quite convinced that Ruby Young would 'be true', he recited the false alibi for the night of the crime.

Two identification parades were held, and Wood was picked out by several witnesses, most of them prostitutes who claimed to have seen him with Phyllis Dimmock during the past fifteen months. He was also identified as having been with the woman in the bar of the Eagle on the Wednesday night. The most unorthodox identification was that of Robert MacCowan (he who claimed to have seen a man leaving 29 St. Paul's Road on the morning of the murder); he was unable to pick out anyone at the parade, but as soon as the men started to move away, he identified Wood by his walk.

Wood was charged with the murder, and almost at once his luck changed, not merely for the better, but for the best. His employers subscribed £1000 to a defence fund, thus enabling his solicitor, Arthur Newton, to spend lavishly in scheming an answer to the prosecution case and to brief Marshall Hall to lead three junior counsel at the trial.

In the period between the committal proceedings and the trial, public sympathy for Wood came close to mass hysteria. Engendered by the belief that he had been betrayed for money by a prostitute, the sympathy was artfully nurtured by Newton who, when cross-examining at the police court, implied that the testimony of the other prostitutes and of MacCowan, who was unemployed, had been purchased by the police.

Ruby Young had to go into hiding, and several other prosecution witnesses received threats. MacCowan complained: 'I might have committed the murder myself. Letters have been sent to me threatening to cut my throat, "blood money" has been chalked over my door, and my children were even told of it at the county council school where they attend. In future, even if I actually saw with my own eyes a man getting his throat cut in the street, I do not think I would give evidence again.'

Wood's demeanour at the trial, which began at the Old Bailey on Thursday 12 December, was that of a rather bored spectator. He whiled away much of the time by drawing sketches and caricatures of the lawyers and of the stage celebrities who filled the seats reserved for distinguished visitors.

At the end of the first day, back in his cell at Brixton Prison, he wrote to his brother:

Dear Charles,
I am just back. So sorry I could not grasp you by the hand today.

I commenced a letter yesterday to Bessie, but it is bundled away among my things.

Of course I have nothing now of my possessions except the things I stand in.

My feelings were strange today. Such that I cannot describe though quite peaceful. Whispers of good cheer came from every direction and even the orderly that tends my room moved silently and with some reverence this morning.

Little did I think that one day I should appear on the capital charge under that beautiful gold figure of Justice (by Frampton, R.A.) that towers above the Old Bailey—I think you have admired it.

I have a memory of sitting with this great sculptor at supper on more than one occasion.

I liked Marshall Hall's manner when he spoke to me today, and he is apparently a splendid man.

I am rather cut off now from Mr. Newton so please call his attention to any point; though I expect they view things differently from us. I mean the legal mind.

Pardon, dear Charlie, if I have omitted any due remarks or thanks.

To be tried for one's life is I think sufficient for the day and I am now weary.

I must ask you all to be of good cheer and to take good care of yourselves.

I understand that there are great odds to face that may end disastrously; but I will carry my head high for I have done no grievous wrong.

Goodbye, with fondest wishes to all.

Bob

Marshall Hall's defence of Wood was a sort of forensic conjuring act; several of his tricks were patently obvious and one or two went wrong, but this didn't really matter because the members of the jury were on his side from the beginning, ready to forgive and forget any mistakes and naiveties in the defence case.

Wood stuck to his story that he had first met Phyllis Dimmock on the Friday before she was murdered—and so, in dealing with the prostitutes who claimed that the acquaintanceship was of far longer duration, Marshall Hall sought more to blacken their characters than to challenge their evidence. Cross-examining Bertram Shaw and Robert Roberts, he implied that *even* if the jury accepted their water-tight alibis, their evidence lacked credibility because, as suspects, they had had every reason to lie to the police in order to exculpate themselves.

Marshall Hall's most spectacular success was in seeming to demolish the evidence of Robert MacCowan, whose poor showing in the witness-box is exemplified by the following extract from his cross-examination:

What sort of morning was it [just before 5am on 12 September]?
It was a drizzly, thick, muggy morning.
Do you know that not a drop of rain fell in London that day?
I call weather like that, when there is dew, 'muggy'. I have not swallowed the dictionary. I am Suffolk (*sic*). That is how we talk in Suffolk.
In Suffolk a morning not raining is drizzly?
Yes.
What kind of a morning was it?
It was a foggy morning.
You have described it before as a drizzly, thick, foggy, muggy morning, getting daylight, but not yet daylight?
Yes. . . .

Have you no regard for human life?

Yes, or I should not have come forward and given evidence. One life is as good as another.

Is that how you behave in Suffolk?

Yes.

The defence cast further doubt on MacCowan's powers of observation by calling as one of their witnesses a member of the electricity department of St. Pancras Borough Council. MacCowan asserted that when he passed through St. Paul's Road at about 4.50 on the morning of the murder, the street lamps had still been alight; according to the electrician, however, the lamps had been switched off ten minutes before. This point was more showy than valid, for it is unlikely that MacCowan's cheap alarm-clock kept perfect time, or that his estimate of how long it took him to walk from his home to St. Paul's Road was accurate to the minute. At all events, neither this point nor any of the others made by the defence explained away MacCowan's identification of Wood by his walk, the peculiarity of which was referred to by other witnesses.

The importance of the charred letter, which proved that a definite appointment had been made, was played down by the defence. In the witness-box, Wood admitted that the handwriting was his, but maintained that the words were not part of a letter. As if this assertion were not ludicrous enough, he suggested that the words were 'fragments of some amusing phrases and sketches' that Phyllis Dimmock had taken from him during one of their meetings at the Rising Sun: 'She had many little things I had written. She looked through my letters and papers which I used to take out of my pocket in pulling out my sketch-book in the bar. Girls like that are very bold. . . . When I pulled out my sketch-book, everything fell out. She was very forward. It may have been written in her presence or it may have been in my pocket. I lay stress on the "may have been". I sent no message to her. . . . I cannot imagine [the object of] a careless scribble like that.'

The jury retired at 7.45 on the evening of the sixth day of the trial. They returned a quarter of an hour later, and Robert Wood earned a place in legal history by being the first defendant in a murder case to be found Not Guilty after giving evidence on his own behalf. He listened to the verdict calmly, with a slight smile, and before being discharged, tidied up a sketch he had made of Mr. Justice Grantham during the summing-up.

The cheers in court that greeted the verdict were taken up by the crowd that thronged the streets around the Old Bailey, and a 'vast cordon' of police was needed to escort Wood and his many relatives to a restaurant in the Strand, where his father made a speech of thanks from the balcony.

Theatrical performances were interrupted to announce the news. At His Majesty's, Mrs. Beerbohm Tree, the actress-wife of the actor who had built the place, received the greatest applause of her career by rushing on to the stage, wearing Edwardian clothes rather than Shakespearian costume, and declaiming: 'I have just arrived from the court!—the court where young Robert Wood stood in peril of his life!! I am glad to be able to tell you that the jury found him Not Guilty!!!'

Ruby Young—sketched from the dock by Robert Wood.

By eleven o'clock, the crowd outside the Old Bailey had dwindled slightly, but only to become a mob, and Ruby Young, the girl who had contributed almost as much to Robert Wood's acquittal as to his arrest, needed to be smuggled out of the building disguised as a charwoman.

DEATH SCENE
Walt Whitman

['The good grey poet', a Long Islander, had many jobs, of several kinds (as clerk, compositor, teacher, newspaper-editor, carpenter), before his first book of verse, Leaves of Grass, was published in 1855, when he was thirty-six. For eighteen months during the Civil War (1861–5), he did volunteer missionary work in hospitals in Washington, DC, supporting himself and raising funds to buy gifts for patients by working as a copy-clerk and by sending war-reports to newspapers in New York and Brooklyn. Perhaps as the result of his wartime experiences, he grew frail; he held a series of clerkships, some of them sinecures, in government offices, and meanwhile published his war-poems as Walt Whitman's Drum-Taps. Following an attack of paralysis in 1873, he moved to his brother's home at Camden, New Jersey, and was kept from poverty (usually some way from it) through the generosity of fellow-writers and other admirers, English as well as American. The tenth edition of Leaves of Grass, published in 1891, is known to bibliophiles as the 'deathbed edition', the reason being that Whitman died in March of the following year; he was buried at Harleigh Cemetery, Camden, in a self-designed tomb.]

THE DAY, 14 APRIL 1865 [Good Friday], seems to have been a pleasant one throughout the whole land—the moral atmosphere pleasant too—the long storm, so dark, so fratricidal, full of blood and doubt and gloom, over and ended at last by the sunrise of such an absolute National victory, and utter breaking down of Secessionism—we almost doubted our own senses! Lee had capitulated beneath the apple-tree of Appomattox. The other armies, the flanges of the revolt, swiftly followed. . . . And could it really be, then? Out of all the affairs of this world of woe and passion, of failure and disorder and dismay, was there really come the confirmed, unerring sign of plan, like a shaft of pure light—of rightful rule—of God? . . . So the day, as I say, was propitious. Early herbage, early flowers, were out. (I remember that where I was stopping at the time, the season being advanced, there were many lilacs in full bloom. By one of those caprices that enter and give tinge to events without being at all a part of them, I find myself always reminded of the great tragedy of that day by the sight and odour of these blossoms. It never fails.)

But I must not dwell on accessories. The deed hastens. The popular afternoon paper of Washington, the little *Evening Star*, had spattered all over its third page, divided among the advertisements in a sensational manner in a hundred different places, *The President and his Lady will be at the Theatre this evening*. . . . (Lincoln was fond of the theatre. I have myself seen him there several times. I remember thinking how funny it was that He, in some respects the leading actor in the greatest and stormiest drama known to real history's stage, through centuries, should sit there and be so completely interested and absorbed in those human jack-straws, moving about with their silly little gestures, foreign spirit, and flatulent text.)

On this occasion the theatre was crowded, many ladies in rich and gay costumes, officers in their uniforms, many well-known citizens, young folks, the usual clusters of gas-lights, the usual magnetism of so many people, cheerful, with perfumes, music of violins and flutes—(and over all, and saturating all, that vast vague wonder, *Victory*, the Nation's Victory, the triumph of the Union, filling the air, the thought, the sense, with exhilaration more than all perfumes.)

The President came betimes, and, with his wife, witnessed the play, from the large stage-boxes of the second tier, two thrown into one, and profusely draped with the National flag. The acts

and scenes of the piece—one of those singularly written compo-
sitions which have at least the merit of giving entire relief to an
audience engaged in mental action or business excitements and
cares during the day, as it makes not the slightest call on either the
moral, emotional, aesthetic, or spiritual nature—a piece (*Our
American Cousin*) in which, among other characters, so called,
a Yankee, certainly such a one as was never seen, or the least like
it ever seen, in North America, is introduced in England, with a
varied fol-de-rol of talk, plot, scenery, and such phantasmagoria
as goes to make up a modern popular drama—had progressed
through perhaps a couple of its acts, when in the midst of this
comedy, or tragedy, or non-such, or whatever it is to be called,
and to off-set it or finish it out, as if in Nature's and the Great
Muse's mockery of those poor mimes, comes interpolated that
Scene, not really or exactly to be described at all (for on the many
hundreds who were there it seems to this hour to have left little
but a passing blur, a dream, a blotch)—and yet partially to be
described as I now proceed to give it. . . .

There is a scene in the play representing a modern parlour,
in which two unprecedented English ladies are informed by the
unprecedented and impossible Yankee that he is not a man of fortune, and therefore undesirable for marriage-catching purposes;
after which, the comments being finished, the dramatic trio make
exit, leaving the stage clear for a moment. There was a pause,
a hush as it were. At this period came the murder of Abraham
Lincoln. Great as that was, with all its manifold train, circling
round it, and stretching into the future for many a century, in
the politics, history, art, of the New World, in point of fact
the main thing, the actual murder, transpired with the quiet
and simplicity of any commonest occurrence—the bursting of
a bud or pod in the growth of vegetation, for instance. Through
the general hum following the stage pause, with the change of
positions, came the muffled sound of a pistol shot, which not
one hundredth part of the audience heard at the time—and yet a
moment's hush—somehow, surely, a vague startled thrill—and
then, through the ornamented, draperied, starred and striped
space-way of the President's box, a sudden figure, a man raises
himself with hands and feet, stands a moment on the railing,
leaps below to the stage (a distance of perhaps fourteen or
fifteen feet), falls out of position, catching his boot-heel in the

copious drapery (the American flag), falls on one knee, quickly recovers himself, rises as if nothing had happened (he really sprains his ankle, but unfelt then)—and so the figure, Booth, the murderer, dressed in plain black broadcloth, bare-headed, with a full head of glossy, raven hair, and his eyes like some mad animal's flashing with light and resolution, yet with a certain strange calmness, holds aloft in one hand a large knife—walks along not much back from the footlights—turns fully toward the audience his face of statuesque beauty, lit by those basilisk eyes, flashing with desperation, perhaps insanity—launches out in a firm and steady voice the words, *Sic semper tyrannis*—and then walks with neither slow nor very rapid pace diagonally across to the back of the stage, and disappears.... (Had not all this terrible scene—making the mimic ones preposterous—had it not all been rehearsed, in blank, by Booth, beforehand?)

A moment's hush, incredulous—a scream—the cry of *Murder*—Mrs. Lincoln leaning out of the box, with ashy cheeks and lips, with involuntary cry, pointing to the retreating figure, *He has killed the President*.... And still a moment's strange, incredulous suspense—and then the deluge!—then that mixture of horror, noises, uncertainty—(the sound, somewhere back, of a horse's hoofs clattering with speed)—the people burst through chairs and railings, and break them up—that noise adds to the queerness of the scene—there is inextricable confusion and terror—women faint—quite feeble persons fall, and are trampled on—many cries of agony are heard—the broad stage suddenly fills to suffocation with a dense and motley crowd, like some horrible carnival—the audience rush generally upon it—at least the strong men do—the actors and actresses are all there in their play costumes and painted faces, with mortal fright showing through the rouge, some trembling—some in tears—the screams and calls, confused talk—redoubled, trebled—two or three manage to pass up water from the stage to the President's box—others try to clamber up—etc., etc., etc.

In the midst of all this, the soldiers of the President's Guard, with others, suddenly drawn to the scene, burst in—(some two hundred altogether)—they storm the house, through all the tiers, especially the upper ones, inflamed with fury, literally charging the audience with fixed bayonets, muskets and pistols, shouting *Clear out! clear out! you sons of*—.... Such the wild scene, or a suggestion of it rather, inside the playhouse that night.

Outside, too, in the atmosphere of shock and craze, crowds of people, filled with frenzy, ready to seize any outlet for it, come near committing murder several times on innocent individuals. One such case was especially exciting. The infuriated crowd, through some chance, got started against one man, either for words he uttered, or perhaps without any cause at all, and were proceeding at once to actually hang him on a neighbouring lamp-post, when he was rescued by a few heroic policemen, who placed him in their midst and fought their way slowly and amid great peril towards the Station House. It was a fitting episode of the whole affair. The crowd rushing and eddying to and fro—the night, the yells, the pale faces, many frightened people trying in vain to extricate themselves—the attacked man, not yet freed from the jaws of death, looking like a corpse—the silent resolute half-dozen policemen, with no weapons but their little clubs, yet stern and steady through all those eddying swarms—made indeed a fitting side-scene to the grand tragedy of the murder. They gained the Station House with the protected man, whom they placed in security for the night, and discharged him in the morning.

And in the midst of that night-pandemonium of senseless hate, infuriated soldiers, the audience and the crowd—the stage, and all its actors and actresses, its paint-pots, spangles, and gas-lights—the life-blood from those veins, the best and sweetest of the land, drips slowly down, and death's ooze already begins its little bubbles on the lips. . . . Such, hurriedly sketched, were the accompaniments of the death of President Lincoln. So suddenly and in murder and horror unsurpassed he was taken from us. But his death was painless.

EDITOR'S NOTE. *Simultaneously with the shooting, William Seward, the Secretary of State, was attacked and severely wounded at his home by Lewis Payne, another of the Confederate conspirators.*

Lincoln was carried, unconscious, to a lodging-house

across the street. He died there just before 7.30 the next morning. Some three hours later, Vice-President Johnson took the oath of office as President.

The assassin, John Wilkes Booth—younger brother of the great actor Edwin Booth, and himself an actor—escaped to Virginia, but on 26 April was traced to a barn near Bowling Green; on his refusal to surrender, the barn was set alight, and, according to the official version, he shot himself. (In the autumn of 1989, a play entitled The Man Who Shot Lincoln, by Luigi Creatore, was produced at the off-Broadway Astor Place Theatre; it was based on the quaint notion that the culprit was actually Edwin Booth.) Of the nine persons arrested in connection with the crimes, four were hanged, four imprisoned, and one acquitted. From Who He?: Goodman's Dictionary of the Unknown Famous (Buchan & Enright, London, 1984): 'The day after the shooting, Samuel Mudd, a general practitioner living near Bryantown, Maryland, fixed a splint to John Wilkes Booth's leg, which was fractured near the ankle. Chiefly because Dr. Mudd was slow in informing the authorities that he had had suspicious visitors, he was charged as a conspirator; found guilty, he was sentenced to life imprisonment, and served about three and a half years before being pardoned. In 1980, President Carter exonerated him of all guilt, but still "his name is mud"—an expression coined before the Civil War but given currency by the doctor's disgrace. It may be that the toast "Here's mud in your eye" comes from the same source.'

Ford's Theatre was closed after the assassination. Its owner, John T. Ford, planned to re-open it two months later, but was forced by a public outcry and political pressure to give up the idea. The Government bought the theatre and turned it into offices, at first for dealing with records of Union soldiers. In June 1893, part of the third floor (presumably, the part that had been built on to the front of the upper circle) collapsed, killing or injuring many civil servants. The building was turned into a warehouse for Government publications; then, in 1932, it became the Lincoln Museum. Starting in 1946, Bills were introduced in Congress to restore Ford's Theatre; after twenty-eight

SURRAT.   BOOTH.   HAROLD.

War Department, Washington, April 20, 1865.

$100,000 REWARD!

THE MURDERER

Of our late beloved President, Abraham Lincoln,

IS STILL AT LARGE.

$50,000 REWARD

Will be paid by this Department for his apprehension, in addition to any reward offered by Municipal Authorities or State Executives.

$25,000 REWARD

Will be paid for the apprehension of JOHN H. SURRAT, one of Booth's Accomplices

$25,000 REWARD

Will be paid for the apprehension of David C. Harold, another of Booth's accomplices.

LIBERAL REWARDS will be paid for any information that shall conduce to the arrest of either of the above-named criminals, or their accomplices.

All persons harboring or secreting the said persons, or either of them, or aiding or assisting their concealment or escape, will be treated as accomplices in the murder of the President and the attempted assassination of the Secretary of State, and shall be subject to trial before a Military Commission and the punishment of DEATH.

Let the stain of innocent blood be removed from the land by the arrest and punishment of the murderers.

All good citizens are exhorted to aid public justice on this occasion. Every man should consider his own conscience charged with this solemn duty, and rest neither night nor day until it be accomplished.

EDWIN M. STANTON, Secretary of War.

DESCRIPTIONS.— BOOTH is Five Feet 7 or 8 inches high, slender build, high forehead, black hair, black eyes, and wore a heavy black moustache, which there is some reason to believe has been shaved off.

JOHN H. SURRAT is about 5 feet 9 inches. Hair rather thin and dark; eyes rather light; no beard. Would weigh 145 or 150 pounds. Complexion rather pale and clear, with color in his cheeks. Wore light clothes of fine quality. Shoulders square; cheek bones rather prominent; chin narrow; ears projecting at the top; forehead rather low and square, but broad. Parts his hair on the right side; neck rather long. His lips are firmly set. A slim man.

DAVID C. HAROLD is five feet six inches high, hair dark, eyes dark, eyebrows rather heavy, full face, nose short and fleshy, feet small, instep high, round bodied, naturally quick and active, slightly closes his eyes when looking at a person.

NOTICE.—In addition to the above, State and other authorities have offered rewards amounting to almost one hundred thousand dollars, making an aggregate of about TWO HUNDRED THOUSAND DOLLARS.

years, a Bill was passed that provided some two million dollars for that purpose. On 12 February 1968, the theatre re-opened with a performance of Stephen Vincent Benet's pageant-style play John Brown's Body. In 'A Welcome', Stewart Udall, Secretary of the Interior, said that 'Abraham Lincoln was drama: every inch of his gangliness, every dimension and fibre of his humanness. A Kentucky log-cabin was Act I; Illinois, Act II; Washington, Act III. Ford's Theatre was an Epilogue we remember only for its long and despairing emptiness. . . . From this moment on, let this place be known more for its living performances than for history. Hereafter, let us not recall "the moment of high fate" which occurred here; rather, let us relive the many treasured moments when—here—President Lincoln found human warmth and laughter. May we, too, learn to love this place as a living memorial to a man. Here some, unhoping, will find hope; some, grieving, will discover gaiety, and many, weary, will rest. I believe Mr. Lincoln would have wanted it this way.'

A PREVALENCE OF VICTIMS
David Bowen

[Emeritus Professor of Forensic Medicine, University of London, MA, MB, B.Chir, FRCP, FRCP(Ed), FRC.Path, DMJ, D.Path. Born at Pontycymmer, South Wales, in 1924, he studied medicine at Cardiff, Cambridge, and the Middlesex Hospital, London, and then worked as an intern while waiting to be called up for National Service. Further hospital posts led to training in clinical pathology and then morbid anatomy at The Royal Marsden Hospital. A chance vacancy at St. George's Hospital opened the way for pupillage under the late Home Office pathologist, Professor Donald Teare. In 1966 he started the Department of Forensic Medicine at Charing Cross Hospital Medical School, subsequently becoming Reader and, in 1977, Professor. He has been involved in some 500 murder investigations, and has written numerous papers on forensic topics.]

DENNIS NILSEN stands four-square with earlier experts at murder, such as Armstrong, Ms Borden, Crippen and Dougal, to mention but an alphabetical few, and has a special niche in the archives, as his tally of victims is the largest in the annals of British crime.

The story is a complicated one, involving the discovery of three bodies in a flat in one part of north London, followed by the discovery of the remains of many more bodies—*skeletal* remains, to be more accurate—in a flat previously occupied by Dennis Nilsen in another part of north London, the latter discovery being entirely due to the accused's information on the subject. Almost all the evidence in the case was based on the accused's own statements, and so virtually the entire investigation, legal and medical, was, curiously enough, in the reverse of that to which one is accustomed. It was necessary for Nilsen's statements to be confirmed very accurately, so as to substantiate charges of homicide: any discrepancy between Nilsen's statements and the medical or forensic findings would throw doubt on the veracity of the whole case, particularly as it is not unknown for persons to confess to crimes they have not committed.

Had Nilsen chosen to remain silent—and he might well have done so but for careful and tactful police handling of his first interviews—the deaths for which he was responsible, particularly the mass-deaths at the earlier address, would have gone undetected. Some idea of his ambitions, and an even better idea of his black sense of humour, can be gathered from his throw-away remark to Detective Superintendent Chambers, in charge of the case, that had he proceeded undetected with his crimes, he would have reduced the population of north London by the year 2000 to such an extent that it would have been the subject of statistical comment.

As a pathologist I was fortunate, if one can use the word in this context, to be able to examine Nilsen's last victim within a week of the man's death; also two other bodies, later identified in his residence in Muswell Hill, which he had been unable to dispose of satisfactorily following dismemberment. However, it soon became apparent that it would be impossible to establish the cause of death in two of the three cases, and even identification would be a problem. It was only in the case of Nilsen's last victim that the cause of death was actually given.

There was, of course, extravagant interest from all sections of the national and international press; such interest brought certain newspapers close to contempt of court; there was inaccurate reporting by some tabloids which seem to prefer lurid fiction to hard evidence. Near the end of Nilsen's trial, one 'news'paper reported that the jury had come to the verdict while, in actual fact, they were still some hours away from it.

The case itself concerns the fact that while Dennis George Nilsen, aged thirty-eight, occupied a ground-floor flat in Cricklewood, north London, from 1976, he disposed of 12 male persons; only because that house was being sold, he moved to Muswell Hill, some eight miles to the east, and there strangled three more men; in addition, over the same period of time (1976–81), he made some seven unsuccessful homicide attempts on men who had been invited, for various reasons, to spend an evening with him or to stay temporarily at his flat. A total of twenty-two homicides, or attempted ones, over the course of five years—an average of one victim every ten weeks. All the men were either strangled or garrotted, usually following a tête-à-tête during which Nilsen listened to rock-music through earphones and drank large quantities of Bacardi and Coke. He is obviously attracted to men; however, there is no evidence that he carried out acts of homosexuality—or of necrophilia—on any of his victims, and at the time of the investigation he claimed that he was asexual. Motives for his crimes have been discussed at length, but psychiatrists remain at odds as to the nature of his mental problems; the majority view seems to be that he is a psychopathic personality with schizophrenic overtones.

There is a chicken-or-egg question regarding the fact that the generality of his victims were poor and/or unemployed: Was that because his work often brought him in touch with such men—or did he, perhaps, feel some revulsion at people who were poorly off, a desire to rid society of their presence? It appears that there was just one exceptional victim: a Canadian student who was unfortunate enough to meet Nilsen the night before he was due to leave the country. His disappearance, which aroused considerable interest and investigation at the time, was not explained until his thumb-print was found in a London road-atlas at Nilsen's flat in Muswell Hill. Reverting to the matter of motive, Superintendent Chambers came to the firm conclusion that Nilsen was an intensely lonely man who, bizarre as it may seem, kept his mute victims at home for long periods because he found them 'companionable'.

Nilsen was born in Fraserburgh, Scotland, in November 1945, the second son of an exiled Norwegian soldier and a Scotswoman.

The marriage broke up and the mother remarried. She remained in contact with Dennis and regarded him with considerable affection. In 1961 Nilsen joined the Army on a 12-year contract, and in 1964 was posted to the Royal Regiment of Fusiliers in Germany; he was then in the Catering Corps, having obtained a City and Guilds catering diploma—hence, possibly, his knowledge of anatomy and skill in dismemberment. He was promoted to lance-corporal in 1965, and, as a cooking aide, went to the Persian Gulf, Cyprus and Berlin, and eventually to Scotland, close to Balmoral; his unit was on one occasion responsible for entertainment facilities for Her Majesty the Queen. He was discharged in 1972, having served his contract satisfactorily and been given a good service-record.

That same year, he joined the Metropolitan Police and, after initial training, was posted to Q Division in north-west London (which included the area of Cricklewood—and, more specifically, Melrose Avenue, where his first series of murders took place). Finding police work unsatisfying, he left the force in 1973 and took a job with the Department of the Environment. Then, in May 1974, he joined the Manpower Services Commission, with which he remained until the time of his arrest. His post had prospects. He showed an interest in trade-union activities, and became a minor union-official.

Before considering the details of his crimes, I should mention a significant difference between his residence in Cricklewood and the one in Muswell Hill: the former had a garden to which he had sole access, whilst the latter was a top-floor, or attic, flat which virtually precluded him from using the garden as a depository for human remains. At Muswell Hill, the flat below his (the middle floor) remained empty, whilst the ground-floor flat, which had been divided into two, was partly occupied by two girls and partly by a barmaid and her boyfriend. At one time, the Victorian house was, in estate-agents' parlance, a quite desirable semi-detached residence; in certain respects, it had deteriorated over the years.

The whole affair should have come to light on Saturday, 5 February 1983, when an unpleasant smell in the drains was reported to that well-known drain-cleaning company, Dynorod. As it was the weekend, and administrative difficulties had been encountered, their representative did not arrive till the afternoon of Tuesday, 8 February. He found himself working in dark, bitterly cold conditions—it had been snowing those past few days. Examining a large drain, he happened upon a mass of flesh-like material which a 'gut-feeling' told him was human. He consulted with head office, and it was decided that, on account of the poor conditions prevailing, further investigations should be delayed until the following morning. By then, to the Dynorod man's great surprise, the drain was virtually empty. (The explanation, it turned out, was related to activity heard during the night by ground-floor residents of the house—sounds of someone coming downstairs and going out into the garden, sounds of the drain-cover being removed and then, some time later, replaced. Needless to say, the sounds emanated from Nilsen's efforts to remove the flesh. Some of it was subsequently found, semi-frozen, in the garden—or rather, wilderness—at the back of the house. Shortly before the SOS to Dynorod, Nilsen had taken the precaution of writing to the landlord, pointing out deficiencies in the accommodation—lack of lighting on the stairs and landings ... and the inability of his toilet to flush satisfactorily, thereby causing those in the lower flats to overflow: this, he maintained, was the result of the drains being blocked, which was also causing the nasty odours permeating the building. The root of all the water-associated evils is, of course, not difficult to fathom.)

As the pathologist involved, I came into the picture on Wednesday, 9 February, when just a few bones and some flesh—the only tissues that Dynorod had discovered on their return—were brought by Detective Chief Inspector Jay to my Department at Charing Cross Hospital. There were three or four strips of skin and subcutanous tissue with fine hairs at one margin; also four small bones of a hand. I thought the skin was human—the fine hairs at one end suggested that it came from the margin of the neck. Noticing indentations on the surface, I remarked that it might well have come from a person who had been strangled.

Mr. Jay promptly returned to Muswell Hill and waited for Dennis Nilsen to arrive home from work. He told him that there had been a complaint that the drains had become blocked by the presence of human remains, and that he had reason to believe that those remains had come from Nilsen's flat. He then asked whether there were any further human remains, and Nilsen allegedly pointed to a locked wardrobe, handing over the key. After being cautioned by Mr. Jay, he agreed to accompany him to the station. En route, Nilsen mentioned that there may have been as many as fifteen bodies for whose deaths he might have been responsible. Later that evening, he made the first of many detailed statements, which involved at least thirty hours of interviewing over the period of a month.

That same evening, I made an initial examination of the flat, where I found a malodorous atmosphere despite the fact that Nilsen always kept his windows open when at work as his dog Blip did not like being cooped up. (The dog, incidentally, was taken away to Battersea Dogs Home, although numerous people had offered to look after it.) The flat consisted of a small kitchen with a bathroom beyond, a bedroom and a sitting-room. In the latter there was a large wardrobe which contained two plastic refuse-bags. In the heavier one was a large black bag, two white bags, and a Sainsbury's carrier-bag. The black bag and one of the white bags contained the entire tissues of both sides of a chest, cleanly dissected from the rib-cage in an expert manner; the other white bag contained a torso from the neck to the lumbar region, and the Sainsbury's bag contained some internal organs. The lighter refuse-bag contained six smaller ones, in each of which were two white bags. (It was rather like a Chinese box-puzzle: when one opened a large bag, several others were found within it.) The lighter bag and its constituents ones contained the upper half of a torso, muscular tissues partially dissected away, arms but no hands. (None of the bodies found had hands or feet.) There was also a decomposed skull, devoid of tissue, and a freshly decapitated head—of Nilsen's last victim—with distinctive haemorrhages, as seen in suffocation or strangulation, on the facial skin. In the sitting-room was a large tea-chest which contained some clothes and newspapers, also a large white and a large black plastic bag. The white bag contained a torso, muscles of a left leg partially dissected away, and most of a right leg from which the muscles were missing. The black bag contained another one and two blue ones which, between them, contained a skull with five neck-vertebrae present, two upper-arm bones, lower-arm bones, and a pelvis or hip-girdle, more or less devoid of tissue. A little later—after two days, in fact—we found, hidden behind makeshift shelving in the bathroom, a large plastic bag which contained a recently-dissected torso.

With some difficulty in orientation, we realised that we had the major components of three bodies, including a virtually complete recently-dismembered one. The latter victim was easily identified by fingerprints. There was no doubt in my mind that he had died from asphyxia: although the head had suffered alteration through being par-boiled in a stockpot which Nilsen kept on his stove, the distinctive petechial haemorrhages were present. The other victims in the flat had, according to Nilsen, died in March and September 1982—the most dissected one first. Identification of that victim was through blood-grouping by Anne Davies, of the Metropolitan Police Forensic Science Laboratory. Blood-group substance remaining in the muscle-tissues was compared with bloodstains in the flat and the hospital blood-grouping of a man who, again according to Nilsen, had stayed in the flat. This was a remarkable feat of serology. The other body was also identified by a fine piece of detective work. A search was made in missing-persons files, with particular regard to men who had not been seen since September 1982. One of the first on the list was a Mr. Allen; his girlfriend confirmed his disappearance about that time, recalled who his dentist was, and remembered that he had fractured his jaw the previous year. He had, in fact, attended Charing Cross Hospital for treatment of the fracture, which had been sustained during a fracas when police were called to arrest him. The fracture had been wired expertly, but Mr. Allen had removed the wires himself, and so, of course, the jaw had not healed entirely normally. The remaining fracture-defect was visible on the victim's lower jaw. Mr. Allen had also visited his dentist for an upper denture which he had never collected; with the collaboration of Bernard Sims, the forensic odontologist, we found that the dentures fitted the skull, and the dental records and the superimposition of dental x-rays were entirely satisfactory. The only other remains at Muswell Hill were in the 'garden', where two shoulder-blades, thrown there by Nilsen, were found.

Cricklewood presented much more difficult problems. The garden of the house was painstakingly staked out and searched, following the erection of the usual protective covering to shield the area from the press; it was divided into plots under the supervision of senior scenes-of-crime officers, the soil to a considerable depth was sifted, and all skeletal remains present were carefully collected into plastic bags; later, the adjacent large area of wasteland was examined by police cadets. In fact, the latter search revealed a remarkable number of bones—quite often of animals, including the complete skeleton of a dog.

The entire collection was removed to the police station, and eventually to Charing Cross Hospital for detailed documentation. It was a matter of painstaking cleansing, of sorting animal from human remains, with an effort made to collate items on an anatomical basis. Difficulties arose on account of Nilsen's method of disposal of his victims. He usually left the body for a day or so, allowing rigor mortis to pass off, then dismembered it, distributed the parts under the floorboards prior to disposing of them, sometimes crudely burying them under surface-soil, sometimes making enormous bonfires which he topped with tyres to disguise the smell of burning flesh, and, after the fires were quenched, using a heavy roller to crush the remaining bones. In fact, the only unburnt bones found were two sets of ankle-bones, one complete in the victim's sock, and a few small complete bones; there were no long bones; the charred fragments amounted to upwards of 2000.

There was no point in trying any of the techniques that have been developed for estimating the age of bones, for we knew that all the victims were young men. It was left to the Senior Lecturer in Anatomy, Dr. Jean Ross, to attempt to identify certain bones. She carried out a remarkable, detailed comparison of specimen bones with bone-fragments, and after many weeks was able to say that there were ten fragments from the upper limb (humerus), six being from the lower end on the left—and so we knew for sure that there were no fewer than six bodies present.

Finally, I tried—more out of interest than for any other reason—a method used by archaeologists to separate co-mingled remains into a number of different skeletons with the use of ultraviolet light; a wide range of colours emanates from most bone-surfaces under exposure to such light, which, it seems, excites certain organic elements which, in turn, fluoresce—the radiated colours are directly related to the elements present on the bone-surface. I wondered if this technique might be useful in gauging the number of bones from different individuals on the site. However, it was not at all successful—partly, I think, because the bones had been subject to unnatural processes: in particular, heat.

Mr. Nilsen's counsel was no more successful with his defence of diminished responsibility. The jury found the defendant Guilty on six charges to which he had confessed. Curiously, it seems to me, Mr. Allen, the penultimate victim at Muswell Hill, was not on the charge-sheet, though the other two were included.

Nilsen is presently imprisoned on the Isle of Wight. Every so often, an anecdote about him escapes—or is created outside the prison-walls. As an example, it is said that he has expressed the wish that if a film is made about his exploits, the list of characters in the credit-titles should be given in the order of their *dis*appearance.

There is a postscript to the scientific investigations. A year or so after the trial, I received a bone-like object which had been found by plumbers dealing with a leak in the water-tank in the attic of the house in Cricklewood. Among the newspapers that somehow learned of the find, one declared: **NILSEN CASE REOPENED IN VIEW OF NEW DISCOVERY**. In fact, although the thing resembled quite closely a bone from the arm, the Natural History Museum at Kew Gardens recognised it as being of a species of South American seaweed—found also, strangely enough, on Scottish seashores, in the region of Aberdeen and around the Shetland Islands (both areas distant from Fraserburgh, Nilsen's place of nativity). An extraordinary quirk of nature that it had somehow found its way first of all to Cricklewood and then into the water-system of that particular house. . . .

David Bowen.

THE KILLER IN THE RYE
Jeffrey Bloomfield

[As you will learn from his essay, he is a still-young New York. I got to know him during trips to America to gather information about the Starr Faithfull case; later, while I was writing a book on the case in London, he worked on my behalf in and around Manhattan, finding answers to questions that I had forgotten to ask and answering questions that had still not occurred to me. Since then, I have coaxed him into putting his talents as researcher, historian and social commentator to literary work; an essay of his appears in an earlier anthology that I edited, The Art of Murder, *and another, on the so-called Amityville Horror, is in a forthcoming collection,* The Supernatural Murders; *his work has also appeared in English journals of forensic science; he has recently completed a book of true-crime stories entitled* Deadly Secrets. *After attending Drew University, New Jersey, he graduated from the New York Law School in 1978; for the past ten years he has been an 'investigator-specialist' for the New York State Crime Victims Board.]*

Opening Bars and the Theme

THE UNITED STATES has been labelled the assassination capital of the world. Four Presidents dead, one wounded, four others shot at, one ex-President wounded, two Senators murdered, one

Governor killed, one ex-Governor blown up, one Governor wounded and crippled, a Nobel Prize-winner gunned down, an outspoken African-American defender killed . . . etc. . . . But there is one name on the list that doesn't quite fit: *John Lennon*. Most of the assassination victims drift off into oblivion together with the dead policies or conflicts they represented. Who cares now about Garfield's fatal fight with the Stalwarts' wing of the Republican Party, or William Goebel's populist struggles with the Kentucky political machine that destroyed him?[1] But Lennon was an artist whose best ballads transcended his time; their youthful clarity and directness will electrify listeners for decades, perhaps centuries, to come. A statesman or a reformer, even a Lincoln or a King, will eventually be followed by another. It is not as easy to replace an artist. Now, having said that, I must admit a paradox: I was never a real fan of Lennon or, speaking more generally, the Beatles. I blame this on my not fitting into their generation so precisely as to appreciate them. John Lennon was born in 1940, and he and his group most directly addressed those born between 1948 and 1952—people who were maturing at the time the Beatles were rising in popular and critical esteem. I was born in 1954, and so I was just under ten when I was first aware of them.

Oh yes, I recall that Sunday in February 1964. My family were visiting some of my mother's cousins that afternoon. One of them, Dave Goldstein, was being reminded by his two daughters, Eileen and Iris, that they had to be home at eight o'clock. Dave kept singing snatches of a number from the popular musical, *Bye-Bye Birdy*, about appearing on the Ed Sullivan television show. My sister Lee was not as excited, but she was interested.

We got home that night, and watched them. Millions watched them. My recollections are mixed. There were the screaming fans in the audience . . . the talent and energy of the performers . . . the *explosiveness* of the whole event. It is proof of the lack of my musical curiosity that I concentrated my attention on the

---

[1] Charles Guiteau, the disappointed office-seeker and nut who shot President Garfield, identified with the Stalwarts, led by Senator Roscoe Conkling of New York. Goebel was elected Governor of Kentucky in 1899, after a heated campaign, but was shot on the day of his inauguration in 1900 (he was sworn in as he lay dying).

drum-playing of Ringo Starr, not on John Lennon or Paul McCartney singing, or the back-up work of George Harrison. The words of their songs drifted away from me—except for the refrains 'I want to hold your hand!' and 'She loves you, yeah, yeah, yeah!'. Then the programme ended, and we watched *Bonanza*. I did not realize that I had been watching history.

My lack of adulation did not prevent me from subsequently taking an interest in one aspect of their careers. In 1968–69 there were rumours that Paul McCartney had been killed in an automobile accident; that the death was covered up. Fan-magazines suggested that weird clues were to be found in odd places. The cover of the album, *Abbey Road*, had Paul bare-footed, while the others wore shoes . . . it was claimed that if the track of one of their songs was played backwards, you could hear a voice saying, 'Paul is dead, Paul is dead!' On such 'clues' was the story spread—and believed. Very few survivors of my generation admit to having followed such nonsense.

The story of Lennon and the Beatles is well-known; that of Lennon's slayer is not. Mark David Chapman was born on 10 May 1955 in Fort Worth, Texas. His father David was a sergeant in the Air Force, and his mother Diane a night-nurse. There was a younger sister too. Eventually his father became an employee of the American Oil Company. The family lived in a comfortable middle-class home in Decatur, Georgia. Although Mark seems to have led a normal life for a southern, white, Protestant boy in the United States, there may have been home-problems. His parents were divorced in 1978. Mark was by then a drug-addict, experimenting with heroin and LSD. However, he became a born-again Christian, and overcame addiction. His father insisted he join the YMCA. Mark was fond of children, and was a camp-counsellor for six seasons.

Fenton Bresler, in his book *Who Shot John Lennon?* (St. Martin's Press, New York, 1989), says that there are misconceptions about Mark, one being that he was a loner: actually he was considered personable. But his record of friendships remains spotty. Bresler made an effort to find his friends, but some refused to talk, and others requested pseudonyms or anonymity. Most eventually lost contact with Mark.

He briefly tried to become a comic in Chicago. Then he tried for a career in the YMCA, which required a college degree;

he could not maintain interest in the courses. He joined the YMCA's International Camp Counselling Programme, which was intended to further international friendships through youth-camps; he hoped to go to the Soviet Union, but was sent to Beirut, Lebanon; arriving there in April 1975, his stay was cut short by the start of the civil war. Six months later, through the YMCA, he got a job helping Vietnamese refugees get used to the United States; they seem to have acclimatised quickly, for he was out of work again by the end of 1975.

Mark had been involved with a girl named Jessica Blankinship for several years. His job-flitting caused the relationship to collapse, but it was resumed when they enrolled at a college in Tennessee, where he was 'determined' to get the degree needed for the career with the YMCA. Due to undisclosed problems (possibly emotional), he dropped out. They split again. One of his friends, Gene Scott, suggested that he should become an armed security-guard. He did, but soon either resigned or was fired.

Then Mark decided to go to Hawaii. He gave no reason. He arrived in January 1977, and for several weeks acted like a tourist at a luxury hotel. Then he began looking for a job. All of a sudden, he phoned Jessica to tell her that he felt very miserable. She told him to come to Atlanta, which he did. He was disillusioned to discover that, although she was concerned about him, she had no intention to resume the relationship.

Mark returned to Hawaii. He later claimed that he tried to kill himself with carbon-monoxide gas from a car. Eventually he went to Castle Memorial Hospital as a welfare patient; his condition was described as 'severe depressive neurosis'.

After his release, he worked at the hospital—first as a main-tenance man and then in 'customer services'. It seems that he pulled himself together. In 1978, he borrowed money from the hospital's credit-union so as to take a trip around the world. At the travel-agency, he met Gloria Abe, a Japanese-American. After his return from the six-week trip, he romanced her, and they married on 2 July 1979. He had lived in a low-class apartment house. Now he and his bride moved to a more expensive building. She got a position at the hospital. He entered a period of bizarre behaviour-switches. He pushed for economies, such as selling their car and using public transportation—yet borrowed large sums of money from his mother, his in-laws, and the credit-union to buy art-works. He resigned his job when he felt that he was passed over for a promotion, and got taken on as a security guard in a vacation complex at Waikiki.

In October 1980, Mark read two books. One, J.D. Salinger's novel *The Catcher in the Rye*, he had read years earlier. The other, Anthony Fawcett's *John Lennon: One Day at a Time*, described the Beatle's wealthy life-style. The first book tells of an unhappy adolescent's hatred of 'phoniness'; the second may have directed Mark's hatred towards Lennon as a rich 'phony'.

He sold his most treasured painting, a Norman Rockwell lithograph, for $7500; after partly repaying his mother and the credit-union, he was left with $2500. On 23 October 1980, having resigned from his job, he signed out as 'John Lennon', but then crossed out the name with a double line.

On 27 October, he purchased a five-shot .38 revolver at a store in Honolulu. He bought a single ticket to Newark, New Jersey, one of the three major airports serving the New York City area. He informed his wife and (by phone) his mother that he was going to New York City to iron out his problems. Gloria did not question his behaviour. His mother did question him, in particular when he told her of his plan to change his name to that of the hero in *The Catcher in the Rye*: Holden Caulfield.

Mark left on 29 October. He made one mistake: he should have bought his ammunition in Hawaii. It was not until he reached Manhattan that he discovered that he could only purchase bullets there if he had a New York City gun-permit. Still, he remained in the city for a few days, at the Waldorf-Astoria no less, and toured the town. On 7 November he left for Atlanta—to seek out Gene Scott, who, being a sheriff's officer, had access to ammunition. Mark explained that he needed the gun to protect himself from muggers. Gene accepted this, and got him dum-dum bullets, which can do more damage than regular ones. Mark visited the Blankinship family too. It seems that he was giving himself a momentary calm before the storm. He returned to Manhattan on Sunday, 9 November, and checked into the Hotel Olcott on West 72nd Street.

John Lennon and his wife Yoko Ono had been living for seven years in a seven-room suite in the famous Dakota apartment-house on Central Park West between 72nd and 73rd Streets.

Mark was only around the corner, and he tried to catch Lennon the next day. The doorman told him that the singer and his wife were away. At a loss, Mark went to the Statue of Liberty and (if we credit his statements) tried to shoot himself but failed.

He called Gloria, and flew back to Honolulu. The total fiasco of the trip depressed him. He went to the Catholic Social Services for counselling, but all he told the social worker was that he was depressed about being unemployed; he failed to keep a second appointment on 26 November.

On 2 December he flew from Honolulu to Chicago. (Fenton Bresler makes a valuable contribution to the chronology of events by showing that Mark spent three days in Chicago, and did not reach New York City until 6 December. This is based on a comparison of ticket information with a return-ticket and baggage-tag found among Mark's possessions by the police.) Why Mark stayed in Chicago is not known. He may have visited a grandmother who lived in the city.

In New York again, he checked into the YMCA at 5 West 63rd Street, and returned to the Dakota. Again his prey was unavailable. At a loss, he walked back to West 62nd Street, briefly entered a building there, then crossed Central Park. At East 62nd Street and 2nd Avenue, he took a cab down to Greenwich Village. Why he went down there is unknown. He returned to the YMCA, and checked out the next morning.[1] Now he checked into the Sheraton Center Hotel at 7th Avenue and 52nd Street. Here he laid out his valuables on the bureau in the room, to be observed by whoever might come in. These items included: a pocket Bible, inscribed 'Holden Caulfield', in which he had added Lennon's name to *The Gospel of St. John* and underlined a reference to 'pharisees' in *St. Mark*; a letter of introduction that he had used to get accommodation at YMCAs during his trip around the world; a tape of his favourite rock-singer, Todd Rundgren; a photograph of himself with immigrant Vietnamese children; a photograph of his first

---

[1] Back in the 1960s, whenever my family visited my mother's friend Jewell Schultz, I had an opportunity to see the back of the YMCA, which faced Aunt Jewell's apartment on West 64th Street. The forbidding structure always looked like a prison to me.

car; a still from *The Wizard of Oz* of Judy Garland wiping a tear off the face of the Cowardly Lion; the return-ticket and baggage-tag.

Mark went out, bought a copy of Lennon's latest album, *Double Fantasy*, and walked back to the Dakota. He could now claim to be seeking an autograph. He spent most of 7 December standing outside the apartment house, but still failed to see his prey. He returned to the Sheraton, had dinner, and picked up a prostitute. Some time later that night, he phoned Gloria to tell her that he loved her.

On Monday, 8 December, the Lennons had a photo-session and an interview to occupy their morning and part of the afternoon. Therefore, they had not come out when Mark reached the Dakota. Two female fans were waiting, and Mark took them to lunch, regaling them with the story of his trip around the world. When he returned to the Dakota, an amateur photographer, Paul Goresh, was there. They watched the Lennons' son Sean leave with his nanny in a station-wagon. Finally, at five, the Lennons appeared. A crowd collected around them, and Mark could only walk over and ask Lennon to sign the album. Goresh took a photograph of the killer with his victim some six hours before the crime occurred. He sold it for $10,000.

A limousine took John and Yoko to the Record Plant near La Guardia Airport, where they worked on tapes for a record. Mark remained at the Dakota for the next six hours, arousing the curiosity of the doorman—and of Goresh, who left at 8.30. John and Yoko had dinner at the Stage Deli, off Times Square, and returned to the Dakota at 10.50.

Yoko left the car first, John following with the tapes. As they entered the archway, Mark called out: 'Mr. Lennon.' John started to turn around. He may have seen the crouched man holding a gun. Mark fired all five shots, hitting his target in the back and left shoulder. John fell on the five steps leading to his offices. I regret to say that he did not die immediately. He was in great pain when a policemen arrived. Mark was the calmest person there. He had removed his topcoat, folded it next to the empty gun, and taken out his copy of *The Catcher in the Rye*. He was engrossed in the story when the policeman arrested him.

Help!

When Mark was taken to the Twentieth Precinct for booking, he began to see how dangerous his position was. His victim was idolised by many persons, any one of whom might be happy to see Mark get similar treatment. This fear turned out to be well grounded, as his court-appointed attorneys discovered. The first one, Mr. Herman Adlerberg, resigned after getting a serious-sounding death-threat; he had lasted just two days on the case. He was succeeded by Mr. Jonathan Marks, who, though he also got death-threats, stuck it out until the end. At least one threat was real: the police in Los Angeles arrested a man who was boarding a plane for New York, expressly to exact retribution. Mark was lodged in a cell in an isolated part of Ryker's Island Prison; whenever he appeared in court, he looked bulky in a bullet-proof vest, and was surrounded by naturally bulky policemen.

The defence contended that Mark was insane. Nine mental experts examined him, and gave nine different opinions about his mental condition. Initially, Mark was willing to plead Not Guilty, but on 8 June 1981 he phoned Mr. Marks to tell that him he was changing his plea to Guilty, as God had told him to. His lawyer was unable to dissuade him. In a second call the same day, Mark labelled the psychiatrists 'all phonies'. His lawyer made no comment.

On 22 June 1981, Mark appeared before Justice Dennis Edwards, to answer questions regarding his reasons for changing his plea. Edwards concluded, to his own satisfaction, that Mark had reached his decision after a serious religious experience, and that his answers to the questions showed that he was normal. Despite the protest of Jonathan Marks, the change in plea was accepted. Final sentencing occurred on Monday, 24 August 1981. Mr. Marks called two witnesses. Dr. Daniel Schwartz, called to show that the defendant was mentally unfit to change his plea, said that he was convinced that Mark had created a private world in which he was absolute monarch over 'little people'. The prosecution demolished that, simply by pointing out that Dr. Schwartz relied solely on what Mark had told him. The other witness, Dr. Dorothy Lewis, suggested a medical cause for Mark's behaviour: a seizure causing psychotic delusions. This did not impress Justice Edwards. Mark was allowed to speak for himself. He had insisted, in several earlier statements, that he was the 'Catcher in the Rye' of his generation. Now he recited the key passage of the novel, where Holden Caulfield tells of his vision of himself in a rye-field, rescuing little children running towards a cliff. After politely listening to that, the judge sentenced Mark to prison for twenty years to life, with a chance of parole.

Later, when Mark had an inkling of what his decision had let him in for, he tried to get the sentence overturned; but on 1 May 1984 it was affirmed by the state appellate division. He was sent to Attica Prison, in upstate New York.

His existence is confined to a small cell in an isolated wing of the prison. He has one hour of outdoor exercises daily, and spends the rest of his wakeful hours reading (mostly religious books, though he has made an effort to become a Salinger expert) or writing. Sometimes he gets a visitor. Once each year, Gloria comes to see him.

A Little Help From His Friends?

That is the basic story of the assassination of John Lennon and the legal punishment of his assassin. The crime (no, certainly not 'of the Century', as some journalists have elevated it) seems to have been committed by an emotionally unstable man—not necessarily a psychotic one.

There is another theory, of course. Fenton Bresler tries to put it across in his book, which is extensively researched, in some areas brilliant. He is determined to make the reader believe that the CIA brainwashed Mark Chapman into killing John Lennon: Mark was initiated into the CIA through his involvement with the YMCA—which, so Mr. Bresler says, is a front organisation for the US spying group.

By all means read the book. It's fun. Not as much fun as *The Catcher in the Rye*, but fun all the same. Never mind the use of unreliable sources, Mr. Bresler's tendency to overlook the obvious, and the fact that, though the CIA does sometimes seem rather like an asylum that has been taken over by the lunatics, it is hard to credit Mr. Bresler's notion that they wanted John Lennon exterminated because he, a left-wing radical, threatened the Agency's very existence: as Mr. Bresler himself admits, only a month before the crime, the majority of registered and active voters in the United States had voted Ronald Wilson Reagan into the Presidency. That vote was in part a reaction against the inept Carter administration, but there was genuine grass-roots support for Reagan in the south, midwest and west. There was no earthly need for the CIA to hire oddballs to swat down their 'enemies'. Their man had won. They knew that for the next four years, maybe longer, The Man in the White House was going to hold their hands.

May I offer a theory of my own? In the light of Mark Chapman's confused antics in the weeks before the shooting—purchasing a gun but forgetting to buy bullets, making pointless trips but rarely getting to his destination, talking suicide but never getting around to it—did he see John Lennon as a substitute for himself? Think of this: Mark was a complete failure. But still, he loved the good life: swank hotels, a round-the-world trip, expensive artwork bought with borrowed money. . . . It was all a pathetic dream—and eventually he *knew* that it was. Seeing himself as a phony, he re-read *The Catcher in the Rye*—and, at about the same time, John Lennon came out of retirement: a multi-millionaire who, all being well for him, would become a multi-multi-millionaire. He was—so it seemed to Mark—prostituting his God-given genius . . . turning (or churning) out mediocre material. Mark had good taste and no money; John was sacrificing his gifts in aid of more and more millions. Mark hated himself for being a failure—but he hated the other phony far more. By killing John, he would destroy two phonies. But he—HE—would have become the Holden Caulfield of his generation.

That is how I see it. I claim no more than that it is easier to accept than any evidence-less conspiracy theory.

Jeffrey Bloomfield

A LIVERPOOL TRIPTYCH
Richard Whittington-Egan

[Born in Liverpool in 1924, he has written several books and countless essays on that city. He wrote, with Geoffrey Smerdon, The Quest of the Golden Boy, *the standard biography of the Nineties poet and man of letters, Richard Le Gallienne, and is presently at work on a critical biography of the poet and dramatist Stephen Phillips (best known for his play* Paolo and Francesca). *He has a great interest in, and considerable experience of, psychical research, and edited five volumes of* The Weekend Book of Ghosts and Horror. *His true-crime writings include* The Ordeal of Philip Yale Drew, The Riddle of Birdhurst Rise, *and* A Casebook on Jack the Ripper, *which is one of the three worth-while books on that person or those persons unknown. He is the only writer who has contributed to all of Jonathan Goodman's previous murder-case anthologies. The great-grandson of Ireland's Crown Pathologist, he originally read medicine, and is a member of the Medico-Legal Society and of Our Society. He is a director of* Contemporary Review.]

I
The Cafferata Poisoning Case

THERE IS, or was until recently, a dark old house situated in the Vauxhall Road area of the fair city of Liverpool. The house, like many another in that quarter, had fallen upon evil times. It had seen change and decay. It flaked and peeled like some sick animal in a neglected zoo.

But the darkness of that house was not entirely a matter of mouldering masonry and soot-grimed bricks. It came as much from the *inside* as the outside.

For dark deeds had been done in that place, and it was, I believe, the legacy of those deeds, staining its atmosphere as surely as the smokes and fogs of a hundred years had stained its brickwork, that imparted to it the forbidding air with which it always seemed enwrapped.

The plain fact is that that old house was once the lair of a secret poisoner. Within those walls had dwelt merciless cunning, and had been enacted scenes of cruelty and great anguish, culminating in murder most foul.

Certainly there had been nothing sinister about it in the year 1854, when Mrs. Ann James arrived from the fresh-blown pastures of her native Devonshire, healthy, happy, and full of hope and ambition, to take up residence there.

A clever, capable woman, Mrs. James had rapidly transformed her new home into a thriving place of business. On the ground-floor she opened up a grocery shop, and a large room where meals and refreshments were served. Several of the upstairs rooms were let to lodgers. Soon, Mrs. James found herself salting away a tidy bit of savings.

Success brought in its wake a train of relatives.

Mrs. James was presently joined by her married sister, Eliza Townsend. With her came her invalid husband and their three sons. The next arrivals were Mrs. James's married niece and her husband, a japanner by trade and Cafferata by name.

And then there were eight . . .

. . . Nine, actually, for there hove upon the scene a gentleman named Thomas Winslow. A former ironworker, he started off in the James household as an upstairs lodger, but achieved rapid promotion—first, as major-domo of the lodging side of the business, and subsequently as manager of the grocery shop also.

This, predictably, led to some degree of ill-feeling among the relatives. They did not take to Winslow. They liked even less what they regarded as the disproportionate influence which he seemed to exercise over Mrs. James.

It soon became a house divided: the Townsends and the Cafferatas on the one hand—Winslow on the other—Mrs. James fair and square in the middle.

The Townsend-Cafferata faction sustained a swingeing blow when, first, Mr. Townsend, and then, in rapid succession, Eliza Townsend and two of her sons died.

That left only one Townsend—young Martin, a bit of a nuisance, forever joining, and having to be bought out of, the army, but not rating as a very significant adversary in the internecine war.

And the two Cafferatas.

Even by the high standards of Victorian mortality rates, the occurrence of four deaths in one family in so short a span of time was suspicious.

In the light of later events, suspicion hardens into near-certainty of multiple foul play.

In January 1860, Mrs. James was seized by several mysterious attacks of illness, during one of which Winslow persuaded her to sign an authority—which he had written —for him to withdraw the £130 she had in the savings bank. He also went to the Gas Company, where she had four gas-shares, valued at £200, and tried to get them entered in his name. On being told that this could not be done without a proper transfer, or by will, he arranged for the solicitor of the Gas Company to see Mrs. James, and draw up such a will. In it, the business and the stock-in-trade were left to Winslow, and the remainder of the property divided equally between Mrs. Cafferata and Martin Townsend.

On 5 February, Mrs. James suffered so severe an attack of the mystery illness that Dr. Cameron, Physician to the Southern Hospital, was summoned. Three weeks later, Winslow wrote to Mrs. Cafferata, who was away in Manchester, telling her that she must come at once if she wished to see her aunt alive. She came, and, for a fortnight, slept in the same bed with Aunt Ann in the back-parlour. She noticed how attentive Winslow was, showing great interest in Mrs. James' fluctuating condition, and insisting on bringing all her meals to her himself.

Very gradually, she seemed to improve.

Then, on 29 March, came a severe relapse. Dr. Cameron was hastily sent for. Again, his patient got gradually better.

Then, more relapses, with the doctor in attendance on 8 May and 25 May.

By now, he was very worried. Four times in less than four months he had been urgently called in. Always the symptoms were the same—violent purging and vomiting.

This time, as he came out of the hushed sickroom, he felt certain of it:

A secret poisoner was at work in that house.

Someone was trying to destroy Mrs. James.

When he left, the doctor had certain samples and specimens in his bag. He was going to have them analysed. Then he would know if he was right.

He had his answer on 10 June. The analyst had found traces of antimony.

Dr. Cameron acted swiftly. He communicated with the police. With them, he went to his patient's home. The police took possession of all the medicine bottles and a number of cups that were in Mrs. James' room. Dr. Cameron had Mrs. James removed to the Southern Hospital.

And there, on 24 June, she died.

A post-mortem revealed the presence of cancer of the intestine. The pathologist gave cancer as the cause of death, but added that death was accelerated by the administration of continual small doses of antimony.

Thomas Winslow was arrested.

He accused the Cafferatas of having poisoned Mrs. James.

Winslow's trial opened at Liverpool on 20 August 1860.

Evidence that he had been trying to obtain antimony was given by Mrs. Ann Foley, a woman who once worked for Mrs. James. She said that he gave her tuppence and told her to go and buy some antimony 'for the dog'. But the chemist would not let her have it.

More damaging was the testimony of a boy named Thomas Maguire, who lodged at Mrs. James's. He said that he had purchased a white powder from a bottle labelled 'Ant.' at William Miller's chemist's shop in Tithebarn Street, and given it to Winslow. He had several times seen Winslow, cutting bread in the kitchen for the mistress, take a white powder in a paper from his pocket, and sprinkle it on the bread before he buttered it.

In his charge to the jury, the judge, Baron Martin, told them that if the prisoner administered antimony with the intention of killing, and the deceased's death from a natural disease was thus accelerated, that was murder—but they must not convict unless the evidence satisfied their minds of his guilt.

Apparently it did not. It took them only a few minutes to bring in a verdict of Not Guilty.

So ... the Liverpool Poisoning Mystery remained—a mystery.

But if not Winslow, who? The Cafferatas? Young Martin Townsend?

The old dark house has kept its secret, but if stones could speak, I am pretty sure of the name they would whisper ...

II
The Gentle Chinaman

THE TALE OF the inexplicable tragedy which overtook the Gentle Chinaman is still told in the Chinese quarter of Liverpool. It is whispered, too, beneath the gay lanterns of faraway Tai-Ping, Shanghai, Hong Kong, and Singapore. What our bald speech debases to a cold and matter-of-fact account of senseless murder is, doubtless, elevated in the lilied tongue of his native land to the level of a parable. As they puff ruminatively at their opium-pipes, the Oriental philosophers will find in the cautionary tale of Lock Ah Tam a deep well of proverbial wisdom ... And to the poor Chinaman it will seem to justify that wistful dubiety with which he is accustomed impassively to regard great wealth ...

It was in the high summer of the year 1895 that Lock Ah Tam, native of Canton, then twenty-three years old, decided to abandon his berth as a ship's steward in favour of a clerk's desk in a Liverpool shipping office.

The move was to prove a wise one, for, a dozen years later, he had become a rich and respected member of Liverpool's Chinese community. Tam it was who became the European representative of what was virtually a Chinese stevedores' trade-union—the Jack Ah Tai organisation, with headquarters in Hong Kong. Who but Tam should represent three important British steamship companies in all negotiations with their Chinese employees? And Tam was the man who was elected President of the Kock Man Tong, the greatest, world-wide Chinese Republican Society. He was also the British agent of Sun Yat-Sen, the leading campaigner for the independence of China.

His prestige and influence among Liverpool's Chinese citizenry was immense.

But power, contrary to the old adage, did not corrupt. The gods had smiled on him, and Tam, not slow to appreciate their favour, tried to share his good fortune with those about him. To share his Chinese luck!

He could always be relied upon to dig his hand deep into his pocket for local charities. No one ever appealed to him for help in vain. Indeed, he had a habit of, when walking in the street, distributing—literally, out of hand—money to the poor of his neighbourhood. As one who knew him well was afterwards to testify: 'I have seen him give half-crowns to little children when we have met them; and then he has said, "Look at these poor people," and we did not know them, and he would give them half-crowns.'

Tam himself lived prosperously in a comfortable, old-fashioned house in Birkenhead, across the Mersey from Liverpool; it was presided over by his charming and affectionate Welsh wife, Catherine, who had borne him a son, Lock Ling, and two daughters, Doris and Cecilia.

He had, you might think, and with every justification, achieved a happy and well-balanced life: gentle man, devoted husband, doting father.

A challenge to those evil gods, those spiteful demons, said by legend to turn the sour eye of envy on those mere mortals who seem to be 'having it too good'?

We are almost come to the moment when the first faint crack appears in the mirror of luck . . .

A question had arisen of founding a club in Liverpool where Chinese sailors could meet their friends and enjoy a drink and a game of billiards in safety from land-sharks and suchlike predators as lurked behind the dusty hanging blankets beyond which fan-tan, pi-kow and pucka-pu are played.

It was Lock Ah Tam who, largely at his own expense, saw to it that that club was provided.

In a strange, ironical way, it seems likely that it was this club of his—the Chinese Progress Club—which was responsible for his downfall.

One February evening in 1918, shortly before the Chinese New Year, Tam went along to the club for a drink and a game of billiards. Suddenly, the door burst open and a gang of drunken Russian sailors came tumbling in. Tam ordered them to leave. They started to swear and shout, and one of them, seizing a billiard-cue, landed Tam a tremendous blow on the head. He slumped to the floor, bleeding profusely; but by the time the police arrived, he seemed to have more or less recovered, and was able to walk to his office in the house next door. And, later still that night, he was able to spend an hour at the police station and accompany the officers to a nearby lodging-house in order to identify the man who had attacked him.

However, as we shall presently see, it appears that the damage done by that chance-struck blow may have been far greater than was realised, for thereafter his whole character underwent a sinister and distressing change.

From being a kindly, acute and lovable man, he became suddenly and unaccountably irritable, absent-minded and morose. Always, hitherto, a moderate drinker, he took to the bottle with a vengeance. Previously, he had confined himself to whisky, of which he could carry a very considerable cargo. Up to the time of his injury, no one had ever seen him drunk; he always attributed its lack of unfortunate effect upon him to the fact that to every glass of whisky it was his custom to add two teaspoonfuls of salt! Now, however, he started to mix his drinks and tottered upon the brink of chronic alcoholism.

He tottered, too, upon the brink of sanity. He began to display sudden uncontrollable bursts of maniacal temper on the slightest real—or imagined—provocation. He would flare-up in an instant, stamp his feet and foam at the mouth, and his bloodshot eyes would bulge out from his empurpled, swollen face like those of a madman.

The most trivial thing could send him off into one of these paroxysms.

For example. On one occasion Tam was entertaining seven or eight friends to supper at his home. One of them, a Mr. Jones—yes, his name really *was* Jones—who had been his close associate for many years, made some completely innocuous remark. The effect on Tam was terrifying. He sprang to his feet, face distorted with rage, gibbering and waving his arms about like one demented. Grabbing all the glasses on the table, he hurled them one after the other into the fireplace, before collapsing into his chair.

And there was the evening when Tam invited a taxi driver into his house for a drink. Thinking to please his generous fare, the driver made some flattering reference to China—whereupon, to the unfortunate taxi-man's considerable alarm, Tam flew into another of his instant rages.

The awful, tragic thing about all this was that Tam really and truly loved entertaining. He was never happier than when he had a houseful of friends enjoying his liberal hospitality.

But, best of all, he loved to entertain children. And the highlight of his year was Christmas. Then it was that he would hold a huge party, to which, irrespective of colour, race or creed, he would delightedly invite a positive horde of the children of Liverpool's poor.

Perhaps this small-bodied, big-hearted, yellow-faced man, with almond eyes, sleek black hair, wax-tipped moustache, and sing-song voice, did not much resemble the Father Christmas of venerable tradition, but there was no man in all of Liverpool who enjoyed the Yuletide frolics more heartily than Lock Ah Tam.

But Christmas 1925 was to be different. Terribly different. . . .

The old psychiatric game of hunt-the-cause is always a tricky one; but there have been those who, looking back from the eminence of hindsight, have noted the fact that in 1922 Tam invested more than £10,000—a lot of money in those days—in a shipping venture. It failed and he lost every penny he had put into it. Moreover, his business in Liverpool had ceased to prosper. In 1924 he was made bankrupt.

A knock in the pocket, they hazard, may be just as likely an aetiology for insanity as a knock on the head. Cynical—but undeniable.

Whatever. . . . The crowning tragedy in the life of the uncrowned King of Liverpool's Chinatown came on the night of 1 December 1925.

It was the twentieth birthday of his son, Lock Ling, who had only recently returned to Liverpool after nine years in China. It was an occasion for much rejoicing, and Tam was giving a select little dinner-party.

All went well. Tam remained sober. He was the proud father. The respected head of the family. Amid bowings, handshakes and good wishes, the last guest departed at a quarter to one in the morning. No untoward incident had sullied the festive pleasantry of the proceedings.

About twenty minutes after the household had retired to bed in, so far as Lock Ling knew, a haze of goodwill, he was startled to hear stampings, shufflings and shoutings coming from his parents' bedroom.

Promptly concluding that his father was ill-treating his mother, Lock Ling leapt out of bed, and, accompanied by his two sisters—Doris, who was nearly twenty-one, and Cecilia, the baby of the family at eighteen—rushed to her aid.

He accused Tam of hitting his mother.

Tam indignantly denied it.

There was a noisy scene.

Lock Ling, much distressed, threatened to take his mother next-door to spend the rest of the night with their neighbours, Mr. and Mrs. Kwok Tsan Chin.

Then Lock Ling, his mother and two sisters all went into the sitting-room, and Lock Ling announced that he was going to fetch Mr. Chin. He begged his mother and sisters to go with him. But his mother wouldn't. So he went off on his own.

Apart from the Lock family, there lived in the house a young woman named Margaret Sing, who had, for the last five or six years, acted as companion to Mrs. Lock. Throughout the trouble, Margaret had remained in her bedroom. Now, she heard Tam shouting her name. She went out on to the landing and he told her to bring him his boots. She did so, and Tam ordered her to get dressed.

Returning, fully dressed, to her employer's bedroom, she found the door ajar, and, peeping inside, she caught a glimpse of Tam's face reflected in a mirror.

It was a twisted mask of fury—and in his hand he held a gun.

With pounding heart, Margaret Sing tiptoed to the sitting-room and whispered a warning.

Swiftly they closed and barricaded the door.

Not a moment too soon.

Seconds later, Tam was battering on it and screaming to be let in.

Then . . . silence.

Ears strained that they might catch even the flicker of a mouse's whisker, the four trembling women heard him moving stealthily back to his room.

Softly, very, very softly, they inched open the door, slipped out, and crept, velvet-footed, along to the kitchen.

There, they found Lock Ling and Mrs. Chin.

Hearing their account of what had just happened, Lock Ling again begged his mother to take his sisters and Margaret Sing to the safety of the next-door house. Still, Mrs. Lock refused to do so. Lock Ling wasted no more time in argument. He ran off in search of a policeman.

The women stood round the kitchen-table whispering for a while. Then Margaret Sing picked up some crockery and carried it through to the scullery. Perhaps she was going to do a bit of washing up. *Anything* would be better than the dead-aired heaviness of just waiting . . . waiting. . . .

The others followed her. The scullery was small. There wasn't room for them all. Margaret stood, together with Doris and Mrs. Chin, behind the widely open door. Cecilia was by the gas-stove and Mrs. Lock remained standing in the doorway.

All at once there was a deafening report—and Tam's wife crumpled up on the floor.

Then the wicked-looking barrel of a shotgun slid round the doorway.

There was a second ear-splitting explosion.

This time Cecilia slumped down. Tam came swiftly and silently, like the veritable shadow of death itself, into the scullery. Spit bubbled and trickled from his mouth. He had a shotgun in one hand and a revolver in the other.

He raised the revolver. Great swamping wing-beats of explosive sound reverberated and reverberated in that tiny room as his other daughter, Doris, was slapped to the ground by the life-smashing force of the bullet.

Leaving the three women splayed in death upon the scullery floor, Tam walked calmly to the telephone, lifted the receiver and said: 'I have shot my wife and children. Please put me on to the Town Hall.' The operator put him through to Birkenhead Central Police Station. . . . 'Send your folks, please. I have killed my wife and child. My house is 122 Price Street.' Then he sat down—the Gentle Chinaman once more—to await the arrival of the police.

They knew the house and the man who owned it. They could scarcely credit that he, the gentle, kindly, charitable Chinaman, could have done this thing. But the ghastly scene of carnage which greeted them on their arrival left them, with distress, in no doubt.

That Christmas, for the first time in many years, there was no children's party at Lock Ah Tam's. The house stood dark and empty, its owner lodged, unmerrily, in Walton Gaol.

His trial opened on 5 February 1926, before Mr. Justice MacKinnon, at Chester Assizes.

He was represented by Sir Edward Marshall Hall—the 'Great Defender'—who put up a tremendous battle for the life of his client, claiming that he had not been responsible for his crime but had killed while in a state of 'epileptic automatism'. It was, said Marshall, the injury which the prisoner had received from the Russian sailor back in 1918 that had caused him to commit the crime: that injury had led to the deterioration of the man's intellectual and moral character, to a craving for alcohol, and to epilepsy.

It took the jury precisely twelve minutes to find the prisoner Guilty.

As the judge passed sentence of death, the dreaded black cap dropping in eerie folds from the crisp horse-hair of his wig, the court was filled with the wailing of Tam's Chinese friends. In that place, at that time, in those circumstances, it made the flesh to creep.

Only Lock Ah Tam remained calm.

He stood there immobile as a graven image, the faint line of a smile upon his heavy features.

Maybe, at the end, some deep, Oriental instinct for philosophy had come to his aid.

Maybe he was already a long, long way from that gloomy, panelled courtroom—back among the smiling lotus-blossoms of his sunlit native land . . . a vision of the lost bluebird of happiness before his eyes . . . waiting for the almond to scatter its petals upon him, and the dew to make tears in the eye of the chrysanthemum. . . .

III
The Deadly Teddy Bear

'OH, TEDDY BEAR,' the widow murmured reproachfully, 'I am dying. You must always take care of your Boofie.'

She smiled at the young charmer who had just strangled her. And died.

Now it was Boofie's turn. He had to take care of her.

He selected a knife from the sideboard. There was always the pajama-cord in his pocket—just in case.

He slipped silently up the stairs of the little house in Liverpool's Northbrook Street. Outside, church bells were ringing, chiming for the Sabbath . . . inside, they were booming in his ears, calling him to a second act of murder.

Softly he turned the handle of Boofie's bedroom-door. He saw that she was dressing for church. He put his hands on her shoulders, looked straight into her face, and said flatly: 'You know how much I love you. That's why I'm going to do this.'

He seized the girl by the throat. She struggled free and screamed for her mother. 'You needn't call for your mother,' he said, '*I've already killed her.*'

The tragedy to which this was the awful climax had started six months before, early in 1928. . . .

It was one of those pouring-wet days that every son and daughter of Liverpool knows so well. A ceaseless deluge. Coming down moggies and dogs, as if a gigantic hand had up-ended the Mersey. Mary Agnes Fontaine, a typist, age nineteen, stood sheltering and shivering in a shop-doorway. A pretty girl—rather frail looking, like a piece of porcelain. But below the frailty was a coolness, a resourcefulness, which was to save her quarter-spent life one nightmare Sunday in the following November.

At first she blushed and pretended to ignore the young man who dashed under the dripping eaves into the haven of the doorway beside her. They were alone, and she was embarrassed. He was like a drowned rat, or a sleek water-vole.

If only she had left him there in the cold.

But she took him into her home and her heart . . . and he devoured everything there within. It was like harbouring a stray puppy that grew into a wolf.

The young man, Joseph Reginald Clark, alias Reginald

Kennedy, was decidedly not shy. He could never resist an opportunity of ingratiating himself with a pretty girl, and long before the fury of the rain had abated, he had introduced himself in the name of Kennedy.

One thing followed another in time-honoured fashion.

Mary lived alone with her widowed mother, Mrs. Alice Fontaine, at 110 Northbrook Street, Princes Park (oddly enough, almost opposite the house from which the 'vanishing MP', Victor Grayson, disappeared). Life was somewhat bare, and they were only too willing to accept this well-spoken, lonely orphan of twenty-one into their home. He infiltrated their cosy cocoon like a deadly virus.

He came, first, for tea; then, as a paying guest—or rather, as an *unpaying* guest, since before long it was they who were doing the paying out—and, finally, as a suitor.

They got engaged. There would have been a wedding—if the gallant fiancé had not been careless with an ardent letter from a former flame who clearly believed that the fire was still burning brightly.

They should have shown him the door then. For their 'Teddy Bear', as the Fontaines pet-named him, was really a grizzly bear of the most evil mien.

'The man with a hundred sweethearts', as the newspapers were later to call him, was a most experienced Don Juan. He lived by his wits, or other people's lack of them, and had made a career of sponging on women. Like the mistletoe—that parasite of love—he clung and he sucked until his host was dry and empty.

His laser-hard, unblinking gaze turned women to jelly. 'Somehow I could not resist him and would do anything he suggested,' one victim confessed later. 'I used to find myself feeling tired and sleepy when he looked into my eyes.'

This sounds as if he had hypnotic powers—and that is exactly what he wanted people to think. Hypnotism was still a novelty, strange and exciting, in 1928. Amateur hypnotists abounded, and their party-tricks were all the rage.

Reginald Clark had a head-start over those who picked it up like Pelmanism from a pamphlet. He had learnt it scientifically in a psychology laboratory at Princeton University, in America, where he acted as a volunteer subject. But do not imagine that he was a student there. He was a pantry-boy. For Joseph Reginald Clark was a fraud from start to finish. He wasn't even an orphan.

He spun many yarns of steaming jungles and coconut islands, but the truth is that he was born in King's Lynn, Norfolk. His parents separated and he was brought up by a woman relative; when he was sixteen, she died, and he sailed to join his mother in Virginia. His stint in the cool pantries of Princeton provided the needed polish. He migrated to Halifax, Nova Scotia, and went too far with the daughter of a rich businessman there. Pursued by threats from the enraged father, he worked his passage back to England—as a pantry boy.

He scarcely had to leave the dockside at Southampton before he entrapped a young shop-assistant who supplied him with a becoming wardrobe out of her meagre savings. He told his new bevy of admirers that he was a wireless operator.

Things became a little hot, and he migrated to Liverpool. His ripest conquest here reads like a story straight out of *Decameron Nights*. He wooed four sisters at once. He stole their mother's ring as he required a trinket for the youngest—his favourite—and produced the purloined birth certificate of one of her older sisters when giving notice to marry her at the Birkenhead Registrar's Office.

His malfeasances discovered, he was banished from his mormonic Garden of Eden. Whereupon he waylaid his favourite in the street. 'If I can't have you, nobody else shall,' he informed the shrinking girl, as he pulled a pajama-cord from his pocket, and tightened it around her neck. But the rabbit broke free from the stoat and ran off down Princes Boulevard, screaming for the police.

If only he had been stowed away safely then.

It was a letter from his old sweetheart in Nova Scotia that shipwrecked his new idyll with the Fontaines in Northbrook Street.

Outraged, they told him to go.

He lurked sullenly in his room and whiled away the time composing dirty anonymous letters to the Fontaines.

Uncuddly Teddy Bear had turned savage.

They went to the police. Detective-Sergeant Tomlin warned them that their sitting-lodger was notorious for 'other girls' and 'other things'.

A paranoid notion grew fast, like a tiny cactus seed into a prickly plant, in Clark's head: Tomlin fancied his girl for himself.

Teddy Bear stayed on, growling and licking his wounds.

They tried to reform him. They nagged and they preached. Oh, how they preached!

And so, it was the mother that he sprang at first on that November Sunday morning as her voice yammered on at him.

He choked Mrs. Fontaine to death in one minute flat.

Mary Fontaine was a tougher proposition. Like a Hydra with many heads, she fought back, defying this bloodied bear. He kept producing more weapons. He used his thumbs . . . pajama-cord . . . some electric-light flex . . . he stabbed at her throat.

There was silence—except for the gonging church-bells, out-side or in his head, he did not know which by now.

Then, suddenly, she was alive again . . . talking persuasively . . . trying to calm him. . . .

Very, very gently, she inched out of the room. He followed her. She forced herself to go slowly, very slowly, down the stairs. The front-door came nearer and nearer. She ran at it. . . .

And she was out in the street, with people pretending not to be staring at her, and with the air full of bells.

When the police arrived, Clark was combing his hair in front of a mirror. He made no attempt to escape. Nor did he defend himself at Liverpool Assizes. His trial lasted four and a half minutes.

He was hanged at Walton Gaol on the bleak morning of 12 March 1929. There was a crowd of some two hundred outside the prison-gates, and most of those sighing figures were young women.

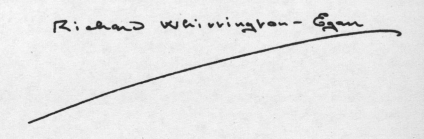

THE CASE OF THE RAGGED STRANGER
Alexander Woollcott

[Drama critic, essayist, and latterly the bell-ringing 'Town Crier' of his own very popular radio show, when he was not working or entertaining at his Manhattan apartment (christened 'Wit's End' by Dorothy Parker), he could often be found at the head, if that is possible, of the 'round table' of performing wits in the Algonquin Hotel. One of his many English friends, F. Tennyson Jesse, said that he was 'half wasp, half honey-bee, but always winged,' and James Thurber dubbed him 'Old Vitriol and Violets'. The grandest of his friends were Franklin and Eleanor Roosevelt; he stayed at the White House during the Washington run of The Man Who Came to Dinner in which he played the eponymous and himself-portraying part of Sheridan Whiteside, and subsequently advised Ethel Barrymore: 'Mrs. Roosevelt runs the best theatrical boarding-house in town.' The drama critic, John Mason Brown, noted that 'his curiosities were themselves curious. . . . His enthusiasms . . . ranged from the American Expeditionary Force [in which he had served, for most of the time as a reporter on The Stars and Stripes] and Dickens, and such dissimilar women as Mrs. Fiske and Lizzie Borden, to Irving Berlin, the four Marxes, Gilbert and Sullivan, Kipling, forgotten murders, Hamilton College

[his alma mater], Thornton Wilder, and, of course, Sir
James M. Barrie.' Woollcott, who had said, 'One day
I shall probably talk myself to death,' suffered a fatal
heart-attack while taking part in a radio discussion-
programme four days after his fifty-sixth birthday in
1943.]

ON THE MORNING of 22 June 1920, Carl Oscar Wanderer awoke to find himself famous. After serving overseas as lieutenant in a machine-gun battalion, this young hero had returned to Chicago, gone to work in his father's butcher-shop, married his pre-war sweetheart, and regretfully settled down to a humdrum existence. Yet here were the newspapers crackling with the details of a melodrama of which Wanderer was the central figure. The setting was the vestibule of the two-family house in North Campbell Avenue, where the bride and groom shared a flat with her mother. It seems, according to the stories which all Chicago read at breakfast, that on the preceding evening the young folks had gone down to the Pershing Theatre to see *The Sea Wolf*,[1] and on the way home had been followed by a tattered young gunman who, on their very doorstep, had attempted a holdup. In the ensuing scuffle, the bride was fatally wounded and Wanderer, drawing his own gun, had shot it out with the tramp. He was still furiously pummelling a body already riddled with bullets when the cop from the corner came running up to see what all the shooting was about.

The coroner's jury not only brought in a verdict against John Doe, the derelict, but so far overstepped the necessities of the occasion as to commiserate with the young husband on his grievous loss and to congratulate him on the red-blooded, soldierly promptitude with which he had spared Illinois the expense of a trial. But the Chicago *Daily News* was already sounding a slightly different note. The day after the shooting, it had sent one of its star reporters—a lad named Ben

[1] EDITOR'S NOTE. *A movie, starring Raymond Hatton and Mabel Juliene Scott.*

Hecht[1]—to interview the hero. The follow-up story which he wrote that afternoon was coloured by the fact that during the interview he had conceived a strong distaste for Wanderer. It had offended the fastidious Hecht, on the morning after the murder of young Mrs. Wanderer, to discover the bereaved husband in the act of pressing his trousers and whistling as he did it. But soon the police developed a distaste for Wanderer based on circumstances quite as alienating and rather more likely to impress a jury. They succeeded in proving that both guns found in that bloody vestibule had been in Wanderer's possession the day before.

Confronted by this evidence, the already tarnished hero at last confessed that he had killed not only the poor schlemiel in the morgue but Mrs. Wanderer as well. She was soon to have borne him a child, and he had longed to escape from the trap of domesticity and go back into the army. So he had picked up the tramp on the street, hired him as an accomplice and planned a bogus holdup, spinning into that luckless ear a tall tale about the great roll of bills which his stingy wife always carried in her purse. It was arranged that after the holdup, the two were to meet down the street and divide the proceeds. What eventually hanged Wanderer, in addition to his using two guns of which both could be traced to himself, was the fact that during the excitement he lost his head, such as it was, and shot his wife and the tramp with the same gun.

The word 'eventually' is used advisedly, for when he was tried for the murder of his wife, Wanderer was defended by foxy lawyers who were capable of maintaining in one breath that the confession had been extracted by brute force, that Wanderer was crazy as a coot, and that anyway it had all been done by a couple of other fellows. These forensic didoes so bemused the jury that, after deliberating for twenty-three hours, they brought

---

[1] *EDITOR'S NOTE. He wrote plays (successfully when he collaborated with Charles MacArthur, e.g.* The Front Page, Twentieth Century), *movie-scripts, and novels (some of which were banned by the Federal Government on the ground of obscenity)—and tried to poeticise the pleasure he derived from the killing of British soldiers by Zionist terrorists/freedom-fighters. Gifted with a talent to abuse, he described Alexander Woollcott as 'a persnickety fellow with more fizz than brain'.*

in a verdict of Guilty but—as was the privilege of juries in Illinois—so limited the penalty that he need only behave himself in Joliet to be turned loose after thirteen years.

As a tart comment on this verdict, the Hearst morning paper came out next day with a photograph of those jurors under the caption 'A Dozen Soft-boiled Eggs'. It also published the names, addresses and telephone numbers of each, together with a broad hint that any disapproving citizen might do well to call them up. Thanks to these tactics, a second jury arrived in court freshly admonished as to its duty. For Wanderer was not out of the woods yet. He could not be tried again for the offence, but he stood accused of another. That was the killing of his forlorn accomplice who still lay unidentified on a slab in the morgue. It took the second jury less than half an hour to reach a verdict which would send him to the gallows.

One of Wanderer's counsel was a sympathetic Portia who bitterly charged the reporters with having achieved this result. This was a true bill, but one must take the bitter with the sweet, and no one watching Wanderer through his ordeal could have doubted that he was hugely enjoying the prominence which the newspapers accorded him. Most murderers, from Ruth Snyder to Bruno Hauptmann, have obviously relished their own trials. Wanderer was so agreeably conscious of the public eye that when the foreman, in tears, announced the verdict, he managed to emit a scornful laugh; and this pattern of behaviour sustained him to the end. On the gallows he elected, as his farewell to the world, to sing a song while the noose was being adjusted. For this occasion he selected a current ballad of which the title was, if memory serves, 'Old Pal, Why Don't You Answer Me?' In his rendition, he had reached the refrain and had just finished the couplet:

> My arms embrace
> An empty space

when the warden pulled the trap and left the singer dangling over eternity. From one of the crowd of reporters watching the execution came the audible comment that Wanderer deserved hanging for his voice alone.

As for his nameless accomplice, he would have been tucked away in Potter's Field had it not been for the intervention of a sentimental saloon-keeper named Barney Clamage, who ordered and paid for a tasty funeral. So he was laid away in Green Oaks Cemetery, and over his grave, for a time, there stood a cross with this inscription:

Here Lies
The
Ragged Stranger.

Alexander Woollcott

THE ETERNAL SUSPECT
Albert Borowitz

[A lawyer practising in Cleveland, Ohio, he is the best of the presently-busy US crime historians; described by a critic as 'a sleuth upon the crossroads between literature and crime', he has explored those crossroads through studies of writers, intellectuals and musicians who confronted crime in their own lives (as criminals, suspects, victims, or observers) or were inspired by criminal cases to create significant works of the imagination. Long before the premiere of Amadeus, *he wrote what remains the most detailed study of the legend of Salieri's murder of Mozart (it can be found in my anthology* The Art of Murder). *In addition to numerous essays, he has written two book-length crime studies,* The Thurtell-Hunt Murder Case *and* The Bermondsey Horror *(about the Mannings case; the book was nominated for a Gold Dagger award by the British Crime Writers' Association). As a mystery novelist, he has created a detective named Paul Prye—who is, like himself, a true-crime aficionado married to an art historian. He and his wife Helen are the joint-authors of a fascinating art-and-crime book,* Pawnshop and Palaces *(Smithsonian Institution, 1991). They have recently established the Borowitz True-Crime Collection, comprising some 6000 volumes, in the Library of Kent State University.]*

ONE ANNOYANCE Moscow police chief Luzhin particularly resented was having to talk business at his club. He was therefore far from pleased when fellow-member Alexander Sukhovo-Kobylin approached him in the late evening of 8 November 1850 to ask, in carefully guarded terms, whether the chief had received any news of a 'traffic mishap involving a woman in a blue cloak'. Luzhin curtly said no, and returned his full attention to his cigar and brandy.

In any event, he had never much liked Sukhovo-Kobylin, though his family was beyond reproach. The thirty-two-year-old man was the son of a veteran of the Napoleonic Wars, Vasily Alexandrovich, who had lost an eye at Austerlitz and retired as a colonel in the artillery; the family proudly claimed common ancestry with the Romanovs. Young Alexander had been a brilliant student at Moscow University, where he won a gold medal for a paper on the application of certain principles of physics to the construction of suspension bridges. After graduation, he studied philosophy in Heidelberg and Berlin, becoming, like many of his generation, a devotee of Hegel. In 1842, he enrolled in the Moscow civil service, rising to the rank of titular councillor, a position that he held at the time of his retirement from the administration in the summer of 1850. His role in the bureaucracy was more formal than active, a fact to which he proudly referred in suggesting that his tomb bear the inscription, 'He never served'. Sukhovo-Kobylin's true calling was not government but business; following the practical bent he had already shown in his university career, he organized wide-ranging enterprises, including forestry, livestock and horse breeding, textiles, sugar, vodka, and Russia's first champagne cellars. At the same time, he was a passionate sportsman, carrying off first prizes in horse-races.

There was much to admire in the young man, but the police chief was not alone in disliking him. Sukhovo-Kobylin was a triumphant womanizer and an acid-tongued gossip, of whom memoirist E. K. Feoktistov has left a predominantly unflattering portrait:

> There is no doubt that he was a very intelligent man. . . .
> He completed a course at Moscow University and even won a gold medal on graduation; he travelled widely and loved serious reading; everything evidently combined in his favour. But meantime, hardly anybody aroused such

general ill-will. The reason was his nature—coarse, impudent, by no means softened by his education; this man, speaking excellent French, having acquired gentlemanly manners, trying to appear a real Parisian, was in reality a cruel savage who did not stick at any abuses of feudal rights; his servants were afraid of him. I have had occasion more than once to note that such people, distinguished in masculine beauty, self-assured to the point of insolence, brilliantly witty but at the same time completely heartless, produce an enchanting impression on women. Alexander Kobylin could congratulate himself on a whole series of amatory adventures, but they also destroyed him.

Police chief Luzhin and just about everybody in Moscow high society knew about Sukhovo-Kobylin's current romantic entanglements. Since 1842, he had maintained an open liaison with Louise Simon-Dimanche, a fashionable red-haired milliner whom he had met in Paris; following her arrival in Moscow (perhaps at his summons), he had appointed her manager of his wine and provisions store and installed her in an apartment where his serfs attended to her housekeeping and he regularly shared her table. His domineering mother, the cigar-smoking saloniste Marya Ivanovna, accepted Louise warmly and treated her like a trusted relative (but not quite a daughter-in-law). The couple's relationship survived periodic storms over Sukhovo-Kobylin's chronic infidelities, never more scandalous than his current intrigue with a captivating married woman, Natalya Naryshkina. In November 1850, Louise lived in the house of Count Gudovich in Tverskaya Street (now Gorky Street); early in the month, Sukhovo-Kobylin had vacated the principal rooms of his family's house at 9 Strastnoy Boulevard to make room for his sister and her husband, and moved into a wing of the same building.

The police chief may have wondered momentarily about the identity of the mysterious 'woman in the blue cloak,' but the next morning, 9 November, Sukhovo-Kobylin visited Luzhin again and was more forthright in disclosing his worries. He now made an official request that the police search for Louise Simon-Dimanche, who had disappeared two nights before. He indicated two possible directions for police inquiries, the Petersburg Chaussee to the northwest of the city (a highway that he had spent much of the day exploring himself without success) and the western road that led to the village of Choroshevo and the Silver Pine Forest.

By the evening of 9 November, police efforts remained fruitless; but from an apparently independent quarter came the grim news of the discovery of a female corpse. Beyond the Presnenski gate in the western perimeter of Moscow, the body, arms folded beneath, lay prone in a snow-covered ravine near the wall surrounding the Vagankovsky cemetery. The beautiful woman, still young, was elegantly attired in a green checked dress, blouse of Dutch linen, sky-blue jacket and veiled silk cap. She wore gold earrings set with brilliants, and rings adorned fingers of both hands. On her feet were velvet half-boots—a strange choice for a wintry night's excursion. Beneath the woman's dress were three petticoats, but the corset that fashion mandated was absent; her drawers were rucked up to the knees.

When the police looked more closely at the woman, horror overwhelmed their admiration of her beauty; a loosened tress of her luxuriant red hair wound around her neck, but failed to cover a yawning wound in her neck, from which some blood, but surprisingly little, had escaped to stain the snow. Near the corpse there were tracks of a sleigh and horses' hooves; everything seemed to proclaim that the body had been carried out of Moscow and deposited in fitting proximity to the cemetery, which lay not far from the Choroshevo road which Sukhovo-Kobylin had mentioned to the police chief.

After the body was brought to Moscow, house serfs of Sukhovo-Kobylin identified the dead woman as the missing Louise Simon-Dimanche. Doctor Tichomirov made an external examination of the body, and that was followed on 11 November by an autopsy in which he participated. The body was of rather strong build and medium height. On the front of the neck, below the larynx, was a five-inch diagonal wound, apparently inflicted with an even-edged instrument; the windpipe, carotid arteries and both jugular veins were completely severed. A groove with the dimension of 'a little finger' was noticeable all around the upper portion of the neck. The doctors also observed a large dark purple swelling, about the size of the palm of a hand, around the left eye.

The entire left side of the body was bloody; on the left arm, from the shoulder to the elbow, was a large dark stain with bruising and an obliquely indented groove ending in a triangular excoriation. Three left ribs were fractured and another smashed. Nothing pathological or abnormal was found in the mouth, alimentary canal or windpipe, and the internal organs showed no sign of bleeding and were otherwise in normal condition.

Only in late January 1851 did the police make a detailed examination of the victim's clothing. The green dress was covered with thick streams of blood from the top to the waist; the first petticoat of white calico was also heavily stained, but there were barely noticeable stains on the exterior of the second petticoat and none closer to the body. The two doctors who performed the autopsy concluded that the death of Louise Simon-Dimanche was caused by extraordinary force—and specifically by 'the unquestionably mortal wound' at the front of the neck.

The report of the murder spread rapidly through Moscow, and, long before the police had a chance to complete an investigation, the public had confidently promulgated its own theory. According to the 'public version,' as adopted and elaborated by literary critic Leonid Grossman in *The Crime of Sukhovo-Kobylin* [*Prestuplenie Sukhovo-Kobylina*] (1928), Sukhovo-Kobylin murdered his French mistress in a fury over her disruption of an amorous rendezvous with Natalya Naryshkina. Simon-Dimanche, the theory went, tracked her rival in the early hours of 8 November to the wing of Sukhovo-Kobylin's house on Strastnoy Boulevard and surprised the two lovers when her presence was least needed. Angered at the intrusion and her abuse of Naryshkina, Sukhovo-Kobylin struck Louise with a candle-stick and cut her throat. He then ordered his servants, whom Leonid Grossman hypothetically identifies as his valet Makar Lukyanov and cook Efim Egorov, to carry the body to the cemetery where it was found.

The police were not as hasty as the public in pronouncing the case solved. Instead, they questioned a large array of witnesses, including Sukhovo-Kobylin and his valet Lukyanov, and the house serfs he had delegated to serve Simon-Dimanche in her apartment on Tverskaya Street. The assigned servants included four who were to be centrally involved in the investigation: two maids—Pelageya Alekseeva, aged fifteen, and Agrafena Ivanova

Kashkina, who was twenty-seven; the cook Egorov, who lived in Sukhovo-Kobylin's house but worked in Louise's kitchen; and a boy from the wine-shop, Galaktion Kozmin, who was serving as coachman at the time of the tragedy because of the illness of the regular driver. Incriminating evidence was found on Egorov's person when he was questioned: under the lining of his vest pocket he had concealed 100 rubles, a sum corresponding to Simon-Dimanche's household funds. Later, police recovered Louise's gold watch in the attic occupied by Egorov in Sukhovo-Kobylin's house; it was wrapped in a letter addressed to the valet Lukyanov. The police placed Egorov, Lukyanov and Louise's three household servants under arrest.

From depositions of the young substitute-coachman Kozmin and other witnesses, the police were able to reconstruct many of the details of Louise's busy last day. Her schedule did not suggest that she was a woman brooding about her lover's infidelity or plotting a melodramatic intervention. Kozmin had driven the Frenchwoman around Moscow on a twelve-hour excursion beginning at nine in the morning. The first stop was at Gazetny Lane to pick up Louise's close friend, Mme. Ernestine Liandert, with whom she proceeded to Ochotny Row (now Marx Prospekt) to shop for provisions. Louise spent an hour chatting at Ernestine's apartment and afterwards returned home alone for about an hour. Then she was back in her sleigh, ordering Kozmin to drive her successively to a bookstore, a business office and her dressmaker's. Stopping at home to change for the evening, she was off again for dinner at Ernestine Liandert's with her friend's lover Lieutenant Sushkov and another tall man with a moustache whom Kozmin didn't know. Then the four left in a pair of sleighs for an evening's ride around the boulevards, ending with a drive across the Kuznetsky Bridge to eat ices at a popular confectioners' shop. When Kozmin brought her home at 9:00 p.m., Louise ordered that the horse, understandably tired, be unharnessed.

Much of Louise's next hour (the last time she was seen before the murder) was devoted to household matters. Efim Egorov told the police that he had gone to see her around 10:00 p.m. 'to ask her what food to prepare for the following day; when he left Dimanche's place, she gave him a note for his master, which he delivered to the valet [because Sukhovo-Kobylin was away].' After Egorov's departure, a clerk, Fyodor Fedotov, arrived 'with expense-accounts for the table, and Dimanche ordered him to tell his master to send an answer to the note she had dispatched to him through the cook Efim. However, Fedotov did not give the message to his master, because he didn't see him: when he returned from Dimanche's, his master wasn't at home.'

Although Louise's note was sealed, the valet Lukyanov stated that she had written to enquire whether Sukhovo-Kobylin planned to dine with her on the following evening (8 November). According to Lukyanov, his master, on his return home early in the morning of 8 November, told him to inform Simon-Dimanche that he had an engagement for the evening, and so only breakfast should be prepared for him.

The housemaid Pelageya Alekseeva stated that, after sending her letter to Sukhovo-Kobylin, Simon-Dimanche waited about half an hour for a response. Then the other maid, Agrafena Kashkina, saw her mistress leave the apartment, wearing a warm cloak and the same apparel in which she had been dressed for the evening. Louise did not tell any of her servants where she was going; she said only that she would soon return, and did not even order them to extinguish the candles. Alekseeva added that about 8.00 the next morning, a tall gentleman with a small moustache called and introduced himself as a friend of Mme. Ernestine Liandert. He asked after Simon-Dimanche and, when the maids told him she had not yet come home, said: 'That's a bad business.' Only after the stranger left did Sukhovo-Kobylin arrive—to find that Louise was missing.

On 16 November, Moscow society (despite its own suspicions) was shocked by the news that Sukhovo-Kobylin had also been placed under arrest. Police cited 'inconsistencies' in his statements. The smooth-talking aristocrat said that he was convinced that robbery must have been the motive and that the murderer was probably either an unidentified hackney-coachman whom Louise had engaged for her mysterious nocturnal errand, or Efim Egorov, who had been found in possession of her money and watch. But if it was robbery that had inspired the crime, why had the killer overlooked the jewelry with which the ears and fingers of the corpse were adorned? The Muscovite gossips had a ready explanation: Sukhovo-Kobylin's accomplice, through stupidity or haste, had neglected to support the robbery 'red herring' by removing the jewelry.

Sukhovo-Kobylin stoutly asserted an alibi for the murder-night: he had been a dinner-guest of the Naryshkins and returned home very late. Some of the Naryshkins' servants supported the story, but the police strangely failed to question either the Naryshkins or their other guests.

It was not only on Sukhovo-Kobylin's depositions that the police based their arrest-warrant but also on discoveries made in the search of the wing he had recently begun to occupy at the family-house on Strastnoy Boulevard. The finds that the police trumpeted were a letter to Simon-Dimanche which they believed established Sukhovo-Kobylin's premeditation of the crime; a pair of daggers; and a number of apparent bloodstains. By contrast with these intriguing clues, searches of Simon-Dimanche's apartment on Tverskaya Street revealed no signs of violence, and neither Prince Radziwill, a student who lodged in a flat above, nor any of the servants in the house had heard any outcries or other suspicious sounds on the night of the crime.

The evidence that the police identified in Sukhovo-Kobylin's rooms was a remarkably weak foundation for a murder-charge against him. The supposedly incriminating letter that the arrested man had sent to Louise was written in a playful tone:

> Chère Maman. It happens that I will stay for several days in Moscow. Knowing that you have remained in the countryside only to play out your farces and to listen to a passion that (alas!) doesn't tell you my name but that of another, I prefer to call you back to my side so as to have an ungrateful and treacherous woman in my sight and within reach of my Castilian dagger. . . .

The investigators were not expert in the literary analysis of love-letters; nor were they able to elucidate such an obvious phallic symbol as a 'Castilian dagger'. Instead, they seized two ornamental daggers as possible instruments of the crime.

Clearly, the police felt more at home with bloodstains. They thought they had found quite a few at Strastnoy Boulevard—but by no means in the copious amount they should have expected to encounter if the throat of a living woman had been cut in the apartment. Still, they carefully catalogued what they had observed. On the wall-plaster of a variously-described antechamber, in the direction of the hallway, two small stains appeared, one in the shape of a spreading oblong drop about two inches long and the other a spatter of the size of a five-kopek silver-piece. In the hall near a storeroom, a seven-inch semicircular spot could be seen on the dirty floor near the base-board and, nearby, blood-coloured streams and splotches partly cleaned. Apparent bloodstains of various sizes were also visible on the back stairs. Floors in all the rooms were painted yellow and recently washed.

Sukhovo-Kobylin found innocent explanations for all those stains. Many people had lived in the wing before him, and he had only recently moved there; he had not yet had occasion to give attention to cleaning or refurbishing his rooms. He told the police that poultry and game from the country were often brought up the back stairs for slaughtering there and in the hallway, where a slop-bucket was kept to catch the blood. He was less certain of the origin of the wall-stains, but he recalled that one of his menservants was inclined to nosebleeds; in view of Sukhovo-Kobylin's admittedly violent treatment of his serfs, it was small wonder.

The police cut away pieces of the wall-plaster and floor, for some reason neglecting to sample the stains on the back stairs, and submitted the evidence for forensic analysis. The Moscow Medical Office concluded that the stains on the floor were dried blood but considered that the determination whether it was of human or animal origin was beyond available scientific means. The appraisal of the wall-stains was even less conclusive: because of the insignificant size of the sample and the impossibility of separating the stains from the plaster without substantial admixture, the composition of the stains could not be determined.

On 20 November, the case took a dramatic turn when the cook Egorov, after being sequestered for intensive questioning, confessed to the murder with the participation of Simon-Dimanche's three other servants, who, in order, confirmed his story in all significant particulars. The servants' motive was revenge for their mistress's cruel treatment, and the theft of the household funds and other valuable objects not kept under lock and key was pretty much an afterthought. One of the main sources of the servants' miseries with their late employer was that Louise had never acquired a sure command of the Russian language. Often the serfs did not fully understand her oral instructions, and when, as a consequence, they did not perform to her satisfaction, she beat them or denounced them to Sukhovo-Kobylin, who had a much heavier hand. When Egorov entered her household, he already had a personal grievance against Louise: his sister Vasilisa had previously served her as chambermaid and left after only three months because of her tyranny.

In his confession (as supplemented by the statements of his confederates), Egorov said that in the days before her death, Simon-Dimanche had become even nastier and more capricious, and he had often talked with the other servants about getting rid of her. About 8:00 p.m. on 7 November, he came to Tverskaya Street to obtain his mistress's instructions about food. She wasn't home yet, so he sat with the maids and they renewed their conversation about how to finish the business they had been discussing; they decided to kill her early the next morning, and he instructed them to pass the word to Kozmin when he came back. He was about to leave when the sleigh returned, so he sought out the young driver in the stable, where he was putting away the horse, and announced the murder-plan directly.

Having made his arrangements for the crime, Egorov calmly presented himself to Simon-Dimanche to discuss his cooking duties. When he arrived home at Strastnoy Boulevard later that evening, he gave Simon-Dimanche's note to the valet Lukyanov and went to sleep in the servants' quarters. At 1:30 in the morning, Lukyanov woke him up with their master's response: Egorov was to tell Simon-Dimanche to prepare only breakfast, for his excellency would be busy for dinner.

Egorov had quite a different errand in mind. He went back to the Tverskaya Street apartment at about 2:00 a.m. and aroused his accomplices. Kozmin took a flat-iron from the kitchen, and the two men proceeded to Louise's bedroom door, which the maids by prearrangement had kept unlocked. Their mistress was sleeping. Egorov, walking to the bed, pressed a pillow over her face. When she woke up, and cried out twice, Egorov gagged her with a handkerchief, then seized her throat and began to strangle her, using a towel as a noose; he struck her once with his fist in her left eye, and Kozmin meantime beat her sides with the flat-iron.

When the woman was dead, the maids dressed her. Kozmin harnessed the horse, and the two men placed the body downwards in the sleigh under a fur cover. After they arrived at the cemetery, Egorov, in sudden panic, thought he heard Simon-Dimanche utter a feeble sound, so he cut her throat with Kozmin's folding-knife; he threw the weapon somewhere nearby. While the men were disposing of the body, the two housemaids put the murdered woman's apartment in order; when Egorov and Kozmin returned from the cemetery, the maids burned Louise's cloak in a Dutch oven. Kozmin located two bottles of wine in the back room and drank with Egorov until six in the morning, when they capped their revels with a visit to a local tavern.

After Egorov's confession, Sukhovo-Kobylin was released; but the investigation of his complicity lumbered on in spite of the disappointing results of the bloodstain analysis. On 8 December 1850, Natalya Naryshkina—pregnant with Sukhovo-Kobylin's child—obtained permission to leave for France, where she later became the mistress and then wife of Alexandre Dumas *fils*. The authorities' apparent belief in Naryshkina's innocence was not shared by Leo Tolstoy, who on 7 December wrote to his relative Tatyana Ergolskaya a garbled account of the case:

> Since you are keen on tragic stories, I'll tell you one which has created a stir in Moscow. A certain Mr. Kobylin was keeping a certain Madame Simon, and he supplied her the services of two men and a maidservant. Now, Mr. Kobylin, before [sic] keeping this Madame Simon, formed a liaison with Madame Naryshkina, née Knorring, a lady from the best Moscow society and a lady very much in vogue, and he had not stopped corresponding with her, although he was keeping Madame Simon. On top of all this, one fine morning Simon is found murdered, and certain evidence indicates that she was killed by her own servants. This might not have amounted to anything much, were it not for the fact that the police, when arresting Kobylin, found among his papers some letters from Madame Naryshkina, in which she reproaches him for abandoning her and threatens Madame Simon, *which only adds to the many other reasons for concluding that the murderers were but the instruments of Madame Naryshkina* (emphasis added).

On 13 September 1851, the Moscow Aulic Court, rendering the first judgment in the case, convicted the four servants and declared Sukhovo-Kobylin Not Guilty. Egorov, Kozmin and the two maids were sentenced to deprivation of all civil rights, public flogging (together with branding for the men), and hard labour in prison, mine or workhouse, for terms ranging from 15 to $22^1/_2$ years. Though Egorov was identified as the ringleader and sent to a prison-camp, Kashkina drew the longest sentence. The judgment was affirmed by the Moscow Criminal Tribunal.

Despite the outward appearance that the trial-proceedings were being resolved in Sukhovo-Kobylin's favour, the case against the servants was in fact beginning to unravel. In May and June 1851, the two maids recanted their confessions, claiming that their depositions had been manufactured by their interrogators. In connection with their appeals to the Senate, Egorov and Kozmin followed suit; the cook claimed that his confession had been coerced by torture, and both men claimed that the police had held out enticements in the form of letters from Sukhovo-Kobylin offering rewards and freedom for them and their families. After a hearing before the Senate in December 1852, three members of the hearing panel voted to affirm the decision of the Criminal Tribunal, but Senator I. N. Chotyaintsev dissented, concluding that Sukhovo-Kobylin's guilt was probable and that the servants were innocent. He thought it impossible that the dead woman's maids would have had time after the murder to dress her in the elegant apparel and adornments found on her body in the cemetery, and he doubted that the neck-wounds could have been inflicted with a small knife.

After the panel's decision was announced, the case was brought before the general assembly of the Moscow departments of the Senate. However, because the views of the senators were divided, the matter was referred to the Minister of Justice, V. N. Panin—who, in his report to the Senate, opined that the confessions of the serfs, because of the 'obvious incompleteness and evident shortcomings of the investigation,' did not satisfy legal requirements and that the statements, in light of their contradictions, were very doubtful and even incredible. Panin also firmly rejected Sukhovo-Kobylin's claim that robbery was the motive. Since neither Prince Radziwill nor the other residents of the victim's house had heard any cries on the murder-night, the minister was persuaded that the crime had not been committed there. Focusing on Sukhovo-Kobylin's actions on 8 November, Panin commented that the nobleman, who had not previously worried about Louise's absences, visited her apartment six times beginning at 9:00 a.m., and that when he returned home that night, he told his valet: 'Dimanche must surely have been murdered.'

In the light of his doubts about the judgments of the courts below, Minister Panin decided that a new, thorough investigation was necessary. This conclusion was confirmed by the State Council on 17 December 1853, and the Tsar's approval followed the next month. By February, an investigative commission was ready to begin work.

The re-investigation brought more sufferings to the beleaguered Sukhovo-Kobylin, who was again imprisoned, from May to November 1854. With the passage of time, there was no new light to be cast on the mystery. The commission questioned three of the servants (Pelageya having died in the course of the proceedings); but, though they professed more vivid memories as witnesses than they had displayed as prime defendants, they had little to contribute to the cause of truth. All the old evidence and issues were re-examined—Sukhovo-Kobylin's alibi . . . the condition of the dead woman's clothing . . . the bloodstains in the house in Strastnoy Boulevard . . . the ability of Prince Radziwill, the Tverskaya Street tenant, to hear sounds from the floor below where Louise had lived and perhaps died.

All the commission's inquiries proved inconclusive, and the case again meandered through the court system. The Moscow Criminal Tribunal issued a new judgment, reconfirming Sukhovo-Kobylin's innocence and upholding prison sentences for the three surviving servants; on 30 June 1855, the Moscow military governor, General A. A. Zakrevsky, approved this judgment and referred the case to the Senate. Once again, however, the senators derailed the case, finding the servants' confessions incredible and the circumstances such as to cast suspicion on Sukhovo-Kobylin of at least indirect involvement in the crime. In the light of these considerations, the Senate reached a bizarre decision: (1) to 'leave Sukhovo-Kobylin under suspicion for participation in the murder'; (2) to free the servants from the responsibility for the crime but to exile them to Siberia for perjury and obstruction of justice.

Ultimately, Sukhovo-Kobylin's mother successfully petitioned the Empress to intervene in favour of her son, who was now running the risk of becoming an eternal suspect. Even with imperial favour, the path to freedom was far from smooth. In an interview with Sukhovo-Kobylin in St. Petersburg in May 1856, Minister Panin informed him that the case would be terminated. But it was not until 25 October 1857 that the State Council, after manoeuvres in the Senate, approved a judgment freeing the serfs from responsibility for the murder and entrusting them to the protection of local authorities against any reprisals from their master; and relieving Sukhovo-Kobylin as well from the murder-charge—but ordering him, 'for his illicit love-affair, to submit to ecclesiastical penitence for the cleansing of his conscience'. The Tsar approved the decree on 3 December 1857, finally bringing Sukhovo-Kobylin's travail to an end.

Sukhovo-Kobylin's experiences in the toils of Tsarist justice inspired him to create one of the monuments of nineteenth-century Russian theatre, the intricately-linked trilogy to which he ultimately gave the name *Pictures of the Past* [*Kartiny Proshedshevo*]. Weaving a tragi-comic theme that has similarities to the unifying idea of Wagner's Ring cycle, Sukhovo-Kobylin recounts a series of struggles by conscienceless men to gain control of the fortune of a wealthy provincial landowner, Muromsky, and the disasters that greed brings to everyone with the ironic exception of the arch-villain. The first play, *Krechinsky's Wedding* [*Svadba Krechinskovo*], of which Sukhovo-Kobylin wrote a large part during his 1854 imprisonment, is a 'well-made' comedy about the nearly successful effort of an upper-class gambler, Krechinsky, abetted by a ridiculously unscrupulous henchman, Rasplyuev, to acquire Muromsky's riches by wedding his naive daughter Lida. Krechinsky's plans are threatened by the pressures of his creditors, but he averts disaster in the nick of time by pledging a worthless copy of a valuable ring belonging to Lida. When his fraud is exposed, Lida, though her eyes are now open to his self-seeking courtship, comes to his rescue by delivering the real jewel to the pawnbroker.

While sharply attacking the degradation of aristocratic morality, *Krechinsky's Wedding* did not directly target the Tsarist regime, and so was passed by the censors, bringing its author great success on the stage at the same time as he remained under suspicion of murder. In a sequel, however, Sukhovo-Kobylin proceeded to a bitter indictment of the Russian court system. In this play, titled simply *The Case* [*Delo*] (completed in 1861, four years after the end of his prosecution), Sukhovo-Kobylin drew on both his own experiences and Gogol's satires of soulless Russian bureaucracy. In his 1862 preface, the playwright took pains to advise his public that the work did not represent the 'fruit of leisure' or a literary exercise, but was 'in all actuality a real case that has been ripped, dripping with blood, from truest life'.

In *The Case*, the Muromskys are enmeshed in an endless criminal prosecution based in part on the false testimony of a servant and designed for the sole purpose of extorting bribes for the benefit of the bureaucrats overseeing the criminal courts. The authorities have concocted the fantastic charge that Lida Muromsky conspired with Krechinsky in his plan to rob her father, asserting that she was motivated by a secret love-affair with her suitor. Although the playwright drew a picture of universal corruption, there seems little doubt that he was drawing a parallel to his own prosecution, and that his audience was to regard Lida's alleged betrayal of her beloved father as no more incredible than the allegation that Sukhovo-Kobylin had murdered his companion of many years. Muromsky, desiring to bring his daughter's martyrdom to an end, is persuaded by Tarelkin, a bribe-taking subordinate of corrupt State Councillor Varravin, to meet with his boss. When Varravin proposes an extremely high bribe for closing the case, Muromsky appeals to the Prince, Varravin's superior. The interview comes to a disastrous conclusion, for the Prince, obsessed with his painful hemorrhoids, quarrels with Muromsky and orders the entire case reviewed. Tarelkin and Varravin are in mortal terror that a re-opening of the investigation will hinder their extortion plans, so Tarelkin decides to bring matters to a head by suggesting that Lida be subjected to a medical examination to supply evidence of her alleged love-affair. To save his daughter's honour, Muromsky offers Varravin the huge sum he had demanded, but the crafty minister, turning back only a small portion of the delivered money, accuses Muromsky of attempted bribery. Muromsky dies of a stroke, but the play ends with a show of dishonour among thieves: Tarelkin inveighs against Varravin, who has kept all the bribe money for himself.

In the finale of the trilogy, a black comedy called *The Death of Tarelkin* [*Smert Tarelkina*] (finished in 1868), the battle between Varravin and Tarelkin over Muromsky's bribe-money resumes, and the focus of Sukhovo-Kobylin's attack shifts from the court administration to the oppressive Russian police. To escape his creditors, Tarelkin assumes the identity of his neighbour Kopylov, who has just died; under his new name, he plans to blackmail Varravin, from whom he has stolen incriminating correspondence. Rasplyuev, Krechinsky's former henchman and newly-appointed police inspector, comes to believe that both Tarelkin and his neighbour have died but have returned to life as a single vampire. Glorying in his police authority to arrest and question people at will, he seeks to extract testimony, however ludicrous, that may support his theory of vampirism. Meantime, Varravin is perfectly aware of Tarelkin's imposture, and, when the moment is right, forces him to return the stolen letters in exchange for permission to keep his new identity forever as a shield from creditors. By the end of the play, vampirism has become a symbol of all Russian society; Tarelkin admits that he is a vampire, and says that his accomplices include the entire populations of St. Petersburg and Moscow.

Unsurprisingly, *The Case* and *The Death of Tarelkin* did not please the censors. *The Case* was first performed in a bowdlerized version in 1882 under a title, *Bygone Days*, that purported to put its events at a safe distance[1]; and *The Death of Tarelkin* was not presented in its original form until 1917. Sukhovo-Kobylin's struggles with censorship caused him to give up drama for philosophical writings; but prior to his death in 1903, in Beaulieu, France, he had the satisfaction of election to the Russian Academy of Sciences.

Under the Soviet regime, the Sukhovo-Kobylin trilogy has been given important theatrical productions, and all three plays were filmed between 1953 and 1966. Still, the ghost of the murder case has proved difficult to appease. In 1928, the publication of Leonid Grossman's *The Crime of Sukhovo-Kobylin* revived the old controversies by affirming the guilt of the famous dramatist. Though valuable for its detailed presentation of the

---

[1] Sukhovo-Kobylin's cautious title for the trilogy, *Pictures of the Past*, served the same purpose. Still, in an afterword to the trilogy, the dramatist maintained that the work was rooted in reality: 'If, after all this, the question were posed to me, "Where have I seen such Pictures?," I would have to respond with my hand on my heart: Nowhere!!! . . . everywhere.'

legal proceedings, Grossman's work failed to examine in detail either the servants' original confessions or the medical evidence. Instead, Grossman relied heavily on nineteenth-century Russian public opinion, strongly unfavourable to Sukhovo-Kobylin, and instances of violent behaviour on the part of Sukhovo-Kobylin and his ancestors. He particularly noted the writer's aggressive support of his mother in opposing what they regarded as a misalliance between one of his sisters and a Moscow university professor.

In 1936, a powerful rebuttal was made by Viktor Grossman in *The Case of Sukhovo-Kobylin* [*Delo Sukhovo-Kobylina*].[1] Grossman believes that Louise Simon-Dimanche was murdered by the servants substantially in the manner detailed by them in their confessions, and that Sukhovo-Kobylin was innocent of the crime. He notes that violent reprisals of Russian serfs against their abusive masters were common, and argues that the sole purpose of Sukhovo-Kobylin's prosecution was to extort bribes, which he regards as the very life's blood of the Tsarist court system.

In the course of his researches, Viktor Grossman submitted the evidence to a forensic scientist, Professor N. V. Popov. The professor concluded that Louise had died of strangulation (probably by a towel, as evidenced by the wide furrow in her upper neck), and that the injuries to her body were consistent with having been inflicted by an angular blunt instrument such as a flat-iron. The lack of bleeding in the windpipe and esophagus was strong proof that Louise's throat had been slit *after* she was dead; and the blood found on the snow at the cemetery was consistent with the post-mortem throat-cutting confessed by Egorov—which, in Popov's view, would have resulted in some blood-flow, perhaps facilitated by the constriction of blood vessels due to the cold weather. Popov rejected the evidence of the so-called bloodstains in Sukhovo-Kobylin's apartment as unreliable, and opined that had the victim's throat been cut there while she was alive, blood would have spurted over a much greater area.

---

[1] The Soviet conductor Gennady Rozhdest-vensky, who first called the Sukhovo-Kobylin case to my attention many years ago, told me that Viktor Grossman was Leonid's brother. If this is true, the literary warfare between the Grossmans over the guilt or innocence of the Russian dramatist presents an example of sibling hostility almost as interesting as the murder they have disputed.

Viktor Grossman also scored heavily against Leonid Grossman's theory that Louise had voluntarily left her apartment late at night without changing any of her dinner apparel. She would never have gone to dinner with two gentlemen without wearing a corset, and her velvet half-boots were not appropriate for a winter sleigh-ride; the maids must therefore have dressed her dead body, but they did not struggle to put on her corset, and left her drawers unfastened. Finally, there was no evidence that Sukhovo-Kobylin, despite his new infatuation with Naryshkina, had lost his regard for Simon-Dimanche, who in any event had told friends that she would soon be leaving for France, with a pension promised by her lover.

After her departure from Russia, Naryshkina bore Sukhovo-Kobylin a daughter, whom he named Louise after his murdered mistress and cherished for the rest of his life. Over his bed he hung a portrait of Simon-Dimanche, and proudly pointed it out to visitors. Leonid Grossman would have us believe that, like the murderer in Browning's 'My last Duchess', Sukhovo-Kobylin was cynically showing off the picture of his victim and that his unwavering protestations of persecuted innocence both in private correspondence and in his masterly trilogy were hypocritical.

Despite the maddening contradictions of the evidence in the case, however, it seems right for posterity to accept the Tsar's final decree and to acquit Sukhovo-Kobylin of the murder-charge. In granting final relief, the Tsar, although probably influenced by the defendant's family connections, belatedly came to the rescue of a persecuted man who had deserved better of his government. Amidst our justifiable enthusiasm for the overthrow of Soviet Communism, Sukhovo-Kobylin's case serves as a reminder that the regard of the predecessor-regime for human rights was far from exemplary.

MY LAST DUCHESS

Robert Browning

That's my last Duchess painted on the wall,
Looking as if she were alive. I call
That piece a wonder, now: Frà Pandolf's hands
Worked busily a day, and there she stands.
Will't please you sit and look at her? I said
'Frà Pandolf' by design, for never read
Strangers like you that pictured countenance,
The depth and passion of its earnest glance,
But to myself they turned (since none puts by
The curtain I have drawn for you, but I)
And seemed as they would ask me, if they durst,
How such a glance came there; so, not the first
Are you to turn and ask thus. Sir, 't was not
Her husband's presence only, called that spot
Of joy into the Duchess' cheek: perhaps
Frà Pandolf chanced to say 'Her mantle laps
'Over my lady's wrist too much,' or 'Paint
'Must never hope to reproduce the faint
'Half-flush that dies along her throat:' such stuff
Was courtesy, she thought, and cause enough
For calling up that spot of joy. She had
A heart—how shall I say?—too soon made glad,
Too easily impressed; she liked whate'er
She looked on, and her looks went everywhere.
Sir, 't was all one! My favour at her breast,
The dropping of the daylight in the West,
The bough of cherries some officious fool
Broke in the orchard for her, the white mule
She rode with round the terrace—all and each
Would draw from her alike the approving speech,
Or blush, at least. She thanked men,—good! but thanked
Somehow—I know not how—as if she ranked
My gift of a nine-hundred-years-old name
With anybody's gift. Who'd stoop to blame
This sort of trifling? Even had you skill
In speech—(which I have not)—to make your will

Quite clear to such an one, and say, 'Just this
'Or that in you disgusts me; here you miss,
'Or there exceed the mark'—and if she let
Herself be lessoned so, nor plainly set
Her wits to yours, forsooth, and made excuse,
—E'en then would be some stooping; and I choose
Never to stoop. Oh sir, she smiled, no doubt,
Whene'er I passed her; but who passed without
Much the same smile? This grew; I gave commands;
Then all smiles stopped together. There she stands
As if alive. Will't please you rise? We'll meet
The company below, then. I repeat,
The Count your master's known munificence
Is ample warrant that no just pretence
Of mine for dowry will be disallowed;
Though his fair daughter's self, as I avowed
At starting, is my object. Nay, we'll go
Together down, sir. Notice Neptune, though,
Taming a sea-horse, thought a rarity,
Which Claus of Innsbruck cast in bronze for me!

DEATH BY LASER-BEAM
Rayner Heppenstall

[The friend—and, all too often, subsequently the enemy—of more-publicised writers, including George Orwell, Dylan Thomas, and C.P. Snow (who described him as 'the master eccentric of English letters'). Novelist, poet, translator, critic, memoirist, playwright—he moonlighted at each of those occupations while despondently earning a living as a BBC radio producer, and did not exploit his study of the Newgate Calendar and of French crimes and criminals till his retirement in 1967. From 1969 till the day before his death, at the age of seventy, in 1981, he kept a journal. Much of the following is taken from it. 'Portrait' = Portrait of the Artist as a Professional Man, his account of his BBC career, published in May 1969.]

Tuesday, 29 April 1969

I looked through the advance copy of *Portrait* again last evening, wondering how it would affect people, wondering how justly I had achieved the various effects I wanted, wondering whether I could have stayed on at the BBC comfortably if I had only played my cards better, musing upon those twenty-two lost years, thinking thoughts, in general charitable, about the many people with whom work in radio had brought me into contact. I missed the company of actors (was very pleased last Saturday to see Stephen Murray again). I missed certain technicians, one or two delightful secretaries, and the studio excitement. I was glad to have no more to do with BBC administrators, but then administrators are frightful all the world over, and those at the BBC had been honourable men in a limited way, with good manners. If they had done me harm, it had been out of stupidity and worry.

With the head of Drama Department, Martin Esslin, I remained on excellent terms, and he was keeping a promise that, after my departure, I should have as much free-lance work as I wanted for the Department. In the past two years, my total income had barely dropped at all and, from BBC free-lance work alone, included sums of £1100 and £950. My view of my former colleagues was therefore rosy, and *Portrait* erred on the side of indulgence to everyone but myself.

Last evening, towards midnight, sitting in my usual chair for a while, perfectly relaxed before going to bed, I thought these thoughts. I forgave all the administrators, even Michael Standing [Controller of BBC Programme Organisation (Sound) since 1957]. So far as I knew, none of them had done me deliberate and malicious harm. The one man who had at least tried to was Joe Burroughs [a producer in Drama Department].

Joe was thin, with features of extreme aquilinity and dark hair worn Hitler-style, his eyes of indeterminate colour, somewhat exophthalmic or at any rate markedly *à fleur de tête*, but inexpressive, curiously jellied, not mirrors of his soul unless this had at one time turned rigid with horror. His thin lips were stretched over large, uneven teeth, later replaced. His hands were filleted, sensitive, and reluctant to feel in his pockets for small change. He walked flat-footedly, his toes turned in.

Although he was good at his job, Joe Burroughs's most marked characteristic was persistent mendacity on a clinical scale. In general, this was harmless in its effects and sometimes amusing, for most of Joe's immediate colleagues were persons of higher intelligence and better education than himself, who soon learned to discount a great part of what he said and either to avoid his company or to be careful about what they said when he was present. He told lies for all the usual reasons, including self-aggrandisement, or for no apparent reason. His purpose was sometimes malicious. His easiest successes were, of course, gained against modest and vulnerable persons, notably young actresses, but he must certainly be credited with the departure in disgrace of one of his more gifted colleagues. Among some actors, technicians, secretaries and other simple, hopeful souls, he enjoyed a positive reputation for kindness, while even those who saw through him were often amused—the actor's picture of life, in particular, being so very largely anecdotal.

Towards the end of 1965, Joe started a campaign against me. This arose from the fact that I had frustrated an attempt by him to sell as his a very promising idea of mine, which he had heard me discussing with Terence [Tiller, another producer], whom also, at much the same time, he estranged by putting about a damagingly untrue account of the latter's behaviour after their joint departure with their wives from my daughter's wedding reception.

That Joe had embarked on a campaign against me I quickly saw for myself, though it was Carleton Hobbs, perhaps the best radio actor of all time, who came and told me one line Joe was plugging, *viz,* that it was I who had stolen *his* idea.

He probably thought he had done me more harm than he had, so that my departure had seemed to him an achievement of his own.

Thinking thus, I became, for a few moments, incandescent with hatred of Joe. The phenomenon appeared to be one not of heat but of intense light. There was none of that rush of blood to the head which might have produced a headache, nothing like that bursting of an artery just outside the brain which, in the same chair fourteen years previously, had been medically described as a sub-arachnoid haemorrhage. I might have imagined that I was emitting a laser-beam directed accurately towards a small house I knew in a Kensington mews.

The phenomenon passed, and I went to bed.

At ten o'clock this morning, I answered the telephone to Administrative Assistant, Drama (Sound), a nice woman called Marie. With the idea, no doubt, of sparing them the possible shock of hearing about the matter in a roundabout way, and perhaps also of alerting them to a funeral they might feel they should attend, she was ringing round to those who had been closely associated with Joe Burroughs to inform them that he had died suddenly as the result of a heart-attack *last evening, towards midnight.*

I experienced no guilt, though I examined myself to see whether I ought to experience guilt . . . Joe was no loss to the world. I did not even feel particularly sorry for his widow, though I had always liked her. No doubt she would be miserable for a while, but it would have been better for her to be rid of Joe earlier, while she was young enough to marry again and be cured of childlessness. She would not be hard up.

From a literary point of view, it would have been a good thing if I had known, while writing my reminiscent volume, that Joe Burroughs would be dead before it came out. An account of some of his more spectacular villainies and discomfitures (the results of him being caught out in reckless mendacity) would have enlivened the book. On the other hand, if I had put them in, I might not have found myself thinking of him with such hatred last night, and so he would still be alive.

WARNER'S WARNING; OR, THE PERILS OF IDENTIFICATION
William Roughead

[Richard Whittington-Egan (whose book William Roughead and His Chronicles of Murder will be published shortly, and who is presently working on a book about the Oscar Slater case) writes: 'Roughead was born in 1870, with a silver-plated spoon in his mouth. His father owned a large drapery shop in Princes Street, Edinburgh. Roughead qualified as a Writer to the Signet, but, being possessed of adequate private means, did not need to earn his living, and was thus able to carve a niche for himself as the recording angel of Scottish matters criminous. From 1889 till the 1940s, he attended practically every interesting murder trial at Edinburgh's High Court of Justiciary. He edited many volumes in the Notable British Trials series (including the one on the Oscar Slater case) and published collection after collection of essays on causes criminal and historical. His wife bore him three sons and a daughter. He seldom left Edinburgh, save for the occasional holiday, often on the Isle of Arran; never abroad. It was his great delight to go swimming in the sea-water baths at Portobello each afternoon and then repair to a Hanover Street cafe for a cup of tea and a rich digestive biscuit. He died in 1952, and

*was cremated, free, at Warriston Crematorium, of which he
had been a director.]*

'Deil tak' me, but like is an ill mark!'
King James the Sixth

AS A DILIGENT READER, and when occasion serves an interested auditor of Scottish criminal trials, I have long marvelled
at the powers of observation and memory displayed in the
witness-box by the most unlikely persons. I have never been
called upon to give evidence in a court of justice; and frankly,
though flattering myself on the possession of the usual mental
faculties common to mankind, I can make no claim to rival
in this regard the rich endowments of the average witness. I
could not, either to save my own life or to endanger that of
a fellow-mortal, swear what I was doing or whom I saw at a
definite hour on a particular day a month ago—unless, of course,
I had chanced then to be knocked down by a taxi, or married, or
had succeeded to a fortune, or otherwise received some equally
pungent and indelible impression. But there would seem to reside
in the very atmosphere of the 'box' a quality which develops in its
transitory occupants a sixth sense, not enjoyed by mere unsworn
humanity. Thus have I heard in a certain celebrated murder trial
[that of Oscar Slater] a little message-girl of fourteen, who, at
7.10 of a dark and rainy December night in a street indifferently
lighted, being brushed against by a man running at full speed
with his hat pulled down over his eyes, was by reason of the
aforesaid powers enabled to give his age as from twenty-eight
to thirty, to describe his figure as tall and thin, his features as
clean-shaven, with the nose twisted somewhat to the right, and
his vesture as a fawn-coloured waterproof, dark trousers, a tweed
cloth or Donegal hat, and brown boots. Modest in the exercise of
her amazing gift, she declined on cross-examination to depone
whether the boots were laced or buttoned. Such scrupulosity, in
view of the temptation to omniscience offered by the occasion,
is commendable. If she failed to notice the condition of the
fugitive's teeth and the state of his fingernails, this was doubtless
due to the fact that his mouth was shut at the time and his hands,
as she observed, were in his pockets.

In the matter of identification, the flair of these Apostles of Truth is even more conspicuous. I recall, for example, in the same case, the evidence of a witness, who, being asked in cross-examination, 'Are you positive of your identification of a man whom you only saw once, he being a man you had never seen before, and of whom you only saw his back at a distance of 13 yards, on a December night at 9.15, that man being upon his trial for murder?', replied, 'Well, I am certain that it is the same man that I saw.' Everyone is susceptible to suggestion; and it is to be regretted that the auto-suggestive methods of the ingenious Monsieur Emile Coué are so largely employed by the police in this business of identification of a suspect. When one reads how they managed the matter in the affair of Oscar Slater; and how, in that of Charles Warner, which we are presently to consider, five perfectly respectable and honest witnesses were prepared positively to swear to his identity with the supposed murderer,[1] and yet were all and each of them proved beyond the peradventure of a doubt to be utterly and entirely wrong, it would appear that in other states than Denmark there is in this connection something rotten. The police are too apt to play Hamlet to the witness's Polonius:

HAMLET. Do you see yonder cloud that's almost in the shape of a camel?
POLONIUS. By the mass, and 'tis like a camel, indeed.
HAMLET. Methinks it is like a weasel.
POLONIUS. It is backed like a weasel.
HAMLET. Or like a whale?
POLONIUS. Very like a whale.

The system, as Mr. Mantalini would say, is a 'demd' system, and ought to be amended. A photograph of the suspect—usually a very poor one from a newspaper—is exhibited to those who have seen, in conditions more or less favourable, the supposed murderer. The 'likeness' is often bad enough to baffle the subject's own mother, were it shewn to her; but that only gives the identifier an ampler margin. In nine cases out of ten, he or

---

[1] One soft-hearted identifier, we are told, actually wept, declaring: 'I know I am putting the rope round his neck, but that's the man!'

she has little difficulty in 'recognising' it. The next segment of the vicious circle consists in the parading of the suspected person for 'identification' by those who have just seen his counterfeit presentment. Naturally, they have still less difficulty in doing this, for, apart from the fact that they have already seen his photograph, the suspect is generally exposed to their view in circumstances, to say the least, propitious. A German Jew like Slater, of flagrantly foreign aspect, is put up among nine plain-clothes Glasgow policemen and two railwaymen, all Scots; a Colonial 'down-and-outer' like Warner, palpably un-English in type, is presented along with ten casual British occupants of the county gaol. In neither case need, nor do, the witnesses for a moment hesitate to pick him out—whether as the original of the photograph or as the murderer is a different matter. The classic example of Adolf Beck's case in this connection is too trite for citation. It is sufficient here to quote, from the Report of the Commission of Inquiry into the circumstances of that most scandalous conviction, the following *dictum* of Lord Collins: 'Evidence as to identity based on personal impressions, however *bona fide*, is perhaps of all classes of evidence the least to be relied upon, and therefore, unless supported by other facts, an unsafe basis for the verdict of a jury.'

But the reader who has proceeded apace upon his pilgrimage through the comedy of errors called life, needs not a Royal Commission to tell him that. Ordinary experience teaches us that we are constantly mistaking other people and being mistaken by them. I have been told that I was seen in certain places when I can truthfully affirm I wasn't there. If it chanced to be a church, so much the better; but it might just as well have been a tavern: which reminds me that I have greeted more than once a perfect stranger as a friend, and this, too, while I was, in the words of Margaret Dods, vintner in St. Ronans, 'fasting from all but sin and bohea'. If ever I were tempted to play the murderer, which, from what I know of the drawbacks attending the performance of that rôle, I am little likely to be, I should carefully make up for the part in the character of some person eminent in the public eye. But then this uncanny gift of 'identification' would surely be too much for me in the end: despite the red wig, false nose, and flowing whiskers of a music-hall celebrity, the skilled—I had almost written *trained*—eye of the witnesses would penetrate my

gingerous ambushment, and with one verifying glance at a press
photograph of the popular comedian, they would exclaim in full
chorus: 'Thou art the man!' And for once, and for a wonder, they
would be right.

On Saturday, 2 November 1912, the postman whose common
task it was to deliver letters at Elmgrove House, Broughty Ferry,
noticed that the letter-box, which for a fortnight before he had
been gradually filling with correspondence, had reached the limit
of its capacity and was overflowing. He accordingly mentioned
the fact to the police, who had a look at the house that night,
but, seeing nothing to arouse their suspicion, refrained from
disturbing the rest of its venerable occupant, Miss Jean Milne.
Once before, upon a false alarm, the guardians of the peace
had entered the premises in that lady's absence, and when she
returned, 'got her opinion of their action,' which was, we may
infer, unfavourable.

The mistress of Elmgrove was no common householder; the
more we learn of her—though we shall never know very
much—the stranger she appears. Sixty-five years of age, sole
sister and heiress of a wealthy Dundee tobacco manufacturer,
Miss Milne had since his death nine years before lived all alone
in the fraternal mansion, a large handsome house of fourteen
rooms, standing in its own grounds of some two acres, well
screened by trees and shrubbery from the observation of the
vulgar. Though enjoying an income of over £1000 a year, Miss
Milne followed stoically the simple life: she occupied but a single
living-room, kept neither servant nor companion, and while not
unsociable when called upon, never returned visits. A love of
gay and girlish clothes, a taste for gardening, a passion for
magazines and, strangely enough in this connection, for devo-
tional literature—these were the harmless foibles of a character
locally dubbed eccentric. Absolutely fearless, she paid no heed to
friendly hints as to the dangers to which her defenceless position
exposed her; and reading late of nights, as was her wont, in
her religious library, she did not even trouble to pull down
the blinds, so that anyone outside in the dark garden could
watch her, unconscious, in the brightness of the candle-lighted
chamber. Candles, by the way, were her only illuminant; gas she
used but for heating and cooking. It was the old lady's habit on

going from home, which she often did, to notify the postman and the constable on the beat; on this occasion she had not done so.

Accordingly, at nine o'clock on Sunday morning, the police returned to the house. Repeated ringing of the door-bell meeting with no response, a joiner was employed to force an entrance. Doors and windows were all securely fastened; so a pane of the kitchen window was broken, the catch undone, and the man got inside to open the front door to the officers. On his way through the hall, he was horrified to see the dead body of Miss Milne, fully dressed, lying at the foot of the stairs, in circumstances pointing but too plainly to foul play. When the officers were admitted, they found the body partly covered with a sheet; there were upon the head several wounds from which blood had flowed freely; beside it lay the sitting-room poker, also bloodstained; the ankles were tightly bound together with a curtain-cord; the wires of the telephone, a few feet from where the body lay, had been cut, obviously with the pair of garden-shears lying on the floor beside it; and the curtains of the glass-door in the hall were so tied together as to prevent anyone seeing into it from without. The appearance of the hall suggested a severe struggle between the assailant and the victim. Nothing appeared to have been taken from the house, so burglary did not seem to be the motive. Such was the sensational setting of what became well and widely known as The Broughty Ferry Mystery.

The local authorities, realising that they were confronted with a case of exceptional difficulty, wisely decided to invoke the skilled assistance of Detective-Lieutenant Trench, of the Glasgow City Police, a criminal officer of great experience, then recognised as the most capable detective in Scotland. His name had come prominently before the public in 1909 in relation to the notable, and since notorious, trial of Oscar Slater, convicted in that year for the murder of an old lady named Miss Marion Gilchrist in Glasgow. The obvious resemblance between the circumstances of the two crimes made Trench's selection for the task peculiarly appropriate ... He was called in on Monday, 4 November. It appears that he had no opportunity to view the body, which was buried in the Western Cemetery, Dundee, on Tuesday, the 5th.

The result of the post-mortem examination of the remains, as reported, was as follows. The advanced stage of decomposition suggested that at least three weeks had passed since death took place; this had occurred soon after the injuries were inflicted, as was indicated by the fact that undigested food was found in the stomach. All over the body were the marks of many blows, plainly caused by a heavy instrument such as the poker; and death was due to cerebral hemorrhage, produced by the injuries to the head which, though numerous, were relatively slight, none in itself sufficiently serious to prove fatal. It was probable that the shock sustained by the elderly victim of the attack contributed to her death.

The uncertainty as to the exact time when the murder was committed increased the difficulties which beset the case. Neighbours testified that no smoke had been seen from the chimneys of Elmgrove for over a fortnight; but as the old lady used only gas and candles, that does not seem very helpful. The earliest of the letters among the accumulated correspondence in the letter-box was dated 14 October. Inquiries shewed that on Sunday, 13 October, Miss Milne was at church as usual; on Monday, the 14th, she attended a Home Mission meeting in Dundee; on Tuesday, the 15th, she was last seen alive and well in Dundee and Broughty Ferry. On Wednesday, the 16th, David Kinnear, an elder of St. Andrews United Free Church, of which Miss Milne was a member, went to Elmgrove with her Communion card, there being a celebration of the Sacrament on the ensuing Sabbath. It was after sunset, and he found the house in darkness: the accustomed candles were all out. He knocked and rang repeatedly, but receiving no response, went away. The absence of Miss Milne from church next Sunday was remarked upon, as she was a regular communicant. On Friday, 18 October, a trunk-call from London for Elmgrove was received at Broughty Ferry. The operator repeatedly rang up Miss Milne, but could get no reply. The police inferred from these facts that the crime was committed on the night of Tuesday-Wednesday, 15-16 October. But presently there appeared one Alexander Troup, sometime gardener at Elmgrove to the deceased tobacconist, and then employed by the Town Chamberlain as a collector for the Broughty Benevolent Trust. In pursuance of his pious purpose, on the forenoon of Monday, 21 October, he called at the house. On entering the grounds, with which he was familiar, he saw at an upper window, partly hidden by the curtain, a woman whom he took to be Miss Milne. He rang the front doorbell twice, but there was no reply. In doing so, he observed that the cover of the lock was down. Unwearied in well-doing, he went back in the afternoon for the due subscription. The woman had vanished from the window; but the cover of the lock, which in the forenoon had been down, was now up, from which he inferred that a key had in the mean season been inserted in the door. That the collector was indeed sent to Elmgrove on the 21st otherwise appears; but that the figure at the window was that of Miss Milne is rendered improbable by the evidence, such as the advanced stage of decomposition. His statement is interesting, however, in view of a theory of the crime later to be noticed.

Even more doubtful than the precise date of the deed was the motive by which it was actuated. Robbery was out of the question; on the fingers of the old lady as she lay dead in the hall were no fewer than seven diamond and other valuable rings; her gold watch and chain were exposed upon the toilet-table in her bedroom, and in a drawer there was her purse, containing £17 in gold. She had drawn from her bank at the end of September £20 in gold, of which this sum was apparently the balance. None of the silver or any other article of worth was missing; and except for the condition of the hall, nothing in the house would seem to have been disturbed. The theory of the casual tramp or peripatetic burglar, so dear to the official mind, had therefore to be discarded.

The respect paid by the assailant to the Eighth Commandment while engaged in violating the Sixth was not the only unusual feature of the crime. Such elements as the binding of the legs and the cutting of the telephone-wires, for example, at once arrested attention. The cord with which the ankles were pinioned had been so roughly torn from the hall-curtains as to break the brass catch that held it; the curtains themselves had been carefully tied together across the glass door with a piece of common twine; the wires had been cut with garden-shears; and the body was decently covered with a sheet, conveyed presumably from the bedroom. The several things which the felon in the course of his employment must have touched, such as the poker, had been since so often handled as to afford no clue from finger-prints; but Trench unearthed a remarkable bit of evidence, previously overlooked: from the ashes of the dining-room grate he recovered the end of a half-smoked cigar. This fact, together with the further one that, despite Miss Milne's notoriously inhospitable habits, the table was laid for high tea for two persons, a twopenny meat-pie being the *pièce de résistance*, suggested that the old lady had expected and received company, and that her visitor was of the male persuasion.

Another strange discovery was made by Trench. As I have said, he did not see the body, which, in approved police fashion, was buried the very day of his arrival to investigate the crime. On examining the deceased's clothes, however, he noticed that the blouse and under-garments worn by Miss Milne at the time of her death were perforated by some instrument which, from the nature and approximation of the two component punctures, he judged to have been a double-pronged fork. Now, the initial survey of the hall had disclosed upon the floor, half hidden beneath a trunk, the carving fork of the household set from the sitting-room sideboard; but this, characteristically, by the authorities 'was not at the time associated with the tragedy'. So significant, however, did the find appear to Trench that he used every effort to have the body exhumed, but without effect. One should think that the point would have been put beyond dispute by the result of the post-mortem examination; as the report of this was not published, the matter is but an added mystery.

Save for the cigar-end in the grate, the fatal visitor might well have been a woman: the relatively slight injuries to the head inflicted by so heavy a weapon as the poker, the fiend-like employment of the fork, and the covering of the body from sight, were deemed by sundry misogynists to signify the feminine touch.[1] Shortly before her death, however, the old lady had ordered from a local dealer a supply of wine and whisky, 'of the same quality as her brother used to get,' volunteering as an explanation of this, for her, unusual purchase that she expected 'a gentleman friend to dinner'. This fact, coupled with the testimony of eye-witnesses shortly to be narrated, seems to dispose of any question as to the assailant's sex.

Among the curiosities of conduct exhibited by the recluse of

---

[1] The woman seen by Troup at the window on 21 October was held to support this view; but as the deed was done not later than the 16th, one fails to see why the performer should linger on the stage for well nigh a week.

Elmgrove, not the least singular was what may be termed a 'Capital' complex, or lust for London. Three times a year did this retiring spinster emerge from her eremitical seclusion, and having put on her brightest bonnet and most frivolous frock, would abandon the dusty chambers and neglected lawns of Elmgrove, and sally forth in quest of those metropolitan joys for which she so unseasonably pined. Thus the authorities ascertained that, the year before her death, Miss Milne had stayed at the Bonnington Hotel, Southampton Row, from 28 November 1911 to 26 February 1912; that she went back to London, putting up at the Strand Palace Hotel, during the months of April, May, and June 1912; and that she expressed the intention to return to town for Christmas. It was also found that in September she went on a tour to the North of Scotland.

It further appeared that the venerable anchorite of Broughty Ferry was, in her new avatar of an antique charmer, not averse from accepting the attentions of male acquaintances. To a lady-friend she remarked on the pleasure she derived from her association with an unnamed gentleman whom she met at the hotel, 'and who, she said, had taken her about and been so kind to her'. The friend received the impression that it was, however unlikely, a love-affair: 'Miss Milne was so kittenish over the matter; she giggled, just like a girl.' Another friend, to whom the old lady announced that 'she was probably to get a companion,' assuming that some indigent gentlewoman was in question, commended so wise and prudent a step; whereupon Miss Milne coquettishly replied that what she meant was 'a companion for life'. Upon such grounds, therefore, it was of late current gossip in the neighbourhood that the spinster had 'got a sweetheart'.

Before following up with the police the clue thus afforded, let us pause for a moment to consider what Lieutenant Trench thought of the affair. The first point— which, though equally important in the Slater case, oddly enough was at that trial unnoticed—is: How did the murderer get into the house? The windows were all hermetically sealed, not having been opened for years; there were no indications of a forced entry; and the clear inference is that the victim with her own hand unbarred the door to Death and herself admitted her assassin. The probability, too, is that the visitor was a stranger. There can be no question that Miss Milne was slain where she was found—namely, on the hall-floor at the foot of the main staircase, the area of the bloodstains being confined to that spot. The murderer must have borne bloody traces of his work, for it appears that he had waited to wash his hands before he left the scene. A table in the hall was overset, and several knick-knacks and small articles were scattered in all directions. The garden-shears beside the telephone, and a rake and hoe nearby, suggest that she may have been gardening before the visitor called. Whatever caused the struggle between them which had such fatal consequences, Trench's view was that the assailant did not intend to kill. Had he meant murder, to dispose at once of a little frail old woman were a simple task.[1] He must have accounted her merely stunned; why, otherwise, should he tie her ankles to prevent her rising to seek for help, and disconnect the telephone by which, on regaining consciousness, she might call the police?[2] The old lady had been seen on occasion in her garden armed with this very poker, wherewith to chastise divers wanton boys who proposed in due time to enjoy the kindly fruits of Elmgrove; and Trench conceived that she might have armed herself with her favourite weapon, which was wrested from her by her adversary and employed in turn against her. The supplementary stab with the fork would seem to indicate personal spite or vengeance. The draping of the body with a sheet is inexplicable. His end achieved, the intruder must have left by the front door, which had a spring-lock, closing it behind him.

It was understood that the correspondence, which consisted chiefly of begging letters, afforded some clue to the identity of the 'gentleman friend' whose acquaintance Miss Milne had so fatally made in London. No details of this discovery were permitted, in the newspaper term, to 'transpire'; but it was reported that the local police, 'assisted by the evidence which the correspondence found in Elmgrove had furnished,' were in communication with

---

[1] The superfluous ferocity of the attack was a striking feature of Miss Gilchrist's murder. There the murderer was plainly determined to 'mak siccar'.

[2] Elmgrove was served by what is termed a 'party line,' so that to disconnect the telephone, it was not sufficient to remove the receiver: the wires must be cut: which suggests that the murderer knew the instrument.

Scotland Yard regarding the whereabouts of a certain 'dashing American'.

The reward of One Hundred Pounds, officially offered for such information as should lead to the taking of the thief of life, exercised upon the public intelligence—or imagination—the wonted stimulus; and divers persons furnished the police with the results of their observations.

Thus Margaret Campbell, a maid employed in the neighbouring house, of which an upper window commanded part of the grounds of Elmgrove, had a tale to tell. One morning in the second week of October—*i.e.* between 6th and 12th—about half-past ten o'clock, having gone upstairs and opened this window, she was surprised to see a tall handsome man of some six feet walking up and down one of the garden paths. His head was uncovered, his hair seemed to be fair, his features round—but whether or not clean shaven she could not see; and, strangely enough at that hour and place, he wore evening dress. He appeared to be meditating, for he paced slowly to and fro with bent head and his hands in his pockets. She watched him for some time with interest, for although she had been two years in her situation, she never before had seen a human being in those grounds. Having exhausted her curiosity, the maid went downstairs to her work, and mentioned the incident to her mistress as an interesting item of news.

At 4.30 on the morning of 16 October, James Don, a scavenger in the employment of the burgh, was attending to his duties in Grove Road, when he saw a man come out of the small door of the main entrance-gate to Elmgrove. The stranger stopped for a moment, then took a few steps forward, the gateway being recessed, and glanced up and down the road. Seeing Don looking at him, he drew quickly back into the shadow. Suddenly he stepped out again and walked briskly away, disappearing at a bend of the road. The morning was not a dark one and there was a gas-lamp at the spot. Don was within ten yards of him and noted that the man was about thirty, tall and well built, his face pale and thin, with a slight fair moustache. He wore a bowler hat and a dark overcoat, with the collar turned up. Don had never seen him before.

On the receipt of this information, a new 'Hue and Cry' was

issued, containing the descriptions of the men seen respectively by the housemaid and the scavenger:

About 10.30 a.m. on a day in the first or second week in October 1912 a man of the following description was seen by a servant-girl from a bedroom window overlooking the ground surrounding Miss Milne's house, walking in the private grounds at the back of Miss Milne's house—from 30 to 40 years of age, about six feet in height; well made and well set up; a handsome-looking man, evidently a gentleman, dressed in an evening suit, showing an extensive starched white shirt front, and was bareheaded.

About 4.20 a.m. on Wednesday, 16 October 1912, a man of the following description was seen leaving the grounds of the house:—Between 30 and 40 years of age, 5 feet 8 or 9 inches in height; approximate weight between 11 and 12 stones; sharp features; very pale complexion; slight fair moustache; carried his head erect and swung his arms when walking. He was dressed in a dark overcoat, which reached a little below his knees, the collar of which was turned up; trousers of a dark colour; of respectable appearance, and looked like a gentleman.

Notice is hereby given that a reward of £100 will be paid by the subscriber to anyone giving such information as shall lead to the apprehension and conviction of the person or persons who committed the murder.

J. HOWARD SEMPILL,
Chief Constable.

I have been thus particular to set forth the exact text of this document because the broadcasting of the bill was, as we shall see, productive of very singular results.

Other witnesses there were who believed themselves privileged to have had a private view of the murderer. The first of these to see the 'mysterious stranger,' as the reporters delighted to term him, was John Wood, in the employment of a jobbing gardener, who had worked occasionally for Miss Milne during the last six years of her life. He was always chosen for the job as he knew how to humour the old lady's peculiarities. 'Others had been sent to Elmgrove,' this disciple of Adam told the Press, 'but they did not understand Miss Milne, and found themselves chased out of the place before they had been long there.' On her return from her last visit to London in August, she had much to tell about a 'German gentleman,' a tea-planter, whom she had met at her hotel in the Strand and from whom she was expecting a letter. On Friday, 20 September, as was otherwise ascertained, Miss Milne left for a tour in the Highlands.[1] The day before her departure, Wood, who had been shutting up the house that afternoon, was about to leave at half-past five when the door-bell rang. He opened the door and was confronted by a gentleman, who asked, 'Is Miss Milne in?' That lady, being apprised by Wood of the fact, jumped up from her chair in the sitting-room, 'and, just like a lassie, skipped along the passage' to the hall, where she welcomed affectionately her guest. 'You have come!' she cried; 'I expected you earlier.' She then presented Wood with two shillings, asking him to keep an eye on the premises while she was away, and ushered the visitor into the dining-room. That was the last Wood saw of the old lady; next day he visited the grounds, but the house was then shut up and deserted. Now, this witness had a most excellent opportunity of observing the man. He was about forty years of age, and 5 feet 8 or 9 inches in height, fairly stout and well made; he had fair hair and a slight fair moustache, cheery face, fresh complexion, and was of smart appearance, being dressed in a dark morning-coat, a deep-cut vest, and dark trousers, with a soft, round tweed hat. He carried a cane, and was altogether of gentlemanly aspect. His voice was deep and guttural, from which Wood inferred that he was the 'German gentleman' of Miss Milne's reminiscences. Identification by such a witness of the wanted man, if and when secured, should surely prove well nigh conclusive.

In the early hours of the morning of Tuesday, 15 October, Frederick Ewing, a Dundee taxi-driver, was waiting at the West Station on the chance of a 'fare' from the South train, due about

---

[1] According to the information of the police, Miss Milne left Broughty Ferry for Glasgow, where she embarked in the *Chevalier* on a cruise round the coast to Inverness, arriving there on the 24th and going home on the 26th. On the return-journey, she was seen and recognised on board the Caledonian Canal steamer, accompanied by a tall handsome man, with whom she left the boat at Fort Augustus.

1 a.m., and his patience was presently rewarded by a peremptory hail from a passenger, who demanded to be driven to Broughty Ferry. The driver asked for the address; 'I will tell you when we get there,' said the passenger shortly; so away they went. He spoke with an English accent. During the journey, though he sat beside the driver, he was very taciturn, and seemed to be fidgety. In the vicinity of Elmgrove, he stopped the cab, paid his fare, with a substantial tip, and walked off. The unknown carried a small handbag, was smartly dressed, and was of good build. He wore an overcoat and a waterproof, and was about 5 feet 9 inches in height. He was of a pale complexion and had a slight fair moustache. Ewing was struck by the sinister aspect of the stranger, whose fierce demeanour and piercing eye made him glad to part company. As this happened on the very morning of the crime, particular importance would seem to attach to the incident; yet we hear no more of the taxi-driver or his testimony.

On Monday, 7 October, being the local Autumn Holiday, two sisters of the name of M'Intosh, who had been calling on a relative in the neighbourhood, were passing the entrance to Elmgrove about 8.30 p.m. when a man emerged from the entrance-gate. Aware of Miss Milne's reclusive habits, they were surprised to see a gentleman leaving the house, and observed him closely, with what results we shall see in the sequel.

On the evening of Friday, 11 October, certain youngsters were disporting themselves in Grove Road, hard by the entrance to Elmgrove, when they noticed a gentleman go in at the gate. Boylike, they were curious to watch the stranger, who, they saw, after walking a few yards up the drive, turned off to the right by a path through the shrubbery—a circumstance from which was inferred his familiarity with the grounds.

There were several other persons who claimed to have seen 'the man'; but those whom I have mentioned were deemed by the police the most positive and important. It will, of course, have occurred to the reader, however gentle, that the gardener's guttural German could hardly be got to tally with the taxi-driver's Anglican 'fare'. But even more disparate descriptions, as the Slater case bears witness, have been made beautifully to combine by the wondrous alchemy of official methods.

*   *   *

Of the criminous grain sown by the Broughty Ferry police, some fell on good ground. In due course, a copy of the reward-bill was delivered to the prison authorities at Maidstone, farther south even than London. It so chanced that there was then and there in custody a mysterious Colonial, who gave his name as Charles Warner and his address as No. 210 Wilton Avenue, Toronto, and who had been for well nigh a fortnight in the enjoyment of His Majesty's hospitality, in respect of having, on 4 November, obtained by false pretence from one Robert Daish, hotelkeeper at Tonbridge, food and lodging to the amount of seven shillings, with intent to cheat and defraud him of the same. It appeared from the evidence upon which he was convicted that Warner had walked into the Rose & Crown one morning, and demanded breakfast and a bed. His luggage—which probably resembled that of Mr. Jingle—was, he averred, coming by express-train. After a hearty meal, the traveller proposed to leave the hostelry for a constitutional; but the waiter demurred to this healthful project, as the bill had not been paid. He pursued the uninviting guest, overtook him as he was about to avail himself of a 'lift' from a passing trap, and delivered him up to an adjacent constable, by whom the stranger was conveyed to jail. Upon subsequent legal proceedings taken, the breakfast was found to be irrecoverable, the prisoner penniless; and the conclusion of the matter was fourteen days.

Having thus fulfilled, so far as circumstances permitted, the charge of Dogberry: 'You shall comprehend all vagrom men,' the Maidstone watch, on perusal of the Broughty Ferry handbill, perceived at once that they had in their very hands the wanted man. Warner was promptly exposed to the camera, and copies of his photograph—which, it was stated in the press, 'were exceptionally bad ones'—were forwarded to Scotland for recognition by the local witnesses. As a result of this exhibition, it was decided to send to England, in order to identify the original in the flesh, the following five witnesses: (1) John Wood, the gardener, (2) Margaret Campbell, the maid, (3) and (4) the Misses M'Intosh, and (5) James Don, the scavenger.

Accordingly, on Friday, 22 November, the chosen ones set out from Broughty Ferry by the morning train for London. At King's Cross they were welcomed by Chief Constable Sempill, by whom they were escorted to the Police Institute, where they were to be accommodated during their stay. Next day, after a brief sight-seeing tour of the metropolis, the party were taken down to Maidstone to interview in the prison the object of their quest.

'The drama within the high walls occupied,' we are told, 'nearly two hours, and the police authorities were at the conclusion naturally extremely reticent as to what had taken place; but from the stories of the various witnesses, a fairly accurate impression was obtained.' The procedure, as appears, was on this wise: the suspect was placed in a row among ten other prisoners, dressed in their outdoor clothes. The witnesses were introduced separately, and their statements afterwards taken down by a warder. John Wood picked out Warner at the first glance; he was unswerving in his recognition, and the prisoner made no comment. John Don had no hesitation in recognising him as 'the man,' of whom he possessed 'a complete and accurate mental picture'; and again the prisoner was silent. Margaret Campbell recognised his features at once, but asked him to remove his cap, as the gentleman she had seen in the garden was bareheaded. 'With pleasure, madam,' said the prisoner, suiting the action to the word. This was unfortunate, for Miss Campbell expressed some doubt as to the hair, which was greyer than she expected; but she added, 'I cannot forget his eyes.' Neither of the Misses M'Intosh had any difficulty in identifying the prisoner as 'the man'. A factor in one sister's recognition was 'the display of gold-filled teeth when the man spoke to her in the yard'. Apparently, the beautiful unanimity of these opinions proved too much for the prisoner's composure. 'It's not fair,' he burst out to the last witness; 'the others have told you where I am standing. It's a farce. Do you, too, wish me to take off my cap?' and he flung his cap upon the ground. 'No, I don't,' retorted Miss M'Intosh; 'I know you quite well without that. I'm quite satisfied.' Having thus discharged their duty, the witnesses, after what must have been for them a stimulating experience—though it was like to prove a sedative one for the suspect—returned, trailing clouds of glory, to their respective homes.

Monday, 25 November, would see the expiry of the prisoner's sentence; but word of the happenings at Maidstone had reached Dundee. A warrant for Warner's arrest on a charge of murder was obtained from the Sheriff during the week-end; and Lieutenant Trench, with that document in his pocket, went

South on the Sunday night to effect the apprehension of the murderer.

For the quiet, old-world county-town of Maidstone, the day was one of unusual bustle and activity. The opening of the Assizes, with an exceptionally heavy calendar, had attracted many visitors; the streets were busy; there was an awakened interest in matters criminal; and when it became known that the stranger within their gates was none other than the much-sought-for Broughty Ferry murderer, as certified by five intelligent natives of that place, and that he was about to be arrested and conveyed to Scotland, there to suffer the extreme penalty of his crime, public excitement was intense, and the moment of his removal eagerly awaited.

As the cab containing the prisoner and his guardians drove out of the prison-gates, a dramatic incident occurred. Warner became at that instant technically a free man; but the Chief Constable produced and read to him the warrant for his arrest upon the murder charge, and he was at once handcuffed to Lieutenant Trench. As was picturesquely noted at the time, 'a battery of cameras clicked in unison with the snap of the cuffs'. The prisoner eyed nonchalantly the corps of pressmen and photographers by whom he was beset. 'Hurry up, boys,' he called to them from the window as the cab, pursued by racing reporters, drove swiftly away; 'come along, or you'll miss it!' At the station, snapshooters lined the platform for a last volley. 'You'll be sorry for this in a few days,' remarked their object; 'I'm an innocent man.' 'I'm sorry now, sir,' said one of the marksmen, who must have been new to his job; 'but we have got to do it, though I'd rather not.'

In London the prisoner was submitted to a further test, with results unexpectedly disappointing. On 26 November, at Scotland Yard, Warner was confronted with six London witnesses who had seen the 'dashing American' in company with Miss Milne at the Strand Palace and Bonnington Hotels, and who thought they recognised the photographs. Not one of them was able to identify him. Thereafter, travelling *incognito* as 'Mr. Brown, Dundee,' he reached Tay Bridge Station, and appeared in due course before Sheriff Neish at Dundee, when, being formally charged, he made no statement, and was committed to prison, pending further investigation.

'Warner,' we read, 'seemed little concerned, and walked with a firm step and almost jaunty air. His cap was worn well down on his head, but a good view of his face was obtainable. His figure indicates great physical strength. He is well set up and broad shouldered, about 5 feet 9 or 10 inches in height, with prominent jaw and small, piercing eyes. He is massive and muscular, of well-groomed, gentlemanly appearance, the only draw-back to his attractiveness being his unshaved condition.'

On 29 November the accused was paraded, among a dozen other men, for identification by no fewer than twenty-two fresh witnesses. These included two ladies who saw 'the man' in Miss Milne's company on her West Coast cruise in September; an employee of Broughty Ferry post office, of whom 'the man' enquired the way to Elmgrove; a pedlar who saw 'the man' in the grounds of that mansion; three boys who saw him entering the gate, as before described; two workmen, who, travelling from Broughty to Dundee by different cars on the morning of 16 October, had each 'the man' as fellow-passenger; a hairdresser who 'removed the moustache of a well-dressed man about the middle of October'; two gentlemen of West Ferry who respectively received that month calls from a mysterious stranger; a steamship official who saw a suspicious voyager embark for Hamburg; a gentleman 'who had dealings with a man in Leith'; as well as divers other vigilant and alert observers. It would have been instructive to learn the result of this inquisition, and whether or not the new identifiers came up to the official scratch.[1] But the prisoner's interests were now in the hands of his legal advisers, and no further information was allowed, in the reporters' phrase, to 'transpire'; so the journalists went empty away.

Lieutenant Trench was, for a policeman, remarkably fair-minded, straightforward, and intelligent. Many officers in his position, pluming themselves on the success of the Maidstone pilgrimage, would have been content to let well alone and the law take its course. But Trench was not satisfied. He had ample opportunity of studying his prisoner, and of forming an opinion as to the

---

[1] As it was repeatedly stated in print that 'a dozen witnesses' identified the accused, it would seem that some of these did so.

character of the man and the likelihood of his story being true; and the conclusion at which he arrived was that Warner, like the Flowers of Spring, had 'nothing to do with the case'. That victim of identification declared, generally, that he had never been in Scotland in his life, and, particularly, was a stranger to the beauties of Dundee. A Canadian by birth, he had voyaged to Europe four months before, and landed at Havre. After visiting Paris, he made his way to England, reaching London in the beginning of September. He next went to Liverpool, where he lived for some time in a boarding-house at Seacombe. Thereafter, resuming his wanderings, he returned to the Continent, visiting Amsterdam, Brussels, and Antwerp. He then went back to London, where he remained till 3 November—the day of the discovery of the murder at Elmgrove—when he set forth upon his ill-fated tramp to Tonbridge. Trench pressed him as to his whereabouts at the crucial date: 16 October. Warner replied that he had lived in Antwerp for a week prior to that date, that he left that city on the 17th, and reached London on the 18th. If this were so, and could be proved, his alibi was irrefragable; but here Trench was met by a difficulty due to the unconventional habits of the wanderer. He had no private address in Antwerp, having slept out of doors in parks and public places. Still Trench sought for some particular that would establish the truth of his tale. At last Warner recollected that at the very time of the murder, he had pawned in Antwerp a waistcoat for a franc. Furnished with this clue, Trench left for Antwerp, found the pawnshop, redeemed the waistcoat, and came back to Dundee with the perfect alibi in a brown paper parcel.

Meanwhile, the Procurator-Fiscal of Dundee having completed his case against the accused, the precognitions (or statements) of about 100 witnesses—extending, we are told, to some 300 pages—were submitted to the Crown authorities in Edinburgh for their information, with a view to framing the indictment upon which Warner would be brought to trial. The Crown Office, being duly apprised of the new dramatic evidence of the alibi,[1]

---

[1] This was stated in the Press to be the granting to Warner, by the British Vice-Consul at Antwerp, of a passport to London on 17 October, the day after the murder. Both versions may be correct; but I am reluctant to discard the waistcoat, as the more picturesque and pleasing.

whereby the guns of the prosecution were so effectually spiked, on 6 January 1913 dispatched to the Fiscal a telegram in the following terms: 'Charles Warner.—Murder.—Crown counsel have considered precognitions and decided evidence insufficient. Please liberate.' Whereupon the Fiscal at once issued a warrant as follows: 'Charles Warner.—Murder.—Please liberate this accused. (Signed) W. F. Mackintosh, Procurator-Fiscal.' This, in turn, was transmitted to the Governor of the Prison, and his involuntary guest was at length at liberty to depart.

But the Dundee authorities, regardless of the instructions of Dogberry, touching such as refuse to stand in the Prince's name: 'Why, then, take no note of him, but let him go; and presently call the rest of the watch together, and thank God you are rid of a knave', were not yet done with Warner. The scene at the prison-gate of Maidstone was re-enacted. No sooner was he a free man than he was again arrested on another charge. This time the matter was less grave, relating merely to the unauthorised acquisition of a topcoat.

At Bow Street, London, whither he had been transferred at the conclusion of the Scottish episode, the prisoner, on 9 January, pleaded guilty to stealing from the Charing Cross Hotel the garment in question. In mitigation of sentence, he told the Magistrate that his brother, from whom he had been receiving an allowance, had lately died in Canada. Being destitute, and suffering much from cold and exposure, he had gone into the lounge of the hotel, where he had formerly been a guest, to spend a few hours in reading. Fearing to face another night of misery, and having only fourpence-ha'penny in his pocket, he yielded to temptation and took the topcoat. His intention was to tramp to Dover and try to get aboard a Red Star liner for Canada; but at Tonbridge his journey was interrupted in the manner already known to us. A detective officer informed the Court that the prisoner was very well connected in Canada. The magistrate said that, in view of the prisoner's late experiences, he would impose no punishment but would bind him over, so that the officer could see him off to Canada. Let us hope that his life in the Dominion was pleasanter than it had been in Britain.

It is a quaint reflection that Warner, having been saved from death by a waistcoat, should have fallen a victim to an overcoat;

and it is also a remarkable coincidence that Slater's tribulations began, as those of Warner ended—in a pawnshop!

The fact that five reputable and worthy witnesses were ready to send to the gallows a man who had no more to do with the crime than you or I, raises some very serious questions. As in the case of Oscar Slater, there was nothing whatever to connect Warner with the deed except his identification by what we may call the casual and transient eye-witness, whose capacity of visualisation is never tested. To such evidence the sole defence would seem to be that upon which the elder Mr. Weller—justly, as appears—placed so great reliance. Slater's alibi was as good a one as his unconventional mode of life could reasonably be expected to furnish; yet it proved insufficient to avoid conviction. Warner's, fortunately for him, was complete, conclusive, and incontrovertible. But without it, he, though innocent, would probably have been hanged, because the evidence of identity was in his case much stronger and more positive than in that of Slater.

The moral which one deduces from these disquieting facts is this: that the recognition of a person by people who have had but a passing glimpse of their man, who have never seen him before, and who have not heard him speak, is practically worthless. Even if greater advantages in this regard be enjoyed, the result, as we have seen in the present instance, is unreliable. Apart altogether from varying powers of observation, such recognition is not to be depended on. If I were called upon to serve as a juryman—a duty from which, unluckily for future subjects of identification, I am professionally exempt—I should refuse to convict a prisoner on testimony of this nature alone. Unless the prosecution was able, by evidence direct or circumstantial, otherwise to establish the panel's connection with the crime, I should acquit him, despite the oaths of any number of unsupported eye-witnesses.

Another point: no witness to identification ought ever to be shewn a photograph of the suspected man. The unfairness of doing so is obvious, and the effect may be, as in Warner's case, disastrous . . .

Finally, when the identifier reaches the witness-box, the stereotyped pronouncement: 'That is the man,' ought not to be accepted as in itself enough. According to the good old practice of our forebears, the evidence of a witness, which was reduced to writing, read over to him, and signed by himself and by the judge—called the Lord Examinator—invariably concluded with the words: *Causa scientiae patet* (This evidence is admissible). In like manner, all identifying witnesses should be made to give reason for the faith that is in them, and to declare specifically how, why, and upon what grounds they are in a position to swear, in the accepted damnatory formula: 'That is the man.'

Having regard to the samples of the system which the affairs of Beck, Slater, and Warner supply, it may, in unofficial quarters, be doubted whether, after all, the game is worth the scandal . . .

Of the Broughty Ferry affair, with which we started and of which we seem rather to have lost sight, there is nothing more to tell. It began in mystery and in mystery it unto this day remains. But if the real murderer were ever caught, it would be comfortable to hear what the Warner witnesses had to say touching his identity with 'the man' of their choice.

Postscript

Since the above was written, I have broken my record; and were it not that it would spoil the paragraph, I should re-write the opening lines. For on Monday, 9 July 1928, within the High Court of Justiciary, in the hour of cause, I was duly sworn as a witness in the successful Appeal: Oscar Slater v. His Majesty's Advocate. And not only so; I testified as within my recollection to facts which occurred well nigh twenty years before! In this I may seem to be inconsistent; but listen to my excuse: as to being called, of course, I had no option; and with respect to my evidence, I spoke to certain written and printed matters still extant. If I did proceed to report a particular conversation, the circumstances at the time were such as indelibly to impress its import upon my otherwise irresponsible memory. This I think it well to explain, lest some discerning critic should seek to condemn me out of my own mouth. To the views I have expressed about *other* witnesses and their ways I still adhere.

William Roughead:

ARNOLD ROTHSTEIN'S FINAL PAYOFF
Damon Runyon

[Born in 1880 in another Manhattan, a then-small town in Kansas (founded, so he said, by his paternal and still slightly French grandfather, William Renoyan), Alfred Damon Runyan followed in the least meandering set of his drunkard father's footsteps by becoming a printer's devil for the Pueblo Evening News; his first reporting assignment, when he was fourteen, was a pre-publicised lynching. A couple of years later, after he had become a reporter for the other Pueblo evening paper, the 'a' of his surname was misprinted as 'o', which he felt looked better; he continued to be by-lined as Alfred Damon Runyon for the next dozen years, during which he worked on papers in Denver and San Francisco (and, again so he said, fought as a teenaged infantryman in the Philippines), and only dropped his first name when he became a sports reporter for the New York morning paper, Hearst's American. By the early 1920s, he was the world's highest-paid reporter: of front- as well as back-page news, including sensational murder trials ('the main events', he called them). His 'Broadway Guys and Dolls' tales, which he began writing in 1929, are not entirely fictional: for instance, 'The Brain Goes Home' romanticises the last days of Arnold Rothstein; Runyon's friend Al Capone is 'Black Mike Marrio', and

*the New York gangster Frank Costello is 'Dave the Dude',
in 'Dark Dolores'. Costello contributed $25,000 to the
memorial cancer-fund that was set up after Runyon's death
in 1947.]*

From the New York *American*
19 November 1929

IF THE GHOST of Arnold Rothstein was hanging around the
weather-beaten old Criminal Courts Building yesterday—and
Arnold always did say he'd come back after he was dead and
haunt a lot of people—it took by proxy what would have been
a violent shock to the enormous vanity of the dead gambler.

Many citizens, members of the so-called 'blue-ribbon panel,'
appeared before Judge Charles C. Nott, Jr., in the trial of George
C. McManus, charged with murdering Rothstein, and said they
didn't know Rothstein in life and didn't know anybody that did
know him.

Arnold would have scarcely believed his ears. He lived in
the belief he was widely known. He had spent many years
establishing himself as a landmark on old Broadway. It would
have hurt his pride like sixty to hear men who lived in the very
neighbourhood he frequented shake their heads and say they
didn't know him.

A couple said they hadn't even read about him being plugged
in the stomach with a bullet that early evening of 4 November a
year ago, in the Park Central Hotel.

Well, such is fame in the Roaring Forties!

They had accepted two men to sit on the jury that is to hear the
evidence against McManus, the first man to pass unchallenged by
both sides being Mark H. Simon, a stockbroker, of No. 500 West
111th Street, and the second being Eugene A. Riker, of No. 211
West 21st Street, a travelling salesman.

It seemed to be a pretty fair start anyway, but just as
Judge Nott was about to adjourn court at four o'clock, Mark
H. Simon presented a complication. He is a dark-complexioned,
neatly-dressed chap, in his early thirties, with black hair slicked
back on his head. He hadn't read anything about the case, and
seemed to be an ideal juror.

But it appears he is suffering from ulcers of the stomach, and this handicap was presented to Judge Nott late in the day. James D. C. Murray, attorney for McManus, George M. Brothers, assistant prosecuting attorney, in charge of the case for the State, and three other assistants from District Attorney Banton's office, gathered in front of the bench while Mark H. Simon was put back in the witness-chair and examined.

The upshot of the examination was his dismissal from service by Judge Nott, which left Riker, a youngish, slightly bald man, with big horn specs riding his nose, as the only occupant of the jury-box. Judge Nott let the lonesome-looking Riker go home for the night after instructing him not to do any gabbing about the case.

The great American pastime of jury-picking took up all the time from 10:30 yesterday morning until four o'clock in the afternoon, with an hour off for chow at one o'clock. Thirty 'blue ribboners,' well-dressed, solid looking chaps for the most part, were examined, and of this number Murray challenged a total of fourteen. Each side had thirty peremptory challenges. Attorney Brothers knocked off nine and four were excused.

George McManus, the defendant, sat behind his attorney, eyeing each talesman with interest but apparently offering no suggestions. McManus was wearing a well-tailored brown suit, and was neatly groomed, as usual. His big, dark-toned face never lost its smile.

Two of his brothers, Jim and Frank, were in the courtroom. Frank is a big, fine-looking fellow who has a nifty tenor voice that is the boast of the Roaring Forties, though he can be induced to sing only on special occasions.

Very few spectators were permitted in the court, because there wasn't room in the antique hall of justice for spare chairs after the 'blue ribboners' were all assembled. A squad of the Hon. Grover Whalen's best and most neatly uniformed cops are spread all around the premises, inside and out, to preserve decorum.

Edgar Wallace, the English novelist and playwright, who is said to bat out a novel or play immediately after his daily marmalade, was given the special privilege of the chair inside the railing and sat there listening to the examination of the talesmen, and doubtless marvelling at the paucity of local knowledge of the citizens about a case that he heard of over in England.

Mr. Wallace proved to be a fattish, baldish man, and by no means as young as he used to be.

A reflection of the average big towner's mental attitude towards gambling and gamblers was found in the answers to Attorney Murray's inevitable question as to whether the fact that the defendant is a gambler, and gambled on cards and the horses, would prejudice the talesmen against him. Did they consider a gambler a low character?

Well, not one did. Some admitted playing the races themselves. One mumbled something about there being a lot of gamblers in Wall Street who didn't excite his prejudice.

Attorney Murray was also concerned in ascertaining if the talesmen had read anything that District Attorney Banton had said about the defendant, and if so, had it made any impression on the talesman? It seemed not. One chap said he had read Banton's assertions all right, but figured them in the nature of a bluff.

Do you know anybody who knew Rothstein—pronounced 'stine' by Mr. Brothers, and 'steen' by Mr. Murray — or George McManus? Do you know anybody who knew either of them?

Do you know anybody who knows anybody connected with (a) the District Attorney's office? (b) the Police Department? Were you interested in the late political campaign? Ever live in the Park Central? Ever dine there? Know anybody connected with the management? Did you ever go to a race-track?

Did you ever read anything about the case? (This in a city of over 4,000,000 newspaper readers, me hearties, and every paper carrying column after column of the Rothstein murder for months!) Did you ever hear any discussion of it? Can you? Suppose? Will you? State of mind. Reasonable doubt—

Well, by the time old John Citizen, 'blue ribboner' or not, has had about twenty minutes of this, he is mighty glad to get out of that place and slink home, wondering if after all it is worth while trying to do one's duty by one's city, county and state.

20 November

A client—or shall we say a patient—of the late Arnold Rothstein popped up on us in the old Criminal Courts Building in the shank o' the evening yesterday. He came within a couple of aces of being made juror No. 8, in the trial of George C. McManus, charged with the murder of the said Rothstein.

Robert G. McKay, a powerfully built, black-haired broker of No. 244 East 67th Street, a rather swanky neighbourhood, was answering the do-yous and the can-yous of James D. C. Murray as amiably as you please, and as he had already passed the State's legal lights apparently in a satisfactory manner, the gents at the press tables were muttering, 'Well, we gotta another at last.'

Then suddenly Robert G. McKay, who looks as if he might have been a Yale or Princeton lineman of, say, ten years back, and who was sitting with his big legs crossed and hugging one knee, remarked in a mild tone to Murray, 'I suppose I might say I knew Arnold Rothstein—though none of you have asked me.'

'Ah,' said Attorney Murray with interest, just as it appeared he was through with his questioning.

'Did you ever have any business transactions with Rothstein?'

'Well, it was business on his part, and folly on mine.'

'Might I have the impertinence to ask if you bet with him?'

McKay grinned wryly, and nodded. Apparently he found no relish in his recollection of the transaction with 'the master mind' who lies a-mouldering in his grave while the State of New York is trying to prove that George McManus is the man who tossed a slug into his stomach in the Park Central Hotel the night of 4 November, a year ago.

Attorney Murray now commenced to delve somewhat into McKay's state of mind concerning the late Rothstein. He wanted to know if it would cause the broker any feeling of embarrassment to sit on a jury that was trying a man for the killing of Rothstein, when Judge Charles C. Nott, Jr., remarked, 'I don't think it necessary to spend any more time on this man.'

The late Rothstein's customer hoisted his big frame out of the chair, and departed, a meditative expression on his face, as if he might still be considering whether he would feel any embarrassment under the circumstances.

They wangled out six jurors at the morning session of the McManus trial, which was enlivened to some extent by the appearance of quite a number of witnesses for the State in the hallways of the rusty old red-brick Criminal Courts Building.

These witnesses had been instructed to show up yesterday

morning with the idea that they might be called, and one of the first to arrive was 'Titanic Slim,' otherwise Alvin C. Thomas, the golf-playing gambling man, whose illness in Milwaukee caused a postponement of the trial a week ago.

'Titanic Slim' was attended by Sidney Stajer, a rotund young man who was one of Rothstein's closest friends, and who is beneficiary to the tune of $75,000 under the terms of the dead gambler's will. At first the cops didn't want to admit 'Titanic Slim' to the portals of justice, as he didn't look like a witness, but he finally got into the building only to learn he was excused.

The photographers took great interest in the drawling-voiced, soft-mannered, high roller from the South, and Sidney Stajer scowled at them fiercely, but Sidney really means no harm by his scowls. Sidney is not a hard man and ordinarily would smile very pleasantly for the photographers, but it makes him cross to get up before noon.

The State's famous material witness, Bridget Farry, chambermaid at the Park Central, put in an appearance with Beatrice Jackson, a telephone operator at the same hotel. Bridget was positively gorgeous in an emerald-green dress and gold-heeled slippers. Also she had silver stockings and a silver band around her blond hair. She wore no hat. A hat would have concealed the band.

Bridget, who was held by the State in durance vile for quite a spell, is just a bit stoutish, but she was certainly all dressed up like Mrs. Astor's horse. She sat with Miss Jackson on a bench just outside the portals of justice and exchanged repartee with the cops, the reporters and the photographers.

Bridget is nobody's sap when it comes to talking back to folks. Finally she left the building, and was galloping lightly along to escape the photographers when her gold-heeled slippers played her false, and she stumbled and fell.

An ambulance was summoned post-haste, as the lady seemed to be injured, but an enterprising gal reporter from a tab scooped her up into a taxicab, and departed with the witness to unknown parts. It is said that Bridget's shinbone was scuffed up by the fall.

Some of the State's witnesses were quite busy at the telephone booths while in the building, getting bets down on the Bowie races. It is a severe handicap to summon a man to such a remote quarter as the Criminal Courts Building along towards post-time.

21 November

Twelve good men, and glum, are now hunched up in the jury-box in Judge Nott's court, and they are all ready to start trying to find out about the murder of Arnold Rothstein.

But the hours are really tough on a lot of folks who will figure more or less prominently in the trial. Some of the boys were wondering if Judge Nott would entertain a motion to switch his hours around and start in at 4 P.M., the usual hour of adjournment, and run to 10:30 A.M., which is a gentleman's bedtime. The consensus is he wouldn't.

George Brothers, one of District Attorney Banton's assistants, who is in charge of the prosecution, will probably open the forensic fury for the State of New York this morning, explaining to the dozen morose inmates of the jury-box just what the State expects to prove against the defendant—to wit, that George McManus is the party who shot Arnold Rothstein in the stomach in the Park Central Hotel the night of 4 November, a year ago.

You may not recall the circumstances, but McManus is one of four persons indicted for the crime. Another is Hyman Biller, an obscure denizen of the brightlights region of Manhattan Island, who probably wouldn't be recognized by more than two persons if he walked into any joint in town, such is his obscurity.

Then there is good old John Doe and good old Richard Roe, possibly the same Doe and Roe who have been wanted in forty-nine different spots for crimes ranging from bigamy to disorderly conduct for a hundred years past. Tough guys, old John and Richard, and always getting in jams. McManus is the only one on trial for the killing of Rothstein, probably for the reason he is the only one handy.

22 November

'Give me a deck of cards,' said 'Red' Martin Bowe plaintively, peering anxiously around Judge Nott's courtroom in the dim light of yesterday afternoon, as if silently beseeching a friendly volunteer in an emergency.

'Get me a deck of cards, and I'll show you.'

You see, Red Martin Bowe had suddenly come upon a dilemma in his forty-odd years of travelling up and down the earth. He had come upon a fellow citizen who didn't seem to savvy the elemental pastime of stud poker, and high spading, which Martin probably thought, if he ever gave the matter any consideration, is taught in the grammar schools of this great nation—or should be.

So he called for a deck of cards. He probably felt the question was fatuous, but he was willing to do his best to enlighten this apparently very benighted fellow, Ferdinand Pecora, the chief representative of Old John Law on the premises, and to show the twelve good men, and glum, in the jury-box just how that celebrated card game was conducted which the State of New York is trying to show cost Arnold Rothstein his life at the hands of George McManus.

But no deck of cards was immediately forthcoming. So Martin Bowe didn't get to give his ocular demonstration to the assembled citizens, though a man came dashing in a little later with a nice red deck, while even Judge Nott was still snorting over Martin Bowe's request.

Possibly if Mr. Pecora can get a night off later, some of the boys who sat in the back room yesterday might be induced to give him a lesson or two in stud poker. Also high spading.

Martin Bowe is a big, picturesque-looking chap, who is getting bald above the ears, and who speaks with a slow drawl and very low. In fact, all the witnesses displayed a remarkable tendency to pitch their voices low, in marked contrast with their natural vocal bent under ordinary circumstances, and the attorneys had to keep admonishing them to talk louder.

'Gambler,' said Bowe, quietly, and without embarrassment, when asked his business. Then he went on to tell about the card game that will probably be remarked for many years as Broadway's most famous joust. It began on a Saturday night and lasted into the Sunday night following. Martin said he previously played five or six hours at a stretch, and then would lie down and take a rest. He stated:

'It started with bridge, then we got to playing stud. The game got slow, and then some wanted to sport a little, so they started betting on the high spade.'

'I lose,' remarked Bowe calmly, when Pecora asked how he

came out. McManus was in the game. Also Rothstein, 'Titanic,' Sam Meyer Boston, Nate Raymond, 'Sol-somebody'. A chap named Joe Bernstein was present, and several others he didn't remember, though Sam Boston later testified Bernstein was 'doing something and he wasn't playing'. It is this Bernstein, a California young man, who 'beat' Rothstein for $69,000 though Bernstein was never actually in the play. He bet from the outside.

As near as Bowe could recollect, Raymond, Rothstein, McManus and Bernstein were bettors on the high card. He heard McManus lost about $50,000. Rothstein was keeping a score on the winnings and losings. McManus paid off partly in cash and partly by check, while Rothstein was putting cash in his pocket, and would give out IOUs. Bowe said he heard Rothstein lost over $200,000. The redoubtable 'Titanic' won between $20,000 and $25,000 from McManus. Pecora asked: 'What about Sam Boston?'

'He wins.'

Under cross-examination by James D. C. Murray, Bowe said he had often known McManus to bet as much as $50,000 on one horse-race and never complain if he lost. He said:

'It's an everyday occurrence with him. He always paid with a smile.'

After the game, he said, Rothstein and McManus were very friendly; they often ate together at Lindy's. Rothstein won something from McManus in the game, but Bowe didn't know how much.

It was a rather big day for the defence. In his opening address to the jury, George Brothers, assistant district attorney, didn't seem to offer much motive for the possible killing of Rothstein by McManus other than the ill-feeling that might have been engendered over the game in which they both lost.

That, and the fact that McManus fled after the killing, seemed his strongest points, while Attorney Murray quickly made it clear that part of the defence will be that Rothstein wasn't shot in room No. 349 at all, and that he certainly wasn't shot by George McManus.

Murray worked at length on Dr. Charles D. Norris, the City Medical Examiner, trying to bring out from the witness that the nature of the wound sustained by Rothstein and the resultant shock would have prevented Rothstein from walking down three flights of stairs and pushing open two or three heavy doors to reach the spot in the service-entrance of the hotel where he was found, especially without leaving some trace of blood.

During the examination of the doctor, the expensive clothes that Arnold Rothstein used to wear so jauntily were displayed, now crumpled and soiled. The white silk shirt was among the ghastly exhibits, but the $45 custom-made shoes that were his hobby, and the sox, were missing. Dr. Norris didn't know what had become of them.

The jurors, most of them businessmen on their own hook, or identified in salaried capacities with business, were a study while Martin Bowe and Sam Boston were testifying, especially Bowe, for he spoke as calmly of winning and losing $50,000 as if he were discussing the price of his morning paper.

You could see the jurors bending forward, some of them cupping their hands to their ears, and eyeing the witness with amazement. That stud and high-spade game had been mentioned so often in the papers that it had come to be accepted as a Broadway fable. Probably no member of the jury, for none of them indicated in their examination that they are familiar with sporting life, took any stock in the tales of high-rolling of the Broadway gamblers.

But here was a man who was in the game, who had lost $5700 of his own money, and who knew what he was talking about. It was apparent that the jurors were astounded by the blasé manner of Bowe as he spoke of McManus dropping $50,000 as 'an everyday occurrence,' and even the voluble Sam Boston's glib mention of handling hundreds of thousands of dollars yearly in bets on sporting events impresses them.

28 November

Nothing new having developed in the life and battles of Juror No. 9, or the Man with the Little Moustache, the trial of George McManus for the murder of Arnold Rothstein proceeded with reasonable tranquility yesterday.

Just before adjournment over Thanksgiving, to permit the jurors to restore their waning vitality with turkey and stuffin', the State let it out rather quietly that it hasn't been able to trace very far the pistol which is supposed to have ended the tumultuous life of 'the master mind' a year ago.

On a pleasant day in June last year—the fifteenth, to be exact—it seems that one Mr. Joe Novotny was standing behind the counter in his place of business at No. 51 West Fourth Street, in the thriving settlement of St. Paul, Minnesota, when in popped a party who was to Mr. Joe Novotny quite unknown, shopping for a rod, as the boys term a smoke-pole.

Mr. Novotny sold the stranger a .38-calibre Colt, which Mr. Novotny himself had but recently acquired from the firm of Janney, Sempler & Hill, of Minneapolis, for $22.85. The factory number of the Colt was 359,946. Mr. Novotny did not enquire the shopper's name, because it seems there is no law requiring such inquisitiveness in Minnesota, and Mr. Novotny perhaps didn't wish to appear nosey.

No doubt Mr. Novotny figured the stranger was a new settler in St. Paul and desired the Colt to protect himself against the wild Indians and wolves that are said to roam the streets of the city. Anyway, that's the last Mr. Novotny saw of pistol No. 359,946, and all he knows about it, according to a stipulation presented by the State of New York to Judge Nott late yesterday afternoon, and agreed to by James D. C. Murray, attorney for George McManus, as Mr. Novotny's testimony.

It may be that some miscreant subsequently stole the gun from the settler's cabin in St. Paul or that he lent it to a pal who was going to New York, and wished to be well dressed, for the next we hear of No. 359,946 is its appearance in the vicinity of Fifty-sixth Street and Seventh Avenue, Manhattan Island, where it was picked up by one Bender, a taxi jockey, after the shooting of Arnold Rothstein. A stipulation with reference to said Bender also was submitted to Judge Nott.

The State of New York would have the jury in the trial of George McManus believe it was with this gun that Rothstein was shot in the stomach in room 349 in the Park Central Hotel, and that the gun was hurled through a window into the street after the shooting. It remains to be seen what the jury thinks about this proposition.

It is not thought it will take any stock in any theory that the gun walked from St. Paul to the corner of Fifty-sixth Street and Seventh Avenue.

If the settler who bought the gun from Mr. Novotny would step
forward at this moment, he would be as welcome as the flowers
in May. But those Northwestern settlers always are reticent.

It was around three o'clock in the afternoon when Mr. James
McDonald, one of the assistant district attorneys, finished read-
ing the 300 pages of testimony taken in the case to date to
Mr. Edmund C. Shotwell, juror No. 2, who replaced Eugene
Riker when Mr. Riker's nerves bogged down on him.

It was the consensus that Mr. Shotwell was in better physical
condition than Mr. McDonald at the conclusion of the reading,
although at the start it looked as if Mr. McDonald would wear
his man down with ease before page No. 204.

Juror No. 9, who is Norris Smith, The Man with the Little
Moustache, whose adventures have kept this trial from sinking
far down into the inside of the public prints long ere this, sat in
a chair in the row behind the staunch juror No. 2, which row is
slightly elevated above the first row. Juror No. 9, who is slightly
built and dapperly dressed, tweaked at his little moustache with
his fingers and eyed the press section with baleful orbs.

Juror No. 9 was alleged to have been discovered by newspaper
men bouncing around a Greenwich Village shushery and talking
about the McManus trial, though he convinced Judge Nott that
he hadn't done or said anything that might impair his status as
a juror in the case. Finally it was learned that juror No. 9 was
shot up a bit in his apartment at No. 420 West Twentieth Street
on February 29, 1928, by a young man who was first defended
by James D. C. Murray, now McManus's counsel.

What juror No. 9 thinks of the inmates of the press section
would probably be suppressed by the censors. And yet, without
juror No. 9, where would this case be? It would be back next to
pure reading matter—that's where.

30 November

Draw near, friend reader, for a touch of ooh-my-goodness has
finally crept into the Roaring Forties' most famous murder trial.
Sc-an-dal, no less. Sh-h-h!

And where do you think we had to go to get it?

To Walnut Street, in the pleasant mountain city of Asheville,
North Carolina. Folks, thar's sin in them hills!

Here we'd been going along quietly for days and days on end with the matter of George McManus, charged with plugging Arnold Rothstein with a .38, and the testimony had been pure and clean and nothing calculated to give Broadway a bad name, when in come a woman from the ol' Tarheel State speaking of the strangest didoes.

A Mrs. Marian A. Putnam, she was, who runs the Putnam Grill in Asheville, a lady of maybe forty-odd, a headliner for the State, who testified she had heard loud voices of men and a crash coming from the vicinity of room 349 in the Park Central Hotel the night 'the master mind' was 'settled'. And that later she had seen a man wandering along the hallway on the third floor, with his hands pressed to his abdomen and 'a terrible look on his face'.

Well, there seemed nothing in this narration to mar the peaceful trend of events, or to bring the blush of embarrassment for this city to the cheek of the most loyal Broadwayer. Then James D. C. Murray took charge of the witness and began addressing the lady on the most tender subjects, and developing the weirdest things. Really, you'd be surprised.

Handing the lady a registration card from the Park Central Hotel and assuming a gruff tone of voice several octaves over the perfunctory purr that has been the keynote of the trial to date, Murray asked, 'Who are the Mr. and Mrs. Putnam indicated by that card as registered at the Park Central on 28 October 1928?'

'I am Mrs. Putnam.'

'Who is Mr. Putnam?'

Mrs. Putnam hesitated briefly, and then replied, 'A friend of mine to whom I am engaged.'

There were subdued snorts back in the courtroom as the spectators suddenly came up out of their dozes and turned off their snores to contemplate the lady on the witness-stand.

Mrs. Putnam wore a rather smart-looking velvet dress, with a grey caracul coat with a dark squirrel collar, and a few diamonds here and there about her, indicating business is okay at the Putnam Grill.

But she didn't have the appearance of one who might insert a hotsy-totsy strain into the staid proceedings. She looked more like somebody's mother or aunt. She described herself as a widow, and here she was admitting something that savoured of social error, especially as the lady subsequently remarked that 'Mr. Putnam' had occupied the same boudoir with her.

The spectators sat up to listen, and mumbled we were finally getting down to business in this trial.

Murray now produced a death certificate attesting to the demise of one Putnam, who died in 1913, and asked, 'The Mr. Putnam who occupied the room with you wasn't the Mr. Putnam who died in 1913, was he?'

At this point Mrs. Putnam seemed deeply affected, possibly by the memory of the late Mr. P. She gulped and applied her handkerchief to her eyes, and the spectators eyed her intently, because they felt it would be a thrill if it transpired that the deceased Putnam had indeed returned to life the very night that 'the master mind' was shot.

But it seems it wasn't that Mr. Putnam, and Mr. Murray awoke some very antique echoes in the old courtroom as he shouted, 'Who was it?'

Well, Mrs. Putnam, doubtless restrained by a feeling of delicacy, didn't want to tell, and Judge Nott helpfully remarked that as long as she didn't deny she was registered at the hotel, the name didn't seem important. Murray argued that Mrs. Putnam's fiancé might be a material witness for the defence, so Judge Nott let him try to show it.

Finally Mrs. Putnam said the man's name was Perry. He is said to be a citizen of Asheville, and what will be said of Mr. Perry in Asheville when the news reaches the sewing circles down yonder will probably be plenty. Not content with touching on Mr. Perry to Mrs. Putnam, the attorney for the defence asked her about a Mr. Elias, and then about a Mr. Bruce, becoming right personal about Mr. Bruce.

He wanted to know if Mr. Bruce had remained with Mrs. Putnam one night in her room at another New York Hotel, but she said no. Then Murray brought in the name of a Mr. Otis B. Carr, of Hendersonville, N. C., and when Mrs. Putnam said she didn't recall the gentleman, the attorney asked, 'Did you steal anything out of a store in Hendersonville?'

Mrs. Putnam said no. Moreover, in reply to questions, she said she didn't steal two dresses from a department store in Asheville and that she hadn't been arrested for disorderly conduct and fined $5. Before Murray got through with her, some of the listeners half expected to hear him ask the lady if she had ever personally killed A. Rothstein.

Mrs. Putnam couldn't have made the State very happy, because she admitted under Murray's cross-examination that she had once denied in Asheville, in the presence of Mr. Mara, one of the district attorney's assistants, and County Judge McCrae, of Asheville, that she ever left her room in the Park Central the night of the murder.

She said her current story is the truth. Mr. Murray asked her if she hadn't said thus and so to newspapermen in Asheville. She replied, 'I did.'

A young man described as Douglas Eller, a reporter of an Asheville paper, was summoned from among the spectators in the courtroom and brought up to the railing, where Mrs. Putnam could see him. The lady was asked if she knew him, and she eyed him at length before admitting she may have seen him before. Mr. Eller retired, blushing slightly, as if not to be known by Mrs. Putnam argues that one is unknown in Asheville.

Murray became very curious about the Putnam Grill in Asheville. Didn't she have curtained-off booths? She did but her waitresses could walk in and out of them at any time—a reply that Mrs. Putnam tossed at Murray as if scorning utterly the base insinuation of his question.

Did she sell liquor? She did not. She had been shown pictures of Rothstein and McManus and Biller, but she couldn't recognize any of them. She was mighty reluctant about telling the name of a lady-friend with whom she dined in her room the night of the killing, but finally admitted it was a Mrs. Herman Popper. She explained her reluctance by saying, 'I don't want to get other people mixed up in this.'

3 December

The most important point to the State in the trial of George McManus yesterday seemed to be the key to room 349 in the Park Central Hotel, which, according to testimony, was found in a pocket of an overcoat hanging in the room.

This overcoat bore the name of McManus on the tailor's label in the pocket.

The prosecution will, perhaps, make much of this as tending to show that the occupant of the room left in a very great hurry and didn't lock the door, besides abandoning the overcoat, though Detective 'Paddy' Flood said the door was locked when he went there with a house-detective to investigate things.

It was Detective Flood who told of finding the key. He was relating how he entered the room and found, among other things, an overcoat with the name of George McManus on the label. He was asked, 'What other objects did you find?'

'A handkerchief in the pocket of the overcoat, with the initials "G. Mc." There were other handkerchiefs in the drawer in the bedroom and a white shirt.'

'Did you find anything else in the coat?'

'A key, in the right-hand pocket, for room 349.'

'A door-key?'

'Yes.'

Aside from that, the testimony brought out that 'the master mind,' as the underworld sometimes called Arnold Rothstein, died 'game'.

Game as a pebble.

In the haunts of that strange pallid man during his life, you could have had 10 to 1, and plenty of it, that he would 'holler copper,' did occasion arise, with his dying gasp.

Indeed, he was often heard to remark in times when he knew that sinister shadows hovered near—and these were not infrequent times in his troubled career, living as he chose to live: 'If anyone gets me, they'll burn for it.'

And cold, hard men, thinking they read his character, believed they knew his meaning. They felt he was just the kind, when cornered by an untoward circumstance, that would squeal like a pig. It shows you how little you really know of a man.

For when the hour came—as the jury in Judge Nott's court-room heard yesterday, with the dismal snow slanting past the windows of the grimy old Criminal Courts Building—when Arnold Rothstein lay crumpled up with a bullet through his intestines, knowing he was mortally hurt, and officers of the law bent over him and whispered, 'Who did it?' the pale lips tightened, and Rothstein mumbled, 'I won't tell and please don't ask me any more questions.'

Then another 'sure thing' went wrong on Broadway, where

'sure things' are always going wrong—the 'sure thing' that Rothstein would tell.

But as the millionaire gambler lay in the Fifty-sixth Street service-entrance of the Park Central Hotel that night of 4 November 1928, with the pain of his wound biting at his vitals, and the peering eyes of the cops close to his white countenance, he reverted to type.

He was no longer the money king, with property scattered all over the Greater City, a big apartment house on fashionable Park Avenue, a Rolls-Royce and a Minerva at his beck and call, and secretaries and servants bowing to him. He was a man of the underworld. And as one of the 'dice hustlers' of the dingy garage-lofts, and the 'mobsters' high and low, he muttered, 'I won't tell.'

A sigh of relief escaped many a chest at those words, you can bet on that.

Detective Flood, who knew Rothstein well, was one of those who bent over the stricken man.

Patrolman William Davis, first to respond to the call of the hotel attendants, also asked Rothstein who shot him, but got no more information than Flood.

The head of the millionaire gambler was pillowed on a wadded-up burlap sack when Davis reached the scene, which was important to the State in trying to show that Rothstein was shot in the hotel, in that it had been said that Rothstein's overcoat was put under his head.

Before the session was completed, the tables in the courtroom were covered with exhibits of one kind and another taken by Flood and other officers from room 349 in the Park Central.

There was a layout of glasses and a liquor bottle, and ginger-ale bottles on a tray. But, alas, the liquor bottle was very empty. Also the State had the dark blue overcoat with the velvet collar that was found in a closet of room 349, said overcoat bearing a tailor's label, with George McManus's name on the label.

Likewise, handkerchiefs found in the room were produced, and these handkerchiefs were elegantly monogrammed. One was inscribed 'g Mc M.,' another like 'GMA' with the 'G' and 'A' in small letters, and the 'M' big. A third was monogrammed 'JMW' with the 'J' and 'W' in small letters on either side of the large 'M', while the fourth bore the marking 'JM'.

A white shirt with collar attached, some race-tracks slips, and a window screen with a hole in it were spread out for the jurors to see. Also the .38-calibre pistol which one Al Bender, a taxi driver, picked up in Seventh Avenue.

This is supposed to be the pistol with which Rothstein was shot, and the screen is supposed to be the screen through which the pistol was hurled out into the street after the shooting, though the point where the pistol was picked up is quite a hurling distance from room 349.

While Flood and some other officers were in the room, Hyman Biller, a cashier at the race track for McManus, and under indictment with McManus for the murder of Rothstein, came in with Frank and Tom McManus, brothers of George, and remained about twenty minutes.

It was the failure to hold Biller on this occasion that brought down much criticism on the heads of the Police Department, for Hymie was never seen in these parts again.

The lights were burning in room 349 when Flood got there. Four glasses stood on the table, which is the basis of the indictment returned against McManus and Biller and the celebrated John Doe and Richard Roe. The State claims four men were in the room when Rothstein was summoned there by a message sent by McManus to Lindy's restaurant. The State inferred that Rothstein was summoned to pay the overdue IOUs given in the high-spade game described by Martin Bowe.

Vincent J. Kelly, elevator operator at the Park Central, testified that he was working on the service elevator the night Rothstein was shot, and saw Rothstein in the corridor, holding his hands across his stomach, and didn't see him come through the service doorway, through which he must have passed to make good the State's contention that he came from upstairs.

He heard Rothstein say, 'I'm shot.'

Thomas Calhoun, of Corona, Long Island, thirty-two, a watch-man on the Fifty-sixth Street side of the hotel at the time of the murder, saw Rothstein at 10:47 standing in front of the time office at the service entrance. Calhoun ran and got Officer Davis.

He heard Rothstein say something to the policeman about taking his money, and it was his impression that Rothstein had his overcoat over his arm and that it was put under his head as he lay on the floor, which impression was not corroborated by other testimony.

Through Calhoun, Attorney Murray tried to develop that Rothstein might have come through the swimming pool by way of Seventh Avenue. While cross-examining Calhoun, Murray suddenly remarked, testily, 'I object to the mumbling to the District Attorney.'

He apparently had reference to Mr. Brothers, of the State's legal display. Everybody seemed to be a bit testy yesterday, except the defendant, McManus, who just kept on smiling. . . .

EDITORS NOTE. McManus knew that he was more than somewhat entitled to smile. After a couple more days of ramshackle testimony, the judge directed the jury to return a verdict of Not Guilty. (Damon Runyon doesn't seem to have stayed till that end.) The district attorney admitted that the State had failed to establish a case; the indictments against Hyman Biller and the figurative Richard Roe and John Doe were dropped. The identity of Arnold Rothstein's killer remains officially unknown.

SOME EXECUTIONS
—AND AN EXECUTIONER

If we are to abolish the death penalty, I should like the
first step to be taken by our friends the murderers.

Alphonse Karr (coiner of the
'Plus ça change . . .' saying,
1808–90

I
GOING TO SEE A MAN HANGED
William Makepeace Thackeray

[Born in 1811 at Calcutta, where his father (who was of
an English family made rich by trade in killed elephants)
held lucrative posts with the East India Company, he was
sent to England when he was fourteen. His guardian-aunt's
consternation that he could wear her husband's hat was
quelled by a doctor's assurance that 'his big head has a
good deal in it'; his having his nose permanently disfigured
in a fight with a fellow-pupil at the Charterhouse added
to the oddity of his appearance. After wasting time at
Cambridge, he pottered around Europe, drew caricatures
for fun, studied desultorily for the Bar, and then bought
an arts magazine which soon went bust; larger losses at
gambling and on share deals dissipated the fortune he had
inherited from his father, and, needing to earn, he went

to Paris, where he published essays and satirical drawings, and acted as correspondent to an ultra-liberal London paper owned by his step-father; returning to England, he married and became an industrious journalist, particularly for Fraser's Magazine, *in which the following appeared in August 1840—about the time when his wife, having borne him a third daughter, lapsed into 'mental languor' from which she never recovered. In 1846–7, his 'Snobs of England' made him famous; while that series was running in* Punch, *his novel* Vanity Fair *was published, increasing his fame. Rich from further journalism and subsequent novels, he died in 1863 of 'an effusion into his brain'—which, weighed post-mortem, tipped the scales at 58½ ounces.]*

X—, WHO HAD VOTED with Mr. [William] Ewart [MP] for the abolition of the punishment of death, was anxious to see the effect on the public mind of an execution, and asked me to accompany him to see Courvoisier killed[1]. We had not the advantage of a sheriff's order, like the 'six hundred noblemen and gentlemen' who were admitted within the walls of the prison, but determined to mingle with the crowd at the foot of the scaffold, and to take up our positions at a very early hour.

As I was to rise at three in the morning, I went to bed at ten, thinking that five hours' sleep would be amply sufficient to brace me against the fatigues of the coming day. But, as might have been expected, the event of the morrow was perpetually before my eyes through the night, and kept them wide open. I heard all the clocks in the neighbourhood chime the hours in succession; a dog from some court hard by kept up a pitiful yowling; at one o'clock, a cock set up a feeble, melancholy crowing; shortly after two, the daylight came peeping grey through the window-shutters; and by the time that X— arrived, in fulfilment of his promise, I had been asleep about half an hour. He, more wise, had not gone to rest at all, but had remained up all night at the club, along with Dash

[1] EDITOR'S NOTE. *The Swiss-born François Courvoisier was hanged at Newgate on Monday, 6 July 1840, for having terminated his employment as valet to Lord William Russell by near enough decapitating that member of the distinguished Bedford family.*

and two or three more. Dash is one of the most eminent wits in London, and had kept the company merry all night with appropriate jokes about the coming event. It is curious that a murder is a great inspirer of jokes. We all like to laugh and have our fling about it; there is a certain grim pleasure in the circumstances—a perpetual jingling antithesis between life and death that is sure of its effect.

In mansion or garret, on down or straw, surrounded by weeping friends and solemn oily doctors, or tossing unheeded upon scanty hospital beds, there were many people in this great city to whom that Sunday night was to be the last of any that they should pass on earth here. In the course of half-a-dozen dark wakeful hours, one had leisure to think of these (and a little, too, of that certain supreme night that shall come at one time or other, when he who writes shall be stretched upon the last bed, prostrate in the last struggle, taking the last look at dear faces that have cheered us here, and lingering—one moment more—ere we part for the tremendous journey); but, chiefly, I could not help thinking, as each clock sounded, what is *he* doing now?—has *he* heard it in his little room in Newgate yonder? Eleven o'clock. He has been writing until now. The gaoler says he is a pleasant man enough to be with; but he can hold out no longer, and is very weary.

'Wake me at four,' says he, 'for I have still much to put down.' From eleven to twelve the gaoler hears how he is grinding his teeth in his sleep. At twelve he is up in his bed, and asks, 'Is it the time?' He has plenty more time yet for sleep; and he sleeps, and the bells go on tolling. Seven hours more—five hours more. Many a carriage is clattering through the streets, bringing ladies away from evening parties; many bachelors are reeling home after a jolly night; Covent Garden is alive; and the light coming through the cell-window turns the gaoler's candle pale. Four hours more! '*Courvoisier*,' says the gaoler, shaking him, 'it's four o'clock now, and I've woke you, as you told me; but there's no call for you *to get up yet*.'

The poor wretch leaves his bed, however, and makes his last toilet; and then falls to writing, to tell the world how he did the crime for which he has suffered. This time he will tell the truth, and the whole truth. They bring him his breakfast 'from the coffee-shop opposite—tea, coffee, and thin bread and butter'. He will take nothing, however, but goes on writing. He has to write to his mother—the pious mother far away in his own country—who reared him and loved him; and even now has sent him her forgiveness and her blessing. He finishes his memorials and letters, and makes his will, disposing of his little miserable property of books and tracts that pious people have furnished him with. '*Ce 6 Juillet, 1840. François Benjamin Courvoisier vous donne ceci, mon ami, pour souvenir.*' He has a token for his dear friend the gaoler; another for his dear friend the under-sheriff. As the day of the convict's death draws nigh, it is painful to see how he fastens upon everybody who approaches him, how pitifully he clings to them and loves them.

While these things are going on within the prison (with which we are made accurately acquainted by the copious chronicles of such events which are published subsequently), X—'s carriage has driven up to the door of my lodgings, and we have partaken of an elegant *disjeune* that has been prepared for the occasion. A cup of coffee at half-past three in the morning is uncommonly pleasant; and X—enlivens us with the repetition of the jokes that Dash has just been making. Admirable, certainly—they must have had a merry night of it, that's clear; and we stoutly debate whether, when one has to get up so early in the morning, it is best to have an hour or two of sleep, or wait and go to bed afterwards at the end of the day's work. That fowl is extraordinarily tough—the wing, even, is as hard as a board; a slight disappointment, for there is nothing else for breakfast. 'Will any gentleman have some sherry and soda-water before he sets out? It clears the brains famously.' Thus primed, the party sets out. The coachman has dropped asleep on the box, and wakes up wildly as the hall-door opens. It is just four o'clock. About this very time they are waking up poor—psha! who is for a cigar? X—does not smoke himself; but vows and protests, in the kindest way in the world, that he does not care in the least for the new drab-silk linings of his carriage. Z—, who smokes, mounts, however, the box. 'DRIVE TO SNOW HILL,' says the owner of the chariot. The policemen, who are the only people in the street, look knowing—they know what it means well enough.

How cool and clean the streets look, as the carriage startles the echoes that have been asleep in the corners all night. Somebody has been sweeping the pavements clean in the night-time surely; they would not soil a lady's white satin shoes, they are so dry and neat. There is not a cloud or a breath in the air, except Z—'s cigar, which whiffs off, and soars straight upwards in volumes of white, pure smoke. The trees in the squares look bright and green—as bright as leaves in the country in June. We who keep late hours don't know the beauty of London air and verdure; in the early morning they are delightful—the most fresh and lively companions possible. But they cannot bear the crowd and the bustle of midday. You don't know them then—they are no longer the same things. We have come to Gray's Inn; there is actually dew upon the grass in the gardens; and the windows of the stout old red houses are all in a flame.

As we enter Holborn, the town grows more animated; and there are already twice as many people in the streets as you see at midday in a German *residenz* or an English provincial town. The gin-shop keepers have many of them taken their shutters down, and many persons are issuing from them pipe in hand. Down they go along the broad bright street, their blue shadows marching *after* them; for they are all bound the same way, and are bent like us upon seeing the hanging.

It is twenty minutes past four as we pass St. Sepulchre's: by this time many hundred people are in the street, and many more are coming up Snow Hill. Before us lies Newgate prison; but something a great deal more awful to look at, which seizes the eye at once, and makes the heart beat, is

There it stands, black and ready, jutting out from a little door in the prison. As you see it, you feel a kind of dumb electric-shock, which causes one to start a little, and give a sort of gasp for breath. The shock is over in a second; and presently you examine the object before you with a certain feeling of complacent curiosity. At least, such was the effect that the gallows first produced upon the writer, who is trying to set down all his feelings as they occurred, and not to exaggerate them at all.

After the gallows-shock had subsided, we went down into the crowd, which was very numerous but not dense as yet. It was evident that the day's *business* had not begun. People sauntered up, and formed groups, and talked; the newcomers asking those who seemed *habitués* of the place about former executions; and did the victim hang with his face towards the clock or towards Ludgate Hill? and had he the rope round his neck when he came on the scaffold, or was it put on by Jack Ketch[1] afterwards? and had Lord W—taken a window, and which was he? I may mention the noble marquess's name, as he was not at the exhibition. A pseudo W—was pointed out in an opposite window, towards whom all the people in our neighbourhood looked eagerly, and with great respect too. The mob seemed to have no sort of ill-will against him, but sympathy and admiration. This noble lord's personal courage and strength has won the plebs over to him. Perhaps his exploits against policemen have occasioned some of this popularity; for the mob hates them, as children the schoolmaster.

Throughout the whole four hours, however, the mob was extraordinarily gentle and good-humoured. . . . What good sense and intelligence have most of the people by whom you are surrounded; how much sound humour does one hear bandied about from one to another. A great number of coarse phrases are used that would make ladies in drawing-rooms blush; but the morals of the men are good and hearty. A ragamuffin in the crowd (a powdery baker in a white sheep's-wool cap) uses some indecent expression to a woman near; there is an instant cry of shame, which silences the man, and a dozen people are ready to give the woman protection. The crowd

[1] EDITOR'S NOTE. *From about 1678 until 1686, shortly before Richard Jacquet died in bed at his home in London, he was the most publicised of England's several public executioners. As is explained in Lloyd's MS Collection of English Pedigrees in the British Museum, 'The Manor of Tyburn, where felons for a long time were executed, was formerly held by Richard Jacquet, whence we have the name Jack Ketch as a corruption.' That nickname, tagged to subsequent executioners, applied in the case of Courvoisier to William Calcraft, who held office from 1829 until 1874.*

has grown very dense by this time, it is about six o'clock, and there is great heaving, and pushing, and swaying to and fro; but round the women the men have formed a circle, and keep them as much as possible out of the rush and trample. In one of the houses near us, a gallery has been formed on the roof. Seats were here let, and a number of persons of various degrees were occupying them. Several tipsy, dissolute-looking young men, of the Dick Swiveller cast, were in this gallery. One was lolling over the sunshiney tiles, with a fierce sodden face, out of which came a pipe, and which was shaded by long matted hair, and a hat cocked very much on one side. This gentleman was one of a party, which had evidently not been to bed on Sunday night, but had passed it in some of those delectable night-houses in the neighbourhood of Covent Garden. The debauch was not over yet, and the women of the party were giggling, drinking, and romping, as is the wont of these delicate creatures; sprawling here and there, and falling upon the knees of one or other of the males. Their scarfs were off their shoulders, and you saw the sun shining down upon the bare white flesh, and the shoulder-points glittering like burning glasses. The people about us were very indignant at some of the proceedings of this debauched crew, and at last raised up such a yell as frightened them into shame, and they were more orderly for the remainder of the day.

The windows of the shops opposite began to fill apace, and a fellow with ragged elbows pointed out a celebrated fashionable character who occupied one of them; and, to our surprise, knew as much about him as the *Court Journal* or the *Morning Post*. Presently he entertained us with a long and pretty accurate account of the history of Lady—, and indulged in a judicious criticism upon her last work. I have met with many a country gentleman who had not read half as many books as this honest fellow, this shrewd *prolétaire* in a black shirt. The people about him took up and carried on the conversation very knowingly, and were very little behind him in point of information. It was just as good a company as one meets on common occasions. I was in a genteel crowd in one of the galleries at the queen's coronation; indeed, in point of intelligence, the democrats were quite equal to the aristocrats. How many more such groups were there in this immense multitude of nearly forty thousand, as some say? How many more such throughout the country? I never yet have been in an English mob without the same feeling for the persons who composed it, and without wonder at the vigorous, orderly good sense and intelligence of the people.

The character of the crowd was as yet, however, quite festive. Jokes bandying about here and there, and jolly laughs breaking out. Some men were endeavouring to climb up a leaden pipe on one of the houses. The landlord came out and endeavoured, with might and main, to pull them down. Many thousand eyes turned upon this contest immediately. All sorts of voices issued from the crowd and uttered choice expressions of slang. When one of the men was pulled down by the leg, the waves of this black mob-ocean laughed innumerably; when one fellow slipped away, scrambled up the pipe, and made good his lodgement on the shelf, we were all made happy, and encouraged him by loud shouts of admiration.

What is there so particularly delightful in the spectacle of a man clambering up a gas-pipe? Why were we kept for a quarter of an hour in deep interest gazing upon this remarkable scene? Indeed it is hard to say; a man does not know what a fool he is until he tries; or, at least, what mean follies will amuse him. The other day I went to Astley's and saw a clown come in with a foolscap and pinafore, and six small boys who represented his school-fellows. To them enters schoolmaster; horses clown, and flogs him hugely on the back part of his pinafore. I never read anything in Swift, Boz, Rabelais, Fielding, Paul de Kock, which delighted me so much as this sight and caused me to laugh so profoundly. And why? What is there so ridiculous in the sight of one miserably rouged man beating another on the breech? Tell us where the fun lies, in this and the before-mentioned episode of the gas-pipe? Vast, indeed, are the capacities and ingenuities of the human soul that can find, in incidents so wonderfully small, means of contemplation and amusement.

Really the time passed away with extraordinary quickness. A thousand things of the sort related here came to amuse us. First, the workmen knocking and hammering at the scaffold, mysterious clattering of blows was heard within it, and a ladder painted black was carried round, and into the interior of the edifice by a small side-door. We all looked at this little ladder and at each other—things began to be very interesting.

Soon came a squad of policemen; stalwart, rosy-looking men, saying much for city-feeding; well-dressed, well-limbed, and of admirable good humour. They paced about the open space between the prison and the barriers which kept in the crowd from the scaffold. The front line, as far as I could see, was chiefly occupied by blackguards and boys—professional persons, no doubt, who saluted the policemen on their appearance with a volley of jokes and ribaldry. As far as I could judge from faces, there were more blackguards of sixteen and seventeen than of any maturer age; stunted, sallow, ill-grown lads, in rugged fustian, scowling about. There were a considerable number of girls, too, of the same age; one that Cruikshank and Boz might have taken as a study for Nancy[1]. The girl was a young thief's mistress evidently;

[1] EDITOR'S NOTE. Thackeray had already criticised Oliver Twist (1837–9) as being, inter alia, of the 'Newgate School' of fiction—a glorification of criminals and a primer for aspiring ones.

Charles Dickens ('Boz') was also in the audience (in a room with a view) at the Courvoisier execution; he caught sight of Thackeray's large head, its crown 6 foot 3 inches above the cobbles, but was unable to attract his attention. He too was distressed by the occasion (as the great Dickens-scholar Philip Collins has pointed out; memories of it seem to affect Barnaby Rudge [1841–2], and Dickens wrote about it explicitly in a letter published in the Daily News of 28 February 1846)—but whereas Thackeray would remain an opponent of capital punishment (at least in public: according to George Saintsbury, an editor of Punch, speaking after Thackeray's death, 'He kept to . . . the anti-capital-punishment fad . . . for some time, but in his later and wiser days admitted that he was wrong'), Dickens, while being uncompromising in his belief that hangings should be done indoors, relatively privately, was equivocal on the question of whether hanging should be done away with altogether.

if attacked, ready to reply without a particle of modesty; could give as good ribaldry as she got; made no secret (and there were several enquiries) as to her profession and means of livelihood. But with all this, there was something good about the girl: a sort of devil-may-care candour and simplicity that one could not fail to see. Her answers to some of the coarse questions put to her were very ready and good-humoured. She had a friend with her of the same age and class, of whom she seemed to be very fond, and who looked up to her for protection. Both of these women had beautiful eyes. Devil-may-care's were extraordinarily bright and blue; she had an admirably fair complexion, and a large red mouth full of white teeth. *Au reste*, ugly, stunted, thick-limbed, and by no means a beauty. Her friend could not be more than fifteen. They were not in rags but had greasy cotton shawls, and old, faded, rag-shop bonnets. I was curious to look at them, having, in late fashionable novels, read many accounts of such personages. Bah! what figments these novelists tell us!

Boz, who knows life well, knows that his Miss Nancy is the most unreal fantastical personage possible; no more like a thief's mistress than one of Gessner's shepherdesses resembles a real country wench. He dare not tell the truth concerning such young ladies. They have, no doubt, virtues like other human creatures; nay, their position engenders virtues that are not called into exercise among other women. But on these an honest painter of human nature has no right to dwell; not being able to paint the whole portrait, he has no right to present one or two favourable points as characterising the whole; and therefore, in fact, had better leave the picture alone altogether. The new French literature is essentially false and worthless from this very error—the writers giving us favourable pictures of monsters (and, to say nothing of decency or morality), pictures quite untrue to nature.

But yonder, glittering through the crowd in Newgate Street— see the sheriffs' carriages are slowly making their way. We have been here three hours! Is it possible that they can have passed so soon? Close to the barriers where we are, the mob has become so dense that it is with difficulty a man can keep his feet. Each man, however, is very careful in protecting the women, and all are full of jokes and good-humour. The windows of the shops opposite are now pretty nearly filled by the persons who hired them. Many young dandies are there, with mustachios and cigars; some quiet, fat, family parties, of simple honest tradesmen and their wives, as we fancy, who are looking on with the greatest imaginable calmness, and sipping their tea. Yonder is the sham Lord W—, who is flinging various articles among the crowd; one of his companions, a tall burly man with large mustachios, has provided himself with a squirt, and is aspersing the mob with brandy and water. Honest gentleman! high-bred aristocrat! genuine lover of humour and wit! I would walk some miles to see thee on the tread-mill, thee and thy Mohawk crew!

We tried to get up a hiss against these ruffians, but only had a trifling success; the crowd did not seem to think their offence very heinous; and our friend, the philosopher in the ragged elbows, who had remained near us all the time, was not inspired with any such savage disgust at the proceedings of certain notorious young gentlemen as I must confess fills my own particular bosom. He only said, 'So-and-so is a lord, and they'll let him off,' and then discoursed about Lord Ferrers being hanged [in 1760, having been tried and found Guilty—by other Peers—of the murder of his Steward, John Johnson]. The philosopher knew the history pretty well, and so did most of the little knot of persons about him, and it must be a gratifying thing for young gentlemen to find that their actions are made the subject of this kind of conversation.

Scarcely a word had been said about Courvoisier all this time. We were all, as far as I could judge, in just such a frame of mind as men are in when they are squeezing at the pit-door of a play or pushing for a review or a lord mayor's show. We asked the men who were near us whether they had seen many executions (most of them had, the philosopher especially); whether the sight of them did any good? 'For the matter of that, no; people did not care about them at all; nobody ever thought of it after a bit.' A countryman, who had left his drove in Smithfield, said the same thing; he had seen a man hanged at York, and spoke of the ceremony with perfect good sense and in a quiet sagacious way.

J. S—, the famous wit now dead, had, I recollect, a good

story upon the subject of executing, and of the terror which the punishment inspires. After [Arthur] Thistlewood and his companions were hanged [in 1820, for the 'Cato Street, Conspiracy' between the eleven of them, the thwarted intention of which was to wipe out the entire British Cabinet at a stroke], their heads were taken off according to the sentence; and the executioner, as he severed each, held it up to the crowd in the proper orthodox way, saying, 'Here is the head of a traitor!' At the sight of the first ghastly head, the people were struck with terror, and a general expression of disgust and fear broke from them. The second head was looked at also with much interest, but the excitement regarding the third head diminished. When the executioner had come to the last of the heads, he lifted it up; but by some clumsiness, allowed it to drop. At this, the crowd yelled out, 'Ah, Butter-fingers!'—the excitement had passed entirely away. The punishment had grown to be a joke—Butter-fingers was the word—a pretty commentary, indeed, upon the august nature of public executions and the awful majesty of the law.

It was past seven now; the quarters rang and passed away; the crowd began to grow very eager and more quiet, and we turned back every now and then and looked at St. Sepulchre's clock. Half an hour, twenty-five minutes. What is he doing now? He had his irons off by this time. A quarter: he's in the press-room now, no doubt. Now at last we had come to think about the man we were going to see hanged. How slowly the clock crept over the last quarter! Those who were able to turn round and see (for the crowd was now extraordinarily dense) chronicled the time—eight minutes, five minutes; at last—ding, dong, dong, dong!—the bell is tolling the chime of eight.

Between the writing of this line and the last, the pen has been put down, as the reader may suppose, and the person who is addressing him gone through a pause of no very pleasant thoughts and recollections. The whole of the sickening, ghastly, wicked scene passes before the eyes again; and, indeed, it is an awful one to see, and very hard and painful to describe.

As the clock began to strike, an immense sway and movement

swept over the whole of that vast dense crowd. They were all uncovered directly, and a great murmur arose, more awful, *bizarre* and undescribable than any sound I had ever before heard. Women and children began to shriek horridly. I don't know whether it was the bell I heard; but a dreadful, quick, feverish kind of jangling noise mingled with the noise of the people and lasted for about two minutes. The scaffold stood before us, tenantless, and black; the black chain was hanging down ready from the beam. Nobody came. 'He has been respited,' someone said; another said, 'He has killed himself in prison.'

Just then, from under the black prison-door, a pale, quiet head peered out. It was shockingly bright and distinct; it rose up directly, and a man in black appeared on the scaffold, and was silently followed by about four more dark figures. The first was a tall, grave men: *'That's he—that's he!'* you heard the people say as the devoted man came up.

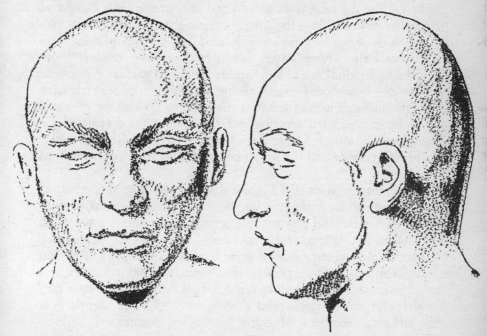

Drawings of Courvoisier's death-mask

I have seen a cast of the head since, but, indeed, should never have known it. Courvoisier bore his punishment like a man, and walked very firmly. He was dressed in a new black suit, as it seemed; his shirt was open. His arms were tied in front of him. He opened his hands in a helpless kind of way, and clasped them once or twice together. He turned his head here and there, and looked about him for an instant with a wild, imploring look. His mouth was contracted into a sort of pitiful smile. He went and placed himself at once under the beam, with his face towards St. Sepulchre's. The tall, grave man in black twisted him round swiftly in the other direction, and drawing from his pocket a night-cap, pulled it tight over the patient's head and face. I am not ashamed to say that I could look no more, but shut my eyes as the last dreadful act was going on, which sent this wretched guilty soul into the presence of God.

If a public execution is beneficial—and beneficial it is, no doubt, or else the wise laws would not encourage forty thousand people to witness it—the next useful thing must be a full description of such a ceremony, and all its *entourages*, and to this end the above pages are offered to the reader. How does an individual man feel under it? In what way does he observe it—how does he view all the phenomena connected with it—what induces him in the first instance to go and see it—and how is he moved by it afterwards? The writer has discarded the magazine 'We' altogether, and spoken face to face with the reader, recording every one of the impressions felt by him as honestly as he could.

I must confess, then (for I is the shortest word, and the best in this case), that the sight has left on my mind an extraordinary feeling of terror and shame. It seems to me that I have been abetting an act of frightful wickedness and violence performed by a set of men against one of their fellows; and I pray God that it may soon be out of the power of any man in England to witness such a hideous and degrading sight. Forty thousand persons (say the sheriffs), of all ranks and degrees—mechanics, gentlemen, pickpockets, members of both houses of parliament, street-walkers, newspapers-writers—gather together before Newgate at a very early hour; the most part of them give up their natural quiet night's rest in order to partake of this hideous debauchery, which is more exciting than sleep, or than wine, or the last new ballet, or any other amusement that they can have. Pickpocket and peer, each is tickled by the sight alike, and has that hidden lust after blood which influences our race. Government, a Christian government, gives us a feast every now and then: it agrees—that is to say, a majority in the two houses agrees—that for certain crimes it is necessary that a man should be hanged by the neck. Government commits the criminal's soul to the mercy of God, stating that here on earth he is to look for no mercy; keeps him for a fortnight to prepare, provides him with a clergyman to settle his religious matters (if there be time enough, but government can't wait); and on a Monday morning, the bell tolling, the clergyman reading out the word of God, 'I am the resurrection and the life,' 'The Lord giveth, and the Lord taketh away'—on a Monday morning, at eight o'clock, this man is placed under a beam, with a rope connecting it and him; a plank disappears from under him, and those who have paid for good places may see the hands of the government agent, Jack Ketch, coming up from his black hole and seizing the prisoner's legs and pulling them until he is quite dead—strangled.

Many persons, and well-informed newspapers, say that it is mawkish sentiment to talk in this way—morbid humanity, cheap philanthropy, that any man can get up and preach about. There is the *Observer*, for instance, a paper conspicuous for the tremendous sarcasm which distinguishes its articles ... 'Courvoisier is dead,' says the *Observer*; he 'died as he had lived—a villain; a lie was in his mouth. Peace be to his ashes. We war not with the head.' What a magnanimous *Observer*! ...

'Peace be to his ashes. He died a villain.' This is both benevolence and reason. Did he die a villain? The *Observer* does not want to destroy him body and soul, evidently, from that pious wish that his ashes should be at peace. Is the next Monday but one after the sentence the time necessary for a villain to repent in? May a man not require more leisure—a week more, six months more—before he has been able to make his repentance sure before

Him who died for us all?—for all, be it remembered—not alone for the judge and jury, or for the sheriffs, or for the executioner who is pulling down the legs of the prisoner—but for him too, murderer and criminal as he is, whom we are killing for his crime. Do we want to kill him body and soul? Heaven forbid! My lord in the black cap specially prays that Heaven may have mercy on him; but he must be ready by Monday morning . . .

Murder is such a monstrous crime (this is the great argument)—when a man has killed another, it is natural that he should be killed. Away with your foolish sentimentalists who say no—it is *natural*. That is the word, and a fine philosophical opinion it is—philosophical and Christian. Kill a man, and you must be killed in turn; that is the unavoidable *sequitur*. You may talk to a man for a year upon the subject, and he will always reply to you: It is natural, and therefore it must be done. Blood demands blood.

Does it? The system of compensations might be carried on *ad infinitum*—an eye for an eye, a tooth for a tooth, as by the Old Mosaic law. But (putting the fact out of the question, that we have had this statute repealed by the Highest Authority) why, because you lose your eye, it that of your opponent's to be extracted likewise? And yet it is just as natural as the death dictum, founded precisely upon the same show of sense. Knowing, however, that revenge is not only evil but useless, we have given it up on all minor points. Only to the last we stick firm, contrary though it be to reason and to Christian law.

There is some talk, too, of the terror which the sight of this spectacle inspires, and of this we have endeavoured to give as good a notion as we can in the above pages. I fully confess that I came away down Snow Hill that morning with a disgust for murder, but it was for *the murder I saw done*. As we made our way through the immense crowd, we came upon two little girls of eleven and twelve years: one of them was crying bitterly, and begged, for Heaven's sake, that someone would lead her from that horrid place. This was done, and the children were carried into a place of safety. We asked the elder girl—a very pretty one—what brought her into such a neighbourhood; the child grinned knowingly and said, "We've koom to see the mon hanged!" Tender law, that brings out babes upon such errands, and provides them with such gratifying moral spectacles.

This is the 20th of July, and I may be permitted for my part to declare that, for the last fourteen days, so salutary has the impression of the butchery been upon me, I have had the man's face continually before my eyes; that I can see Mr. Ketch at this moment, with an easy air, taking the rope from his pocket; that I feel myself ashamed and degraded at the brutal curiosity which took me to that brutal sight; and that I pray to Almighty God to cause this disgraceful sin to pass from among us and to cleanse our land of blood.

II
FAREWELL PERFORMANCES
Jonathan Goodman

IN 1866, a Royal Commission on Capital Punishment, under the chairmanship of the Duke of Richmond, recommended the passing of an Act to end Public executions.

On 22 May of that year, a Tuesday, the last *entirely* public execution in Scotland took place against the south wall of Perth Prison, on a scaffold borrowed from Aberdeen. The condemned man was Joseph Bell, who twelve days before had been found guilty of the murder of Alexander M'Ewan, a baker's vanman who had been shot to death—'his head veritably riddled with pellets'—in furtherance of the theft of his takings and pocket-money (amounting to £10s.0d[1]. near Vicars Bridge, Blairingone. Bell, who protested his innocence till the end, had been a potter by day, a poacher by night, and in time spared from those occupations, an unrewarded poet. When condemned, he turned to poetry full-time, filling blank spaces in books of an uplifting nature brought to him by a clergyman of Perth. On the title page of a book he bequeathed to his parents, he wrote:

> Dear Father and Mother, it is the 12th of May,
> I wrote these lines for you today;
> Sad news they will have to tell,
> About our parting. Joseph Bell.

---

[1] The 1991 purchasing power of the 1866 £ is reckoned to be about £34.

In remembrance of me pray keep this book,
With earnest eyes do on it look,
For this day we must take farewell.
Your loving son, Joseph Bell.

And he inscribed a book earmarked for an uncle:

I cannot help speaking without amaze;
See how the Court did on the jury gaze
When the verdict of guilty did sound it knell
Upon your nephew, Joseph Bell.

It was estimated that about 2000 people surrounded the barricades when William Calcraft, on one of his comparatively infrequent excursions across the border, drew the bolt on the borrowed scaffold.

On 11 May 1868, a Monday, the Capital Punishment Within Prisons Bill, embodying the recommendation of the Royal Commission, received its third reading in the House of Lords and was sent to the Queen for her assent. Next day, up in Scotland, Robert Smith, who was nineteen, was hanged outside Dumfries Prison for the sexually-motivated murder of a little girl named Scott near the village of Cummertrees. Half-bowing to the wish of the Provost of Dumfries that the hanging should be the first done privately, the governor of the prison arranged for the barricades to be erected more for the purpose of restricting the spectators' view of what they had come to see (many having trudged long distances to do so) than to make breathing-space for those directly involved in the event. Rather a shame, that, for the hanging was more suspenseful than most: a *Scots Black Kalendar* records that 'the execution, which was the last public one in Scotland, was, however, not carried through with dispatch, as the rope had to be taken off and readjusted before the bolt was drawn. (Askern, of York, officiated.)'

On Tuesday, 26 May, three days before the Capital Punishment Within Prisons Bill received the Royal Assent, a twenty-seven-year-old Irish stevedore named Michael Barrett, convicted of having played a leading part in a Fenian bombing of the Clerkenwell House of Detention on 13 December 1867 that had killed a dozen people, five instantly (and injured 120 more), was hanged outside nearby Newgate by Calcraft, performing publicly for the last time.

Barrett should have become the last person to be hanged publicly in the British Isles earlier than he did. His execution had been postponed for a few days, giving time for an extra-judicial inquiry into his contention—from the moment he was arrested and charged in Glasgow, and throughout his trial—that he was nowhere near Clerkenwell around the time of the explosion; the morning after he was eventually hanged, *The Times* suggested that, far from being upset at this treatment, he should have been grateful to British justice for having given him what amounted to two trials—'It is rare in the history of our criminal jurisprudence that Government allows a sort of special commission to inquire into the validity of a jury's verdict and the judge's approval.' (Nearly forty years passed before, in 1907, a Court of Criminal Appeal was established.)

If some people had had their way in 1917, Barrett's place in the history of capital punishment would have been undermined by Sir Roger Casement, condemned to death for treachery on behalf of aims similar to those of Barrett and his fellow-Fenians: it was seriously suggested that as the Act of 1867 referred only to the hanging of murderers, Casement should be executed in some large public place—Hyde Park, perhaps. No one influential took any notice, and Casement was hanged in the privacy of Pentonville Prison. (In 1965, remains said to be his were dug from the Pentonville graveyard and shipped to Eire, a token of the British Government's desire for Anglo-Irish détente. There is a suspicion that a mistake was made and that the remains disinterred were those of Dr. Crippen.)

On Thursday, 13 August 1868, the first private execution in Great Britain was carried out in Maidstone Prison, Kent—of Thomas Wells, aged eighteen, the murderer of Edward Adolphus Walshe, the station-master at Dover, in the same county. Next morning, *The Times* reported that 'at the moment of the drop there were very few, if any, strangers in the vicinity of the prison, and the town of Maidstone presented quite its usual appearance, presenting a marked extraordinary contrast to that which it exhibited on the occasion of a public execution'; but the *Morning Star*, after breathing a sigh of relief that 'the citizens [have been] freed from the odious accompaniment of an execution', rambled towards a conclusion about a 'spectacle' that wasn't: 'No, the English people cannot long tolerate the spectacle of criminals put to death in a private pit.'

Presumably there was strict obedience to ancillary provisions of the causative Act, most of which were meant to allay concern that capital punishment might turn into a hole-and-corner pursuit, not only deficient in moral lessons but seeming (among those who needed such lessons) to be something to be ashamed of doing. The sheriff, the gaoler, the chaplain, and the prison surgeon had to be present; local Justices of the Peace could attend if they wished, but it was left to the sheriff or visiting justices of the prison to decide whether or not to admit relatives of the prisoner or anyone else. (Passes were almost invariably given to journalists—some of whom, fiction writers in their spare time too, contributed much to a mythology of private executing that would have grown substantial even if they had been uncreative. Abolitionists who before the Act had prophesied that some papers would vie with some others for 'exclusives' on the private hangings of celebrated criminals were only too happy to be able to lament when it happened. 'The cheap newspapers carry the account of the final scene of disgrace and pain far and wide,' wrote one of the reformers, 'and it is eagerly read by all who are eagerly attracted by baneful excitement.' Twenty years elapsed before the Home Office ordered that the press were to be excluded, at the same time reminding sheriffs that, as signatories to the Official Secrets Act, they were not allowed to give information about executions to outsiders.) Directly after a hanging, the surgeon had to ensure that its practical purpose had been fulfilled, and once he had signed a declaration that he had done so, the sheriff, gaoler, and chaplain had to sign a declaration to the effect that he was satisfied; no more than hours after a hanging, a coroner's inquest had to be held on the body, which then had to be buried within the precincts of the particular prison.

III
A BAKING AT SING SING
Anonymous

'I always thought it was a ridiculous name for a prison
—Sing Sing, I mean. Sounds more like it should be an
opera house or something.'
   Lines spoken by Audrey Hepburn in the movie Breakfast
   at Tiffany's *(1961); screenplay, based on the novella by*
                        Truman Capote, *by George Axelrod*

EDITOR'S NOTE. William Kemmler eloped with Tillie Ziegler, another man's wife; but in 1899, when they were living at Buffalo, New York State, he, having grown tired of Tillie, sought to dispel his ennui by murdering her with an axe. As a result of his unsubtle crime, he became the first victim of 'electrocide'—a word coined by the New York World, *an organ owned by Joseph Pulitzer that had supported the campaign against the replacement of hanging by electrical execution. On Thursday, 7 August 1890, the day after the inaugural event at Sing Sing, the* World *was pleased to report that things had not gone at all neatly:*

THE FIRST EXECUTION by electricity has been a horror. Physicians who might make a jest out of the dissecting room, officials who have seen many a man's neck wrenched by the rope, surgeons who have lived in hospitals and knelt beside the dead and dying on bloody fields, held their breaths with a gasp, and those unaccustomed to such sights turned away in dread.

The doctors say the victim did not suffer. Only his Maker knows if that be true. To the eye, it looked as though he were in a convulsive agony.

The current had been passing through his body for fifteen seconds when the electrode at the head was removed. Suddenly the breast heaved. There was a straining at the straps which bound him; a purplish foam covered the lips and was spattered over the leather head-band.

The man was alive. Warden, physicians, everybody, lost their wits. There was a startled cry for the current to be turned on again. Signals, only half understood, were given to those in the next room at the switchboard. When they knew what had happened, they were prompt to act, and the switch-handle could be heard as it was pulled back and forth, breaking the deadly current into jets.

The rigor of death came on the instant. An odour of burning flesh and singed hair filled the room. For a moment a blue flame played about the base of the victim's spine. One of the witnesses nearly fell to the floor. Another lost control of his stomach. Cold perspiration beaded every face. This time the electricity flowed four minutes.

Kemmler was dead. Part of his brain had been baked hard. Some of the blood in his head turned into charcoal. The flesh at the small of his back was black with fire . . .

The electric execution law ought now to be repealed on all accounts. So long as it stands, convictions for capital offences will be difficult to the point of impossibility. Juries will not willingly condemn men to death by torture. So long as capital punishment is maintained, old-fashioned hanging is good enough, provided it is administered by trained and skillful hangmen.

But the New York Times *(same date) felt differently:*

No doubt the advocates of this method of executing the death penalty are for the moment put upon the defensive, but they have not a failure of method to face. Nothing that they have claimed has been refuted. The first trial was of necessity an experiment and was not conducted with that care and coolness that was requisite to ensure success. But it was made clear that with the current that had been recommended for the purpose, with appliance free from defect in construction and operation, and with a firm and confident application of the process, there could hardly be any question of instant and painless death. It would be absurd to talk of abandoning the law and going back to the barbarism of hanging, and it would be as puerile to propose to abolish capital punishment, because the new mode of execution was botched in its first application.

The first authorised use of a gas-chamber for killing a human being was at the Nevada State Prison, Carson City, on 8 February 1924, when a Chinaman called Gee Jon was executed for the murder of a member of a rival tong-gang; a timekeeper noted that death ensued some six minutes after hydrocyanic gas had been admitted to the chamber.

It was not, however, the first time a gas chamber had been used for this purpose. In 1891, Herman Webster Mudgett (who used at least eleven aliases, his favourite being Henry Howard Holmes) opened an hotel, built to his own specifications, in Chicago; local people dubbed the Gothic-style building 'Holmes's Castle'. Some of the guests never checked out. Five years after the opening, police visited the hotel, intending to quiz Mudgett about an insurance fraud; but he had fled—to Philadelphia, as it transpired. Searching the building, the police found that it contained all modern murderous conveniences, including air-tight rooms with gas inlets. Mudgett conducted his own quaint defence at his trial for the murder of a business associate, Benjamin Pitezel; found guilty and sentenced to death, he confessed to twenty-seven killings. Considering the venue of his execution, by hanging, on 7 May 1896—Moyamensing Prison, Philadelphia

—it is safe to say that he would have taken strong exception to the sentiment expressed in W. C. Fields's self-chosen epitaph: 'On the whole, I'd rather be in Philadelphia.'

IV
THE BEHEADING OF BLUEBEARD
Webb Miller

[A remarkably honest press-reporter, he was born in 1892 on a run-down tenant-farm in the hamlet of Pokagon, Michigan. He 'wanted to write more than anything else'—and so, after finishing high school, he taught at a primary one till, at the age of twenty, he had saved enough to support himself in Chicago while seeking a job on a newspaper. He was taken on by the Chicago American (the news-room of which is among those said to be the original of the news-room scenes in the play The Front Page*). The first execution he witnessed was a hanging in the county jail in 1914 ('It is horrible and sickening, but there is also something repellantly fascinating about watching a man die'—reminiscent, that, of Dickens' 'attraction of repulsion'). He left the* American *in 1916, to be a freelance reporter with the US expedition into Mexico in pursuit of the bandit, Pancho Villa; returning to Chicago shortly before the US entry into the Great War, he joined the United Press agency, who almost immediately posted him to Europe. He remained a UP foreign correspondent ('in 41 countries') for some twenty-five years—'but I still write laboriously. I have to pull out every sentence by the roots.']*

EDITOR'S NOTE. *In his verse, 'They Don't Read De Quincey in Philly or Cincy', Ogden Nash remarks that Henri Désiré Landru, 'When shedding his prospective brides / In multiple uxoricides, / Just combed his beard and shined his hat / And led them to the Landrumat'. On 30 November 1921, at the Court of Assize, Versailles, Landru was found guilty of, among many other crimes; the murder (for profit) of ten women who had answered his widower-seeks-a-wife small ads.*

*   *   *

ON THE NIGHT of Friday, 24 February 1922, together with half a dozen French reporters, I caught the electric train to Versailles. We went to the courthouse, obtained crudely mimeographed green *laissez-passers* for the execution, and retired to the Hôtel des Réservoirs with five bottles of cognac to await dawn.

At 4 a.m. word came that Monsieur Deibler, the famous executioner who performed all the executions throughout France, had arrived with his apparatus. Anatole Deibler, shy, wistful, goat-bearded, had performed more than 300 executions. His salary was 18,000 francs per year (a little over $1000 at the 1936 rate of exchange). He suffered from a weak heart and could not walk upstairs, but this did not seem to interfere with his gruesome vocation. He lived in a small house near Versailles under the name of Monsieur Anatole, consorted very little with his neighbours, and led a retiring existence. He kept the guillotine in a shed outside his house. When performing an execution, he wore white gloves and a long white 'duster'.

We hurried to the prison. Four hundred troops had drawn cordons at each end of the street and permitted only the possessors of the little green mimeographed tickets to pass. According to the French law, executions had to occur· in the open street in front of the prison door. On the damp, slippery cobblestones beside the streetcar tracks, workmen were rapidly erecting the guillotine a dozen feet outside the towering gate of Versailles prison. It was still quite dark. The only light came from the workmen's old-fashioned lanterns, with flickering candles, and the few electric street-lights. The workmen bolted the grisly machine together and adjusted its balance with a carpenter's level. Deibler hauled the heavy knife to the top of the uprights.

Nearly one hundred officials and newspapermen gathered in a circle around the guillotine; I stood about fifteen feet away. News arrived from inside the prison that Landru, whose long black beard had been cut previously, had asked that he be shaved.

'It will please the ladies,' he had said to his gaolers.

His lawyer and a priest went into his cell. He refused the traditional cigarette and glass of rum always offered just before executions.

Landru wore a shirt from which the neck had been cut away, and a pair of cheap dark trousers. That was all—no shoes or socks. He would walk to the guillotine barefooted.

As his arms were strapped behind him, his lawyer whispered, 'Courage, Landru.' 'Thanks, Maître, I've always had that,' he replied calmly.

Just as the first streaks of the chilly February dawn appeared, a large closed van drawn by horses arrived and backed up within a few feet of the right side of the guillotine. Deibler's assistants, wearing long smocks, pulled two wicker baskets from the van. They placed the small round basket carefully in front of the machine, where the head would fall. Two assistants placed another basket about the size and shape of a coffin close beside the guillotine. Into that the headless body would roll.

The cordon of troops halted a streetcar full of workmen on their way to work. They decided to open the cordon to permit the car to proceed, and it slowly rumbled past within a few feet of the grim machine. Staring faces filled the windows.

The guillotine underwent a final test. Deibler raised the lunette, the half-moon-shaped wooden block which was to clamp down upon Landru's neck. Then he lowered it, and the heavy knife shot down from the top of the uprights with a crash which shook the machine. The lunette and knife were raised again. All was ready.

Suddenly the huge wooden gates of the prison swung open. The spectators became silent and tense. Three figures appeared, walking rapidly. On each side, a gaoler held Landru by his arms, which were strapped behind him. They supported and pulled him forward as fast as they could walk. His bare feet pattered on the cold cobblestones, and his knees seemed not to be functioning. His face was pale and waxen, and as he caught sight of the ghastly machine, he went livid.

The two gaolers hastily pushed Landru face-foremost against the upright board of the machine. It collapsed, and his body crumpled with it as they shoved him forward under the wooden block, which dropped down and clamped his neck beneath the suspended knife. In a split second the knife flicked down, and the head fell with a thud into the small basket. As an assistant lifted the hinged board and rolled the headless body into the big wicker basket, a hideous spurt of blood gushed out.

An attendant standing in front of the machine seized the basket containing the head, rolled it like a cabbage into the larger basket, and helped shove it hastily into the waiting van. The van-doors slammed, and the horses were whipped into a gallop.

When Landru first appeared in the prison courtyard, I had glanced at my wrist-watch. Now I looked again. Only twenty-six seconds had elapsed.

V
THE CULPRIT
A. E. Housman

[1859–1936: a classical scholar and an unprolific but wonderfully hair-raising poet, much of whose work evokes the county of Shropshire; there has been speculation, some of it by salacious persons, about his 'poetic urges', but he himself explained that he seldom wrote poetry unless he was rather out of health.]

EDITOR'S NOTE. This poem was quoted by Clarence Darrow during his closing speech for the defence (or rather, against capital punishment) at the trial in Chicago, in 1924, of the teenaged 'thrill killers', Nathan Leopold and Richard Loeb, for the kidnapping and murder of fourteen-year-old Robert Franks.

The night my father got me
   His mind was not on me;
He did not plague his fancy
   To muse if I should be
   The son you see.

The day my mother bore me
   She was a fool and glad,
For all the pain I cost her,
   That she had borne the lad
   That borne she had.

My mother and my father
   Out of the light they lie;
The warrant would not find them,
   And here 'tis only I
   Shall hang so high.

Oh let not man remember
  The soul that God forgot,
But fetch the county kerchief
  And noose me in the knot,
    And I will rot.

For so the game is ended
  That should not have begun,
My father and my mother
  They had a likely son,
    And I have none.

Clarence Darrow's success in saving Leopold and Loeb from execution ranks as one of the worst miscarriages of justice of pre-abolition times. His clients had committed a despicable, savage crime for pleasure; they felt no remorse—only regret at having left so many clues that even the Chicago police were able to solve the case. If they did not deserve execution, then no one did.

The trial, like far too many others, demonstrates that the interests of truth, clarity and justice would be better served if psychiatrists were not permitted to air their views from the witness-box but, if allowed to appear at all, were treated as formal rather than expert witnesses, called only to prove transcripts or tape-recordings of interviews with defendants; interpretation could be left to the judge and jury, who, with no pecuniary or egotistical reason for favouring one theory against another, would not feel duty-bound to make inferential mountains out of traumatic molehills.

Illustrating the quaintness of American arithmetic, both Leopold and Loeb were sentenced to imprisonment for life plus ninety-nine years. And yet Leopold was released in 1958, thirteen years before his death from natural causes (rather perplexing, this: he left a widow). In 1936, Loeb had been killed by a fellow-convict, who claimed that he had acted in self-defence, Loeb having sought entry to one of his bodily orifices—a statement instantly accepted by the Chicago Daily News, *which reported that 'Richard Loeb, a brilliant college student and master of the English language, today ended a sentence with a proposition'.*

'A. E. Housman' by Humbert Wolfe (1886–1940), a lesser poet who ought not to be generally forgotten:

> When lads have done with labour
> in Shropshire, one will cry,
> 'Let's go and kill a neighbour,'
> and t'other answers 'Aye!'

> So this one kills his cousins,
> and that one kills his dad;
> and, as they hang by dozens
> at Ludlow, lad by lad,
> each of them one-and-twenty,
> all of them murderers,
> the hangman mutters: 'Plenty
> even for Housman's verse.'

VI
BLOOD CARNIVAL
Anonymous

EDITOR'S NOTE. The Allied Intelligence Bureau played a major part, gathering information and carrying out sabotage, in the war against Japan. In the course of 264 sorties into enemy-held territory, 164 members of AIB were killed, and 178 'disappeared'. Following the Allied invasion of New Guinea in April 1944, the discarded diary of a Jap soldier was found. The title 'Blood Carnival' was written above the entry for Monday, 29 March 1943. . . .

ALL FOUR OF US—Kurokawa, Nishiguchi, Yawate and myself—assembled in front of Headquarters at 1500 hours. . . . The 'Tai' commander Komai, who came to the observation-post today, told us personally that in accordance with the compassionate sentiments of Japanese *Bushido* ['the code of the warrior'], he was going to kill the prisoner himself, with his favourite sword. So we gathered to observe this. After we had waited a little more than ten minutes, the truck came along.

The prisoner, who is at the side of the guard-house, is given his last drink of water. The surgeon, Major Komai, and the Headquarters Platoon Commander come out of the Officers' Mess, wearing their military swords.

The time has come.

The prisoner, with his arms bound and his long hair now cropped short, totters forward. He probably suspects what is afoot, but he is more composed than I thought he would be. Without more ado, he is put on the truck and we set out for our destination.

I have a seat next to the surgeon. About ten guards ride with us. To the pleasant rumble of the engine, we run swiftly along the road in the growing twilight. The glowing sun has set behind the western hills. Gigantic clouds rise before us and dusk is falling all around. It will not be long now. As I picture the scene we are about to witness, my heart beats faster.

I glance at the prisoner. He has probably resigned himself to his fate. As though saying farewell to the world, he looks about as he sits in the truck, at the hills, the sea, and seems in deep thought. I feel a surge of pity and turn my eyes away. The truck runs along the seashore now. We have left the Navy guard sector behind us and now come into the Army sector. Here and there we see sentries in the grassy fields, and I thank them in my heart for their toil, as we drive on; they must have 'got it' in the bombing the night before last; there were great gaping holes by the side of the road, full of water from the rain.

In a little over twenty minutes, we arrive at our destination and all get off.

Major Komai stands up and says to the prisoner, 'We are going to kill you.' When he tells the prisoner that, in accordance with *Bushido*, he will be killed with a Japanese sword and that he will have two or three minutes' grace, he listens with bowed head. He says a few words in a low voice. He is an officer, probably a flight-lieutenant. Apparently, he wants to be killed with one stroke of the sword. I hear him say the word 'one'. The Major's face becomes tense as he replies, 'Yes.'

The prisoner is made to kneel on the bank of a bomb-crater, filled with water. He is apparently resigned. The precaution is taken of surrounding him with guards with fixed bayonets, but he remains calm. He even stretches his neck out. He is a very brave man indeed. When I put myself in the prisoner's place and think that in one minute it will be goodbye to this world, although the daily bombings have filled me with hate, ordinary human feelings make me pity him.

The Major has drawn his favourite sword. It is the famous *masamune* sword which he has shown us at the observation station. It glitters in the light, sending a cold shiver down my spine. The Major taps the prisoner's neck lightly with the back of the blade, then raises it above his head with both arms and brings it down with a powerful sweep. I had been standing with muscles tensed, but in that moment I closed my eyes.

A hissing sound—it must be the sound of spurting blood, spurting from the arteries. The body falls forward. It is amazing —he has been killed with one stroke.

The onlookers crowd forward. The head, detached from the trunk, rolls forward in front of it. The dark blood gushes out. It is all over. The head is dead-white, like a doll's. The savageness which I felt only a little while ago is gone, and now I feel nothing but the true compassion of Japanese *Bushido*.

A corporal laughs: 'Well—he will be entering Nirvana now.' A seaman of the medical unit takes the surgeon's sword and, intent on paying off old scores, turns the headless body over on its back and cuts the abdomen open with one clean stroke. They are thick-skinned, these *keto* [hairy foreigners—term of opprobrium for white men]; even the skin of their bellies is thick. Not a drop of blood comes out of the body. It is pushed into the crater at once and buried.

Now the wind blows mournfully, and I see the scene again in my mind's eye. We get on the truck again and start back. It is dark now. We get off in front of Headquarters. I say goodbye to the Major and climb up the hill with Technician Kurokawa.

This will be something to remember all my life. If I ever get back alive, it will make a good story to tell; and so I have written it down.

VII
THE LATE MR. ELLIS
Charles Duff

[Author of, among other books, A Handbook on Hanging *(from which the following is taken), the 'satirical essay' which was, and is, the most successful piece of propaganda against capital punishment. First published in London in 1928, between 1934 and 1961 there were seven revised*

editions, each from a different London publisher; a German edition, Henkerfibel, *the translation supervised by Berthold Brecht, appeared in 1931, and had the honour of being burned by the Nazis two years later. Duff, who was born in a southern part of Ireland in 1894, turned out to be a problem-child but a linguistic prodigy; after leaving a school that he had often run away from, he became a purser on an ocean-liner, did a flit from it because of an uncontrollable impulse to travel with Spanish gypsies and learn their languages, joined the British Army during the Great War and was awarded the Military Medal, worked at the Foreign Office (at first in MI5: counter-intelligence) till, in 1936 or thereabouts, he fell out with his boss over the Spanish Fascists, resigned, and spent the remaining thirty or so years of his life writing and lecturing on, among other things, linguistics, Irish and Spanish history, and, of course, capital punishment.]*

MR. JOHN ELLIS resigned his post as Hangman of England in March 1924 after holding it honourably for twenty-five years, during which time he assisted or presided at some 200 executions, all of which were, in accordance with the Home Office instructions (not to divulge facts to the contrary), carried through with expedition.

Mr. Ellis was a man of towardly parts, homely manners, renowned for his proficiency and art. It is melancholy to have to record of such a man, of whom it has been written that he was too tender-hearted to wring the neck of one of his own fowls, that his experience in hanging Mrs. Edith Thompson—who was carried unconscious from her cell to the hang-house on 9 January 1923—drove him to attempt to commit suicide. The account of it given in the *News of the World,* 29 August 1924, is this. Shortly after one o'clock in the morning, his family were awakened by the noise of a revolver-discharge, and poor Mr. Ellis was found lying on the floor of his living-room, bleeding from the neck. A revolver lay beside him. He was brought before the magistrates and charged with attempting to commit suicide. The Chairman asked him if he was prepared to give an undertaking that he would not again attempt suicide; and to this Mr. Ellis agreed.

The Chairman of the Bench then replied in well-chosen words, as follows:

> 'I am sorry to see you here, Ellis. I have known you for a long time. If your aim had been as true as some of the drops you have given, it would have been a bad job for you. Your life has been given back to you, and I hope you will make good use of it, and lead a good life in atonement.'

Very fine sentiments, too, except that the logic seems to be wrong; a life which has not been taken away can hardly be given back. Mr. Ellis said on this occasion that he had 'some drink taken'. One can understand why. Throughout his career, he was forbidden to stay at public-houses, as his sojourn might 'attract custom'. Why not? Now, a hangman has a thirst like other men, and it is quite conceivable that Mr. Ellis was enjoying the freedom of retirement, and had had 'one over the eight'. There is an old saying, *in vino veritas*, and this is an interesting case in human psychology, if human is the correct word.

It was the very great privilege of this writer to make the personal acquaintance of the late Mr. Ellis, who in his day endeared himself to the public and was so much loved by candidates for the gallows that they would say, 'I hope Ellis hangs me.' It was at Great Yarmouth, when in retirement he was giving his famous lecture on hanging, with a demonstration of the working of a gallows and his own part in an execution. 'You can't beat English hanging,' this eminent hangman said to me, as we chatted on the beach one summer's day, while he allowed the grains of Yarmouth sand to trickle through his fingers as if to symbolize a gravitational flow of life towards death. Those other ways of putting away murderers—he always used the verb 'to put away', never 'to execute', and rarely 'to hang'—were either mean or messy. Whenever he spoke of hanging, he would run his tongue round his lower lip as if he could taste the flavour of it, and once he paused to look me up and down as if mentally taking my weight and measure for a drop. With a convincing finality, and pointing an index-finger heavenwards, Mr. Ellis looked me straight in the neck and exclaimed: 'Now, sir, hanging is *clean*. It's the cleanest way of all of putting them away. In fact, it's English—as English as cricket or plum pudding or Worcester Sauce.'

He was contemptuous of electrocution, which he said was a c-r-u-e-l business because the client was sometimes part-cooked like a herring on a griddle. Terrible!— especially for 'them present', that is.

Ellis's chief anxiety seemed to be for 'them present', and the man hanged was to him a mere abstraction who (or which) did not matter. 'In hanging,' said he, looking at me sideways with a smile like the Mona Lisa, 'it's all over in a second or two, before you could say Jack Robinson. No mess either—or very rarely. A touch of the lever and *squonk*, a few kicks and maybe wheezes and'—he snapped his fingers—'it's all over bar the inquest and collect the dough.' To illustrate how expeditious it is, he laughingly told me an anecdote. A hangman on one occasion by mistake whipped the white cap over the prison-chaplain's head, adjusted the rope, and was about to give him the drop when suddenly—and only just in time—the parson's cassock was spotted. 'Which just shows you!' he added, lighting a cigarette.

Guillotining? Too messy! Asphyxiation? Ellis lowered his head, looked at me under his eyelids, showing the whites of his eyes, and commented sadly that one day it might come to that. But asphyxiation is *too soft;* and useless as an example to the public. The public would 'get no kick out of it' as they do from hanging. Imagine picking up a Sunday newspaper and reading that So-and-so, the murderer, had been put away by asphyxiation! Why, it would be as if somebody had passed out under an anaesthetic! And what use was that?

Ellis warmed up: 'It's the *good example* in it that makes British Governments stick to hanging,' he said, 'and they are wise. How could you make a better example of anybody than by hanging him?' I suggested drawing and quartering, to which he immediately replied: 'Out of date. The humanitarians and the squeamish would object; and maybe even the bishops and judges would protest.' Ellis was not averse to beheading with an axe, but 'only for high-ups', as in the past. In a democracy, hanging was best every time: especially when 'done proper'. As for him, he'd never bungled a hanging.

All the same, women were a great nuisance. When they hanged Edith Thompson, everybody present was upset to vomiting-point. Hanging women upset most hangmen; and you just shouldn't do that.

'We don't make mistakes nowadays,' he assured me; 'it's all taped and worked out, and even if there should be some slight mishap, the whole government machine goes all out to save the hangman's face. *They have to.*' Again he looked me straight in the neck and said, 'No one ever had to save *my* face.' I could well believe it.

That fine High Hangman of England, the reader will be distressed to learn, has gone to the great beyond.[1] But he has left a fragrant memory. We may leave him to deal with the problem which will face him on the other side if he should run into some of his earthly clients. It would hardly be surprising if some of those clients awaited his ascension (or descension, as the case may be). Here is an aspect of the subject deserving of contemplation, and it seems a great pity that, as on some other aspects of life after death, we are lacking in precise information. The theologians are no great help, even when they expand the boundaries of their own belief and ours.

I had almost omitted to mention that Mr. Hangman John Ellis had some business correspondence with a Sir John Samuel (an important official) in February 1922, in which he quoted his fees: 'You can rely on me being at Glasgow on Tuesday morning. : . . My fees are £15 for each execution, first-class return railway fares and cab fares. In the event of a reprieve, half-fees, £7 10s.'

In Scotland, as in England, they hang women, when necessary. In 1923 they hanged a woman named Susan Newall. Of this Ellis wrote: '*It is more difficult to execute a woman than two men*, and I propose that Mr. R. Baxter, of Hertford, goes with me, as he was one of the assistants who was with me at Mrs. Thompson's execution. . . . Will you please ask the Prison Commissioners to send the special body-straps made for Mrs. Thompson?' You may remember that there was considerable public outcry about the hanging of Mrs. Thompson. It leaked out that this was altogether a rather horrible business, and Ellis himself did not like it because

---

[1] *EDITOR'S NOTE. Surprisingly, the author does not mention the fact that John Ellis, a barber by full-time trade, succeeded in taking his own life (in September 1932) by slitting his throat with a razor that he had often used unblemishingly in his barber-shop in Rochdale, Lancashire.*

of the anguish it caused to the onlookers. He was not taking any risks with Susan Newall. Of the hanging of Mrs. Thompson, Major Lloyd-George was able to assure the House of Commons that 'the proprieties were observed'.

An afterthought. Before we finally part from the good Ellis, I remember one strong impression I had at the time of the interview: Ellis's pride in his profession and his conceit in personal publicity relating to it. I asked him whether he kept notes of his executions, and he said, 'No need—I used to keep press-cuttings about them,' on which I remarked, 'You must have a very valuable collection.' An expression of acute agony came over his cheerless features, and he said mournfully: 'No! It was like this. One evening, after a good session in a pub, I was sorting them out for an autobiography I intended to write. I was sitting at home by the fire at the time, and must have fallen asleep. For I woke up on the floor and saw the last flames of the very best of my fine collection dying out before my eyes. I don't mind telling you that I cried—yes, *cried*. Just imagine! The record of a long career—gone up in flames!' Tears again trickled down his cheeks. I asked him whether the autobiography would ever be written, and he said, 'Although a Sunday paper made me a good offer, I just can't face it. I remembered *everything* by those cuttings, and now I feel so lost that I could never do the job justice.' All I could say in the circumstances was that it would be a great loss to posterity and leave an irreplaceable gap in the national history: to which he nodded in solemn acquiescence.

Ellis never gave up his belief in hanging, but he was no hypocrite about it. He did not believe in it as a deterrent but merely as retributive justice in the Old Testament sense. He was at heart a fundamentalist.

Vale Ellis. In omni labore emolumentum est.

Charles Duff

THREE LIFERS
Horatio Bottomley

[*The founder and editor of* John Bull, *used that mass-circulation weekly magazine, and other periodicals that he controlled, in aid of many swindles; eventually, in 1922, he was sentenced to seven years' penal servitude for just one of the fleecings, a nice large earner called* The Victory Bond Club. *While in prison, and under the influence of 'The Ballad of Reading Gaol', he dashed off sufficient poems to make a book that was larger than most poetry-books; introducing it, Lord Alfred Douglas, sometime friend of Oscar Wilde, applauded Bottomley (as poet) for his 'perfect sincerity'.*]

He worked in the prison printing shop,
   His sentence being Life;
His crime that in a fit of rage
   He'd shot and killed his wife.

Already twelve long years in gaol,
   Cut off from all the world,
He might as well, it seemed to me, •
   Have been to Hades hurled.

One day he came in happy mood,
   And told us all with glee,
'They've answered my petition, boys,
   And cut it down to three.'

'That's fifteen years in all to do,
   And three years yet,' I said;
'Lord bless you, guvnor,' he replied,
   'I'll do it on my head.'

The second Lifer was a man
   Who eighteen years had done;
He never spoke about his case—
   They say he'd killed his son.

'I've seen the Guvnor, mates,' he said,
   'And what d'you think about?
It's solemn truth I tell you, though—
   Next week I'm going out.

'My God! I'm going out next week;
   I can't believe my eyes,
But there it is, in black and white'—
   And like a child he cries!

And now a third I'll introduce:
   A Lifer just come in—
A poor, consumptive-looking chap;
   No matter what his sin.

They put him in the garden gang,
   To hoe, and weed, and delve,
And joyfully he told us all,
   'I shan't do more than twelve.'

Ah, happy lags, I envy them,
   Insensible to time;
Who count not weeks, nor months, nor years—
   Oblivion sublime!

And yet not Neptune's solar course
    Could span a single day
Of coffined, suffocating life
    Of him who sings this lay.

THE AFFAIR AT VILLA MADEIRA
F. Tennyson Jesse

[*The F stands for Fryniwyd, which she shortened to 'Fryn'.
Born in Kent in 1888, a great-niece of Alfred, Lord
Tennyson (whose favourite bed-side book was a Newgate
Calendar), she studied art, but in 1911 took up journalism;
during the Great War, she was one of the few women
who reported from the battle-areas in France. In 1918 she
married H.M. ('Tottie') Harwood, cotton-spinner, doctor,
playwright and screen-writer; separately or together, they
wrote many plays that were produced in the West End.
She also wrote novels, short stories, poems, essays . . .
and a history of Burma. Unintendedly—as Harry Hodge,
founder of the* Notable British Trials, *assumed before
meeting her that she was a man—she became the first
woman to edit a volume in that series; and she edited
five more, including the bumper-volume on the respective
trials of Evans and Christie (in private conversation, she
called the happenings at 10 Rillington Place 'The Feast of
Corpus Christie'). Referring to her book* Murder and Its
Motives *(in which she coined the term 'murderee'), one of
her many American friends, Alexander Woollcott, wrote to
her in 1941: 'I have just been going over the library at the
White House (that's our Buckingham Palace, dear), and I
am glad to see that classic . . . in its rightful place on those*

shelves.' She died, and was glad to, in 1958; her husband Tottie, who, being a gentleman, had waited for her to go first, died soon afterwards.]

ON 25 SEPTEMBER 1934, the following advertisement appeared in *The Bournemouth Daily Echo*: 'Daily willing lad, 14–18, for housework. Scout-trained preferred.'

This advertisement had been inserted by a Mrs. Rattenbury, of Villa Madeira, Manor Park Road, and was answered by a youth called George Percy Stoner. Since he was of an age to drive a car, and his previous employment had been in a garage, he was engaged as chauffeur-handyman.

On Monday, 27 May 1935, Alma Victoria Rattenbury and George Percy Stoner were charged at the Central Criminal Court, Old Bailey, with the murder of the woman's husband, Francis Mawson Rattenbury. Both the accused pleaded Not Guilty.

Mrs. Rattenbury was thirty-eight years old, and Stoner had attained the age of eighteen in November of 1934. Mrs. Rattenbury and Stoner had become lovers soon after Stoner was taken into Mr. Rattenbury's employ in September of that year.

Both Mr. and Mrs. Rattenbury had been previously married; he once and she twice. Mr. Rattenbury had a grown-up son; and Mrs. Rattenbury, a little boy called Christopher, born in 1922. The marriage of Francis Rattenbury and Alma Victoria took place about 1928, and a boy, John, was born a year after. Since the birth of this child, Mr. and Mrs. Rattenbury had not lived together as husband and wife. Mr. Rattenbury was sixty-seven years old and not a young man for his age. He was an architect of distinction, and had lived most of his working life in Canada, but when he retired in 1928, he and his wife came to live in Bournemouth.

Eventually, they took a little white house called Villa Madeira in a pleasant suburban road near the sea, shaded by pines. A companion-help, Miss Irene Riggs, came to live with them. Little John went to school but came home every week-end, and Christopher, the child of Mrs. Rattenbury's second marriage, spent his holidays at Villa Madeira.

When Stoner was first employed at Villa Madeira, he lived at home and went to his work by day, but in November he took up residence in the house. He had become Mrs. Rattenbury's lover before that.

On the night of Sunday, 24 March 1935, Mr. Rattenbury was attacked from behind as he sat sleeping in an armchair in the drawing-room. It was never in dispute that the weapon employed was a carpenter's mallet which Stoner had fetched from his grandfather's house that afternoon.

The events that night, as they first were made known in the newspapers, were as follows:

Mrs. Rattenbury declared that at about 10.30, after she had gone to bed, she heard a groan from the room below, and that she went downstairs and found her husband in the easy-chair, unconscious, with blood flowing from his head. She called Irene Riggs and told her to telephone for Dr. O'Donnell, who was her doctor. He arrived and found Mrs. Rattenbury very drunk, and Mr. Rattenbury unconscious, with blood flowing from his head. Mrs. Rattenbury said: 'Look at him—look at the blood—someone has finished him.'

Dr. O'Donnell telephoned for Mr. Rooke, a well-known surgeon. Mr. Rooke arrived and found it impossible to examine the patient as Mrs. Rattenbury was very drunk and excitable and kept getting in his way. The ambulance was sent for, and the patient removed to Strathallen Nursing Home. After his head had been shaved in the operating theatre, Mr. Rooke and Dr. O'Donnell saw three serious wounds that could not have been self-inflicted; accordingly, they communicated with the police.

Mr. Rooke operated on Mr. Rattenbury; and between 3.30 and 4 a.m., Dr. O'Donnell returned to Madeira Villa. He found Mrs. Rattenbury running about, extremely intoxicated, four or five police officers in the house (some of whom she was trying to kiss), the radio-gramophone playing, and all the lights on. He gave Mrs. Rattenbury half a grain of morphia, and put her to bed. During the hours of progressive drunkenness, Mrs. Rattenbury had kept on making statements to the effect that she had killed her husband. The next morning, she repeated her assertions in a slightly varied form, and she was taken to the Bournemouth Police Station and charged with doing grievous bodily harm with intent to murder. When she was charged, Mrs. Rattenbury said: 'That is right—I did it deliberately, and would do it again.'

Such was the terrible case for the prosecution against Alma Victoria Rattenbury. The picture that had inevitably formed itself before the public mind was revolting.

There was probably no one in England—and no one in Court when the trial opened, save Mrs. Rattenbury, her solicitor and counsel, Stoner and his solicitor and counsel, and Irene Riggs—who did not think that Mrs. Rattenbury was guilty of the crime of murder. In everyone's mind, including my own, there was a picture of Mrs. Rattenbury as a coarse, brawling, drunken and callous woman.

But life is not as simple as that, and very often an accurate report fails to convey truth, because only certain things have been reported. The form of the English oath has been very wisely thought out—'the truth, the whole truth, and nothing but the truth'. It is possible to give an erroneous impression by merely telling the truth and nothing but the truth. The 'whole truth' is a very important factor. The whole truth about Mrs. Rattenbury came out during the trial, and the woman, who at first seemed so guilty, was seen to be undoubtedly innocent. This was not merely because there proved to be no evidence beyond her own drunken utterances, but because of her own attitude in the witness-box. For there is no test of truth so relentless as the witness-box—it is deadly to the guilty, and it may save the innocent.

In most criminal trials, the pattern is set at the beginning and merely strengthens as the trial progresses. In the Rattenbury case, the evidence—which seemed so damning on the first day—completely altered in character; what had seemed to be undoubted fact proved to be an airy nothing, and the whole complex pattern shifted and changed much as the pattern of sand changes when it is shaken—and, like sand, it slipped away between the fingers, leaving a residue of grains of truth very different from the pile that the prosecution had originally built up. Even at the end of the trial, so rigid is the English fashion of thinking (or rather feeling, for it is not as careful or accurate a process as thought) on sexual matters, that many people still considered Mrs. Rattenbury morally damned. That worst of all Anglo-Saxon attitudes, a contemptuous condemnation of the man and woman—but more particularly the woman—unfortunate enough to be found out in sexual delinquency, never had finer scope than was provided by the Rattenbury case.

*   *   *

Mrs. Rattenbury was born Alma Victoria Clark, in Victoria, British Columbia, and was the daughter of a printer in quite humble circumstances. She was extremely talented musically. The cheap strain in her came out in the lyrics of songs she wrote, but she was a really fine pianist. She grew up to young womanhood just before the Great War, already well known in Western Canada as a musician, and, although not strictly speaking pretty, very attractive to men. In the witness-box she still showed as a very elegant woman. She was well and quietly dressed in dark blue. She had a pale face, with a beautiful egg-like line of the jaw, dark grey eyes, and a mouth with a very full lower lip. She was undoubtedly, and always must have been, a *femme aux hommes*. That is to say that, although she had women friends and was a generous, easy, kindly, sentimental creature, she was first and foremost a woman to attract men and be attracted by them.

She first married a young Englishman called Caledon Dolly, who joined the Canadian forces on the outbreak of war and was transferred to England. She followed him and obtained employment in Whitehall. She was very devoted to her husband, but he was killed in action. This was the only completely happy relationship with a man which Mrs. Rattenbury was ever to know. She joined a Scottish nursing unit, and then became a transport driver, and worked hard throughout the war. After the Armistice, she married a man whose wife had divorced him, citing Alma Victoria Dolly. She married this second husband in 1921, and the child of that union was born the following year. The marriage was unhappy, and she returned to the house of an aunt in Victoria, and there met Mr. Rattenbury. He, married at the time, fell very much in love with Alma Victoria, and his wife divorced him, citing her. At this time Mr. Rattenbury was about sixty years of age, and Mrs. Rattenbury thirty-one. Life was not too easy for Mr. Rattenbury and his new wife in a country where everyone knew of the scandal of the divorce, and this was the chief reason why the Rattenburys came to England to settle in Bournemouth.

Mrs. Rattenbury was a highly-sexed woman, and six years of being deprived of sexual satisfaction had combined with the tuberculosis from which she suffered to bring her to the verge of nymphomania. Now, nymphomania is not admirable, but neither is it blameworthy. It is a disease. In spite of the urgency of her desires, which must have tormented her, Mrs. Rattenbury had not, so far as is known, had a lover since the birth of little John. She certainly had had none during the four years she had lived in Bournemouth, and she had no abnormal tendencies. She was fond of her husband in a friendly fashion, and he was devoted to her, very interested in her song-writing and anxious for her to succeed. He would often talk to Irene Riggs about his wife, dwelling on the unhappy life she had led, and he never in these conversations said anything against her. Miss Riggs, one of my informants as to these matters, also said that Mrs. Rattenbury was very kind to her husband—that she was, indeed, kind to everyone.

The household was not an unhappy one, but neither was it happy. For one thing, Mrs. Rattenbury was a gregarious creature, and her husband was of an unsociable frame of mind. He knew hardly anyone of his own station in life, except Dr. O'Donnell and Mr. Jenks, a retired barrister who had an estate at Bridport. But Mrs. Rattenbury was very different from her husband; she had that lavish, easy friendliness which one associates with music-hall artistes, and she could not live without affection. When she made a friend of Irene Riggs, she did so because it was her nature to be friendly with the people who surrounded her. She was fond of Irene Riggs, who, on her side, was devoted to her employer, in spite of the latter's impatient temper. Any little outing to London, any treat such as a visit to a theatre, Mrs. Rattenbury shared with Irene Riggs, and the girl has remained attached to the memory of the kindest person she ever met, who helped anyone in need that she came across. But the chief devotion of Mrs. Rattenbury's life was for her children. No one denies that she was a good and loving mother. Dr. O'Donnell and Miss Riggs both say that Mrs. Rattenbury thought nothing too good for her children, and that there was nothing she would not have done for them. She was forever thinking and talking about them, and occupying herself in practical ways for their welfare.

The Rattenburys lived peaceably as a rule, but sometimes they had quarrels—these were about money. Mr. Rattenbury, like a great many men, was generous in big matters but difficult in small ones. He allowed his wife £1000[1] a year, and many newspapers reported this fact in such a manner that the reading public might easily have imagined that this sum was hers for herself alone. As a matter of fact, out of it she paid for the food for herself, her husband, the domestics and the children when at home, and for one of the boys' schooling. She also paid for Mr. Rattenbury's clothes and for her own, and she paid the servants' wages. Mr. Rattenbury was a heavy drinker of whisky, and every few weeks Mrs. Rattenbury would drink more cocktails than would be good for her, so that the bill for drinks alone must have amounted to a good deal. Mrs. Rattenbury had very little money sense, and her husband had every reason to fear her lavish spending. About twice a year she would coax an extra sum out of him: a large sum, over £100, but this he parted with much more easily than he would have parted with small sums more often. Mrs. Rattenbury did not pretend that she told her husband true stories to induce him to give her this extra money. She admitted that she invented whatever story would be the most likely to achieve the desired result. Mr. Rattenbury was frequently very depressed about financial matters; like everyone else, he had suffered in the slump, and he was apt, during his moods of depression, to threaten suicide. One day in July 1934, he harped on this threat at greater length than usual, and his wife lost her temper and told him it was a pity that he did not do it instead of always talking about it. Mr. Rattenbury in his turn then lost his temper and hit his wife, giving her a black eye. She sent for Dr. O'Donnell, who found her very agitated and upset. Her husband had left the house, and she feared that he really had gone to kill himself. Mr. Rattenbury did not return till about two in the morning, by which time Dr. O'Donnell also was extremely anxious. Mrs. Rattenbury was by then so ill that he injected a quarter of a grain of morphia, and she slept for twelve hours. After that, life went on as usual with the Rattenburys. She bore him no grudge for having struck her. She was a person of quick temper herself, but generous in what children call 'making it up'. This was the only serious quarrel between the Rattenburys that Dr. O'Donnell or Irene Riggs knew of in four years. In the

[1] EDITOR'S NOTE. *The 1992 purchasing power of the 1935 £ is reckoned to be just over £27.*

witness-box, Mrs. Rattenbury was asked whether her married life was happy, and she answered: 'Like that . . .!' with a gesture of her hand. A gesture that sketched the married life of the larger part of muddled humanity.

Life might have gone on in the usual pedestrian fashion at Villa Madeira for ever; but George Percy Stoner joined the household, and Mrs. Rattenbury fell in love with him.

The expression 'falling in love' is an attempt to define something which escapes definition. Mankind has a natural weakness for labels, for they simplify life, and though this particular label is one of the most pernicious which have been evolved, it must be remembered that it covers not only a multitude of sins, but of virtues. Perhaps no two people would give quite the same definition of its meaning. Very few people trouble to try.

Mrs. Rattenbury herself was a woman who dealt in labels, and she accepted the expression 'falling in love'. She was 'in love' with Stoner, who, except for his virility, was not a particularly interesting or attractive person. Indeed, lack of taste is one of the chief charges against Mrs. Rattenbury, both in her work and in her life. She was very uncontrolled emotionally. Her lyrics were appalling. She was subject to drinking bouts, which added to her natural excitability. She had not scrupled, twice, to take other women's husbands away from them, and she seems to have been, to use a slang phrase, a natural-born bad picker. When she took Stoner as her lover, she said to Dr. O'Donnell: 'There is something I want to tell you. I am afraid you will be shocked and never want to speak to me again.' Dr. O'Donnell replied that there were very few things he had not been told in the course of his life, and that he was not easily shocked. She then told him the step she had taken, and he spoke to her seriously, warning her that she was probably being very unwise. But she was too far gone in love by then to heed any advice he gave her. She merely reiterated that she was in love with Stoner.

One of the things that told most strongly against Mrs. Rattenbury's moral character was that, in the witness-box, she admitted that she had had connexion with her lover when little John was asleep in his bed in the same room. This was to many people in Court, including myself, a very shocking statement. However, it must be admitted in fairness that there are unfortunately thousands of families in England where the same thing goes on. I myself have come across such families, and I consider the practice to be nonetheless shocking because the parents happen to be married. There is no doubt that an innocent child, awakening and seeing what was going on, would get an impression of something ugly and terrifying, even unnatural, which might do him harm for the rest of his life. But it is only fair, also, to add that Dr. O'Donnell has assured me that he never knew a child who slept as soundly as little John. If the Doctor and Irene Riggs were attending Mrs. Rattenbury when she happened to be ill, John would sleep undisturbed throughout the visit. I should also add that relations of Mr. Rattenbury, who took Mrs. Rattenbury into their house after her acquittal, told me that she said: 'I can't think what made me say that in the witness-box about Stoner making love to me when little John was in the room. He didn't. I got bewildered, and lost my head, and heard myself saying it.' There is, of course, no means of knowing whether Mrs. Rattenbury was speaking the truth when she made this remark. I can only say that I think it unlikely: she gave the impression throughout her evidence of being a witness of truth, of being so terrified of what might be the result if she diverted from the truth that she dared not do so, even when it told against her. It may be thought that the solution to the riddle is that, generally, she did go into Stoner's room when little John was at home, but that on some occasions connexion took place in the room where the child was. If so, Mrs. Rattenbury's bad taste is again manifest.

The obvious answer to the question as to what love meant for her is that it meant physical satisfaction. Yet, if it had meant only this, it would have deserted her when she stood in peril of her life. It did not do so—and neither did Stoner's love for her. Stoner refused to go into the box, and told his counsel that he did not deny having attacked Mr. Rattenbury. The woman for weeks insisted, to her solicitor and counsel, that she wished to take the blame, so as to save Stoner. Mr. Lewis-Manning, her solicitor, made it clear to her that, if she lied, her story would not stand the test of the witness-box and that she would only hang herself without saving Stoner. But not till Christopher, the little boy of her second marriage, was sent to her in prison to plead with her to tell the truth did she give way. And afterwards, in the witness-box, she said as little against her lover as possible, making light of certain alleged attacks of violence towards herself, attacks which had frightened her so much that, long before the murder, she had consulted Dr. O'Donnell about them.

One of the most interesting points in this case is that it is the only one, so far as I am aware, where two people have been charged together on the capital indictment when neither of the accused has abandoned the other in a scramble for safety. Milson and Fowler, Field and Gray, Gabrielle Bompard and Eyrand, Mr. and Mrs. Manning, Ruth Snyder and Judd Gray, to remember only a few at random, all tried to throw the blame on the partner in crime. In 1922, Mrs. Edith Thompson, terrified and conscious of her own innocence of murder, never gave a thought to the safety of her lover, Bywaters. But Mrs. Rattenbury was willing and anxious to take the whole blame if by so doing she could save her lover. It is Mr. Lewis Manning's considered opinion that she was not merely in a condition of exaltation that would have failed her at the last pass, but that she would have hanged without a tremor if by so doing she could have saved Stoner.

The story of Mrs. Rattenbury's life is a mingling of tragedy and futility. It is easy to be sentimental and see only the tragedy. It is easy to be stupid and see only the futility. The truth is that it is always easy to label people—but because a thing is easy, it is not necessarily accurate. No human being is simple. Stoner may have seemed simple enough to his family; he had always been a quiet boy who did not make friends, but his quiet appearance concealed stormy adolescent yearnings. He had the dramatic instincts natural to the young, and, unfortunately, circumstances thrust him into real drama before he could tell the difference between what was real and what was make-believe. Physically, he was very passionate, and nothing in his mental training had equipped him to cope with the extraordinary life to which it had pleased Mrs. Rattenbury to call him.

Francis Rattenbury, that outwardly quiet man, is a pathetic figure in retrospect. Mr. Justice Humphreys referred to him as being 'that very unpleasant character for which, I think, we have no suitable expression, but which the French call a *mari complaisant*. A man who knew that his wife was committing adultery, and had no objection to it.' Mrs. Rattenbury said, in the box, that she thought her husband knew because she had told him she was living her own life. But she may well have told him that without his taking in the meaning of her words. He was completely incurious, and he lived not in the present but in regrets for the past and anxieties for the future.

Irene Riggs, Dr. O'Donnell, and, indeed, everyone acquainted with the household to whom I have spoken, was of the opinion that Mr. Rattenbury was not aware that his wife and his chauffeur were lovers. But when I saw Villa Madeira, I thought this difficult to credit. It is so small as to be remarkable, small as the witch's cottage in *Hansel and Gretel*. On the ground floor are the kitchen, drawing-room, dining-room, and a room that Mr. Rattenbury used as a bedroom, and which opened off the drawing-room. Is it possible that a man, in a house as small as Villa Madeira would not hear the footsteps over his head whenever Stoner went into Mrs. Rattenbury's room, and that he would not hear the occasionally loud quarrels which took place between them? Looking at Villa Madeira, the answer would seem to be that it would be quite impossible. And yet Mr. Rattenbury's known character and habits supply a different answer. Every night, he drank the best part of a bottle of whisky. He was a man brilliant in his profession, with many excellent qualities, and he was not a drunkard; but he was not a young man, and he was very deaf. The alcohol which he consumed every night explains why he no longer lived with his wife, why he was completely incurious as to her doings, and why he heard nothing of what was going on over his head. He was not, in the opinion of all who knew him—the doctor, his own relations, and Irene Riggs, who lived in the house—the character stigmatised by Mr. Justice Humphreys as a '*mari complaisant*, not a nice character'. He was a quiet, pleasant man whose finances worried him, and whose emotional relationships had disappointed him.

A man in Mr. Rattenbury's condition, and of his age, is apt to forget the power that the natural inclinations of the flesh had over him in youth and middle age, and he may fail to realise that it is still a factor in the life of anyone else. So far as he knew, he was a good husband to his wife. He admired her, was genuinely fond of her. There was nothing within his power that he would not have done for her, and Mrs. Rattenbury was astute enough to take advantage of this whenever possible. In regard to his wife, his chief anxieties were financial, and after he had started to take his prolonged night-cap each evening, the rest of the world existed very little for him. The passions, the jealousies, of a decade earlier had ceased, not only in the present, but even as a memory of the past. The chief tragedy in life is not what we are but what we have ceased to be, and Mr. Rattenbury was an example of this truth. It is easy to say that a man who knows that his wife is committing adultery and has no objection is not a nice character. But it is not necessarily the truth. It is possible that a man who no longer leads a normal life with his wife yet thinks of her, not as his property, but as a human being who belongs to herself, with a right to a normal life. I do not say that this was Mr. Rattenbury's attitude (although Mrs. Rattenbury said that it was): I merely say that it would not necessarily have been a despicable attitude. But, of course, the judgment of the man in the street is the same as that of Mr. Justice Humphreys. It is an Anglo-Saxon attitude.

Another Anglo-Saxon attitude, accepted by the learned Judge, by counsel on both sides, and by the British public, was that, because of her greater age, Mrs. Rattenbury dominated her young lover. It was this same assumption which hanged Edith Thompson. There has been a growing consensus of public opinion ever since the Bywaters-Thompson trial that the female prisoner was wrongly convicted; and the memory of the earlier trial haunted the courtroom like a ghost. The Rattenbury case seemed like an echo of that tragedy, and it is not fanciful to say that Mrs. Thompson's fate did much to save Mrs. Rattenbury. A judge who knew how to point out firmly and clearly to the jury that a woman must not, because of her moral character, be convicted of murder, and a jury who were determined that no confusion of thought or prejudice should lead them into giving a wrong verdict, were two great safeguards for Mrs. Rattenbury, and the uneasy memory of Edith Thompson was yet a third. Nevertheless, the assumption of the Bywaters-Thompson case, that an elderly woman dominates her young lover, still obtained at the Rattenbury trial. The actual truth is that there is no woman so under the dominion of her lover as the elderly mistress of a very much younger man. The great Benjamin Franklin knew this, and there is extant a letter of advice written by him to a young man, which is a model of clear thinking. The original belongs to the US Government, and is in the custody of the Librarian of Congress at Washington, DC. This copy was taken from the original letter, and has not hitherto been published in England.

June 25th, 1745.

My Dear Friend,

I know of no medicine fit to diminish the violent nocturnal inclinations you mention, and if I did, I think I should not communicate it to you. Marriage is the proper remedy.

It is the most natural state of man, and therefore the state in which you are most likely to find solid happiness. Your reasons against entering it at present appear to me not well founded. The circumstantial advantages you have in view of postponing it are not only uncertain, but they are small in comparison with that of the thing itself—the being married and settled.

It is the man and woman united that make the complete human being. Separate, she wants his force of body and strength of reason; he, her softness, sensibility and acute discernment. Together they are most likely to succeed in the world. A single man has not nearly the value he would have in a state of union. He is an incomplete animal; he resembles the odd half of a pair of scissors. If you get a prudent healthy wife, your industry in your profession, with her good economy, will be a fortune sufficient.

But if you will not take this counsel, and persist in thinking a commerce with the sex inevitable, then I repeat my former advice, that in your amours you should prefer OLD WOMEN TO YOUNG ONES. You call this a paradox, and demand reasons. They are these:—

First. Because they have more knowledge of the World, and their minds are better stored with observations; their conversation is more improving and more lastingly agreeable.

Second. Because when women cease to be handsome, they study to be good. To maintain their influence over men, they supply the diminution of beauty by an augmentation of utility. They learn to do a thousand services, small and great, and are the most tender and useful of all friends when you are sick. Thus they continue amiable, and hence there is scarcely such a thing to be found as an old woman who is not a good woman.

Third. Because there is no hazard of children, which, irregularly produced, may be attended with much inconvenience.

Fourth. Because, through more experience, they are more prudent and discreet in conducting an intrigue to prevent suspicion. The commerce with them is therefore safe with regard to your reputation, and with regard to theirs. If the affair should happen to be known, considerate people might be rather inclined to excuse an old woman who would kindly take care of a young man, form his manners by her good counsels, and prevent his ruining his health and fortune among mercenary prostitutes.

Fifth. Because, in every animal that walks upright, the deficiency of the fluid that fills the muscles appears but on the highest part. The face first grows lank and wrinkled, then the neck, then the breast and arms—the lower parts continuing to the last as plump as ever; so that, covering all above with a basket, and regarding only what is below the girdle, it is impossible of two women to know an old from a young one. And as in the dark all cats are grey, the pleasure of corporal enjoyment with an old woman is at least equal and frequently superior; every knack being, by practice, capable of improvement.

Sixth. Because the sin is less. The debauching a virgin may be her ruin and make her life unhappy.

Seventh. Because the compunction is less. The having made a young girl miserable may give you frequent bitter reflections, none of which can attend the making an Old woman Happy.

Eighth and Lastly. They are so grateful.

This much for my paradox, but still I advise you to marry immediately, being sincerely,

Your affectionate friend,

B. FRANKLIN.

'Eighth and lastly' is worthy of the consideration of English lawyers and the English public when a Thompson-Bywaters or Rattenbury-Stoner case is under consideration. Once Stoner had become Mrs. Rattenbury's lover, she worshipped him. It was before the consummation of her desire that she was the dominating character, and to that extent she was responsible for the whole tragedy; but to that extent only. She felt this responsibility deeply, and it was remorse as well as love that made her eager and willing to save Stoner even at the cost of her own life. It was, indeed, a terrible responsibility in view of the events. She could not know that Stoner would be wild with jealousy, but she must have known, had she paused to think, that a lad of Stoner's age and antecedents would lose all sense of values when he became the lover of his social superior, who dazzled him with a whole new mode of life. If Stoner's first love-affair had been with a girl of his own class, no ill need have come of it. Nevertheless, another strange assumption was made—that it is somehow harmful for a young man of eighteen to have sexual connexion.

Dr. Gillespie, physician for psycho-medicine at Guy's Hospital, a witness for the defence, was asked in cross-examination by Mr. Croom-Johnson, whether 'regular sexual intercourse with a member of the opposite sex by a boy of eighteen or onwards would be likely to do him good or harm?' Dr. Gillespie replied that it would not do him good 'if a moral point of view were meant'. Mr. Croom-Johnson said that he was not talking from a moral point of view, that he was asking him as a doctor. Still Dr. Gillespie wisely refused to commit himself. 'Do you think it would likely be good for his constitution—a boy of eighteen—just think what you are saying, Doctor?' 'I am not saying that it is good for his constitution, but I am saying that if it were occurring with such frequency ... as nature would permit, it would not necessarily show the effects in his external appearance.' 'Take the ordinary case—the ordinary boy, not somebody very strong, talking about the ordinary English youth of eighteen—do you really find yourself in any difficulty in answering the question?' 'I find difficulty,' replied the Doctor, 'in answering the question as I believe you expect it to be answered.' Doctors, as a rule, make excellent witnesses, and in this little cross-examination, Dr. Gillespie was no exception to the rule—but with what frank, Homeric laughter the question would have been greeted in a Latin country! In England it is apparently impossible to admit the simple truth that a young man of eighteen is an adult who would normally take a mate, were it not that economic conditions render it impossible.

Mrs. Rattenbury was a good witness, and in nothing more notably so than in her simple acceptance of the values of life as she knew it. 'You have told us that on the Sunday night Stoner came into your bedroom and got into bed with you. Was that something that happened frequently?' asked Mr. Croom-Johnson in cross-examination. 'Oh, yes,' replied Mrs. Rattenbury simply. And later on: 'Did it occur to you that if you went to Bridport, Mr. Rattenbury might want to treat you as his wife?'—'No, if I had thought it was going to happen like that, I would never have suggested going.' 'It never occured to you?'—'No.' 'You know what I mean by saying "treat you as his wife"?' 'Yes, exactly,' replied Mrs. Rattenbury, as though mildly surprised that there could be any mistake about it.

Mrs. Rattenbury's vagueness about money matters and her lavish spending came out as clearly in the witness-box as did her attitude towards sensual matters. In answering to a question as to her habit of giving away cigarette-holders, she said: 'That is nothing for me. If anyone sees a cigarette-holder and likes it, I always say "take it". It is my disposition'; and later: 'I am very vague about money.' This was certainly true. Mr. Croom-Johnson asked her how much money her husband let her have in the course of a year, to which she replied that she 'really couldn't say'. 'Hundreds?' 'I suppose so.' 'About how much a year did he let you have?' 'He used to give me regularly £50 a month, and I was regularly overdrawn.' '£50 a month would be £600 a year?' 'I see,' said Mrs. Rattenbury; and one received the impression that she had not worked out this fairly simple sum for herself. 'In addition to that,' went on Mr. Croom-Johnson, 'about £150 on each of two occasions?' 'Yes, I daresay.' Later, cross-examining her about the clothes she had lavished on Stoner in London, Mr. Croom-Johnson said: 'You used the words "that he required clothes"?'—'Yes, I considered so.' 'Silk pajamas at sixty shillings a suit?'—'That might seem absurd, but that is my disposition.' And certainly it was her disposition.

So, as we have seen, Mr. Rattenbury was reserved, kindly, but rather mean in money matters. Mrs. Rattenbury was unreserved, also kindly, but in a more indiscriminate fashion than her

husband, and her generosity was indiscriminating also. Irene
Riggs liked both of them, but her loyalty was naturally for the
mistress who had been kinder to her than any human being she
had ever met.

Irene Riggs was not as happy after Stoner's arrival as she had
been before. When Mrs. Rattenbury told her about the liaison,
Irene was too fond of her to blame her, but nevertheless felt
uneasy about the affair, and sorry that she could not have
found happiness with someone more of her own age and class.
Though Miss Riggs and Stoner did not like each other, they got
on together well enough. He was a very quiet boy; she also was
quiet. And she was self-effacing and efficient. She was shocked
when Mrs. Rattenbury first told her the truth, but human nature
quickly adapts itself to knowledge, and she very rightly felt that
it was not for her to praise or to blame. She stayed behind when,
on 19 March, Mrs. Rattenbury arranged to take Stoner with her
on a trip to London, because Stoner was very jealous of any third
person, and the charm of the little friendly expeditions that had
been the highlights in Irene Rigg's life before the coming of Stoner
was gone.

In London, Mrs. Rattenbury and Stoner stayed at the Royal
Palace Hotel, Kensington, and spent their days in shopping and
going about town. Mrs. Rattenbury explained this trip to her husband by saying that she was going to have an operation (she had
had several minor operations in the preceding years), and he gave
her the generous sum of £250 for that purpose. Mrs. Rattenbury
used a large part of the money to pay outstanding housekeeping
bills, and the rest she spent wildly upon the London trip and
presents for Stoner. The importance of the expedition to London
lies in the fact that, for four or five days, Stoner was accepted by
the little world about him as Mrs. Rattenbury's social equal. He
did not go to the Royal Palace Hotel as her chauffeur, but as her
brother. They had two rooms opposite each other, and he had
free access to his mistress. He was called 'Sir' by the servants,
and every day Mrs. Rattenbury bought him presents which to his
simple mind must have appeared equivalent to Danae's golden
shower. Crêpe-de-chine pajamas at three guineas a pair and a
made-to-measure suit must have seemed to the young man, who
was a labourer's son, most exciting luxuries.

The learned Judge referred to the 'orgy in London'. It is

difficult to imagine an orgy at the Royal Palace Hotel at Kensington; I have indeed, never been able to discover of what an 'orgy' consists. It is associated, more or less vaguely, in the popular mind with the 'historical' productions of Mr. C. de Mille; glasses of wine, dancing girls, tiger-skins and cushions are some of its component parts. The private coming together of a pair of lovers and their normal physical ecstasies, however reprehensible these may be morally, do not seem well described by the word 'orgy'. Even shopping at Harrods does not quite come under this heading. However, in this trial, as in all others of the same nature, the stock phrases were used of which most people are heartily tired. 'Adulterous intercourse,' 'illicit union,' 'this wretched woman' and the like: they all have a very familiar ring. They are clichés, and come to the lips of those concerned in the administration of the law as inevitably as the adjective 'fashionably dressed' is attached to the noun 'woman' in any reporter's account of the female spectators at a murder trial. Leaving these clichés, the fact, nevertheless, remains that Stoner's trip to London must have thoroughly unsettled him. He was happy enough at Villa Madeira, where the social régime was easy and pleasant for such as he.

Mrs. Rattenbury affected no superiority with anyone in humbler circumstances of life than her own, and Mr. Rattenbury had lived for years in the democratic country where Mrs. Rattenbury was born. Stoner often played cards with him in the evening, and Mr. Rattenbury, Stoner, and Miss Riggs took their meals together. Therefore, merely to have returned to Villa Madeira, to continue its pleasant, easy life, would not necessarily have upset Stoner. But this was not exactly what happened. The lovers arrived back late on Friday evening. Mr. Rattenbury, already having imbibed his night-cap, asked no questions; even next day, according to Mrs. Rattenbury, and so far as Irene Riggs's knowledge went, he never enquired about the operation his wife had ostensibly been to London to undergo. The Saturday found him in one of his worst fits of depression. A scheme for building some flats, of which he was to have been the architect, was hanging fire, owing to the financial depression, and Mrs. Rattenbury tried to cheer him up in vain.

On the Sunday, he was still more depressed. In the morning Mrs. Rattenbury took him for a drive. After lunch he slept. They had tea together, little John with them. He had been reading a book, a novel in which there was a perfect holocaust of suicides, and, according to Mrs. Rattenbury, he expressed his admiration for anyone who had the courage to make an end of himself. Mrs. Rattenbury suggested that she should ring up their friend, Mr. Jenks, at Bridport, and ask whether they could go over on the Monday. She did indeed telephone, and Mr. Jenks said he would be pleased to see them, and asked them to spend the night, an invitation which they accepted. The telephone was in Mr. Rattenbury's bedroom, which opened off the drawing-room. Mr. Rattenbury remained in the drawing-room, but Stoner came into the bedroom, and overheard the arrangements which Mrs. Rattenbury was making. He was frightfully angry and threatened her with an air-pistol, which he was carrying in his hand, and which she took to be a revolver. He told her that he would kill her if they went to Bridport. She, nervous lest her husband should overhear the conversation (though, as she said, 'He never really took very much notice') urged Stoner into the dining-room, and went there with him.

Once there, he accused her of having had connexion with her husband that afternoon—an accusation entirely baseless—and said that, if the Bridport plan were carried out, he would refuse to drive. Stoner said that at Mr. Jenks's house the Rattenburys would have to share a bedroom, but Mrs. Rattenbury assured him that that would not be so—and what she said she knew to be the truth, for she and her husband had stayed with Mr. Jenks before, and had had two rooms. Stoner, though he appeared to be pacified, continued to brood over the matter, and at about eight o'clock that evening, he went to the house of his grandparents, sat and chatted, apparently normally, with his grandmother for some time, and borrowed a carpenter's mallet, but borrowed it perfectly openly. He went back to Villa Madeira, and Mrs. Rattenbury noticed nothing abnormal about him.

That same evening, Mrs. Rattenbury sat and played cards with her husband, kissed him good-night, and went upstairs. It was Irene's evening out, and Mrs. Rattenbury passed the time by getting together her things for Bridport. She had already put out Mr. Rattenbury's clothes in his bedroom downstairs. Irene came in at about 10.15, and went straight to her room. Some ten minutes later, she went downstairs, either to see if all was well or to get something to eat—there seems a slight discrepancy in her evidence here. When she was in the hall, she heard a sound of heavy breathing, and putting her head into Mr. Rattenbury's bedroom, she switched on the light. He was not there. The sound of breathing came from the drawing-room, the door between that and the bedroom being open. Miss Riggs concluded that he had, as he so often did, fallen asleep in his chair, and she went back to her bedroom. A few moments later, she went out again to go to the lavatory, and found Stoner leaning over the banisters at the head of the stairs, looking down. She said, 'What is the matter?' He replied, 'Nothing; I was looking to see if the lights were out.'

About a quarter of an hour later, Mrs. Rattenbury came to Irene's room and told her about the expedition to Bridport. Mrs. Rattenbury then went to her own room, and about ten minutes later Stoner came and slipped into her bed. He seemed very agitated and upset. She said, 'What is the matter, darling?' He replied that he was in trouble, but that he could not tell her what it was about. She said that he must tell her, that she was strong enough to bear anything, and he then said, 'You won't be going to Bridport to-morrow.' He went on to say that he had hurt 'Ratz'. He said that he had hit him over the head with a mallet, which he had since hidden in the garden. Mrs. Rattenbury definitely conveyed the impression from the box that it was possible that the idea in Stoner's head was merely to injure Mr. Rattenbury, so that the proposed expedition could not take place. 'I thought,' she said, 'he was frightened at what he had done, because he had hurt Mr. Rattenbury. . . . I thought he'd just hurt him badly enough to prevent him going to Bridport, and when I said "I'll go and see him," he said "No, you must not; the sight will upset you," and I thought all I had to do was to fix Ratz up, and that would put him all right.'

It may be that this was the only idea in Stoner's unbalanced and ill-educated mind, but that he found it impossible to stop after the first blow and administered two more. Or it may be that, in his disturbed and jealous state, he would have done anything sooner than allow the Bridport trip to take place. If Stoner had driven the Rattenburys to Bridport, he would have had to do so in his capacity of chauffeur; he would have stayed there in the same capacity, eaten in the servants' hall, not had access to his mistress, and ranked as a domestic with the other domestics. The thought of the expedition to Bridport, coming directly after the 'orgy' in London, was unbearable.

It may be argued that, as a motive, this distaste for going to Bridport was very inadequate. But all motives for murder are inadequate. Men have murdered for smaller sums than an embezzler would plot to obtain.

Directly the sense of what Stoner was telling her penetrated to Mrs. Rattenbury's mind, she jumped out of bed and ran downstairs as she was, in her pajamas and bare feet. A minute later, Irene Riggs, who had not yet fallen asleep, heard her mistress shrieking for her. Miss Riggs ran downstairs and found Mr. Rattenbury leaning back in an armchair, as though he were asleep. There was a large pool of blood on the floor; one of his eyes was very swollen and discoloured, and she thought he had a black eye, but this was, in reality, 'contrecoup'—the effect upon his eye of the blows on the back of his head. Mrs. Rattenbury asked Irene to telephone for the doctor at once, telling her to hurry and, to use Miss Riggs's own expression, went 'raving about the house'. 'Oh! poor Ratz. Poor Ratz!' she kept repeating, 'can't somebody do something?' She drank some whisky; she was violently sick, and drank more whisky. She kept on telling Miss Riggs to wipe up the blood because, she said, little John must not see any blood.

Now, there is no doubt that Mrs. Rattenbury knew from the moment she set eyes on her husband that Stoner's talk upstairs had not been a mere attempt to attract her interest and attention. She knew that he had injured her husband in a terrible fashion, and that tragedy, which she could not control, had suddenly taken possession of her life. Her first thought was for her husband, her second for little John. Her third was for Stoner, and this thought persisted, and deepened in intensity, during the hours that followed.

Dr. O'Donnell arrived at Villa Madeira at about 11.45. Mrs. Rattenbury was, in his opinion, already very drunk. Mr. Rooke, the surgeon, arrived at the house about five minutes after midnight, and he also was of the opinion that Mrs. Rattenbury was drunk. Dr. O'Donnell and Mr. Rooke decided that, largely owing to her excited condition, the only proper place for her husband was in a nursing home. They took him there, shaved his head, and discovered three wounds. Dr. O'Donnell telephoned the Central Police Station, about ten minutes' walk from the nursing home and two minutes by car, and said: 'Dr. O'Donnell speaking from Strathallen Nursing Home, Manor Road. Mr. Rooke and myself have just taken Mr. Rattenbury from 5 Manor Road to the nursing home. On examination, we find three serious wounds on the back of his skull, due to external violence, which will most probably prove fatal.' Central Police Station replied: 'You want an officer?' Dr. O'Donnell said 'Yes, at once.' But it was half an hour before a constable arrived. The constable then said he must get an inspector, and at about 3.15 a.m. Inspector Mills, who had already been at Villa Madeira, arrived. At 3.30 Inspector Mills, Mr. Rooke, and Dr. O'Donnell left the nursing home. Stoner was sleeping peacefully outside in the Rattenbury car, and he drove Dr. O'Donnell back to Villa Madeira, following the police car.

When Dr. O'Donnell got out of the car, he was struck by the fact that every light in Villa Madeira was on, the door was open, and the radio-gramophone was playing. There were four police officers in the house. Mrs. Rattenbury was by now extremely drunk. A constable, who had arrived at 3 o'clock, had observed then that Mrs. Rattenbury was under the influence of alcohol, but, as he put it, 'to a mild extent'. One has, of course, to realise that the police standard of drunkenness is very high; as Mr. Justice Humphreys phrased it—'drunk in the police sense seems to mean hopelessly drunk.'

At 3.30, according to Dr. O'Donnell, Mrs. Rattenbury was past knowing what she was thinking or saying. Dr. O'Donnell, very shocked, turned off the radio-gramophone, and tried to explain to Mrs. Rattenbury the gravity of her husband's condition, but she could not take in what he was saying. Inspector Mills agreed that Mrs. Rattenbury was more under the influence of drink than when he had seen her at 2 a.m. He said to her: 'Your husband has been seriously injured and is now in the nursing home,' and she asked: 'Will that be against me?' Inspector Mills then cautioned her, and apparently was satisfied that she understood the meaning of the caution.

Then she made a statement: 'I did it. He has lived too long. I will tell you in the morning where the mallet is. Have you told the Coroner yet? I shall make a better job of it next time. Irene does not know. I have made a proper muddle of it. I thought I was strong enough.'

Dr. O'Donnell, who considered that Mrs. Rattenbury was unable to understand what was said to her, or to know what she was saying, pointed out that she was in no fit condition to be asked anything, and took her up to bed. He administered half a grain of morphia—a large dose—and went downstairs again. After a few minutes he went into the sitting-room and found that Mrs. Rattenbury had managed to get downstairs again and was again being questioned by the police. Inspector Mills said to her: 'Do you suspect anyone?' and she replied: 'Yes. I think so. His son.'

Dr. O'Donnell, who was aware that Mr. Rattenbury's son lived abroad, said to the Inspector: 'Look at her condition—she is full of whisky, and I have just given her a large dose of morphia. She is in no condition to make any statement.' He then took her by the arm and helped her upstairs again. Then (it was by now after 4 a.m.), Dr. O'Donnell went home. At 6 a.m. Inspector Carter arrived at the house, where some members of the police had remained all night. He stated in evidence that he went into Mrs. Rattenbury's room and she woke up. This was not unnatural, in view of the fact that the police had been in that tiny house all night, perpetually going up and down stairs. Inspector Carter realised that Mrs. Rattenbury was ill, and he told Miss Riggs to prepare some coffee. When the coffee came, the saucer shook so in Mrs. Rattenbury's hand that she could not hold it. She managed to swallow it, but retched and said that she wanted to be sick. The Inspector telephoned for a police-matron, who arrived and helped Mrs. Rattenbury downstairs to her bath and helped her to dress. This matron was not called as witness, but it is reasonable to conclude that she thought Mrs. Rattenbury a sick woman. Yet, according to Inspector Carter, Mrs. Rattenbury, who had been drinking steadily from about 11 o'clock the night before till 3.30 in the morning (quite undeterred by the police), and who had then been given half a grain of morphia which she had not been allowed to sleep off, was by 8.15 competent to make a statement! The statement which she then made to him, after being duly cautioned, and which he wrote down in his notebook, read as follows:

'About 9 p.m. on 24 March I was playing cards with my husband when he dared me to kill him, as he wanted to die. I picked up a mallet and he then said: "You have not the guts to do it!" I then hit him with the mallet. I hid the mallet outside. I would have shot him if I had had a gun.'

Inspector Carter deposed that Mrs. Rattenbury read the statement over aloud and clearly before signing it. He then took her to Bournemouth Police Station, where she was charged. Before she left the house, she had a moment alone with Miss Riggs and said: 'You must get Stoner to give me the mallet.' This is important; it is quite clear, on reading Mrs. Rattenbury's statements all through the night, that, even in her befogged condition, there was one thread of continuity—a desire to help Stoner, and to get hold of the mallet with which he had told her he had hit Mr. Rattenbury and then hidden in the garden. At the Police Station, about 8.45, Mrs. Rattenbury was formally charged, and said: 'That is right. I did it deliberately, and would do it again.'

The police did not, at the hearing at Petty Sessions, mention the fact that Mrs. Rattenbury had been drunk, and Mr. Rooke, noticing this omission, communicated the fact to Mrs. Rattenbury's solicitors. Had it not been for Mr. Rooke and Dr. O'Donnell, the fact that Mrs. Rattenbury had been in no fit condition to make a statement, to know what was said to her, or to know what she herself was saying, would not have been given in evidence. At the trial, her counsel, Mr. O'Connor, in his cross-examination of Inspector Carter, said: 'Dr. O'Donnell has told us in his evidence that no reliance can be placed on any statement made by Mrs. Rattenbury at 8.15 in the morning.' 'No,' agreed the Inspector. 'Do you say she was normal at 8.15?'—'Yes. She was not normal when she first woke up, but I waited till 8.15.' 'Do you know that the medical officer at Holloway Prison has reported that she was still under the influence of drugs three days later?'—'He has never reported it to me.' 'Is your evidence to the jury that, from the time you began to take her statement until she left your charge, she did not appear to you to be under the influence of drugs?'—'She did not.' 'Not at any time?'—'Not at any time.' Yet Mrs. Rattenbury was, during the whole of the time Inspector Carter had to do with her, *non compos mentis* from morphia!

Later in the trial, Mr. Justice Humphreys, turning over the

pages of Inspector Carter's notebook, was struck by the fact that there was an entry that had not been put in evidence. This consisted of a statement that Mrs. Rattenbury had made directly she woke up at 6 o'clock. Mr. O'Connor was handed the notebook, read the entry through to himself, and expressed his gratitude to the Judge. Indeed, Mr. Justice Humphreys had made one of the most important points for the defence that were made in the case, as was shown when Inspector Carter was recalled to the box.

By the Judge: 'Did Mrs. Rattenbury make any statement to you about this alleged crime before 8.15?'—'No statement to me, my lord. Mrs. Rattenbury said the words that I have written in that book, while she was lying on the bed, directly she woke up. I did not put them down in statement form. I did not refer to it in my evidence for this reason. When Mrs. Rattenbury woke up, I said in my evidence that, in my opinion, she was not then in a normal condition and I did not caution her, and for that reason I made no reference at all to these remarks that I put down in my book that she said. That is why I omitted to say anything at all about it in my evidence-in-chief. I was not entitled, in my opinion, to give anything in evidence if I had not previously administered a caution, and, in my opinion, she was not in a condition normally to make a statement.' *By the Judge*: 'Then in your opinion she was not in a condition to make a statement at 6.15?'—'At 6.10, no, my lord.' *By the Judge*: 'Then what was said at that time was something said by a woman who was not in a condition to make a statement that can be acted upon?'—'Not in my opinion, my lord.'

There was no doubt that Inspector Carter was actuated by an admirable sense of fair play, and the Judge, in his summing-up, said: 'I think there is no ground for complaining of his conduct or saying that he acted improperly here, although, I think, he was mistaken. . . . He made a mistake in not informing the Director of Public Prosecutions that that statement had been made by the accused, and that he had it in his notebook. It is not for the police officers to decide . . . what is admissible in evidence and what is not, or what should be given or what not. Their duty is to give all material to the authorities, and let them decide.'

Now, the important point about the first entry in Inspector Carter's notebook—the entry he did not put in evidence, that he wrote at 6.15—and the one which he wrote down after cautioning her at 8.15, is this: the two statements are practically identical. At 6.15 when, according to Inspector Carter, she was not fit to make a statement, she said: 'I picked up the mallet and he dared me to hit him. He said "You have not guts enough to do it." I hit him. I hid the mallet. He is not dead, is he? Are you the Coroner?' At 8.15 she said: 'He dared me to kill him. He wanted to die. I picked up the mallet, and he said "You have not the guts enough to do it." I hid the mallet outside the house.' It will be seen at once that, with the exception of the words, 'He is not dead, is he? Are you the Coroner?' the statements are the same, except that at 8.15 she used the word 'kill', and at 6.15 the word 'hit'. To put it concisely: she made the same statement when, according to the Inspector, she was fit to make a statement that she had made two hours earlier, when even he had considered her totally unfit! The importance of this is obvious—Mrs. Rattenbury no more knew what she was saying at 8.15 than she did at 6.15, and the second statement was of no more value than the first. At one o'clock of that day, when Dr. O'Donnell saw her at the police station, he says that she was supported into the room, that she could not stand without swaying, and that she looked dazed and had contracted pupils as a result of the morphia. Three days later, Dr. Morton of Holloway Prison considered that she was still suffering from 'confusion of mind, a result of alcohol, and possibly a large dose of morphia. She kept repeating the same sentences over and over again.' From 28 March, she was better and appeared to have forgotten what she had said and how she had behaved on the previous days since her reception. It is perfectly obvious that police officers are not fit judges of when a person is under the influence of morphia or not. There is no reason why they should be. But they *are* judges of drunkenness, and Mrs. Rattenbury should not have been allowed to go on drinking—or have been questioned during the Sunday night. As the Judge pointed out, Dr. O'Donnell knew much more of these matters than the police officer, and much later on Monday, after she had been taken to the Police Court, he declared that it would still be unsafe to attach any importance to anything that Mrs. Rattenbury said.

Now, Mrs. Rattenbury was not used to drugs, in spite of suggestions made to the contrary; she had, indeed, a horror of drugs, and the only time previously in her life that any had been administered to her was in July 1934, when Dr. O'Donnell had administered a quarter of a grain of morphia, as she was ill and excited. On that occasion she was allowed to have her sleep out, and she had indeed slept for some twelve hours. When the stronger dose of half a grain of morphia was given to her on the night of Sunday, 24 March, she had no chance of sleep. It is not suggested for a moment that the police tried to awaken her. But Stoner and the police were up and down and about the house all night long. Now, anyone who has had to have morphia knows that if he is not allowed to sleep off the effects, his condition is far worse than if it had never been administered. This was the case with Mrs. Rattenbury, and, according to the experienced Dr. Morton, she was still suffering from the effects of the morphia three days later. Many people felt that even if Mrs. Rattenbury did not know what she was saying when she was drunk and when she was drugged, what she said came from her subconscious self, and hence was true. This is an error, as any doctor knows. What does come through all her statements, if they are carefully analysed, is her anxiety for Stoner, and her wish to take the blame.

Another strong point for the defence, besides the undoubted one that Mrs. Rattenbury was quite unfit to make statements, was the complete blank in her memory when she emerged from her drugged state into ordinary consciousness at Holloway Prison. Mrs. Rattenbury remembered nothing from the time when she began to drink after discovering her wounded husband until 28 March at Holloway Prison. Many people, as a result of drinking, 'pass out'. Mrs. Rattenbury did so, and the result of the morphia's effect being thwarted was that she stayed 'out' for a very long time. She remembered nothing from when she first became drunk on the Sunday night. So far as her mind was concerned, she knew nothing about the interrogations, nothing about the injection of morphia, nothing about the police-matron having helped to get her up. She did not remember being taken away from Villa Madeira in a car by the police; the only thing that swam up at all in her recollection was Stoner's farewell-kiss in her room, and the face of little John at her door. Mr. Croom-Johnson, in cross-examination, asked her: 'About conversations, your mind is a complete blank?'—'Absolutely.'

'About incidents?'—'Yes. It might be somebody else you are talking about.' 'Is your mind a complete blank about making the statement to Inspector Carter which he wrote down in this little book?'—'I cannot remember that. I have tried and tried and tried yesterday, and last night I tried to remember again.' The notebook was handed to her, and Mr. Croom-Johnson asked her whether the signature at the bottom of the statement was hers. She said that it was: 'It is my signature, but I do not remember it.' Now, it is natural for the layman to feel that loss of memory is a convenient form of defence, but Mrs. Rattenbury could not have deceived medical men as highly trained and as astute as Mr. Rooke, Dr. O'Donnell, and Dr. Morton—the last-named accustomed to all the tricks of delinquent women.

The prosecution took the unusual step of allowing the defence to recall one of the Crown witnesses, Mr. Rooke, and this courteous gesture was a great help to Mrs. Rattenbury. Mr. Rooke deposed that in his experience patients often talked long and lucidly when under morphia, but when the effects of the drug had worn off, their minds were a complete blank regarding anything they had said. When it is considered that Mrs. Rattenbury was not only suffering from the morphia, but that before the morphia had been administered she had temporarily lost her mind through drink, I think it is clear that no reliance can be placed on anything that she said.

Mrs. Rattenbury was removed to Holloway Prison in London, and Stoner and Miss Riggs were left in the house at Manor Road. But Miss Riggs had no intention of being left alone with Stoner. She knew that Mrs. Rattenbury was innocent—not only of striking the blows, but of complicity in the assault. One of Mrs. Rattenbury's most striking characteristics was her horror of cruelty; she could not have hurt anything. Therefore Irene Riggs thought that either a burglar had broken in or that Stoner must have been Mr. Rattenbury's assailant.

Irene's mother and brother moved into Villa Madeira and stayed there with her until Stoner was arrested on Thursday, 28 March. The story of those days between the commission of the crime and the arrest of Stoner is a curious one. Dr. O'Donnell had been asked by relations of Mr. Rattenbury to keep Villa Madeira under his eye, and the Doctor accordingly called there on the Monday, Tuesday, Wednesday and Thursday. On the three first days he tried to see Miss Riggs alone, but found it impossible as Stoner did not leave them. On Wednesday Miss Riggs was nearly distracted with anxiety, and felt she must talk about the case to someone. She still believed herself to be the custodian of Mrs. Rattenbury's secret love-affair, and she never discussed her even with her relations. Although not a Catholic, she went to see a priest, because she knew that what she told a priest would be safe. She came back at about 10.30 that night and her mother opened the door to her. Mrs. Riggs told her that Stoner was very drunk, that he had been going up and down the road, shouting: 'Mrs. Rattenbury is in jail, and I've put her there.' He had been brought back by two taxi-drivers. Irene Riggs telephoned to the police, and two plain-clothes men arrived. Stoner was in bed and seemed very drunk. This was most unusual for him, for he not only never drank himself, but objected to Mrs. Rattenbury drinking, and had a good influence on her in this respect.

On the morning of Thursday, 28 March, Dr. O'Donnell called at Villa Madeira. Irene Riggs opened the door. It had always been Stoner who had opened it up to then. Dr. O'Donnell asked where Stoner was, and she told him that he had gone to Holloway to see Mrs. Rattenbury. Dr. O'Donnell then said that Mrs. Rattenbury was the best mistress that Miss Riggs had ever had, or that she was ever likely to have, and if there was anything she could tell the police, it was her duty to do so. Poor Miss Riggs, still loyal to her employer, said she could not let Mrs. Rattenbury's secret out, but Dr. O'Donnell very sensibly said that a secret was nothing when a life was at stake. He pointed out that if she was put in the witness-box, and then had the story of Mrs. Rattenbury's liaison dragged out of her, she herself would be implicated for having concealed her knowledge. He asked her whether she thought Mrs. Rattenbury had murdered her husband, and Irene Riggs replied: 'I know she did not do it.' Dr. O'Donnell asked her how she knew, and she said that Stoner had confessed it to her: he had told her that there would be no finger-prints on the mallet as he had worn gloves. Dr. O'Donnell rang up Bournemouth Police Station, and said that Miss Riggs wished to make a statement; that Stoner had confessed to her. Dr. O'Donnell added that Stoner had left for London and that no time should be lost in taking the statement. At 2.30 the police arrived and Irene Riggs told them what she knew. Stoner was arrested at the station on his return to Bournemouth that evening—and this time the charge was murder, for Mr. Rattenbury had died.

The very fact that both Stoner and Mrs. Rattenbury refused to inculpate each other was a source of great difficulty to their defenders. Stoner further complicated his counsel's task by injecting into his defence the curious suggestion that he was a cocaine addict, which there was no evidence to bear out, and which Mr. Justice Humphreys disposed of in no uncertain fashion in his summing-up. The Judge pointed out that there was one human being, and one only, who knew whether Stoner was in the habit of taking cocaine, and whether he took it on the afternoon of Sunday, 24 March, and that was Stoner himself. Stoner was an available witness, and had he wished to prove that he had ever taken cocaine, or was under the influence of cocaine, he could have gone into the box to say so. 'What,' remarked the Judge, 'seems to me in the circumstance of this case a fact of the utmost significance is that Stoner prefers not to give evidence.' Stoner had told Mrs. Rattenbury a long time before the murder that he took drugs. She was so worried about this that she confided it to Dr. O'Donnell, although she was not at all sure—for, in spite of her headlong infatuation, she had a certain shrewdness—that Stoner had not invented the whole thing so as to make himself interesting to her. Dr. O'Donnell, at Mrs. Rattenbury's request, had interviewed Stoner and asked him what drug he was taking. Stoner had told him that it was cocaine, and that he had found it in his father's house. To anyone who had seen Stoner's father in the witness-box, the suggestion was not only cruel but absurd. Mr. Stoner was a self-respecting, honest, hard-working man. It detracts somewhat from what has been called the chivalry of Stoner's conduct that he should have been able to make such a suggestion about his father. Stoner was certainly not a drug-addict. Whether he was a cinema-addict I do not know, but this fantastic story might well have emanated from a cinema-nourished mind. Had he not confused his defence by insisting on this fairy-tale, his counsel would have been able to present a much more sympathetic picture of a boy crazy with love and wild with unreasoning jealously, who had hit without knowing what he did. The cocaine story was too far-fetched. When Stoner was asked to describe what cocaine looked like, he replied that it was brown with black specks in it, evidently describing the only sort of things he knew, such as household pepper or influenza snuff.

During the trial, Stoner sat unmoved in his corner of the dock, with his elbow on the ledge, his cheek on his hand. His eyes were downcast and his face remained immovable. Mrs. Rattenbury also was perfectly calm, but it was a frozen, and not an apathetic, calm. Her physical aspect changed, without any movement on her part, in a curious manner. By Friday she looked twenty years older than she had on Monday. On the last day, even her hands changed colour: they were a livid greenish white.

She was an excellent witness. Her voice was low and rich. She gave a great impression of truthfulness, and she was astonishingly self-controlled. Only a nervous tick in the side of her face, which jerked perpetually, betrayed the tension of her mind. Mr. R. Lewis-Manning, her solicitor, was impressed throughout all his conversation with her, by her veracity. He, as did Mr. O'Connor, felt a terrible responsibility. Mr. Lewis-Manning was certain that Mrs. Rattenbury was not pretending when for several weeks she insisted that she would not implicate Stoner but preferred to hang rather than that he should come to any harm. Unlike Mrs. Thompson, she had immense physical courage. It was the thought of her children, and what a fearful heritage would be theirs if she were found guilty, that eventually made her tell the truth. It is easy to say that all this could have been a pretence on her part, but it would not have been possible for her to make this pretence appear the truth to Mr. Lewis-Manning and Mr. O'Connor.

The behaviour of a certain section of the press during the course of the trial, had it been made public, which for obvious reasons it was not, would have caused an uneasy feeling in the public mind. Someone engaged in the case was telephoned on the Monday when the case opened, and offered £500 as his 'rake-off' if he would get Mrs. Rattenbury to write her life-story. Then, as the unexpected angle that the case was assuming became visible, the offer was raised. By Thursday, this gentleman engaged in the case, who was a man of honour, was offered £3500 as his 'rake-off,' and one paper was foolish enough to put this offer in writing! It is needless to say that none of the offers was considered for a moment, and would not have been if the wealth of the world had been offered.

Mr. Casswell was handicapped in his defence of his client Stoner by the fantastic nature of the story which Stoner had told. Mr. O'Connor was in no such invidious position; he had a very clear notion of the mentality of his client, and he was able to give full play to his sympathetic interpretation of that mentality. There were cases, Mr. O'Connor pointed out, when the accused person had a record and history which might inspire the jury with a revulsion against that person's character. 'It is in this case, perhaps,' he continued, 'that the task of the jury is most difficult of all—the task of separating from their minds the natural revulsion they feel against behaviour which nobody would seek to condone or commend. I am not here to condone, still less to commend, her conduct. I am not here to cast one stone against that wretched boy whose position there in the dock may be due to folly and self-indulgence on her part, to which he fell a victim.' Mr. O'Connor went on to say that the jury must not imagine that the two defences had been arranged in concert—were connected in any way. Each defence was in its water-tight compartment. 'I will say no more,' continued Mr. O'Connor, 'about what is past in Mrs. Rattenbury's life. I would only say that if you are tempted to feel that she has sinned, and that her sin has been great and has involved others who would never otherwise have been involved, then you should ask yourselves whether you or anybody of you are prepared first to cast a stone.'

Having pleaded one of the greatest of speeches for the defence ever uttered—and the deathless words 'cast a stone' sounded through a hushed Court—Mr. O'Connor went on to give a very good description of the mentality of Stoner: 'Can you doubt seduced; raised out of his sphere; taken away to London; given a very high time there—a lad who was melodramatic and went about with a dagger, violent sometimes, impulsive, jealous, his first love; a lad whose antecedents had been quiet, whose associations had been prosaic; never mixed with girls; flung into the vortex of this illicit love; unbalanced enough, and, in addition to all these things, either endeavouring to sustain his passion with cocaine or already an addict of drugs. You may, as moral men and women, as citizens, condemn her in your souls for the part she has played in raising this position. She will bear to her grave the brand of reprobation, and men and women will know how she has acted. That will be her sorrow and her disgrace so long as she lives. You may think of Mrs. Rattenbury as a woman, self-indulgent and wilful, who by her own acts and folly had erected in this poor young man a Frankenstein monster of jealousy which she could not control.'

Mr. Justice Humphreys's summing-up was a brilliant exposition of the law. There was no judge more capable of weighing evidence, and the right value was given to every piece of evidence that had come before the Court. But the Anglo-Saxon assumption still is that women, whatever their circumstances, want to be married; and Mr. Justice Humphreys was no exception in making that assumption. He spoke of the period (the 'orgy') which Mrs. Rattenbury and Stoner spent in Kensington: 'Do you believe that while they were in London, the future was not discussed? What they were going to do when they got back? Could life go on in the same way? Would not something have to be done with—or to—Mr. Rattenbury? Would he not ask: "What about my £250? How much did the operation cost you? Did you have the operation? If so, where? I hope you are better for it." Or, if he was so callous and disinterested a husband that he would not be expected even to ask about the operation, at least as a mean man would not you expect him, and would not they expect him—that is the point—to make some enquiries about the money? Do you think that these two persons in London imagined that life could go on just the same after their return, after an absence of four days, as before?'

The Judge went on to quote Mrs. Rattenbury's account of the events of Saturday—'I think we played cards. I think it was just the same as any other night.'—and asked: 'Do you believe that? Do you believe that after an absence of four days, Mr. Rattenbury never asked a question as to what happened in London?'

Let us consider the history and mentality of these people as we know them through the medium of the trial. Ill-balanced as she was, Mrs. Rattenbury was a woman of the world. The last thing she would have wanted was to have married a chauffeur, twenty years younger than herself; she was—again to use a slang expression, but slang fits Mrs. Rattenbury's career—'sitting pretty'. She had a kind husband who allowed her to live her own life. She had a young and ardent lover who satisfied her emotionally and physically. She had two children to whom she was passionately devoted. She was being supported as extravagantly as she could have hoped for, all the circumstances considered. She was, as she rather pathetically said in evidence, 'happy then'. For her husband, she had a maternal affection—it must be remembered that in all her loves Mrs. Rattenbury was essentially maternal. She spoiled and protected Stoner; she adored her children; she comforted her husband; she tried to give Irene Riggs as good a life as possible; she was kind to every stranger who came within her gates. The one thing that would have been impossible to Mrs. Rattenbury, amoral, casual, unbalanced, and passionate as she was, would have been to take part in harming another human being. Mrs. Rattenbury, both as a humane woman and as a completely amoral woman, did not desire her husband's death, and did not wish to marry her lover; there is no evidence that she had ever desired either of those things.

The unfortunate Stoner, with a much simpler experience of life and with that adolescent urge to heroics which is a hang-over from infantilism, could not see that there was no need for any drama of jealousy at all. The boundary-line between drama and reality was obscure for him, and, living entirely in an unintelligent world of crude emotion, he hit out almost blindly. And this gesture, conceived in an unreal world, materialised in a world of actual facts. Our prisons are, of course, full of sufferers from infantilism: what goes on in their heads bears no relation at all to real life, as it has to be lived, though it could not possibly be said that they are not sane.

The jury were out for forty-seven minutes, and they returned the only possible verdicts to which they had been directed upon the evidence. They found Mrs. Rattenbury Not Guilty, and Stoner Guilty, adding a recommendation to mercy. Mrs. Rattenbury stood immovable while the verdict of Not Guilty was returned; but when the foreman pronounced the word 'Guilty' in respect of Stoner, she gave a little moan and put out her hand. She was led away, and Stoner received his sentence without flinching. He spoke for the first time when asked by the Clerk of the Court whether he had anything to say why the Court should not give him judgment of death according to law. He replied in a low voice: 'Nothing at all.' He was then taken below, and Mrs. Rattenbury was brought back to plead to the accusation of being an accessory after the fact. She could not speak—she could not make any sound at all—her mouth moved a little and that was all. The Clerk of the Court informed the jury that the prisoner at the Bar had pleaded Not Guilty. The prosecution said that they proposed to offer no evidence, and Mr. Justice Humphreys instructed the jury to return a verdict of Not Guilty, which they did. Mrs. Rattenbury was discharged.

She had had an admirably fair trial. She was not, of course, bullied by the prosecution, as she would have been in France or the United States. In fact, Mr. Croom-Johnson could, even within the limits allowed to the Crown, have been more severe than he was. Mr. Justice Humphreys told the jury unmistakably that even though they might feel that they could not possibly have any sympathy for the woman, it should not make them any more ready to convict her of the crime: it should, if anything, make them less ready to accept evidence against her. This was admirable, and in the best tradition of the English law.

Unfortunately, there is a custom in the Courts that is not nearly so admirable: to animadvert upon the *moral* qualities, or lack of them, in a person accused of a crime. I am, of course, using the word merely in the only sense that Anglo-Saxons seem to use it, with reference to sexual morality. Though Mrs. Rattenbury was a woman at the extreme edge of what it was possible to bear and go on living, she had to listen to the dread voice of the Judge, as he said: 'Members of the jury, having heard her learned counsel, having regard to the facts of this case, it may be that you will say that you cannot possibly feel any sympathy for that woman; *you cannot have any feeling except disgust for her.*' More could hardly be said of George Joseph Smith, or of a systematic poisoner, or of a baby-farmer.

This may show a very lofty viewpoint, but we are often told that a criminal court is not a court of morals. In this trial apparently it was. And strange as it may seem, there are some of us, though apparently regrettably few, who are so constituted that we cannot see a fellow-human in the extreme of remorse, shame and despair, without feeling pity as well as disgust. Indeed, it is quite possible for the disgust to cease to exist because of the overwhelming nature of the pity. Mrs. Rattenbury was in some ways a vulgar and a silly woman, but she was a generous, kindly, lavish creature, capable of great self-sacrifice. She was innocent of the crime of which, entirely on the strength of her own drunken maunderings, she was accused—but, nevertheless, though her life was handed back to her, it was handed back to her in such a shape that it was of no use to her. 'People'—that dread judgment-bar of daily life known as 'people'—would always say: 'Of course, she told him to do it. And, anyway, she was a dreadful woman.' For the world has progressed very little since Ezekiel wrote: 'And I will judge thee as women that break wedlock and shed blood are judged, and I will give thee blood in fury and jealousy.' Such was the judgment of society on Mrs. Rattenbury, and she knew it.

Her husband's relatives took her away with them, but the press besieged the flat where they gave her refuge. She was removed to a nursing-home, pursued by newspaper men, one of whom called out to the doctor escorting her: 'If you take her to Bournemouth, we'll follow you.' A horrible example of what the demands of his newspaper can do to a young man who probably started as a decent human being.

Mrs. Rattenbury was by now very ill, physically and mentally. And, in her fear and grief for Stoner, in her misery for her children, in her remorse and shame, she wanted to be alone. She left the nursing-home; and of what she did during the nightmare hours that followed we only know from the tragedy that followed. She must have bought a knife and taken a train down to that part of the world where she had been happy in what was stigmatised as an 'adulterous intercourse'. And there, beside the placid waters of a little stream, she sat and wrote, feverishly and passionately, on the backs of envelopes and odd bits of paper, the reasons for the terrible deed that she was about to do. She referred to the assumption that she dominated Stoner, and declared that no one could dominate him, and that whatever he wanted to do he always did. She repeated that if she had not been made to tell the truth, she would never have given Stoner away. She complained about the press dogging her footsteps, and she wrote of the scathing attack on her character. How, indeed, was it possible for her ever to make a home for her little boys, to watch them at play, to invite other children to play with them? She must have known that it would be worse for her children if she lived than if she died.

Her writing finished, she thrust the knife six times into her breast. The blade penetrated her heart thrice. She fell forward into the water, dead. When an ancient Roman killed himself, he inserted the tip of the sword between two ribs, and fell upon it; he called it 'falling upon his sword'. He knew that the shrinking of the flesh was such that it was almost impossible to drive a knife steadily into the breast. Mrs. Rattenbury drove it in six times.

The Rattenbury case had revealed a strange and unlovely mode of life; but the woman's last act raised it sharply to higher issues. Most people in England, especially women, seemed easily able to feel superior to Mrs. Rattenbury. She had had 'adulterous intercourse'; she had taken for her lover a boy young enough to be her son; and the boy was a servant. That out of this unpromising material she had created something that to her was beautiful and made her happy was unforgivable to the people of England. Her life had been given back to her, but the whole world was too small a place, too bare of any sheltering rock, for her to find a refuge.

Stoner lost his appeal, but he was reprieved, and the sentence of death commuted to penal servitude. Blind and muddled humanity had been even more blind and muddled than usual, and everyone concerned had paid a terrible price for the sin of lack of intelligence.

EDITOR'S NOTES. 1. From 1932 till a few days before his death in 1947, James Agate—who was, first and foremost, a dramatic critic—kept a journal which was published (by Harrap, London) in nine volumes, all entitled Ego, *followed by a series-number. Here are extracts from some entries:*

Wednesday, 29 May 1935. The *Daily Express* asked me to do an impression of the Rattenbury trial at the Old Bailey. . . . It was all very like the three French major novelists. The way in which the woman debauched the boy so that he slept with her every night [*sic*] with her six-year-old son in the room, and the husband, who had his own bedroom, remaining cynically indifferent—all this was pure Balzac. In the box Mrs. Rattenbury looked and talked exactly as I have always imagined Emma Bovary looked and talked. Pure Flaubert. And last there was that part of her evidence in which she described how, trying to bring her husband round, she first accidentally trod on his false teeth and then tried to put them back into his mouth so that he could speak to her. This was pure Zola. The sordidness of the whole thing was relieved by one thing and one only. This was when Counsel asked Mrs. Rattenbury what her first thought had been when her lover got into bed that night and told her what he had done. She replied, 'My first thought was to protect him.' This is the kind of thing which Balzac would have called sublime, and it is odd that, so far as I saw, not a single newspaper reported it. . . .

Friday, 31 May. Mrs. Rattenbury acquitted and Stoner condemned to death. The second must not happen. . . . In its account of the last scene, *The Daily Sketch* has this cryptic sentence: 'A mere boy, but it may be that he behaved as a man behaves.' What a rum thing is the mind! This trial has moved me immensely. . . . Meanwhile, the Rattenbury verdict, happening in the afternoon, has given an immense fillip to Emlyn Williams's *Night Must Fall*, a good, highly imaginative play about a murder in an Essex bungalow.

Wednesday, 5 June. . . . As we were setting off in the car, the newspapers came out with the placard: 'MRS RATTENBURY STABBED AND DROWNED'. Reggie Arkell said this was the most dramatic thing he had seen in the streets since 'TITANIC SINKING'. The two things of this kind which have shocked me most have been the arrest of Crippen, about which I read on the pier at Llandudno—I can still point out the exact plank on which I stood—and the newspaper placard announcing the death of Marie Lloyd. I remember how this rooted me to the pavement in Tottenham Court Road.

2. *Tennyson Jesse is contemptuous of Mrs. Rattenbury's songs (which she wrote under the pen-name of Lozanne), calling the lyrics 'cheap'—but remember that Noel Coward, more of an expert on the matter, had a character in* Private Lives *say: 'Extraordinary how potent cheap music is.' While Mrs. Rattenbury was awaiting trial, she composed a song entitled 'By Some Mistake,' and told a friend: 'I kept repeating the extraordinary words over and over again to help keep my mind sane':*

> By some mistake, my spirit held you, dear,
> But now I wake to agony and fear,
> To fading hope and thought distressed and grey;
> With outstretched hand I put your face away.

> By some mistake, you filled my empty days,
> But now I wake to face the parting ways.
> I see your smile, I hear the words you say;
> With no reply I hush your voice away.

> By some mistake, by some divine mistake,
> I dreamed awhile, but now I wake, I wake.
> Yet, dying, dream you kept my vision true;
> I seem to climb to heav'n in loving you.

3. Extracts from Mrs. Rattenbury's last letters, found in the handbag she left on the bank of the tributary of the Avon near Christchurch, a few miles from Bournemouth:

I tried this morning to throw myself under a train at Oxford Circus. Too many people about. Then a bus—still too many people about ... If I only thought it would help Stoner I would stay on, but it has been pointed out to me all too vividly I cannot help him. That is my death sentence. . . . Eight O'clock. After so much walking I have got here. Oh to see the swans and spring flowers and just smell them. What a lovely world we are in. And how singular I should have chosen the spot Stoner said he nearly jumped out of the train once at. It was not intentional, my coming here. I tossed a coin, like Stoner always did, and it came down Christchurch. It must be easier to be hanged than to have to do the job oneself, especially under these circumstances of being watched all the time. One must be bold to do a thing like this. Pray God nothing stops me tonight. . . . God bless my children and look after them. . . . It is beautiful here and I am alone. Thank God for peace at last.

4. Stoner, a model prisoner, was released in 1942, when he was still only twenty-six. He joined the army, and took part in the Normandy Landings; after the war, he returned to Bournemouth, married, and settled down in his parents' house, which is still his home. I am aware that he was again in the news in the autumn of 1990; but as the 'newsworthiness' had far more to do with who he was than with what he had recently done, I don't think it would be fair to him to say what that was.

JUDD'S STORY
Judd Gray

[One fine day in June 1925, Henry Judd Gray, a bespectacled little man of thirty-two, whose job as a traveller
for the Bien Jolie Corset Co. meant that he was often
away from his wife and daughter in New Jersey, popped
into Henry's smörgasbord restaurant, in Manhattan, for
a quick lunch. Already there, sitting in a booth with two
friends, a man and a woman, was a blonde woman of
twenty-eight. Her name was Ruth Snyder. She had come
into town from another borough of New York City,
Queens, where she lived in a new, clapboard house, 9327
222nd Street—incompatibly with her husband Albert, who
was the art editor of Motor Boating magazine, lovingly
with their seven-year-old daughter Lorraine, and resignedly
with her recently-widowed mother, Mrs. Josephine Brown,
who helped pay for her keep by doing those domestic
chores that Ruth hated doing, which was practically all
of them.

Ruth's male lunchtime-companion, a lingerie salesman
who was acquainted with Judd Gray, invited him to 'make
a foursome', and he did so, taking the one spare seat. That
seat was next to Ruth's—and so, while her two friends
covertly talked business of some kind to each other, she
and Judd engaged in small talk; and by the time that
Olaf, the globular waiter, presented the bills, Judd was
captivated by Ruth . . . and she was—well, it seems true

to say that she, aware of his captivation, was considering certain possibilities.

A month or so went by; neither Judd nor Ruth tried to get in touch with the other. Meanwhile, most of Judd's sales-calls were in places distant from New York City; the Snyders went away on holiday, but after a specially fierce row between Ruth and Albert, she, with Lorraine, returned home early. She was still unpacking when the phone rang. It was Judd, inviting her to dine at Henry's with himself and the man who had introduced them. She accepted. Afterwards, she went with Judd, he alone, to his office, where he spieled the peculiar merits of the Bien Jolie range of corsets (or, as he insisted on calling them, 'intimate garments' or 'corselets'), and she then burst into tears and said what a brute her husband Albert was, and he tried to comfort her by offering a complimentary corselet, adding that he would be only too pleased to fit it for her, and, she having wiped her eyes and powdered around them and said thanks, they both undressed and, uncomfortably on the linoleum-covered floor, became adulterers. During the following eighteen months, they copulated frequently (though, because of Judd's itinerant occupation, not regularly)—never again, it appears, in his office, but at hotels in and around Manhattan, sometimes the swank Waldorf-Astoria, always unexpensively for Judd, who included the outgoings among the business expenses he submitted to Bien Jolie.

He had been happily married. In a funny sort of way, he still was. But he was no longer merely captivated: he was captive. He said all the things that he thought Ruth ('Momie' to him) wanted him ('Bud' to her) to say; was desperately careful not to say anything that might, just might, make her wonder whether he really believed all her tales, every single component of them, concerning Albert the Wife-Beater, the Drunkard, the Skinflint, the Stay-at-Home . . . and so on, down the line from most dreadful to simply cranky, ending up with Albert the Perpetual Mourner of a fiancée who had died ages before he had proposed to Ruth at Christmas-time 1914, and she, then working clerically at his office, had been swayed into saying yes by the generous

*size of the diamond in the engagement ring he had bought
on approval (she often, while horizontal, sighed to Judd at
the grab-the-diamond-and-wed reason for her subsequent
misery, illustrating the moral of the tale by shimmying
her stretched left hand, thereby sparking facets of the
once-corrupting stone against the background of rumpled
bed-linen).*

*After a while, not a long one, she spoke of her day-dreams
of escape—of marital bliss with Judd (taking it for granted
that if she were free to re-marry, he would divorce his wife
so as to make himself available); and after a further while,
not a long one, she began to talk, if not practically, then
determinedly, of ways of 'getting rid of the governor'. And
then, since Judd ummed and ahed whenever she pleaded
for his help in making her dreams come true, she told
him of her solo efforts. At first he lied when he said
he believed her accounts of ham-handed or half-hearted
attempts at murder; but (perhaps after she had used him
as guinea-pig in an experiment with a Scotch-and-sedative
cocktail which left him comatose for fifteen hours) the time
came when he understood that she was not romancing
about attempts respectively employing carbon-monoxide,
domestic gas, and knockout drops as an ingredient of
Albert's favourite dessert, something called prune whip.
She may or may not have mentioned to Judd that she had
tricked Albert into signing life-assurance policies with the
Prudential. The most beneficial of the policies, basically for
$45,000, contained a double-indemnity clause, agreeing
to double the pay-out if Albert died as the result of an
accident or in the course of a crime. (James M. Cain's
novel* Double Indemnity, *loosely based on the Snyder-Gray
story, is itself the firmer basis of Raymond Chandler's script
for the excellent movie of the same title that was made by
Billy Wilder in 1944; another screen-version of the story,
called* Body Heat, *was released—as if recklessly from an
asylum—in 1981.) Ruth pleaded with Judd to obtain
murder-materials—chloroform and chloral-hydrate, for
instance—on her behalf . . . or rather, their behalf, so
she told him. He always promised to, but always needed
to invent excuses for having let her down. That brings us*

*to about the second week—the Ides—of March 1927: to
Judd's story.]*

AT THIS TIME I was not yet drinking in the day-time, but
steadily at night. I could not sleep otherwise. I had to progress
with my work—some kind of sleep was a necessity. As it was,
it seemed a constant uphill fight to even keep going. Worry over
home conditions, lack of physical stamina—liquor. The last few
trips I made I can recall only in spots at best.

Awaiting me in Rochester was a letter from Ruth, saying her
husband was ill with hiccoughs and had been for two or three
days. I happened to be selling to a customer that day who
mentioned two cases of the same illness in town: one man
passing away and the other man being cured with pineapple
juice. I wrote her of these.

As I recall, I travelled into New York over the week-end to
see a customer, and I am under the impression that I saw her for
luncheon—my memory seems a bit vague here. I do recall her
telling me that at the time of the hiccoughs she used bichloride
of mercury and an anodyne; and I commented, 'That is a hell of
a way to cure hiccoughs.' She said she never saw anyone in her
life so very ill and yet pull through. . . .

That she endeavoured to take life and I sat by in sympathy for
her is incredible—certainly I would have given more consideration to an imperilled dumb animal. I can only account for it as
having sunk so low in soul, mind, and body that whatever pleased
her was unquestionable in my eyes. Of course, when she related
it I was always under the influence of liquor—and she was most
affectionate.

Why I never had manhood enough to warn the man by an
anonymous letter, or strength enough to prevail upon her, I do
not know. I asked her if she had made any progress towards
divorce, and she answered, 'No.' She said she kept bichloride of
mercury in the house in a Midol box, so no one would know the
difference—she had marked a small cross on it. As to size and
so forth, they were akin.

My mind was bending more noticeably under the strain. I
could no longer depend on my memory, and wrote down
everything that I did or had to do. In fact, there almost

seemed two persons inside my skin—one constantly striving to act normal, the other constantly doing foolish things. Such as shaving two or three times in the morning, looking for things I had already dressed myself in, turning on the water in the boiler, as I did at home, and leaving it to flood the cellar. I remember once meeting my wife Isabel—taking her to the theatre and thinking all the time that she was a stranger. Another time I was met at my suburban station by Isabel and my daughter Jane, and I was in such a haze that I was unable to impress it on myself that they belonged to me—hardly that I had ever seen them before. Life for me was chaos.

And the next time I met Ruth for dinner, she wept, and I comforted her, stroking her lovely, smooth hair.

That night, I might say, ended my life. We dined at a restaurant, dancing afterwards. Trying to enjoy it, yet there was something, some undercurrent, different from anything I had experienced. Ruth was deep in thought, loving yet aloof. And I can never tell how it happened, but I vowed that my love was great enough that I would go to infinite depths for her—give her my life. She said I must plan, plan—do something.

The only thing I could think of was to meet him and have a fight—have it out. Quickly Ruth said, 'No, you are not strong enough.' I drank myself into unconsciousness that night. The next morning she reminded me: 'You are going to keep your promise?' I answered that I would try—though I did not know how I could.

I had reached the verge of I know not what, whether travelling or at home. I thought only of the horror of that promise. My thoughts kept reverting to my home—to Isabel—Mother—Jane. And life there seemed as strange as the stranger I felt to myself. I accomplished everything by instinct rather than thought or forethought. And I was scarcely able to keep my fire burning.

Ruth asked me to luncheon—she said I must have some plan—I had none. She waited, expecting me to say something, was angry; so I said, why not a burglary? She suggested that I could strike him with a hammer. I said I could not. She asked me to buy chloroform and coloured handkerchiefs, and I said 'All right'. She had served several drinks, and when I was about to leave for home, she put on her coat and hat and came with me, saying she would wait while I bought everything. We walked around to a number of stores in the locality of the station I was leaving from, but I could find none of the things she told me to purchase. She waited outside the stores while I went in. So I left for my trip. I realized I was facing a terrible situation, yet could not convince myself that I would have any part in it. I knew I could never take part in such a thing.

I arrived in Albany, had a bite to eat and a few more drinks. It was there I bought the chloroform, handkerchiefs and a pair of rubber gloves. Then I sat down and wrote her I had bought the things but could do no more, could not go through with it. In Kingston I purchased the sash-weight and more chloroform, and took the train for New York City. I left the things at the office. Through this period my memory is blank towards much. However, certain moves and details stand out boldly. I remember securing a piece of green felt and a reducing roller from my cellar and taking them to New York with me. I wrapped everything in a bundle together. I gave it to Ruth when she and Lorraine met me at Henry's for luncheon. I was in a trance. I remember Ruth said to me: 'You look terrible.' She had never spoken to me in that cutting tone before. I replied that 'I *felt* terrible'. I could not eat, could only think of that bundle under Ruth's chair. I did try to swallow a little food.

We wrote a couple of notes and handed them across the table. I think I said I would see her Monday. She wrote that she was trying to get chloral hydrate. That stuff seemed to be on her mind.

Finally I said I must make a train, and left them. If I had possessed any mind at all, I certainly would have followed the knowledge of wrong that was being evidenced in my very soul and would have come out like a man and told her so. But I never recall it coming to my mind: this is right or wrong to do. It was simply a question of 'I didn't think I could go through with it,' or hoping something would happen to prevent it.

Ruth arranged to meet me at Jamaica station, a mile or so from her home, that Monday evening. We went to a nearby Chinese restaurant—a low-ceilinged place, black with the shadows of screens and lit by cup-shaped orange lanterns. And over the chop-suey and coffee, I said, 'I must leave for a trip, but I will come out tonight.' She instructed me to buy some rope, and impressed on me that if there was a light in her mother's room I was to come in the kitchen where she would meet me. Then I went back to New York to the office. I stayed in the office. I was afraid to move. On every side of me yawned an abyss—try as I might I could find no bridge that would bear me over and away. The best I could hope, and it seemed the most logical thought to cling to, was that Ruth would never demand such a thing of me. She was a woman, tender, humane; at the last moment she could not go through with it herself—and I would be free. If worse came to worst, I would take my own life.

I packed my bags, eating no dinner. Filled a flask to take with me, though goodness knows I did not need it. I took picture-wire from the office in place of the rope she told me to bring. Then I rode out to Queens Village.

There was a light in the cellar of her home. It started to rain. I walked and drank until eleven o'clock. I do not remember much where I went, as I seemed to have difficulty at times in walking. I had impressed on myself two things—'see a light upstairs'—and the time my train left.

When I passed the house once again, I heard someone knocking on a window. It was Ruth motioning me from the kitchen. I went to the rear door. She gave me some more to drink—said her husband had been working in the cellar, and 'would I go through with it?' I said, 'I must make my train.' She said, 'Shall I take the things?' I said, 'No, I'll keep them.' Yet I cannot tell why I wanted to cart those things around with me. . . .

That week is hazy to me—the week prior to the tragedy—I would come, I wrote, on Saturday next. She wrote that they were going to a party; that her mother would be away.

I was living on alcohol then. I did not much care what happened—the real me seemed dead anyway. I was a blank wall—a failure. I was positive that I was mad. . . .

When I reached Syracuse [about 250 miles north-west of Queens], I sat down in my room and spent the early evening in writing, paid my bills, arranged my personal affairs, cleaned out my wallet and papers. Thinking, thinking. What road was there now to freedom? Help her—then become free—hoping, always hoping, something might happen.

It is hard to live over those days or put down any picture of my state of mind or condition. Somehow I cannot express it as I am today. It was more like living in a semi-coma—and the awful cold sweats I suffered—constantly it was necessary to change to dry clothes.

That morning in Syracuse I stopped to see my boyhood friend Haddon Gray. I had no alibi plans. Still hoping I would not have to go through with it. We had luncheon together. I was tempted to confide in him—ask his aid—but did not dare. So then and there I decided to go. Asked him if he would attend to some mail for me, as I planned to go to Albany to meet someone. I told him I might not return until some time on Sunday and to hang a 'do not disturb' sign on my door in case anyone—there were some boys I knew staying in the hotel—tried to see me. Then I thought the sign should be off in the afternoon, so asked him to remove it if it was not too much trouble.

I filled a flask—took two more drinks before I made my train at four o'clock. . . . I remember little of the trip down to Manhattan. I know that I ate nothing. I drank enough to keep half-conscious.

When I left the train, I walked down either Park or Fifth Avenue. It was drizzling rain. Why I walked to the Penn Station I do not know, unless it was to kill time. I had quite a wait there. Bought a newspaper, but could not read it. The station seemed very brightly lighted, and inside me everything seemed to hum. When I walked, I listened for my step—no sound seemed to follow. On the train, I picked up a scrap of Italian newspaper. It fell from one of the passengers' bundles.[1] I placed it in my briefcase alongside my rubbers, a pair of rubber gloves, a comb, chloroform, some waste I had picked up on the street in Rochester, and two pieces of picture-wire.

Ruth had written me that if a packet of cigarettes was on the kitchen-table, they would not be at home—if there was none

[1] EDITOR'S NOTE. *Well, perhaps—but he would leave the scrap of newspaper in the house, as a false lead to an* **Italian** *burglar.*

there, to wait in the kitchen. The side-doors would be open for me.

When I reached the inside of the kitchen, I could not remember what the cigarettes meant—home or vice-versa. I sat down awhile. My head was numb and hurt me. I had to rest. Finally I went up to her mother's room, as she had directed. I removed my coat and threw it in the closet. I sat down in a chair. Again that feeling of trance. Truly no longer did I know the purport of my visit. . . .

Ruth had written me to look under the pillow and find the sash-weight, a bottle of whisky, and cutting-pliers (the telephone-wires were supposed to be cut). I took a drink from the small bottle she had left for me. I finished it in one drink. I started to perspire, took off my coat and was so dizzy I had to sit down on the floor. What was in the bottle I do not know, but my head went round and round—and the room seemed to expand—into space. My legs felt as if they were stilts—wood. I cannot tell how long I sat there—I had an impulse to go. I picked up my briefcase and coat, forgetting my overcoat and hat, and started downstairs. I heard an automobile, and turned and fled up the stairs again. I say fled—stumbled, rather, on those long wooden pegs of mine. I flopped unnerved on the floor—lay there. I reached out and took a drink from the quart-bottle. Again I had that wild impulse to run—and made the landing facing the front door. Their car drove up, and I just reached the room again as Ruth and Lorraine entered the house. I dropped on the rug—motionless.

Ruth took Lorraine to her room, then came to the room I was in and whispered: 'Are you there, honey?' I mumbled, 'Yes, go away.' Evidently she put Lorraine to bed—as she passed the door she murmured, 'I'll be in shortly.' I lay on the floor panting, while her husband came upstairs and went to his room. Then she came in and kissed me, asking me if I had found everything. And questioned me as to when I had arrived. She accused me: 'You have been drinking.' I answered 'Plenty' and again told her to go away.

Later she came in and said he was sleeping. She asked me: 'You are going through with it, aren't you?' I answered, 'I don't think I can.' She asked me where I was when they came in. I said, 'Almost out of the house.' She said, 'Isn't it funny, one of the men at the party tonight said he would kill my husband if he did not treat me better.' Then she remarked: 'How long do you think we should wait?' I said, 'I don't know.' We stood there whispering quite a while. I did not have a watch on (she was wearing hers), so I do not know about the time. The door was slightly ajar, and she would go to it occasionally. I had removed my glasses—the next thing I knew, I was holding the sash-weight, and had on rubber gloves. She had the chloroform, waste, and the handkerchief. I know Ruth had not been drinking. I remember she took me by the hand and went to the door with me, and stood there while I entered the room.

At the first blow, I think he sat up, fighting—this is all jumbled. I was caught by the necktie—I know I screamed to Ruth 'For God's sake help me!' I was being choked—I do not remember what happened then. Next I remember she handed me a tie to secure his feet. Next I knew, I was down in the living-room, trying to leave without coat, overcoat or anything. The next thing I recall was going to the bathroom, where Ruth had discovered that the front of her kimono and gown were covered with blood. I had a spot directly over my own heart about the size of a silver dollar. Somehow I had injured my leg, a wrench at the knee, causing me to limp.

As to the wire about Mr. Snyder's neck. . . . I have not the slightest recollection of that part of the deed, if I did it, and I would hate to think of placing the blame of it anywhere, for God knows the rest of it was bad enough. I may have done it—Ruth alone can tell. I am willing to accept every bit of the guilt that is mine. . . .

I recall Ruth asking me if the stains could be washed out, and I answered 'No'. She brought me in a shirt of her husband's. I was unable to fix the studs in it, so she attended to them. As I was struggling to put it on, she went down to the cellar and burned the gown, the kimono, and my shirt in the furnace.

The next thing I recall, we were sitting on the davenport in the living-room, and I heard the tinkle of a milk wagon. She said we must muss up the house to make it look like a robbery—or had that been done? Then we were upstairs, and I asked about the gun. It was not under his pillow; she took it from a dresser and handed it to me. I broke it, throwing some of the cartridges out, after I had put it in his hand. I have a hazy recollection that at this time she asked me if he was dead. I answered 'No'. I believe I felt his pulse. She said, 'He must be or I am ruined.' I answered that I was 'already ruined, and through'. Strange how these snatches filter back into my mind as if from a dream. Just like a dream where you wake and can only remember bits of it here and there. You recall this and that, but whether it happened in your dream you cannot say.

I recall taking a bottle of liquor from the sideboard downstairs. And that she endeavoured to find the chloroform container which one of us finally found on the bed or under the bed-covers. . . .

I remember she gave me a route-list of mine, eight or ten sleeping powders, her watch, and a box containing bichloride of mercury—to take away with me. Although my nerves seemed paralyzed, I did things super-acutely in some respects. For instance, when I reached the cellar I picked coal from the bin lump by lump—so it would make no noise. Then I brushed up where I had stepped. She had shown me where she had hidden the sash-weight in a box of tools and I sprinkled ashes in the box.

My mind must have been alert to some things while dead to others—I have no relative scale of time regarding my movements.

Suddenly glimmers of grey dawn like curls of smoke started to trail through the window. Soon it would be light. I made an attempt to pull myself together. She cut the shirt-band into a longer buttonhole. Her daughter's room was locked. She asked me to hit her on the head, but I said I could not, so bound her loosely and left her on her mother's bed with a fur-coat over her. I took my briefcase, the empty chloroform-bottle and my rubbers. It was almost light. She asked me to take her jewelry, which I refused. She gave me her husband's wallet. I extracted the money and scattered the remainder of the contents on the floor. I asked her if she would hide the money as I did not want it. She said 'Take it'. I did not count it but think there were seven ten-dollar bills.

Then I kissed her—good-bye—and said, 'You will not see me for a month—two months—perhaps never.' I said, 'I have nothing to protect myself with if I am apprehended before I get back to Syracuse.' She interrupted me: 'I would die before giving up one word against you. I have a poison capsule—enough in it to kill a dozen people. If necessary, it is for myself.'

She said: 'Unlock Lorraine's door as you go out.' I stumbled down the stairs—closed the street-door gently behind me. Nothing, not a word of the future, had been mentioned—no syllable of plans as to what we would do if the deed became known. All I can say is that there had occurred a deed the hideousness of which made my blood run cold, as it does now while writing this. I have never forgotten the feeling in the hundreds and hundreds of times I have lived it over. I can only think that neither of us was aware of what we were doing. There was no thought in my mind of lawlessness, detectives, or electric chair. The crime just seemed something that had to be accomplished for her sake.

I do not set this down in the spirit of trying to explain anything away—that cannot be done. Neither am I trying to alleviate any of the guilt through insanity. All I can truthfully say is that I was not in my normal mind—if that would account for it.

I walked a considerable distance for a bus and stopped on the corner of the Turnpike to await it. From there I went to Jamaica, where I found I could not get a train into Manhattan. Then I took a taxi to 59th Street and Broadway, where I changed to a bus that took me to 42nd Street and Fifth Avenue. My mind was too foggy to permit me to walk, and I was so weary that I could hardly stand up. I had not slept virtually for days. On my arrival at the Grand Central Station, I endeavoured to eat breakfast but could only swallow a few mouthfuls of coffee. I then boarded the train. I could get a seat only as far as Albany. I dropped the brief-case in the Hudson River where it runs near the tracks.

I could not sleep on that long trip. When I arrived in my hotel, I washed, shaved and changed my clothes—then called up my friend. He invited me to his home for supper. I asked him to come and get me. Before he came, my mind cleared enough for me to think in a hazy way. I realized that I could not go on with a thing like that on my soul. Withal, it seemed like a dream. So I took three tablets of bichloride of mercury and put them in the bottle of whisky

I had brought from her home. The other tablet I placed in my vest-pocket.

Then I planned that the next day (Monday) I would hire a car, take the contents of the bottle, and drive over the embankment on the way to Auburn or on the way to Skaneateles. Simple, yet what a queer track for my mind to take! I had a dozen sleeping powders she had given me and enough poison to kill six men without a trace, yet in my mind was implanted the fact that it must be done with a car and appear an accident. Why? I do not know, for the other way would have been quick and painless. I knew I could never go back home. I thought of my family—remote—I was remote—

My friend Haddon Gray came to the hotel and I told him the story. I asked him what to do, little realizing what I was getting him into—this man I had always held as dear as a brother. I showed him the bottle and told him I thought of drinking it. He said, 'Pour it out.' Then he told me not to worry.

After I left his house that evening, I stopped at a nearby hotel to see a man. And when I left the hotel I was so dazed that I could not find my way back to my own hotel, try as I would. Finally I asked my way, though it was but a few blocks.

When I arrived in my room, I endeavoured to write a letter but could not. I recall, though, mailing something in the mail-chute—what it was I do not know. I returned to my room and was partially undressed when a knock, sharp and unmistakable, came on my door. My mind was not functioning; the only thought I had was that it was a bell-boy for my laundry.

I opened the door to a group of detectives—and without a word went to the Syracuse Police Headquarters with them.

What had happened was this: Early on the Sunday morning, Lorraine, woken by noises outside her room, found her mother lying bound and gagged. The child fetched neighbours, and they called the police. Ruth told the invented tale; but negative evidence in the house contradicted it. The police found an address-book containing the names of 28 men, including that of Judd Gray; also a tie-pin with the initials JG. A detective read out the names to Ruth—who appeared flustered or frightened when he came to the G pages. *She stuck to the tale throughout twelve hours of questioning, and then fell for an old trick: told, untruly, that Judd Gray had been traced and that he had confessed, she broke down and admitted that she had helped to plan the murder; she insisted, however, that she had done her level best to dissuade him from committing the crime and that she had played 'no active part' in the murder. She handed over a snapshot of Judd, and—presumably aware by now that she had been fooled by the police—said that he was staying at the Onondaga Hotel in Syracuse.*

During nearly twenty-four hours of questioning—first, at the Syracuse Police Headquarters, then on a train to New York City—Judd insisted that he was innocent, that he had a watertight alibi. But then, having been shown a newspaper with a front-page headline announcing that Ruth had confessed and implicated him, he told his side of the story—apparently with great relief, 'like water from a hose'.

On Wednesday, 23 March, he and Ruth were indicted for murder in the first degree. Each of them pleaded Not Guilty. The trial, which began little more than three weeks later, was covered by star reporters—among them, Damon Runyon, who began his first account:

A chilly looking blonde with frosty eyes and one of those marble, you-bet-you-will chins, and an inert, scare-drunk fellow that you couldn't miss among any hundred men as a dead set-up for a blonde, or the shell game, or maybe a gold brick.

Mrs. Ruth Snyder and Henry Judd Gray are on trial in the huge weatherbeaten old court house of Queens County in Long Island City, just across the river from the roar of New York, for what might be called, for want of a better name, The Dumbbell Murder. It was so dumb.

On 7 May, two days before the end of the trial, The New Yorker *published 'Clytemnestra: Long Island Style' by 'A Reporter at Large' (Elmer Davis):*

By the time you read this, the jury will probably have

decided who killed Albert Snyder, or who did not, as the case may be, and the newspapers will have a lean and hungry look—till the next good murder comes along. In this lull between the gusts of the typhoon, then, let us pause a moment to examine this Snyder murder which used up so much newsprint paper. Why was it a good story?

For quite a while I persisted in the stubborn belief that it was not a good story at all, that it was an inflated, an oxygenated, a pumped-up story. It was a good story, certainly, for the first two days; but after the confessions were published, the only solid interest lay in the question whether they would stand up in court. Logically, the trial ought to have been worth about three sticks a day till the defendants went on the witness-stand.

Besides this, the story failed to meet the first and most obvious criterion of a good murder. If Genevieve Forbes Herrick covers it for the Chicago *Tribune*, it is a good murder, otherwise not; and while all this alleged excitement was occurring in Long Island City, Mrs. Herrick remained in Chicago, writing three sticks a day about a girl who had drilled her lover in a back alley on the South Side. So, I reasoned and argued, it was not a good story; and yet I presently found myself getting up early in the morning and making the long and onerous journey from Morningside to Long Island City in time to throw somebody out of my seat before court opened. And towards the end of the trial everybody was talking about it; so whether or not it should have been a good story, it seems that it was.

On the day Ruth Snyder went on the stand, every seat in the largest courtroom I have ever happened to see was being claimed by anywhere from two to six people, and standees were packed in thick. Spectators had to pass a police barrier at every turn in the corridor; a mere card from a district leader was worth nothing. For everybody who was inside, at least three persons, I should say, were turned back at the gate.

Well, that interest was legitimate and explicable enough; it was precisely the interest that brought Roman

crowds to the Colosseum to see a Christian blonde try
to dodge the lions. This time—I have it on the word
of Dr. John Roach Straton [the loudly holier-than-thou
Minister of the Calvary Baptist Church, near Carnegie
Hall], who ought to know—it was a pagan in the arena,
while the Christians licked their chops on the benches;
but the principle is the same. For here was the climax
of the king of sports, the end of a manhunt; better still,
the end of a womanhunt; a human victim tracked down,
putting up the last fight for life in plain sight of the
customers. And in this case public sentiment was so
overwhelmingly against the defendants that the average
citizen could lean back and give three cheers for the lions
with no perceptible qualms.

For that matter, our enlightened age has rather
improved on the Colosseum pastimes. A prisoner equipped with counsel as diligent as Mr. Edgar Hazelton (who
is defending Ruth Snyder) is in the happy position of a
Christian who might have had a good police-dog to help
her stand off the lions; and, with a possibly unconscious
instinct of showmanship, our two victims improved the
act by turning on each other. So it was as if you had two
Christians, each trying to throw the other to the lion and
climb out of the arena while the king of beasts was busy
with his prey.

There you have an act that will draw a crowd anywhere,
in any age. But it drew the crowd, partly, because it had
already been well advertised, so that the whole town
knew about it; and this day-by-day news value of the
Snyder case still requires some explanation. My guess
may be wrong, but it is hereby offered to start the ball
rolling.

In the first place, this is the only murder I can
remember in which the overwhelming majority of public
sentiment, from the first, was with the victim. Usually,
nobody cares a hoot about him; he is dead already and
the only interest lies in the efforts of the defendants to
go on living. Now the late Albert Snyder, whatever his
merits, does not appear to have been an exceptionally

winning personality; any number of people who have publicly expressed the hope that his killers would go to the chair would have felt no great fellowship with him in his lifetime. Take this guess for what it's worth; a good deal of that goes back to one simple, inconspicuous touch in the first-day story. Whoever killed him slugged him while he was sleeping on his good ear. Six hundred thousand husbands must have read that and reflected: 'Thank God, mine are both good.' What with whiskey and chloroform, he would probably have never known what hit him, anyway; it does not appear that either his wife or Judd Gray considered the fact that he was sleeping on one side rather than the other; but this small detail somehow put the finishing touch on the picture.

Any further chance for general sympathy that the defendants might have had was destroyed, I suspect, by the promptitude with which they squealed on each other. It was no way for Paolo and Francesca to treat each other; it rather kills their chance of figuring as one of the great pairs of lovers in history, despite the encomiums which each defendant's counsel bestowed on the other defendant's irresistible sex appeal.

I have heard experts suggest that the story owed its popularity to the fact that all the characters so closely approximated the divine average. The newspapers exploit the rich and give plenty of publicity to the poor, but the middle class rarely makes the front page. Here you had hundred-dollar-a-week people figuring as principals in a crime of passion; small commuters, members of a class which has received perhaps less attention than any other group in the country. Fiction and news alike had neglected them; news stories about them had the same novelty interest as the first fiction written about South Sea Islanders or Carolina mountaineers or similar folk. . . .

To be sure, this story was not devoid of its incidental merits. It produced some good lines, chief among them this priceless pearl from Mr. Hazelton's opening for the defendant Snyder: 'A woman is just as God intended her, but for some man.' Mr. Hazelton deserves recognition, too, for the subtlety of his original theory, later discarded, that Mrs. Snyder was in the conspiracy before the murder, in it after the murder, but not in it at the moment of the murder. This derives, visibly, from the doctrine of marriage by which the Sacred Rota is guided in its annulment proceedings: that if there were any flaws in your intention of being one hundred per cent married at the moment of making the promise, it does not make any difference how long and faithfully you may have lived afterwards in the married state; but Mr. Hazelton has the distinction of having refined upon even this master product of the Vatican's metaphysicians.

There is a genuine human interest, in the true sense of that much misused term, in many of the details of the case; precisely the interest that can be found in anybody's affairs if they are exposed, flung wide open to the public view. Give eight columns a day to any murder, at least any love-murder, and you would find just about as much human interest. But one item deserves more attention than it has received—the contents of the suitcase that the couple checked at the Waldorf.

A study of the inventory of these paraphernalia of middle-aged passion would do a good deal, I surmise, to keep impressionable young people on the straight and narrow path; for it certainly takes the edge off romance. Run over this list and you will find no fewer than twelve kinds of cosmetics, which Ruth Snyder apparently needed to keep herself presentable for twenty-four hours. To while away the tedium of the night of love there was a deck of cards and a copy of *Gentlemen Prefer Blondes*; there was that unromantic adjunct to the sense of well-being, bicarbonate of soda. And don't forget the four cakes of soap from an up-state hotel and the shoe-horn from the Allerton House hotel, which the thrifty Judd Gray had brought along with him—the same Judd Gray who gave a taxi driver a nickel tip for a three-dollar-and-a-half ride, and thereby made sure that one vital witness would never forget his face.

Altogether, one might say that the newspapers have cooked up a pretty good story out of rather unpromising material. Yet one bit of material was inexplicably good; inexplicably, because no one has yet satisfactorily analyzed the interest that attaches to Ruth Snyder. A commonplace woman to all appearance; her irresistible charm is visible only to Judd Gray. A woman accused of a peculiarly atrocious crime, of course; but neither that, nor her position at the apex of the triangle, accounts for the fact that she has dominated this story from the very first day. Nothing that she has done, nothing that she has said, accounts for the impression she has made; even before she went on the stand, she had pretty well established herself as (I borrow a phrase from Mr. Alexander Woollcott) one of the great ladies of our time. She overshadows even that virtuoso of the law, Mr. Hazelton; she towers far above Judd Gray. It was a tribute to the impact of her personality, ominous as it may have been for her prospects of survival, that, when Hazelton pictured her as the helpless, frightened tool of her lover, the audience frankly laughed.

But there she runs true to type; Clytemnestra traditionally has to put up with whatever she can get in the way of an Aegisthus.

The jury retired at twenty minutes past five on 9 May, and returned with two verdicts of Guilty exactly a hundred minutes later. Judd continued his reading of a prayer book; shortly after seven, Ruth, on her way to the cells, caught sight of a priest and got him to accept her as a convert to Roman Catholicism. On 13 May, they were sentenced to be electrocuted at Sing Sing Prison. Their separate appeals were denied. And Ruth's claim against the Prudential was turned down. John Kobler, in his fine introduction to the trial-transcript (Doubleday, Doran & Co, New York, 1938), notes that

at least two serial biographies of Ruth appeared in print, one purporting to have issued from her pen. . . . While not occupied [if she ever was] with her autobiography, she gave attention to her now greying hair, permitting it to grow long and dyeing it. She was distressed over her failure to lose weight in prison and requested a tennis ball to bounce in the exercise yard. Another source of grievance was her matron's refusal to supply her with chewing gum, but ever since a condemned desperado fashioned a deadly weapon—not unlike a sash-weight—by rolling up the pages of a magazine and gluing them together with 'Juicy Fruit', this delicacy had been forbidden inmates of the death house. Ruth consoled herself for this deprivation—she was a rabid gumchewer—by making a pet of a white mouse. On visiting days her mother and brother, Andrew Brown, brought magazines of the true-confession variety, but candy and fruit were not allowed. She craved, as she confided in a letter to a friend, 'a bird and a cold bottle like in the old days.'

Her intellectual habits took a curious turn and she began penning verse, of which the following is an example:

> So many unkind words have been spoken,
> Each with a hurt in its aim,
> All over the globe they keep travelling,
> Causing us sorrow and pain.
>
> These words have crushed my dear mother,
> Changed happiness to despair,
> Lined her dear face with more wrinkles
> And added more silver to her hair.
>
> The bowed head of my only brother
> To his sister brought many a tear,
> For the little this world gave
> Her pleasures, she's truly paid dear.
>
> My baby, God's treasure, He gave me,
> Has suffered in her innocent bliss
> From a wrong befallen her mother,
> Who longs to have her to kiss.

Only you who have scattered these words
Know well they are untrue;
Still you keep sending more along,
Not knowing when they'll return to you.

You've blackened and besmeared a mother,
Once a man's plaything—A Toy—
What have you gained by all you've said,
And has it—brought you Joy?

And the hours when 'Babe' needed my love,
You've seen fit to send me away—
I'm going to God's home in heaven,
Ne'er more my feet to stray.

Someday—we'll all meet together,
Happy and smiling again,
Far above this earthly span,
Everlastingly—in His reign.

Ruth was not without her sympathizers, for close upon the publication of this poem she received 164 offers of marriage, should she be released.

Much of the time Ruth was paralyzed with terror, and in the long nights her screams would rattle the windows. During her calmer moments she managed flashes of her old vaudeville wit, as when she remarked, 'I always wanted an electric heater, but my husband was too stingy to buy me one. Now I guess I'm going to get one.'

The determinedly conscientious Judd, having signed a contract with a book-publisher to write the story of his life from start to, excepting a few minutes, finish, slaved to ensure that he would have left nothing important out when the immutable deadline arrived—an hour or so away from Friday the Thirteenth of January, 1928:

12 January 1928.

Like two doomed ships that pass in storm,
We had crossed each other's way:
But we made no sign, we said no word,

We had no word to say;
For we did not meet in the holy night,
But in the shameful day.

OSCAR WILDE

My will is made. The newspapers give in detail the process we must endure tonight to step from this life. . . . I order my dinner, anything I wish; what irony, when I have a thousand things to think of besides food. Everyone is kindness itself. Offer me their outdoor periods—I must stay within and write. First to my little girl, Jane—Oh! Jane, try and think lovingly of me sometimes—may the blessings I have denied you fall richly on your head. And now Communion. I have sponged my soul—Concealed nothing. It is a clean slate—it feels clean.

It gives me happiness and courage to meet my family— they will be more comfortable, too, with indecision about a stay of execution in the air. As for me, I *know* it will be today. They will not have to see me with that shaved spot on top of my head. I pinch myself to know it is not all a dream and that I will wake up just recovering from a long illness. Sometimes it seems—

My family, long hours together. One by one the lights are lighted— those bright spots that will make a beacon of this hill tonight. A beacon that all the world may see and read 'finale'.

All afternoon and until early evening we have talked in low tones—the three that have always loved me and have been with me to the last—The guards turning their sympathetic, harassed eyes away from us. The guards who gave them hot tea, cheered them with talk of a 'stay'. We talked of where I will lie after tonight—of every small thing we had forgotten until now, passing lightly over subjects that hurt too much—forgiving all—understanding all. Clinging with our glances until they hurt like a physical wound. Promising faith and love and blessings forever—recalling faith and love and blessings from the past—Giving me messages from friends—'Bon voyage.' And 'God bless you'—as my boat is pulling out from shore, never to anchor on this side again. From time to time I would have to pause and glance at the telegrams and letters sent me—the last telegram—'Good-bye, boy—God bless you.'

The Doctor arrives. The Keeper gently motions my family—

through the bars we may say farewell. We clasp each other's hands in turn—again—clasp and cling. What can we say in words? 'Be my brave,' I murmur—The guard is weeping. We turn from each other—how can life hurt so—And the innocent ones—Outwardly calm, inside we are crucified—

I cannot be alone—my head is shaved in the round spot that is necessary. I am bathed. The Chaplain arrives. My lawyer, broken by emotion, wrings my hand—good-bye—He dashes out. The Warden, a splendid man, shakes me by the hand—The Chaplain and I sit down—We start the Twenty-third Psalm—somewhere between here and New York my mother is repeating this with me, will continue to do so every night of her life. Faintly I hear the boys in the cells singing 'Onward, Christian Soldiers'—and now 'The Pilgrims of the Night'. That is what we are—pilgrims of the night. Slinking out of the world, forced out into the night to make our way by steep and unknown paths—somewhere. A prayer on our lips for those we leave behind; for ourselves; for those who must travel this way in the future.

We start, the minister and I, to repeat together, 'Blessed are the pure in heart'—the Beatitudes—I have always loved them—full of promises. God has kept all His promises to me—made me whole again—smoothed the path today. He will be with me to the end—'I shall fear no evil, His rod and staff, they comfort me'—Just a little longer, measuring the minutes—

And at last I am sure of Christ—I will be free. I know. I have bought this all with my own coin—and paid with my body. . . . In death I shall smile. Somehow they will know—I will write that to my family—that in death I shall smile—

It is twenty minutes past ten. When the eleven o'clock train whistles under the prison wall, bodily I will be no more—The letters my dear ones left with me I will save until the last moment, and their kisses will go with me into the Beyond. I take up my pen and paper, and write 'My own dearest little family' for the last time.

John Kobler continues the story:

After supper, Ruth's spirits revived somewhat. When Warden Lawes, whose anomalous duty it was to attend the dying agonies of condemned prisoners while disapproving capital punishment, offered the usual last services, she held herself fairly steady. At eleven o'clock, with no word forthcoming from Governor Smith, two matrons led her from her cell along the twisting corridor, through the green door and into the death chamber. She walked unsupported. As guards adjusted the electrodes and wired casque, Ruth delivered herself of her oft-quoted last words. "'Father, forgive them, for they know not what they do.'" (Did Ruth ever study the life and works of Johann Hoch? Herr Hoch, the most monstrous of American 'Bluebeards'—he murdered upwards of thirty-eight women—uttered the same words on his way to the gallows.)

Among the twenty-four witnesses, twenty were news-papermen. One of them, a Mr. Thomas Howard, was staff photographer for Pacific and Atlantic Photos on special assignment for the New York *Daily News*. Posing as a reporter, this gentleman of highly individualistic ethical principles carried concealed in his trouser leg a tiny 'ankle camera'. He secured a front seat in the death chamber, twelve feet distant from the chair. The room was lighted by an indirect system providing him with excellent illumination.

As the state's gaunt, dour executioner, Robert Elliott, shot the current through Ruth's body and it heaved against the leather straps, Howard clicked the shutter. Saturday's edition of the *News* carried on its front page a blurred picture of a woman from whose body electricity was blasting the last breath of life. It stirred furious controversy, with the *News* editors defending Howard's action as the most literal translation of War-den Lawes's warning to reporters to record only what they saw, and with others denouncing it as a vile and nauseating violation of human decency. Photographer Howard received a bonus of $100 and an important Washington assignment.

The process of destroying Ruth Snyder, the third woman to die in the electric chair,[1] consumed seven minutes. At 11.07, her body was wheeled into the autopsy room adjoining the death chamber and the brain excised. Mrs. Brown was allowed to remove the remains and bury them in Woodlawn Cemetery.

At 11.10, Judd Gray entered. He made no speech and, but for an almost imperceptible tremor, held himself rigid. Four minutes later he was dead.

And in the autopsy room the two lovers shared their last intimacy—on a pair of stone slabs.

[1] EDITOR'S NOTE. *The third in New York State. The predecessors were Mrs. Martha Garretson Place, found guilty of murdering her stepdaughter Ida, and executed on 21 March 1899 (nine years after the very first electrocution, of William Kemmler for the axe-murder of his mistress, Tillie Ziegler), and Mrs. Mary Farmer, found guilty of murdering a next-door neighbour, Sarah Brennan, and executed on 20 September 1909.*

REMARKS ON RIPPEROLOGY
Jonathan Goodman

Has anyone seen him? Can you tell us where he is?
If you meet him, you must take away his knife.
Then give him to the ladies. They'll spoil his pretty fizz,
And I wouldn't give you tuppence for his life.
From a broadsheet, September 1888

JACK THE RIPPER has been credited—if that is the word—with
as many as eleven murders in the Whitechapel area, but it is
now generally reckoned that his actual tally of 'women of the
unfortunate class' was merely five:

Mary Ann Nicholls—Friday, 31 August 1888
Annie Chapman—Saturday, 8 September 1888
Elizabeth Stride and Catherine Eddowes—
Sunday, 30 September 1888
Mary Jane Kelly—Friday, 9 November 1888

Though he certainly cannot have believed that the pen is mightier
than the sword, he seems to have been as prolific as a letter-writer
as he was extravagant as a murderer. Dr. Thomas Dutton, a
friend of the rippings-investigating Chief Inspector Frederick
Abberline, and a dab-hand at microphotography, examined 128
letters and postcards purporting to come from the killer himself,
and concluded that at least 34 were genuine. The correspondence
was addressed to the Central Press Agency, to the police, and
to individuals. (George Lusk, a member of the Whitechapel
Vigilance Committee, received a 'ginny' kidney by parcel-post;

with it was a note which read: 'Mr Lusk, sir, I send you half the kidne I took from one woman, prasarved it to you, tother piece I fried and ate it; was very nice.' Charming.)

Many—too many—identity-of-the-Ripper theories have been concocted, but none succeeds in fitting all the facts: indeed, few of the theorists, so-called Ripperologists, allow facts to interfere with their illogic. A random sample of 'culprits':

Joseph Barnett, a porter at Billingsgate fish-market who at one time lived with Mary Jane Kelly; *Prince Albert Victor, Duke of Clarence*; *Dr. Thomas Neill Cream*—or a doppel-gänger, since Cream appears to have been in an American prison when the murders were committed; *Frederick Bailey Deeming*, who murdered elsewhere— suspected simply because he, like Dr. Cream, is said to have waited till the executional noose was adjusted before starting to brag that he was the Ripper, only to have the pretentious sentence curtailed by the legal one; *Montague John Druitt*, a cricket-playing lawyer turned schoolmaster who committed suicide a month or so after the murder of Mary Jane Kelly; *Sir William Withey Gull*, physician-in-ordinary to Queen Victoria, and accomplices in the persons of *Sir Robert Anderson*, the head of the Criminal Investigation Department of the Metropolitan Police, and *John Netley*, who had been the Duke of Clarence's carriage-driver; '*Jill the Ripper*', a psychopathic midwife; *Severin Klosowski*, otherwise known as *George Chapman*, an inn-keeper who was hanged for triple-murder by poisoning in 1903; *Alexander Pedachenko*, also known as *Vassily Konovalov*, *Andrey Luiskovo* and *Mikhail Ostrong* (or *Ostrog*), a crazy Russian doctor working for the Okhrana, the Tsarist secret police; *Jack Pizer*, or *Kosminski* ('Leather Apron'), a syphilitic Polish Jew; an unnamed secretary of General William Booth, founder of the Salvation Army; an unnamed shochet, employed to slaughter animals by the Jewish ritual method; '*Dr. Stanley*', a Harley Street surgeon who was angry with all prostitutes because one of them had given his son VD; *James Kenneth Stephen*, a writer of parodies and doggerel (a few bits of which are rather bloodthirsty), and, incidentally, a relative of Virginia Woolf; the artist, *Walter Richard Sickert*—accused because (I promise you that this quotation is accurate:) 'none of the other [Ripper] candidates had his acquaintance with Hogarth'—the artist, not the same-named publishing firm founded by Virginia Woolf and her husband; a black magician named (with all sorts of variations) *Roslyn D'Onston Stephenson;'* L. *Forbes Winslow,* a crackpot psychiatrist. . . .

In a book called *Who He?* (1984), which the excellent publishers, Buchan & Enright, subtitled *Goodman's Dictionary of the Unknown Famous,* I included a spoof entry for the 'real' Jack the Ripper:

HARPICK, PETER J.
A transvestite sculptor, innovative in his use of Plasticine, whose mother Adascha Harpick, *neé* Schmidt, was a keen cricketer (collections of sport statistics, though not *Wisden,* record that she scored a half-century on behalf of a Women of Kent XI during a friendly match with The Ladies of South Kensington at Fontwell Park in 1860) and whose father Wally is said to have been descended from the Romanovs by way of a Brighton peer. In early manhood, after studying under Dr. Wilhelm Bunbury at the Chorlton-cum-Hardy Polytechnic, Harpick developed an obsession that his mother was a surrogate, standing in, as it were, for a woman of Whitechapel's unfortunate class who had actually borne him. In the autumn of 1888, he determined to put an end to all prostitutes in the area, and, being methodical, started off with those who were unfortunate enough to have an 'a' in their names. After doing away with some half-dozen, between times writing provocatively to the press, signing the messages with an anagram of his name, he became bored with the whole idea, and retired to south-east London, where he died in obscurity soon after publishing his monumental work, *Statues to be Observed in Penge and Its Environs: a Rambler's Guide* (1903), which was dedicated to 'my only true begetter, Mr W.H.' (his late father, of course).

I meant that to poke fun at the 'Hunt the Ripper' game: I assumed that all readers would understand that the name of my 'candidate' was an anagram of the alias, that the potted biography was a fiction—therefore, I was surprised to receive a letter from a Ripperologist, requesting further information about Peter J. Harpick, and I remain astonished that a dozen other people subsequently wrote me similar letters. I must say, I found it rather hard to compose polite replies. The fact that I, not intending to fool a single reader, fooled a number of them just goes to show how easy it is for Ripper writers who aim to deceive readers into accepting their particular candidates to achieve partial success: the simple trick is to put forward a few biographical truths that do not conflict with the notion that the candidate fills the bill, add some assumptions in the guise of truths, and omit—or think up a way of discounting—proof that the theory is nutty.

Early in 1988, the Ripper Centenary Year, the *Daily Telegraph* gave considerable publicity to a new hare-brained assertion that Jack had been identified. The paper published a letter of mine to the editor, pointing out objections to the theory, and ending: 'Let us agree that Jack the Ripper was Peter J. Harpick, and leave him at that.' And again I received tell-us-more-about-Harpick mail.

Later in the year, when the Centenary Celebrations were in full swing, I wrote this verse, which was published in the monthly *True Crime Detective*:

WHITECHAPEL BLUES

(To be ho-hummed to the tune of 'These Foolish Things'—or what you will.)

A hundred years since Ripping Jack—
Forgive me if I don't look back;
I'm tired of Clarence, Chapman, Druitt—
None of them had the nous to do it.
Another thing: we can't be sure
If there was one Jack, two, or more:
Copy-cat killings have been known
To be ascribed to one alone.
There's all the talk of 'Jill' as well—
Lily Langtry, Ethel M. Dell:
Maybe it *was* a fatal femme,
But frankly, I don't give a damn.
So far as I'm concerned, the rippin'
May all have been done by Dr. Crippen.
I know he wasn't even here; he
Was in the States. It's just a theory—

Along the lines of those I've heard
From Ripper buffs, and quite as absurd.
There you behold my boredom's root:
Hunt the Ripper is a trivialised pursuit.

Save for one salient fact, the following essay makes a better stab at unmasking the culprit than any of the seemingly serious attempts I have read—or rather, skipped through. And, unlike nearly all of those, it presents the 'evidence'—quotes and all—with entire honesty. As a bonus, it entertains.

CHARLES THE RIPPER . . . ?
Ivan Butler

[If he had been born, not in 1909, but a couple of years earlier, Ivan Butler might well have been among the first who learned that the fugitive Dr. Crippen and his mistress Ethel Le Neve were on board the S.S. Montrose—for the message to that effect from Captain Kendall was picked up by the wireless installation at the nautical training school at Heswall, near Liverpool, which Butler's father superintended. He spent most of his working life in the theatre, as actor, director and playwright; in the 1920s he was with Hamilton Deane's travelling repertory company, during which time Deane was presenting his original version of Bram Stoker's Dracula *(from which the Bela Lugosi movie was derived), and he played a part in the birth of the same manager's* Frankenstein *(written by Peggy Webling), which was influential in the making of the Boris Karloff movie. Since his retirement from active work in the theatre, he has written more than a dozen books, most of them on cinematic subjects, but including the original, and still best, 'murder gazeteers',* Murderers' London *and* Murderers' England; *he also edited the* Brian Donald Hume *volume in the 'Celebrated Trials' series.]*

I RECENTLY COMPLETED a study of the life and crimes of Jack the Ripper, the main purpose of which was to set the murders against the background of their surroundings and contemporary events. I had no intention of putting forward yet another 'solution' as to his identity: enough, I thought, was enough.

To create a pleasant and accurate picture of the ordinary daily life of the period, I decided to make use of the Diary of that industrious and respectable Everyman, Mr. Charles Pooter, the first entry of which appeared in the pages of *Punch* on 7 July 1888, coinciding closely (by a lucky chance, as I thought) with the start of the murders.[1] On reading through the Diary to see what the author was up to in his quiet way during the Autumn of Terror, I was disappointed to find that a large section had been 'wilfully torn out' by an unknown hand. It took some time for the true significance of this to dawn on me: when realisation came, it came like a thunderbolt. The missing pages covered the period, 30 August to 29 October—the months of September and October 1888! During that very period—when no record could be found of Mr. Pooter's activities—occurred the murders of Mary Ann Nicholls, Annie Chapman, Elizabeth Stride and Catherine Eddowes—four crimes definitely attributed to the Ripper.

With a hand that, I admit, trembled slightly, I looked up an earlier date—6 August. The body of Martha Turner, thought by many to be the first Ripper victim, was found early on the 7th. 6 August, I discovered, brought Mr. Pooter a terrible shock. His son Lupin, to whom he was devoted but whose irresponsible behaviour had been causing him great concern, was staying with his parents in their new house. On the morning of the 6th, the young man lay in bed and refused to come downstairs until a quarter to three, despite repeated summoning. He then announced to his appalled father, 'Look here, Guv'nor, it's no use beating about the bush. I've tendered my resignation at the Bank'.

---

[1] The *Punch* entries, with others, were subsequently published as a book, *The Diary of a Nobody* (of which there have been many editions). The *Diary* was written on behalf of Mr. Pooter by George and Weedon Grossmith. The former, who died in 1912, was a prolific writer of sketches and songs, and a star of Gilbert & Sullivan operas. The latter, who died in 1919, was a popular comedy-actor and a playwright; as well as sharing in the writing of the *Diary*, he did the drawings.

Let Mr. Pooter continue in his own words. 'For a moment I could not speak. When my speech came again, I said: "How dare you, sir? How dare you take such a serious step without consulting me? Don't answer me, sir!—you will sit down immediately and write a note at my dictation, withdrawing your resignation and amply apologising for your thoughtlessness." Imagine my dismay when he replied with a loud guffaw: "It's no use. If you want the good old truth, I've got the chuck!"'

Such a calamity was enough to push any father over the edge, let alone so scrupulous a parent as Pooter. The entry for the following day is extremely brief, as if he was completely exhausted. He says he persuaded his employer to allow him to postpone his holiday at Broadstairs for a week because the usual rooms were not available. A more probable reason (in the light of what is to be revealed) is that he did not dare leave the safety of his home, The Laurels, in the North London borough of Holloway, until he had recovered from the previous night's activities. There is then a gap in The Diary of four days—as if the writer, suffering from delayed shock, felt unable (or too frightened) to put pen to paper.

By now I felt I was on a most sinister trail. I looked up the date for the murder of Emma Smith, a possible Ripper victim whose body was discovered on the morning of the previous 3 April. Pooter *started* his Diary, as published in book form, on that very day, having just moved into The Laurels. He spent (if he can be believed) an innocuous day, the only noteworthy point being his friend Mr. Gowing's remark that there was 'an infernal smell of paint'. Emma Smith is generally regarded as being outside the Ripper canon, but I was now convinced that I was on to something pretty ominous. Then, as if to clinch matters, I came across the entry for 29 April, when Mr. Pooter suffered an experience so horrifying as to unbalance a mind far steadier than his own. Devotees of the Diary (now to be so rudely awakened) will remember that it was on this day that, having shown 'strong symptoms of a cold,' he decided to have a bath 'as hot as I could bear it'. He continues: '. . . very hot, but very acceptable. I lay still for some time. On moving my hand above the surface of the water, I experienced the greatest fright I ever received in the whole course of my life; for imagine my horror on discovering my hand, as I thought, full of blood.' And not only his hand. On stepping out of the bath, he found he was 'perfectly red all over, resembling the Red Indians I have seen depicted at an East End theatre'. (Note that he was familiar with the East End.) The unfortunate man had completely forgotten that a few days previously he had painted the entire bath red—an odd thing to do, in itself.

The whole, dreadful picture was now clear. Mr. Pooter, a typical convention-bound, frustrated, over-genteel product of his times, had taken a step up the ladder of respectability by moving into his new house. That respectability meant everything to him. Beneath that apparently fastidious exterior, however, seethed a monstrous madness. Close scrutiny of the Diary, with eyes opened by this appalling realisation, reveals a dozen details of aberrant behaviour. Take, as only one example, his insane obsession with enamel paint. In three days he painted, in addition to the bath, the flower-pots, the servant's washstand, towel-horse and chest-of-drawers (the servant Sarah, according to her master, 'evinced no sign of pleasure'), the coal-skuttle, the backs of his *Shakespeare*, the fender, picture-frames, an old pair of boots, and his friend Gowing's walking-stick.

Here, at last, lies the truth. Pooter may well have murdered Emma Smith (though it is not essential to the theory) as a mark of disapproval of her calling, a sign of his final emancipation from the lower rungs of Society. Shortly afterwards, he had the appalling experience of finding himself marked—as he thought, literally—as a man of blood, totally immersed in it. This started to topple his already unsteady sanity, which then collapsed completely under the weight of Lupin's disgrace. On August Bank Holiday night, he creeps out of the Laurels unheard by his wife Carrie (who was obviously a heavy sleeper, for he remarks that the noise of the trains at the bottom of the garden never disturbed her), makes his way quickly through the three miles or so of deserted streets—perhaps indulging in a hansom for part of the way—to Whitechapel, and there kills poor Martha Turner. His blood-lust aroused, increasingly distracted by worry over Lupin and by such infuriating mysteries as finding a large brick flung into his geraniums, he starts on the orgy of September and October. Doubtless he confided veiled hints of his activities to the Diary—and then, realising they might incriminate him, tore out (note how, in his earlier reference to the incident, Mr.

Pooter carefully—perhaps subconsciously—avoids the use of the more graphic verb 'ripped') the whole two months, and tried to blame the charwoman for their disappearance by pretending he had found a torn piece of paper in the grate, and accusing her of using the pages to light the fire.

On 31 October the Diary proper recommences—practically the whole of the previous day's entry is given over to the 'loss' of the vital section. Significantly, the entries start with a piece of good news: a job has been found for 'our dear boy, Lupin'. Perhaps at last, Mr. Pooter hopes, things will quieten down—sanity will return. He even has the nerve to declare, the following day, that he would willingly give ten shillings to find out who 'tore' his Diary.

Worse, however, much worse, was in store. To his utter dismay, on 5 November, Lupin, 'without consulting us or anything', announced that he was engaged to a Miss Daisy Mutlar—a woman seemingly about eight years his senior.

Lupin said : " I'm engaged to be married."

On 8 November (a fatal date) Mr. Pooter met, not Daisy herself, but her younger brother, a 'gawky youth' who spent most of the evening playing tricks that 'sent Carrie into fits' and eventually took Lupin out with him—'to my utter disgust'— although it was well past midnight. The emotions surging through Mr. Pooter's mind can well be imagined. It was enough to drive even a reasonably sane man beyond the reach of moderation, and it was only too clear what followed. Mr. Pooter went after his son—to what dreadful dens of vice we do not know—keeping himself well hidden, and later, in a frenzy of despair, committed his climactic murder, that of the young prostitute Mary Jane Kelly, in the filthy Court off Commercial Street.

The Diary entry for the following day is extremely brief and non-committal. He dared not risk pretending to lose more pages from it: in fact, most significantly, the entry starts with a reference to the previous 'loss'.

The Miller's Court horror was in all probability Mr. Pooter's last effort. He had, in his own self-justifying mind, struck a blow against the fleshly temptations that might destroy his easily-led son, and played a small part in sustaining the pillars of respectable society. He had, at a deeper level of the subconscious, purged himself of his blood-bath. There were many troubles ahead, with Lupin and others, but he learned to live with them and—his Ripper days behind him—found a measure of peace, and even prosperity.

So there it is at last. If there is one definite fact among all the shifting mysteries of Jack the Ripper, it is that the murderer must have been an unnoticeable man—someone able to walk the East End streets without attracting attention. He was not the dark, looming, sinister figure of legend, or he would very quickly have been recognised and apprehended. He was, in fact, to all appearances, a Nobody.

THE BLOODTHIRSTY BUTLER
H.B. Irving

[The elder son of Henry, the first actor-knight, and himself a distinguished actor-manager (he was the original Admirable Crichton—and, incidentally, his wife, Dorothea Baird, was the original Trilby), he derived pleasure from studying, writing about, and discussing crimes—French ones being his favourites. By hosting a dinner-party, attended by other connoisseurs, at his London home in 1903, he unwittingly founded Our Society, sometimes called 'The Crimes Club', which presently dines at the Imperial Hotel, close to where he lived: 7 Gordon Place, Bloomsbury. He died at the age of forty-nine in 1919. (Five years before, his brother Laurence, also an actor-manager, had been drowned when The Empress of Ireland, on which he was travelling home after touring Canada in a play called Typhoon, was rammed by a collier in dense fog, and sank within a few minutes.) Hesketh Pearson comments that 'though both of the brothers were famous in their day, neither appears to have impressed the editor of The Dictionary of National Biography. In one of his biographical studies, Harry Irving complains that "the greatest and most naturally gifted criminal England has produced", Charles Peace, is omitted from that compilation, which includes many less remarkable law-breakers. The same fate has overtaken the Irving brothers, for both of whom space should have been found in the 1912–21 volume between the not more notable

*names of Elsie Maud Inglis, physician and surgeon, and
Henry Jackson, Regius Professor of Greek at Cambridge.']*

ON THE EVENING of 23 March 1905, Mr. William Munday, a
highly respected citizen of the town of Tooringa, in Queensland,
Australia, was walking to the neighbouring town of Toowong
to attend a Masonic gathering. It was about eight o'clock, the
moon shining brightly. Nearing Toowong, Mr. Munday saw
a middle-aged man, bearded and wearing a white overcoat,
step out into the moonlight from under the shadow of a tree.
As Mr. Munday advanced, the man in the white coat stood
directly in his way. 'Out with all you have, and quick about
it,' he said. Instead of complying with this peremptory summons,
Mr. Munday attempted to close with him. The man drew back
quickly, whipped out a revolver, fired, and made off as fast as
he could. The bullet, after passing through Mr. Munday's left
arm, had lodged in the stomach. The unfortunate gentleman was
taken to a neighbouring hospital, where, within a few hours, he
was dead.

In the meantime a vigorous search was made for his assailant.
Late the same night, Constable Hennessy, riding a bicycle, saw a
man in a white coat who seemed to answer to the description of
the assassin. He dismounted, walked up to him and asked him
for a match. The man put his hand inside his coat. 'What have
you got there?' asked the constable. 'I'll soon show you,' replied
the man in the white coat, suddenly producing a large revolver.
But Hennessy was too quick for him. Landing him one under the
jaw, he sent him to the ground and, after a sharp struggle, secured
him. Constable Hennessy little knew at the time that his capture
in Queensland of the man in the white coat was almost as notable
in the annals of crime as the affray at Blackheath, London, on
an autumn night in 1878, when Constable Robinson grappled
successfully, wounded as he was, with Charles Peace.

The man taken by Hennessy gave the name of James Wharton,
and as James Wharton he was hanged at Brisbane. But before his
death it was ascertained beyond doubt, though he never admitted
it, that Wharton was none other than one Robert Butler, whose
career as a criminal and whose natural wickedness may well
rank him with Charles Peace in the hierarchy of scoundrels. Like

Peace, Butler was, in the jargon of crime, a 'hatter', a 'lone hand', a solitary who conceived and executed his nefarious designs alone; like Peace, he supplemented an insignificant physique by a liberal employment of the revolver; like Peace, he was something of a musician (the day before his execution, he played hymns for half an hour on the prison organ); like Peace, he knew when to whine when it suited his purpose; and like Peace, though not with the same intensity, he could be an uncomfortably persistent lover when the fit was on him. Both men were cynics in their way, and viewed their fellow-men with a measure of contempt.

But there the parallel ends. Butler was an intellectual, inferior as a craftsman to Peace, the essentially practical, unread, naturally gifted artist. Butler was a man of books. He had been schoolmaster, journalist. He had studied the lives of great men, and, as a criminal, had devoted especial attention to those of Frederick the Great and Napoleon. Butler's defence in the Dunedin murder trial was a feat of skill quite beyond the power of Peace. Peace was a religious man after the fashion of the mediaeval tyrant; Butler an infidel. Peace, dragged into the light of a court of justice, cut a sorry figure; here Butler shone. Peace escaped a conviction for murder by letting another suffer in his place; Butler escaped a similar experience by the sheer ingenuity of his defence. Peace had the modesty and reticence of the sincere artist; Butler the loquacious vanity of the literary or forensic coxcomb. Lastly, and it is the supreme difference, Butler was a murderer by instinct and conviction; 'a man's life,' he said, 'is of no more importance than a dog's; Nature respects the one no more than the other, a volcanic eruption kills mice and men with the one hand. The divine command, "kill, kill and spare not," was intended not only for Joshua, but for men of all time; it is the example of our rulers, our Fredericks and Napoleons.'

Butler was of the true Prussian mould. 'In crime,' he would say, 'as in war, no half measures. Let us follow the example of our rulers whose orders in war run, "kill, burn and sink, and what you cannot carry away, destroy."' Here is the gospel of frightfulness applied almost prophetically to crime. To Butler, murder was a principle of warfare; to Peace, it was never more than a desperate resort or an act that was the outcome of ungovernable passion.

Ireland can claim the honour of Butler's birth. It took place at Kilkenny about 1845. At an early age, he left his native land for Australia, and commenced his professional career by being sentenced under the name of James Wilson —the same initials as those of James Wharton of Queensland—to twelve months' imprisonment for vagrancy. Of the sixteen years he passed in Victoria, he spent thirteen in prison, first for stealing, then in steady progression for highway robbery and burglary. Side by side with the practical and efficient education in crime furnished by the Victorian prisons of that day, Butler availed himself of the opportunity to educate his mind. It was during this period that he found inspiration and encouragement in the study of the lives of Frederick and Napoleon, besides acquiring a knowledge of music and shorthand.

When, in 1876, Butler quitted Australia for New Zealand, he was sufficiently accomplished to obtain employment as a schoolmaster.

At Cromwell, Otago, under the name of 'C. J. Donnely, Esq.,' Butler opened a 'Commercial and Preparatory Academy,' and in a prospectus that recalls Mr. Squeer's famous advertisement of Dotheboys Hall, announced that the programme of the Academy would include 'reading, taught as an art and upon the most approved principles of elocution, writing, arithmetic, Euclid, algebra, mensuration, trigonometry, bookkeeping, geography, grammar, spelling and dictation, composition, logic and debate, French, Latin, shorthand, history, music, and general lectures on astronomy, natural philosophy, geology, and other subjects'. The simpler principles of these branches of learning were to be 'rendered intelligible, and a firm foundation laid for the acquirement of future knowledge'. Unfortunately, a suspicion of theft on Butler's part cut short the fulfilment of this really splendid programme, and Butler left Cromwell hurriedly for the ampler field of Dunedin. There, less than a fortnight after his arrival, he was sentenced to four years' hard labour for several burglaries committed in and about that city.

On 18 February 1880, Butler was released from prison. With that consummate hypocrisy which was part of the man, he had contrived to enlist the sympathies of the Governor of the Dunedin Jail, who gave him, on his departure, a suit of clothes and a small sum of money. A detective of the name of Bain tried to find him employment. Butler wished to adopt a literary career. He acted as a reporter on the Dunedin *Evening Star*, and gave satisfaction to the editor of that newspaper. An attempt to do some original work, in the shape of 'Prison Sketches,' for another newspaper, was less successful. Bain had arranged for the publication of the articles in the *Sunday Advertiser*, but when the time came to deliver his manuscript, Butler failed to appear. Bain, whose duty it was to keep an eye on Butler, found him in the street looking wild and haggard. He said that he had found the work 'too much for his head,' that he had torn up what he had written, that he had nowhere to go, and had been to the end of the jetty with the intention of drowning himself. Bain replied somewhat caustically that he thought it a pity he had not done so, as nothing would have given him a greater joy than going to the end of the jetty and identifying his body. 'You speak very plainly,' said Butler. 'Yes, and what is more, I mean what I say,' replied Bain. Butler justified Bain's candour by saying that if he broke out again, he would be worse than the most savage tiger ever let loose on the community.

As a means of obviating such an outbreak, Butler suggested that, intellectual employment having failed, some form of manual labour should be found him. Bain complied with his request, and got him a job of levelling reclaimed ground in the neighbourhood of Dunedin. On Wednesday, 10 March, Butler started work, but after three hours of it relinquished the effort. Bain saw Butler again in Dunedin on the evening of Saturday, 13 March, and made an appointment to meet him at half-past eight that night. Butler did not keep the appointment. Bain searched the town for him, but he was nowhere to be found.

About the same time, Butler had some talk with another member of the Dunedin police force, Inspector Mallard. They discussed the crimes of Charles Peace and other notable artists of that kind. Butler remarked to Mallard how easy it would be to destroy all traces of a murder by fire, and asked the inspector whether if he woke up one morning to find some brutal murder had been committed, he would not put it down to him. 'No, Butler,' replied the inspector. 'The first thing I should do would be to look for suspicious circumstances—and most undoubtedly, if they pointed to you, you would be looked for.'

In the early morning of this Saturday, 13 March, the house of a Mr. Stamper, a solicitor of Dunedin, had been broken into, and some articles of value, among them a pair of opera glasses, stolen. The house had been set on fire, and burned to the ground. On the morning of the following day, Sunday the 14th, Dunedin was horrified by the discovery of a far more terrible crime, tigerish in its apparent ferocity. In a house in Cumberland Street, a young married couple and their little baby were cruelly murdered and an unsuccessful attempt made to fire the scene of the crime.

About half-past six on Sunday morning, a man of the name of Robb, a carpenter, on getting out of bed, noticed smoke coming from the house of a neighbour of his, Mr. J. M. Dewar, who occupied a small one-floored cottage standing by itself in Cumberland Street, a large and broad thoroughfare on the outskirts of the town. Dewar was a butcher by trade, a young man, some eighteen months married, and father of a baby girl. Robb, on seeing smoke coming from Dewar's house, woke his son, who was a member of the fire brigade. The latter got up, crossed the street, and, going round to the back door, which he found wide open, entered the house. As he went along the passage that separated the two front rooms, a bedroom and sitting-room, he called to the inmates to get up. He received no answer, but as he neared the bedroom he heard a 'gurgling' sound. Crawling on his hands and knees, he reached the bedroom door, and two feet inside it his right hand touched something. It was the body of a woman; she was still alive, but dying. Robb dragged her across the passage into the sitting-room. He got some water, and extinguished the fire in the bedroom. On the bed lay the body of Dewar. To all appearances, he had been killed in his sleep. By his side was the body of the baby, suffocated by the smoke. Near the bed was an axe belonging to Dewar, stained with blood. It was with this weapon, apparently, that Mr. and Mrs. Dewar had been attacked. Under the bed was a candlestick belonging also to the Dewars, which had been used by the murderer in setting fire to the bed. The front window of the sitting-room was open, there were marks of boot nails on the sill, and on the grass in front of the window a knife was found. An attempt had been made to ransack a chest of drawers in the bedroom, but some articles of jewellery lying in one of the drawers and a ring on the dressing-table had been left untouched. So far as was known, Mr. and Mrs. Dewar were a perfectly happy and united couple.

Dewar had last been seen alive about ten o'clock on the Saturday night, getting off a car near his home. At eleven, a neighbour had noticed a light in the Dewars' house. About five o'clock on the Sunday morning, another neighbour had been aroused from his sleep by the sound as of something falling heavily. It was a wild and boisterous night. Thinking the noise might be the slamming of his stable-door, he got up and went out to see that it was secure. He then noticed that a light was burning in the bedroom window of the Dewars' cottage.

Nothing more was known of what had occurred that morning until, at half-past six, Robb saw the smoke coming from the Dewars' house. Mrs. Dewar, who alone could have told something, never recovered consciousness and died on the day following the crime. Three considerable wounds sufficient to cause death had been inflicted on the unfortunate woman's head, and five of a similar character on that of her husband. At the top of the bed, which stood in the corner of the room, there was a large smear of blood on the wall; there were spots of blood all over the top of the bed, and some smaller ones that had, to all appearances, spurted on to the panel of the door nearest to the bed.

The investigation of this shocking crime was placed in the hands of Detective Bain, whose duty it had been to keep an eye on Robert Butler; but he did not at first associate his interesting charge with the commission of the murder. About half-past six on Sunday evening, Bain happened to go to a place called the Scotia Hotel, where the landlord informed him that one of his servants, a girl named Sarah Gillespie, was very anxious to see him.

Her story was this: On the morning of Thursday, 11 March, Robert Butler had come to the hotel; he was wearing a dark-lavender check suit and carrying a top-coat and a parcel. Butler had stayed in the hotel all Thursday, and slept there that night. He had not slept in the hotel on the Friday night, and Sarah Gillespie had not seen him again until he came into the house about five-and-twenty minutes to seven on Sunday morning. The girl noticed that he was pale and excited; he seemed worried and afraid, as if someone were coming after him. After giving her some money for the landlord, he went upstairs, fetched his top-coat, a muffler, and his parcel. Before leaving, he said he would have a pint of beer, as he had not breakfasted. He then left, presumably to catch an early train.

Butler was next seen a few minutes later at a shop near the hotel, where he bought five tins of salmon, and about the same time a milk-boy saw him standing on the kerb in Cumberland Street in a stooping position, his head turned in the direction of Dewar's house. A little after ten the same night, Butler entered an hotel at a place called Blueskin, some twelve miles from Dunedin. He was wearing an overcoat and a light muffler. He sat down at a table in the dining-room and seemed weary and sleepy. Someone standing at the bar said, 'What a shocking murder that was in Cumberland Street!' Butler started up, looked steadily from one to the other of the two men who happened to be in the room, then sat down again and, taking up a book, appeared to be reading. More than once he put down the book, and he kept shifting uneasily in his chair. After having some supper, he got up, paid his reckoning, and left the hotel.

At half-past three the following morning, about fifteen miles from Dunedin, on the road to Waikouaiti, two constables met a man whom they recognized as Butler from a description that had been circulated by the police. The constables arrested and searched him. They found on him a pair of opera glasses, the property of Mr. Stamper, whose house had been burgled and burned down on the morning of the 13th. Of this crime Butler acknowledged himself to be the perpetrator. Besides the opera glasses, the constables took from Butler two tins of salmon, a purse containing four shillings and sixpence, a pocket-knife, a box of matches, a piece of candle, and a revolver and cartridges. The prisoner was carrying a top-coat, and was dressed in a dark coat and grey trousers, underneath which he was wearing a white shirt, an under-flannel and a Rob Roy Crimean shirt. One of the constables noticed that there were marks of blood on his shirt. Another singular feature in Butler's attire was the fact that the outer soles of his boots had been recently removed. When last seen in Dunedin, Butler had been wearing a moustache; he was now clean-shaven.

The same evening, a remarkable interview took place in the lock-up at Waikouaiti between Butler and Inspector Mallard. Mallard, who had some reason for suspecting Butler, bearing in mind their recent conversation, told the prisoner that he would be charged with the murder in Cumberland Street. For a few seconds, according to Mallard, the prisoner seemed terribly agitated and appeared to be choking. Recovering himself somewhat, he said, 'If for that, you can get no evidence against me; and if I am hanged for it, I shall be an innocent man, whatever other crimes I may have committed.' Mallard replied, 'There is evidence to convict you—the fire was put out.' Butler then said that he would ask Mallard a question; but, after a pause, decided not to do so. Mallard, after examining Butler's clothes, told him that those were not the clothes in which he had left the Scotia Hotel. Butler admitted it, and said he had thrown those away in the North East Valley. Mallard alluded to the disappearance of the prisoner's moustache. Butler replied that he had cut it off on the road. Mallard noticed then the backs of Butler's hands were scratched, as if by contact with bushes. Butler seemed often on the point of asking questions, but would then stop and say, 'No, I won't ask you anything.' To the constables who had arrested him, Butler remarked, 'You ought to remember me, because I could have shot you if I had wished.' When Mallard later in the evening visited Butler again, the prisoner, who was then lying down, said, 'I want to speak to you. I want to ask the Press not to publish my career. Give me fair play. I suppose I shall be convicted, and you will see I can die like a man.'

A few days after Butler's arrest, a ranger on the Town Belt, a hill overlooking Dunedin, found a coat, a hat and a silk-striped cravat, and a few days later a pair of trousers folded up and placed under a bush. These articles of clothing were identified as those which Butler had been seen wearing on the Saturday and the Sunday morning. There were a number of blood-stains on them, not one of them larger in size than a pea, some almost invisible. On the front of the trousers, about the level of the groin, there were blood-spots on both sides. There was blood on the fold of the left breast of the coat and on the lining of the cuff of the right arm. The shirt Butler was wearing at the time of his arrest was examined also. There were small spots of blood, about fourteen altogether, on the neck and shoulder-bands, the right armpit, the left sleeve, and on both wristbands. Besides the clothes, a salmon tin was found on the Town Belt, and behind a seat in the Botanical Gardens, from which a partial view of the Dewars' house in Cumberland Street could be obtained, two more salmon tins were found; all three were similar to the five purchased by Butler on the Sunday morning, two of which had been in his possession at the time of the arrest.

Such were the main facts of the case which Butler had to answer when, a few weeks later, he was put on his trial before the Supreme Court at Dunedin. The presiding judge was Mr. Justice Williams, afterwards Sir Joshua Williams and a member of the Privy Council. The Crown Prosecutor, Mr. Haggitt, conducted the case for the Crown, and Butler defended himself.

To a man of Butler's egregious vanity, his trial was a glorious opportunity for displaying his intellectual gifts, such as they were. One who had known him in prison about this time describes him as a strange compound of vanity and envy, blind to his own faults and envious of the material advantages enjoyed by others. Self-willed and arrogant, he could bully or whine with equal effect. Despising men, he believed that if a man did not possess some requisite quality, he had only to ape it, as few would distinguish between the real and the sham.

But with all these advantages in the struggle for life, it is certain that Butler's defence would have been far less effective had he been denied all professional aid. As a matter of fact, throughout his trial Butler was being advised by three distinguished members of the New Zealand bar, now judges of the Supreme Court, who, though not appearing for him in court, gave him the full benefit of their assistance outside it. At the same time, Butler carried off the thing well. Where imagination was required, Butler broke down; he could not write sketches of life in prison; that was too much for his pedestrian intellect. But given the facts of a case, dealing with a transaction of which he alone knew the real truth, and aided by the advice and guidance of trained intellects, Butler was unquestionably clever and shrewd enough to make the best use of such advantages in meeting the case against him.

Thus equipped for the coming struggle, this high-browed ruffian, with his semi-intellectual cast of countenance, his jerky, restless posturing, his splay-footed waddle—'like a lame Muscovy duck,' in the graphic words of his gaol companion—stood up to plead for his life before the Supreme Court at Dunedin.

It may be said at the outset that Butler profited greatly by the scrupulous fairness shown by the Crown Prosecutor. Mr. Haggitt

extended to the prisoner a degree of consideration and forbearance, justified undoubtedly towards an undefended prisoner.
But, as we have seen, Butler was not in reality undefended. At
every moment of the trial he was in communication with his
legal advisers, and was being instructed by them how to meet
the evidence given against him. Under these circumstances, the
unfailing consideration shown him by the Crown Prosecutor
seems almost excessive. From the first moment of the trial, Butler
was fully alive to the necessities of his situation. He refrained
from including in his challenges of the jury the gentleman who
was afterwards foreman; he knew he was all right, he said,
because he parted his hair in the middle—a 'softy,' in fact.
He did not know, in all probability, that one gentleman on the
jury had a rooted conviction that the murder of the Dewars was
the work of a criminal lunatic. There was certainly nothing in
Butler's demeanour or behaviour to suggest homicidal mania.

The case against Butler rested on purely circumstantial evidence. No new facts of importance were adduced at the trial. The
stealing of Dewar's wages, which had been paid to him on the
Saturday, was the motive for the murder suggested by the Crown.
The chief facts pointing to Butler's guilt were: his conversation
with Mallard and Bain previous to the crime; his demeanour after
it; his departure from Dunedin; the removal of his moustache and
the soles of his boots; his change of clothes, and the bloodstains
found upon them—added to which was his apparent inability to
account for his movements on the night in question.

Such as the evidence was, Butler did little to shake it in cross-
examination. Many of his questions were skilful and pointed,
but on more than one occasion the judge intervened to save him
from the danger common to all amateur cross-examiners: of not
knowing when to stop. He was most successful in dealing with
the medical witnesses. Butler had explained the bloodstains on
his clothes as smears that had come from scratches on his hands
caused by contact with bushes. This explanation the medical
gentlemen with good reason rejected. But they went further,
and said that these stains might well have been caused by
the spurting and spraying of blood on to the murderer as he
struck his victims. Butler was able to show by the position of
the bloodstains on the clothes that such an explanation was open
to considerable doubt.

Butler's speech in his defence lasted six hours, and was a creditable performance. Its arrangement is somewhat confused and repetitious, some points are over-elaborated, but on the whole he deals very successfully with most of the evidence given against him, and exposes the unquestionable weakness of the Crown case. At the outset, he declared that he had taken his innocence for his defence. 'I was not willing,' he said, 'to leave my life in the hands of a stranger. I was willing to incur all the disadvantages which the knowledge of the law might bring upon me. I was willing, also, to enter on this case without any experience whatever of that peculiarly acquired art of cross-examination. I fear I have done wrong. If I had had the assistance of able counsel, much more light would have been thrown on this case than has been.' As we have seen, Butler enjoyed throughout his trial the informal assistance of three of the most able counsel in New Zealand, so that this heroic attitude of conscious innocence braving all dangers loses most of its force. Without such assistance, his danger might have been very real.

A great deal of the evidence as to his conduct and demeanour at the time of the murder Butler met by acknowledging that it was he who had broken into Mr. Stamper's house on the Saturday morning, burgled it, and set it on fire. His consciousness of guilt in this respect was, he said, quite sufficient to account for anything strange or furtive in his manner at that time. He was already known to the police; meeting Bain on the Saturday night, he felt more than ever sure that he was suspected of the robbery at Mr. Stamper's; he therefore decided to leave Dunedin as soon as possible. That night, he said, he spent wandering about the streets half-drunk, taking occasional shelter from the pouring rain, until six o'clock on the Sunday morning, when he went to the Scotia Hotel. A more detailed account of his movements on the night of the Dewars' murder he did not, or would not, give.

When he comes to the facts of the murder and his theories as to the nature and motive of the crime—theories which he developed at rather unnecessary length for the purpose of his own defence—his speech is interesting. It will be recollected that on the discovery of the murder, a knife was found on the grass outside the house. This knife was not the property of the Dewars. In Butler's speech, he emphasized the opinion that this knife had been brought there by the murderer: 'Horrible though it may be, my conclusion is that he brought it with the intention of cutting the throats of his victims, and that, finding they lay in rather an untoward position, he changed his mind, and, having carried out the object with which he entered the house, left the knife and, going back, brought the axe with which he effected his purpose. What was the purpose of the murderer? Was it the robbery of Dewar's paltry wages? Was it the act of a tiger broken loose on the community? an act of pure wanton devilry? or was there some more reasonable explanation of this most atrocious crime?'

Butler rejected altogether the theory of ordinary theft. No thief of ambitious views, he said, would pitch upon the house of a poor journeyman butcher. The killing of the family appeared to him to be the motive: 'an enemy hath done this.' The murderer seems to have had a knowledge of the premises; he enters the house and does his work swiftly and promptly, and is gone. 'We cannot know,' Butler continues, 'all the passages in the lives of the murdered man or woman. What can we know of the hundred spites and jealousies or other causes of malice which might have caused the crime? If you say some obscure quarrel, some spite or jealousy, is not likely to have been the cause of so dreadful a murder, you cannot revert to the robbery theory without admitting a motive much weaker in all its ruthless, unrelenting, determined vindictiveness. Every blow seemed to say, "You shall die—you shall not live."'

Whether Butler were the murderer of the Dewars or not, the theory that represented them as having been killed for the purpose of robbery has its weak side—all the weaker if Butler, a practical and ambitious criminal, were the guilty man.

In 1882, two years after Butler's trial, there appeared in a New Zealand newspaper, Society, published in Christchurch, a series of 'Prison Portraits,' written evidently by one who had himself undergone a term of imprisonment. One of the 'Portraits' was devoted to an account of Butler. The writer had known Butler in prison. According to the story told him by Butler, the latter had arrived in Dunedin with a quantity of jewellery he had stolen in Australia. This jewellery he entrusted to a young woman for safe-keeping. After serving his first term of two years' imprisonment in Dunedin, Butler found on his release that the young woman had married a man of the name of

Dewar. Butler went to Mrs. Dewar and asked for the return
of his jewellery; she refused to give it up. On the night of the
murder, he called at the house in Cumberland Street and made a
last appeal to her, but in vain. He determined on revenge. During
his visit to Mrs. Dewar, he had had an opportunity of seeing the
axe and observing the best way to break into the house. He
watched the husband's return, and decided to kill him as well
as his wife on the chance of obtaining his week's wages. With
the help of the knife which he had found in the backyard of an
hotel, he opened the window. The husband he killed in his sleep;
the woman waked with the first blow he struck her. He found
the jewellery in a drawer, rolled up in a pair of stockings. He
afterwards hid it in a well-marked spot some half-hour before
his arrest.

A few years after its appearance in *Society*, this account of
Butler was reproduced in an Auckland newspaper. Bain, the
detective, wrote a letter questioning the truth of the writer's
statements. He pointed out that when Butler first came to
Dunedin, he had been at liberty only a fortnight before serving
his first term of imprisonment, very little time in which to make
the acquaintance of a woman and dispose of the stolen jewellery.
He asked why, if Butler had hidden the jewellery just before his
arrest, he had not also hidden the opera-glasses which he had
stolen from Mr. Stamper's house. Neither of these comments is
very convincing. A fortnight seems time enough in which a man
of Butler's character might get to know a woman and dispose of
some jewellery; while, if Butler were the murderer of Mr. Dewar
as well as the burglar who had broken into Stamper's house, it
was part of his plan to acknowledge himself guilty of the latter
crime and use it to justify his movements before and after the
murder. Bain is more convincing when he states at the conclusion
of his letter that he had known Mrs. Dewar from childhood as a
'thoroughly good and true woman,' who, so far as he knew, had
never in her life had an acquaintance with Butler.

At the same time, the account given by Butler's fellow-prisoner,
in which the conduct of the murdered woman is represented as
constituting the provocation for the subsequent crime, explains
one peculiar circumstance in connection with the tragedy: the
selection of this journeyman butcher and his wife as the victims
of the murderer. It explains the theory, urged so persistently by

Butler in his speech to the jury, that the crime was the work of an enemy of the Dewars, the outcome of some hidden spite or obscure quarrel; it explains the apparent ferocity of the murder, and the improbability of a practical thief selecting such an unprofitable couple as his prey. The rummaged chest of drawers and the fact that some trifling articles of jewellery were left untouched on the top of them are consistent with an eager search by the murderer for some particular object. Against this theory of revenge is the fact that Butler was a malignant ruffian and liar in any case: that, having realized very little cash by the burglary at Stamper's house, he would not be particular as to where he might get a few shillings more: that he had threatened to do a tigerish deed, and that it is characteristic of his vanity to try to impute to his crime a higher motive than mere greed or necessity.

Butler showed himself not averse to speaking of the murder in Cumberland Street to at least one of those with whom he came in contact in his later years. After he had left New Zealand and returned to Australia, he was walking in a street in Melbourne with a friend when they passed a lady dressed in black, carrying a baby in her arms. The baby looked at the two men and laughed. Butler frowned and walked rapidly away. His companion chaffed him, and asked whether it was the widow or the baby that he was afraid of. Butler was silent, but after a time asked his companion to come into some gardens and sit down on one of the seats, as he had something serious to say to him.

For a while, Butler sat silent. Then he asked the other if he had been in Dunedin. 'Yes,' was the reply. 'Look here,' said Butler, 'you are the only man I ever made any kind of confidant of. You are a good scholar, though I could teach you a lot.' After this gracious compliment, he went on: 'I was once tried in Dunedin on the charge of killing a man, woman and child, and, although innocent, the crime was nearly brought home to me. It was my own ability that pulled me through. Had I employed a professional advocate, I should not have been here today talking to you.' After describing the murder, Butler said: 'Trying to fire the house was unnecessary, and killing the baby was unnecessary and cruel. I respect no man's life, for no man respects mine. A lot of men I have never injured have tried to put a rope round my neck more than once. I hate society in general, and one or two individuals in particular. The man who did that murder in Dunedin has, if anything, my sympathy, but it seems to me he need not have killed that child.' His companion was about to speak. Butler stopped him. 'Now, don't ever ask me such a silly question as that,' he said. 'What?' asked his friend. 'You were about to ask me if I did that deed,' replied Butler, 'and you know perfectly well that, guilty or innocent, that question would only be answered one way.' 'I was about to ask nothing of the kind,' said the other, 'for you have already told me that you were innocent.' 'Good!' said Butler, 'then let that be the end of the subject, and never refer to it again—except, perhaps, in your own mind, when you can, if you like, remember that I said the killing of the child was unnecessary and cruel.'

Having developed to the jury his theory of why the crime was committed, Butler told them that, so far as he was concerned, there were four points against him on which the Crown relied to prove his guilt.

Firstly, there was the fact of his being in the neighbourhood of the crime on the Sunday morning; that, he said, applied to scores of other people besides himself.

Then there was his alleged disturbed appearance and guilty demeanour. The evidence of that was, he contended, doubtful in any case, and referable to another cause; as also his leaving Dunedin in the way and at the time he did. He scouted the idea that murderers are compelled by some invisible force to betray their guilt. 'The doings of men,' he urged, 'and their success are regulated by the amount of judgment that they possess, and, without impugning or denying the existence of Providence, I say this is a law that holds good in all cases, whether for evil or for good. Murderers, if they have the sense and ability and discretion to cover up their crime, will escape, do escape, and have escaped. Many people, when they have gravely shaken their heads and said "Murder will out," consider they have done a great deal and gone a long way towards settling the question. Well, this, like many other stock formulas of Old World wisdom, is not true. How many murders are there that the world has never heard of, and never will? How many a murdered man, for instance, lies among the gum-trees of Victoria, or in the old abandoned mining-shafts on the diggings, who is missed by nobody, perhaps, but a pining wife at home, or helpless children, or an old mother?

But who were their murderers? Where are they? God knows, perhaps—but nobody else ever will.' The fact, he said, that he was alleged to have walked up Cumberland Street on the Sunday morning and looked in the direction of the Dewars' house was, unless the causes of superstition and a vague and incomplete reasoning were to be accepted as proof, evidence rather of his innocence than of his guilt.

He had removed the soles of his boots, he said, in order to ease his feet in walking; the outer soles had become worn and ragged, and in lumps under his feet. He denied that he had told Bain, the detective, that he would break out as a desperate tiger let loose on the community; what he had said was that he was tired of living the life of a prairie dog or a tiger in the jungle.

Butler was more successful when he came to deal with the bloodstains on his clothes. These, he said, were caused by the blood from the scratches on his hands, which had been observed at the time of his arrest. The doctors had rejected this theory, and said that the spots of blood had been impelled from the axe or from the heads of the victims as the murderer struck the fatal blow. Butler put on the clothes in court, and was successful in showing that the position and appearance of certain of the blood-spots were not compatible with such a theory. 'I think,' he said, 'I am fairly warranted in saying that the evidence of these gentlemen is, not to put too fine a point on it, worth just nothing at all.'

Butler's concluding words to the jury were brief but emphatic: 'I stand in a terrible position. So do you. See that, in your way of disposing of me, you deliver yourselves of your responsibilities.'

In the exercise of his forbearance towards an undefended prisoner, Mr. Haggitt did not address the jury for the Crown.

At four o'clock, the judge commenced his summing-up. Mr. Justice Williams impressed on the jury that they must be satisfied, before they could convict the prisoner, that the circumstances of the crime and the prisoner's conduct were inconsistent with any other reasonable hypothesis than his guilt. There was little or no evidence that robbery was the motive of the crime. The circumstance of the prisoner being out all Saturday night and in the neighbourhood of the crime on Sunday morning only amounted to the fact that he had an opportunity shared by a great number of other persons of committing the murder. The evidence of his agitation and demeanour at the time of his arrest must be accepted with caution. The evidence of the blood-spots was of crucial importance; there was nothing save this to connect him directly with the crime. The jury must be satisfied that the blood on the clothes corresponded with the blood-marks which, in all probability, would be found on the person who committed the murder. In regard to the medical testimony, some caution must be exercised. Where medical gentlemen had made observations, seen with their own eyes, the direct inference might be highly trustworthy; but when they proceeded to draw further inferences, they might be in danger of looking at facts through the spectacles of theory; 'we know that people do that in other things besides science—politics, religion, and so forth.' Taking the Crown evidence, at its strongest, there was a missing link; did the evidence of the bloodstains supply it? These bloodstains were almost invisible. Could a person be reasonably asked to explain how they came where they did? Could they be accounted for in no other reasonable way than that the clothes had been worn by the Murderer of the Dewars?

The summing-up was distinctly favourable to the prisoner, and after three hours' deliberation the jury returned a verdict of Not Guilty.

Later in the session, Butler pleaded Guilty to the burglary at Mr. Stamper's house, and was sentenced to eighteen years' imprisonment. The severity of this sentence was not, the judge said, intended to mark the strong suspicion under which Butler laboured of being a murderer as well as a burglar.

The ends of justice had been served by Butler's acquittal. But in the light of after-events, it is perhaps unfortunate that the jury did not stretch a point and so save the life of Mr. Munday of Toowong. Butler underwent his term of imprisonment in Lyttleton Jail. There his reputation was unenviable. He was described by a fellow-prisoner as ill-tempered, malicious, destructive, but cowardly and treacherous. He seems to have done little or no work; he looked after the choir and the library, but was not above breaking up the one and smashing the other, if the fit seized him.

In 1896, Butler was released from prison. The news of his release was described as falling like a bomb-shell among the peaceful inhabitants of Dunedin. In the colony of Victoria, where Butler had commenced his career, it was received with an apprehension that was justified by subsequent events. It was believed that, on his release, the New Zealand authorities had shipped Butler off to Rio. But it was not long before he made his way once more to Australia.

From the moment of his arrival in Melbourne, he was shadowed by the police. One or two mysterious occurrences soon led to his arrest. On 5 June he was sentenced to twelve months' imprisonment under the Criminal Influx Act, which made it a penal offence for any convict to enter Victoria for three years after his release from prison. Not content with this, the authorities determined to put Butler on trial on two charges of burglary and one of highway robbery, committed since his return to the colony. To one charge of burglary, that of breaking into a hairdresser's shop and stealing a wig, some razors and a little money, Butler pleaded Guilty.

But the charge of highway robbery (which bore a singular resemblance to the final catastrophe in Queensland), he resisted to the utmost, and showed that his experience in the Supreme Court at Dunedin had not been lost on him. At half-past six one evening, in a suburb of Melbourne, an elderly gentleman found himself confronted by a bearded man, wearing a long overcoat and a boxer hat, and flourishing a revolver, who told him abruptly to 'turn out his pockets'. The old man did as he was told. The robber then asked for his watch and chain, saying: 'Business must be done.' The old gentleman afterwards identified Butler as the man who had taken his watch. Another elderly man swore that he had seen Butler soon after the robbery in possession of a fine gold watch, which he said had been sent him from home. But the watch had not been found in Butler's possession.

On 18 June, he was put on trial in the Melbourne Criminal Court before Mr. Justice Holroyd, charged with robbery under arms. His appearance in the dock aroused very considerable interest. 'It was the general verdict,' wrote one newspaper, 'that his intellectual head and forehead compared not unfavourably with those of the judge.' He was decently dressed and wore pince-nez, which he used in the best professional manner as he referred to the various documents that lay in front of him.

He went into the witness-box and stated that he had spent

the evening of the crime, according to his custom, in the Public Library. For an hour and a half he addressed the jury. He disputed the possibility of his identification by his alleged victim—'an old gentleman of sedentary pursuits, and not cast in the heroic mould'. Such a man would be naturally alarmed and confused at meeting suddenly an armed robber. Now, under these circumstances, could this recognition of a man whose face was hidden by a beard, his head by a boxer-hat, and his body by a long overcoat, be considered trustworthy? And such recognition occurring in the course of a chance encounter in the darkness, that fruitful mother of error? The elderly gentleman had described his moustache as a slight one, but the jury could see that it was full and overhanging. He complained that he had been put up for identification singly—not with other men, according to the usual custom. The police had said to the victim: 'We have here a man that we think robbed you, and, if he is not the man, we shall be disappointed,' to which the victim had replied: 'Yes, and if he is not the man, I shall be disappointed too.' For the elderly person who had stated that he had seen a gold watch in Butler's possession, the latter had nothing but scorn: he was a 'lean and slippered pantaloon in Shakespeare's last stage'—and he, Butler, would have been a lunatic to confide in such a man.

The jury acquitted Butler, adding as a rider to their verdict that there was not sufficient evidence of identification. The third charge against Butler was not proceeded with. He was put up to receive sentence for the burglary at the hair-dresser's shop. Butler handed the judge a written statement which Mr. Justice Holroyd described as a narrative that might have been taken from those sensational newspapers written for nursery-maids, and from which, he said, he could not find that Butler had ever done one good thing in the whole of his life.

Of that life of fifty years, Butler had spent thirty-five in prison. The judge expressed his regret that a man of Butler's knowledge, information, vanity, and utter recklessness of what evil will do, could not be put away somewhere for the rest of his life, and sentenced him to fifteen years' imprisonment with hard labour.

'An iniquitous and brutal sentence!' exclaimed the prisoner. After a brief altercation with the judge, who said that he could hardly express the scorn he felt for him, Butler was removed. The judge subsequently reduced the sentence to one of ten years.

Chance or destiny would seem implacable in their pursuit of Mr. William Munday of Toowong.

After his trial, Butler admitted that it was he who had robbed the old gentleman of his watch, and described to the police the house in which it was hidden. When the police went there to search, they found that the house had been pulled down; but among the debris they discovered a brown-paper parcel containing the old gentleman's gold watch and chain, a five-chambered revolver, a keen-edged butcher's knife, and a mask.

Butler served his term of imprisonment in Victoria—'an unmitigated nuisance' to his custodians. On his release in 1904, he made, as in Dunedin, an attempt to earn a living by his pen. He contributed some articles to a Melbourne evening paper on the inconveniences of prison discipline, but he was quite unfitted for any sustained effort as a journalist. According to his own account, with the little money he had left he made his way to Sydney, thence to Brisbane. He was half-starved, bewildered, despairing; in his own words, 'if a psychological camera could have been turned on me, it would have shown me like a bird fascinated by a serpent, fascinated and bewildered by the fate in front, behind, and around me'. Months of suffering and privation passed, months of tramping hundreds of miles, months of hunger and sickness; 'my actions had become those of a fool; my mind and will had become a remnant guided or misguided by unreasoning impulse.'

It was under the influence of such an impulse that on 23 March Butler had met and shot Mr. Munday at Toowong. On 24 May he was arraigned at Brisbane before the Supreme Court of Queensland. But the Butler who stood in the dock of the Brisbane Criminal Court was very different from the Butler who had successfully defended himself at Dunedin and Melbourne. The spirit had gone out of him; it was rather as a suppliant, represented by counsel, that he faced the charge of murder. His attitude was one of humble and appropriate penitence. In a weak and nervous voice, he told the story of his hardships since his release from his Victorian prison; he would only urge that the shooting of Mr. Munday was accidental, caused by Munday picking up a stone and attacking him. When about to be sentenced to death he expressed great sorrow and contrition for his crime, for the poor wife and children of his unfortunate victim. His life, he said, was a poor thing, but he would gladly give it fifty times over.

The sentence of death was confirmed by the Executive on 30 June. To a Freethought advocate who visited him shortly before his execution, Butler wrote a final confession of faith: 'I shall have to find my way across the habour-bar without the aid of any pilot. In these matters I have for many years carried an exempt flag, and, as it has not been carried through caprice or ignorance, I am compelled to carry it to the last. There is an impassable bar of what I honestly believe to be the inexorable logic of philosophy and facts, history and experience of the nature of the world, the human race and myself, between em and the views of the communion of any religious organisation. So instead of the "depart Christian soul" of the priest, I only hope for the comfort and satisfaction of the last friendly goodbye of anyone who cares to give it.'

From this positive affirmation of unbelief, Butler wilted somewhat at the approach of death. The day before his execution, he spent half an hour playing hymns on the chapel-organ in the prison; and on the scaffold, where his agitation rendered him almost speechless, he expressed his sorrow for what he had done, and the hope that, if there were a heaven, mercy would be shown him.

MAJOR ARMSTRONG,
MASTER OF ARTS
Robin Odell

[*He began working in the true-crime genre in the 1960s, with an examination of the Whitechapel Murders; unusually, he sought to establish the occupation rather than the identity of the Ripper. His book* Exhumation of a Murder *(1975), about the Armstrong case, was described by one reviewer, C.P. Snow, as 'perhaps the most thorough investigation that has ever been devoted to any of the classical murders'. There followed a partnership with Joe Gaute, the late crime-bibliophile, which produced a trilogy of excellent reference works:* The Murderers' Who's Who *(which won an 'Edgar' from the Mystery Writers of America),* Murder Whatdunit *and* Murder Whereabouts. *Since then, and following a further foray into Ripperland, Robin Odell has concentrated on post-war cases: he and Christopher Berry Dee are the authors of* Dad, Help Me, Please *(1990), in which they tell the story of Craig and Bentley, and argue for an official pardon for the latter on the ground that he was hanged for a murder that was committed by Craig; and their second collaboration,* A Question of Evidence, *about the 'Babes in the Woods' murders at Brighton, has just been published.*]

THE LAST DAY of December 1921 was bitingly cold. In the little market-town of Hay-on-Wye, on the England/Wales border, there was a hint of snow to come as Herbert Rowse Armstrong began the walk from his home to his office.

Armstrong was a solicitor; a retired Army-officer with the rank of major. He was a Master of Arts and held the Territorial Decoration. Nature had created this man in a small mould. At the mature age of fifty-one, he weighed 7 stone and stood 5 feet 6 inches tall. His features were also small. His passport description read: '. . . nose, *small*; chin, *small*; mouth, *small* . . .' He sported a heavy, waxed moustache, and his intensely blue eyes surveyed the world through gold-rimmed spectacles.

He carried himself very upright, with his back straight as a ramrod. His military appearance on this particular day was enhanced by the clothes he was wearing—breeches, trench boots, and an Army officer's British-warm overcoat. He was every bit a pocket-soldier.

He could not realise it then, but that morning was his last as a free man. Within hours, he was under arrest, and the secret crimes of one of Hay's most respected citizens were laid bare.

Armstrong went to Hay in 1906, having been up at Cambridge, later qualifying as a solicitor. He began his professional career in Liverpool and then worked in the West of England, where he met Katharine Friend, his wife-to-be. He saw prospects at Hay, where he took a position as managing clerk to one of the town's old-established solicitors.

The following year, he married Katharine Friend, and shortly afterwards he was made a full partner in the firm of solicitors. The Armstrongs moved to a house in the fashionable area of Cusop, just outside Hay. Their new home was called 'Mayfield'. It was a fine-looking house, set back from the road and approached by a broad, gravelled drive.

The early days at Mayfield were happy ones. The Armstrongs had three children; Herbert was promoted to Captain in the Territorials and to Senior Deacon in the Loyal Hay Lodge of Freemasons; and Katharine's life was smoothed by a staff of servants so that she could devote her time to such pursuits as piano-playing.

Armstrong's office was in Broad Street, Hay's main thorough-fare. From there, he and his elderly partner conducted a modestly successful business. There was only one other firm of solicitors in the town, run by Robert Griffiths, and between them the two firms carried out virtually all of the legal business for a widespread, thriving farming community. Armstrong was also Clerk to the local Justices. His social status was high, and he was in every respect an eminent man in the life of Hay.

The life of this successful man had but one blemish upon it—his wife nagged him. Katharine looked tall beside her husband, and for that reason the couple were known to local youths as 'Mutt and Jeff'. But there was more than physical disparity. Katharine had an uncontrollable desire to dominate her spouse, and their acquaintances were well aware that Herbert was a mouse in his own home.

He seemed to accept his wife's domination without complaint, and his forbearance was admired. Then outside events crowded in. In the spring of 1914, both Armstrong's aged partner and the partner's wife died suddenly; on consecutive days. Armstrong thus became sole heir to the legal practice. Before he could really grasp this new situation, however, England was at war with Germany.

Caught up in the swirl of mobilization, Armstrong was posted to 'depot duties' in Southern England. The closest he got to the Western Front was a three-month spell at a base-camp in France in 1918. Major Armstrong, as he now became, undoubtedly enjoyed army-life. He could drink and smoke as he wished and was probably freer in the officers' mess than he was in his own home. But all good things must come to an end, and in 1919 he was demobilized.

Armstrong returned to Hay, but soon experienced difficulty in settling down to the old life. For one thing, he was on his own now in the legal practice; and he probably missed service-life—the more so since his wife's attitude had become more repressive, not to say cranky.

Katharine became increasingly hypochondriacal and took to dosing herself with homeopathic medicines. She did not like to be touched— even avoided brushing against people in the street. But most difficult to bear was the constant humiliation to which she subjected poor Herbert.

She abhorred tobacco and allowed her husband to smoke in only one room of the house; never out of doors. Herbert was fond of a pipe when he was out, but was always quick to hide it away if Katharine chanced to be in the vicinity. And he was kept on a tight rein at dinner parties. Servants filling glasses were abruptly dismissed by Katharine with the command: 'No wine for the Major.' On one occasion, she rebuked him in front of the servants for being a few minutes late at the meal-table. 'How can you expect the staff to behave if the Master is late?' she snapped. Another time, she appeared at the tennis-courts where Herbert was playing with some friends, declaring that it was his bath-night and he should come home at once. Racket at the droop, Armstrong tamely followed her back to Mayfield.

Katharine Armstrong first became seriously ill in August 1920. The family-doctor, Tom Hincks, was called, and found her in a poor mental condition. Eight days later, she was certified and admitted to Barnwood Asylum near Gloucester. The doctors there noted that she was in a weak state: her muscles were wasted, there was a loss of power in her hands and feet, there was albumen in her urine, and she was depressed. The cause of her condition was thought to be 'probably toxaemic'.

During the next two months, Mrs. Armstrong's health improved; she regained some of her strength. After she had been in the asylum for five months, the Major applied to have her released and brought home. The asylum doctors were surprised by this request, for they did not consider that Mrs. Armstrong was sufficiently fit to be discharged. They suggested that she should be given leave of absence for three months, thereby leaving the way open for her to be re-admitted to the asylum without re-certification. But Armstrong insisted that his wife be discharged as 'recovered'. Though the doctors would not agree to this, Armstrong had her home anyway. He wrote to the asylum, thanking the medical staff for looking after his wife, and adding, 'I have been able to disabuse her mind of some absurd ideas, and no doubt the others will also vanish.'

So, after all the wrangling, Katharine Armstrong returned to the bosom of her family. The Major got a nurse in to look after her and she appeared to be making fairly good progress. On 8 February 1921, she celebrated her forty-eighth birthday. Three days later, she was complaining to the doctor of feelings like 'springs pressing her up from the ground'. Dr. Hincks noticed that she had a high-steppage gait. On 16 February, in the words of her housekeeper, 'Mrs. Armstrong's health changed for the worse'. On that day, she took to her bed. She did not come downstairs again until she was borne on the shoulders of undertakers.

Her body became emaciated through constant vomiting and diarrhoea, her skin became copper-coloured, and she could do virtually nothing for herself. She died exactly a month after returning from the asylum. Major Armstrong's diary-entry for that day read simply: '22nd February—K died.'

Dr. Hincks certified the cause of death as gastritis, but also mentioned heart disease and nephritis. Katharine Armstrong was buried at Cusop without fuss. The card on her husband's wreath bore the words: 'From Herbert and the Chicks.'

After his wife's death, the Major, according to his housekeeper, was 'nervy and unable to work'. He decided to take a few weeks' holiday on the Continent 'to help dispel his grief'.

It seems that he had quite a jolly time. At any rate, a new mood was expressed in his diary. Whereas previous entries had been on such riveting matters as when he weeded the rosebeds and what articles he sent to the laundry, he now noted social engagements with a number of women. 'Susan', 'Miss McRae', and 'Miss B' featured quite often, and there is one intriguing entry which runs: '15 April—Billeted with Miss B'.

On returning from his holiday, the Major received news that probate had been granted on his late wife's will: he inherited all her money, which amounted to over £2000.[1] With cash in the bank and no nagging wife at home, the future for Major Armstrong looked set fair. There were just two things which bothered him—the weeds in his garden and Oswald Martin, his rival solicitor's new partner. He declared war on the weeds with arsenic bought from the local chemist, but what was he to do about Martin?

The latter, a serious-minded young man, was going from

[1] EDITOR'S NOTE. The 1992 purchasing power of the 1921 £ is reckoned to be just over £17.

strength to strength in the legal practice across the street from Armstrong's. The simple fact was that he was doing very well by attracting custom at the Major's expense.

The relationship between the two men was cool at the professional level and practically non-existent socially. However, their interests were brought together in August 1921 over a property deal in which Martin acted for the purchasers and Armstrong, who was stakeholder for the purchaser's deposit money, had failed to complete the deal, which was more than a year overdue.

The solicitor originally acting for the purchasers died suddenly and Martin was asked to act in his stead. He wasted no time in pressing Armstrong to complete the sale. The Major dillied and dallied, speaking of difficulties and further delays. This went on for several weeks, and Martin finally threatened to rescind the contracts unless completion was carried through by 20 October. Armstrong failed to meet that deadline—no explanation was offered.

At this most tense moment, Armstrong invited Martin to tea.

After a little difficulty in fixing dates, Martin accepted the Major's invitation to take tea with him at Mayfield on the following Wednesday, 26 October.

On the appointed day, the two men sat in Mayfield's drawing-room, making polite conversation. No reference was made to the important issue that was between them. They drank tea, and Armstrong handed Martin a buttered scone, with the apology, 'Excuse Fingers.' More pleasantries followed, and after about ninety minutes, Martin took his leave. He drove home, where he set to work on some papers he had brought back from the office.

He felt slightly unwell and did not have much appetite for his supper. Later in the evening, he felt really ill. Throughout the night, he was in great pain, vomiting frequently and shivering. His wife, fearing a haemorrhage as his retching was so violent, wanted to call the doctor. But Martin delayed the call until the following morning. By then, the worst of the vomiting had ceased, although he had diarrhoea. Dr.Hincks examined him and diagnosed that he had had a bad bilious attack.

Martin's father-in-law, John Davies, was the Hay chemist. He rather doubted the doctor's diagnosis—and said as much to

Hincks himself. He knew that Martin had been up at Major Armstrong's for tea, and he made no bones about the fact that he wouldn't trust Armstrong a yard. Furthermore, he pointed out that the Major had recently bought arsenic from his shop.

Thus were the seeds of suspicion sown.

Only then, in that climate of apprehension, with Martin recovering from his severe purging, did other people around him begin to suspect that he had been poisoned. And only then did Mrs. Martin connect in her mind two previous incidents. The month before, Martin had received a parcel containing a box of chocolates from an anonymous sender. Apart from being puzzled at the unexpected gift, the Martins had thought no more about it. But, weeks later, when they had visitors, they remembered the box of chocolates and put some in bon-bon dishes for after dinner. During the night, one of the guests, Dorothy Martin, was very unwell—she suffered a bout of diarrhoea and vomiting. She quickly recovered, and it was not necessary to call the doctor. Her indisposition was attributed to a chill.

But now, standing around Martin's bed, these events came into sharp focus. Perhaps the chocolates were poisoned? This clinched John Davies's suspicions. He consulted Dr. Hincks and they agreed to send the remaining chocolates and a sample of Martin's urine to a clinical research laboratory for analysis.

Armstrong never knew how nearly he escaped. When the laboratory sent their quotation for carrying out the analysis, Dr. Hincks decided that he was not prepared to meet the fee, and so he brought the matter to the attention of the Home Office. The file containing his letter was passed from desk to desk, and it was suggested that as the doctor was not prepared to talk to a uniformed policeman, the Secretary of State wold be unable to take any action. The whole question of doing an analysis for arsenic thus very nearly foundered. But, finally, it was pointed out that as the Home Office paid a yearly retainer of £500 to its official analyst anyway, it wouldn't cost anything if he were to do the analysis requested by Hincks.

After six weeks of waiting, the doctor and the chemist were given their answer—the urine sample contained 1/33rd of a grain of arsenic, and two of the chocolates were found to contain 2 grains of arsenic.

Now it was the turn of the Director of Public Prosecutions

and the Scotland Yard detectives. Chief Inspector Crutchett and Detective Sergeant Sharp were despatched to Hay on 10 December. Their brief was simply to get the facts—without alerting Armstrong.

The Major suspected nothing. He met Martin in the street after his illness and asked how he was. Martin said that he was getting better, to which Armstrong replied, 'It seems a queer thing to say, but you'll be ill again soon.' Shortly after this, Armstrong began a strange cat-and-mouse game. Sitting at a desk by the window of his first-floor office, he could almost see into Martin's office across the street. From this vantage point he telephoned Martin, inviting him to tea. Not surprisingly, Martin was reluctant to accept the Major's hospitality again; he made polite excuses and declined the invitations.

But the Major was persistent. The invitations came thick and fast, several times in some weeks. Poor Martin had such a wretched time thinking up and uttering polite and plausible excuses that his nerves became quite shattered. But his misery was ended on Saturday, 31 December, when the investigating officers marched into Major Armstrong's office.

Armstrong made a statement to the police and, protesting his innocence of the attempted murder of Martin, was then arrested. He was searched, and among the perfectly ordinary contents of his pockets were a folded piece of paper bearing his handwriting, three love-letters addressed to him, and a paper packet containing a white powder. Each of these items contributed in some measure to his subsequent downfall.

With the formality of arrest completed, Hay's Clerk to the Justices found himself locked away in a police-cell. Meanwhile, a search was conducted at Mayfield (a packet of arsenic was found in a bureau) and arrangements were under way to have Mrs. Armstrong's body exhumed. Digging began on Monday, 2 January 1922, the day that her husband was brought before the Magistrates' Court.

The news that the Major had been arrested hit Hay like a bombshell. Most people were unbelieving at first, but there was no doubting the truth of the matter when the little man was brought into the tiny court-room to face the magistrates, some of whom were his friends. It was a brief appearance, for the court was adjourned, the question of 'other matters' being mentioned.

One of the 'other matters' was the exhumation. Sir Bernard Spilsbury, the celebrated Home Office pathologist, was present when Mrs. Armstrong's body was removed from the ground for post-mortem examination. Spilsbury found the body to be '. . . unusually well-preserved'. It appeared to be undergoing mummification rather than putrefaction, despite having been in the ground for more than ten months. Laboratory tests on parts of various organs showed that the corpse contained 208 mg of arsenic—described by the Senior Home Office Analyst as '. . . the largest amount of arsenic I think I have found in any case of arsenical poisoning'. The liver alone contained 138 mg—the equivalent of a fatal dose.

Another charge was now preferred against Major Armstrong— that of murdering his wife. After a rather protracted magistrates' hearing at Hay, during which some unsavoury information about Armstrong was made public, he was committed for trial at Hereford Assizes.

At the hearing, a protesting Dr. Hincks was forced to admit that he was treating Armstrong for syphilis; he was giving him injections of *Novarsenobillox*. Later during the hearing, the doctor recalled a conversation he had had with Armstrong during a treatment session. The Major had asked what was in the injection. On being told that it was an arsenical preparation, he had enquired the amount of a fatal dose. The doctor had answered, 'Two or three grains,' to which Armstrong had asked: 'Wouldn't one be sufficient?'

A sheet of paper found on Armstrong when he was arrested contained his handwritten notes on the progress of his syphilis. These covered a period of ten months, and showed that he was being treated during the weeks of his wife's fatal illness. A sore had first been noticed on 23 November. Syphilis has an incubation period of 9 to 90 days, which means that in all likelihood the Major contracted the disease while his wife was in the asylum. Strangely, he mentioned that the rash irritated—that is uncharacteristic of syphilis.

It has been suggested from time to time that Armstrong's behaviour could be accounted for if he were suffering from General Paralysis of the Insane (GPI), a late stage of syphilis which destroys brain-tissues and leads to progressive insanity, and can cause acts of violence, even murder. But that stage is usually only manifest after ten to fifteen years from the time of infection. This would seem to rule it out in Armstrong's case.

It appears that Mrs. Armstrong was a cold fish at the best of times. The Major therefore sought warm embraces elsewhere, and there is no doubt that he was generous with his favours. When his house was searched, the detectives found two soiled French Letters in the washstand drawer in his bedroom. As Chief Inspector Crutchett put it: '. . . that will show you the kind of man he is morally.'

The Major was certainly something of the gay dog after his wife died. His diary had a number of references to dances held in Hay—dances at which, according to Dr. Hincks, he was not above pestering teenage girls. Not surprisingly, there were those who thought it out of place for the Justice's Clerk to appear at the local hops. But, as one of Armstrong's contemporaries said, 'The Major was a bit of a dasher, you know!'

Together with the list of venereal-disease symptoms, there were three love-letters in Armstrong's pocket when he was arrested. The sender, 'Your Loving Marion', was the mysterious 'Madame X' who appeared both at the hearing and at the trial. Her name, which Mr. Justice Darling ordered to be kept out of the case, was Marion Glassford Gale.

She was a fifty-year-old widow who lived with her mother and niece near Bournemouth. Armstrong's relationship with her was on a different plane to the rest of his amorous affairs. They first met in 1915, when Armstrong was serving with the Royal Engineers at a camp near Christchurch. He visited Marion and her mother at their home, Ford Cottage. They knew that he was married and had children. Like many decent folk during the war years, they welcomed into their home a soldier whom circumstances had taken from his family.

A friendship developed between Armstrong and Marion, and when he was posted away from the area, they corresponded. In July 1920—after he was demobilised, and a month before Mrs. Armstrong was taken to the asylum—they met in London. They did not see each other again until after Mrs. Armstrong's death, and then the scent of marriage was in the air.

In August 1921, Armstrong made a definite proposal of marriage; but Marion was unsure. She was strongly influenced by her feelings of duty and responsibility towards her mother and niece. However, Armstrong was not discouraged. They decided to reconsider the matter after a few months had elapsed. They met a few more times before the end of the year, and Marion stayed at Armstrong's house on one occasion.

There is no doubt that marriage was discussed in a very practical context. Armstrong mentioned the possibility to his housekeeper and asked when it would be best to tell the children. In a letter to Armstrong, a family-friend spoke of the prospect of his 'going into double-harness again'.

The Major would have been quite a catch for Marion. After all, he was a prominent man in Hay, and the prospect of becoming mistress of his house, with servants to do her bidding, must have been attractive. However, it was all inconclusive, and the last expressions of the relationship were contained in the three letters from Marion found on Armstrong on 31 December 1921.

These were not read out in court, and 'Madame X', or Marion Glassford Gale as we now know her, was simply asked to acknowledge that she had written them. This she did. All the letters contained grumbles about her dreary life. There is a feeling that her desire to be taken away from it all caused her to overplay her hand, for there is a suspicion that Armstrong's ardour was cooling. Her tone at times is almost accusatory—'Why this heavy silence?' she asks, and '. . . don't you want to see me? Your last letter was rather casual.'

Perhaps Armstrong realised that the prospect of marriage to this woman, torn between family loyalties and the thought of making a new life, was too remote. But Marion was plainly still talking about the possibility of marriage in the last lines of her letter.

An odd topic for discussion in their correspondence was Armstrong's inoculations. It is unlikely that he told her that he was being treated for syphilis, but perhaps he was hinting at a health problem which would be a reason for breaking off the relationship.

The last words addressed by Marion to Armstrong were New Year greetings. Unfortunately she was in error with the year—it should have been 1922, *not 1921*. This might have been an omen, for unbeknown to Marion the police were already on the Major's track; within a day or two of receiving this letter, he was arrested.

Marion was interviewed by the police. She said that she had only heard of Major Armstrong's arrest by reading of it in the newspapers. She was obviously shocked. The police expected to find a strong whiff of intimacy between the widow and Armstrong, but all Marion would say was: 'Major Armtsrong was to me everything a gentleman ought to be.'

Disappointed at the first attempt, the police questioned Marion again. The nature of the questions is obvious from the replies given. She was at pains to make it quite clear that she had not slept with Armstrong.

Marion was one of those people whom life seems repeatedly to injure. She had been a widow for many years, unselfishly making a home for her mother and niece. Then Armstrong stepped into her life and her prospects brightened. Her niece remembered seeing Marion sat at the kitchen-table with her head in her hands—spread before her, a newspaper containing the news of Armstrong's arrest. It must have been a bitter blow.

In murder, as in any other enterprise, it is wise to be prepared. When he walked to his office on that cold Saturday morning in December, Major Armstrong was prepared. In his jacket-pocket was a small paper packet. It measured $1^1/_2$ inches by $^3/_4$ of an inch and contained white powder. It might have passed as a chemist's headache-powder. In fact, it was a lethal dose of arsenic.

At his trial, Armstrong was given a gruelling time by Mr. Justice Darling regarding the account he had given of his methods for using arsenic as a weed-killer. His story was that he had divided up the bulk quantity of arsenic into twenty little paper packets; he put the packets into his jacket pocket and went into the garden, where he used one packet per dandelion; he only treated nineteen dandelions on this particular occasion, which accounted for the one packet left in his pocket.

It was, to say the least, an eccentric way to go about killing weeds. That seemed to be Mr. Justice Darling's view. Just as Armstrong was preparing to stand down from the witness-box at the end of a six-hour ordeal of questioning, the judge requested a few more answers.

'Why go to the trouble of making twenty little packets, one for each dandelion, instead of taking out the ounce you had got and making a hole and giving the dandelions something from the ounce?'

Armstrong replied: 'I do not really know.'

'Why make up twenty little packets, each a fatal dose for a human being, and put them in your pocket?'

Armstrong answered lamely: 'At the time, it seemed to me the most convenient way of doing it. I cannot give any other explanation.'

The Major had done quite well in the witness-box up to this point. He was calm, and answered questions without hesitation. But he fell at the last fence. He could not find a convincing reason to account for that menacing packet of arsenic in his pocket. The irresistible conclusion was that the poison was ear-marked for another attempt on Oswald Martin's life.

The contents of his pockets contributed tangibly to Armstrong's downfall. But there were other factors too. For example, the part he played in making his wife's Last Will and Testament. That was in June 1917. The will contained thirteen clauses, and the main provisions were for her three children; there were also bequests to her sister and housekeeper, and an annuity of £50 for her husband. This document, the First Will, had four executors, including Major Armstrong.

On the day of Mrs. Armstrong's funeral, the Major let it be known that his wife had left everything to him in a will dated 8 July 1920—that is, a few weeks before she was admitted to the asylum. This will, which was written in Major Armstrong's hand, contained no provisions for the children and made no bequests—everything went to the Major, who was also sole executor. This was the Second Will.

Probate was granted on the Second Will in March 1921, and Major Armstrong inherited the sum of £2278. Mrs. Armstrong's sister was most surprised at the changes in the provisions. So was the Director of Public Prosecutions when he considered the papers shortly after Armstrong's arrest. He asked Chief Inspector Crutchett to get a specimen of Mrs. Armstrong's signature and to question the two women who had witnessed the will. Both signatories were servants in Major Armstrong's household. Their statements to the police made it perfectly obvious that the witnessing procedure had been highly irregular.

Emily Pearce, the elderly housekeeper, remembered signing a document in the presence of Major and Mrs. Armstrong, but she did not recall if the other witness was there. Lily Candy, a housemaid, was quite certain that she had not been asked to witness Mrs. Armstrong's will. But she did remember signing a paper in the Major's study—she was not told what it was but thought at the time that it was someting to do with her National Insurance.

An important clue regarding Mrs. Armstrong's intentions was provided by the lady herself while in the asylum. On 11 January 1921, six months after the Second Will was made, she wrote to her sister, asking the whereabouts of her will, and saying, 'I think *all* executors ought to know.' Surely she was referring to the four executors of the First Will and *not* to the sole executor of the Second?

Chief Inspector Crutchett reported that two friends of Mrs. Armstrong who were familiar with her writing were of the opinion that the signature on the Second Will was not in her hand. The Chief Inspector concluded that if this view was correct, then the Second Will had been forged by Armstrong in order to get his wife's money.

This imputation was not put directly at the trial. Questioned about the drawing-up of the Second Will, Armstrong said, quite blandly: 'I think one does things rather more irregularly for one's own family.'

There is no doubt whatever that Armstrong was in deep financial difficulties and that his wife's money would have been of great help. He was pretty sharp on small money matters; for instance, he had the nerve to ask the asylum authorities who looked after his wife to give him interest on the fees which he had paid. Still, penny-pinching is not a crime; indeed, there are many who consider it a virtue.

However, the Major's handling of some of his client's affairs was far from virtuous. He handled £300 compensation awarded to one of his servants who had lost her husband in an industrial accident. Armstrong gave the young woman £17 to meet the funeral expenses—but she saw nothing of the remainder. Armstrong's own bank-manager was of the opinion that 'some enquiry would appear to be desirable in this matter'.

It was the larger business transactions that got Armstrong into trouble. He borrowed from one client to pay another, and left a legacy of muddle wherever he went. One client owed him £4500, and this was to be an important factor in the Major's subsequent behaviour.

The fruits of Chief Inspector Crutchett's inquiries were contained in a report which he sent to his superior at Scotland Yard: '. . . we are generally accumulating evidence which shows that Armstrong's affairs are in great disorder, that he is insolvent and has been improperly using his client's money.' Despite this view, the question of the wills was not pursued at Armstrong's trial. It was perhaps not of central importance, but the thought that Armstrong inherited his wife's money improperly has always been an intriguing possibility.

The late Mr. Henry Rhodes, a highly regarded document-examiner, made an appraisal of the validity of Mrs. Armstrong's signature on the Second Will. The standard signatures of Major Armstrong and Mrs. Armstrong were compared with Mrs. Armstrong's questioned signature on the Second Will. Mr. Rhodes noted that the 'line-quality' of certain parts of this signature were poor, especially the K, M and terminal g. More significantly, he found that the pen-movements associated with the base of the t and with the o were not consistent; particularly in the case of the o, the writing was more consistent with that of Major Armstrong.

The most important part of the analysis was the measurement of the heights of the minuscules, or small letters. Metrical analysis, a standard authentication procedure used in document examination, consists of measurements expressed in terms of the proportional heights of each character; these can be shown in graphical form. Mr. Rhodes concluded that the metrical values of Mrs. Armstrong's true signature 'are quite inconsistent with those of the questioned writing'. Those of Major Armstrong, on the other hand, were substantially consistent with the values of the questioned signature. In other words, it is a virtual certainty that Major Armstrong forged his wife's signature on the Second Will and had it improperly witnessed by two servants.

One of the great mysteries of the Armstrong case has always been the property sale which brought the Major into confrontation with Oswald Martin. It has long been thought that this rivalry, coupled with his dislike for Martin, created the Major's motive for the attempted poisoning. But the way in which he bungled the attempt has an air of desperation about it, and contrasts so sharply with the careful way in which he disposed of his wife as to suggest that there were other reasons.

In the tangled mess of Armstrong's business accounts, one name crops up again and again. That name is John Williams Vaughan. There is much to indicate that the affairs of Armstrong and Williams Vaughan were inextricably mixed.

Williams Vaughan was a landowner who had been one of Armstrong's clients since 1910. His account was frequently in arrears. At the end of 1919, he decided to sell some of his property. The Velinnewydd Estate was broken up into lots, and two of these were sold to local farmers, who paid deposits amounting to £500 to Major Armstrong, solicitor acting for Williams Vaughan.

Completion of the deal was fixed for February 1920, but that date came and went without the contracts being finalised. The Brecon solicitor acting for the purchasers pressed Armstrong for completion. But all the Major would say was that there were some difficulties which he was having to clear away. The affair dragged on for over a year. Then, in July 1921, the Brecon solicitor died—strangely enough, after a visit to Armstrong—and Oswald Martin was asked to act in his place. The first thing the new solicitor did was to ask Armstrong why 'completion had been delayed such an excessively long time'. No direct answer was forthcoming—only talk of continuing difficulty which might delay completion for another day or two.

Martin made several representations to Armstrong, but each time came away empty-handed. Finally he told the Major that unless the matter was settled by 20 October, he would rescind the contracts and demand repayment of the deposits, together with costs and expenses.

A few days before this deadline was due, Armstrong was still talking of difficulties. On the day set for completion, Martin was in his office with the two farmers, who had in their pockets the balance of the purchase money. Armstrong did not appear, and so Martin telephoned him. Incredibly, there was still some impediment which prevented him from completing. He asked Martin to allow him to speak personally with the two farmers.

Martin was present when the Major, in a state of some distress, pleaded with the purchasers for a further week in which to finish the deal. They refused. On the following day, over eighteen months since the original completion date, Martin notified Armstrong that the contracts were to be withdrawn—and he asked for the return of the deposit-money.

That same day, Armstrong extended his first tea-invitation to Martin. They settled for Wednesday of the following week, 26 October, with the result that we know so well.

The only reason ever offered by Armstrong for not completing the sale was at the trial, when the question was put to him directly. He replied: 'Several questions had arisen on the title.' Martin's understanding of the matter bore this out. 'I believe,' he said, 'that there was some complication with the Yorkshire Penny Bank, who were mortgagees of this property.' But Armstrong's agitated behaviour, especially his plea to speak with the purchasers, led Martin to think that the affair in some way affected Armstrong personally.

The Major's actions were both extraordinary and, to a degree, unprofessional. Pleading for time with another solicitor's clients was a little unusual, and not giving satisfactory answers to his own client's repeated enquiries was unprofessional. Although fading memories of an unimportant legal tangle have combined with incomplete files to frustrate the researcher, it does become clear that Armstrong was fighting for his business and for his professional life. He was on a desperate merry-go-round, and the person sharing the ride was his landowner-client, John Williams Vaughan.

The landowner was not, as it turned out, the best kind of client for a solicitor in Armstrong's position. His assets were heavily mortgaged, and he did not keep his solicitor properly informed about his legal and financial arrangements. But despite the fact that Armstrong was himself in financial difficulty, he continued to lend money to Williams Vaughan. On occasions, when he had no money of his own to lend, he handed out other people's, and, of course, repercussions followed. When the police inquired into Armstrong's business affairs, they had no difficulty in getting statements from irate clients whose money the Major had loaned without their permission.

The result of these tangled transactions was that the Williams

Vaughan estate owed Armstrong over £4000. The Velinnewydd sale, for which Armstrong held the deposits amounting to £500, would gross £4500 on completion. This would easily enable Armstrong to recoup his losses from Williams Vaughan. In fact, the Major's position had become so precarious that his sole source of financial salvation lay in the successful completion of the deal.

The only obstacle in the path to success was the problem over the mortgages. Armstrong had waged a stalwart stalling campaign to keep the deal alive for over eighteen months. The intending purchasers had shown considerable patience—but then, when perhaps a little more time would bring the deal to completion, Oswald Martin entered the scene.

Caring for nothing other than the clearing up of a messy deal, Martin began to hustle and harry. The pressure was on, and the Major knew that he would be ruined if the deal fell through. He would have to repay the deposit-money and say goodbye to his chance of regaining his money from Williams Vaughan. He could not cover a loss of nearly £5000 from his own resources, for he was on the verge of insolvency, and even the money gained by forging his wife's will was inadequate. He would be finished.

What could he do? The only possible course was to gain more time in the hope that the legal difficulties blocking completion would be finally cleared away. When his plea to Martin's clients failed, he could think of only one further manoeuvre: to stay Martin's hand and gain a little breathing-space.

The thought of going bankrupt, with all the attendant disgrace in a small town like Hay, must have given Armstrong nightmares. It certainly lent desperation to his plans. He didn't like Martin anyway, so the prospect of poisoning him presented no difficulty, Moreover, he was already an experienced poisoner—he alone knew the dark secret of his wife's demise, and that probably gave him confidence. But his anxiety was so great that he did not anticipate the problems involved in secretly administering poison to someone outside his own household. The trick was to create the right opportunity. Tea at Mayfield, with the one poisoned scone unerringly directed to Martin, must have looked right. But he had reckoned without the younger man's strong constitution.

Having failed to do more than put Martin in bed for a few days, Armstrong's cunning was usurped by his desperation.

Everything that followed—the warning to Martin of 'another attack soon', the incessant further invitations to tea—inevitably drew suspicion to himself.

Armstrong did not give up hope of completing the property deal. He declared that he was ready to finalise on 6 December. Even if this was genuine, it was far too late, as Martin had long since closed negotiations. But on 13 December the Major appeared at Martin's and served him with High Court writs for specific performance. This really was an about-face for Armstrong. It was a most unusual course for a solicitor to take in such a dispute, and can only be interpreted as a last-ditch effort to retain a slender grasp on his legal right to costs from his own client. But it was too late.

The Velinnewydd sale had still not been completed by the time Armstrong was put on trial. It was further complicated by a legal argument over the priorities of Williams Vaughan's mortgages. And then his estate, like Armstrong's, went into bankruptcy.

The thesis, then, is that Armstrong murdered his nagging wife and forged her will to help finance his freedom. The poisoning was done with care and deliberation—for ten months it was a 'perfect murder'. His diary shows a new man emerging with the prospect of marriage to the widow, Marion Glassford Gale. But his syphilis shows a kind of philandering far removed from the relationship that might have been cemented with Marion. Her love-letters clearly indicate that their affair was going off the boil.

Then Armstrong's business finances began to collapse like a pack of cards—the joker who started it seems to have been John Williams Vaughan. The only escape for Armstrong was to complete the property deal and use the money earned from it to offset his losses to the landowner.

It was sink or swim for the Major. He decided to swim—but his strokes were frantic ones. In his anxious efforts to buy time after Oswald Martin's intervention, he merely gave the game away. For a man who set such great store on etiquette, there was surely no better way of focusing attention on his actions than the 'Excuse fingers' episode. Sir Archibald Bodkin, the Director of Public Prosecutions, is said to have fallen about with laughter when his children used the expression 'Excuse fingers' at the meal-table. It really was inexcusable for the assured poisoner to highlight his method so evidently.

Armstrong's attempts on Martin's life—there were two if we count the box-of-chocolates incident—were not simply acts of pique against a rival. They were the efforts of a desperate man to stave off financial ruin. Martin's initiative in the property deal triggered off that malignant area of Armstrong's brain wherein lurked the idea of murder. From that moment on, his ruin was assured.

The extraordinary events surrounding the Martin affair are thus no less amazing—but perhaps the Major can now be seen in a slightly different light.

Herbert Rowse Armstrong was a small man, vain and egotistical. He was such a stickler for details that he would write sheaves of letters about a rubber-stamp missing from the office. He revelled in his accomplishments; one might almost say that he wallowed in them. He sprinkled his beloved title of 'Major' all around—on his cheques, on the records of his arsenic purchases . . . even on his wife's lunacy petition.

In their different ways, the papers found on him when he was arrested each contributed something to his downfall. The list of syphilis symptoms toppled him from his proud perch as a respected citizen of Hay, the love-letters showed his disregard for the warm feelings expressed by Marion—but the tiny packet of arsenic, carried in readiness for the moment of opportunity, surely damned him. After Mr. Justice Darling's devastating questioning, that packet of poison was Armstrong's death-warrant.

But he was not without courage at the end. He behaved with dignity, exhibiting good manners to all who came into contact with him. He made gifts to Sir Henry Curtis Bennett and his lesser defenders, and he wrote a letter of warm thanks to his solicitor, T.A. Matthews.

The last word should be left to Armstrong himself. The day before the execution, the Governor of Gloucester Prison said to the condemned man: 'I don't like this hanging business, Armstrong.'

The Major nodded sympathetically and commented: 'Yes, I'm sure it must be most unpleasant for you.'

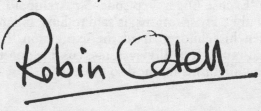

THE LIZZIE BORDEN SONG
Michael Brown

[He claims that although he was born in Texas, he is often broad-minded. He is a man of many talents (some of them 'prodigious', according to The Hollywood Reporter): composer, lyricist, producer and director in the commercial and 'business' theatre, author of children's books (sales of his 'Santa Mouse' series run into millions), and performer. His very first engagement as a singer of his own songs was at the famous Manhattan cabaret, Le Ruban Bleu, where he broke the house-record by being kept on for more than a year; this phase of his career culminated at the Savoy Hotel, London, where his act was enjoyed by many discerning critics, one of whom dubbed him 'the American Noel Coward'. He has contributed to several musicals and revues since 1952, when his hoe-down version of the Borden case invariably stopped the New Faces show on Broadway (there is an 'original-cast recording': RCA CBM1–2206). He and his wife, the dancer Joy Williams (who, so far as I know, has never appeared in Agnes de Mille's Borden-case ballet, Fall River Legend), live near Broadway.]

One hot day in old Fall River,
Mister Andrew Borden died,
And they booked his daughter Lizzie
On a charge of homicide.

Some folks say, 'She didn't do it,'
Others say, 'Of course she did;'
But they all agree Miss Lizzie B.
Was quite a problem kid.

'Cause you can't chop your poppa up in Massachusetts,
Not even if it's planned as a surprise.
No, you can't chop your poppa up in Massachusetts;
You know how neighbours love to criticise.

Now, she got him on the sofa,
Where he'd gone to take a snooze,
And I hope he went to heaven,
'Cause he wasn't wearing shoes.
Lizzie kind of rearranged him
With a hatchet, so they say.
And then she got her mother
In that same old-fashioned way.

But you can't chop your momma up in Massachusetts,
Not even if you're tired of her cuisine.[1]
No, you can't chop your momma up in Massachusetts;
If you do, you know there's bound to be a scene.

Now, it wasn't done for pleasure
And it wasn't done for spite,
And it wasn't done because the lady
Wasn't very bright.
She had always done the slightest thing
That mom and poppa bid.
They said, 'Lizzie, cut it out,'
And that's exactly what she did.

But you can't chop your poppa up in Massachusetts,
And then get dressed to go out for a walk.
No, you can't chop your poppa up in Massachusetts;
Massachusetts is a far cry from New York.

[1] EDITOR'S NOTE. 'Mrs. Borden [Lizzie's step-momma]
appeared about seven [on Thursday, 4 August 1892], and
her husband and Mr. Morse [a visiting in-law] soon following, the three breakfasted together. This breakfast was

subsequently discussed at more than one legal investigation, so it may be said that, according to Mr. Morse, it consisted of mutton, bread, coffee, "sugar cakes" and bananas. The Irish housemaid [Bridget Sullivan,] who prepared the food, said that there was mutton-broth, as well as mutton itself, johnny cakes, coffee and cookies. Bridget insisted, in answer to the specific question, that to the best of her belief, they had no bananas that day. At all events, for a hot morning in mid-summer it was a breakfast well adapted to set the stage for a tragedy. One trembles at the thought of beginning a day in August with mutton-soup.'—Edmund Pearson, Studies in Murder, Macmillan, New York, 1924.

Curiously, so it seems to most people who have read the trial-transcript, Lizzie Borden was acquitted of the double-murder—which meant, among other things, that she was entitled to her share of the estate of her murdered father and step-mother. She used comparatively little of it to buy a mansion at a desirable edge of Fall River, and, sanguine at the gossip about both her axewomanship and her association with certain unconventional persons of her own sex, remained there, insisting on being called Lizbeth, till her death in 1927.

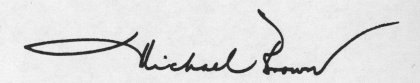

A SPIN ACROSS
LONDON BRIDGE
Richard D. Altick

[Born in Pennsylvania in 1915, he began teaching at the Ohio State University in 1945, and is now that university's Regents' Professor of English, Emeritus. Much of his writing—which is always lucid, witty, and alive—is about British literature and society in the Victorian Age. Indicating the range of his interests, his books include The Presence of the Present: Topics of the Day in the Victorian Novel; The English Common Reader, *which is the standard history of the English reading public; a history of popular entertainments,* The Shows of London; Paintings from Books, *on the use of literary subjects in British art between 1760 and 1900; and the Penguin edition of Browning's* The Ring and the Book *(which was partly inspired by a murder case). And, of course, there are his books on true crimes:* Victorian Studies in Scarlet *and* Deadly Encounters *(re-titled* Evil Encounters *by its English publisher), his brilliantly-crafted and wonderfully entertaining account of two London 'sensations' of 1861. His collection of stories of literary detective-work,* The Scholar Adventurers, *has acquired a cult-following since it was first published in 1950; the fact that it has never been published in England is a dreadful reflection on English publishers.]*

> You cannot carry with any degree of safety, either in a cab or by
> any other mode, a dead body along the streets of London.
>
> *The Lord Chief Justice, Sir Alexander Cockburn*

SATURDAY, 11 SEPTEMBER 1875, was a warm, butter-turning
day in London, and the mortgagee had taken possession of Henry
Wainwright's brushmaking warehouse in the Whitechapel Road.
Wainwright had lately been unscathed by prosperity; some ten
months earlier, his salesroom across the road had burned down,
and the insurance company, exercising the option it reserved in
cases of reasonable doubt, had delayed paying his claim. Now,
in taking leave of the warehouse, he was about to remove such
chattels as remained on the premises to a new location, a building
called the Hen & Chickens, just south of the Thames near the
junction of Southwark Street and the Borough High Street. Here
his brother Thomas had briefly been in the ironmonger's trade,
but Thomas too had recently failed and his stock had been sold
at auction. However, he still had the key to the building, whose
deep and solid foundations, forming a cellar with remote and
inaccessible corners, were well adapted for Henry's purposes.
Henry had therefore borrowed the key.

The property he proposed to transfer this day consisted of two
large and unwieldy bundles wrapped in black 'American cloth'
(oilcloth). He was then at a grain warehouse in the New Road,
where, by the generous permission of the proprietor, he was
carrying on his brush business until he could get back on his
financial feet. Wainwright asked Alfred Stokes, who had been
with him as a brushmaker for seventeen or eighteen years, 'Will
you carry a parcel for me, Stokes?'

'Yes, sir, with the greatest of pleasure.'

They went to the Whitechapel Road warehouse, and Stokes
shouldered the two large bundles Wainwright drew from underneath some straw, not without complaint over their weight
and strong odour. Outside the warehouse, Wainwright relieved
Stokes of the lighter one and, so encumbered, they trudged a
quarter-mile down the road, at which point Wainwright went
in search of a cab, leaving Stokes to guard the awkward
freight. Yielding to normal curiosity, he began to open one
parcel—and quickly learned that he was in charge of, at the

very least, one severed human hand. He did not venture to probe further.

While Stokes was pondering the possible significance of this disquieting discovery, Wainwright arrived with a cab he had found at a nearby rank. He was then smoking a large cigar. Stokes helped him load the bundles on to the cab. He thanked Stokes for his trouble and said he would see him later. Then, as he was about to drive off with his bulky packages, Wainwright happened to see a young ballet-dancer of his acquaintance emerging from a tavern and, to complete his enjoyment, asked her to go along for a ride on this nice Saturday afternoon. 'I don't mind if I do,' we can hear her answering as he gallantly handed her up. Off went the cab, laden with Wainwright, theatrical person, and bundles. It probably struck her as odd that, as soon as they were under way, he gave her a newspaper and invited her to read it while they rode. He said he wanted to think.

Stokes, left behind on the sidewalk, now sensed that something was decidedly wrong. He therefore took off in pursuit of the cab as it headed westward through Commercial Road, Aldgate High Street, and Leadenhall Street, en route to London Bridge. On seeing two policemen in Leadenhall Street, he stopped, caught his breath, and urged them to join in the chase. 'Man, you must be mad,' said they, laughing. So, panting and perspiring, he resumed his run. Across London Bridge, the refuse-swollen river gleaming dully in the sun. Past old St. Saviour's, later to become Southwark Cathedral, its tower grazed by a looming railway viaduct. Into the Borough High Street: the brisk clop-clop of the horse's hoofs, the ever more laboured puffing of Stokes in pursuit. 'I was so exhausted that I felt I should drop,' he later told the court. Before he did so, however, the cab stopped at the Hen & Chickens. Not far away stood another policeman, whom Stokes desperately accosted. This co-operative guardian of the peace agreed to have a look into the matter. He went up to where Wainwright was unloading the parcels with the cabbie's assistance, and, like Stokes earlier, began to open one. A horrified glimpse, and he summoned a fellow constable, who joined him in declining the £200 bribe[1] Wainwright promised to have ready for

---

[1] *EDITOR'S NOTE. The 1992 purchasing power of the 1875 £ is reckoned to be about £35.*

them in twenty minutes. Wainwright was arrested on the spot.

Since Stokes, the lonely long-distance runner, does not appear again in the case, it may be noted here that after he testified to the strenuous part he played in Wainwright's apprehension, the judge awarded him £30 from the public funds for his 'perseverance'. He had earned every shilling of it.

The prisoner Wainwright, custodian of those grisly bundles, was a man of some consequence in the East End of London. The son of a churchwarden who left an estate of £11,000, he had been a member of Christ Church Institute of St. George's-in-the-East, where he had been active in musical and elocutionary classes. He also had participated in private theatricals and in 1867 was lecturing, as far away as Leeds, on 'The Wit and Eccentricity of Sydney Smith'. In earlier years he had promoted temperance from the platform, but he seems subsequently to have lost his convictions in this regard. His sociable inclinations as well as his enthusiasm for the stage had brought him into the intimate company of the management and artistes at the Pavilion Theatre, next door to his brush shop, and at their suppers a favorite recitation of his—an ominous choice—was Thomas Hood's famous poem, 'The Dream of Eugene Aram'.

Well-filled and satisfying though his leisure had been, his personal and business fortunes had declined. In 1872, being already in possession of a wife and several children, he had acquired a mistress, Harriet Lane, whom he set up in lodgings under the name of 'Mrs. Percy King,' and by whom he had two more children. By September 1874, however, his interest in this arrangement had faded, along with his ability to support it in the style to which it was accustomed. It was at this time that Harriet vanished from her place of residence, from which she was due soon to be evicted anyway, for drunk and disorderly conduct on the pavement outside.

The following month, whatever misgivings Harriet's friends and relatives may have entertained over her sudden disappearance were allayed by Henry's announcement that she had eloped to the continent for 'a spree' with one Edward Frieake. Telegrams and letters were received to the same effect, signed by Frieake. This happened to be the name of a respectable Whitechapel auctioneer and longtime friend of Wainwright, who, upon learning of the unauthorized misappropriation, protested to Wainwright. In light of Frieake's current engagement to a young lady, who could be expected to take an intolerant view of his being romantically linked with another, we may well believe that those representations were fairly heated. Wainwright, amused, told his friend that he wasn't the fellow at all—the Teddy Frieake involved with the former Harriet Lane, more recently the *soi-disante* Mrs. King, was a younger man, a hanger-on in billiard saloons and similar places of entertainment. He was also a figment of Wainwright's imagination, except insofar as Henry had prevailed upon his brother Thomas to impersonate the said Teddy in his strategy of inducing Harriet to disappear.

The truth was that Harriet, in the flesh, had never left Whitechapel. Since approximately the day she was last seen at her lodgings, she had been reposing, with three bullets in her head and her throat cut, under the flagstone paving of the paint room in the brush warehouse. Wainwright had thought to erase her totally from the local scene by interring her with fifty pounds of chloride of lime—purchased, it was proved at the trial, the day before she left her lodgings.[1] He was one more victim of the vulgar error which assumes that, when liberally applied to a dead body put in earth, lime—any kind of lime—will quickly decompose it. In 1849, Fred and Maria Manning had been on the right track when they covered Patrick O'Connor with *quick*lime, although the quantity used was insufficient for their purposes, and when the kitchen floor was dug up, enough identifiable evidence of O'Connor survived to hang them. Wainwright, despite what one must assume was a superior education, chose chloride of lime, which, far from destroying flesh, has the quite opposite, and certainly undesirable, effect of preserving it. It must have been a dark moment in his life when, after all the trouble to

---

[1] This purchase, and the inquiries leading thereto among wholesalers, acquired the sweet smell of legitimacy because in his line of work ('brush-making' seems to have embraced the sort of merchandise now classed as janitors' supplies) Wainwright was interested in providing 'small stores' to various purchasers, including, of all people, the police. In the last months of his independent existence as a brushmaker, just after he killed Harriet, he actually won a contract to provide the police with chloride of lime.

which he had gone to dispose of Harriet, he finally had to face the necessity of moving her stubbornly existing remains from Whitechapel to Southwark. That his well-laid plan had failed through a mere ignorance of elementary chemistry must have rendered additionally disagreeable the chore of separating her into ten pieces for convenience of packaging and shipping.

Even his misguided reliance upon chloride of lime, however, might not have betrayed Wainwright, because if all else had gone well, he might have transferred his bundles to the former ironmongery and buried them there without anyone the wiser. His crucial miscalculation amounted to no more than failure to light his cigar soon enough. Had he done so the moment he extracted the bundles from beneath the straw, it is possible that Stokes would not have become inquisitive enough to examine one of the bundles while awaiting the cab; especially if (as the editor of the trial,[1] H. B. Irving, sensibly observes) he had given Stokes a cigar to smoke himself.

The record of Wainwright's trial, which led to his execution, is of substantial and variegated interest. Among the most curious of its aspects is the appearance of William Schwenck Gilbert's name as one of the barristers instructed for the defence in the police-court hearing. Actually, it was Gilbert's way of getting out of jury duty. At this date he was no longer at the bar but was hard at work on *Broken Hearts*, a sentimental drama in blank verse. Having been called to jury service, he persuaded a friend to get him a nominal two-day brief in the Wainwright case so that, as a 'practising' lawyer, he could be excused. *Broken Hearts*, produced in December, was such a disaster that modern Gilbertians agree that he could have spent his time better doing his duty as a citizen.

There could be no more vivid and authentic record than the trial provides of the physical and social ambience of an East London neighbourhood at a moment in history. The whole drama, as reconstructed from the witness-box, occurs

---

[1] *Trial of the Wainwrights* (Hodge, Edinburgh, 1920).

in perfectly ordinary houses, shops, and pubs, indistinguishable from a hundred thousand other ones in the Victorian metropolis except for the accident that they were somehow associated with a particularly macabre crime. The warehouse where Harriet was buried, a typical small-time business establishment, is portrayed with a detail impossible even to contemporary photography; for no photography could do justice to the Cockney complaints about the faulty drains and unremoved refuse-piles which were the putative source of the disagreeable odour that had hung about the premises since Wainwright had deposited Harriet under the floor—nor could it explain the sudden disappearance of a dog which had persisted in nosing in the vicinity of the paint room. Curiosity has been known to kill more than cats.

And there is much information about occupational routines of the time. From several post-office clerks, for example, we hear of the exact manner in which the GPO filed its daily accumulation of telegrams handed in at each office, numbering and docketing them. After being kept for a month, they were sent to be pulped. From a pawnbroker we learn that it was the custom to write only the last name of the customer on the ticket, then prefixing it with the generic 'John' if it was a man, 'Ann' if it was a woman. Tickets of goods that were redeemed were filed day by day and kept for two years.

We are enabled, also, to follow a perfectly unexceptional person, living in London in 1875, on a daily itinerary, just as Pepys enables us to do for the rounds of a quite exceptional person living in London in the 1660s. At 12:30 p.m. on 10 September, Thomas Wainwright, the erstwhile 'Mr. Frieake' who a year earlier had taken Harriet Lane on a fictitious spree to the continent, lunched with friends at the Black Lion, Bishopsgate Street. He was, as we have noted, out of employment, his iron-mongery at the Hen & Chickens having been sold up. After lunch, he went round to call on Henry, at work in the grain warehouse. Henry asked him to go and buy a garden-spade and cleaver ('for chopping wood') at Mr. Pettigrew's nearby shop. The transaction at this (solvent) ironmongery was extended to a half-hour or forty-five minutes by his going out for a drink with Mr. Pettigrew. Mr. Pettigrew paid. Thomas then went by the warehouse to deliver the implements, charging his brother five shillings for what he had bought, at trade discount, for three shillings. It was now 2:30 p.m., time for a spot of sherry at another public house. After this, to another place for dinner (a meal eaten in the middle of the afternoon at this date in some social circles), following which, back to the Black Lion; then to 1 Racquet Court, Fleet Street, at 4:30, and finally to the Surrey Gardens, a popular amusement spot, where he was with at least a dozen friends until 10:45 p.m. And so, Pepys-like, to bed. So minute a rendering of his movements that day supplied Thomas with an impervious alibi, for it was during those later hours that brother Henry was performing his butchery on Harriet's remains with the brand-new tool he had received, at a fraternal markup of sixty-six per cent, from Mr. Pettigrew's.

To the archaeologist, shards from a midden—prehistoric rubbish—are precious evidence of man's way of life before he learned to write. To the social historian, similarly, the contents of a man's pockets may illustrate the life of the time in a way no formal records do. What did a Whitechapel man in a small and unsuccessful way of business carry with him on the day he took a theatrical lady on a ride across the Thames? This is the inventory made at the police station: £3 10s. in gold, 12s. 8d. in silver, some coppers, foreign coin, pawnbrokers' checks, twenty-seven keys, a silver watch and metal chain, a tape measure, spectacles and case-knife, rule, pencil case, two cigars (another had been consumed during the cab-ride), a memorandum book, and a handkerchief.

Details of mid-Victorian female costume: Harriet wore her hair 'done up in the back, with a large pad. . . . Her hair was frizzed over the pad.' The surgeon who inspected her remains marvelled—perhaps he was not a family man—at the formidable contrivance the unfortunate lady bore, under the dictates of fashion, on her head. In addition to a bullet embedded in it, 'There were also in the pad an immense quantity of hairpins. . . . The hairpins in the pad were bent, broken, and rusty. They were innumerable all over the pad, and sufficient to have arrested the progress of a bullet.' History does not record what effect, if any, this testimony had on the vogue for chignons.

Graphic vignettes of scene, habit, and character:

The testimony of an oilman neighbour in Whitechapel Road who kept a pistol with him to practice marksmanship in odd moments: 'I fired at anything I took it into my head to fire at.' The Lord Chief Justice: 'Was it with the view of practising to make yourself a shot, or at little birds hopping about, or had you any particular mark to fire at?' Witness: 'I had no particular mark.' (This in the midst of a crowded city!)

The sudden grim scene of shirtsleeved policemen digging for evidential odds and ends at Harriet's late grave: 'On the first day,' testified one of them, 'we had candles and lanterns. In the daytime it was perfectly light there from the skylight. Sometimes children came round the door and looked through the keyhole and watched us. There were fissures in the shutters, through which they looked when we were there.' Slum children's free entertainment, a peep-show with live actors.

And, by way of contrast, the delightful business of the third champagne glass: When Harriet was visited, shortly before her disappearance, by a gentleman (Thomas Wainwright, posing as M. Frieake), they sent her landlady, Mrs. Foster, across the street to a pub to buy champagne and borrow glasses.

Defence counsel, recalling the episode in his closing speech: 'Mrs. Foster went and borrowed three glasses, and only two were used. There were only two persons for whom the wine came, and why did she get three? Possibly she thought they would ask her to take a glass.'

Lord Chief Justice: 'The same thought occurred to me.'

Counsel: 'I am happy to be confirmed by the Lord Chief Justice. Mrs. Foster was not asked to drink, and whether or not she thought the rising generation less polite than in her younger days, the disappointment was one likely to impress the matter upon her memory, and she said the bottles came upon two separate occasions, thereby flatly contradicting Mrs. Humphries' evidence.' A landlady who has been pointedly not asked to share a bottle of champagne, even when she has brought her own glass, is not likely to have forgotten the incident or the surrounding circumstances.

From the human-interest point of view, then, Wainwright's is a most instructive case. Aesthetically, however, it is less satisfactory.

Edward FitzGerald[1] complained to the actress, Fanny Kemble, that it was 'a nasty thing, not at all to my liking'. Like other spectators, he regretted that the Whitechapel brushmaker bore the same family name, less the medial *e*, that had been made famous many years earlier by the cunning activities of the art critic, Thomas Griffiths Wainewright. There was a world of difference between an accomplished forger-poisoner and a hacker-up of a woman's body. So also thought Algernon Swinburne, who wrote in indignation to William Michael Rossetti: 'I must express to you the deep grief with which I see the honoured name of Wainwright associated with a vulgar and clumsy murder, utterly inartistic and discreditable to the merest amateur. It is as though William Shakespeare were charged with the authorship (*pace Laureati*) of [Tennyson's] "Queen Mary".' This was a most unkind double-edged cut on Swinburne's part—but who can say that, strictly on the technical level, Henry the bungling brushmaker did not deserve it?

Richard D. Altick

---

[1] Poet and translator (of, inter alia, *The Rubáiyát of Omar Khayyám*). He liked to quote to his correspondents, as evidence of his delight in murder trials, the lines in *The Beggar's Opera*: 'The charge is prepared; the Lawyers are met; The Judges all ranged, a terrible show!' Once, remarking on his having ordered a copy of the *Newgate Calendar*, he wrote, 'I don't ever wish to see and hear these things tried; but when they are in print I like to sit in Court then, and see the Judges, Counsel, Prisoners, Crowd: hear the Lawyers' Objections, the Murmur in the Court, etc.' FitzGerald's early biographer, Thomas Wright, describes his delicate discrimination: 'Murders whose incidents were picturesque or suggestive of chiaroscuro, or which exposed the bed and secret recesses of the soul, whether of the assailer or the victim, excited his deep and perennial interest; whereas a brutal common murder, unaccompanied by startling psychological accessories, only disgusted him.'

THE DEATH OF A DESPERADO
Anonymous

'As our late and great editor, Dutton Peabody, used to say:
"... This is the West. When a legend becomes a fact, print
the legend."'

*Lines spoken by Carleton Young, playing a
newspaper reporter, in the movie* The Man Who
Shot Liberty Valance *(1962); screenplay by
James Warner Bellah and Willis Goldbeck*

Dispatches to the Chicago *Tribune*:

KANSAS CITY, Missouri, 3 April [1882]—Here the James
boys, Frank and Jesse, were reared, and here has ever been
their harbour of refuge when chased from pillar to post and
State to State by detectives. Here many of their old guerrilla
comrades of the Civil War are living, and here, too, they have
friends and relatives residing.

The James boys were raised in Clay County, within twelve
miles of Liberty; the other outlaw brothers, the Youngers, in
Jackson County, within four miles of Independence. There is
something suggestive in the names of their homes, for liberty and
independence with them have been carried beyond the limits of
criminal license.

Frank James joined Quantrell's guerrillas in 1863, when he
was twenty years old. He soon became noted for his daring and
murderous ferocity. Jesse, only fourteen years old, sought service
at the same time, but was rejected as too young. Returning home,

he became serviceable as a spy for the guerrillas infesting Clay and adjoining counties. His stepfather, Dr. Reuben Samuels, was a pronounced Secessionist, and old Mrs. Zerelda Samuels gave unbridled license to her tongue in advertising her sympathy for the South. The family, thus making themselves conspicuous, were marked for vengeance by the Union militia of the State.

In William Quantrell's command the James boys found congenial spirits in Cole and Jim Younger, John Jarrette, Clell Miller, George Shepherd, and others who have been partners in their robberies since the War. Both were in Quantrell's band of twenty when Lawrence, Kansas, was sacked, burned, and nearly every male inhabitant ruthlessly murdered. Jesse James boasted at the time to have shot down thirty-six.

Probably no horror of equal enormity or atrocity was ever perpetrated than the massacre on 27 September 1864, at Centralia, Missouri, in a way station on the Wabash Railroad. Here, Bill Anderson, assisted by Jesse and Frank James, first raided the village and sacked the stores. Then, waiting for the east-bound train, they stopped it and robbed the passengers of their money. Among the passengers were thirty-two sick soldiers en route from St. Joseph to St. Louis for better hospital accommodations. These poor wretches were marched out and aligned by Frank and Jesse James, and Bill Anderson, with his own hands, shot and killed every man of them, a pistol being handed him by either Frank or Jesse as fast as he emptied the one in hand.

Scarce had the diabolical massacre been finished before a company of Iowa volunteers appeared in the distance, and they, too, became victims of the unerring aim of these bandits. Thus within two hours eighty slain were piled up about the village. Such scenes as these hardened the James boys, and made their latter-day crimes merely trivial in comparison.

St. Joseph [fifty or so miles north of Kansas City], 3 April [1882]—A great sensation was created in this city this morning by the announcement that Jesse James, the notorious bandit and train-robber, had been shot and killed here. The news spread with great rapidity, but most people received it with doubts until an investigation established the fact beyond question. Then the excitement became more and more intense, and crowds of people rushed to that quarter of the city where the shooting took place, anxious to view the body of the dead outlaw and to learn the particulars.

The body is that of a man of magnificent physique, who in the pride of health and strength must have been a commanding figure, six feet tall, and weighing 175 pounds, with every muscle developed and hardened by active life. It is a body that would fill with delight the surgeon seeking material for demonstrating anatomy.

The features, but little disturbed in death, are not unpleasing, and bear the imprint of self-reliance, firmness and dauntless courage. To look upon that face is to believe that the wonderful deeds of daring ascribed to Jesse James have not been exaggerated. The hair is dark brown, the eyes half-opened, glazed, a cold steel grey; upon the upper lip is a close-cropped moustache, stained by nasal hemorrhage, and the lower part of the face is covered by a close brown beard about four inches long.

Over the left eye is the blackened wound caused by the bullet of Robert Ford, the beardless boy whose cunning and treachery, animated by greed of gold, brought to an ignoble end the desperado who has so long snapped his fingers contemptuously at the law and its myriad of agents.

A superficial examination of the body would alone afford strong proof that the dead body is that of Jesse James. He has been literally shot to pieces in his daring exploits, and his old wounds would have killed anyone cast in a less rugged mould. Two bullets have pierced the abdomen, and are still in the body. There is a bullet-hole in the right wrist, and another in the right ankle. Two more disfigure the left thigh and knee. The hands are soft and white and unstained by manual labour, and the middle finger of the left hand has been shot away at the first joint.

Hundreds of people have passed before the body, and while there was a unanimous expression of relief that the country was rid of so formidable a desperado, there were not a few who did not hesitate to condemn the manner of his taking off. Nevertheless, the young Ford brothers are undeniably the heroes of the hour. As they sat in the County Clerk's office this afternoon awaiting their call before the Coroner's inquest, then progressing in an adjoining room, they were the coolest and most unconcerned persons present, and the very last that a stranger would pick out as the slayers of Jesse James.

It was Robert E. Ford, the younger brother, who fired the fatal shot, but his brother Charles was at his side with cocked revolver in hand to second his attempt. Charles is twenty-four years old, with black hair banged over the forehead, heavy black eyebrows, a faint and foppish moustache, high cheek bones, sunken cheeks, and square jaw, denoting great firmness. Robert, the killer, is but twenty years of age, five feet ten and a half inches tall, and weighs 135 pounds. His hair is brown and close-cropped, and his round, ruddy face is smooth-shaven. He has hazel eyes, as sharp as a hawk's, which constantly move about with restless and penetrating gaze. There was not the faintest trace of excitement in the young man's manner as he detailed the story of his act.

'There is nothing to conceal,' he said, 'and I am proud of what I have done. I was born in Richmond, Ray County, Missouri, and raised on a farm until seventeen, when I clerked for two years in a country store. Then I went back on the farm.

'So they say the dead man isn't Jesse James, do they? Then they are mistaken. I first met Jesse James three years ago, and I have made no mistake. He used to come over to the house when I was on my oldest brother's farm. Last November he moved here to St. Joe and went under the name of Thomas Howard. He rented a house on 31st up on the hill back of the World's Hotel, a quiet part of town and not thickly settled.

'My brother Charley and I had known nearly all of the gang, but had never worked with any of them otherwise. I was in collusion with the detectives, and was one of the party that went to Kentucky and arrested Clarence Hite for robberies last February. Hite got twenty-five years in the penitentiary.

'Jesse never suspected that we were false to him, and as his gang was all broken up, he wanted new material and regarded us favourably. Two weeks ago, he came to Clay County to see his mother, Mrs. Samuels, who lives forty miles east of Kansas City. Charley and I told him then that we wanted to join him and become outlaws, and he said all right. Charley came here with him a week ago Sunday and I followed last Sunday night. We both stayed at his house, a one-storey building with seven rooms. Governor Thomas Crittenden had offered $10,000 reward for Jesse, dead or alive. We knew that the only way was to kill him. He was always cool and self-possessed, but always on the watch.

'During the day he would stay around the house, and in the evening he would go down town to the news depot and get the papers. He said there were men here who ought to know him, but they never did. He took the Chicago *Tribune*, Cincinnati *Commercial* and Kansas City *Times*, and always knew what was going on all over the world. About a week ago he read a piece in one of the papers that Jesse James's career was over, and Charley said he was awful mad about it. He said he would show them before long that Jesse James was not done yet. He had not done any job since the 'Blue Cut' train robbery last September, and I don't believe he had over $700 or $800 in money. He was thinking of robbing some bank nearby and then running in under close cover. It was for this he wanted our help.

'Well,' continued the youth, calmly relighting his cigar, 'we knew we had to kill him. But there was no chance to get the drop on him until this morning. His wife, and boy of seven and girl of three, were in the kitchen. Jesse was in the front sitting-room where he slept.

'I never knew him to be so careless. He commenced brushing the dust off some picture-frames, but stopped and took off his weapons and laid them on the bed. There was a Colt's revolver and a Smith & Wesson, each .45 calibre. He also had in the room a Winchester repeating rifle, fourteen shots, and a breech-loading shotgun.

'As he turned away from the bed, we stepped between him and his weapons and pulled on him. I was about eight feet from him when he heard my pistol cock. He turned his head like lightning. I fired, the ball hitting over the left eye and coming out behind the right ear. Charley had his finger on the trigger, but saw he was done for and did not shoot. He fell dead at Charley's feet.

'We got our hats, went to the telegraph office and telegraphed Governor Crittenden, Police Commissioner Henry Craig of Kansas City, and Sheriff Timberlake of Clay County. The latter replied: "I will come at once. Stay there until I come."'

Bob Ford told this story in the most matter-of-fact and unimpassioned way, without a particle of the dramatic in the delivery.

EDITOR'S NOTE. People (I don't exclude myself) need heroes; and, perhaps because of the insufficiency of real ones, some people are willing—eager—to accept counter-feits. The quaint notion, quite widely held before Jesse James's death, that he was a sort of updated Robin Hood, forced by Big Business, The Establishment, The System (any or all of the above) to commit crimes (or rather, to retaliate), was given a tremendous fillip by Bob Ford: the suddenly late psychopath's life was twisted into required fiction—by dime-novelists masquerading as historians (fore-runners of those persons called drama-documentarists), composers of folk-songs (a sample: 'Jesse James was one of his names,/Another it was Howard./He robbed the rich of every stitch./You bet, he was no cow-ard.'), and eventually, and most influentially, Twentieth Century-Fox.

James's mother, who said that she had an almighty dread of grave-robbers, buried his body in her back-yard, and then charged for admission through the gate. Foremost among her merchandising sidelines was the selling of pebbles from the grave. The very fact that these went like hot cakes indicates a geological miracle: though by closing time on a good day the hallowed hummock was picked clean of pebbles, by opening time next morning it was pebble-strewn again (meanwhile, an opposite kind of phenomenon occurred in nearby creeks, the beds of which gradually became pebble-less). Part of one day's profits was spent on a marble memorial column which, when firmly planted at the head of the grave, was visibly less than nine feet tall. After twenty years in business, Mrs. Samuels (ex-James), clearly a sentimental old soul, had the casket and the column transported to the family plot in a cemetery at Kearney, halfway between St. Joseph and Kansas City; by the mid-1930s, the column, even the foundational part of it, was gone, chipped away by memento-obsessional pilgrims, many of them fully-paid-up members of one or another of the umpteen Jesse James fan-clubs. Later in that decade, an entrepreneur bought The House Where Jesse Met His Maker and removed it to an open site on what was then the edge of St. Joseph; so far as I know, it is still there, centrepiece of a 'Jesseland' theme-park, a major money-spinner for Jesse James Enterprises, Inc.

Six months after the death of his brother, Frank James surrendered—to Governor Crittenden in person. His belief that jurors would consider the murder of Jesse a fine excuse for saying that he, Frank, was innocent of all the murders, etc., that he had committed, was justified—not just once, but at a series of events called trials. It appears that, not wishing to push his luck, he thereafter led an honest life; he died naturally in February 1915, soon after his seventy-second birthday. As worried about the security of his remains as his mother had been about Jesse's, he had left instructions that his ashes were to be deposited in a bank-vault till they could be mixed with his wife's; though she outlived him by thirty years, his instructions were followed to the letter, and then the combined ashes, his and hers, were interred in a cemetery in Kansas City.

A fortnight after the shooting of Jesse James, both of the Ford brothers pleaded Guilty to murder in the first degree and were sentenced to be hanged; but as soon as Governor Crittenden heard about that, he granted them unconditional pardons. Certainly Bob Ford received a substantial slice of the long-promised reward (which, according to Crittenden, 'did not exceed $20,000, not one cent of which was drawn from the State'—meaning, presumably, that it was all contributed by railroad companies and banks), and Charles Ford received a lesser sum; but details of the pay-outs were never divulged. If it is true that Charles soon became paranoid from fear of being shot in the back (or, for that matter, in the front), his incapacity is understandable; at any event, one night in May 1884 he drank even more than he customarily did and then used a six-gun to silence his brain. After doing an act on the vaudeville circuit, Bob Ford opened a saloon for the silver-rushers in Creede, Colorado; in June 1892, E.O. Kelly, a far-distant in-law of the outlaw Youngers who had been on-and-off allies of the Jameses, considered that tenuous link a sufficient motive for entering the saloon and emptying his shotgun into the proprietor.

THE FATAL BARNEY
Peter Cotes

[Born in Berkshire, the eldest of four sons (two of the others, John and Roy, made a joint-name for themselves as the movie-producing Boulting Brothers), he was educated at the Italia Conti Stage School and by private tutor, and then became an actor, considered by many critics to be an infant prodigy. In 1947 he married Joan Miller, the distinguished Canadian-born actress, with whom he was also in professional partnership till her death in 1988. During that time, they ran the New Lindsey Theatre Club and the New Boltons Theatre, in London, and the Library Theatre, Manchester, presenting many new plays and revivals of plays by, among others, Strindberg, O'Neill, Ibsen and Shaw; Cotes's production of the premiere of his friend F. Tennyson Jesse's A Pin to See the Peepshow (based on the Bywaters-Thompson murder-case), in which Joan Miller seemed to become Edith Thompson, caused many supporters of capital punishment at least to consider changing sides. He has directed other murderplays in London, including Finishing School (based on the Adelaide Bartlett case) and The Mousetrap (of which he was the original director). He was a pioneering producer of television drama, both in England and abroad. He has written a number of books, including biographies of Charlie Chaplin and George Robey, and is presently writing his own life-story.]

Why shouldn't I have fun? I died young, didn't I?
'Elvira' in Noël Coward's Blithe Spirit

ONE WAY AND ANOTHER, Elvira Barney has been cropping up in my life since the time when, as a very young actor (in Charles B. Cochran's production of Noël Coward's *Cavalcade* at Drury Lane), I was first made aware of her through the evening newspapers I would regularly take into the dressing-room. I have often wondered since whether Coward read about her, too, and decided to call one of his best-known characters after the woman with the unusual name who proved to be such a great 'attraction' during her rather limited run at the Old Bailey.

Later I was to meet two of the three daughters of Elvira's defending counsel, one of whom I got to know well; and later the great man himself when, lunching at the Ritz in the late 1940s at the invitation of Philip Barry, whose play *The Animal Kingdom* I had just directed in the West End, my host invited 'Pat' Hastings, who was also a playwright, to join us for a liqueur.

Later still, in rapid succession, I was to meet three further members of the cast of that Old Bailey 'production'. First there was Arthur Jeffress, with whom my wife and I shared a day at the home of a mutual friend, Beverley Nichols, and then a dinner at our own home in Chelsea after we had driven him back to London from Surrey. During the day we had heard a little about Elvira, and I guessed when we invited him in for a drink that later, if he stayed to dine (which he invited himself to do), we should hear more. He was, as I remember him, both witty and wistful and, as befitted the last person but one to see Michael Stephen alive, a mine of information about the fateful night at Williams Mews. It was a pity we never saw Arthur Jeffress again. Like his friend Elvira, he was to die in Paris—not long after leaving us, but over a score of years later than her. Unlike her, he died by his own hand.

Then there was the trial judge. In 1951 I directed a dramatisation of the Tennyson Jesse novel, *A Pin to See the Peepshow*, which dealt with the Thompson–Bywaters case, and the elderly, though still alert, Sir Travers Humphreys accepted my invitation to honour a matinee performance with his presence. He had been junior counsel for the Crown in Rex *v.* Thompson and

Bywaters (1923). After the performance, over tea, he expressed his fascination at having seen the Edith Thompson story re-enacted, and subsequently penned a congratulatory letter, which I proudly pinned on to the backstage notice-board for the benefit of the cast.

Subsequently I made the acquaintance of Judge H. C. Leon, better known to the reading public as Henry Cecil. But although Judge Leon as a young barrister attended the Barney trial 'on behalf of an interested party', I never enquired who the interested party was. I have an idea that such a query would have produced no satisfactory reply from a lawyer who, though he sometimes poked good-natured fun at certain aspects of the law, would have regarded the identity of his 'interested party' as some sacred trust, to be treated in the strictest professional confidence.

On the night the Barney trial ended, I went, together with several other occupants of my dressing-room at Drury Lane, to a small drinking club that was then open for after-the-show refreshments in a cellar in Gerrard Street, off Piccadilly Circus. It was called by the somewhat exotic name of Smokie Joe's, and I had made its acquaintance through its proximity to both the London Hippodrome and the Queen's Theatre, where I had recently played.

Shortly after midnight, down the steps clattered a trio— two women and a man—who immediately ordered drinks. There was a heaviness about the jowl and a tired brightness in the eyes of one of the women in the party that made her face appear familiar. But the lighting was subdued, and it was not until later, when she unexpectedly lurched over to our table and, with what passed for a flashing smile, invited me to dance with her, that I knew for certain who she was. We danced, or rather walked, to a blues, and after a few minutes around that little dance floor, I felt very tired indeed. The solitary jazz-pianist finished his number, and I remember (there are some things you simply cannot forget) that Elvira staggered back to her table, calling over her shoulder for me to join her party. But I went home to bed. I shall never know what prompted her gesture; nor shall I forget it. As I recall the memory of that brief early-morning encounter, made less distant as I write, it would seem, upon reflection, that Elvira Barney danced no better than she shot.

* * *

On 1 June 1932, the following brief report appeared, inconspicuously featured, on an inside page of a London newspaper:

Tragedy after a Cocktail Party

Michael Stephen, the handsome son of a distinguished father, was found lying dead with a wound in his chest on the landing of an exotically-furnished little house in Williams Mews, Lowndes Square, Knightsbridge, while Mrs. Elvira Dolores Barney, the beautiful daughter of Sir John and Lady Mullens, stood distractedly above him, moaning and sobbing.

The tragedy has presented the police with a difficult and delicate problem. It is understood that their investigations have not established how the fatal shot came to be fired. It is probable that further investigation will be left to the coroner and his jury, who will have to decide in what way the young man met his death.

This was followed three days later by a front-page item that read:

Mrs. Elvira Dolores Barney, the beautiful daughter of Sir John and Lady Mullens, was arrested last night in the house of her parents in Belgrave Square, S.W.

She was taken to Gerald Road police station and charged with the murder of Mr. Michael Scott Stephen, who was found shot dead on Tuesday morning.

When Mrs. Barney appeared at Westminster Police Court on 6 June, charged with the murder, it was merely to hear evidence of formal arrest. Her reply to the charge was: 'I did not shoot him. I am not guilty.'

From these bare reports was to emerge a murder trial such as had not been before the courts for years, according to Mrs. Barney's counsel, Sir Patrick Hastings. It was certainly 'the murder of the year'; the most vivid and controversial; the most theatrical because it was the most dramatic. Its worldwide audience had no difficulty in appreciating its topicality, for, outside that period in time, perhaps the very events that stirred so many to debate the character of the woman on trial for her life would never have happened. Julian Symons has written in *Between the Wars*:

> In retrospect the whole period looks like an interregnum between the savage realities of two wars, but again, of course, it was not like that for those who lived through it. The pictures as one turns them over are optimistic, sad, nostalgic, unbelievable. Were there actually Bright Young Things?

'There was a terrible barney at No. 21,' neighbours told the police after the shooting, using the word in the sense of a rowdy jollification and without being conscious of the pun. It was Elvira's party that caused it, of course; that was what the barney was all about. Such parties were dangerous: lavish but sleazy, and often frequented by drug-takers. In those days you had to be a member of a select coterie to get the 'stuff'. At one such party, held in a house in Chelsea Church Street a short time earlier and attended by Elvira, a young man named Philip Carew had hurled himself out of a top-floor window while 'high' on cocaine. He was dead when they found him. His death caused no widespread comment, few questions. The pushing and taking of dope was rarely seen by bystanders, as it is today, in public lavatories, at hippie carnivals, and outside West End chemists, when the sight of addicts fixing themselves, and sometimes selling the stuff to anyone whose needs—or finances—are greater than their own, provides a gruesome spectacle. At the time of the Barney case, such things were not done publicly; drug-taking was an activity reserved for private gatherings.

The type of party favoured by Elvira Barney was only one of many given by the rich. In the squares of St James's, Belgrave, Portman, Grosvenor and Berkeley, the glittering parties were thrown by and for the mighty of the land. And some of the children of the mighty concocted novel party-formats: there were circus parties, pajama and nightdress parties, Swiss/Greek/Russian parties, Royal Flying Corps/ nautical/marine parties, fireworks parties, bathing parties, adults-dressed-as-kiddies parties; for a Mozart party given by David Tennant, the bill came to over £3000, which in today's accounting—with service *and* VAT—would amount to thirty times that figure. One wonders what the unemployed and the destitute thought about such extravagance.

It is doubtful whether Elvira Barney ever thought about what anybody, irrespective of class, thought of anything or anybody. She seems to have believed that her riches meant that she could afford to be selfish; she wanted her own way and was usually able to get it.

She was the elder, by three years, of two sisters. In October 1925 the younger sister, Avril, then only sixteen, married Prince George Imeretinsky, a member of a noble White Russian family. The wedding was held at St Margaret's, Westminster; the bride received from her father a flat in the then still exclusive Park Lane, a settlement of £4000 a year, and a string of individually expensive pearls.

Sir John Ashley Mullens had been created a knight a few years before Avril's wedding. An Old Etonian, he was a trustee of the Stock Exchange and held the position of Chief Government Broker. The tall and striking Lady Mullens was said, with some justification, to look as young as her two daughters. In the 1920s and early 1930s, before the distressing events in which the whole family became helpless participants, the Mullens did much entertaining at their sumptuous town residence, 6 Belgrave Square, and at their country estate, the Manor House at Haslemere, Surrey.

When Avril won her Prince, Elvira—who had been receiving stage training at Lady Benson's Acting Academy for some months past—decided to turn what was perhaps a teenage whim and an amateurish exercise into a rather more professional pursuit. Hence her appearance in *The Blue Kitten*, which opened at the Gaiety Theatre in the West End on 23 December 1925. The programme did not list the young 'Dolores Ashley' (she had taken both her own and her father's second Christian name as a theatrical pseudonym), but she is said to have been 'a pleasant kid' by a member of the cast, whose memory, though blurred, still recalls her polite manner and the pre-production publicity that resulted from the theatrical début, though in a tiny part, of the elder daughter of such influential social lights as the Mullens.

Apparently, at the end of the run of *The Blue Kitten*, it was decided that Elvira was to return to the conventional life of a well-bred and well-heeled young woman. She was seen at first nights, smart restaurants and royal garden parties. She engaged in the social round of hunt-balls, Henley, Ascot, Goodwood, the Eton & Harrow match at Lords, and weekend shooting-parties. She helped her mother entertain throughout the year and especially during the 'season' at the fine London house.

Late in 1927, at one of the gatherings at 6 Belgrave Square, she first met the man she was destined to marry. John Sterling Barney was an American entertainer who had appeared in the revue *Many Happy Returns* at the Duke of York's Theatre, and had played in cabaret and on the music-hall stage in a singing act, 'The Three New Yorkers'. It was a good little trio—top-hat-white-tie-and-tails in style—and Barney's partners were later to continue as a double-act under the name of Ross and Sergeant, becoming well-known in cabaret and on gramophone records. 'The Three New Yorkers' were popular entertainers at society functions, and after they had performed their act at a party given by Lady Mullens, Barney danced with Elvira, who seems to have at once succumbed to his facile charm. They arranged to meet again, and before long a close relationship developed. On 2 August 1928 they were married at Princes Row Register Office, a venue which, in comparison with St Margaret's, Westminster, suggests that the Mullenses questioned whether it was a fair exchange to lose Elvira as a daughter and gain John Sterling Barney as a son.

The marriage was a failure from the start. At the trial, Sir Patrick Hastings referred to Barney as a 'brute'. Although no evidence was produced to substantiate that description, it seems to be confirmed by the recollection of Effie Leigh, one of Elvira's friends, and the only person, apart from Lady Mullens, whom she wished to see while awaiting trial in Holloway Prison: 'One day she held her arms in the air, and the burns she displayed—there and elsewhere—were, she insisted, the work of a husband who had delighted in crushing out his lighted cigarettes from time to time on her bare skin.'

The violent rows started in earnest within weeks of the marriage. A few months later, the cabaret-artist left Elvira and returned to the United States; 'the beautiful blonde', who was so quickly to go to seed, and the singing American, who had so quickly stopped singing, never saw each other again. (Four years later, his wife about to stand trial, Barney was to send a cable to Lady Mullens; apart from a brief newspaper paragraph later still, this was the last that was heard of the former member of 'The Three New Yorkers'.)

After the parting, Elvira's life-style grew even more rackety. She started 'sniffing the snow', along with Brenda Dean Paul's set, whose kicks came from a wide variety of drugs. She threw parties, frequented night-clubs and bars, and became the demanding but generous mistress of a number of disorientated and sexually-odd lovers. After a succession of such affairs, she was to be found at the start of 1932 living with Michael Scott Stephen, a good-looking man of twenty-five who described himself as a dress-designer.

If Stephen appeared more worthless than Elvira, it was only because she was rich and he was not. His father, the London manager of the North of Scotland Bank and a Justice of the Peace, had grown so disgusted with his son's mode of living that he had cut off his allowance and barred him from the family-home; his mother, however, continued to send him small sums of money. He had two brothers and a sister. All three sons had been educated at Shrewsbury; in 1932, Stephen's sister was studying domestic science.

Stephen shared Elvira's banking-account as well as her bed, at 21 Williams Mews, which had been a garage before being converted into a four-roomed maisonette. The Mews itself was a narrow cobble-paved cul-de-sac leading off the Knightsbridge end of Lowndes Square, and was mainly comprised of garages with living-quarters above them for chauffeurs and their families.

Whether Elvira derived most pleasure from the dope, the alcohol or the wild parties is anybody's guess. Whether she experienced a vicarious thrill from her lover's activities with other men, which were additional to his heterosexual behaviour with her, cannot be ascertained at this late date. What we do know, from subsequent disclosures, is that much of the fighting and screaming that went on between them was intended to whet the appetite of each partner in what was a perverse sexual relationship. But however odd their liaison, there is no doubt of Michael's contentment in being kept and Elvira's contentment in keeping him. 'I was more in love with him than with any of the others,' she was to say later. Many of her remarks must be viewed with suspicion, but not that one.

*   *   *

The day and night of Monday, 30 May 1932, proceeded in a manner that was more or less normal, if one can apply that word to such a relationship. Elvira and Michael lunched in the West End after staying in bed until nearly noon, sleeping off the effects of a party; more drinks were consumed before, during and after their meal. Then they returned to Williams Mews to prepare for the party they were giving that night.

From about six o'clock until past ten, a babble of voices and the strains of jazz records sounded through the open windows; cars of the open-carburetter type, fast and noisy mechanical monsters in lurid colours, came and went. If the time passed quickly for the party-goers, it must have dragged for the neighbours. However, Elvira's last party at 21 Williams Mews was allowed to run its course: on earlier occasions during the year or so that she had lived in the Mews, some of the chauffeurs and their wives had called in the police to stop the pandemonium, but there were no interruptions tonight.

According to Arthur Jeffress, the last arrival, he stayed on and accompanied Elvira and Michael to the Café de Paris for 'supper' and then to the Blue Angel Club in Soho for drinks. It was after 2 a.m. when they left Jeffress and returned home. He said later that they had *appeared* to be friendly.

At about 4.40 a.m. the telephone rang at the home of Dr Thomas Durrant, a well-known West End physician, who had attended Mrs. Barney for certain maladies whose nature was never disclosed. Crying hysterically, Mrs. Barney said that there had been a terrible accident at 21 Williams Mews, and begged the doctor's wife, who had answered the call, to get her husband to come at once. A few minutes later the telephone rang again. Mrs. Barney, more incoherent than ever, was now demanding to know why the doctor had not arrived. Dr Durrant arrived at the maisonette, in fact, less than ten minutes later, but by that time Stephen was dead. He was lying on the stairs, shot in the chest at short range. Elvira was sobbing and screaming in turn, every so often moaning and kissing the dead man. She kept repeating: 'He wanted to see you to tell you it was only an accident.'

The doctor called the police, who arrived within a few minutes. Despite her hysteria and dazed condition, the story Mrs. Barney told the first officers on the scene was the same that she was to tell throughout the subsequent interrogations. In bare outline, it was that when she and Michael had returned from the night-club and gone to bed, an argument had started. He had got out of bed, threatened to walk out on her, and dressed with the intention of doing so. There had been an argument about a revolver that Elvira kept on the premises and Michael was taking with him. He left the bedroom with it and she followed in an attempt to regain the weapon. There was a struggle, during which Michael was accidentally shot.

Sir John and Lady Mullens were telephoned. The police, anxious to question Elvira further, made preparations to take her to the police station before her parents arrived. What was left of her self-control snapped and she clouted the officers' faces, struggled as they tried to hold her, and threatened them with dire consequences if they put her in a cell. 'You foul swine,' she screamed at one of the detectives. 'Now you know who my mother is, perhaps you will be more careful what you say and do to me.'

It is a curious aspect of the case that the police did little or nothing to restrain Elvira in the face of great provocation, though a violent attack upon any of their number, especially under the shadow of what was suspiciously akin to previous violence resulting in death, should have been sufficient reason for doing so. What is more surprising is that, immediately after making her statement at the police station, she was allowed her liberty *unconditionally*. The police may have felt that their suspicions were not strong enough to justify a charge being preferred; even so, a woman suffering such strain and having already displayed violence in their presence might surely have been regarded as too dangerous to be let loose at that time.

Elvira Barney made three statements within a few hours of the shooting, but as they hardly differ, we shall concentrate on one only, which reads as follows:

> I am twenty-seven years of age and of no occupation. I have been residing at the above address alone for about a year. I am a married woman living apart from my husband, who is at present in America. The last I heard of him, he was a singer. He left me about two and a half years ago. I have known a man named Michael Scott Stephen for about a year. I was introduced

to him through friends.

We were great friends and he used to come and see me from time to time. He had no occupation. He always used to see me home, and last night he did so as usual. We arrived home at 2 a.m. Immediately we got in, we had a quarrel about a woman he was fond of. He knew I had a revolver in the house. I have had it for years. I do not know where it came from. It was kept in various places. Last night it was under the cushion of a chair in the bedroom, near the bed. I was afraid of it and I used to hide it from time to time. He knew where it was last night. He took it from under the chair saying, 'I'm going to take it away for fear you will kill yourself.' He went into the room on the left. I ran after him and tried to get it back. There was no struggle in the bedroom. He was outside in the spare room in the doorway. As we were struggling together—he wanted to take it away and I wanted to get it back—it went off. Our hands were together, his hands in mine, for a few minutes. I did not think anything had happened. It seemed quite all right.

I did not think anything serious. He went into the bathroom and half-shut the door. He said, 'Fetch a doctor.' I asked, 'Do you really mean it?' I did not have the revolver then. I think it had fallen to the ground.

I saw he looked ill. I rang up the doctor and no one answered. I went upstairs and saw him sitting on the floor. I was upset and began to cry. I again rang up the doctor and he said he would come. I went upstairs again. Stephen said, 'Why does not the doctor come? I want to tell him what has happened. It was not your fault.' He repeated that over and over again. I tried to cut his tie off. I put a towel on his chest and got pillows. I again rang up the doctor and they said he was leaving. I again went upstairs and saw he was dead and just waited. I don't remember what I did afterwards, I was so frantic. I am sure, as far as I know, there was only one shot fired.

Stephen and I had quarrelled on previous occasions, but not often.

(*Signed*) ELVIRA DOLORES BARNEY
31.5.32

After making the statement, Elvira went to her parents' house, where she was put to bed and heavily sedated.

During the rest of that day and the following one, there was much police activity at 21 Williams Mews—and, for that matter, in the mews itself. Before long, items of information began coming in from many quarters—reports from forensic experts, and statements from neighbours and from acquaintances of Elvira and Stephen. But there was silence from most of those who had attended the party. Arthur Jeffress, the last person but one to see Stephen alive, was interviewed, and a statement was taken from Hugh Wade, who had been at the party and later played the piano at the club where Elvira, Jeffress and Stephen had finished up their night with drinks. The rest of the party-goers were bashful about coming forward. One man telephoned but was not prepared to give his name; he arranged to meet the police but failed to turn up.

The tenants of the mews were agog with excitement: a man had been shot by one of their number, and they knew more about it than anybody else. Some of them claimed that they had heard not only the noise of the quarrel, but Mrs. Barney shrieking, 'I will shoot you.' Some of them insisted that there had been more than one shot. (There was apparent corroboration of this from the fact that two chambers of the five-chambered pistol had been fired, and the mark of a second bullet had been found by the police in the wall where the stairs turned.) Some people living a good distance from No. 21 claimed to have heard a quarrel on a previous night. Stephen, they said, had walked out of the maisonette and Elvira had leaned out of a window, screaming, 'Laugh, baby, laugh for the last time,' and then produced a gun and fired at him.

It seemed to the police that statements like these— coupled with information contained in the preliminary reports of Sir Bernard Spilsbury, the pathologist, and Robert Churchill, the gunsmith—provided adequate evidence for charging Mrs. Barney with murder. She was arrested four days after the shooting and brought before Mr. Boyd, the magistrate at Westminster Police Court.

Her first appearance only served the purpose of ensuring that she would have expert legal representation. Walter Frampton, one of the most able criminal lawyers of his day, represented her at the second police-court appearance, when she was bound over for a further week. The police utilised the time to complete their case and make Elvira's committal a foregone conclusion. Sir John and Lady Mullens took the opportunity to prevail upon a reluctant Sir Patrick Hastings to lead Frampton in the defence. She was fortunate in this respect, if in little else.

The only recollection of the police-court proceedings to stay in Sir Patrick's memory was Elvira's appearance. She was less composed than at any other time since her arrest, and her face was ashen. Although described as a beautiful member of a smart set, she was anything but beautiful now; her mode of life in recent years had coarsened her looks. Her present ordeal was doubtless a contributory factor in determining her counsel's verdict on her lack of charm. He said in his autobiography:

> My first view of Mrs. Barney was slightly depressing. ... her appearance was not calculated to move the hearts of a jury; indeed, she was a melancholy and somewhat depressing figure as she stood in the dock with a wardress upon each side of her.

But if the memory of Sir Patrick remained clear about his client's appearance in his autobiography, he was less sure about his own part when cross-examining those two star witnesses, Sir Bernard Spilsbury and Robert Churchill: the former the Home Office's most distinguished pathologist, and the latter a renowned fire-arms expert. When both cast doubts on the prisoner's version of the shooting, Sir Patrick had to break his own rule that it is better not to cross-examine in a police court when the criminal charge is a serious one. This rule was based on his belief that the barrister, when engaged for the defence in a case that was almost certain to be sent to a higher court, should act as an observer, the silent friend at court, holding a watching brief rather than behaving as an active advocate. Writing about the case, Sir Patrick recalled: 'The proceedings in the police court were not unduly prolonged as there was no cross-examination.' But memory played him false. He did, in fact, examine witnesses, including Spilsbury, and gave the latter a foretaste of the type of long and searching cross-examination to which he might be subjected later on. There was more than one sharp passage of words, and when Spilsbury attempted to qualify a statement regarding the likelihood of both

Stephen's and Mrs. Barney's hands being on the trigger of the gun when it went off, and refused to give Hastings an unqualified 'Yes' or 'No' reply, he was told: 'I will now ask you the same question over again. I would like you to answer my question, yes or no.' Spilsbury replied that perhaps he could put it another way, to which came the retort that counsel would rather he put it in *his* way.

So much for the great advocate's memory regarding the tactics to be employed at police-court proceedings. His lapse here was less odd than when reading aloud one of Elvira's letters. He had got well into this before realising that it was the wrong one to read at that time:

> Michael darling, at last I have got your sweet little letter. It was not very long was it? If only I had received it last night I should have slept well. As it was I wondered if you really love me and it kept me awake all night.

This was part of a letter that was carefully noted by the magistrate—but at the trial it was never submitted as evidence. The only one of Elvira's 'passionate' letters that was read aloud then stated that her belief that Michael loved her was never in serious doubt.

The star performer of the Barney Case was, without a doubt, Sir Patrick Hastings. A man of the drama in the theatre (he had written a number of plays, none of them lucky enough to enjoy really long runs), he was the opposite of the old-style courtroom orator and fiery advocate. By the time the Barney Case arrived, he was in his early fifties and at the height of his fame as a King's Counsel. When he sat in court, a lithe, intense figure, with arms folded and wig slightly tilted over his brow, his eyes looking ahead or occasionally glancing at the dome of the court, his gold pencil continually rolled by thin nervous fingers, it was he who attracted the most interest. He did not seek the audience and the applause; they came to him as if by natural right. He invariably held the centre of the stage.

This was the man whom Sir John Mullens begged to defend his daughter. Sir Patrick hesitated. He was up to his eyes in work, with more than a score of expensively marked briefs in his chambers. Apart from the demands on his time, there was his well-known dislike of participating in trials involving a capital charge. It was said later by his daughter Patricia that his sole reason for accepting this particular case was his wife's persuasiveness. There had been a curious, though remote, link some years earlier, when the Hastings children had had a governess who had formerly been in the employ of Sir John and Lady Mullens. The governess had called her former charge '*dear* little Elvira', and Lady Hastings, remembering this term of endearment when she read about the arrest, felt acutely distressed for the parents of such a paragon. It was highly providential for 'little Elvira' that the wife of the man who was to plead her case so brilliantly remembered her as such.

From the start, the case was treated on a highly emotional level by the press, with purple passages galore:

> The door of the police court opened to admit a Mrs. Barney whose step was steady and gaze alert. Pale, perhaps, the rouged lips accentuating the pallor, yet with her emotions obviously under control. The hand of the matron rested lightly and guidingly upon one black swathed arm, but Mrs. Barney gently but firmly released herself. She passed me so close that I heard her husky murmur, 'I can manage, thank you.' And before a well-meaning court official could reach her side, she passed into the dock, which is more like a gang-way, and settled herself comfortably with her feet upon the lower rail. The tiny green bottle of smelling salts which was handed to her she dropped into her lap with a repeated, 'I am all right, thank you.' Then she looked across to Lady Mullens with the smile of a child who wishes to assure her mother that all is well with her. Occasionally she dabbed at her eyes and sometimes the shoulders shuddered, but she displayed no other emotion. There was no warning of the collapse which came at the end of an hour . . .

Michael's will was reported soon afterwards. It was very short, but anything to do with the case was compulsive reading, and when an evening newspaper printed the fact that '£5 was the sum left by Michael Stephen (real name William Scott Stephen), described as a dress designer, aged 25, whose address in his will was given as the Park Lane Hotel, Piccadilly, W.1.', it was as front-page news.

Voices were heard calling for the estranged husband. 'Where is John Barney?' demanded *The Daily Telegraph*. When he received news of Elvira's arrest, he suddenly left his New York apartment. Rumours started flying around that he was on his way to London, but even if he ever intended to stand by Elvira, he never arrived. His only reaction was to send two cables. The first, to Elvira, read: 'PETTY SQUABBLES ARE FORGOTTEN NOW'; the second, to Lady Mullens, 'STAND BY AND DO EVERYTHING FOR ELVIRA'S DEFENCE.'

Special teams of reporters were assigned to analyse the leading players in the drama. 'A Woman Reporter' took a close-up of Elvira from 'the woman's angle'—sob-stuff that has rarely been equalled:

> A young woman sobbing. Her gold shingled hair grown so long that it straggles outside her smart hat. . . . She is dressed in a simple black dress and coat and a close-fitting black hat encircled with a wreath of black and white camellias. . . . Her shoulders twitch the whole time. Her fingers are nicely manicured and she wears on one of them a huge sapphire ring. Her face is dead pale, but she has used her lipstick before coming to the court. . . . Everyone leans forward except the impersonal wardress and her change, who appears to be slipping sideways off the bench. It is by those twitching shoulders and the angle of the head that you can see how the ordeal is telling upon her. The clothes of the dead man are being examined. At the sight of his coat and canary-coloured pullover, Mrs. Barney bursts into sobs. . . . The last witness has been called. Mrs. Barney is asked to stand. She runs her fingers through her side curls, and as she is helped to her feet the contents of her handbag fall out, and coppers go spinning over the floor of the court. Then, supported by the wardress, she is led away. . . .

The bare facts were that a woman accused of shooting her lover had been committed to stand her trial at the Old Bailey. But 'bare facts', however dramatic, have rarely endeared themselves to popular newspapers, whose principal aim, in order to beat their nearest rival's circulation figure, seems to be to transform drama into melodrama. The press of the year 1932 had had murder in *low* places. Now it was to be murder in *high* places. As Edgar Lustgarden has said in *Defender's Triumph*:

> In contrast to the Borgias of fourteenth-century Italy and to the Medicis of sixteenth-century France, the well-to-do classes of twentieth-century Britain did not go in for killing, except with motor cars. . . . [A] great murder trial which did involve the rich came to many as a bolt out of the blue.

It is small wonder that large sections of the country looked forward to an exposure of high society as the trial drew near—an even bigger, better, more dramatic *crime passionnel* than any of its predecessors down the years. Admittedly, there was then no television to take the scenes, described by a newscaster, into the sitting-room; possibly the written word of the journalist who excelled in the 'purple passage' was superior in entertainment value. The morning and evening papers vied with each other in composing the most lurid banner-headlines, and on the placards were to appear such appetising morsels as 'Love Hut Letters', 'Amazing Notes in Barney Case', 'Mrs. Barney Sensation', 'Barney: More Revelations', and 'Elvira Collapses'.

The trial opened at the Central Criminal Court, Old Bailey, on Monday, 4 July 1932, before Mr. Justice Humphreys, who was later to be described by Sir Patrick Hastings as almost, if not quite, the best criminal judge he had ever known. Sir Ernle Blackwell, Permanent Under-Secretary at the Home Office, occupied a seat next to the Clerk of the Court, and the Director of Public Prosecutions, Sir Tindal Atkinson, was also in Court. Sir Percival Clarke and Mr. L.A. Byrne appeared for the Prosecution; Sir Patrick Hastings, KC, Mr. Walter Frampton, and Mr. Maurice Alexander for the Defence.

Elvira's leading counsel had refused to see her before the trial, although she had sent several messages begging him to visit her in prison. Hastings says in his autobiography that his decision was based on his fear that he would be 'hampered in the conduct of her defence either by something the defendant may have said or by something she may have thought her counsel may have wished that she would say. I am afraid that Mrs. Barney was disappointed at my refusal to see her.'

The Crown's case looked strong. Mrs. Hall, a neighbour, had testified at the Police Court that before the fateful shot, she heard Mrs. Barney shouting, 'Get out, I'll shoot you.' The experts in the case, Sir Bernard Spilsbury and Robert Churchill, had thrown serious doubts on the version that it was an accident; Churchill, the gunsmith, had described the weapon as one of the safest made and had spoken of the heavy pull of the trigger. It would be Hastings' task to shake the formidable battery of expert opinion and, if possible, discredit those who thought they had seen—and heard—so much.

Sir Percival Clarke opened the case for the Crown fairly and with restraint. Warning the jury that unlawful killing was murder unless otherwise proved, he urged them to look for any evidence consistent with innocence that would permit them to know how Stephen could possibly have died by means other than by the prisoner firing a pistol at him. He enumerated points that told against the prisoner, such as her unrestrained outburst against the police after the tragedy and her firing from the window of No. 21 at Stephen when he was leaving about three weeks earlier.

The Crown's first witness was on the point of being called when Hastings rose to make an application to the Judge that all Crown witnesses should leave the Court until they were needed to give evidence. *Not* including Sir Bernard Spilsbury, the Judge's expression seemed to say—but what he was *heard* to say was, 'Including Sir Bernard Spilsbury?' and then, 'Be it so.' And out they all trooped.

The Crown's first witnesses dealt with routine matters: Stephen's brother with evidence of identification, the police with the finding of the body. They were followed by the two intimates—Jeffress and Wade—who had been present at the party and later at the Café de Paris and the Blue Angel. Then came the witness who lived opposite No 21: Mrs. Hall, a chauffeur's wife, who told of watching the comings and goings at the cocktail party, of seeing Mrs. Barney and her friends leave afterwards, and of hearing Mrs. Barney screaming at four o'clock in the morning.

'I . . . heard Mrs. Barney say she was going to shoot. She said it twice. . . . I heard a shot. . . . I heard Mr. Stephen shout: "What have you done?" Mrs. Barney was screaming out, "Chicken, come back to me; I will do anything I can for you."' Mrs. Hall went on to say that there had been some shooting about three weeks before; Mrs. Barney had fired out of the window.

SIR PERCIVAL CLARKE: Where was Mr. Stephen?—He was at her door talking and calling and asking her for money.

Did she give him any?—She told him to go and fish for it. Mr. Stephen went away in the taxi-cab in which he had arrived and then returned, walking. I saw Mr. Stephen going away from the house, and Mrs. Barney looked out of the window and said: 'Laugh, baby—laugh for the last time,' and she fired.

How was she dressed?—I don't think she had anything on.

How do you know she fired?—I saw her and heard the shot.

Did you see in which hand she held the pistol?—The left.

Where was Mr. Stephen standing?—Practically outside my door.

Did he appear to be hit?—No. He told Mrs. Barney not to be so foolish, as everybody was looking at them.

Did she go inside?—She fell as though she had fainted.

Where did Michael go?—He got into a greengrocer's van standing in the mews.

Have you heard quarrelling between them before?—Many times.

In his cross-examination, Sir Patrick Hastings asked the witness:

Do you happen to know that the name by which Mrs. Barney frequently addressed Stephen was Mickey?—It might have been.

Are you prepared to pledge your oath that the words she used were not 'Mickey, Mickey, don't leave me'?—I am quite sure the word she used was 'Chicken'.

If you are wrong about that, and the word was

'Mickey', do you think you are as likely to be wrong about anything else you heard?—I still say the word she used was 'Chicken'.

Mrs. Kate Stevens, also a chauffeur's wife, who lived at No. 8, was then called. She said that she had heard two shots fired, and then two more. By this time it was about half-past four. 'I went to bed again, and then I heard a final shot . . . much louder. . . . It seemed to me from the bedroom.' She had heard Mrs. Barney and Stephen quarrelling but did not recognise the man's voice at first; after the last shot she heard Stephen say, 'What made you do it?' and then Mrs. Barney say, 'Michael, Michael, come back. I love you.' The witness then repeated, almost verbatim, Mrs. Hall's account of the previous shooting episode.

Dr Durrant, who had arrived before anybody else, in answer to Elvira's SOS over the telephone, confirmed that he had talked to her before she had had time to prepare any story that was untrue to suit her own ends. After talking the doctor through the telephone calls for help, his arrival and discovery of the body and the prisoner's behaviour throughout, Sir Patrick Hastings went on to ask: 'Did she appear to be passionately devoted to this dead man?'

DR DURRANT: Oh, yes.
HASTINGS: Did she kiss him after he was dead?
DR DURRANT: Yes, several times.
HASTINGS: And did her actions appear to you, so far as you could judge, to be absolutely sincere and genuine?
DR DURRANT: Certainly.

At the end of the long day, a weary Mrs. Barney—'I can still see her agonised face as she stood in the dock,' her counsel was later to recall—was escorted down to the cells while the fashionable sightseers restarted their chattering as they made for the exits, many of them more concerned as to which smart summer frock they could wear for the second day of the entertainment than with the predicament of their 'friend'.

The first part of the police evidence on the opening of the second day was of a formal nature. Detective Inspector Winter described the scene when he arrived, the position of the corpse at the top of the stairs, the revolver's proximity to the dead man's hand, the state of the drawing-room with its dirty bottles and glasses.

While cross-examining the inspector, Hastings sought to reduce the impact of the evidence of the two chauffeurs' wives regarding the earlier shooting incident:

> HASTINGS: As a result of your inquiries, can you tell me whether anyone complained to the police about an attempted murder in the mews about a fortnight previously? ... Or a report of any shooting? ... No complaint of any sort or kind?
> INSPECTOR: Not to the police.

The inspector admitted that no trace of any bullet-marks had been found in the mews, despite a very thorough search.

> HASTINGS: Was this revolver examined for fingerprints?
> INSPECTOR: Yes.
> HASTINGS: Was it found that the marks on it were so blurred that no fingerprints were decipherable except one?
> INSPECTOR: That is so.
> HASTINGS: Whose was that one?
> INSPECTOR: That was mine.

The Defence was holding its own. But now it was the turn of the experts, and the most notable of them, Sir Bernard Spilsbury, entered the witness-box to answer Sir Percival Clarke's questions about the cause of death. Spilsbury said: 'The wound was 2¾ inches below the left collar-bone and 3 inches to the left of the middle line of the front of the body. It was horizontal from back to front.'

The famous pathologist was the least histrionic of witnesses. However, the clinical details, calmly spoken, for some reason seemed to tickle the 'smart set' present, and that evening Hastings was to confide to his daughter Patricia that he had never in all his experience witnessed such repulsive behaviour in a court of law.

Clarke asked Spilsbury about suicide, and his admission that at the post-mortem on Stephen he had had to take such a possibility into account.

> SPILSBURY: Such a possibility did not appear to be a

reasonable one. In the first place, the bullet had not been fired from close to the body in the sense of touching it, at any rate as is usual in suicide injuries; it was also unlike suicides in that the aim was at the chest instead of the heart. There was also an absence of any attempt to draw aside the clothing. These things rendered suicide very improbable.

Clarke handed the revolver to Spilsbury, who said that it had a long and heavy pull and was impossible to discharge if pointed at the left side of the chest of the person holding it. 'With the wrist bent as it must be bent, I could not get enough power to discharge the pistol off at all.'

Hastings got to his feet, and the moment that so many had been waiting for had arrived. The pathologist was asked three short technical questions on bone formation. They were casually put; the great expert was in fact treated like a first-year medical student, and then dismissed. That was all. Spilsbury left the box, Hastings sat down. A murmur of surprise and speculation went around the court, but was quickly silenced by an usher.

Then came expert No. 2, Robert Churchill, to answer Sir Percival's questions concerning the weapon. Churchill said that it was of strong make, in good working order, with a strong trigger pull.

When he rose to cross-examine, Sir Patrick's response to this flat statement was to smile, point the weapon at the ceiling and pull the trigger over and over again. Someone jumped, and Sir Patrick reassuringly said, 'There's no danger.' This drew a laugh, the only one in the trial. Anyone who witnessed the 'demonstration' must have thought that even a child could have handled such a toy; the impression conveyed was that in any struggle the gun might have gone off. The expert's expression, as he watched the pantomime, was as tight as the gun was supposed to have been. He was about to step down when—apparently as an afterthought—Hastings casually continued:

HASTINGS: If two people were struggling to get possession of a revolver, and the pressure exerted was not strong enough to fire it at first, the cylinder might be turned around?

CHURCHILL: It might spin round.

HASTINGS: If the struggling persons are close and one has the revolver in her hand, and the other seizes the hand, it would go off?

CHURCHILL: It might.

HASTINGS: When the finger, not of the person killed, is on the trigger?

CHURCHILL (after a pause): Yes.

This evidence concluded the case for the Prosecution. The Defence then called a *Crown* witness, Dr. Morton, the Governor and Medical Officer of Holloway Prison, who had examined Mrs. Barney after her admission. He stated that he had found bruises on the prisoner, and agreed that they could have been caused during the alleged struggle over the revolver. Sir Patrick's next question was to help dispel rumour: 'Has there been, while the prisoner has been under your charge, the slightest indication that she has ever been addicted to drugs?' Dr. Morton answered 'No'.

Then Sir Patrick quietly called the prisoner at the bar. Without hesitation, Elvira walked almost languidly to the witness-box, accompanied by the two wardresses who had been her constant companions in the dock for the last day and a half. Although only twenty-seven, she looked at least twice her age—a raddled woman in her fifties. It was difficult to believe that only a few short years ago she had been appearing on the stage at the Gaiety Theatre, more for her physical appearance and position in society than for her histrionic ability. The courtroom was hushed as she replied to the first questions gently put to her by her counsel. The failure of a short marriage, the ill-treatment suffered at her husband's hands, her loneliness before taking a lease of the house in the Mews, the relationship with Stephen, her wish to marry him as soon as she could get a divorce from John Barney.

Elvira's voice trembled several times at the start of the examination, and the Judge told her that she could sit. Her counsel watched patiently, making no attempt to hurry the examination. When he addressed her, his voice was soft and sympathetic.

HASTINGS: Had Stephen any means, so far as you know, of earning his living?

MRS BARNEY: No.

She agreed, in answer to Sir Patrick's questions, that she became very devoted to Stephen, was anxious to marry him, and supported him almost entirely. He was not always kind to her; she was sometimes frightened of him, on one occasion so much so that she called the police.

When Stephen came to your window in May and asked for money, what did you say or do?—He stayed outside the house for some time.

Do you remember what you did?—I was so unhappy that I thought I would make him think I was going to commit suicide. I got the revolver and fired at random. I thought he would think I had killed myself, and would fetch people, the police possibly, so I looked out of the window and he saw me and realised, I suppose, that I was all right and nothing more was said or done at the time.

On the left wall of your bedroom are the marks of a revolver-bullet. When were they made?—On that occasion.

Was that the only occasion you fired the revolver before the day of Stephen's death?—Yes.

Then she was asked detail by detail about their return to the flat on the night of 30 May.

I am afraid you must tell us this, Mrs. Barney. Where did you go when you came back to the flat?—We went into the bedroom.

And at first, while you were in your room, was Michael Stephen kind to you, or was he not?—First of all, yes.

And what happened after you had been there for some time? Did he continue kind? Just tell us what he said to show how he changed.—He made love to me but was very angry because I did not respond in the way he wanted, and he said perhaps my feelings had changed. I told him that it was only because I was so unhappy at what had happened during the day—about money—and I could not forget it. That made him all the more angry. He said he was not pleased with the way things were going, and he wanted to go out the next day and not see me at all.

In other words, he was not either loving or kind at that time?—No.

What did Stephen do—did he stop in bed or get up?—He got up after some time. He dressed. I asked him not to leave me. I said if he did I should kill myself.

When you said you would kill yourself, did he say or do anything?—Yes, he got up from the dressing-table and made a dash for the armchair, and said: 'Well, anyway, you won't do it with this.'

Do you know how he knew the revolver was there?—I don't know exactly how, but he knew everything.

When he said: 'You won't do it with this,' what did he do?—He picked up the revolver. He ran out of the room towards the spare room. I ran after him.

At that time, in whose hand was the revolver?—Michael's.

Did you come up to him?—Yes. In the doorway of the spare room.

Will you now tell us as much as you can remember of what then happened?—We struggled with the revolver. He had it and I wanted it back. I kept saying, 'Give it to me.' I don't know whether he said, 'No', but the more I tried, the more he tried to get it away. The struggle became more and more hard. We were moving about. I cannot remember all our positions. I was so unhappy. I was crying. I don't remember, but I know we were struggling and suddenly I heard a shot.

Stop there. Have you ever in your life desired to shoot Michael Stephen?—Never.

Has there ever been in your life anybody you were fonder of than Michael Stephen?—Never.

Did you shoot him that night?—No.

Had you any motive for shooting him?—None.

In his cross-examination, Sir Percival Clarke strongly suggested jealousy as a motive for the shooting. This was the first suggestion of that emotion and Elvira looked surprised at the line of questioning, though agreeing without hesitation that there *was* another woman.

Sir Percival went in for the prepared 'kill', suggesting that she was consumed with jealousy of that other woman. No, Elvira replied wearily, the rows had been about gambling and not about sex. Later, in reply to Sir Percival's question: 'Did you say: "Get out, I'll shoot you"?' (which elicited a protest from the Defence that the words were, in fact, 'I'll shoot'), Mrs. Barney stated that what she actually said was, 'Don't leave me, don't leave me. If you do, I'll shoot myself.'

Sir Patrick rose to re-examine. He studied the prisoner, nearly at the end of her tether, and told her to stand, then asked that the pistol be placed on the ledge of the witness-box. For a moment or two, it seemed an eternity, there was silence. Hastings turned slightly away, then wheeled rapidly round to suddenly thunder: 'Pick up that revolver, Mrs. Barney!' She picked it up—spontaneously—with her *right* hand. 'Have you ever picked up a revolver with your left hand in your life?' 'No', replied Mrs. Barney. Not a soul in the court did not believe that the prisoner had been taken by surprise and had acted without forethought; not a soul in the court did not remember that Mrs. Hall had sworn that she saw the prisoner fire the revolver with her *left* hand.

Elvira's ordeal was over. The two stalwart wardresses helped her from the witness-box back to the dock.

The Crown's final address was forcefully put by Sir Percival Clarke, who made great play with motive (jealousy) and the indications that the prisoner was a woman of uncontrollable temper. He pointed out that the hands of the dead man were clean, whereas they would surely have been blackened had he been holding the gun when it was fired.

The Judge refused the Defence application to make its *entire* speech before the court rose, and Sir Patrick therefore elected to commence the next day.

After the court rose, Elvira's parents were again granted permission to visit her in the cells below.

It was the second-act curtain for that highly theatrical audience, and as they exited, talking and laughing, jostling and nudging each other, arranging where to meet that night—which party and at what time?—Pat Hastings surveyed the scene with ill-concealed loathing for those who had tried to turn a court of justice into a vulgar peepshow and peacock parade.

Immediately the court assembled for the last day, he was on his feet, laying about him with cutting scorn. It was the only emotion he displayed in what the Judge was later to term 'a remarkable forensic effort, certainly one of the finest speeches I have ever heard at the Bar'. Hastings flayed the sightseers and the curiosity-seekers; he showed his contempt in his manner as well as his words, referring to the strange amusement found by those who came to witness another person's agony. With more constraint, he scathingly referred to the Crown's contention that only 'slight provocation' had made his client strike a policeman.

Dispassionate but convincing, Elvira's defender spoke brilliantly and at length in his fight to save her from the gallows. His closing speech was perfectly audible everywhere, but, being *pianissimo*, it could not command the applause of the laymen. In the years ahead it was to draw from the Bar itself many tributes, and Mr. Justice Humphreys, who had sat grave and immobile throughout the address, was able, in summing-up, to tell the jury that the speech would assist them the more easily to reach the correct verdict because it had consisted of a careful analysis of the evidence and was free from anything like an appeal to sentiment.

After two hours, the jury returned a verdict of Not Guilty. The Crown's decision not to press a further indictment (that of shooting at Stephen with intent to murder him or do him grievous bodily harm) was agreed to by the Judge. The woman who had been the prisoner at the bar was one no longer; sobbing uncontrollably, she was resting her head on her arms, both supported by the dock's ledge. Meanwhile, Lady Mullens was being attended to by a physician, having collapsed on the floor as the verdict was being announced.

In the streets outside, the news of the verdict spread rapidly, and several hundred people were singing 'Three Cheers for Mrs. Barney' and 'For She's a Jolly Good Fellow' as Sir Patrick Hastings unobtrusively left the Old Bailey.

'C. H. Rolph', who, as Chief Inspector Hewitt of the City of London police force, was on duty at the time, remembers the occasion well: 'I was in Court throughout the trial and now stood in the Judge's Corridor at the Old Bailey when the court rose on the last day. As Mr. Justice Humphreys passed me, he said to his Clerk, "Most extraordinary! Apparently we should have given her a pat on the back!"'

Elvira, although acquitted of murder by the jury, was found guilty by the press of being loose, vicious and immoral. A free press, we have been reminded, performs a vital role in exposing wrongdoing and corruption. But a press that becomes the public prosecutor rarely serves justice. Elvira's life-style was played up for all it was worth; the implication was that the company she kept was wholly appropriate to a fortunate murderess.

Elvira joined that company while the tanks rumbled, the dictators ranted and many people wondered where the next meal was coming from. With three million unemployed, the not-so-bright-young-things, left over from the twenties, were still living a rainbow-coloured dream-life; they pursued their idle lives with a relentless purpose that concealed its purposelessness.

As Macdonald Hastings has pointed out in *The Other Mr Churchill*:

> Half of West End society smirked that it had been present at the cocktail party which preceded the event, and the other half were accused of it. In fact, it was attended by not more than thirty people; and it is notable that there were as many to risk their reputations as that. Elvira was rich and generous; but her converted stable house hardly invited a second visit. Even the police, when they saw the place, were as shocked as it is possible for policemen to be.
>
> Over the cocktail bar in the corner of the sitting-room there was a wall painting which would have been a sensation in a brothel in Pompeii. The library was furnished with publications which could never have passed through His Majesty's Customs. The place was equipped with the impediments of fetishism and perversion. The revolver which killed Michael Scott Stephen, Mrs. Barney's lover, may well have had a sexual association, too. There is reason to suppose that it wasn't the first time it had been fired.
>
> But that is only one speculation among many in a case of which [Robert] Churchill's considered conclusion

was: 'I never held that it was deliberate murder, but it was manslaughter and *sexually odd*.' The jury, at the trial, took a different view.

So many of the circumstances of the Mrs. Barney affair are enveloped in question marks that . . . it is worth noting that even the bare account of the facts reveals, between the lines, that it was treated by the prosecution and the police with what might be regarded as the utmost, indeed almost inexplicable, restraint. Why, is anybody's guess.

When Dr. Morton was asked whether he thought that Elvira was addicted to drugs, he answered 'No'. Probably all he meant was that he had found no syringe-marks on her body. As stated previously, Elvira was a 'sniffer'; her addiction to cocaine bore no tell-tale signs. In cocaine-addicts there is increased physical and mental power as part of the effect, and there may be perpetual disturbance and occasional paranoia. Many addicts carry weapons to respond to such stimulation.

Michael Scott Stephen was most likely a pusher; we know for a fact that he was an addict. Beverley Nichols wrote: 'He was a very unpleasant little gigolo, who once offered me cocaine, which I threw back in his face.' And from a diary supposedly written by Stephen, excerpts from which were published in a popular Sunday newspaper a few days after the trial, it would appear that Mr. Nichols's low opinion of Stephen was shared by Stephen himself:

> Women have loved me too much . . . I say this in no conceit, but rather with bitterness. It is just a plain statement of fact—women loved me too much. And how avaricious and all-demanding some of them can be. For many young men to be loved too much by women is bad—often fatal. Such love brings with it that worst of all curses—jealousy. Bright Young Things . . . I will say something of the *queer* slumming parties that we arranged, our ridiculous gambles, drugging sessions, the strange fashions that we initiated . . . I have played my sorry part in these affairs and will doubtless do so again. Sometimes I am happy and revel in the fun. But there are times when our way of life looks to me like one sickening

round of illicit love, of furtive and shameless passion, jealousy, quarrels, drink and tragedy ... I sometimes think that it is easier for the drug-addict to renounce his pet poison than for one of us to break away from this circle; easier for a prisoner to escape from behind stone walls and iron bars than for one of us to escape from this prison of the senses ... But there were always cocktails to arouse a false sense of hilarity.

But what of the centre of this 'storm-in-a-court'? Elvira Barney was a woman of no importance who had been endowed with meretricious notoriety as the daughter of a rich and powerful father, the sister of a 'royal', and the recipient of a considerable family-allowance. A good-time girl, cleared of murder after a brawl at her 'love nest' during which a gun had gone off, killing the man whose mistress she was, and leaving the Court in a state of collapse, she had sufficiently recovered by the following day to be photographed in a dozen different poses. And during that day she signed a contract with a Sunday newspaper for the publication of a series of articles. 'My Life' started with the words 'I write in tears', and continued in that vein for the better part of the two whole pages of its first instalment. But enough was enough, and after that splurge of miserable self-revelation, the newspaper and Elvira decided to cancel the rest. If Elvira's 'Life' had continued as it had started, it would just have been another piece of unadulterated journalistic exhibitionism parading under the cover of a 'human document'.

After this, she spent much of her time abroad. It was in France that she very nearly killed the man who had saved her from the gallows. Sir Patrick Hastings recalled in his autobiography:

> I saw her once more in my life ... I was driving my car up the steep hill from Boulogne on the Paris road when a long low car, driven by a woman, dashed round the corner on the wrong side, nearly killing me and my chauffeur who was sitting beside me. As he indignantly picked up his cap, he said: 'Did you see who was driving that car, sir? It was Mrs. Barney!'

Dr. Johnson remarked that 'in human nature there is a general inclination to make people stare; and every wise man has himself to cure of it, and does cure himself'. Elvira, with her fast cars, bright-coloured clothes, promiscuous sex, wild parties, and emphatic nuisance-value, never cured herself of wanting to 'make people stare'. This was an unfortunate trait in 'dear little Elvira' from the time she started to play at amateur theatricals. It was to lead her into that brief flirtation with the professional theatre, far too disciplined in those days for her emotional instability, and finally into the midst of the Bright Young Things following the break-up of her marriage. She was a 'bawler' who, in a different stratum of society from that into which she was born, might have won for herself an award for The Best Billingsgate Fish-Wife.

During the last years, she changed her name: she wanted to forget, she said, that she was the notorious Mrs. Barney. But she did little to change her mode of life—in Corfu, Majorca or Paris, or wherever else she went, with the Bairds, the Dean Pauls, Anna Wickham, and others who moved in her set. The same company, the same pastimes, all round the clock. She who shouted on the dance-floor of the Café de Paris, 'I am the one who shot her lover—so take a good look,' was the same woman who was to drink to excess and drive to the public danger. She was 'news' to the bitter end. The elegant and effeminate young man named René Cady 'who had proposed to her but had his plans cancelled and the ceremony postponed', gave interviews to the newspapers, in the course of which he said that she was depressed by both the postponement and the lack of ready cash.

Elvira's last hours were true to form. Her end was a fitting conclusion to a theatrical play that had all the overtones of *grand guignol* and the undertones of a morality tale. She had, it appears, spent the early evening of Christmas Eve, 1936, in Montparnasse, the gay Latin Quarter where Mimis and Trilbys of Murger and du Maurier mingled with the exotic world that was Paris after dark. She went to the Coupole, the well-known Bohemian café, and later to the apartment of her more or less permanent escort, the said Monsieur Cady. While with friends at this flat, she insisted on listening to a Midnight Mass broadcast from a Paris church. She was much affected by the singing, and cried bitterly. Her friends tried to cheer her up, and then all left for Montmartre. She was seen in several restaurants and cocktail bars, where she sat laughing and talking, surrounded by gaiety, cocktails and music. Sitting on a high stool at the bar, she suddenly fainted;

upon regaining consciousness, she said she felt ill; she went back alone to her hotel. As she passed the night-porter on the way to her room, she told him she felt very cold. He heard the key turn in her door.

Monsieur Cady had arranged to see his fiancée on Christmas afternoon in his flat. When she did not come, he felt anxious, and with some of her friends went to her room. There was no answer to their knocking, and so they broke the door down. They found her lying half on her bed and half off. There were signs of haemorrhage round her mouth. She had been dead many hours. Elvira was still clad in the black-and-white check dress and fur coat she had worn in Montmartre.

'She is a young woman with the rest of her life before her,' her counsel had said at her trial. Four years later, she was dead.

Peter Cotes

HARVARD AND HOMICIDE
Thomas M. McDade

[Several inches more than six feet tall, he is also a big man in unvisible respects. For five years from 1934, he was an FBI agent, specialising in cases of kidnapping and bank-robbery (his hair-raising funny account of his road-race with Baby-Face Nelson appears in an earlier anthology that I edited, The Vintage Car Murders; *other essays of his are in other anthologies of mine). After wartime service in the Pacific as a lieutenant-colonel, during which he helped re-organise the police department of Manila, he became controller of one of America's largest corporations; when he retired, he acted as lawyer and accountant to the poor. He is President of the Society of Connoisseurs in Murder and a long-standing member of the Baker Street Irregulars. When he was compiling his remarkable bibliography,* The Annals of Murder: . . . American Murders From Colonial Times to 1900 *(University of Oklahoma Press, 1961—out of print for far too long), he scarcely needed to leave the library in the house he called Scotland Yard. His wife Bea makes beautiful furniture, some pieces a lot larger than she is, and is mistress of the delightful little art of turning literally common-or-garden stones into sculpture.]*

WHEN PROFESSOR JOHN WHITE WEBSTER was hanged in 1850 for the murder of Dr. George Parkman, he was assured of immortality among his Harvard peers, and his fame, though ignoble, is more memorable than many of his more scholarly colleagues'. So great indeed has been his personal fame that succeeding Harvard homicidal dons have long been forgotten while the memory of Professor Webster stays evergreen. It is therefore proper that we pay credit to another of those talented murderers of Cambridge, Massachusetts. We must pass over Charles R. Eastman, the Harvard instructor tried in 1900 for shooting to death Richard H. Grogan, for his acquittal renders him ineligible in the Harvard homicidal sweepstakes. I refer instead to Erich Muenter, a German instructor who, before passing from public view, had his name, photograph, and academic attainments on the front pages of all the principal newspapers of America.

In 1906, Muenter, his wife, and three-year-old child lived within a ten-minute walk of the campus, though he more frequently made the journey there by bicycle. Even in the scholastic world, he was a mild eccentric, though his peculiarities were not readily describable. Born in Hanover, Germany, thirty-five years before, he had but a bachelor's degree obtained from the University of Chicago at the advanced age of twenty-eight. Minor teaching posts had culminated in a year at the University of Kansas, and in 1904 he had come to Harvard as an instructor in German.

Of medium height, spare, dark-haired, first moustached and then letting his beard flower into a Vandyke, he had nothing noticeably unusual about him. But he was, in modern terminology, a loner. If he had few friends, he made no enemies. On 6 April, Mrs. Muenter gave birth to a child, another girl. She was attended in her labour and in the days to follow by a Christian Scientist midwife. Despite her ministrations, both immediate and at times absent treatment, Mrs. Muenter grew visibly weaker. Muenter telephoned a Dr. McIntire, who came but refused to handle the case when he learned of the Christian Scientist. On the fourteenth, Muenter tried a Dr. Fred Taylor, but he likewise refused to take the case. On the following night, Muenter told the nurse to rest, that he would watch his wife. At six o'clock the next morning, he called the nurse and said that his wife had died in the night.

When Muenter summoned a local undertaker, A. E. Long, he was told that nothing could be done with the body until a death certificate had been obtained from a doctor. The instructor's call to Dr. McIntire was unavailing; he was told to call the medical examiner. In the end, a conclave of doctors, including Taylor, McIntire, Swan, the medical examiner, and a Dr. Durrell, came to the apartment which the Muenters occupied, and, after removing the stomach and intestines, which were sent to Harvard Medical College for analysis, a certificate of death was prepared, indicating the cause of death as 'gastro-duodenitis'. Now able to proceed with the burial, Muenter, who had spoken previously of burying his wife in nearby St. Auburn Cemetery, made plans to take the body to Chicago, where his wife's parents resided, and he left the next day, hiring a Mrs. Derrick to accompany him to care for the two children on the trip. On arrival in Chicago, the body was cremated, and the German instructor turned the children over to their grandparents.

In Cambridge, the police received a report from Professor Whitney of Harvard describing his findings of substantial quantities of arsenic in the stomach and intestines, and the police quietly began to inquire when Muenter was expected back. The University had been notified that he did not plan to return; he had asked to be relieved of his duties. A lodger in his apartment house had received two letters, one incoherent, the other explaining that his sister would care for his effects.

On 28 April, the collegiate calm was shattered by the appearance of a police circular charging Muenter with poisoning his wife and giving his description. Tired of waiting, the police were now convinced he was not planning to return.

The academic world of Cambridge was aghast. His few friends thought some terrible mistake had been made and that he would return and clear himself. His sister attributed his disappearance to his anguish over the death of his wife and even placed an advertisement in the papers urging him to return to face the charge. The newspapers described him as an instructor teaching German while working towards his doctorate in philosophy. The subject of his doctoral thesis raised a few eyebrows—'Insanity as described in German romantic literature.' He was also said to have been trying to construct a universal language—a combination of German and Scotch.

The police offered as a possible motive a $1000 insurance policy on Mrs. Muenter's life. It seemed hardly sufficient incentive;

but, strangely enough, Muenter, before he disappeared, had tried to collect on the policy at the Chicago office of the New York Life Insurance Company, where he was told they would have to refer it to their Eastern office.

The deceased woman's family, now anti-Muenter, added items on his background. Walter Krembs, her brother, claimed that the German government had sought Muenter in connection with his marriage to a Miss Rosalie Kratz of Biberich. Others claimed he had been charged with bigamy in Maine. In addition, John M. Crowe, who had lived in the same house with the Muenters in Chicago, reported that on no fewer than three occasions the gas in the Muenter apartment had blown out, and that once Mrs. Muenter had been overcome by the fumes.

On 30 April, Bertha Muenter, the fugitive's sister, arrived in Cambridge, sold off much of the contents of the apartment, and returned to Chicago with no visible contact with her brother.

No one ever saw Muenter—as Muenter—again, though one last curious missive from him appeared at Harvard. Early in June, a number of his former associates received in the mail, apparently posted from New Orleans, a printed pamphlet of 36 pages which bore on the first page the single word, 'PROTEST'. On the reverse and for the next thirteen pages, there was reported a wild tale, a macabre caricature, which began as follows:

> Sensation! Scandal! Autopsy! Cremation! Assfixiation! [*sic*].
>
> Brutal murder of four prominent citizens by Oxford Profesor [*sic*] Nurse and baby killed by gas.
>
> Assassin escaped. Killed eighteen wives before. Oxford, April 25, 1906.
>
> Ten days ago, Mrs. Smith, wife of head Professor Smith, had given birth to a baby in the top flat No. 9 Rue Morgue. Dr. Macinwitch (with the Scotch bilabial pronunciation of the w), though not present, asserted an easy birth. Because Mrs. Smith was a Christian Scientist, having employed besides the doctor a Christian Science healer and nurse, Dr. Vulture, the medical examiner insisted on an autopsy when Mrs. Smith died.

In the ensuing pages, Smith shoots the four doctors while they are performing the autopsy on his wife, and generally goes berserk.

At this point, a new section of the pamphlet starts, and we apparently have Muenter addressing us directly: 'Having read so far, compare this story with the silly lies in half a dozen Chicago and Boston newspapers. . . .' He proceeds to revile the press for its distortion of the facts. In a long, rambling article on religion, sociology, and crime, Muenter wanders about, threatens his brothers-in-law and finally states that an ad in the newspapers of 22 July 1906 will reach him with a message.

The police, after sending out their wanted notice on Muenter, had numerous secret inquests but issued no further bulletins. A letter to a Kansas friend from one of Muenter's Harvard associates gave a strange view of the household just before the child had been born. 'The friends of Muenter here,' he wrote, 'are praying that the baby may be a boy, as they are afraid Muenter will be in a mood to do something rash if there is another girl in his home.'

The usual arrest on mistaken identity occurred, this time in Appleton, Wisconsin, but Muenter had disappeared for good.

From our vantage-point in time, we can now trace his movements. Proceeding to Mexico City, Muenter, under an alias, easily procured a job as secretary in the office of the Krupp Munitions Company in that city. How long he stayed there we do not know; we can only say that he next appeared in Fort Worth, Texas, where he registered as a student at Polytechnic College in February 1908 under the name of Frank Holt. At about the same time, the Cambridge police, after a lapse of two years, were preparing a new wanted notice on Muenter, to be printed in eight languages and distributed around the world. What academic history he claimed at Fort Worth is unknown, but his capacity and learning were sufficiently demonstrated for that school to give him a Bachelor of Arts degree in 1909. That same year, he married Lena Sensabaugh, who had been in his class at Polytechnic. From Fort Worth, he moved on to Norman, Oklahoma, where, for the school year 1909–10, he taught German at the University of Oklahoma. His contract was not renewed, as he had differences with his superiors;

nor did he remain long at any institution. A year teaching French and German at Vanderbilt University, Tennessee, was followed by two years at Emory and Henry College, Virginia. In 1913, he moved to Cornell University, New York State, where he spent two years, and in that time completed the work towards his doctor of philosophy degree, which he received in June 1915.

Nine years had elapsed since Muenter had disappeared. The clean-shaven Holt, with his new scholastic background, a wife, and two children, seemed safe from detection.

With the end of the 1915 academic year at Cornell, there also ended Holt's career at that Ithaca institution. His father-in-law, a Methodist minister and educator, had been selected as the president of the new Southern Methodist University, to open in Dallas in the fall. Holt had an appointment there as head of the department of romance languages. As a full professor, he would attain the rank which he had long felt was his due. In anticipation of his removal there, his wife and children went ahead; Holt remained a few days in Ithaca, and on 2 June went to New York City, where he registered at the Mills Hotel on Seventh Avenue at 36th Street. The charge for a night was thirty cents; it was a dormitory-type hostel for the poor and homeless. On the same day, he wrote a letter to President Wilson.

The war in Europe had been raging for more than nine months. While among his colleagues Holt had assumed a neutral position, he had written at least one letter to an Ithaca paper protesting the American policy which permitted shipments of munitions to flow from our ports to England and France. His letter to the President protested that such a policy was hardly neutral and urged the banning of shipments to all belligerents. On 5 June he wrote to the Kaiser, but the contents of that letter are not known.

On the eleventh, he returned briefly to Ithaca to despatch some articles to his wife in Dallas; by the fourteenth, he was again registered at the Mills Hotel. At this time, his conduct took on a much more bizarre character. On the seventeenth, in Jersey City, he bought two revolvers—a .38 in one shop, a .32 in another. On the nineteenth, he appeared at Central Park Station, near Syosset, Long Island, and, under the name of Patton, rented a two-room bungalow. For some days, he made the neighbours uneasy with his target practice at the back of the house. Had they known of his activities inside, their simple annoyance would have turned to panic. On the twenty-first, he ordered two hundred sticks of dynamite, as well as fuses and dynamite caps, from the Aetna Explosives Company, to be shipped to C. Hendricks at Syosset.

The fuses and caps arrived on the twenty-third, but, as railroad regulations limited the shipment of dynamite to Mondays, the sticks did not arrive in Syosset until the twenty-eighth. Holt, alias Patton, picked up the two cases (weighing 120 pounds) with a buggy and drove to his temporary home.

For the next few days, he was busily occupied in the cottage, meanwhile eating out of cans. He next appeared on Friday, 2 July, to catch the 7:09 a.m. train from Syosset to Pennsylvania Station in New York City. A heavy trunk, which he routed through to that station, was taken to a livery stable to be stored for F. H. Henderson. By noon, he had departed for Washington, D.C., carrying a small handbag, and later that afternoon he rented a room on D Street near the Union Station. What remained of the afternoon he spent visiting public buildings. Unobserved, he left a parcel in a phone-booth in a reception room of the Senate Hall of the Capitol.

The composition of this package he later explained: 'I took three sticks of dynamite and bound them together. Then I took my knife and hollowed out a place in one of the sticks. I put some match-heads into the hole—three or four. I then took a little bottle of sulphuric acid and put a regular cork in the neck. I turned the bottle upside down and fastened the cork to the hole just above the match-heads. I had timed the sulphuric acid in my tests and I knew just how long it would take to eat through the cork and get to the match-heads.'

Holt then returned to his room, picked up his bag, and left. In the long twilight, he walked about the city, seeing the sights and no doubt consulting his watch at frequent intervals.

He also posted a letter to each of the four principal Washington newspapers, in which he made plain the reason for his actions:

> Unusual times and circumstances call for unusual means.
> In connection with the SENATE affair, would it not be well to stop and consider what we are doing?
>
> We stand for PEACE and GOODWILL to all men, and yet, while our European brethren are madly setting out to kill one another, we edge them on and furnish them more effective means of murder. Is it right?

After disclaiming that his act was prompted by the Germans, he went on:

> Sorry, I too had to use explosives. (For the last time, I trust.) It is the export kind and ought to make enough noise to be heard above the voices that clamour for war and blood money. This explosion is the exclamation point to my appeal for peace.

The letters were signed R. Pearce and dated 1 June, showing how long this had been in conception. The word 'Senate' in the first passage was handwritten and had been inserted after the bomb was placed, as Holt had had a number of places under consideration and did not make up his mind until he had visited the Capitol.

By ten o'clock, he had retired to a berth on the midnight train leaving for New York. Shortly before the train pulled out, he was assured of the success of his venture by the distant thump of the explosion.

While the physical damage done by the bomb was small, Holt had correctly estimated its reverberation as a news event. Screaming headlines the next morning proclaimed that a 'tremendous explosion' had wrecked the east reception room, bringing down part of the ceiling and side-walls and shattering a crystal chandelier. A door to the office of the Vice-President, Thomas Marshall, which had not been unlocked for forty years, was blown open and the mirrors and windows blown from their frames.

Holt's letters did not reach the newspapers until after the morning editions were out, and the press could only conjecture on the reason for the bombing; most papers ascribed the work to a crank, although there were some who muttered about spontaneous combustion. When the letters were received, the police made a Sherlockian observation of entirely no consequence by noting that, as there were two originals and two carbon-copies, the writer had probably had to make two typings as he had but one piece of carbon paper.

Arriving at Pennsylvania Station in New York at 6:00 a.m., refreshed by his Capitol success, Holt was in plenty of time to catch the 7:30 a.m. for Glen Cove, Long Island, where he had plans for another busy day. He entered the taxi of a Myron Ford and asked to be driven to the home of J. P. Morgan, the financier. The estate was located on East Island, reached by a causeway bridge several hundred feet long. Ford stopped in front of the house and then for the first time became suspicious of his passenger when Holt, after telling him to wait, returned, saying, 'I forgot to get my card.' He opened a suitcase, took out what appeared to be a revolver and, slipping this into his pocket, approached the front door.

Holt was greeted by the Morgan butler, a man with the marvellous name of Henry Physick.

'I want to see Mr. Morgan,' said Holt, handing a card to Physick. The card read: 'Summer Society Directory. Thomas C. Lester, representing.'

'What is your business with Mr. Morgan?' asked Physick, and, when Holt declined to tell him, insisted that he must know. Holt's patience being exhausted, he drew a revolver with each hand from his two coat-pockets and, pressing them against the servant, exclaimed, 'Don't try to stop me!'

Physick displayed the presence of mind one would expect in Mr. Morgan's butler. 'You will find Mr. Morgan in the library,' he said, turning and walking in that direction.

Actually, the banker, with his wife and the British Ambassador, Sir Cecil Spring-Rice, was breakfasting in the opposite direction on the same floor. As Holt entered the library, Physick ran down the hall, shouting to his employer, 'Upstairs, Mr. Morgan, upstairs!' His intention, as he later explained, was to get the Morgans to the second-floor, and, fearing to reveal Morgan's whereabouts, he did not go to the breakfast room. As a result, there was a confused rushing about of people. The Morgans ran up a back stair, the great J.P. seeking a burglar he believed to be there. Of one of the nurses he met upstairs, he asked in a loud voice what had gone wrong. 'Nothing at all,' he was told, so he continued moving from room to room. Suddenly, the nurse at the head of the front stairs spied Holt coming up, attracted by the loud voices, and she shouted to Mr. Morgan.

Holt, a revolver in either hand, reached the top of the stairs just in time to come face to face with the banker, and greeted him with the words: 'Now, Mr. Morgan, I have got you.' *Mrs.* Morgan attempted to throw herself between the two men, but her husband, whose steely gaze had made many a stronger man turn away, closed with his attacker. As tall as Holt and perhaps half again as heavy, the banker bore down on his quarry. Two shots sounded. Holt was borne to the ground, where Morgan flattened him by lying on top of him and wrung the pistol from his left hand. Holt's right hand was pinned under Morgan, and, when he was finally able to work it free, Morgan and the nurse promptly seized it and disarmed him. At this point, Physick, the perfect butler, arrived, armed with a large lump of coal picked up from a fireplace, and, crashing it down on Holt's head, rendered the German teacher *hors de combat*. More servants arrived, and Holt was trussed with rope and held for the police.

Morgan, satisfied of the security of the prisoner, then went to the telephone and called a Dr. Zabriskie, who lived nearby, to reveal that he had two bullet-wounds, one in his thigh and the other in his abdomen. Calm as one would expect of him, he next called his mother in Utica to tell her that she might hear he had been injured but that it was not serious. The Glen Cove police soon arrived and carried off a battered Holt, grimy and bloodstained, his two pistols, and three sticks of dynamite which he had had with him.

At police headquarters, Holt disclaimed any intention of injuring Morgan. All he had wanted to do, he said, was to talk to the financier in an effort to persuade him to help in discontinuing arms sales to Europe.

'He came running towards me angrily as soon as he saw me and I shot to frighten him,' was Holt's explanation. 'I wanted to go to every manufacturer personally and persuade him to stop this traffic. It was physically impossible for me to do this, but Mr. Morgan, with his great influence, could do what was impossible for me, and I decided to apply to him.'

The reporters, who by this time were swarming about the Glen Cove police station, found Holt's manner quiet and didactic.

When he told them that he had a Ph.D. degree, one of them asked the subject of his thesis and got a prompt rebuff. 'Oh, that is wandering very far from the subject.' When asked what other things he had done to further his views, he replied, 'I have done what I can. I have argued with people to keep them neutral. I have written to the press. I wrote several letters which were printed in the Ithaca press.'

Of Mr. Morgan, Holt had this to say: 'I admire his courage. If he would display a quality of moral courage equalling the physical courage which he showed towards me, he would go down in history as a very great man.'

Concerned as to what his wife might be feeling in Dallas, Holt wrote the following telegram, which the authorities allowed him to send:

> MAN PROPOSES, GOD DISPOSES. DON'T COME HERE TILL YOU GET LETTERS. BE STRONG. FRANK.

Holt's connection with the Washington bombing was not long in coming out. The letters which he had posted to the Washington papers contained the sentence, 'We would, of course, not sell to the Germans if they could buy here, and since, so far, we have sold only to the allies, neither side should object if stopped.' In his confession to the police at Glen Cove, Holt had written, 'If Germany should be able to buy munitions here, we would, of course, positively refuse to sell to her.' Taxed with the similarity, Holt admitted that he had set the bomb in the Capitol. His letters, he claimed, explained all.

Almost immediately after the news of Holt's activities reached Cambridge, the police in that city announced the suspicion that the man seized in Glen Cove might be the missing Harvard professor, Erich Muenter. A college professor of German, given to violence, whose description was similar to their fugitive's, seemed a likely subject of investigation, and Holt's pictures were exhibited around Cambridge to those who had known Muenter. But the first photos of Holt showed him clean-shaven, blood- and coal-streaked from Physick's blows, and not too easily recognized as the bearded Muenter. Holt refused to admit the charge, and there was a great scramble for persons who could surely identify Muenter.

In the meantime, Morgan had been examined by a squad of

doctors who pronounced his wounds painful but not too serious. His abdomen had not been pierced, and the wound in his thigh was superficial. But even the momentary doubt about the nature of the injuries had caused a seismic shudder to run through the financial world, as well as through other circles. Prayers for his speedy recovery were offered in churches of all denominations. His neighbours and business associates paid their respects at his home, which had suddenly become an armed camp, patrolled by thirty guards with rifles and shotguns, where before there had been none.

While Holt recovered from his physical injuries, he declined in spirit and energy. He appeared withdrawn and depressed. On Monday, 5 July, he made a small cut in his wrist with the metal eraser-holder on a pencil, and it was decided to place a guard in his cell to prevent him from taking his own life. However, on Wednesday night, the guard went off to investigate a noise from some of the other prisoners, and the scholar quickly slipped from the cell, the door of which had been left unlocked, and threw himself head-first to a concrete floor twenty feet below. The noise of his skull cracking sounded like a pistol-shot—thus leading to a report that he had destroyed himself by biting a dynamite cap. Death was instantaneous, and the authorities were left with the tangled ends of his trail and with recriminations and charges of carelessness.

His death, instead of ending the case, only quickened the investigation. The police had already located the trunk which Holt had sent to be stored in a livery stable on 38th Street, Manhattan. It contained 134 sticks of dynamite, along with fuses, wires, and many other devices. It was estimated that about fifty sticks of dynamite were still unaccounted for. The harried detectives were further beset by the fact that the two hundred sticks of dynamite sent by Aetna Explosives to Syosset had been 40% dynamite while the 134 found in Manhattan were 60%. Were there two shipments, or was there a mistake in the Aetna consignment?

For several days before his death, Holt had made cryptic statements which worried the police. On Sunday, he had talked of everything except the dynamite and, when pressed, had replied, 'I will tell you all about that on Wednesday, but on Wednesday the whole world will know.'

On the sixth, Mrs. Holt, in Fort Worth, received a letter which the mad instructor had sent off after he had returned from Washington and before his foray in Glen Cove. In this letter he told of his plan to hold the wife and children of Morgan as hostages until the banker himself had gone to Europe to stop the arms deliveries. Furthermore: 'A steamer leaving New York for Liverpool should sink, God willing, on the 7th. It is the Philadelphia or the Saxony [Saxonia] but I am not sure, as these left on the 2nd or 3rd.' In the margin of the letter was the admonition: 'Tear this off until after this happens.'

Mrs. Holt communicated this information to a family friend, who advised the authorities. The Navy Department immediately sent out wireless messages to the two ships, suggesting a search for bombs. None was found.

Holt, however, had been correct in his timing. Only in the name of the vessel was he in error. At 4:15 p.m. on the seventh, an explosion occured on the *Minnehaha*, an ammunition ship bound for England which had sailed from New York on 3 July and was 580 miles southeast of Halifax. The *Minnehaha* immediately turned to make for port. A fire, in Hold No. 3, was controlled by live steam, which helped to suffocate it. Hold No. 3 contained small shipped parcels, and it was surmised that Holt had addressed a package containing a bomb to a fictitious person in England.

During the two-day race to Halifax, the crew fought to confine the fire to the one hold, and, although the bulkhead into Hold No. 4 collapsed under the heat, the danger had passed by the time the ship reached port.

With the safe arrival of the *Minnehaha*, the Holt case promptly lost its full-spread headlines and in a few days passed from public view, leaving a trail of bits and pieces. Frustrated Justice berated the guard whose ineptitude had allowed Holt to escape the law. Some men of Harvard formally identified the corpse of Holt as that of Muenter. And it turned out that Holt's disguise had been pierced at least once.

In November 1914, Professor Chester Nathan Gould, of the Germanic Department of the University of Chicago, visited Cornell to do some research. While there, he was introduced to Holt and thought he reminded him of someone. Later, after several meetings with Holt, Gould became convinced that he was the man whom he had known as Erich Muenter at Harvard ten years before. Though he felt a little nervous for his own safety, he decided not to disclose what he knew. 'He seemed to be getting along nicely and to be a credit to the department. Everything I knew about him was good, except the charge, unproven so far as I knew, of killing his wife. I thought it better to let well enough alone.' Later, when a Professor Bennett had spoken to Gould about Holt, saying that the latter had applied for membership in the Masons, Gould had in confidence revealed to him Holt's background, and Bennett had made sure that Holt was not admitted to the order.

Holt's wife decided to have his remains shipped to Dallas for burial. Before they departed, however, the brain was removed for scientific study. It was delivered to Dr. Carlos MacDonald, a noted alienist who had seen Holt while he was alive in prison and who had pronounced him a paranoiac. The brain was said to be unusually large and heavy. The whole episode smacks of the days of phrenology, when the standard for large brains was set by Daniel Webster.

One among many residual uncertainties concerned the rather important question of the criminal's identity. The death certificate insisted that the remains were those of Frank Holt, born on 25 March 1875—the same day and month as, but four years later than, the birthdate of Erich Muenter.

Tom McDade.

CIRCUIT MURDERS
Lord Cockburn

[*Born in 1779 at Hope Park, Edinburgh, one of the eleven children of Archibald Cockburn of Cockpen, who eventually became a Baron of Exchequer, Henry rose to leadership of the Scottish Bar, together with Francis Jeffrey, whose biography he wrote. (One of his five brothers founded the still-flourishing firm of wine-merchants bearing their name.) A dedicated Whig, he was made Solicitor-General for Scotland in 1830. Shortly afterwards, he wrote this 'personal message': 'I hope you are aware that, whatever Mr Cockburn was, His Majesty's Solicitor-General is a decorous person, arrayed in solemn black, with a demure visage, an official ear and evasive voice, suspicious palate, ascetic blood, and flinty heart. There is a fellow very like him who traverses the Pentland Hills in a dirty grey jacket, white hat, and with a long pole. That's not the Solicitor-General, that's Cocky, and you may use all freedom with him.' In 1834 he was appointed, as Lord Cockburn, a judge of the Court of Session (two of his wife's sisters each married a judge, and so at one time, perhaps uniquely, three judges were truly brothers-in-law); in 1837 he became a Lord of Justiciary. The posthumously-published* Memorials of His Time, *Cockburn's sketches of life in Edinburgh in the 1820s, is wonderfully entertaining; his* Journal, *being too much about politics, is not. Even more entertaining than* Memorials, *it seems to me, is his diary of* Circuit Journeys, *from which most of the following entries are culled.]*

BONALY [Cockburn's home, at Colinton, near Edinburgh], *28 March 1838.*—I have got this volume (prepared under the personal directions of Thomas Maitland, the first of gentlemen binders) in order to record anything remarkable that may occur in my Circuits. It will be my fate to perform these journeys, being a Criminal Judge, as long as I am fit for anything.

But first, looking back: A deep sensation of horror was excited at the end of 1828 by the exposure in Edinburgh of what are called 'The West Port Murders'. It was only for a single murder that William Burke and his woman, Helen Macdougal, were tried; but it was nearly certain that, within a year or two, Burke and William Hare had murdered about sixteen people, for the sale of their bodies to anatomists; and after his conviction Burke confessed this. Sir James Moncreiff and I were drawn into the case by the junior counsel. The evidence against Burke was far too clear to be shaken by even Moncreiff's energy and talent; but the woman, who had been assigned to my care, escaped, because there were some material doubts in her favour. (It is stated in vol. xliv of the *Quarterly Review* that at the moment I was addressing the jury, I whispered 'Infernal hag!'—'the gudgeons swallow it!' and I suppose that a credulous Quaker, whose work [on the principles of morality] was reviewed in that article, believes this, and, as I understand, comments upon it as a piece of professional fraud. It is utterly untrue. No one could be more honestly convinced of anything than I was, and am, that there was not sufficient legal evidence to warrant a conviction of Helen Macdougal. Therefore, no such expressions or sentiment *could be* uttered. At any rate none such, and none of that tendency, *were* uttered.)

We carried two important points, after a battle with the Court, which would probably have been decided otherwise if the leaning of their lordships had been feebly resisted. These were: our right to have each murder tried separately; and to impeach the credit of the accomplices by questioning them about their accession to other murders or crimes.

No case ever struck the public heart or imagination with

greater horror. And no wonder. For the regular demand for anatomical subjects, and the high prices given, held out a constant premium to murder; and when it was shown to what danger this exposed the unprotected, everyone felt himself living in the midst of persons to whom murder was a trade. All our anatomists incurred a most unjust, and a very alarming, though not an unnatural odium; Dr Knox, in particular, against whom not only the anger of the populace, but the condemnation of more intelligent persons, was specially directed. But tried in reference to the invariable, and the necessary practice of the profession, our anatomists were spotlessly correct, and Knox the most correct of them all. Had it not been for the evidence exhibited in Burke's case of the necessity of providing a cheap, safe, and legal mode of supplying anatomical subjects, it is more than probable that the Anatomy Act would not have passed so soon, if ever.

Except that he murdered, Burke was a sensible, and what might be called a respectable, man; not at all ferocious in his general manner, sober, correct in all his other habits, and kind to his relations. Though not regularly married, Helen Macdougal was his wife; and when the jury came in with the verdict convicting him but acquitting her, his remark was: 'Well, thank God you're safe!'

30 March 1838.—My first Circuit was the West, which began at Stirling on 16 September 1837. Lord Moncreiff was my colleague.[1] On Monday the 18th, he and I parted. He went to Inveraray, I to Renfrewshire. I got to my brother-in-law's at Barr, by Lochwinnoch, to dinner. Stayed there till Tuesday night, when I went to Glasgow, and tried civil causes from Wednesday morning till Saturday evening, when I returned to Barr and remained there till Monday the 25th, when I went to Possil, near Glasgow, the residence of Archibald Alison, the Sheriff of Lanarkshire, where I met Moncreiff, and where we continued all night.

Next morning, we made a grand procession into the Court, the grandest I ever saw at a Scotch Circuit; there were four carriages

[1] *EDITOR'S NOTE. In 1829, the year after he defended Burke, Sir James Moncreiff, Bt., had been made a judge of the Court of Session.*

and four, besides four or five with two horses—plenty Lancers, in all their bravery of men and steeds—rows of well-drilled police—music— gazers, etc. It took us till the evening of the next Tuesday to dispose of the criminal cases.

There were two convictions for murder—one against a woman for drowning her child, and one against a man, a tobacco-spinner, who first married a woman whom he knew had several illegitimate children, and then, *from jealousy*, killed her by repeated stabs. They were both sentenced to be executed at Paisley on the same day. The woman's sentence was commuted into the strange substitute of imprisonment for four years, but the man's was carried into effect.

I tried his case, and consequently had to pronounce the sentence—the first capital one I ever pronounced, and I hope the last. It is a very painful duty.

There is a great art in pronouncing sentences. The old judges used generally to abuse the prisoner. The feelings of a later age would not tolerate this. But they have introduced a sermonising system which it requires some courage in any judge to avoid. Even in the slightest case—not extending beyond imprisonment—the prisoner must always be reminded of his latter end and of his immortal soul, and two present judges very rarely ever fail to point out the way to salvation by actually naming Redemption and the Redeemer. There are others (*inter quos ego*) who think that more direct and practical expositions of the personal and immediate consequences of crime are more likely to operate on worldly audiences and worldly villains. The misfortune of the religious plan is that, as adherence to it is thought a duty, it is apt to lose its effect by being applied indiscriminately to every case. A proper mixture of the two would be the best thing.

Moncreiff, the most excellent of men, and one of the most admirable of judges, but whose piety and simplicity sometimes give him odd views, has signalised himself twice, in passing sentence, by principles which have greatly diverted his friends, and produced much speculation among English lawyers, as I heard his friend Lord Brougham, when Chancellor [1830–34], tell him.

Once was in dooming a man to die for murdering a female who lived with him. It was altogether a shocking case, but his Lordship found out, and debated upon this peculiar atrocity, that the woman he had killed was *not* his wife, but *only* his mistress—because, as he explained, if she had been your wife, there might possibly have been some apology for you, on account of the difficulty of getting quit of a wife in any other way. But this unfortunate woman being only your associate, you might have freed yourself from her whenever you chose. How Brougham revelled over this discovery, that it was a lesser crime to murder a wife than to murder a mistress!

If I were a culprit, I would rather be sentenced by Moncreiff than by any judge I have ever known. He is, in general, very sensible, and always very kind, and never dreams of making it an occasion for display, but addresses the prisoner almost as if he were an unfortunate friend, for whose temporal and eternal welfare he had a deep anxiety, to whom he pointed out penitence and the formation of better habits as the only means of reaching future happiness, and of whose reformation he rarely despaired.

NORTH CIRCUIT. AVIEMORE, *12 April 1838.*—My studies in the chaise have been the new number of the *Edinburgh Review*, and the last volume of Lockhart's *Life of Scott*. The review is not just yet published. The striking article is the first, on the abuses of the press, *by Brougham*. It is a curious performance, and will produce much discussion. The portraits of his contemporaries are worthy of Clarendon. They are all too favourably drawn. Lockhart mentions Scott as having gone to see my old client, Mrs. Smith, who was guilty, but acquitted, of murder by poison. The case made a great noise. Scott's description of the woman is very correct. She was like a vindictive masculine witch. I remember him sitting within the bar, looking at her. Lockhart should have been told that as we were moving out, Sir Walter's remark upon the acquittal was: 'Well, sirs! all I can say is that if that woman was my wife, I should take good care to be my own cook.'

INVERNESS, *Friday Night, 13 April 1838.*—We left Aviemore to-day at eleven, and got here about three. A beautiful day. There are three interesting things in this part of the road—the wood of Scotch firs (I forget its name) near the Bridge of Carr, the branches being more gnarled and tossed about like those of forest trees than any fir branches I ever saw; the long, deep, pastoral descents and rises of the road; and the glorious bursts of the Moray Firth, and the Ross-shire and other hills when the height, about five miles from Inverness, is gained. Yet some monsters are *improving* the country (as they no doubt call it) by planting out these magnificent prospects, by lining the road with abominable stripes of wretched larch trees. Our only hope is in the boys and the cattle.

My heart will ever warm at the mention of the Bridge of Carr. The first time I was ever at Relugas, the Paradise formerly possessed by my friend Sir Thomas Dick Lauder, now above twenty years ago, he joined the late excellent Dr. Gordon, Mr. Macbean, and me, who had come from Edinburgh there; and what a day!—and how many happy days succeeded that meeting! After an alarming breakfast—alarming both from its magnitude and its mirth—we rolled along in two gigs, on a splendid autumnal day, till we annihilated the twenty-two miles between us and Eden; where began the first of a course of almost annual visits, hallowed in my memory by scenery and friendship, by the society and progress of a happy family, and, above all, by the recollection of Gordon. The Bridge of Carr brings them all to my eye, and to my heart.

HUNTLY, *Tuesday, 17 April 1838, Night.*—On Saturday the 14th, I was in Court till midnight.

The only curious case was that of Malcolm M'Lean, a fisherman from the isle of Lewis, who is doomed to die upon 11 May for the murder of his wife. He admitted that he killed her, and intentionally, but the defence by his counsel was that he was mad at the time. There was not the slightest foundation for this, for though he was often under the influence of an odd mixture of wild religious speculation, and of terrified superstition, he had no illusion, and in all the affairs of life, including all his own feelings and concerns, was always dealt with as a sound practical man.

One part of his pretended craziness was said to consist in his making machinery to attain the perpetual motion, and his believing that he had succeeded. This shows that this famous problem is not in such vogue as it once was. But the thing that seemed to me to be the oddest in the matter, was the perfect familiarity with which the common Celts of Lewis talked and thought of the thing called the perpetual motion, whatever they fancied it. Their word for it, according to the common process of borrowing terms with ideas, was, 'Perpetual Motion,' pronounced and treated by them as a Gaelic expression. The words 'Perpetual motion,' were used in the middle of Gaelic sentences without stop or surprise, exactly as we use any Anglified French term.

This man's declaration, which told the whole truth with anxious candour, contained a curious and fearful description of the feelings of a man about to commit a deliberate murder. He had taken it into his head that his wife was unkind, and perhaps faithless to him, and even meant to kill him, and therefore he thought it better, upon the whole, to prevent this by killing her—which accordingly, on a particular day, he was determined to do. He went to work on a piece of ground in the morning, thinking, all the time he was working, of going into the house and doing the deed, but was unwilling and infirm. However, he at last resolved, went in, sat down, she at the opposite side of the fire, the children in and out—but still he could not, and went to work again. After reasoning and dreaming of the great deed of the day, he went to the house again, but still could not, and came out; and this alternate resolving and wavering, this impulse of passion and this recoiling of nature, recurred most part of the day—till at last, sitting opposite to her again, he made a sudden plunge at her throat and scientifically Burked her by compressing the mouth and nose; after which a sore fit of sated fury succeeded, which gave way, when people began to come in, to an access of terror and cunning, which made him do everything possible for his own safety, till tired of wandering about, and haunted by some of his religious notions, he went towards Stornoway to redeliver himself (for he had been previously taken, but escaped), when he was discovered. He is now low and resigned, and says he has not been so comfortable for years, because he has got the better of the Devil at last, and is sure of defying him on 11 May.

I went officially to church on Sunday, and was again in Court yesterday till twelve at night. Today we came here, amidst a strong bitter wind, loaded with driving snow, which has been our fare since Tuesday morning, this being the end of our last vernal month.

PERTH, *Monday, 23 April 1838.*—We reached Aberdeen on the 18th, through clouds of snow and bitter blasts. There were three wreaths between Huntly and Pitmachie, which really alarmed me.

Moncreiff joined me at Aberdeen, and we were three days in Court there, from morning till past midnight. There was nothing curious in any of the cases. The weather was so bad that we had no public procession, but went to Court privately and respectably. The dignity of justice would be increased if it always rained. Yet there are some of us who like the procession (though it can never be anything but mean and ludicrous) and who fancy that a line of soldiers, or the more civic array of paltry police-officers, or of doited special constables, protecting a couple of judges who flounder in awkward gowns and wigs through the ill-paved streets, followed by a few sneering advocates, and preceded by two or three sheriffs, or their substitutes, with white swords, which trip them, and a provost and some bailie-bodies trying to look grand, the whole defended by a poor iron mace, and advancing each with a different step, to the sound of two cracked trumpets, ill-blown by a couple of drunken royal trumpeters, the spectators all laughing—who fancy that all this ludicrous pretence of greatness, and reality of littleness, contributes to the dignity of justice. Judges should never expose themselves unnecessarily—their dignity is on the bench.

We have had some good specimens of the condition of jails. One man was tried at Inverness for jail-breaking, and his defence was that he was ill-fed and that the prison was so weak that he had sent a message to the jailor that if he did not get more meat, *he would not stay in another hour* and he was as good as his word. The Sheriff of Elgin was proceeding to hold a court to try some people, when he was saved the trouble by being told that they had all walked out. Some of them being caught, a second court was held, since I was at Inverness, to dispose of them; when the proceedings were again stopped from the very opposite cause. The jailor had gone to the country taking the key of the prison with him, and the prisoners not being willing to come forth voluntarily, *could not be got out*. Lord Moncreiff tells me that when he was Sheriff of Kinross-shire, there was an Alloa culprit who was thought to be too powerful for the jail of that place. So they hired a chaise and sent officers with him to the jail of Kinross, where he was lodged. But before the horses were fed for their return, he broke out, and wishing to be with his friends a little before finally decamping, he waited till the officers set off, and then returned to Alloa, without their knowing it, *on the back of the chaise* that had brought him to Kinross, *with them in it*.

EDINBURGH, *30 April 1838*.—We had tough work at Perth, which it took four and a half days to get through. We were only free yesterday about three, and got home in the evening, and a clear, beautiful, though cold evening it was.

We had an example of that horrid piece of nonsense, invented within these twenty years by the Court of Justiciary, and called by the inventors '*The option*'. The absurdity cannot possibly last long,[1] and for the edification of posterity it may be as well to tell what it was.

Some people think it cruel, and conducive to perjury, to compel parents or children to give evidence against each other; others—of whom I am one—admit it to be painful, but think that everything must yield to the necessities of justice, and that nothing is so cruel as that an innocent man should be convicted because a son is indulged in protecting his father by silence, which may happen in many ways. What is thought the humane side prevails at present in our criminal law. But it occurred to some of the judges, about twenty years ago, that, as the indulgence was granted solely from delicacy to these relations, it was competent to them to reject it if they chose. They therefore introduced *The option*, by which parents and children might hang each other or not, just as they pleased, unless they happened to be under pupillarity, in which case, being held incapable of discretion, they are always rejected.

The practical operation of this folly is this: A mother is on trial for her life. Her daughter is called as a witness against her. The Court tells her she has the option. She is a person of right feelings, and declines to testify. The possession of such feelings is a proof that she is worthy of being credited, even in the case of

[1] *EDITOR'S NOTE. I am grateful to Professor W.A. Wilson, Dean of the Faculty of Law at the University of Edinburgh, for telling me that '"the option" was abolished with most of the other rules about relationship, by the Evidence (Scotland) Act 1840 s 1 (3 and 4 Vic c 59)'.*

a parent. Nevertheless, truth is defied, and the claims of justice disregarded, for her comfort. But if she had been a monster, to whom hanging her mother was a luxury—that is, if she had been a person who exercised this option by preferring to give evidence—then she proves herself to be utterly incredible. Yet, just on this account, she is admitted to be sworn. And if the whole family be true to each other, as is commonly (but not always) the case, then all the light depending on parents and children is utterly excluded. A father may cut his wife's throat with complete safety, provided he takes care to perform the operation before nobody but her ten grown-up sons and daughters.

In the case at Perth, a man called Murray was charged with having forged his son's name. But the son, who alone could prove the forgery, took advantage of this notable option, and refused to answer, on which the witness and the accused walked out of the Court arm in arm.

This tissue of nonsense is no part of the law of Scotland. The fear of perjury—a foolish principle, but one that was not unnatural to superstitious barbarians, played on by cunning churchmen—made our old law reject such testimony altogether and without distinction. But the option, by which its reception is made to depend on the pleasure or profligacy of each witness, is the production of a few judges, not at all qualified to legislate on such a subject, within these few years.

The true principle is to disregard relationship, except that of husband and wife, as an objection to the competency of any witness.

Perth is the only place I have ever seen where, in the arrangement of the spectators in a public court, there is an entire separation made between the ladies and the gentlemen. The gallery is divided into a male and a female compartment. It looks very odd, but it seems to conduce to silence. The eyes flirt more silently than the tongue. I don't understand, however, that this was the object.

I have long been accustomed to watch for my first swallow towards the end of the Spring Circuit, and almost always to find it. This year I looked for it in vain; no swallow has been so foolish as to appear yet.

WEST CIRCUIT BONALY, *11 May 1840*.—I went with my daughter Jane and Rosa Macbean to Stirling, visiting Linlithgow Palace by the way, on Monday, 27 April. Before dinner that day, I went and visited Lord Abercromby at Airthrie. He had been very ill, but was then better, and his place was in the perfection of young vernal beauty. It has been the finest spring ever vouchsafed to Scotland. There are few Julys like this April. And the verdure of Abercromby's grass, the bright, fresh, tenderness of his foliage, the clearness of his lake, the mirth of his lambs and water-fowl, and the softened richness of his rocks and hills were all blended into a scene of singular loveliness.

I was in Court the whole of the three next days, the 28th, 29th, and 30th. There was nothing particular in any of the cases, except that in one of them we had an excellent specimen of that beautiful option. Four people were under trial for theft, and two for reset [the receiving of stolen property]. A villain, who would have cut the throats of all his relations for a shilling, was called as a witness by the prosecutor. It was objected that, being the son of one of the thieves, he was not bound to give evidence. The prosecutor (Cosmo Innes) endeavoured to make the objection inapplicable by saying that he only called him *against the two resetters*. But the reply, that still his parent was one of the accused, and that he was in the same position as a wife called to testify in a case where her husband was one of the accused, is at present deemed sound by the Court. So I was obliged to disgrace the law by explaining to him the respect paid to his sensibilities, and that in order to spare his filial piety, he had the option of defeating justice by telling the truth or not, just as he chose. No censure of this modern piece of judge-made legal nonsense could be severer than the grotesque and villainous leer with which he said: 'Odd! a' like that hoption, ma Lord!'—on which he retired amidst the laughter of the prisoners, and the amazement of the jury, and saved the two resetters.

The Lord Advocate (Rutherfurd) and I made out a Bill lately, which has just passed the Commons, for preventing the repetition of such disgraceful scenes by abolishing the objection of relationship. But its passage through the Peers is by no means certain, for a majority of the Faculty of Advocates is actually opposing it. They call such a blackguard's declining to speak, 'the voice of nature'. The opponents always take the case in which nothing worse can happen than that a guilty man escapes. But under this rule an innocent one may be convicted. Take this case. A is on his trial along with B for a murder, which *B alone* committed. He calls B's son, who saw his father alone do it. In this case the life of the innocent person is sacrificed to what, at the very best, is the filial injustice of the guilty one's relation.

We had five days of work, from nine in the morning till six or seven in the evening, having been liberated, however, on Saturday the 9th in time to reach home that night.

There was nothing particular in the cases, the great mass of them being aggravated thefts, followed by seven years' transportion, *ad nauseam*. There was one capital conviction, for murder. But even this was commonplace: the common Scotch case of a brute, excited by his own liquor, and pretending to be provoked by that of his wife, and finding himself alone in his own house with his helpless victim, proceeding to beat her to death. This man seemed to think it a sort of defence that it was a Saturday night, when 'he was *always worst*, it being his payday'. His wife was perfectly sober, and though 'she *could* take a dram,' was not of dissipated habits generally, and was never known to show any violence towards her husband. Yet though the proof could not have been clearer if the jury had seen him murder her, they unanimously recommended him to mercy on the ground of *provocation*, of which there was not a tittle, either in evidence or in truth. Such is the modern aversion to capital punishment. His name was Thomas Templeton.

There was also a shocking case of a poor child, scarcely eight years old, a climbing boy, who was compelled by threats to go up, or down, thirty-eight new chimneys successively, and without any interval for rest or food, though he was quite exhausted, cold, wet, and excoriated, and imploring that he might not be sent down the thirty-eighth vent, in which he died. The labour and danger were greatly increased by the vents being new, and the object being to clear them, by a chisel, of the lime and rubbish that adhered to their sides, a task requiring time and strength, and the rubbish greatly obstructing the passage at every turn. It was only charged as a culpable homicide, and the master had rather an affection for the boy, and worked him to death from no anger or selfishness, but merely from the general brutality of his craft. We longed to transport him, and will be abused by the benevolent for not doing so; but, in the circumstances, we could not go beyond imprisonment.

Our public breakfast was a substitute for the public dinner, and has been tried twice at Glasgow with success. It does not supersede one or two small, rational, dinners, of eight or twelve friends or respectable connections of the Court, but only the abominable gathering of all the monsters who, as a matter of right, have long been permitted to scandalise Scotch Circuits. Though often sorely grudged, the old judges deemed these festivals indispensable to the dignity of the law. They were deemed essential for the preservation of Church and State. But for some years past, much business, the want of the judges, picking the jurors, the cessation of the attendance of the gentry, and the weakness of the modern stomach, have introduced a distaste among most of us for these judicial and stately feasts.

There are only two of us who now don't loathe them; Moncreiff, who enjoys the refreshment of meat and drink, and the Justice (Lord Boyle) who, besides the conviviality, still deludes himself with the notion that the Circuit dinner exhibits him and the law in an imposing attitude. These two delight to sit down at two in the morning to salmon and roast-beef, though they have to return to Court at nine, and to do Provosts the honour of taking bumpers of claret or mulled port with them; every shut eyelid in the house starting open at the sound of the glorious trumpets, as they drink the royal health. When these two shall be gone, there will not be a judge of such bad taste as to endure these horrid and mirthless meetings.

But how [Lord] Hermand would have despised this. With him the jollity of the Circuit was the only thing respectable about it. Nothing made it contemptible, even judicially, except sobriety. I once heard the servant of his serene colleague Pitmilly, who had a strong taste for decorum and law, and none whatever for laughter or liquor, tell the chambermaid at Perth to bring his master a large kettle of warm water. Hermand, who was passing to his dinner at midnight, said, 'God bless me, sir, is he going to make a *whole kettle* of punch—and before supper too!' 'No, no, my Lord, he's going to his bed, but he wants to bathe his feet first!' 'Feet, sir?' exclaimed Hermand, 'what ails his feet? Tell him to put some *rum* among it and to give it all to his stomach!'

SOUTH CIRCUIT. LANGHOLM, *Saturday Night, 10 April 1841.*—I left Edinburgh on the morning of Wednesday last, with

Mrs. Cockburn and my niece Graham Maitland. Meadowbank is to go to Ayr; I have been at Jedburgh, and am proceeding to Dumfries.

After being dragged up, with our backs to the glories of Edinburgh, to Middleton Moor, we swept down, amid the silent peacefulness of the Gala, to Melrose. It was about thirty years since I had gone into the Abbey, and I was very glad that the necessity of showing it to Graham compelled me to see it again. It is greatly improved in keeping, being really, at last, decently clean and respectable. But they have allowed a brewery to get up within, I should suppose, 100 yards of the principal window. John Bowers, who has shown it for about forty years, and who even makes drawings of it thought worthy of being engraved, though, I dare say, a worthy man, has two faults—one that somebody has told him to eschew plain Scotch, and so he called the ruin 'a grand *Rowen*,' and gave it as his opinion that if the great window were to be destroyed, it would 'create a vast *vacuum*', the other that, though for anything I know he may be qualified for the Presidency of the strictest Temperance Society, he has a very whiskyfied visage.

NORTH CIRCUIT. ABERDEEN, *12 April 1842*.—Moncreiff joined me at Stonehaven, and we processed into Aberdeen grandly.

FOCHABERS, *Saturday Night*, *16 April 1842*.—We were in Court in Aberdeen all Wednesday, Thursday, Friday, the 13th, 14th, and 15th, and I was there today till eleven, when I came away in order to get to Inverness with as little of what is now called 'Sabbath desecration,' which chiefly means travelling on Sunday, as possible. I left Moncreiff yoked to a long case of fire-raising, by a black-looking fellow called Rosenberg, a Prussian Jew, and his wife, at one time an actress in London; and got here about six.

The only unusual bar scene at Aberdeen was in the *lifting* in of a prisoner, the only one I ever saw so introduced to be tried. She was an otherwise respectable woman, who if she had not directly murdered her infant, had caused its death by wilful neglect at bringing it into the world. And remorse, as was said, had deprived her of the use of her limbs, and prevented her from being capable of being tried till her crime was three years old, and she had become a truly pious woman. As it was necessary to get quit of her case one way or other, she, though not small, was lifted like a big child into Court, in the arms of an herculean porter, who, after she had pleaded guilty and had been sentenced to a short imprisonment for the neglect, put his left arm under her as a nurse does to a child, and (she steadying herself by placing her right arm over his neck) carried her away.

The only person I ever saw absolutely and entirely *lifted* into Court, was one Smith, who, because he chose to work for less wages than they thought proper, was shot by those scoundrels the cotton-spinners on the street, in Glasgow, in open day. The ball shattered his spine, and paralysed him all over, but left his mind unimpaired. He was brought in as a witness, lying in bed, the bed (without any posts or curtains) being laid on a flat wooden frame, and placed on the table of the Court. He was pale and emaciated, with a fallen chin and feeble voice, but with a clear eye, though obviously dying. I scarcely ever felt more than when he lay before us and, raising up his thin hand, swore, in answer to the absurd initiatory question, of which we have only last year got quit, that he had no malice or illwill at the prisoner, John Kean, to whom he owed the painful and lingering death which closed his sufferings in a few days. My client would have been hanged if the law had allowed it, but unfortunately the statute which makes shooting, though not fatally, capital, had not then [1825] been extended to Scotland. This miscreant had the merit of getting it done.

We had a premature sort of a villain at Aberdeen, an advocate's clerk aged only nineteen but who was old enough to conceive and execute the sending of three threatening letters in order to extort money. They were well-written and well-contrived letters for his purpose, for each of them held out to a different person the certainty of utter ruin by having crimes imputed to them if they did not comply with his demands—which demands were always made very slender, but if once yielded to, would of course have risen. We cordially transported the heartless dog for ten years.

We went to an evening party at Aberdeen. If their usual society be, as I am told it is, in the same style with any I have ever seen, they are a kindly, hospitable, unceremonious, happy people.

Marischal College is finished. If they do not succeed in getting the front of it cleared, they have been wasting their money. And even though they do, the building will be poor, and the attempt to maintain two Universities in such a place absurd. 'For you must know, Mr. Speaker,' as somebody said a few years ago in the House of Commons, 'that England has two Universities, and so has Aberdeen.' They should have made the old, venerable, well-placed, academic-looking King's College the single seat of their science. It is in vain to speak of anything so reasonable to either of these two parties, each of whom would rather see its favourite establishment, and science besides, extinguished than yield to the other. But their folly ought to have been disregarded.

GLASGOW, *Wednesday Night, 14 September 1842.*—I went this forenoon to Lochwinnoch, to attend the funeral of my brother-in-law, Lieut.-Col. Laurence Macdowall. After which I came here, where I found my colleague, Lord Mackenzie, who has been at Inveraray. And so nothing of this Circuit remains, except the comfortable prospect of having to try about one hundred criminal cases, besides some civil ones, and to dispose of some appeals.

But I have forgot Ardrossan. It is above, or about, thirty years since I last saw it. It was then a sort of poor fishing-village, with no harbour, and no fashion as a bathing-place. The late Earl of Eglinton was just beginning the attempt to realise his vision of glorifying and enriching his family by carrying a canal from Glasgow, by Paisley, to this part of his property, and thus making Ardrossan Tyre and Saltcoats Sidon. The canal, after being bankrupt, reached Johnstone, and now, with its railway rival, it will certainly never advance an inch further. But his lordship succeeded in compelling the sea to submit to be a small port, and in alluring genteel invalids, by a large bad inn and small bad baths, to resort there in summer. So Ardrossan is a town, and has a harbour. The whole place is respectably clean.

The ladies' bathing is conducted on the genuine Scotch principle of not being at all ashamed of it, as why should they? Is it not pure? and healthy? and ordered by the doctor? and anything wrong in it? So the ladies emerge, in full day, from their flats, in their bathing-dresses, attended by a maid, and a sister or aunt, the maid carrying a small bundle containing a towel and some dry clothes, the friends tittering. The bather crosses the road and goes to the sea, which is never more than a few yards, or inches, beyond the road's edge. She then enters the water, and shivers, or splashes, according to her taste, conversing or laughing or screaming all the while with her attendants ashore. But it is on coming out that the delicate part of the operation begins; for as they don't walk home wet, and then dress in their own rooms, they must change their *whole* raiment before the public. For this purpose the maid holds a portion of the dry vestment over the dripping lady's head, and as the soaked gown descends to the heels, the dry *is supposed* to descend over the head as fast, so that the *principle* is that, between the two, the *lady* is never seen. Ignorance is sometimes bliss, and it is very wise in the assistants never to tell the patient anything about it. But I wonder how, when they happen to be looking at a fellow-exhibitor, and observe the interest taken from every window, and by all the street, in the proceeding, they can avoid discovering that such feats are seldom performed without revelations, and that a single fold of wet linen adheres too accurately to the inner surface to require any other revelation.

But I never saw bathing performed by ladies in Scotland even with common decency. Why the devil can't they use bathing-machines, or go into retired places, or wall or pale off enclosures? There was *one* bathing-machine on the beach at Ardrossan, which was rarely used, and two in the inn court, which the landlord told me were never used at all. Portobello, however (the most immodest spot in Scotland), shows that machines may be used so as to be no protection, but the reverse, for there they are used, nearly touching, by men and women indiscriminately.

BONALY, *Saturday, 24 September 1842.*—We began at Glasgow on the morning of Thursday the 15th, and ended yesterday at four o'clock p.m. We had exactly 99 cases to dispose of—about 15 or 20 more than were ever on the list at any of our Circuits—and, one way or other, every one of them was disposed of. None, I mean, that could have been tried were not tried. There was no capital case, and the whole batch was utterly uninteresting, the great majority being commonplace thefts. The exile of about 60 of our fellow-creatures is upon our souls.

One of the days was a Sunday, a very serious thing in Glasgow. To avoid its horrors, Lord Mackenzie spent the day at Possil. He is a very old acquaintance, and one of the best possible colleagues. A weak, awkward, and apparently timid manner gives him an outward appearance almost directly the reverse of the real man. For beneath this external air of helplessness, there works an acute, resolute, and original understanding; combined with great intelligence and a very amiable heart. Not very practical, and wanting tact, he seems to be constantly engaged with his own speculations, the intrepidity of which make an amusing contrast with the feebleness of his manner. He is a most excellent man, a singularly agreeable companion, and an admirable judge—except that, on the Bench, whenever there is anything to be done which requires force, or impressiveness, his poverty of manner makes him fail. But in private life this outside awkwardness makes him only picturesque.

WEST CIRCUIT. GARSCUBE, *Tuesday Night, 25 April 1843.*— We came here to-day, through wind and rain, from Tarbet. I have been invited to this hospitable house for above thirty years, but never made it out till now. A very comfortable place, with the air and the reality of luxury in everything about it. Considering the odious manufacturing country that surrounds it, its principal excellence is its singular seclusion within the dressed ground of the place. A stranger could never suspect while admiring its trees, beautiful grass, well-kept walks, its garden, stream, and mansion-house, that if he ventured to raise his head above the slopes that enclose him, he would see groves of chimneys, the obelisks of manufacturers, polluting the atmosphere on every side.

BONALY, *3 May 1843.*—Meadowbank and I left Garscube on the morning of Wednesday, 26 of April, and processed into Glasgow. Whether it was our error or theirs I do not know, but the magistrates and we took different roads, and for about half an hour we chased each other, to the great diversion of the people. We had our public dinner on that day, and were quiet, though not absolutely solitary, every day afterwards. On Saturday evening I came to Edinburgh, and went back on Monday morning.

There were 82 indictments and 142 prisoners. Some of these cases were so long that if they had all gone on, they could not have been disposed of till the end of this week. But a doubt occurred about the citations of about twenty of the longest of them, which prevented these being proceeded with, and it has had a similar effect at Perth. This misfortune, for it is wrong not to dispose of all the business, and it generally recurs at some less convenient season, liberated us suddenly yesterday at two, and at five we were in Edinburgh.

There was one capital sentence, a murderer's, a brute who after fatiguing himself by beating his half-drunk wife, at last sharpened a knife on the hearthstone, and stabbed her, all because she would not give him breakfast, which his blows made her incapable of doing, but which was done for her by another woman. She was an intolerable wife, insomuch that he had often said that 'one of us would certainly swing for the other'. But they had gone out this morning about nine on good terms, and had returned in about an hour, both more stupefied than excited by whisky; and after taking all his blows without any other resistance than an appeal to 'Charley, dear,' the wretched woman was bled to death by a fierce cut of the femoral artery, on no other provocation than that of being disabled by his violence from feeding the beast with her own hands. This scene occurred on a Sunday—a day sacred, with a part of our population, to whisky and brutality. The convict's name is Charles Mackay.

There was also the case of a woman accused of murdering her husband, but it was one of the twenty, and did not come on. She first committed the capital offence of giving her husband a dose of arsenic, which very nearly killed him, but he survived it. Thinking (truly) that it was her unskilfulness in administering that made this dose fail, she resolved to improve herself by a little practice, and then to renew the attempt. She therefore experimented upon a neighbour, whom she killed. And having now ascertained how to proceed, she gave another dose to her spouse, and killed him too. She was indicted for the two murders and the abortive administration, an awkward accumulation of charges. It being in her case that the motion to put off all the trials was made, she was brought to the bar; and, whether it was fancy or not, struck me as having a very singular expression. She was little, apparently middle-aged, modest and gentle looking, with firm-set lips, a pale countenance, and suspicious restless eyes. Her name is Mary Macfarlane or Taylor.

A band of five horrible women—real Glasgow faggots—incorrigible devils—were sent to Botany in a batch, for a ferocious robbery committed on a decent stranger they had

438

inveigled into their den. I was greatly diverted by overhearing the account which one of them gave, in a soliloquy, of her learned judges as she was leaving the bar: 'Twa d—d auld grey-headed blackguards! They gie us plenty o' their law, but deevilish little joostice!'

GLASGOW CIRCUIT. BONALY, *8 January 1844.*—I left Edinburgh by the half-past seven o'clock train on Tuesday last, the 2nd, and was in time for the Winter Circuit procession at ten. Medwyn was my colleague. The job lasted till Saturday evening the 6th, sitting generally from nine till about eight. There were 64 cases, and we left not one untried that the prosecutor could proceed with.

My strolls, whether before breakfast or after dinner, being all in the dark and generally under heavy rain, I saw nothing.

The cases were a mass of commonplace trash.

It seems to me to augur worse and worse for the effect of long imprisonments. We had about twelve thieves, all of whom had been imprisoned by the Court of Justiciary for at least one year, and several more on whom the benevolence of long and religious incarceration had been wasted by Sheriffs. I suppose that, including the last Spring and Autumn Circuits at Glasgow, I have seen about fifty such cases in the last ten months.

One handsome-looking young woman, called Mary Boyle, had been in the Penitentiary at Perth, the very school of penal virtue, and had come out with a great character, a thoroughly reformed creature, their best swatch. Well, after being a month free, *and employed*, she engages in a daring burglary with a gang of male villains; and then on being sentenced to transportation threw off in an instant the decorous air which had made people first doubt the evidence, and then pity her, and broke out into a paroxysm of the most cordial fury I ever saw at the bar: cursing prosecutor, judges, jury, her own counsel, and all concerned, in the coarsest terms, and in the manner of the best brimstone, and dealing effective blows on all the enemies within her reach, not omitting even the poor macer, who had had nothing to do with it. But crime—nay, the particular sort of it—runs in families like everything else, and this lady belongs to a race of thieves. She has a father and mother and two brothers or sisters already in Australia, and the only two that remain have already gone through what seems to be the first stage of the transporting process—a short imprisonment. It is to be hoped that the strength of the hereditary tendency saves the reputation of Perth.

Thank God, no other Court will ever be held in the abominable internal structure which, for above thirty years, has disgraced Glasgow and impeded the administration of justice, to say nothing of its smiting judges, who were exposed to its bitterest gale, with lumbago, sciatica, and all manner of colds. The wit of no devil could devise a more atrocious composition. Posterity will scarcely believe that so recently as about the year 1810, a large sum was expended in a great city on a Courthouse so constructed that the judges sat (literally) on the top of a staircase, separated from the street only by a folding door; that their only room for robing or taking refreshment was a closely adjoining water-closet; that there was not a single apartment of any kind for counsel, or anybody, except two that were got for the occasion of each Circuit, one for the jury to be enclosed in, and one of about 15 feet square for as many as perhaps 1000 witnesses as could be squeezed into it without respect to age, sex, or station, and that for all concerned, except judges, witnesses, and prisoners—that is, for counsel, agents, jurymen, and mob coming and going—there was only *one door*, and it placed at the greatest attainable distance from the greatest number of people. This cursed door made the Court just a street. There was a constant stream of jostling comers in and goers out, whose noise, from tongue and from feet, the thumbscrew itself could not have checked. The Court is still to be held in the same place, but totally changed in all its arrangements. How these will turn out will be seen in September.

A good Court-room must have innumerable apartments close at hand, a separate place—and each place with a separate access—for each class of the members of the Court, judges, counsel, agents, jurors, witnesses, and distinguished spectators; and though there ought to be due and comfortable accommodation for the public, it is an error to suppose that it is necessary to admit the whole public at once.

Of all the judicial spectators in Scotland, those of Glasgow are the worst. They are the least attentive, and by far the most vulgar. But I observe that the attention is always in proportion to the facility of hearing.

The only bad fact that I know for the new Court is that John Hope[1] has taken the chief charge of the plan, and declares it to be perfect.

NORTH CIRCUIT. BRIDGE OF TILT, *Tuesday Night, 18 April 1848*.— Left Aviemore at nine and were here by five. The day cold but bright, and the long, silent range in an excellent state. There is no better drive for a contemplative man.

When I left home, I thought of devoting these pages to anecdotes connected with famous trials, chiefly those in which I have been professionally engaged. But I find that it would not do, without far more detail than anybody would care to follow. Let me therefore just tell three stories, which are all simple and curious.

In July 1800 a person of the name of Elliot was convicted of a capital offence—either horse-stealing or forgery—and was doomed to die. Owing to some legal doubt, he was pardoned only a day or two before he was to have suffered; but another man, who had been condemned to be executed on the same day, was not so fortunate. Lord Medwyn (who is my informer) was caught, by accident, on the Lawnmarket of Edinburgh, and could not escape from the crowd which he found assembling to witness the execution of the law's remaining victim, but he got into a remote spot at the upper end of the street. A man came there hurriedly, and in intense agitation, and stood out most part of the scene. His eyes were strained towards the scaffold, as if they would burst, his hands clenched in agony, his chest heaving, the very picture of horror. *It was Elliot*. Medwyn had seen him in court, and knew him. Instead of flying, he felt it irresistible to witness the proceeding in which he himself had so nearly been an actor; and probably suffered far more in seeing the position of his associate, and in sympathising with *himself*, than he would have done if he had been the spectacle and not the spectator. It was a strange feeling that forced him there, yet not an incomprehensible one.

I had a client called David Haggart, who was hanged at Edinburgh for murdering his jailor in Dumfries. He was young, good-looking, gay, and amiable to the eye; but there never was

<hr>

[1] *EDITOR'S NOTE. Lord President of the Court of Session.*

a riper scoundrel, a most perfect and inveterate miscreant in all the darker walks of crime. Nevertheless, his youth (about twenty-five) and apparent gentleness, joined to an open confession of sins, procured him considerable commiseration, particularly among the pious and the female. He employed the last days of his existence in dictating memoirs of his own life to his agent, with a view to publication. The book was published, and my copy contains a drawing of himself in the condemned cell, by his own hand, with a set of verses, his own composition, which he desired to be given to me in token of his gratitude for my exertions at his trial. Well, the confessions, and the whole book, were a tissue of absolute lies—not of mistakes, or of exaggerations, or of fancies, but of sheer and intended lies. And they all had one object: to make him appear a greater villain than he really was. Having taken to the profession of crime, he wished to be at the head of it. He wanted to die a great man. He therefore made himself commit crimes of all sorts—none of which, as was ascertained by inquiry, were ever committed at all. His guilt in these deathbed inventions was established by as good evidence as his guilt in the act for which he suffered was. A strange pride. Yet not without precedent—and in nobler walks of criminal ambition.

Mrs. Mackinnon was convicted of murder on 13 March 1823. Jeffrey and I were her counsel. Her family had been respectable. It was sworn that her deceased father was a captain in the army. But by misfortune after misfortune, or more probably by successive acts of misconduct, she was at last, when not much above thirty, reduced to the condition of being the mistress of a disorderly house in Edinburgh. But still she was not all bad; for a strong and lofty generosity, by which she had been distinguished before she fell, neither the corruptions nor the habits of her subsequent life could extinguish. She had stabbed a man with a knife, in a brawl in her house, and it was for taking his life that her own was forfeited. If some circumstances which were established in a precognition (taken after her conviction by the orders of Sir Robert Peel, then Home Secretary) had transpired on the trial, it is more than probable that Jeffrey—whose beautiful speech is remembered to this hour—would have prevailed on the jury to restrict their conviction to culpable homicide. But, in law, it was a murder, and Peel, though moved, was advised that she could not be spared.

So she died publicly, but gracefully and bravely; and her last moment was marked by a proceeding so singular that it is on its account that I mention her case. She had an early attachment to an English Jew who looked like a gentleman, on the outside at least; and this passion had never been extinguished. She asked him to come and see her before her fatal day. He did so; and on parting, on her last evening, she cut an orange into two, and giving him one half and keeping the other herself, directed him to go to some window opposite the scaffold, at which she could see him, and to apply his half to his lips when she applied her half to hers. All this was done; she saw her only earthly friend, and making the sign, died, cheered by this affection.

Here the anecdote ought to have ended; and if it had been an invention, it would have ended here. But see how nature's wonders exceed those of art. She had left everything she had, amounting to four or five thousand pounds, to her friend. He took the legacy, *but refused to pay the costs of her defence*, which her agent only screwed out of him by an action.

PERTH, *Sunday Night, 23 April 1848.*—Getting on slowly; and dull, commonplace work. The audience was *relieved* yesterday by a murder. But it was a poor one. An infant suffocated in its clothes by its natural father. He was condemned, but won't be hanged. (PS, 21 May: But he has been, though.)

We went to church today in state. A grand oration, from the same mouthy declaimer we had on 27 April 1845. His fancy goods are of a bad pattern, and want body.

NORTH CIRCUIT CASTLETON, *Saturday Night, 22 September 1849.*—The Aberdeen criminal business exhausted four days, Tuesday, Wednesday, Thursday, and yesterday. There were not more cases than usual; but they happened to be of a worse description. In particular, there were four capital cases: two murders, one murder combined with raptus [rape], and one raptus alone. One of the murders ended in an acquittal—and very properly, because though the guilt was certain and savage, the evidence was not satisfactory. In another murder, a plea of culpable homicide produced twenty years' transportation. The simple raptus ended in a conviction, and in transportation for life. The murder and raptus combined caused a sentence of death. This last was a horrid case.

The prisoner was James Robb, a country labourer of about twenty-five, a known reprobate, and stout. His victim was Mary Smith, a quiet woman of sixty-two, never married or a mother, who lived by herself in a lonely house by the wayside. There was a fair held at a village in Aberdeenshire called Badenscoth, which sometimes, though in no eminent degree, produced some of the disorderly scenes natural to fairs.

Mary Smith, though not the least alarmed, happened to observe casually that 'she was not afraid of anybody, except that lad Jamie Robb'. That very night (9 April 1849) Robb left the fair about ten, vowing that he was determined to gratify his passion on somebody before he slept. He had then no thought of this old woman; but, unfortunately, her house lay in his way. He asked admittance, upon pretence of lighting his pipe. She refused. On this he got upon the roof and went down the chimney, which consisted of a square wooden box about 5 feet long by $2^1/_2$ wide, placed about 8 feet above the fire. Its soot streaked his corduroy dress, which helped to identify him. Having got in, the beast fell upon its prey. She was thought in good health, but after death was discovered to have an incipient disease in the heart, which agitation made dangerous but which might have lain long dormant. The violence of the brute, and the alarm, proved fatal. She was found dead in the morning, and the bed broken and in the utmost confusion. A remarkable composite metal button, broken from its eye, was found twisted in what a witness called 'a lurk,' or fold, of the sheet. Buttons of exactly the same kind, with the same words and figures engraved on them, were found on his jacket, all complete except that one was awanting. But its eye remained; and this eye, with its bright recent fracture, exactly fitted the part of the button that had been found. These circumstances would have been sufficient to have established his having been in the house. But his declaration admitted the fact. Consent was excluded by its being obvious that it was the energy of her resistance that had killed her.

It is difficult to drive the horrors of that scene out of one's imagination. The solitary old woman in the solitary house, the descent through the chimney, the beastly attack, the death struggle—all that was going on within this lonely room, amidst silent fields, and under a still, dark sky. It is a fragment of hell, which it is both difficult to endure and to quit.

Yet a jury, though clear on both crimes, *recommended the brute to mercy!*—because he did not *intend* to commit the murder! Neither does the highwayman, who only means to wound in order to get the purse, but kills.

Within a few hours after he was convicted he confessed, and explained that the poor woman had died in his very grip. (He was executed, solemnly denying his guilt in respect of raptus!)

BONALY, *Thursday Night, 27 September 1849.*—We got free from Court today at one, and into the Scottish Central Railway at about four, and, after a pause in Edinburgh, were here by nine. Her Majesty passed through the Perth station while we were there, on her way home. She left Balmoral by the highway this forenoon; got on the railway at Cupar Angus, and was in Edinburgh, by Stirling, in two and a half hours. All the stations were crowded with people, panting for a sight of her; and her gracious condescension was expressed by whisking past them at the rate of about thirty miles per hour, with all her windows shut. Immense folly! When I'm a queen, I shall hold it to be my dignity to go slow.

EDINBURGH, *17 January 1850.*—On Tuesday the 8th, Lord Ivory and I began the Glasgow Winter Circuit. It was not over till the night of Tuesday the 15th, being seven Court days.

It was an unusually black tribunal, there being 79 cases, involving about 125 culprits; among whom seven were charged with murder, and many with other serious crimes. Of the murders, one, a female poisoner, was doomed to die; two were transported for life, and one for seven years, one was acquitted, one escaped, and one was imprisoned.

The poisoner had first stolen a bank deposit-receipt; finding that she could not get the money without the owner's signature, she forged it, and then, having committed these two offences, murdered the victim in order to hide them. She was tried for the whole three crimes. The forgery, and the administration of arsenie, were very clearly proved. But there was a doubt about the theft, and therefore the jury found it *not proved*.

Yet upon this fact a majority of them grounded by far the most nonsensical recommendation to mercy that any jury known to me ever made themselves ludicrous by. They first recommended without stating any reason; on being asked what their reason was, they retired, and after consultation, returned with these written words, viz: that they gave the recommendation 'in consequence of the first charge, of theft, not having been proved, which they believe in a great measure led to the commission of the subsequent crime'! Grammatically, this means that it was their *acquittal* of the theft that did the mischief, but what they *meant* was that the murder was caused by a theft *not proved to have existed*. It is the most Hibernian recommendation I have ever seen.

The preceding recommendation, though backed by the whole force of the very active party opposed to capital punishment, failed, and the poor wretch died.

Of the 125 accused, about 122 were tried, and of these only six were acquitted, a fact honourable to the criminal practice of Scotland. Eighty-five were transported.

The peculiarity of this Circuit was that, *for the first time at any Circuit in this country*, the two judges sat, generally, each in a separate Court, of course doing double work. A statute was passed to sanction this about two years ago, but it had never been acted upon. Ivory and I were glad to set the example. It was very popular with everybody, as it saved time and expense.

This was the first time I had seen Ivory as a criminal judge. He is excellent. His law and agreeable manner could not be doubted. But, like other good lawyers, he is apt to be beset by nice doubts, and loves them in civil adjudication; and many people were afraid that he might be troubled by this infirmity on the criminal bench. But if he was—which, however, I saw no symptom of—necessity made him shake it off. He was as decided and hardy as needed to be. A most excellent man.

NORTH CIRCUIT. KNOCKOMIE, *Friday night, 16 April 1852.*— On Tuesday the 13th, the Court opened at Inverness, and the business lasted till yesterday about two.

The only interesting case was that of Mrs. and Mr. Fraser, a mother and her son (a lad), who had chosen to poison their father, a shopkeeper in Ross-shire. They thought him a useless creature, and that they would be better without him, especially as the wife had forged his name to bills, in reference to which his removal, before they became due, would be convenient. I never saw a couple of less amiable devils. The mother had cold, hard eyes and a pair of thin resolute lips, producing an expression very fit for a remorseless and steady murderess. She saw her daughter, a little girl, brought in as a witness, and heard her swear that there were no rats in the house, and that her father's sufferings were very severe, with a look of calm, severe ferocity which would have done no discredit to the worst woman in hell.

They were both convicted, but I fear that the gallows won't get its due. A legal doubt occurred, on which we held ourselves bound to consult the Court before pronouncing sentence; and if this doubt be resolved in the prisoners' favour, they will escape altogether; and even if it be decided against them, the delay will probably save their lives, which will be a pity.

We came here again yesterday evening. I was taken to visit an old lady in Forres, called Miss Macpherson, certainly a person well worth seeing. She called herself eighty, but is said to be eighty-four, and has a face which must have once been beautiful, and is still very handsome. She is in perfect preservation, and in great talk; has known, and recollects, every person and every event in the north of Scotland in her day; is always in excellent spirits, and has a delightful northern accent and dialect, with a willing flow of strong sense and acute observation, generally of a cheerful character. A most enviable specimen of old age. She twice made use of an expression which struck me as very descriptive. I had asked who a particular Grant and a particular Fraser were, and she, meaning to describe them as just of their respective clans, said of each, 'Hoot, he's just the *growth of the ground.*' She goes to Edinburgh in a few days to get her tusks repaired. '*Not from vanity*, but because I can't eat well.'

I went to Altyre to see Sir William Cumming, a far more curious creature than any that his son Roualeyn encountered in Africa.

PERTH, *Thursday Night, 29 April 1852.*—I enjoyed the hyacinths for two days, having gone to Bonaly on Friday the 23rd, and stayed there on Saturday and Sunday, and returned here to breakfast on Monday the 26th, where Ivory rejoined me. There was one *buff* hyacinth that, of itself, was worth the whole journey. I was just in time to catch their dying odours.

We are here still, but shall return to peace and Eden tomorrow.

This has been the most murderous Circuit I have ever known. Besides the two Frasers at Inverness, we have had three Cains here: Thomas Lyneham, who beat his sister-in-law so as to cause her to die; Mrs. Blyth, who broke her old mother's head with the tongs; and Charles Fancoat, who plunged a butcher's knife literally *through* the body of a fellow-workman who had struck him with the fist some time before. However, there was only one capital sentence.

The sister-in-law was in such bad health that this raised one of the doubts at which juries are, justly, so apt to catch, and Lyneham was treated as an assaulter.

Mrs. Blyth was proved to have been insane when she did her deed, and was disposed of accordingly. She was a hard, sensible-like woman, who lived in a village in Fife with her mother, to whom she was much attached. But her reason had been gradually leaving her for two years, till at last it was gone, and she passed her time in visionary misery in bed. One of her prevailing alarms was for her nose, which seemed a very respectable article; but she was convinced that it had got black and was going to fall off. When told that she had killed her mother, she said, 'Weel, had she no lived lang eneuch?' Nevertheless, she was clearly of opinion that she herself ought to be hanged, and was disappointed when the ceremony was avoided.

Fancoat, though strongly recommended to mercy by the jury, will probably suffer. His was a clear murder. He and his victim had been quarrelling throughout the day, and in these half-drunken conflicts he had been ill-used. At last they had parted, and he was safe—but instead of being quiet, he went and borrowed a long and mortal knife, and proceeded in quest of the other man, and meeting him, gave him a strong stab, which produced death in a few minutes. He is a young Englishman of excellent character; his good feelings were evinced to those who, like me, observed his emotion when some of his native villagers came forward to attest his peaceableness and humanity of disposition. I cannot help wishing that his life may be spared. It was whisky and groundless fear that, for the moment, overthrew his better nature. (PS. He has only been transported.)

BONALY, *Saturday Night, 1 May 1852.*—Ivory left me yesterday morning. Only one case, but a most brutal one, remained at Perth, and in a couple of hours it ended in a transportation for life.

I need scarcely say that it came from Dundee—certainly now, and for many years past, the most blackguard place in Scotland. Perth and its shire are always remarkably innocent. Nearly the whole guilt at this place proceeds from the two counties of Fife and Forfarshire, and, of course, chiefly from their towns. Of these towns, Kirkcaldy, Cupar, and Montrose seem well behaved enough. Arbroath is not good; Dunfermline (always meaning *the district*) very bad; Dundee a sink of atrocity, which no moral flushing seems capable of cleansing. A Dundee criminal, especially if a lady, may be known, without any evidence about character, by the intensity of the crime, the audacious bar air, and the parting curses. What a set of she-devils were before us! Mercy on us! If a tithe of the subterranean execration that they launched against us, after being sentenced, was to be as effective as they wished it, commination never was more cordial.

Our weather could not have been better for our purposes, if we ourselves had had the choice of it. How beautifully Inverness and Perth lay, in the mornings, amidst their calm rising smoke, their bursting verdure, and their soft, glorious rivers.

EDINBURGH, 2 MANOR PLACE [Cockburn's town-house], *19 January 1853.*—I had nearly forgotten the late Glasgow Circuit— *the last winter one I shall last to go.*

I went to Glasgow *alone* (!) on the morning of Monday, 3rd January, and, after the usual proceedings, *I* got home in the forenoon of Thursday the 6th. Ivory's cases detained him in Court for some hours upon that day.

I have little else to record.

The whole four days and nights were one ceaseless torrent of rain, which fell through one unbroken mass of cold, thick, wet, palpable fog, through which carts, cabs, vans, drays, and all sorts of manufacturing conveyances roared, as usual, without above two hours' cessation in the twenty-four. These two hours of truce were, and in Glasgow are, between two and four in the morning, before and after which neither London nor hell contains any vehicular roar more accursedly magnificent. Indeed, even these two hours are not always safe. For when I was deluding myself, in my second night-watch, with the hope of silence and Elysium, the roar went on till the chimes of four o'clock roused the whole host of labour to the toil and the noise of the day. And what caused this exception? A *ball*, in the *college*, by the professors of *divinity!* The least offensive sort of theological turmoil.

There were two cases of murder, with convictions in both. One was a mere commonplace affair of a woman drowning her illegitimate infant. About 2500 decent women have petitioned the Crown for a commutation. (PS. And they succeeded.)

The other was the case of a fellow who, in hatred of his stepmother, *intimated his determination* to kill the child which she was soon to be delivered of, and kept his word by cutting off its head. His defence was insanity. And no doubt he was as mad as gusts of passion could make him, but not nearly mad enough to cut off heads with impunity. However, I did not discourage the jury from convicting him, recommending him to mercy on the ground of his intellect being *defective*. This they did, and his life has been allowed to proceed. But as the public reason on this question has been returning of late, the next half-crazy murderer will probably fare worse.

NORTH CIRCUIT CASTLETON, BRAEMAR, *Wednesday Night, 28 September 1853.*—Ivory took Inverness, which I escaped.

The business at Aberdeen was finished yesterday by three o'clock. Another unlicensed doctor had poisoned a child by an absurd dose. This Circuit is the first occasion on which we had to expound and apply the recently introduced punishment of '*Penal Servitude*' in place of short transportations. I augur no good of it.

We had a beastly Circuit dinner, *on a sanded floor*, and came eagerly away this morning from the stinking Royal Hotel; breakfasting at Banchory, we were here about five—Ivory, his daughter, and daughter-in-law, being with us.

I have nothing more to say about beautiful Deeside. But below Ballater it is not improving. Up to Banchory it is polluted by a railway; the wood is disappearing, and agriculture is encroaching. Above Ballater it is unchanged, and I hope unchangeable, and the whole eighteen miles are glorious. The new house being built for the Queen at Balmoral may be better than the old one for residence, but I don't anticipate that it will equal the old one in picturesque beauty. The day was excessively cold, with too much wind, and some surly showers. But on the whole there was a prevalence of bright light, and Lochnagar never shone in greater splendour.

I think it my duty to record the unmatched merits of a leg of mutton which we had today at dinner. It was a leg which stands out even amidst all the legs of my long and steadily muttonised life. It was glorious. A leg of which the fat flats of England can have no idea, and which even Wales, in its most favoured circumstances, could only approach. It was a leg which told how it had strayed among mountains from its lambhood to its death. It spoke of winter straths and summer heights, of tender heather, Alpine airs, cold springs, and that short sweet grass which corries alone can cherish. These were the mettle of its pasture. It left its savour on the palate, like the savour of a good deed on the heart. And then the room was so breezy, and we were always heaping so much wood on the fire, and had so much true wit with an old body of a waiter who said his name was Malcolm, and who was pleased by being dubbed the king, and the brandy and hot-water were so satisfactory, and the evening closed by such a comfortable drowsiness, that, joined to the leg, it was a worthy close of a worthy day.

BONALY, *22 April 1854.*—A most contemptible Circuit; short, solitary, expeditionless.

It has been the South. Ivory was again fixed for Dumfries, and I hoped to soothe myself under the pensive silence of venerable and fading Jedburgh. But a cold prevented me; so Ivory, with his usual kindness, took that too, and I went only to Ayr, the last town of the Circuit, where he joined me.

The only interesting case was that of Alexander Cunninghame, charged with murdering his wife, and convicted on the clearest possible circumstantial evidence. It was a singularly atrocious proceeding. He was about thirty-five, a strong, resolute-looking, dogged scoundrel. She had been a well-conditioned, good woman, whom he had been twice punished for assaulting, and who was obliged, for the preservation of herself and her four children, to cease living with him. She was twice or thrice persuaded to go back, but was always obliged to fly again, and they had been entirely parted for about a year. During all this time the children were maintained solely by her labour. He often said that he would like to kill her, and that he would shoot her as easily as he would 'that gull'. An acquaintance to whom he once disclosed this inclination warned him against 'letting such thoughts enter his heart,' as they would certainly lead to his being hanged. No intimation of these threats, or rather indications, was ever made to the authorities, because they were believed to be mere sulky words.

Though they were both in so small a place as Girvan, he for nine months did not know where she was working. At last he found this out, and next day borrowed a gun, powder, and shot. That evening about seven—a calm, dark evening last December—he got into the garden behind the house she was working in, and saw her sitting, with a candle, at her loom. She was not sitting quite right for receiving the full effect of his shot. He therefore threw a little gravel against the window. This made her look up. He fired and she was dead.

Yet, though the evidence was quite clear, and the jury said nothing of lenity, I expect an exertion to be made by the idiots who have got into a habit of distinguishing themselves on such occasions, to save the life even of this miscreant. They have luckily made their efforts somewhat ridiculous of late, not so much by the folly of their reasons as by their shameless fecundity in the creation of false evidence.

The prisoner was very attentive to the proceedings, and understood everything that was going on. But he got into a very odd speculation. I observed him make a sign to his counsel to come to him. The counsel did so, and resumed his seat, with a look in which I thought I saw some horror and a little mirth. I afterwards asked him what his client had said. It was this: 'If they hang me, what will they do wi' ma clothes?'

This was our last criminal case. It was over about two p.m. of Thursday the 20th.

I left Ivory to try a civil cause, and, passing by the back of the Court, found myself on the seashore. It was one of the finest days of even this unsurpassed spring. The beautiful bay of Ayr could scarcely have been more beautiful. The advancing sea was insinuating its clear waters irresistibly, yet gently, into the innumerable little hollows and channels of the dry sand. Few people were out, but there were plenty of sea-fowls playing on the beach, and in the air, and with the long soft waves. Three white-skinned boys were bathing. No ship, not even a boat, was visible. There was no sound, except of an occasional hammer by a few lazy masons who were pretending to be repairing the point of the pier; the ring of their implements only deepened the silence. The picture of repose was completed on reaching the pier, every projecting point of which was occupied by one or two old bodies of rod-fishers, who were watching the bobbing of their corks as attentively as slumber would allow. They caught nothing, and said that they would not till it should rain, which it had not done for six weeks. So the very fishes were at rest too. It was all a refreshing contrast to the heat and the crowd of that horrid Court.

I went to Glasgow that evening, stayed there all night, and came here yesterday forenoon.

H. C. Cockburn.

Next day, Sunday the 23rd, Lord Cockburn was seized with serious illness; rapidly sinking, he died at Bonaly on the morning of the following Wednesday, 26 April 1854, in his seventy-fifth year. On the first of May, he was (in a strictly private manner, according to his directions) buried in the Dean Cemetery, Edinburgh, close to the resting-places of his friends, the Lords Jeffrey and Rutherfurd.

41313 NY
Jared L. Manley

[That is one of the pen-names that James Thurber used when working part-time for The New Yorker, *which he had joined as a full-time employee—not as a writer or a cartoonist but as business manager—in 1927, when he was thirty-two and the magazine had been running—or rather, stumbling along—for two years. A native of Columbus, Ohio (a State that has provided more than its fair share of contributors to this collection: Richard D. Altick and Albert Borowitz live there), Thurber is thought of by most readers as a great humorist, but by far fewer as a brilliant 'straight' writer (see his essay, 'A Sort of Genius', on Willie Stevens, who, with siblings, was acquitted of the Hall-Mills murders at New Brunswick, New Jersey, in 1922), and by fewer still as a clever parodist (see his* New Yorker *'filler' in which he reports the Snyder-Gray case in the respective styles of Gertrude Stein, James Joyce, and a sports reporter). He was blind, though still writing and drawing, for some years before his death in 1959.]*

From The New Yorker, 27 March 1937:

JUST A FEW MINUTES before two o'clock on the hot, sticky morning of Tuesday, 16 July 1912, a man sauntered up to a table in the café of the old Hotel Metropole on Forty-third Street near Broadway and spoke to another man who sat there. 'Somebody wants to see you outside, Herman,' he said. In that casual sentence was spoken the doom of the famous and flourishing Hotel Metropole; it closed its doors not long afterwards because of what happened in the next minute. The man at the table got up and walked briskly out on to the street, the other man following him. The one who had been addressed as Herman stood under the bright lights of the hotel's marquee, looking around for whoever it was wanted to see him. He didn't have to wait long. Four short dark men jumped out of a grey automobile standing at the curb, closed in on him, and fired six shots. That was the end of Herman Rosenthal, the gambler, and the beginning of one of the most celebrated murder cases in our history. Two days before this happened, Rosenthal had become known to the reading public. The *World* had printed an affidavit of his on that day, charging that a police lieutenant named Charles Becker had exacted 'protection money' from him and had then raided and closed his gambling house. It had also been intimated in the newspaper that Rosenthal would go before the Grand Jury and involve Becker even more deeply in corruption.

The murderers hadn't bothered to remove or obliterate the licence plates of the grey touring car, because, as it transpired later, they had been told that 'the cops are fixed' and nobody would do anything to them on account of their little job. But they reckoned without the *World*, District Attorney Charles S. Whitman, and a man named Charles Gallagher, a cabaret singer, who had just happened to be passing by. Gallagher caught the licence number of the car: 41313 NY. He went immediately to the West Forty-seventh Street police station, reported the number, and was instantly thrown in jail for his pains. His information might have been completely ignored (the police had licence numbers of their own to report, all of them wrong) had not a *World* reporter rung Whitman out of bed. The District Attorney got to the police station at 3.25 in the morning, learned about Gallagher, demanded his release, and got men to work on that licence number. Before dawn the driver of the grey car, a man named Shapiro, was arrested in his bed in a room near Washington Square. Shapiro told Whitman his car had been hired that night by a man known as Billiard Ball Jack Rose.

Born Jacob Rosenzweig, in Poland, Jack Rose, thirty-five years old, was known in certain circles as the slickest poker player in

town and as graft collector for Lieutenant Becker, head of the
Strong Arm Squad, which, among other things, 'looked after'
gambling joints in the city. There were hundreds of such places.
A very popular one, on the second floor of a building at the
north-west corner of Forty-second Street and Sixth Avenue, was
run by a suave gentleman called Bridgie Webber. Rosenthal's
place was nearby, at 104 West Forty-fifth Street, in the building
now occupied by John's Chop House. The Forties writhed with
gambling joints running wide open. They all paid tribute to
Charles Becker. His salary was only $2200 a year, but it came
out later that he had, in one nine-month period, banked almost
$60,000. All his graft money was collected for him by Baldy Jack
Rose (he had several nicknames). Becker lived in a mansion of a
house he had built on Olinville Avenue in the Bronx. It still stands
there; Judge Peter Sheil lived in it until his death some years ago,
and his widow died there last fall.

Two days after the assassination, Rose turned up at Police
Headquarters, and the case's most unusual figure thus made
his formal advent. Soft-spoken, a snappy dresser—his ties and
shirts and socks always matched—Rose's physiognomy was not
unlike that of Peter Lorre, the movie actor, in Lorre's more
familiar makeup. Rose had not a hair on his head; even his
eyebrows and eyelashes were gone, the result of typhoid in
infancy. He admitted, lightly, that he had hired Shapiro's car;
he had hired it to go uptown and visit a relative. He was put
in a cell in the Tombs, where he was shortly joined by two
other suspects, Bridgie Webber and another gambler named
Harry Vallon. Webber had sent the widow Rosenthal $50 to
help towards the funeral of Herman. All three men protested
their innocence; they all had alibis.

The Rosenthal murder case bloomed blackly on the front pages
of all the papers. Here was a more exciting story than even the
story of the Titanic, which had sunk three months before. Various curious characters began to come into the case, enlivening it.
There was a tough gangster chief named Big Jack Zelig (it was
at this time that the word 'gangster' was coined). There was a
strange, blinking little man named Sam Schepps. One week after
the murder, the harried Whitman, who was to become Governor
because of his prosecution of this case, announced he would give
immunity to anyone who named the 'real culprit'. Rose, Webber,

and Vallon, all good poker players, knew when it was time to quit bluffing. They made prompt confessions. They charged that Lieutenant Becker had commissioned them to arrange the murder of Herman Rosenthal. They told who the actual killers were, the men for whom Rose had hired the car, and four unforgettable names were added to the annals of American crime: Lefty Louie, Gyp the Blood, Whitey Lewis, Dago Frank. We can dismiss briefly this infamous quartet, each of whom appears to have got $250, a big price at the time, for croaking Rosenthal. They were henchmen of the gang leader, Big Jack Zelig, who obeyed Becker but hated him. People were eager to hear a gangster chief testify, but they never got the chance; just as the case was about to come to trial, Big Jack Zelig was found one day shot to death. So was the proprietor of a small café who had squealed on Dago Frank, the first of the four killers to be found and arrested. But Rose, Vallon, and Webber lived to testify; the District Attorney saw to it that they were carefully guarded. They lived in style in their cells. Lefty and Gyp and Whitey and the Dago were convicted in November 1912, and speedily sentenced to death, although they weren't executed until a year and a half later. It was Becker, and not the four gunmen, who most interested the public—and Whitman. The case against the big, suave policeman was harder to prove.

Becker's first trial took place three months after the murder. Billiard Ball Jack Rose, neatly dressed in a dark blue suit, his shoes brightly shined, was the State's star witness. He told the jury that Becker had said to him, 'Have Rosenthal murdered—cut his throat—dynamite him—anything!' Rose testified that Becker had advanced Rosenthal the money to open his gambling house, had quarrelled with him, and finally raided the place. Rosenthal, unable to interest Whitman at the time, had taken his plaint to the *World*. Things looked black for Becker, but the testimony of the three gamblers who had turned State's evidence was, under the law, not enough to convict. There had to be a corroborating witness, somebody entirely outside the crime. It was here that Sam Schepps, a cocky little man peering through spectacles, was brought forward by the State. Rose had told about a remarkable meeting, held in a vacant lot far uptown in Harlem and attended by himself, Vallon, Webber, and Becker, at which, Rose said, the police lieutenant had commanded them to get rid of Rosenthal. Schepps, a kind of hanger-on and toady of the gamblers, had witnessed this meeting, it was claimed, but at a distance. He swore he had had no idea what the four men were talking about; he had merely seen them talking together. On this extraordinary evidence about an extraordinary conference, Becker was sentenced to death. His lawyers appealed. Sixteen months went by, and then the Court of Appeals rejected the decision of the lower court, attacking the reliability of Schepps' testimony, declaring that he was obviously an accomplice of the three gamblers.

On 6 May 1914, almost two years after Rosenthal's death, Becker went on trial again. At this trial a defence attorney turned on Rose and said, sharply, 'When you were planning this murder, where was your conscience?' Rose answered, agonisedly but promptly, 'My conscience was completely under the control of Becker.' That seems to have been the truth about Baldy Jack Rose. Like many another gambler, and many a gangster, he lived in abject fear of the cold, overbearing, and ruthless police lieutenant. It was dangerous to cross Becker; he had railroaded dozens of men who had. Becker's lawyers claimed that the gamblers had killed Rosenthal on their own, afraid of what he might reveal about them. Nobody much believed that.

At this second trial—presided over by the youngish Samuel Seabury—a new corroborating witness was somehow found, a man named James Marshall, a vaudeville actor. He testified that he had seen the gamblers and the lieutenant talking in the vacant lot on the night in question. His testimony was accepted; the defence failed to break it down. Becker was sentenced to death again, and this time the higher court did not interfere. He was executed, a maundering, broken hulk, on 30 July 1915, a little more than three years after the slaying of Herman Rosenthal. Charles S. Whitman was then Governor of New York.

Whitman, long out of politics, practises law from an office downtown. Sam Schepps died a few years ago, Bridgie Webber only last July. What happened to James Marshall, the vaudeville actor, and to Charles Gallagher, the cabaret singer, it would be hard to find out. Many of the figures in the Rosenthal case have gone to their graves; others have drifted away. Webber, after the trials, went to live in New Jersey. He became, finally, vice-president and secretary of the Garfield Paper Box Company of Passaic. He had lived in Fairlawn, New Jersey, and worked in Passaic, for twenty years as William Webber, a man without a past, until, four years ago, he appeared as a witness in a trial over there. A lawyer asked him on the stand if he was not the Bridgie Webber of the Rosenthal case. He admitted that he was. It seems to have made little difference to his friends and business associates. He died on 30 July 1936. There may have been some, reading of his end, who found ironic significance in the fact that Charles Becker also died on 30 July, twenty-one years before.

Jack Rose and Harry Vallon are still alive. We have seen them and talked with them. Men verging on to old age, quietly attempting to bury their past, they live and work within an hour's ride of New York City, but they rarely come here. They have spent almost twenty-five years going straight and have good records as law-abiding citizens. Most of their friends and associates know of their past but never mention it. Rose and Vallon work together, or rather Vallon works for Rose. Billiard Ball Jack, now known simply as Jack, lives in a fourteen-room house in a quiet suburban community with his wife. There they brought up two sons who are now in business for themselves in the metropolitan area. Rose operates a chain of roadside restaurants between Milford, Connecticut, and Lynbrook, Long Island. He is sixty years old. He gets up early, dresses as nattily as ever, pulls on a sweatshirt if the morning is cool, always covers his famous bald head with a cap—he has never worn a toupee), and takes a jog around the neighbourhood before driving to this restaurant or that in an old-model Chevrolet. He is mostly to be found in the restaurant nearest his home. When he visits New York, he makes his headquarters at the millinery shop of a relative. It is not very near his old haunts. Rose, we are told, is a favourite of the youngsters in his community. Some of the neighbours chase the kids off their lawns, but Rose invites them to play on his. He likes to talk about his interest in children. He says that it was his ludicrous baldness as a child that led him into fights with other youngsters, and finally, a toughened, embittered boy, into a reform school, where he first made contact with the underworld. Before he came to New York in the Becker regime, he had had a varied career in Connecticut. He ran a hotel in Bridgeport for a while, promoted prize-fights in Hartford, managed the Danbury baseball team, and became part-owner of the Norwich baseball team, gambling and playing the races on the side.

Rose's restaurants are large and impressive and well run. The one we found him in seats, he told us, two hundred and forty-eight persons and can serve three thousand meals a day. Chicken and waffles are a specialty. Another of the restaurants is managed by Harry Vallon, a small, grey, dignified man, who doesn't want to talk about the past. The day we went up to see Rose, Vallon drove up in a little grey car with his aging wife. He excused himself politely when he found out the nature of our visit, and drove away again.

Jack Rose is full of plans for his restaurants. He is always adding a new wing here, a new pavilion there. He is going to install a twelve-piece orchestra at one place. He took us out into a sunken garden under construction at the restaurant where we found him and explained how nice it was going to be when it was finished. He wouldn't talk about his New York past except to say that he and his associates never used to regard gambling as an evil; everybody was gambling then—in stocks, real estate, wheat, or something. He avoided the year 1912 and began to talk about his tour of the Army camps during the war under the auspices of the YMCA. Shortly after the second Becker trial, Baldy Jack Rose announced that he had reformed. He appeared on platforms here and there. When the United States got into the war, he went from camp to camp, lecturing the solders on the evils of gambling and other vices. During that period he started a motion-picture company of his own (he has always been able to get financial backing; friends of his, businessmen, invested $150,000 in his restaurants and realty holdings). He called his film company the Humanology Motion Picture Corporation. 'Humanology' was a word he had invented in his lecturing days; he says it means 'the sense of being human'.

The movie venture, never successful, ended in 1917, but not before Rose had made, among others, six pictures based on poems of his favourite poet, Ella Wheeler Wilcox. Rose used to visit her—at Short Beach, Connecticut—during the days he was making those pictures. He showed us a jewelled ring on a finger of his left hand. 'That was Ella Wheeler Wilcox's,' he said. 'She was given it by an Indian rajah she met on a world tour. I used to admire that ring, and after she died a niece of hers brought it to me one day. She said, "Aunt Ella wanted you to have that ring because you were always admiring it."' Rose has a touch of his old Chautauqua manner now and then. He explained, with the ardour of his Army-camp days, how he had long ago determined that living an honest and upright life was the only thing. 'I try to do so,' he said, 'because I feel I owe a debt of gratitude to all my friends who have stood by me so loyally.'

Before we left, Rose took us back into the restaurant to show us a mechanical device he is very keen about. It's a machine, all bright and nickelled, which makes handburgers. It grinds a chuck of beef, shapes it, shoots it on to a griddle, cooks it; all the counterman has to do is put it on the customer's plate. Jack Rose's eyes sparkled. 'It takes the mystery out of hamburgers,' he told us, proudly.

THE SECRET OF THE MOAT FARM
Edgar Wallace

[John A. Hogan, Organiser of the Edgar Wallace Society, writes: Born in 1875, the illegitimate son of a small-time actress, he became world-famous—as a prolific writer of short stories and articles, author of 183 books (in one year alone, 1929, 25 of them were published), 24 plays (including On the Spot, the central character of which was based on Al Capone), a hundred sketches and nearly as many songs for West End revues . . . and he even found time to ghost an autobiography of the wife of the mad murderer, Harry K. Thaw. More than 170 movies are accredited to his material, and he himself founded British Lion Films; in 1931 he went to Hollywood to write scenarios (among them, King Kong) for RKO. In 1932, when the news of his death reached London, the lights outside theatres were switched off as a token of respect. He had debts of £64,000, but his estate subsequently paid creditors in full. Now, in Ludgate Circus, where he was a newspaper boy, a plaque notes that 'He knew wealth and poverty, yet had walked with Kings and kept his bearing. Of his talents he gave lavishly to authorship—but to Fleet Street he gave his heart.']

AT THE AGE of fifty-six, a spinster may well be resigned to an old maid's life. Camille Cecille Holland had never known romance, though it was inevitable that she should possess her dreams. For she was a woman of imagination. She scribbled sentimental little stories, and painted in water-colours sentimental little landscapes: mills and ponds and green woodlands—pleasant, pretty scenes.

Camille Holland did not look her years: most people thought she was forty. A certain refinement of face and trimness of figure, an exquisite smallness of foot (her chief pride), lent to her an attractiveness which is unusual in women who have passed through many loveless years, 'living in boxes,' having no home but the boarding-house and cheap hotels which she frequented, and no human recreation but the vicarious acquaintanceships she formed in her uneventful journeyings.

She could afford an occasional trip to the Continent; she could afford, too, other occasional luxuries, for her aunt, with whom she had lived many years at Highbury, in north London, had left her the substantial fortune of £7,000, invested in stocks and shares, which brought her from £300 to £400 a year.[1] Amongst her investments was £400 invested in George Newnes Limited, whose shares were to play an important part in the detection of one of the cruellest crimes of the century.

Living as she did, it was natural that she had few friends. There was a nephew in Dulwich, who saw his aunt occasionally; there was a broker to whom she was known, and a banker on whom she sometimes called. Very few tradesmen knew her, because she ran no accounts, buying in whatever town she happened to be, and paying cash.

It was in the early days of the Boer War, when military men had acquired the importance which war invariably gives to them, that a smart-looking, bearded man called at the boarding-house in Elgin Crescent, Bayswater, west London where Miss Holland was in residence. He had evidently met her, for he sent up a card inscribed 'Captain Dougal,' and was immediately received by the lady in her hostess's drawing-room. He appeared a great

[1] EDITOR'S NOTE. The 1992 purchasing power of the 1900 £ is reckoned to be about £45.

friend; he came again and again, took the lady out for long strolls in Hyde Park, and once they went to dinner and to a theatre together.

The devotion of Captain Dougal must have brought to realisation one of the dreams of this spinster whom love had passed by, and she warmed to his subtle flattery, his courtesy and his obvious admiration. When, in his manly way, he confessed to her that he was unhappily married and there could be no legal culmination to their love, she was shocked but did not dismiss him. Life was passing swiftly for her, and she was confronted with the alternatives of going down to oblivion starved of love, or accepting from him the ugly substitute for marriage.

There was undoubtedly a great struggle, sleepless nights of heart-searching, before she surrendered the principles to which she had held, and let go her most cherished faiths. But, in the end, the surrender was complete. One afternoon she met him at Victoria Station, and together they went to a little house at Hassocks, near Brighton, the house having been rented for two months by her imperious lover.

His scruples, his fairness, his very misfortunes, were sufficient to endear him further to this infatuated woman of fifty-six, who for the first time in her life was experiencing the passion about which she had read and heard, and about which, in her mild and ineffective way, she had written. And those first months at Hassocks brought her a joy that fully compensated her for the illegality of the union.

The adventure was no novelty to Samuel Herbert Dougal, sometime quartermaster-sergeant of the Royal Engineers. Nor was it the first time that he had described, in his soft Irish tongue and in the most glowing colours, the happiness in store for his victim. His very brogue, so attractive to the ears of women, was an acquisition, for he had been born in the East End of London, a neighbourhood which had grown a little too hot for him at a very early age, and had made him accept the Army as an alternative to prison.

In a very short time he had gained promotion, for he was a remarkable draughtsman—and so clever with his pen that he earned for himself amongst his comrades the name of Jim the Penman. From his earliest days he had preyed on women, for he had been one of those parasitical creatures to whom a sweetheart meant a source of income.

At twenty-four he married, taking his wife with him when his regiment was moved to Halifax, Nova Scotia. She died there, with suspicious suddenness. Pleading that her death had upset him, he was allowed a short furlough in England, and returned with a second wife, a tall, young and good-looking woman, who tended his children and seemed to be possessed of some means of her own, for she had a quantity of jewellery. Nine weeks after their arrival, she also was seized with a sudden illness, and, like his first wife, died and was buried within twenty-four hours, the death being due, according to Dougal, to her having eaten poisonous oysters. Under military regulations, it was not necessary to register the death in the town of Halifax, and beyond the fact that Dougal seemed to be very unfortunate in the matter of his wives, no notice was taken.

There was in Halifax at the time a girl who had been a friend of both the Mrs. Dougals. Though no marriage ceremony occurred, Dougal, by his very audacity succeeded in imposing upon his comrades to the extent of their accepting her as his wife. He went to the trouble of forging a marriage certificate—which, however, did not deceive the officer commanding, whose signature was necessary to secure her a free passage to England. She and Dougal eventually came to England, but their union was a short one: the man's brutality and callousness were such that she decided to return to Canada.

'What excuse shall I offer my friends?' she asked tearfully. To which he replied, with that cynicism which was part of the man:

'Buy yourself a set of widows' weeds and tell them that your husband is dead.'

Dougal left the Army with twenty-one years' service, the possessor of that good-conduct medal which is the scorn of most military men, and some three-shillings-a-day pension—an amazing end to his military career, considering that during his period of service he served twelve months' imprisonment with hard labour for forging a cheque in the name of Lord Wolseley, Commander-in-Chief of the Forces in Ireland.

Scarcely had the Canadian woman left than another girl was installed in his home—only to flee in the middle of the night from his violence.

He was successively steward of a Conservative club at Stroud Green, Essex, and manager of a smaller club at the seaside; and he held numberless other positions for a short length of time. Invariably, his terms of employment ended abruptly, and, as invariably, the cause had to do with his treatment of women with whom he was brought into contact.

First and foremost, Dougal was a forger. He could imitate handwriting with such remarkable fidelity that even those he victimised hesitated to swear to the forgery.

When he met Miss Camille Holland, he had lost his youthful slimness; the fair, curling moustache was touched with grey, and he had added the pointed beard which lent him a certain sobriety of appearance that so ill accorded with his character. He was a man versed in the arts and wiles of wooing. The life at Hassocks was a dream of happiness to his dupe, and her own nature and predilections assisted him to the fulfilment of his plans.

There can be little doubt that Dougal was a poisoner; the circumstances attending the deaths of his first and second wife almost prove his responsibility. But many years had elapsed since those tragedies; at least two great poisoning cases had been tried in the courts; and he must have learnt how dangerous it was, in so law-abiding a country as England, to repeat the crimes of Halifax.

Moreover, the death of Miss Holland could not in any way benefit him, since he had no legal claim upon her. There is some slight evidence that he tried to induce her to make a will in his favour, but Miss Holland, despite her infatuation, displayed an unusual acumen when the question of placing her signature to a document arose.

The life at Hassocks, delightful as it was, was not exactly the kind of life that the woman desired. She did not want to rent a house; she wanted to settle down, to have a permanent home of her own; and Dougal, to whom she expressed her wishes, agreed with her. When she told him that she would like to buy a farm, he instantly became an authority on farming. Nothing would please him better than to live the simple, rustic life, he said. Accordingly, they began a search for a suitable habitation; the columns of the newspapers were carefully perused.

Eventually a suitable property was found. This was Coldham

Miss Camille Holland

Farm, in the parish of Clavering, in Essex. Negotiations were begun with Messrs. Rutter, of Norfolk Street, Strand, for the acquisition of the house and acreage. If the property had a disadvantage, it was that it was remote and lonely, the nearest village being Saffron Walden, and the equivalent to 'town' the town of Newport, a quaint and ancient place which all people who motor from London to Newmarket pass through without giving it a further thought.

The price of Coldham Farm was £1550, and Dougal, who had charge of all the arrangements, settled with Messrs. Rutter that a conveyance should be made in his name, Miss Holland selling off some of her stock in order to secure the money for the purchase. One day she called with Dougal at Norfolk Street, and the necessary documents were placed before her for her signature. Instead of being perfectly satisfied with the arrangements as he had made them, she read through the conveyance with a frown, and shook her head.

'The property is conveyed to you,' she said. 'I don't like that. It must be conveyed to me.'

'It doesn't make any difference; it is only a matter of form,' pleaded Dougal, who seems to have made no secret of their relationship, even to Rutter's clerk. 'If we are to be known as Mr. and Mrs. Dougal, how can you have the conveyance in your maiden-name? Everybody will know our secret.'

Apparently Miss Holland was superior to the malignant tongues of gossip.

'It must be conveyed in my name,' she said stubbornly, and, despite all Dougal's protests, despite his private interview with her, when he must have urged more intimate considerations, she had her way. The conveyance was torn up, a fresh document was prepared, and Coldham Farm was transferred to her.

The pair left Hassocks at the end of January 1899, and took lodgings at the house of a Mrs. Wiskens in Saffron Walden, where they remained until 22 April. Mrs. Wiskens added to the income she derived from 'lets' by doing odd dressmaking jobs, repairs, etc., incidentally serving Miss Holland in this capacity.

Their life at Saffron Walden seems to have been a pleasant time for Miss Holland. Dougal was still the attentive and devoted 'husband,' and nobody in that respectable little place dreamt that the formality of a marriage ceremony had been overlooked.

Front view of the lonely Moat House Farm

From time to time they drove over to their new home, the purchase of which had not yet been completed, and Dougal simulated a knowledge of farming which must have been very comforting to Miss Holland.

It was a smallish house, surrounded by a moat, and, to the romantic eye of the aged spinster, possessed many attractions. It was she who decided to rename Coldham Farm, which became the 'Moat House Farm,' the Post Office being notified of this change.

They moved into Moat House Farm in April, soon after the purchase was completed. The former owner left behind him a small staff of labourers, cowmen, etc., which Dougal re-engaged for the work of the farm.

He purchased a horse and trap, threw himself with vigour into his new work, and devised changes, including the filling in of certain parts of the moat; whilst Miss Holland, who did not disguise her pride in her new possession, set about the furnishing of the house, and brought from London a grand piano to beguile the tedium of the long evenings. She was something of a musician, just as she was something of an artist, and she may well have looked forward to a life of serene happiness with the man who had come so strangely into her life, and whose love had changed every aspect of her existence.

It would have been remarkable if Dougal, after his adventurous career, could be satisfied with the humdrum of farming. He might be amused and interested for a month or two, but after that the restrictions which the woman imposed, the necessity for keeping up the pretence of devotion, and the various petty annoyances which her shrewdness produced, must have its effect. Change was vital to him—not necessarily change of scene, but change of interest. No one woman could satisfy him, and he took an unusual interest in the choice of the girl-servant that Miss Holland engaged.

This proved to be Florence Havies, who took up her situation three weeks after the Dougals had gone into their new home. On the very morning of her arrival, Dougal came into the kitchen, looked at the girl, and, finding her attractive, put his arm around her waist and kissed her. The girl, to whom such attentions were only alarming, complained immediately to her mistress. It was the first hint that Miss Holland had received of the man's character, and when, trembling with hurt vanity, she demanded an explanation, Dougal tried to laugh the matter away.

Whether he succeeded in allaying the woman's suspicions is not known, but he did not give her time to forget the incident. That night, when Miss Holland was in bed and Dougal was supposed to be in the kitchen downstairs, a terrified scream broke the silence, and Miss Holland, jumping out of bed, made her way to the servant's room, to find her in a condition bordering upon hysteria. After a while the girl was calmed, and told her story. She had been awakened by hearing Dougal at the door, demanding admission in an undertone. The door was bolted, but he had flung his weight against it and was on the point of bursting in when the girl had screamed.

Bewildered, horrified by her discovery, Miss Holland went back to her room, to find Dougal in bed and apparently asleep. She was not deceived, however. She charged him with his offence and ordered him from the room; the girl slept with her that night.

The scene that followed in the morning, when the man and the outraged woman met, was one of intense bitterness. Throughout breakfast, she reproached him—reproaches which he bore with extraordinary meekness. Either he had intended making a breach by his act, or else he had utterly misjudged her complacence. At any rate, he seemed startled by her vehemence and impressed by her sincerity.

It is possible he had never met a woman of her type—and certainly he was a terrible experience to her. The discovery shocked her, threw her for the moment off her balance, and left no definite view but one that the man must go. There was no question of her taking her departure and leaving her property in his hands; she had made it very clear to him, when the conveyance was signed, that she was entirely devoid of that form of quixoticism.

Dougal himself did nothing during that morning except wander disconsolately about the farm. He was seen, with his hands in his pockets, looking thoughtfully at the moat: at one of the half-filled trenches which served to drain the farmyard. His attempt to make up the quarrel was the signal for a fresh outburst, until she was so exhausted by the violence of her anger that she sat down on the stairs and, covering her face with her hands, gave herself up to a fit of passionate weeping. Thus Florrie Havies saw Miss Holland and tried to comfort her.

The girl had not been idle. Realising that she could no longer stay in the house with Dougal, she had written to her mother, asking her to come and fetch her the next day; and, as she told her mistress, she was looking forward anxiously to her parent's arrival.

To the girl, Miss Holland confided her sorrows and her contrition for the folly which she had been led into committing. At the moment she had no definite plan, except that Dougal must leave the farm and their relationship must be broken.

Dougal had no illusions on the subject, and throughout the day was facing the prospect of returning to his precarious method of living. All his plans had come undone; the prospect of an easy life had vanished; his scheme for getting the farm into his own hands had failed. He had no hold whatever on the woman except her goodwill, which he had exhausted by his folly.

To a man of his avaricious nature, the prospect of losing all hope of handling his 'wife's' money was maddening. It is certain that he had already tried to induce her to make a will in his favour, but his failure in this respect would not greatly have troubled him, for an opportunity would arise, if he were given sufficient time, either to forge such a will, or by some trick to induce her to sign a document which would give him control of her wealth after her death. His precipitate action and her resentment destroyed his chances in this respect.

Camille Holland was not a young and inexperienced girl, to be cajoled. She might be ignorant of lovers and their ways, but she had a remarkably good idea of her rights, as she had already shown him, and a reconciliation seemed beyond hope.

What passed between them in secret will never be known, but from subsequent happenings it is certain that she agreed to allow a period of grace, possibly a day or so, to find other quarters. That she gave, or intended to give him, any monetary assistance is doubtful; she neither communicated with her bankers, nor was any cheque drawn in his favour.

Possibly his retention on the farm was a matter of expediency so far as she was concerned. She had to go into Newport that night to do some shopping, and she may have needed him to drive her there. The fact that they subsequently left the farm together does not prove that there was any reconciliation, but rather that she was making use of him, as she herself was not able to drive.

People living in the country did most of their shopping on Fridays, and undoubtedly it was to visit Newport for that purpose that Miss Holland dressed herself at about half-past six on the night of Friday, 19 May, and, going into the kitchen, asked her servant if there was anything she required.

There is a theory that she was taking Dougal to the railway station and intended returning alone; but as she made no statement to the girl, who would be mostly affected by this action, the probability is that the more simple explanation is the true one.

The girl went out and saw that Dougal had harnessed the horse and was awaiting the arrival of his wife. She saw Miss Holland get up by the man's side, and as he flicked his whip and the trap drove over the moat bridge, she heard Miss Holland say:

'Good-bye, Florrie. I shall not be long.'

Nobody else saw them depart. It was quite light, and very unlikely that Dougal offered the woman any violence at that moment. It is certain that the trap did not go into Newport, and that Miss Holland did no shopping whatever. What is more likely is that Dougal employed the drive, following unfrequented roads, to secure from his mistress her forgiveness for his act, and that his efforts were unsuccessful. It is probable that the time occupied by his attempt to bring about a reconciliation was such that it was too late to go into Newport, and that, at her request, he drove her back to the farm.

At half-past eight, Florrie Havies heard the sound of cart-wheels crossing the bridge, and a few minutes later Dougal came into the kitchen. At half-past eight in the middle of May, before the introduction of summertime, it would be almost dark. The girl looked up apprehensively and, seeing him arrive alone, asked:

'Has Mrs. Dougal gone upstairs?'

'No,' replied Dougal; 'she has gone up to London by train. She will be back tonight. I am going to fetch her.'

On the face of it, the story was palpably false, for there was no train from Newport to London until eleven o'clock in the evening, the previous one having departed a few minutes after the pair left the farm together. This, however, Florence Havies did not know, and she accepted the story, which in all probability confirmed some statement Miss Holland had made in the course of the day to the effect that she would consult her solicitors or her nephew, or somebody whom she could trust, about the terrible position in which she found herself.

What happened was that Dougal had returned to the farm half an hour before he came into the kitchen, and, having induced Miss Holland to descend, had shot her dead by means of a revolver which he had placed just below the right ear, and had dropped the body into one of the half-filled trenches he had made in his work on the moat. It is certain that he did not bury her at once, and that when he made his excuse that he was going out to meet her by a later train, he carried a spade to the spot and occupied the time in filling in the ditch so that the remains of the unfortunate woman were hidden from view.

Again he came back, to say that Mrs. Dougal had not arrived and probably would not be back until the midnight train; then he went out again and continued his dreadful work, before he returned, at a quarter to one, with the news that she would not come that night.

'You had better go to bed,' he said, and the frightened girl went up to her room, locked, bolted and barricaded the door as well as she could with a few articles of furniture in the room, and spent the night standing at the window, fully dressed, starting at every sound.

She did not hear Dougal come upstairs, and, so far as she could tell, he did not go to bed that night. As soon as the dull dawn light appeared in the sky, Dougal had returned to the scene of his crime, and by the light of day had searched for and removed all suspicious traces of his deed, throwing more earth into the trench and levelling it down so that the notice of the farm-labourers should not be attracted. When the girl came down early in the morning, she was surprised to find that Dougal was in the kitchen and had already prepared his breakfast. He greeted her with a cheerful smile.

'I have just had a letter from Mrs. Dougal,' he said (a surprising statement, considering the earliness of the hour and the fact that the post was not delivered until eight o'clock). 'She says she is going away for a short holiday, and she will send another lady down.'

It is curious that Dougal had indeed arranged for a lady to come to the farm: some days previous to the occurrence, he had written to his third wife, telling her to come to Stanstead, a village in the neighbourhood, and had rented a small cottage for her, where she took up residence on the day before the murder. This, however, is no proof that the murder was long premeditated. Dougal was now a landed proprietor, and thought he could afford the luxury of another establishment, especially since the rent of the cottage was no more than six shillings and sixpence a week. The knowledge that his wife was there, added to the fact that he knew the girl was leaving that same day, was seized upon by him as a heaven-sent coincidence, for he guessed the girl would talk, and the appearance of another woman at the farm would thus be accounted for.

That same day, Florence Havies' mother arrived and took her away—not without expressions of regret on the part of Dougal that the girl should have so misrepresented his action, his contention being that he had knocked at the door, intending to wind up a clock that was in the room!

The mentality of Dougal is not impressive. The crude lie he told about the letter having arrived before it could possibly have been delivered, the lie he told the girl's mother, no less than the stupidity of making advances to a girl who was a perfect stranger to him and who had previously repulsed him, speak very little for his intelligence, though they point to the queer egotism which is the peculiar possession of the professional murderer.

Scarcely had the servant disappeared than a new Mrs. Dougal, and this time the real Mrs. Dougal, arrived. He must have written on the morning following the murder, telling her to come. In the next four years, the Moat Farm saw many mistresses. The real Mrs. Dougal came and went; new and attractive servants arrived, and became victims to the man's unscrupulous desire for novelty. Amongst these were two sisters, one of whom became the mother of his child.

His financial position was now assured; he had gained from Miss Holland a very complete knowledge of her possessions; he knew the name of her broker, and copies of their letters and of all previous stock and share transactions were available.

Ten days after the murder, the Piccadilly branch of the National & Provincial Bank received a letter, written in the third person, asking for a cheque-book. One was sent, addressed to Miss Camille Holland, The Moat House, and on 6 June a letter was received by the bank, enclosing a £25 cheque and asking for payment in £5 notes. The bank sent the money on in the usual way, but the manager, noticing some slight discrepancy in the signature, asked that this demand should be confirmed. In reply came a letter:

> The cheque for £25 to Dougal is quite correct. Owing to
> a sprained hand there may have been some discrepancies
> in some of my cheques lately signed.

Dougal now set himself the task of converting Miss Holland's securities into cash, and her brokers, Messrs. William Hart, received instructions to sell. It is probable that she had sufficient money on her person or in the house at the time of her death to carry him on for a month or two, for it was not until September that he instructed the brokers to sell stock to the value of £940, which was duly paid into Miss Holland's account. This was followed a month later by a smaller cash payment, and a year later by a payment of £546. In addition to these, on 18 September a letter purporting to be signed by Camille C. Holland instructed the bank to forward certificates of £500-worth of United Alkali shares and £400 of George Newnes' Preference.

Dougal went about his work with care. All the monies that were paid on account of Miss Holland went into her bank and remained in the current account until he withdrew it by cheque in her name.

A year later, at the same time as he was instructing Hart, he forwarded a request that the bank should send to Hart a number of other shares for sale.

The skill with which the forgeries were executed may be illustrated by the fact that when, three years later, Miss Holland's nephew denounced a certain cheque as a forgery, he was equally emphatic that other documents bearing her signature were forgeries, though they were proved by the bank to have been signed by Miss Holland herself on the bank premises.

Nor did Dougal stop short at forging cheques; whole letters in her handwriting were sent to the brokers and bankers, the writing so cleverly imitated that both parties were satisfied that they were genuine. In all, Dougal secured in this way nearly £6000.

During the three years that followed the death of Camille Holland, nobody seems to have had the slightest suspicion that she had come to a violent end. Nor is this remarkable, for the only person who knew of their relationship, the servant, Florence Havies, had long since left the neighbourhood and married, whilst Miss Holland's only living relative, the nephew, was not in the habit of receiving any kind of communication from his aunt. The house agent who had heard the little breeze which followed Dougal's attempt to get the property transferred to himself, had ceased to take any interest in Moat Farm after it had been removed from his books as a saleable proposition.

Dougal's path was by no means a smooth one. He had to face police-court proceedings brought by Kate Cranwell, a servant, in regard to her child. In the early part of 1902, one of Dougal's victims, who had been admitted into closer confidence than her predecessors, was spurred by jealousy, and a desire to get even with the man who had wronged her, to make a statement to the

A corner of the Moat at the Moat Farm

police regarding Miss Holland's disappearance. She could not have known the facts; it is probable that Dougal, in an unguarded moment, had boasted that he was enjoying the income of the dead woman, and imagination had supplied the informer with a garbled version of what had really happened.

It was at first believed that Miss Holland was alive, locked up somewhere by Dougal, and forced from time to time to sign cheques on his behalf. This at least was the theory of Superintendent Charles Pryke, in charge of the district, who called at the farm and had a talk with Dougal. The latter, as usual, was frankness itself.

'I know nothing about her, and have not seen or heard from her since I took her and left her at Stanstead Station three years ago. I drove her there with her luggage, consisting of two boxes.'

'But don't you know her relations or friends?' asked the superintendent.

Dougal shook his head. 'She left nothing behind her in the house. We had a tiff, in consequence of the servant telling her that I wanted to go into the girl's room.'

'Have you seen any papers bearing the name of Miss Holland, or any letters addressed to her?'

'None,' replied Dougal—a somewhat rash statement to make, in view of the fact that letters addressed to Miss Camille Holland had been continuously delivered at the house.

'It is said she is shut up in the house,' said the superintendent. 'Will you let me have a look round?'

Dougal laughed and said:

'Certainly—go where you like.'

The superintendent made a careful inspection of the house, but found nothing. He returned to ask if it was true that Dougal had given away some of Miss Holland's clothes to his own wife and to a servant, and that they had had them altered.

Dougal answered: 'I couldn't do that, because she left nothing behind her.'

He had an account at the Birkbeck Bank, and the day that Superintendent Pryke saw him he drew out practically the whole of his balance, £305. This fact was learned by a shrewd detective inspector, Alfred Marden, who did not share the superintendent's complete faith in Dougal's *bona fides*. Undoubtedly, Superintendent Pryke was gulled by the seeming frankness of the master of Moat Farm, and his report was creditable to the man whom he had examined.

Marden began searching for a relative, and presently found the nephew, who was taken to see certain cheques which had been drawn and had apparently been signed by Miss Holland. He declared them—without too close an inspection—to be forgeries. This was all that Marden required. He was satisfied that Camille Holland had been done to death, but it was absolutely necessary that he should have Dougal in safe keeping while he made a leisurely examination of the property; and though the grounds for the warrant were very slight (and, indeed, the evidence of the nephew would have been absolutely worthless to secure a conviction for forgery), the warrant was granted.

A cheque had been drawn by Dougal in Miss Holland's name, and the bank had paid him the sum in £10 notes. These notes were immediately stopped. As though he were knowingly playing into the hands of the police, Dougal went to the Bank of England to change the £10 notes into £5 notes, signed a false name on the back of one—and was immediately arrested on a charge of forgery.

Had no further charge followed, it is certain that Dougal would not have been convicted, for the evidence against him was of the flimsiest kind; the fact that both the broker and the banker were satisfied that the signatures were genuine would have disposed of the prosecution's case. But the arrest served its purpose: no sooner was Dougal in the hands of the police than Scotland Yard descended upon the Moat Farm and took possession.

Thereafter followed days and weeks of search which will not readily be forgotten, either by the police or by those journalists, like myself, whose duty held them to this bleak spot. Week after week, Dougal, handcuffed and between warders, was marched from the railway station to the little courthouse at Saffron Walden to hear the scraps of evidence and the invariable request for a remand. Week after week, the police probed and pried, dug up floors and examined outhouses, in the hope of finding something which would solve the mystery of Miss Holland's disappearance.

What complicated the search was the discovery in the first day or two of a skull in one of the sheds. It had the appearance of having been burnt, and at first it was thought to be a portion of the remains of the woman. But it afterwards transpired that the skull had been at the farm when Miss Holland was still alive.

It is a curious fact that, though the general opinion amongst the reporters present was that the body of the woman was in the moat, and although it was also known that in the early days of Dougal's occupation there were open trenches leading to the moat, no attempt was made to investigate these 'leads' until every other possible hiding-place had been examined. The police were giving up the search when one of the journalists present said to the detective in charge:

'Why don't you open one of these trenches that Dougal filled up?'

The idea 'occurred simultaneously' to Detective Inspector Marden, and a labourer was given instructions to dig steadily. His work had not proceeded far when his spade turned up a boot. Very soon afterwards, the body of Miss Holland was exposed, and Dougal's secret was a secret no more.

With some difficulty, the body was brought to ground-level and taken to a summer-house. A jury was hastily summoned, and the first sitting of the inquest was held in a great, stark barn on the property.

Heavily guarded, Dougal was brought there, and the scene was one which will long linger in the memory of the witnesses. The old barn, with its thatched roof, was crumbling away with age and neglect. The only light was that admitted by the door, which had been swung back. Here, under the twisted beams and crooked rafters, the court arranged itself as best it could, and Dougal, led past the open grave of his victim, came into the gloom.

The work of the police, however, was not finished with their terrible discovery. Was the body that of Camille Holland? The face was unrecognisable; there were no peculiar marks by which she could be identified. The rotten remnants of a dress might be sworn to by Mrs. Wiskens of Saffron Walden, who had stitched some braid upon it, but it was not sufficient evidence to convict Dougal.

The dress was like thousands of other dresses; the hair-shape, the bustle, the various other wisps of clothing which were found, might have been worn by any other woman. All that was known was that she had been a woman and that she was murdered, for there was a bullet-hole in the skull, and the bullet itself had been discovered at the post-mortem examination.

Still, there was sufficient evidence to commit Dougal for trial on the capital charge. There was one witness, and one witness alone, who could hang him. This was George Lee Mold, a bootmaker of Edgware Road, London.

Miss Holland had patronised Mold regularly. Her feet were so small that her boots had needed to be specially made for her, and Mr. Mold had built a last and made a number of pairs of boots of one pattern. They were half a size *smaller* (2½) than she required, and were lined with lamb's-wool. Mold invariably made these himself, working his initials with brass tacks in the heels of each pair.

There might be in the world thousands of women with small feet, thousands who wore tiny boots; there might be many who wore tiny boots lined with lamb's-wool, as those found were lined; but the 'M' in brass tacks in the heels was undoubtedly Mold's work, and he had only had one customer who wore shoes of this kind. That customer was Camille Holland.

Dougal's trial ran its course. He stood up in the quaint assize court at Chelmsford and received sentence of death from the lips of Mr. Justice Wright; and on a bright July morning, he stood up again, this time to meet the executioner. For a second he flinched; somebody handed him a glass of brandy and water, and he drank it down. Then, without a word, he submitted to the strapping and paced the short distance to the scaffold. There was a tense and deathly silence, broken by the agitated voice of the chaplain:

'Dougal, are you guilty?'

There was no reply.

The hangman, William Billington, fingered the lever nervously and looked almost imploringly at the pastor as though he were asking him not to prolong the agony of the man on the drop.

'Dougal, are you guilty or not guilty?' asked the clergyman again, and in a low but clear voice came the muffled reply:

'*Guilty.*'

As he spoke the word, Billington pulled the lever.

OLD MAN BENDER'S ORCHARD
William Bolitho

[A dictionary of biography describes him as 'English journalist and miscellaneous writer (1890–1930)'; but he was born William Bolitho Ryall in South Africa, the son of a man who seems to have been Dutch and who was certainly a poorly-paid preacher of the Plymouth Brethren. The Ryalls fought on the side of the Boers, and so the British burnt down their home; while the family lived in the slums of Cape Town, the son did any work he could find, meanwhile reading the Elizabethan dramatists and, having taught himself to, Cicero and Racine. He went to a university, and played rugby for South Africa. Having worked his way to England as a stoker on a liner, arriving after the outbreak of the Great War, he enlisted in the British Army and was posted to France, where, in 1916, he was buried alive in a trench cave-in; in hospital, someone gave him entrée into the newspaper world, and, after being demobilised, he acted as Paris correspondent for the Manchester Guardian and as a European correspondent for the New York World, which in 1928 brought him to New York to write a thrice-weekly column. He and his wife moved to the south of France, and it was there that he wrote most of his books—among them the classic Murder for Profit. His friend Noel Coward told him of a novel he *intended to write: 'rather a neurotic novel about a man who committed suicide because he was bored. William whacked his nose with his finger (a trick of his) and said, almost sharply: "Be careful about Death, it's a serious business, big and important. You can't go sauntering towards Death with a cigarette hanging from your mouth!" ' He died within a month or so, of peritonitis following an operation for appendicitis.]*

A *variation on a proverb*: The family that slays together stays together.

IN THE KANSAS PAPERS on 18 June 1872, the following advertisement appeared:

> Professor Miss Kate Bender can heal disease, cure blindness, fits and deafness. Residence, 14 miles east of Independence, on the road to Osage Mission.

Behind it lay a story like those which still make the peasants of remote corners in Europe shiver as they sit round the fire. The sting of folklore, of witches, cannibals, evil innkeepers, and werewolves is somewhat dulled by intervening centuries. The story of the Benders is comparatively brand new, and the details are not blurred by generations of oral transmitters, but preserved on ice in matter-of-fact police records.

Kate Bender was a rectangular, red-faced woman of twenty-four. Her father, Old Man Bender, and her brother were 'large, coarse-appearing men'. Her mother was a masculine, savage creature who, although sixty years old, could still do the work of a horse. They were a family of northern primitives, out of place where law and order were settled, pre-civilized, properly belonging to some age before man gave up the right to kill.

They lived off the beaten track, eighteen miles from the boundary of Kansas State, in a ramshackle frame-house, with a small half-acre orchard behind it. In the front of the house was a room where meals were served to wayfarers. The whole family had truck with ghosts and spirits, and neighbours, seeking a modern name for what with the Benders was a thing as old as savagery, called them 'Spiritualists'. Miss Kate was the youngest, and the leader of the family. They were naturally not popular, and no one of the surrounding district would have stayed a

night in the Benders' Tavern for a fortune. The few who
passed the remote shanty late at night had tales of the evil
sounds that came from within. The place was so far from the
beaten track, however, that rumour did not occupy itself often
with the Benders. People had something more to do in Kansas in
those days than to go worrying about a ghost-ridden family like
the Benders.

Apparently the advertisement did not attract many to the inn.
The journey was long and difficult, and it is not recorded that
more than two or three sufferers came to try the supernatural
powers of Professor Kate. Occasionally a stray voyager ate a meal
there; but most, when asked, referred to the forbidding ways of
the family, their habits of peeping and muttering together, and
the surliness which seemed to possess the whole family.

In 1873, in the spring, Doctor William York left Fort Scott
on horseback, on his way back to his home in Independence,
Kansas, and disappeared. He was rich, and the leader of the little
community where he lived. His family and the citizens, knowing
his cheerful disposition, were certain that he had not committed
suicide, and feared foul play. Search-parties were sent out for him
without any result. His brother happened to be a Senator, and
spared no expense in hiring detectives, who scoured the whole
country. In the course of their wanderings they came to the
township of Cherryvale, five miles from the Benders' Tavern,
where they had news of the doctor.

At Cherryvale most maintained that the doctor had likely
fallen in with border bandits and come to some misfortune.
No suspicion seems to have fallen on the Benders; the visit a
party of mounted men made to the tavern seems to have been
intended simply to ask if the family had seen the doctor pass. To
their surprise, however, when they rode up to the door, there was
no sign of life. The Benders seemed to be away, all the windows
were shuttered. This party rode on, but another, some days later
on the same road, was curious enough to go round to the back of
the house to see what was to be seen. There a most curious and
ill-omened sight met them.

In a little paddock at the back were the dead bodies of several
calves and hogs, dead of thirst and hunger. Before the Benders
could have let this happen, something strange indeed must have
occurred. It is hard for townspeople to understand the instinctive

care which peasants give to their stock—at once their capital and their livelihood. The Benders must have left not only for a grave reason, a reason of life and death, but in a most inexplicable hurry, not to have stopped to take down the fence-gate and give the beasts a chance for their lives.

With foreboding, the party made further search, though still not daring to break door or window to enter the deserted house. It had been raining hard. In the small orchard they noticed that in a certain place the ground had settled very noticeably, and that the depression was in the form of a grave. They set to work and dug up the badly decomposed body of Doctor York. The skull had been crushed and the throat cut in a peculiar manner—somewhat, it was later discovered, as animals are slaughtered in certain rituals.

Before nightfall, seven other bodies were exhumed, and some were later identified as follows: a horse-dealer, a lawyer, a tramp, an immigrant and his infant daughter. In each case the skull was battered to a pulp and the throat cut from ear to ear; the little girl bore no marks of violence, and appeared to have been thrown, living, into her father's grave. The next day another girl's body was found, with long yellow hair. She had apparently been about eight years old. She had been butchered with extreme violence, and her bones were nearly all crushed. Later other bodies were found but not identified.

The officers then entered the house by force. They were met by an overpowering stench. It was easy to see how the crimes had been committed. A little booth was formed by an American-cloth screen or partition, in which a bench and rough table were set. Here the wayfarers took their meals. The table was set so near the partition that the guest was forced to lean his head against the cloth and so allow the shape and position of it to be seen from behind. The brother or the father would then creep up with a stonemason's hammer (also found in the house) and slay. In the middle of the floor was a trapdoor and a great hole from which the smell came. This was opened, and found drenched in congealed blood. Bodies were thrown into this after their throats had been cut—with what strange rites and observances only the Benders could have revealed.

This they never did. Their fate is mysterious. The waggon in which they fled was tracked miles into the waste lands, and at last found, but empty. The hood was riddled with bullet-holes, and splashes of blood were everywhere, but no trace of the family.

While the detectives were searching for them, the crowd back in Cherryvale was doing ugly things, in its frenzy. They had caught a Mr. Brockmann, at one time a partner of Old Man Bender. As both were Germans, and once close friends, the crowd took him to the woods; there attempted to make him reveal the whereabouts of the horrible family. This he was unable to do. At any rate he was hanged and revived three times, and then allowed to go away. He is said eventually to have recovered.

A letter, received by a criminological investigator in San Francisco, seems to throw as much light on the fate of the family as will ever appear. It runs:

> Cherryvale, Kansas,
> 1910
>
> Dear Sir,—Yours received. It so happened that my father-in-law's farm joins that of the Benders and he helped to locate the bodies of the victims. I often tried to find out from him what became of the Benders, but he only gave me a knowing look and said he guessed they would not bother anyone else. There was a vigilance committee organized to locate the Benders, and shortly afterwards Old Man Bender's waggon was found by the roadside riddled with bullets. You will have to guess the rest.—I am, respectfully yours,
>
> J. KRAMER, *Chief of Police.*

The mystery of their deaths remains. It is easier to unravel than that of their precipitate flight. They were under no suspicion, and their precautions were such that no trace, had they remained, would ever have been found of their victims. Why did they kill? Sometimes, but not always, for money, for one or two of the bodies were tramps with nothing to give for the trouble of their slaying. The strange cuts in the throats of some of their victims were perhaps only a refinement of cruelty. Was it the Ghosts that drove the Benders away, leading to their discovery and ruin? The family were fervent, real believers in their own powers of evoking the dead. In that lonely house, with that smell, with those memories and the thought of what lay in the orchard, life must have been difficult for even the nerves of the Benders. Enigmatic, disquieting, primitive people—reminders that the race of ogres, witches, or traps for the unwary traveller, or pure wickedness, are not over. Europe in the 1870s was throwing up its depths; remote corners, never touched by the quick race of civilization, in morals or nature, were being rediscovered, to the amazement of humanity, as the sudden droughts may reveal the bed of a river. Some day a greater than Gibbon will write the sociological history of the United States after the Civil War, in the Middle and Far West. Traces of European savages like the Benders, appear from time to time in Europe. But the gigantic experiment of shipping the 'backwoodsmen' of an old continent to a new virgin country, where they are freed suddenly from the repression of multiple authority, where everything still has to be organized and created, is something which strikes some imaginations as much as the long death-throes of an Empire.

THE WALLACE CASE
Jonathan Goodman

AUTHOR'S NOTE. The occasionally colloquial tone of this essay is due to its being, for the most part, the transcript of a talk I gave to Our Society, at what was then called the Piccadilly Hotel, in 1968; and subsequently to other audiences—most recently, in 1988, to the West London Medico-Chirurgical Society, at the Postgraduate Medical Centre of the Charing Cross Hospital Medical School. I did wonder if I should amend the transcript so as to make it less chatty, but decided not to.

'THE WALLACE CASE is unbeatable. It will always be unbeatable.' So said Raymond Chandler, the writer of fictional tales of crime. And James Agate, the drama critic, wrote in one of his *Ego* diary-books: 'Either the murderer was Wallace or it wasn't. If it wasn't, then here at last is the perfect murder.' Mr. Justice Wright, while summing up at the trial, said: 'This murder, I should imagine, is almost unexampled in the annals of crime.'

At twenty minutes past seven on the evening of Monday, 2 January 1931, the telephone rang at the City Café in the centre of Liverpool. A waitress took the call, and after some delay a man's voice came on the line, asking: 'Is Mr. Wallace there?' The waitress didn't know anyone of that name; but, assuming that Wallace was a member of the Central Chess Club which met at the café on Monday and Thursday evenings, she asked the captain of the club, Samuel Beattie, to speak to the caller.

Beattie had been acquainted with William Herbert Wallace for eight years—nearly as long as Wallace had been a member of the chess club. He knew that Wallace—tall, grey-haired, bespectacled—was a Prudential Insurance agent, and he guessed before he picked up the receiver that the call had something to do with his work.

He told the caller that Wallace was not at the café, and suggested that he should ring up later, as Wallace would be arriving shortly to play a game in the club's Second Class Championship.

The caller said that he couldn't telephone again: 'I'm too busy. I have my girl's twenty-first birthday on, and I want to do something for her in the way of his business. I want to see him particularly. Will you ask him to come round to my place tomorrow evening at 7.30?'

Beattie, having agreed to do that, took a note of a name and an address: *R.M. Qualtrough—25 Menlove Gardens East, Mossley Hill.* That was the end of the conversation.

Some time later, about ten minutes to eight, Beattie noticed that Wallace had arrived and was already engrossed in a game of chess. He gave him the message from Mr. Qualtrough, and Wallace looked puzzled.

'I don't know the chap,' he said. 'Where is Menlove Gardens East? Is it Menlove Avenue?'

Beattie, who happened to live in Mossley Hill, said that he was pretty sure that it was, and another member of the club agreed with him.

'I've got a Scotch tongue in my head,' Wallace said. 'I can enquire.' He noted the name and address in his diary, continued his game (which he won), and, at about ten o'clock, went home to 29 Wolverton Street in the Liverpool suburb of Anfield, and to his wife Julia, to whom he was apparently devoted.

Wallace spent the following day collecting insurance-money. None of his clients noticed anything at all odd in his demeanour. He arrived home just after six, and left the house *no later than* eleven minutes to seven, to keep the appointment with Mr. R.M. Qualtrough.

It was an awkward journey from Anfield to Menlove Avenue; Wallace needed three trams to get there. No one afterwards remembered seeing him on the first tram, but the conductors of the second and third trams—and a ticket inspector—remembered him well, because of his persistent reminders that he wanted Menlove Gardens East and that he was a stranger in the district.

The conductor of the third tram pointed out where Menlove Gardens West entered Menlove Avenue, and Wallace started to search for the home of Mr. R.M. Qualtrough.

He searched in vain. After about half an hour—after wandering the streets and asking for assistance from at least four people, including a policeman—Wallace came to the conclusion that, though there was a Menlove Gardens North, South and West, there was no such place as Menlove Gardens East. He started on the journey home.

At about quarter to nine, Wallace's next-door neighbours, the Johnstons, were getting ready to go out. As Mrs. Johnston tidied her hair in front of the kitchen-mirror, she heard someone knocking at the back door of number twenty-nine. She and her husband left their house by the back door and walked through to the alley which ran along the back of Wolverton Street. As they opened the back-yard door, Wallace hurried past them towards his own yard-door, which was standing open.

He asked if they had heard anything unusual that night. Neither of them had. He explained that he had been out; that he had recently returned, to find the front and back doors of the house apparently locked. Mr. Johnston told him to try the back door again.

Wallace walked across the yard. 'Julia won't be out,' he said. 'She has such a bad cold.' He twisted the door-handle and, almost at once, turned back to them. 'It opens now,' he murmured.

Johnston said that he and his wife would wait while Wallace had a look round. Wallace went into the house. A couple of minutes passed. Then he returned.

'Come and see,' he said. 'She has been killed.'

The murder was committed in the parlour—the front room of

the house—the 'best room'—a room measuring thirteen feet by eleven. The body of Julia Wallace was lying face-down on the hearth-rug, her feet not quite touching the fender, her battered head, haloed by a great oval of blood, by the corner of the rug nearest the door. Protruding from beneath her right shoulder was a bloody and shapeless mass of material which was later identified as Wallace's old mackintosh.

The report on the post-mortem examination, made the following day by John Edward Whitley MacFall, Professor of Forensic Medicine at the University of Liverpool, reads as follows:

> The body was that of a lightly-built woman of about 55 years of age. [*Julia Wallace was, in fact, fifty-three—two years younger than her husband.*] The height was about five foot two.
>
> There was a small recent bruise mark on the inside of the left upper arm. There were no other external marks of violence on the trunk or limbs.
>
> 2 inches above the zygoma was a large lacerated wound measuring 2 inches by 3 inches from which brain and bone was protruding. On the back of the head, towards the left side, were ten diagonal, apparently incised wounds. The appearance was as if a terrific force with a large surface had driven in the scalp, bursting it in parallel lines, with the appearance of several incised wounds.
>
> Death was due to fracture of the skull by someone striking the deceased eleven times upon the head with terrific force. My opinion is that one blow was harder and more severe than the rest. That is the blow which produced the front, open wound, and caused death. Death took place in less than one minute.

As well as the blood around the head, there were two large over-lapping clots on the rug, at the side nearest the door. The room—which prosecuting counsel was to call 'a jam-pot'—was stippled with blood. The majority of the splashes on the walls were no more than four feet high, but a few had reached a height of seven feet.

None of the furniture in the room appeared to have been

disturbed; even the rug on which the body lay was uncreased and set exactly parallel to the fireplace.

The police were called, and the investigation got under way at ten minutes past nine, with the arrival of a police constable on a bike. It was past ten o'clock before the first detective arrived, but by eleven the place was swarming with detectives, uniformed policemen, and forensic experts. The investigation was haphazard, uncontrolled. With no specific duties assigned to them, the detectives scampered about the house in search of clues, each man conducting a separate investigation, without reference to the activities of his colleagues.

Sitting in the kitchen with Mrs. Johnston, Wallace said: 'Julia would have gone mad if she had seen all this.'

Very little real evidence was found in the house.

In the kitchen, suggesting that robbery might be the motive, the door of a small cabinet had been broken. And—according to Wallace—about four pounds was missing from the cash-box in which he kept his insurance-collections. He explained that the box usually contained far more than that, but he had been ill with influenza the previous week and had not collected on Friday and Saturday.

It was discovered that the locks at the front and back of the house were defective—and so, if Wallace was at all agitated, anxious, suspicious when he returned from Menlove Gardens, this could explain why he was unable to open the doors at the first attempt. According to Wallace, the front door was actually locked. He said that he unlocked it to admit the first policeman.

The medical examination by Professor MacFall provided no reliable evidence. Evidence was there if he had looked for it, but he didn't bother to. As to the time of death, for instance: Within ten minutes of his arrival at the house, he stated his opinion that Julia Wallace had been murdered at about 6 p.m. That was a guess—he gathered no facts to support it. He did not take the temperature of the room, let alone that of the body . . . he made no notes of the progress of rigor mortis . . . he did not consider the muscularity of the body or the medical history of the victim . . . he did not examine the stomach-contents. None of those things. At the trial, during a brilliant cross-examination, MacFall was forced to retract virtually all of the statements he had made in his examination-in-chief.

Probably the biggest mystery facing the police was this: that, apart from a couple of small spots of blood found upstairs—which were almost certainly deposited during the investigation—there was no sign of any blood outside the murder-room. That despite the fact that the murderer must have been splashed with blood from head to toe.

There was not the slightest trace of blood on Wallace's body or his clothing.

Even so, the police were quick to suspect Wallace of the murder. Several reasons for that. There was, of course, the statistical reason that, nine times out of ten, the killing of a married woman in her home is proved to be the husband's doing. Another reason was that Wallace seemed so calm and collected. Detective Inspector Gold, the second-in-command of the investigation, said that he saw Wallace sitting in the kitchen:

> He had the cat on his knee and was stroking the cat. I didn't see any sign of emotion in him at all at the death of his wife.

And Professor MacFall, not the most reliable observer, said that he was 'very much struck' with Wallace's demeanour:

> It was abnormal. He was too quiet, too collected, for a person whose wife had been killed in the way that he described. He was not nearly so affected as I was myself. I think he was smoking cigarettes most of the time. Whilst I was in the room examining the body and the blood, he came in, smoking a cigarette, and he leant over in front of the sideboard and flicked the ash into a bowl. It struck me at the time as being unnatural.

But perhaps the most important reason why police suspicion fell upon Wallace was that story of his about a telephone-call, a man named Qualtrough, a street that didn't exist. It sounded . . . well, fishy. . . .

Wednesday, the day after the murder, was one of mixed fortune for the police. They obtained two apparently important pieces of information—the first of which came from the Wallaces' charwoman, who said that an iron bar, about a foot long and as thick as a candle, was missing from the hearth in the parlour. It was used, she said, for raking cigarette-ends and spent matches from beneath the gas-fire.

The police at once assumed that the missing iron bar was the murder-weapon, and a search was started. Dozens of officers from other divisions were brought in, and the Sanitation Department helped by searching dustbins, drains and sewers. The fact that the search was confined to four areas indicates that the police believed that Wallace was the murderer. The areas searched were

1. The Richmond Park district of Anfield, between Wolverton Street and the tram-stop where Wallace must have boarded the first tram to Menlove Gardens.

2 and 3. The areas around the tram-stops at which he alighted from one tram and boarded the next.

4. The Menlove Gardens district.

The search for the iron bar lasted several days, but it was not found.

The discovery of the second Wednesday clue seemed—seemed—to be the result of an astonishing piece of luck.

The waitress at the City Café remembered that, just before R.M. Qualtrough spoke to her, a telephone operator had said: 'Anfield calling you. Hold the line.' The police at once got in touch with the Anfield exchange, in the hope—the forlorn hope, it seemed—of learning from which phone the call had been made. Within a couple of hours, they were presented with a bumper-bundle of information.

Two operators, *plus* the exchange supervisor, remembered the call, because the caller had made such a commotion: about not being able to get through to the City Café ... pressing button A and losing his tuppence ... and goodness knows what else. The supervisor had even made a note of the call, giving the time the caller was eventually connected—7.20—and the number of the call-box from which he was speaking—*Anfield 1627.*

That was the number of the outside call-box closest to Wallace's house. 400 yards away.

With that information, the police suspicion of Wallace became certainty that he was his wife's murderer. Now everything was clear. It was Wallace who had made the call, as the prelude to a cunningly-contrived alibi. His persistent reminders to the tram-conductors, his questioning of passers-by in Menlove Gardens—they had been intended to establish that he was away from his house at a time when his wife *might* have been murdered. In fact, he had killed her before he left the house.

Good news for the police was quickly followed by some very bad news indeed.

On Wednesday evening, a group of children who delivered milk and newspapers in Anfield were talking in the street. Like everyone else, they were talking about the murder. A girl—a milk-girl—said that the son of the couple who owned the dairy had delivered milk at 29 Wolverton Street—and had spoken to Julia Wallace—at a quarter to seven on the night of the murder. While the children were talking, digesting that choice bit of news, the boy himself, fourteen-year-old Alan Close, joined them. Yes, it was true, he said. He *had* spoken to Mrs. Wallace at a quarter to seven. He even remembered the slight conversation they had had.

The other children insisted that he tell the police. He wasn't keen on that idea. He didn't want to get involved, he said. But eventually he agreed to accompany them to 29 Wolverton Street. He treated the whole thing as rather a joke. As they walked, he stuck his thumbs under the lapels of his jacket, swaggered, and declared: 'I am the missing link.' He was so pleased with that remark that he kept repeating it.

He was taken inside the murder-house, where he told his story to the police.

It was a bombshell, of course. There was no doubt that Alan Close had spoken to Julia Wallace *some time* on the night of the murder. If he was right about the time—a quarter to seven—then it was plain that Wallace was innocent. The evidence of the tram-conductors, together with a series of 'tram time-tests' carried out by the police, showed that Wallace must have left for Menlove Gardens by 6.49 at the latest. There just wasn't time for him to have done the murder and all the post-murder chores.

End of police-case against Wallace? No. The following Sunday,

Alan Close was taken to Anfield Police Station. And now he suddenly remembered something.

On the night of the murder, during his milk-round but before delivering at 29 Wolverton Street, he had looked at the illuminated dial of a church-clock and noticed that the time was twenty-five minutes past six.

Accompanied by two detectives carrying stop-watches, the milk-boy retraced his steps over the route of the milk-round so as to establish the time that had elapsed between when he passed the church and when he left 29 Wolverton Street, after delivering the milk to Mrs. Wallace. It worked out at six minutes.

So . . . assuming that the milk-boy's delayed-action memory was reliable, and that the detectives' timing was accurate, Julia Wallace was still alive at 6.31. . . .

. . . Which meant that Wallace had had, *at most*, eighteen minutes in which to kill his wife, get rid of any trace of the crime upon his person, carefully clean or wrap stain-resistant material around the murder-weapon—which, for some reason, he didn't want to leave in the house—fabricate evidence of robbery, and do a few other small, post-murder chores.

Eighteen minutes. At most.

Not long.

Long enough, though, the police decided. Working fast—and Wallace certainly wouldn't have dawdled—he could have done all that was necessary, and still have had a couple of minutes to spare before starting out for the 'alibi area' of Menlove Gardens.

Forsaking strict chronology for a moment, I must mention that it is virtually certain that Alan Close was with Mrs. Wallace some time later than 6.31. An examination of the route from the church and of the things the boy had to do during his milk-round shows that, in order to leave Mrs. Wallace at 6.31, he must have walked at an average speed of at least 5 miles an hour—which is pretty good going for a fourteen-year-old, considering that the average *adult* walking speed is between $3^1/_2$ and 4 miles an hour and that the boy was carrying a cumbersome and quite heavy crate of cans and bottles.

Also, Wallace's solicitor found two witnesses who threw considerable doubt on the time of 6.31. The milk-*girl* had seen Alan Close walking in the direction of Wolverton Street at about twenty to seven. And there was the evidence of yet another newspaper-boy. In the course of his round on the night of the murder, he too had glanced at the church-clock. It was twenty-five to seven. It took him two minutes to get from the church to Wolverton Street. In a statement, he said:

> When I delivered the paper at 27 Wolverton Street, it would be about twenty-two or twenty-three minutes to seven. The door of No. 29 was wide open and a milk-boy was standing on the top step with two or three cans in his hand. When I left, he was still standing there. He was wearing a Collegiate cap.

Alan Close was a pupil at the Liverpool Collegiate School. He was wearing his cap on the night of the murder.

Having established—to their own satisfaction, at least— that Wallace had had time to commit the murder, the police concentrated on removing the last big obstacle in the path to his arrest.

Everyone who had visited the parlour at 29 Wolverton Street was convinced of one thing: the crime could not have been committed without the murderer being heavily splashed with blood. How was it possible to reconcile the idea that Wallace had committed such a brutal and messy crime with the fact that there was no trace of blood on his body or clothing?

A retired Liverpool policeman told me: 'I remember one of my colleagues remarking that if Wallace was the criminal, he had not only committed a crime but performed a miracle. To have escaped from the murder-room as clean as when he went in was like taking a shower-bath and not getting wet.'

Till now, hardly any thought had been given to the old mackintosh —Wallace's mackintosh—which was found beside, and partly beneath, Julia Wallace's right shoulder.

The Liverpool City Analyst had examined the garment and noted that 'it was extensively and heavily stained with human blood, inside and out'. He had also noted that 'a considerable portion at the bottom of the right side had been recently burnt away'. In his opinion, the burning had occurred on the night of the murder.

Now, it was discovered that the front of Julia Wallace's skirt was also severely burnt. The fact that both the mackintosh *and* the skirt were burnt lent support to Mrs. Johnston's impression that Julia was wearing the mackintosh over her shoulders when she was struck down. There was no doubt that the burn on the skirt was caused by contact with the gas-fire, probably by her falling against it after the first blow was struck. And it was reasonable to assume that the burn on the mackintosh was caused in the same way.

The defence used Mrs. Johnston's impression as the basis of their theory that Julia, who was suffering from a cold, had thrown the mackintosh over her shoulders before answering the door to someone. She had taken the visitor into the parlour—a room that was rarely used except for entertaining guests or for musical evenings—and had been murdered as she knelt to light the gas-fire.

That seems a reasonable theory. Far more reasonable than the one thought up by the police.

Their idea was that *Wallace* had worn the mackintosh—as protection from the blood which gushed from the arterial wounds. The burns on the mackintosh, they said, were the result of a deliberate act of arson. After killing his wife, Wallace took off the mackintosh—then, realising that the police would wonder how it came to be so bloodstained, decided to destroy it ... *by burning it on the gas-fire.* Then, as it began to smoulder and catch light, he changed his mind and stuffed it under the body.

That was the theory put forward at the committal proceedings; but by the time the trial began, it had been varied slightly—because someone had pointed out that the mackintosh would not have protected Wallace's trousers from the knees down, nor his boots. And so, at the trial, the suggestion was that Wallace had worn the mackintosh over his naked body, and washed his legs and feet afterwards. Prosecuting counsel, in his opening speech, told the jury that 'the history of our criminal courts shows what elaborate precautions people can sometimes take'. A pause, prelude to the punch-lines:

> One of the most famous criminal trials was of a man who committed a crime when he was naked. A man might perfectly well commit a crime wearing a raincoat, as one might wear a dressing-gown, and come down, when he is just going to do this, with nothing on on which blood could fasten, and, with anything like care, he might get away, leaving the raincoat there, and go and perform the necessary washing if he was very careful.

No doubt the reference to 'a famous criminal trial ... of a man who committed a crime when he was naked' was inserted because it was felt that the less original the 'nude-murderer' theory could be made to appear, the more chance there was of the jury's accepting the idea.

It seems a pity that defence counsel did not ask for the trial to be identified—because the only famous trial in which a similar theory was adumbrated was that of Robert Wood (*see page 55*). The jury in that case returned a verdict of Not Guilty, and so Wallace's prosecutor can't have been talking of Rex *v.* Wood ... or if he was, he shouldn't have been.

The generally accepted view is that he was referring to the trial of François Courvoisier (*see page 191*). If so, one can only say that he was quoting an extremely dubious example. Although it seems probable that Courvoisier was naked when he slit his master's throat, literally from ear to ear, there is no real evidence of it.

Another week passed while the police waited hopefully for some stronger evidence to connect Wallace with the murder. None came.

On Monday, 2 February, 13 days after the murder, he was arrested.

The next morning, he appeared at the magistrates' court. The prosecuting solicitor of Liverpool, summarizing the evidence, made 18 misstatements of fact—an average of one for every eighty words, which must be something of a legal record. The speech was an inflammatory mixture of innuendo, unsupported supposition, and opinion. It was reported verbatim by the three

Liverpool papers, and was undoubtedly read by at least some of the people who later served on the Wallace jury.

Several of the ersatz ingredients of the speech were used to concoct new rumours and theories about the case. Heaven knows, there were enough of them already. Many of the stories and theories are still believed. Talk to anyone in Liverpool who remembers the case, and you are almost sure to hear at least one of the rumours presented as a fact.

Only recently, one of the amateur theories was used as the basis of an article in a quite reputable journal. The suggestion is that, when the milk-boy called at the house, Julia Wallace was already dead. The person who answered the door was none other than Wallace himself—whose daring as a criminal was matched only by his brilliance as a female-impersonator. After murdering his wife, Wallace put on some of her clothes—which must have been a rather tight fit, since he was a foot taller than Julia—and mimicked her voice so successfully that the milk-boy, who had been calling at the house for three years, was completely taken in.

One of the briefest and yet most evocative stories came from a spiritualist lady, who claimed to have heard Julia Wallace's disembodied voice complaining: 'Herbert, how *could* you?'

Wallace chose a young solicitor named Hector Munro (who was the star-player at the Central Chess Club) to represent him. Munro worked like a beaver—not only collecting evidence but also finding the money for the defence-costs.

Eventually, he got in touch with the Prudential Staff Union, and soon after the committal proceedings, a mock trial was held at the union's headquarters in Gray's Inn Road, London. Officials from all over the country heard the evidence for and against Wallace, and were asked for a verdict. They voted unanimously in his favour, and the union guaranteed the defence-costs. It was the first time such a thing had happened; so far as I know, it has never happened since.

The real trial, at St. George's Hall, Liverpool, began on Wednesday, 23 April 1931. The prosecutor was Edward Hemmerde, KC, the Recorder of Liverpool. Roland Oliver, KC, led for the defence.

Before the trial started, the judge, Mr. Justice Wright, called

the two barristers into his room and told them that he wanted
to give the case to the jury by Saturday at the latest, as he was
due at Manchester Assizes the following week.

The deadline was met. The jury were sent out at twenty
minutes past one on Saturday afternoon. They returned an hour
later with the verdict of Guilty.

There are a number of facts which suggest that some members
of the jury had decided the verdict before the trial began—and
which suggest that some of them didn't bother to listen to the
evidence and that some of those who did listen simply rearranged
their prejudices. They all paid attention while the judge recited
the sentence of death.

Wallace appealed, but his position now seemed hopeless.
Though there were ten grounds of appeal, only one of them
really mattered— the one which asserted that 'the verdict was
unreasonable and could not be supported having regard to the
evidence'.

If the appeal was to succeed, the Judges would have to go
against the jury's decision, say that the jury had made a terrible
mistake—and that was something they had never done since
the Court of Criminal Appeal was set up in 1907. Only twice
in the history of the Court had appeals against convictions
carrying the death penalty been allowed. In 1911, Charles
Elson, found guilty of the murder of a woman in Clerkenwell,
London, was released on the ground of misdirection of the
jury by Mr. Justice ('Acid-Drop') Avory. And during the First
World War, H.A. Ablers, the German Consul at Sunderland,
had had the sentence of death for high treason set aside on
the ground that the defence had not been properly presented to
the jury.

On Sunday, 17 May, the day before the appeal, something
happened in Liverpool which created a religious precedent:

The Church of England took a hand in a murder case.

Many times since Wallace's conviction, Hector Munro had
thought, 'Heaven help him. . . .' But none too hopefully. Now
the Church said the same thing; made it official. Special prayers,
described as 'intercessions extraordinary', were offered at Liverpool Cathedral by the Vice-Dean—who, as Sheriff's Chaplain,
had been present throughout the trial.

The appeal, which lasted two days, was heard by the Lord

Chief Justice, Lord Hewart of Bury; Mr. Justice Branson, and Mr. Justice Hawke.

On the second afternoon, after a retirement of three-quarters of an hour, Lord Hewart gave the judgment.

It seems that he did not relish what he had to say. He took 14 minutes to pronounce just over 300 words. (The usual speaking speed is 180 words a minute.)

Sydney Scholefield Allen, the junior defence counsel, thought that the manner in which Hewart delivered the judgment was 'completely sadistic'. He was not alone in that view.

But at last Hewart got to the crucial words:

'The conclusion to which we have arrived'—*pause*—'is that the case against the appellant, which we have carefully and anxiously considered'—*pause*—'and discussed'— *pause*— 'was not proved with that certainty which is necessary in order to justify a verdict of Guilty. . . . The result is that this appeal will be allowed.'

And so the Wallace case, which had already made trades-union and church history, made legal history too.

After a brief holiday, Wallace returned to 29 Wolverton Street and to his old job with the Prudential. But not for long. Every post brought poison-pen letters. He was shunned by people who had been friendly with him; many of his insurance-clients refused to open the door when he called. People came from all over Liverpool to gawp at the murder-house, to scream threats through the letter-box.

Within three weeks of his return, he had had enough. He accepted an indoor job with the Prudential and moved to a small bungalow at Bromborough, in Cheshire.

Around about Christmas, 1932, he had a recurrence of the kidney trouble that had plagued him for most of his adult life. His condition rapidly worsened; the pain increased; he was forced to give up his job. But despite the pain, despite the pleas of his few remaining friends, he refused to take treatment.

He told his housekeeper that he had no wish to remain alive, and it seemed to her that he was 'committing slow suicide'.

On 26 February 1933, twenty-one months after the appeal, he died.

Before I started research into the Wallace case, I wasn't sure whether he was guilty or innocent. Indeed, it was that uncertainty which caused me to start the research. I suppose that, like most people, I thought he was probably guilty.

But gradually, as I picked up bits and pieces of information—from all over the country, not just from Liverpool—I began to think that he was innocent. By the time I was ready to write a book about the case, I was sure of it.

There are—literally—dozens of points in Wallace's favour. I shall refer to just two or three.

At the trial, it was taken for granted that the iron bar missing from the parlour-fireplace was the murder-weapon.

But if it was, why on earth did the murderer bother to remove it? Strangely, that question was never asked. Neither side at the trial was interested in *why* the iron bar had been taken away—but there was much discussion as to *how* and *where* it could have been hidden. As you know, there was an intensive search of the places where Wallace could have hidden it outside the house.

In 1935, the new tenants of 29 Wolverton Street had some alterations made, including a change-over from gas to electricity. The gas-fire in the parlour was removed, and it was noticed that there was a gap between the back wall of the fireplace and the hearth—a gap about two inches deep and roughly the width of a candle. A workman used a screwdriver to scoop out the dirt—and prised up the iron bar that had been lying in the gap since the beginning of January 1931. So far as he could see, there were no stains on it; there was nothing to suggest that it had been used as a murder-weapon.

He informed the police of his find; handed the iron bar over to them. And, once again, it disappeared. But I located three people—two of them ex-detectives—who vouched for the fact that it was found at the back of the fireplace. Some time between the charwoman's last visit to the house on 7 January and the night of the murder, the iron bar must have rolled under the gas-fire and down the gap.

The discovery of the iron bar is a strong point in Wallace's favour. If he was the murderer, and if he took the murder-weapon with him when he left the house, what did he do with it?—how and where did he get rid of it?

But if the murderer was Qualtrough, the problem of how the

weapon was disposed of is no problem at all—he brought it with him to the house, and afterwards had all the time in the world, the whole of Liverpool, in which to get rid of it.

Now a point about the telephone-call—and one which Hector Munro admitted to me 'could be the most important point in the case, but I am afraid that the defence may not have appreciated it'.

The caller, far from being ultra-discreet, as one would expect, seems to have gone out of his way to make the call as unusual as possible, so as to have it recorded in the minds of the operators and in the notebook of the exchange supervisor.

He first got through to the exchange at 7.15. By 7.18, he was causing a small commotion, with the first operator so confused by what he said that she was asking another girl for assistance and shouting for the supervisor.

'I have pressed button A,' he said, 'but have not had my correspondent yet.'

An odd statement, that. Had he never used a public telephone before? Did he not know that there was no need to press button A to hear the 'correspondent'?

What makes the statement even more odd is that he *had not* pressed button A. An automatic device at the exchange showed that he had pressed button B and got his money back.

One would have thought that a prospective murderer would have more important things on his mind than the diddling of the GPO of tuppence. By saving himself tuppence, he made absolutely sure that the call was remembered, recorded.

It seems unbelievable that Wallace would have done such a thing.

But what if the caller was not Wallace? What if it was someone who *wanted* the call to be recorded? What if that person was thinking of killing two birds with one stone—setting in motion the plan for the crime he would commit the following night, and at the same time throwing suspicion upon Wallace?

There are two possible reasons for the caller wanting to lay a false trail of suspicion towards Wallace. Revenge is one of them. If he had been harmed by some action of Wallace's in the past, perhaps this was his idea of getting his own back. If so, then it was repayment a thousand times over.

The other possible reason, more practical and therefore more believable, is that he would have known that the most dangerous period for the perpetrator of a crime is the forty-eight hours or so directly following. If an investigation goes the wrong way at the start, the criminal has good reason for feeling confident, because by the time the police get back to square one, many of the clues have gone cold. The odds in favour of the criminal shorten with each hour that passes. Whoever was responsible for the killing of Julia Wallace was one of the most fastidious planners in the history of crime, and I think it is quite likely that the seemingly odd behaviour of the caller was an integral part of the plan, the criminal's method of insuring against unwelcome police interest during the early days of the investigation. The premiums were paid by Wallace.

As I have said, Hector Munro considered that the behaviour of the caller may have been the most important point in the case. I am inclined to disagree with him, however.

I would say that a more important point is this—*that if Wallace had made the call, he would not have been able to get to the City Café at the time he did.*

So much emphasis was placed upon the time-factor on the night of the murder that it seems to have been forgotten that there was a time-factor on the Monday night as well. Clearly, the police did not attach any importance to it; there were no 'tram tests' to establish how much time was needed to get from the telephone-box to the City Café. At the trial it received only two brief mentions: once when a junior detective agreed with defence counsel that the journey *from the house* to the café would take about half an hour—'or perhaps less'; and once during the direct examination of Inspector Gold, who said that the journey from the telephone-box to the café 'would take twenty to twenty-five minutes at the outside, from my experience on that route'.

Just those two vague references; no more. Yet the time-factor on the Monday evening was of paramount importance.

In examining it, there are two main times to be taken into account: the time the Qualtrough telephone-call ended and the time of Wallace's arrival at the City Café.

We know that it was 7.15 when the caller first tried—if that is the right word—to get through to the café; we know, too, that it was 7.20 before he succeeded. That time is definite, recorded by the exchange supervisor in her notebook, which was produced as a case exhibit.

Having got through, the caller had a short conversation with the waitress, and asked if Mr. Wallace was there.

After telling the caller to hold the line, the waitress walked through to the section of the café reserved for the chess-players, and spoke to Samuel Beattie, who listened to what she said, looked round the room, told her that Wallace was not there, and then agreed to speak to Qualtrough.

Beattie got up from the chess-table and crossed to the phone.

His conversation with Qualtrough consisted of about two hundred words; then he told Qualtrough to wait a moment while he poked around in his pockets for a used envelope and a pencil; having found them, he wrote the name as it was spelt out for him, the address as it was dictated to him.

End of call.

How long did it take, from beginning to end? Even if everything was done in jig-time, which it was not, the call must have lasted at least four minutes. Say four. And so the receiver was put down at 7.24—and if the caller was Wallace, he then went rushing across to the tram-stop in Townsend Lane, Anfield.

Now, how long would he have had to wait for a tram?

Several writers have suggested that the answer to that question is: No time at all. They say that, while Wallace was talking to Beattie, he could have been watching for the arrival of the tram, and, as soon as he saw it coming, finished off the conversation and run to board it. That is all very well as a theory, but there are no facts to support it. The call was not truncated; the last part of it was taken up with spelling the name and dictating the address—and that was definitely not hurried. A further drawback to the theory is that, in order to accept it, one has to believe that Wallace either had wonderful hearing or the power to see around corners. From the call-box, the tram-stop was visible, and so were a few yards of Townsend Lane beyond—but that was all.

Another suggestion is that Wallace could have found out the exact time of the tram's arrival by referring to a timetable. That is nonsense, too. Quite apart from the fact that tram and bus schedules are never more than approximate guides—affected by traffic conditions, the varying number of passengers, etc.—the tram schedules in Liverpool during the middle weeks of January

1931 were made meaningless by a subsidence in the Mersey Tunnel which caused traffic diversions and hold-ups in the centre of the city.

There was a tram service of 8–9 minutes on the route connecting Townsend Lane with North John Street, the location of the City Café. Therefore, if Wallace had left the call-box at 7.24 and been unlucky enough just to miss a tram, he would have had to wait until well after 7.30 before the next tram came along. But suppose fortune smiled upon him—that he crossed from the call-box to the tram-stop in a quarter of a minute and that he waited only three-quarters of a minute for a tram to take him to the City Café. A minute altogether. And so he left Townsend Lane at 7.25.

Turning to the time of his arrival at the café: the first person to observe his presence there afterwards stated, 'I arrived at the City Café . . . at about twenty-five to eight. I saw Mr Wallace approximately ten minutes later.'

The witness's estimate may be accepted. But the fact that he saw Wallace at about a quarter to eight must not be taken to mean that he saw him as soon as he arrived.

On that Monday evening, Wallace was due to play a match in the Second Class Championship. One of the club's rules was that tournament matches had to begin by 7.45. 'They might start earlier than that by arrangement,' Samuel Beattie explained at the trial, 'but you can penalize anyone if they do not start before a quarter to eight.'

Wallace had a reputation for punctuality. Indeed, it was almost a fixation with him. His favourite saying was the one about punctuality being the politeness of kings, the duty of gentlemen, and the necessity of men of business. He was always quoting it. Therefore, if Wallace was Qualtrough, it was almost as vital that he arrive in good time for his match as it was to get the telephone-message through beforehand. If he kept his opponent waiting after the 7.45 deadline, he would have a lot of explaining and apologizing to do—and his uncharacteristic unpunctuality would be remembered . . . would be turned into an important item of suspicion against him when the investigation into his wife's murder began.

As it happened, Wallace arrived at the café to find that the man he was due to play was not present. After chatting with a friend, he arranged to play an outstanding match in the Second Class

Championship with a Mr McCartney. The club's rule concerning the pre-7.45 start still applied to this rearranged fixture, and at about 7.50, when Beattie went over to deliver the message, Wallace and McCartney were deeply involved in the game.

Almost certainly, then, Wallace was at the City Café before 7.45. The important question is: How long before? Surely no one—not even the most ardent of anti-Wallaceites—can complain that two minutes is extravagant?

Now to the sum:

If Wallace waited only three-quarters of a minute for the tram at Townsend Lane, and if he arrived at the City Café at 7.43, the journey occupied eighteen minutes.

But the minimum time for the journey (indeed, one could go so far as to call it the all-time record for the journey) *was twenty-one minutes.*

In other words, Wallace could not have got from the telephone-box to the City Café in the time available.

A point that was practically ignored at the trial is that Wallace's so-called alibi was completely dependent upon the evidence of the milk-boy, Alan Close. If Close had not called at the house and seen Julia alive at whatever time it was—somewhere between half-past six and twenty to seven—Wallace would have had no alibi at all. There is doubt concerning the boy's veracity as a witness, but no doubt whatever that he delivered the milk some time after half-past six, proving that the maximum time at Wallace's disposal for committing the murder and clearing up afterwards was only eighteen minutes.

It has always been assumed—and, indeed, it *has* to be assumed, if the alibi theory is to hold water—that if Wallace was the murderer, the time of the milk-delivery was an integral part of his plan to kill Julia and get away with it.

An alibi is 'a plea which avers that the accused was in another place at the time of the commission of the offence, and therefore cannot be guilty'. Clearly, Wallace could not provide himself with an alibi as water-tight as the legal definition demands: all he could hope to do was (a) imply that some other person, either mythical or real, was guilty of the offence, (b) invent an excuse for being in another place at a time proximate to the offence, (c) after committing the offence, leave the scene as quickly as possible and establish his presence in another place at the earliest possible moment, and (d) commit the offence and destroy the connecting evidence *in a period of time so short as to suggest that, though not impossible, it was unlikely that he could have completed the task in the time available.*

Now suppose that, for some reason or other, Alan Close had not called at the house that night, would Wallace still have carried out the plan to murder his wife?

The answer, surely, is: No, definitely not.

No milk would have meant no time-factor. The last person to have seen Julia alive would have been a baker's boy, at half-past four in the afternoon. Wallace would have returned from work at about five minutes past six; with no one calling at the house after that time, he would have had nearly *three-quarters of an hour* (until 6.49) in which to commit the murder. Three-quarters of an hour—long enough, and allowing for a tea-break, for him to have committed half a dozen murders, if the victims had been available and if he had felt so inclined.

Can it be said, then—and with confidence—that

(1) Alan Close was more important to the plan than either of the tram-conductors, any of the people who spoke to Wallace in Menlove Gardens, or the Johnstons, his next-door neighbours;

(2) Wallace knew, or assumed, that the milk-boy always started delivering at the same time after coming home from school and having his tea, always followed the same route, and therefore always arrived in Wolverton Street at about the same time each evening, never varying more than five minutes or so either way;

(3) Wallace worked out how quickly he could commit the murder and tidy up afterwards . . . he also worked out the time needed to get from Wolverton Street to Menlove Gardens . . . he then added the two periods together—murder and tidying-up plus travelling—and added the sum-period to *the latest time* he expected the milk-boy to call and speak to Julia, thus arriving at the final and vital answer: the time of the appointment with Qualtrough;

(4) if the milk-boy had not called at all on the Tuesday, or if he had called before five minutes past six or within a few minutes of the time Wallace returned from work, Wallace would not have carried out the murder-plan, for without the time-factor his alibi was so tenuous as to be almost non-existent?

Can all that be said with confidence? (Remember, before answering, what Mr Justice Wright said—that if Wallace was the murderer, he could only have done all the things that needed to be done in the short time available to him—maybe less than ten minutes—if he had given the matter a lot of thought and done some preparation beforehand. And remember, too, that if Wallace had not *expected* the milk-boy to call, he would have murdered Julia long before; he would not have considered giving much, if any, thought to a tidying-up timetable.)

I think all fair-minded people must agree that at least three of the four points are indisputable. I shall assume that, anyway—and go on to ask, how is it possible to reconcile those points with the following facts?

The usual time for the milk-delivery to 29 Wolverton Street was about six o'clock. (That is Alan Close's own estimate.)

Normally, Close used a bike for the milk-round.

The reason for his being half an hour later than usual on the evening of Tuesday, 20 January, is that, the day before, something had gone wrong with the front wheel of the bike, making it unrideable, and he had to deliver the milk on foot.

But for the bike being out of order, he would have called at 29 Wolverton Street while Wallace was on his way home from work.

That there was any time-factor at all was completely fortuitous. But for a few bent bicycle-spokes, Wallace's 'alibi'—and it truly deserves those inverted commas— would not have been worth the tuppence saved from the telephone-call.

If Wallace didn't do it, who did?

That question became almost a catch-phrase in Liverpool during the first few months of 1931. It was asked so often, and by so many people, that it even came to the ears of Mr Justice Wright, who considered it necessary to warn the jury:

'. . . The question is not: Who did this crime? The question is: Did the prisoner do it?—or, rather, to put it more accurately: Is it proved to your reasonable satisfaction and beyond all reasonable doubt that the prisoner did it? It is a fallacy to say: "If the prisoner did not do it, who did?"'

The question was asked rhetorically, of course. Most people, while agreeing that Wallace had no apparent motive for killing his wife, were unable to think of a good enough reason for anyone else's doing it.

The defence suggested robbery as the motive; and certainly the evidence of the rifled cash-box, the broken door of the locker, lent support to that theory. But it was pooh-poohed by the prosecution. Was it likely, they asked, that anyone would commit murder for a few pounds?

As a matter of fact, it was; it is. There are any number of examples of murders that were committed for ridiculously small sums. I have not done any statistical research on the subject, but I think it would be true to say that the vast majority of murderers for gain receive incommensurate reward for their troubles—or rather, *apparently* incommensurate reward. If a man is broke, a fiver seems like a fortune.

In any event, the murderer in the Wallace case may have anticipated finding far more in the cash-box than was actually there. The fact that he got away with only a few pounds does not mean that he did not expect more. Normally, the cash-box would have contained about £30,[1] and if the crime had happened during the week of Wallace's monthly collection, at least twice as much. To say that the motive for the murder cannot have been robbery because the reward was too small is like saying that an organized gang of criminals who blow open a safe, only to find it empty, are nothing more than vandals.

And so the robbery motive must not be ruled out.

And neither must the sex motive. Just because Julia was middle-aged, unattractive to most men, does not necessarily mean that she was undesirable to *all* of them. Indeed, to a pervert, to a man whose Oedipus complex had gone completely haywire in a mess of distorted sexual urges, the very fact that she *was* middle-aged and unattractive might have made her irresistibly desirable.

Murders have been committed for the oddest of reasons. Sometimes (and the crime of Leopold and Loeb is a case in point) for no reason at all . . . at least, for no reason connected with the individual victim. Like climbers who scale mountains 'because they are there', some murderers have killed simply to

---

[1] The 1992 purchasing power of the 1931 £ is reproduced to be just over £26.

prove that it could be done, or have slain for the sheer thrill of it, the experience.

Wallace himself thought he knew the answer to the question: *If he didn't do it, who did?*

Two days after the murder, he made a statement at the request of Inspector Gold, naming the people 'who would be admitted by my wife without hesitation if they called while I was out'. Among the fifteen men referred to in the statement were a Prudential superintendent, Joseph Crewe; Wallace's violin-teacher, and his tailor.

Asked if he suspected any of the men, Wallace hesitated a moment, and then told the inspector what he knew about one of them:

Richard Gordon Parry.

Wallace described Parry as 'a single man about 22 years of age [he was born in Liverpool on 12 January 1909], about 5 ft 10, slimmish build, dark hair, rather foppish appearance, well dressed and wears spats, very plausible'. For about two years, until the beginning of 1930, Parry had worked as an agent for the Prudential, under the supervision of Joseph Crewe. Wallace mentioned that, during that time, Parry had 'once called at my house on business and left a letter for me which he wrote in my front room. I was not in at the time but my wife let him in.'

When Wallace was ill, Parry did part of his collecting: 'He called very frequently to see me about business, and he was well acquainted with our domestic arrangements. He had been in the parlour and kitchen frequently, and had been upstairs in the middle bedroom a number of times to see me while I was in bed. . . . Parry knew the arrangements of my business with regard to the system of paying in money collected to the head office, Dale Street. I have had the cash-box from which the money was stolen for about 16 years. . . . Parry knew I kept the money in the box because while he worked for me I always put the money into it when he called to pay over to me his collection. He had seen me take it down and put it back to the top of the bookcase in the kitchen often.'

Wallace knew that Parry was either careless with money or dishonest. And so did Joseph Crewe, who had discovered that he was collecting payments from certain clients and not including the cash in the returns. Crewe had spoken to Parry's parents, and they had paid the deficiency of about £30[1]. When Parry was doing part of Wallace's collection, Wallace had noticed mistakes in the accounts; he had pointed them out to Parry and been told that 'it was an oversight'. Later, noting further discrepancies, he had informed Crewe. Probably as a result, Parry had been given the choice of resigning or getting the sack; he had chosen to resign.

'I have often seen him since he has been working for his new company [first, for a short time, the Standard Life Assurance Co., then the Gresham Life Assurance Society], and have spoken to him,' Wallace stated. One of the last of those encounters took place shortly before the murder: a very brief encounter—'I said good evening and he returned my greeting.'

It occurred at the City Café, on a Thursday evening when the chess club was occupying one part of the premises and an amateur dramatic society, of which Parry was a star-member, was using another.

As well as visiting the City Café for meetings of the society, Parry frequently lunched there.

Wallace recalled that he had met Parry in Missouri Road, part of Wallace's premium-collecting area, round about Christmas-time: 'He had a car then which he was driving.' Almost certainly, the reason Parry was in Missouri Road was that he was visiting his fiancée, Miss Lily Lloyd, who lived with her parents at No. 7.

Wallace made his statement to Gold on Thursday morning, 22 January. Later that day, he was told that the police were satisfied that Parry had no connection with the murder, since he had a perfect alibi, supported by the testimony of a person who was in his company the whole of the Tuesday evening.

But, perfect alibi or no perfect alibi, Wallace was still not satisfied. During the next few months he had plenty of time to think. And the more he thought about the motive for the murder, the identity of the murderer, the more suspicious he became of Parry.

After his release from prison, he learned two additional facts concerning Parry. First, that he was more than usually hard-up at the time of the murder—heavily in debt and pleading with friends for financial aid; second, that he had a police record.

---

[1] See previous footnote.

On 14 September 1931, Wallace wrote in his diary: 'Just as I was going to dinner, Parry stopped me, and said he wanted to talk to me for a few minutes. It was a desperately awkward position. Eventually I decided not to hear what he had to say. I told him I would talk to him some day and give him something to think about. He must realize that I suspect him of the terrible crime. I fear I let him see clearly what I thought, and it may unfortunately put him on his guard. I wonder if it is any good putting a private detective on to his track in the hope of something coming to light. I am more than half persuaded to try it.'

But he never did. And, so far as is known, he never found out any more about Parry.

What else is known about him?

Quite a lot. For instance:

Parry was well-connected in more than one respect. His uncle, George Parry, was the Liverpool City Librarian; following his death in 1933, laudatory letters and poems were published in the local press, and a memorial service was held at the cathedral. Parry's father, William John, was a senior employee of the Liverpool Corporation; in 1948, after forty-three years' service, he was appointed Assistant City Treasurer. At the time of the Wallace case, his secretary was the daughter of the head of the Liverpool CID.

Parry's criminal record was longer, more varied, than Wallace thought. Both before January 1931 and afterwards, he was charged with theft, causing malicious damage, embezzlement, and indecent assault. However, he seems to have had a charmed life: the only time that he was sent to prison was in September 1934, when he was in the army, stationed at Aldershot; he was sentenced to three months' imprisonment with hard labour for stealing a car (a year before, he had appeared in the same court on a similar charge, but the owner of the vehicle had not turned up, and so no evidence was offered). On all the other occasions when he was charged, he was either fined, bound over, or acquitted. In 1936—back in Liverpool and employed as the manager of a shop—he was charged with committing indecent assault on a girl whom he had met in a temperance bar. At the Prescot police court, the prosecution case was that he had offered to drive the girl home, but instead of doing so had driven her to Rainhill, on the outskirts of Liverpool, where, after threatening to murder her, he had committed the assault; one of the girl's ear-rings was found at the scene. (There is a series of small mysteries concerning the reporting—or rather, non-reporting—of this case. A diligent search has failed to find any mention in any newspaper of the outcome of the committal proceedings. It may be that the magistrate's decision came too late to be included in either of the Liverpool evening papers and that the case was considered too sordid to be reported by the staid morning paper, the *Daily Post*—but what can one make of the fact that, though the *Prescot District Reporter* gave coverage to the early hearings, it did not report the outcome? Parry was definitely committed for trial at the Liverpool Summer Assizes—but there is no trace of a report of the trial. If one discounts the notion of a cover-up, a sort of 'D notice' being put on the Liverpool press, then the only explanation seems to be that an account was squeezed out by full coverage of a locally-sensational civil case at the Assizes involving the directors of the Aintree racecourse.)

Turning to Parry's alibi for the night of the killing of Julia Wallace: when he was interviewed by the police, he said that he had spent the material time in the company of his fiancée, Lily Lloyd; separately interviewed, she confirmed that that was so. The police accepted the slender story. The fact that they did not bother to test the strength of the alibi shows that they were not interested in finding other suspects. It is all very well for people with ombuds-mentalities to say that a person's past mistakes should not be held against him, but when a man named as a possible suspect has a criminal record, any alibi he puts forward should not only be checked, but double-checked—even treble-checked.

Two years later, in the summer of 1933, Parry jilted Lily Lloyd, and the scorned young woman went to see Hector Munro, saying that she wished to make a statement to the effect that she was not with Parry at the time of the murder—indeed, couldn't possibly have been with him, since she was working as the pianist at the Cosy Cinema, in the Liverpool suburb of Clubmoor, until late in the evening. Parry had asked her to support his story, and she had done so, though she knew full well that the simplest of inquiries would reveal the lie. The solicitor's response may surprise readers outside the legal profession, and even some within it: he advised Miss Lloyd against making a statement, and hustled her out of his office. Many years later, he gave two reasons for adopting that negative attitude: first—and most important, he said—Wallace had died a few months before, and so he no longer had a client to instruct him; second, as the result of the publicity from the Wallace case, he was far too busy to take on unpaid work. So far as is known, Lily Lloyd did not go to another solicitor—but in 1980 she confirmed what she had told Munro. A couple of years after the ending of her relationship with Parry, she probably felt glad that she had been jilted, for she met and soon afterwards married a wealthy businessman. The marriage lasted for forty years, until her husband's death in the mid-1970s. She is now, and has been for some time, a pillar of the establishment on the Isle of Man, one of the United Kingdom's offshore tax-havens. It would not advance this account to give her married name and address, but the information is available to the Liverpool police if they are interested.

In 1966, after collecting a good deal of information about Parry, I was left with the task of finding out whether he was still alive: if he was, then the laws of libel would prevent me from naming him in the first edition of my book, and I would have to be extremely circumspect in giving any details about 'Mr X'. I went to the central registry, at Somerset House, to consult the death registers. Arriving there early in the morning, I assumed that I was the first customer. I ascended the steps to the circular gallery, on one side of which was a continuous working-surface, and on the other the shelves of registers. As I walked round the gallery to the place where the post-1939 section began, I noticed a register lying open on the working-surface. Glancing at the page, I saw what at first seemed to be the record of my own death. A second, extremely hesitant glance reassured me that the Jonathan Goodman referred to had died before I was born. Even so, having consulted the registers and found no reference to Parry, I took extra care in crossing the street and from then on made sure that the doors of my flat were locked at night.

Eventually, through Thomas Alker, the Liverpool Town Clerk, I learned that Parry's father was still alive and residing at the family home in the suburb called Stoneycroft. I travelled to Liverpool the next day and rang the bell of 7 Woburn Hill. William Parry opened the door. Though it was a hot Sunday morning, he was wearing a black jacket and striped trousers, with a ready-made bow-tie circling a butterfly collar. Several cats sidled and mewed around his feet—which, incidentally, were shod in bedroom-slippers topped by spats—and his whole clerical outfit was given a tweedy appearance by feline hairs. I had decided that there was no point in inventing an excuse for wanting to discover the whereabouts of his son, and so I told him that I was writing a book about the Wallace case and that his son's name had arisen during my research. After wondering why I was 'raking up dead embers', he said that, yes, Gordon had known the Wallaces—but quickly added that at the time of the murder 'the boy' was having the battery of his car charged; that, he said, was established by the police. Without hesitation, he told me Parry's address.

The next evening, back in London, I was accompanied by Richard Whittington-Egan (acting as both witness and body-guard) to 39 Grove Hill Road, a small Victorian terrace-house in an upper-working-class part of the suburb of Camberwell.[1] The front door was open, and Parry was standing on the

---

[1] Late in 1990, I learned of an article on the Wallace case that had appeared in at least two recently-published 'true'-crime books. The writer states that a man, now dead, who in 1966 was employed by the eventual publishers of the first edition of my book, *The Killing of Julia Wallace*, 'had been curious about Parry's present [1966] whereabouts, and had casually looked him up in the London Telephone Directory. It was a long shot, but it paid off. Parry was listed at an address in south London. The author Jonathan Goodman, who was writing his book on the Wallace case, and another crime expert, Richard Whittington-Egan, went to call on him.' 'A long shot . . .'—well, yes: extravagantly long, considering that until I located and spoke to Parry's father, no one who knew that I was searching for Parry had any idea whether he was alive or dead—or, supposing that he was alive, where in the world he was living. There is also the matter of Parry's forenames. He was known only as Gordon Parry to Wallace and to acquaintances whom I had interviewed—and he was referred to as such in press reports of his court appearances, on employment documents, and even in police records. It was not until I spoke to his father that his first name, Richard, reappeared. And so, if the employee of the publishers had looked for his name in the London Telephone Directory, he would have looked for 'Parry, G.' rather than 'Parry, R.G.'. I have substantial evidence, and numerous witnesses to the fact, that the 'long-shot' tale is tosh. The writer has apologised for his error and has undertaken not to repeat the tale.

step, apparently simply enjoying the last of the sun. A van cruised in the road, the driver giving amplified exhortations to vote for a candidate in a local government election.

I introduced myself.

'Is it about the election you want to see me?' Parry asked blandly. As we learned later, he knew quite well who I was, since his father had phoned him, telling him of my call and warning him to expect me.

Here are extracts from Whittington–Egan's notes of the interview:

> Parry, who now works for 'the government' I afterwards found out that he was a GPO telephone-operator, is married to a plump woman who appears some years younger than himself, and has a daughter who is just about to go to university.
>
> We found him a plausible man who was not made in any way uncomfortable by our questioning. He has grey hair, smoothed sleekly back, and a military-style moustache. He is wiry and well-preserved. He is of reasonably powerful build, has noticeably large hands, and a fleshy handshake. His eyes are penetrating and alternately shifty and too-candid. He exudes a false, trowel-laid-on charm, which can easily beguile but which is as bogus as the bonhomie of a used-car salesman; this manner masks, in our opinion, considerable firmness. He is evasive, manipulative, sharp, and very clever. He is quite well-spoken, and throughout the interview kept a self-satisfied and often inappropriate smile on his face.
>
> Parry hinted that, if he chose, he could reveal much about Wallace, whom he described as a 'very strange man'; he implied that Wallace was sexually odd.
>
> He described Julia Wallace as a 'very sweet, charming woman'. He said that he used to sing as a young man, and would often go to tea at 29 Wolverton Street, where Julia would accompany his singing on the piano.

He was quite ready to admit that, as a young man, he was what he called a 'tearaway'. But he made little of the criminal charges against him: just youthful high spirits, no real harm done. 'It was very awkward for me, having my little misdemeanours dragged up at the time of the case,' he remarked. The police, he said, were satisfied as to his innocence of the Wallace murder when he produced some people with whom he had spent the evening 'arranging a birthday celebration'. (This new professed alibi may be significant in view of the fact that R.M. Qualtrough spoke of being busy with his girl's twenty-first birthday-party.) He did not remember the 'new alibi' (that he was having his car-battery changed) mentioned by his father when JG spoke to him.

He refused to talk about his part in the case—'Not if you were to offer me £2000'—because, he said, he had promised his father that he would not speak about it. He added that, when his father died, he might be prepared to talk, subject to proper financial arrangements being made. He suggested that JG had acted less than honestly in his endeavours to trace him, and had upset his father and endangered his heart. But even this was done in an oblique sort of way by saying that 'someone' had called on his father and upset him.

He claimed that the Wallace case broke up his engagement to Lily Lloyd. He refused to talk about Miss Lloyd, apart from saying that he was still in touch with her and that she is now living in Llandudno [the latter piece of information was afterwards discovered to be a lie].

He said that Joseph Crewe, the Prudential superintendent— now conveniently dead—was utterly convinced of Wallace's guilt (this we know to be untrue). It was surprising to learn that he knew of the deaths of Crewe, Alan Close, and Wallace's nephew Edwin. (The latter's death in North Borneo was not at all widely reported, which suggests that Parry watches everything that appears in connection with the case.)

*　　　*　　　*

A week or so after the interview, I telephoned Parry. He was viciously angry at my doing so, and I was taken aback by the breadth of his vocabulary of foul language: many of the obscenities were new to me. The odd thing, though, was that I all the time had the feeling that he was *enjoying* his outburst.

Parry retired from the GPO in 1969, and he and his wife (his second, I later learned) moved to a bungalow, 'Ty'n-y-Fynnon', on Waterloo Hill in the village of Llangernyw, North Wales. He did part-time work as a switchboard-operator in various local hospitals.

Over the next ten years—during which two editions of my book appeared, both using the 'Mr X' device—I occasionally checked up on whether Parry was still living at Llangernyw. I was helped by my friends, Philip and Diane Chadwick, who on one occasion, posing as house-hunters, were invited into the bungalow by Mrs Parry when her husband was out; she told the Chadwicks that he was receiving treatment for a broken ankle, and when Philip Chadwick asked if he was insured, replied: 'Oh, no, he doesn't believe in insurance.'

There were no developments until Radio City, the Liverpool broadcasting station, decided to prepare a programme on the case, lasting two and a half hours, for transmission on the fiftieth anniversary. I agreed to act as consultant and to take part in both the dramatisation (which was based on my book) and the discussion/phone-in parts of the programme. I told the producer, Roger Wilkes, what I knew about Parry, and a representative was sent to Llangernyw. He learned that Parry had died from a heart-attack on 14 April 1980, leaving a will of £18,000.

Knowing that Parry's wife had predeceased him (I am convinced that she knew nothing of his murky past), I had no qualms in agreeing to name him on the programme and to sketch my reasons for believing that he killed Julia Wallace. That I did, and as a result a 'middleman' telephoned Radio City, offering to put them in touch with a man called John ('Pucka') Parkes who had further details about Parry. The middleman said that Parkes wanted payment for the information, and subsequent telephone conversations were chiefly taken up with bartering over 'the right price'. While this was going on, however, information came in from another source which led to the middleman's being bypassed. Parkes, who was a long-term patient in a Liverpool hospital, was interviewed, and he made a statement, the salient parts of which are as follows:

In January 1931, when he was twenty-two, he was employed at night as a cleaner and general hand at Atkinson's Garage in Moscow Drive, a couple of blocks from Woburn Hill, where Parry lived with his parents. Parkes knew Parry well; he had been at school with him, and Parry was a frequent visitor to the garage, not only to have repairs done to his Swift car but also to use the 'social centre' in the flat upstairs, where customers were welcomed for a drink and a chat. Parry was not one of the most welcome customers: he was dilatory in paying his bills, and he had been caught going through a wardrobe in which money was kept. Parkes had once told him off for using the telephone in the flat to make calls to complete strangers: 'he could alter his voice like changing a shilling.'

Late on the night of the murder—or it may have been in the early hours of the following day—Parry drove into the garage. Parkes, who was alone, noticed that he was agitated. Parry told him to wash the car, and, though the vehicle looked clean, Parkes went over it with a high-powered hose. When he had finished the bodywork, Parry—who stood over him all the time—told him to use the hose on the inside as well. Before doing so, Parkes noticed a bloodstained glove protruding from the glove-compartment; he started to remove it, but Parry snatched it from him, saying: 'If the police found that, it would hang me.' Parry was muttering to himself, and at one point he said that he had hidden an iron bar down a drain in Priory Road (which runs beside Anfield Cemetery). The job completed, Parry gave Parkes five shillings and drove away.

The next morning—by which time everyone was discussing the murder in Wolverton Street—Parkes told William Atkinson, the owner of the garage, about the incident; he was advised to say nothing more about it and was told to keep the five shillings. But when Wallace was convicted, Parkes again spoke to Atkinson, who telephoned the police. The head of the Liverpool CID came to the garage, listened to Parkes's story, said simply, 'I think you've made a mistake,' and left.

Parkes had an explanation as to why Parry was not covered with blood. He had spoken to a driver for Ellis's, a local grocery firm, who had informed him that, shortly before the murder, Parry had borrowed from him a pair of thigh-boots, saying that he was going fishing. And a policeman-friend had mentioned to Parkes that he had lent Parry an oilskin coat for a fishing expedition.

Radio City obtained some slender corroboration of the main part of Parkes's story from the widow of one of William Atkinson's sons: she said that she recalled Parkes telling her and her husband about the car-washing episode the morning after it happened.

Even if one discounts Parkes's statement, one is left with a good many facts which, added together, form a sum greater than its parts—great enough, I submit, to support the assertion that Richard Gordon Parry was the killer of Julia Wallace. He may have had any, or all, of three motives for the crime—financial gain, revenge, and/or sex. He knew that Wallace was a member of the Central Chess Club, and, as a frequenter of the City Café, could have looked at the notice-board to see when Wallace was due to play a match. Being an amateur actor, he would probably have had little difficulty in assuming the role of R.M. Qualtrough. He knew of Wallace's insurance business; he knew his way around the house; he knew where the cash was kept. Unknown to Wallace, he was friendly with Julia and often visited her when Wallace was at work; she would have had no hesitation in letting him in while Wallace was searching for Menlove Gardens East. Before the police called on him—fewer than forty-eight hours after the crime—he fabricated an alibi and persuaded his fiancée to break the law by supporting it. He had a diverse criminal-record, some components of which suggest that he was the type of man who *could* have committed the murder. He may have believed that his connections with top people in Liverpool would help him to escape retribution—and perhaps they did.

Within the framework of the Wallace case are several separate tragedies. The killing of a seemingly innocent woman—that, of course, is one of them. Another is the way in which Wallace was martyred, not only during the case but afterwards, until the day he died. There is the tragedy of prejudice sneering at justice, spitting in its blind face. And there is the tragedy of a mishandled investigation—tragic twice over, for by expending all their energies on building the case against Wallace, the investigators ignored or overlooked evidence that could have established the identity of the true culprit.

ACKNOWLEDGMENTS AND SOURCES

Other than those given in the text: 'Rules for Murderesses', first published in *Vanity Fair* (USA), was expanded to make a chapter in *Instigation of the Devil* (Scribners, New York, 1930). 'Scenes From a Murder Trial', a Liverpool *Daily Post* abridgment of part of *Shall We Ever Know?* (Hutchinson, London, 1971), is published by permission of the author of that book. 'Robert and Ruby', a chapter of *Posts-Mortem: The Correspondence of Murder* (St Martin's Press, New York, 1971), is published by permission of the author. 'Death Scene', from *Memoranda During the War*, appears in several Whitman collections. 'A Prevalence of Victims' is published by permission of the author. 'The Killer in the Rye' is published by permission of the author. 'A Liverpool Triptych' is published by permission of the author. 'The Case of the Ragged Stranger', from *Long, Long Ago* (© 1943 by Viking Penguin, Inc), is used by permission of Viking Penguin, a division of Penguin Books USA, Inc. 'The Eternal Suspect', originally published by the Kent State University Libraries as *Occasional Paper, Second Series No. 6*, is published by permission of the author. 'Death by Laser-Beam', from *The Master Eccentric*, edited by Jonathan Goodman (Allison & Busby, London, 1986), is published by permission of Mrs. Margaret Heppenstall. 'Warner's Warning', a chapter of *Malice Domestic* (Green, Edinburgh, 1928), is published by permission of Mrs. Marjorie Roughead. 'Farewell Performances', a section of *The Black Museum* (by Jonathan Goodman and Bill Waddell [Curator]; Harrap, London, 1987), is published by permission of the author. 'The Beheading of Bluebeard' is from *I Found No Peace* (Gollancz, London, 1937). 'Blood Carnival' is quoted in *MacArthur, 1941–51: Victory in the Pacific* by Major-General Charles A. Willoughby and John Chamberlain (McGraw-Hill, New York, 1956). 'The Late Mr Ellis' is published by permission of Mrs. Viva Marie Duff. 'Three Lifers' is from *Songs of the Cell* (Southern, London, 1928). 'The Affair at Villa Madeira', the Introduction to *Trial of Alma Victoria Rattenbury and George Percy Stoner* (Hodge, Edinburgh, 1950), is published by permission of Joanna Colenbrander, for the Harwood Will Trust. 'Judd's Story' is mainly composed of extracts from *Doomed Ship* (Liveright, New York, 1928). 'Remarks on Ripperology', a section of *Bloody Versicles: The Rhymes of Crime* (revised edition: Kent State University Press, Ohio, 1992), is published by permission of the author. 'Charles the Ripper . . . ?', which first appeared in the *Literary Review* (London), is published by permission of the author. 'The Bloodthirsty Butler' is a chapter of *A Book of Remarkable Criminals* (Cassell, London, 1918). 'Major Armstrong, Master of Arts' is published by permission of the author. 'The Lizzie Borden Song' is published by permission of the author. 'A Spin Across London Bridge', a chapter of *Victorian Studies in Scarlet: Murders and Manners in the Age of Victoria* (Dent, London, 1970), is published by permission of the author. 'The Fatal Barney' a combining of the Editor's Note and the Introduction to *Trial of Elvira Barney* (David & Charles, Newton Abbot, 1974), is published by permission of the author. 'Harvard and Homicide', which first appeared in *The Armchair Detective* (USA), is published by permission of the author. Of 'Circuit Murders', the comments on the trial of Burke and Macdougal are from *Memorials of His Time* (Foulis, Edinburgh, 1910), and the remainder from *Circuit Journeys* (Douglas, Edinburgh, 1899); there are other editions of both books. 'The Secret of the Moat Farm' is from *Great Stories of Real Life*, edited by Max Pemberton (Newnes, London, n.d.). 'Old Man Bender's Orchard' is from *Leviathan* (Chapman & Hall, London, 1923). Much of the latter part of 'The Wallace Case' is from *The Killing of Julia Wallace* (Headline, London, 1987); in 1991, the first US edition of that book (Scribners, New York, 1976) was republished, in facsimile, as a 'Time-Life

Classic' by Time-Life Books, Alexandria, Virginia, but all of the essay is published by permission of the author. If any copyright-holder has not been traced or has failed to respond to communications, he or she should write to the editor, who will make amendment in any future edition.